THE OXFORD HANDBOOK OF

ORGANIZATIONAL IDENTITY

THE OXFORD HANDBOOK OF

ORGANIZATIONAL

IDENTITY

Edited by

MICHAEL G. PRATT

MAJKEN SCHULTZ

BLAKE E. ASHFORTH

and

DAVIDE RAVASI

OXFORD
UNIVERSITY PRESS

OXFORD
UNIVERSITY PRESS

Great Clarendon Street, Oxford, OX2 6DP,
United Kingdom

Oxford University Press is a department of the University of Oxford.
It furthers the University's objective of excellence in research, scholarship,
and education by publishing worldwide. Oxford is a registered trade mark of
Oxford University Press in the UK and in certain other countries

Published in the United States of America by Oxford University Press
198 Madison Avenue, New York, NY 10016, United States of America

British Library Cataloguing in Publication Data
Data available

Library of Congress Control Number: 2016950871

ISBN 978–0–19–968957–6

Printed and bound by CPI Group (UK) Ltd, Croydon, CR0 4YY

Contents

List of Figures   ix
List of Tables   x
List of Contributors   xi

Introduction: Organizational Identity, Mapping Where
    We Have Been, Where We Are, and Where We Might Go   1
MICHAEL G. PRATT, MAJKEN SCHULTZ, BLAKE E. ASHFORTH,
AND DAVIDE RAVASI

SECTION I MAPPING THE ORGANIZATIONAL IDENTITY (OI) FIELD

1. Great Debates in Organizational Identity Study   21
DENNIS A. GIOIA AND AIMEE L. HAMILTON

2. Measuring Organizational Identity: Taking Stock
and Looking Forward   39
PETER O. FOREMAN AND DAVID A. WHETTEN

3. Organizational Identity, Culture, and Image   65
DAVIDE RAVASI

4. Organizational, Subunit, and Individual Identities:
Multilevel Linkages   79
BLAKE E. ASHFORTH

5. Organizational Identity Change and Temporality   93
MAJKEN SCHULTZ

6. Hybrid and Multiple Organizational Identities   106
MICHAEL G. PRATT

SECTION II CRITICAL PERSPECTIVES ON OI

7. Organizational Identity and Organizational Identity Work
   as Valuable Analytical Resources   123
   TONY J. WATSON

8. Organizational Identity: The Significance of Power and Politics   140
   KATE KENNY, ANDREA WHITTLE, AND HUGH WILLMOTT

9. Organizational Identity: A Critique   160
   MATS ALVESSON AND MAXINE ROBERTSON

SECTION III INTEGRATIVE MODELS OF OI

10. Optimal Distinctiveness Revisited: An Integrative Framework
    for Understanding the Balance between Differentiation and
    Conformity in Individual and Organizational Identities   183
    EZRA ZUCKERMAN

11. Bridging and Integrating Theories on Organizational
    Identity: A Social Interactionist Model of Organizational
    Identity Formation and Change   200
    JOEP P. CORNELISSEN, S. ALEXANDER HASLAM,
    AND MIRJAM D. WERNER

SECTION IV HOW INDIVIDUALS RELATE TO OI

12. How Do We Communicate Who We Are? Examining How
    Organizational Identity Is Conveyed to Members   219
    BETH S. SCHINOFF, KRISTIE M. ROGERS, AND KEVIN G. CORLEY

13. Mobilizing Organizational Action against Identity Threats: The
    Role of Organizational Members' Perceptions and Responses   239
    JENNIFER L. PETRIGLIERI AND BETH A. DEVINE

14. Organizational Identity and the Undesired Self   257
    KIMBERLY D. ELSBACH AND JANET M. DUKERICH

15. Organizational Identity Work   276
    GLEN E. KREINER AND CHAD MURPHY

SECTION V   SOURCES AND PROCESSES OF OI

16. Re-Membering: Rhetorical History as Identity Work   297
    ROY SUDDABY, WILLIAM M. FOSTER,
    AND CHRISTINE QUINN TRANK

17. Materiality and Identity: How Organizational Products,
    Artifacts, and Practices Instantiate Organizational Identity   317
    LEE WATKISS AND MARY ANN GLYNN

18. Making Sense of Who We Are: Leadership and
    Organizational Identity   335
    DAAN VAN KNIPPENBERG

SECTION VI   OI AND THE ENVIRONMENT

19. Organizational Identity in Institutional Theory: Taking Stock and
    Moving Forward   353
    NELSON PHILLIPS, PAUL TRACEY, AND MATT KRAATZ

20. Institutional Pluralism, Inhabitants, and the Construction
    of Organizational and Personal Identities   374
    RICH DEJORDY AND W. E. DOUGLAS CREED

21. Organizational Identity and Institutional Forces: Toward
    an Integrative Framework   396
    MARYA L. BESHAROV AND SHELLEY L. BRICKSON

SECTION VII   IMPLICATIONS OF OI

22. Organizational Identity and Innovation   417
    CALLEN ANTHONY AND MARY TRIPSAS

23. Planned Organizational Identity Change: Insights from Practice   436
    MAMTA BHATT, CEES B. M. VAN RIEL, AND MARIJKE BAUMANN

24. Identity Construction in Mergers and Acquisitions: A Discursive
    Sensemaking Perspective   455
    JANNE TIENARI AND EERO VAARA

25. Fostering Stakeholder Identification through Expressed
    Organizational Identities   474
    Caroline A. Bartel, Cindi Baldi, and Janet M. Dukerich

Conclusion: On the Identity of Organizational Identity. Looking
    Backward toward the Future   494
    Michael G. Pratt, Blake E. Ashforth, Majken Schultz,
    and Davide Ravasi

Author Index   501
Subject Index   505

LIST OF FIGURES

0.1   Peer-reviewed articles, dissertations, and theses on organizational identity from 1985 to 2015   2

2.1   Temporal comparison of qualitative v. quantitative analyses   53

3.1   Interrelations between organizational identity, image, and culture in past research (a simplified visual representation)   74

4.1   Organizational identity emergence and cascades   80

6.1   A classification scheme for multiple organizational identity management responses   111

11.1   A social interactionist model of organizational identity formation and change (SIMOI)   209

12.1   A typology of organizational identity communication   226

14.1   A framework relating organizational identity affirmation and the undesired self   268

17.1   Instantiating an organizational identity by different elements of materiality   325

20.1   Organizational identity in a pluralistic institutional context   379

20.2   Personal identity in a pluralistic institutional context   381

20.3   Interactions of personal and organizational identities   382

20.4   Composite model of personal and organization identity in a pluralistic institutional environment   383

21.1   The filtering role of OI and institutional structure in influencing how institutional forces shape OI content   405

22.1   Identity-enhancing innovation   421

22.2   Identity-stretching innovation   424

22.3   Identity-challenging innovation   425

23.1   Implementation of planned organizational identity change   439

24.1   The discursive sensemaking approach to identity construction   464

LIST OF TABLES

2.1	Representative list of selected articles	43
2.2	Article coding scheme	44
2.3	Clusters of organizational identity research	49
2.4	Major characteristics of OI research clusters	52
2.5	Additional descriptive statistics of OI research clusters	54
5.1	Dominant views on identity change	95
6.1	Hybrid vs. multiple organizational identity conceptualizations	113
8.1	Framework for analyzing power and organizational identity	146
9.1	Is OI conceptually different from OC?	172
11.1	Metaphors of organizational identity	205
19.1	Summary of organizational identity in institutional theory	354
22.1	Studies of identity-enhancing innovation	422
22.2	Identity-stretching innovation	423
22.3	Studies of identity-challenging innovation	426

List of Contributors

Mats Alvesson is Professor of Business Administration at the University of Lund.

Callen Anthony is a PhD student at the Carroll School of Management, Boston College.

Blake E. Ashforth is the Horace Steele Arizona Heritage Chair in the W. P. Carey School of Business, Arizona State University.

Cindi Baldi is Assistant Professor in the College of Business, Southeastern Louisiana University.

Caroline A. Bartel is Associate Professor of Management in the McCombs School of Business, University of Texas at Austin.

Marijke Baumann is Senior Communication and Research Manager at Rotterdam School of Management, Erasmus University.

Marya L. Besharov is Assistant Professor of Organizational Behavior at the ILR School, Cornell University, Ithaca.

Mamta Bhatt is Assistant Professor at the IESEG School of Management.

Shelley L. Brickson is Associate Professor of Managerial Studies at the University of Illinois at Chicago.

Kevin G. Corley is Professor in the management department at the W. P. Carey School of Business, Arizona State University.

Joep P. Cornelissen is Professor of Corporate Communication and Management at Rotterdam School of Management, Erasmus University (RSM).

Rich DeJordy is Assistant Professor of Management and Organizational Development at the D'Amore-McKim School of Business, Northeastern University.

Beth A. Devine is a PhD student at INSEAD.

W. E. Douglas Creed is Professor of Entrepreneurial Management & Law at the College of Business Administration, University of Rhode Island.

Janet M. Dukerich is Senior Associate Dean for Academic Affairs, Harkins & Company Centennial Chair in the McCombs School of Business, University of Texas.

Kimberly D. Elsbach is Associate Dean and Professor of Organizational Behavior and Stephen G. Newberry Endowed Chair in Leadership in the Graduate School of Management, University of California, Davis.

Peter O. Foreman is Associate Professor at the College of Business, Illinois State University.

William M. Foster is Associate Professor at the University of Alberta.

Dennis A. Gioia is Professor of Organizational Behavior in the Department of Management and Organization, The Pennsylvania State University.

Mary Ann Glynn is the Joseph F. Cotter Professor of Management & Organization at the Carroll School of Management, Boston College.

Aimee L. Hamilton is Assistant Professor in the Department of Management, University of Denver.

S. Alexander Haslam is Professor of Psychology and ARC Laureate Fellow at the University of Queensland.

Kate Kenny is Reader in Management at Queen's University Management School, Queens University Belfast.

Matt Kraatz is Professor of Business Administration at the College of Business, University of Illinois.

Glen E. Kreiner is Associate Professor of Management at the Smeal College of Business, The Pennsylvania State University.

Chad Murphy is Assistant Professor of Management in the College of Business, Oregon State University.

Jennifer L. Petriglieri is Professor of Organisational Behaviour at INSEAD.

Nelson Phillips is Professor of Strategy and Organizational Behaviour at Imperial College Business School.

Michael G. Pratt is the O'Connor Family Professor in the Carroll School of Management, Boston College.

Davide Ravasi is Professor of Strategic and Entrepreneurial Management at the Cass Business School, City University London.

Maxine Robertson is Professor of Innovation and Organisation at the Queen Mary University of London.

Kristie M. Rogers is Assistant Professor at the School of Business, The University of Kansas.

Beth S. Schinoff is a PhD Student in Management at Arizona State University.

Majken Schultz is Professor of Organization and Management at Copenhagen Business School.

Roy Suddaby is the Winspear Chair of Management and the Director of Research at the Peter B. Gustavson School of Business, University of Victoria.

Janne Tienari is Visiting Professor at the Stockholm Business School, Stockholm University.

Paul Tracey is Professor of Innovation & Organisation in the Judge Business School, University of Cambridge.

Christine Quinn Trank is Associate Professor of the Practice of Organization Leadership, Vanderbilt University.

Mary Tripsas is Associate Professor at the Carrol School Of Management, Boston College.

Eero Vaara is Professor of Organization and Management at Aalto University School of Business.

Daan van Knippenberg is Professor of Organizational Behavior at Rotterdam School of Management, Erasmus University.

Cees B. M. van Riel is Professor of Corporate Communication at Rotterdam School of Management, Erasmus University.

Lee Watkiss is a PhD student at the Carrol School of Management, Boston College.

Tony J. Watson is Emeritus Professor at the University of Nottingham.

Mirjam D. Werner is Assistant Professor in the Business-Society Management Department at Rotterdam School of Management, Erasmus University.

David A. Whetten is Professor of Organizational Studies at Brigham Young University.

Andrea Whittle is Professor of Management and Organization Studies at Newcastle University.

Hugh Willmott is Research Professor in Organisational at Cardiff Business School, Cardiff University.

Ezra Zuckerman is the Alvin J. Siteman Professor of Strategy and Entrepreneurship at MIT Sloan School of Management.

INTRODUCTION:
ORGANIZATIONAL IDENTITY

mapping where we have been,
where we are, and where we might go

MICHAEL G. PRATT, MAJKEN SCHULTZ,
BLAKE E. ASHFORTH, AND DAVIDE RAVASI

WHAT happens when you take one of the most fundamental concepts in social science and apply it to one of the most ubiquitous forms of human collectives? This handbook strives to answer this question by exploring what has become a "root construct" (Albert, Ashforth, and Dutton, 2000: 13) in our field: organizational identity (OI). From its rich heritage in the fields of psychology (e.g., Erikson, 1968), social psychology (e.g., Tajfel and Turner, 1979; Brewer and Gardner, 1996) and sociology (e.g., Mead, 1934; Goffman, 1959), the concept of identity has travelled to organization studies. While the term itself is credited to Albert and Whetten's (1985) *Research in Organizational Behavior* chapter by the same name, similar notions have been part of our field for a very long time. To illustrate, some scholars have noted similarities between OI and Selznick's (1948) notion of "organizational character" (see also Phillips, Tracey, and Kraatz, Ch. 19). The term "identity" has been used more directly, albeit briefly, in relation to organizations as well. One classic example can be found in Zald and Denton's (1963: 233, emphasis ours) work on the evolution of the YMCA:

> These changes, if and when they come, may require changes in the financial structure of the organization and in the recruitment of staff... They may also affect the *basic identity of at least part of the organization*, and are likely to be resisted by staff and boards alike.

Echoes of OI also resound in Clark's (1972: 183, emphasis ours) discussion of organizational sagas, especially more bottom-up views of the concept; here he notes, "With

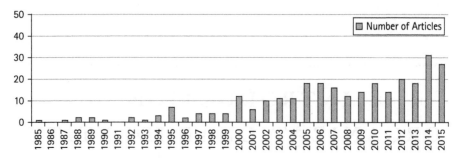

FIGURE 0.1 Peer-reviewed articles, dissertations, and theses on organizational identity from 1985 to 2015

Business Source Complete, ProQuest Dissertations, and Theses Global

deep emotional commitment, believers define themselves by their organizational affiliation, *and in their bond to other believers they share an intense sense of the unique.*"

Since its conceptualization as a concept in its own right in 1985, there has been a proliferation of scholarly treatments of "organizational identity." To get a conservative count of its growth, we examined peer-reviewed journal articles, dissertations, and theses appearing in Business Source Complete, ProQuest Dissertations, and Theses Global (see Figure 0.1) that had the terms "organizational identity" in either their titles or abstracts. As noted in this figure, despite a slow start, research in OI has grown over the years, with most interest occurring since the turn of the century. The steady rise since that time may have been due, at least in part, to a special issue on "Organizational Identity and Identification" in the *Academy of Management Review* in 2000. In addition, during this time, there have been many book chapters, books, and dissertations dedicated to identity in organizations and organizational identity more specifically.

Apart from articles directly on the topic, OI research has played a bigger role in influencing research on a variety of topics in a number of disciplines. Indeed, type "organizational identity" as a single concept into Google Scholar with a range from 1985 to 2015, and you will get about 16,800 hits, not only in organizational theory, but also in studies of organization behavior, corporate communication, marketing, and related fields.

With this growth, we've also seen a dizzying array of how OI is conceptualized, how it is managed, how it forms and changes, and what the implications of its existence (real or metaphorical) are for everything ranging from navigating an organization's place within broader institutions, to its role in establishing a firm's strategic focus, to its use in leadership and in capturing—or alienating—the hearts and minds of employees. The term is also being "appropriated" (albeit not consistently) in other theoretical traditions, such as population ecology and institutional theory, as well as by practitioners in areas such as corporate branding, corporate identity and values-based management, and onboarding. The Gallup organization, for example, now promises to help you with problems stemming from your organization's identity (http://www.gallup.com/services/170918/organizational-identity.aspx [last accessed March 10, 2016]).

Here OI is conceived as a fundamental concept underpinning "purpose, culture and brand." While in our field this description may be more akin to corporate identity, it nonetheless reminds us how OI connects with other concepts central to organizations. What makes the notion of OI so appealing? We believe there are at least four related reasons.

First, we believe that OI is appealing because it addresses an *essential question of social existence: Who are we as a collective?* All major branches of social sciences (including anthropology, sociology, political science, psychology—and even economics, e.g., Akerlof and Kranton, 2000), as well as philosophy and other areas of the humanities address the issue of identity. And most (if not all) also talk about the identity of a collective, be it a nation (or state or city), demographic group, or constituent group. Even mathematics refers to the relationship between or among some variables in terms of identity (e.g., trigonometric or exponential identities).

At its core, *organizational* identity is about how a collective defines itself. To "define" can mean to "to determine or identify the essential qualities or meaning of" or it can mean to "to fix or mark the limits of" (http://www.merriam-webster.com/dictionary/define [last accessed March 10, 2016]). Organizational scholars have taken both meanings to heart. In terms of the first use of "defining," some conceptualizations focus on what members believe is the core, distinctive, and more or less enduring characteristics of their organization. In terms of the second, other conceptualizations of OI focus more on the categories organizations claim to signal similarity or differences (or both—see Zuckerman, this volume, Ch. 10) from others in their institutional environment. In this usage, the clarity and porousness of the boundaries between categories are seen as important. The first way to define OI has been central to social constructivist conceptualizations of OI, while the second way has been used more by institutionalists, sociologists, and those adopting a social actor perspective (see Gioia and Hamilton, this volume, Ch. 1; Foreman and Whetten, this volume, Ch. 2).

Although the core question of "how does a collective define itself?" has remained the same since OI took hold in organizational studies, the answers to the question keep changing as organizations are continuously faced with new stakeholders, new members, and new circumstances for creating meaningful distinctions vis-à-vis other organizations. Indeed, one fundamental trend we noted in this handbook is that there has been movement away from viewing OI as a metaphor or as a relatively fixed property of an organization, toward a more process-oriented view (see Schultz, this volume, Ch. 5). That is, scholars are increasingly viewing identity over time, and noting the steps organizations have to take, not only to change conceptualizations of who they are, but also to create and maintain them (e.g., Cornelissen, Haslam, and Werner, this volume, Ch. 11; Kreiner and Murphy, this volume, Ch. 15; Suddaby, Foster, and Quinn Trank, this volume, Ch. 16; DeJordy and Creed, this volume, Ch. 20).

Second, *organizational identity is at its heart a relational construct* connecting concepts, ideas, and fields—even those that are often viewed as oppositional or antithetical, such as "past" and "future," "similar" and "different," "us" and "them". The relational nature of OI is found with respect to others, to time, and to levels of analysis.

Drawing on early conceptualizations by G. H. Mead (1934) of interrelations between the "I" and the "me," OI emerges from relations between "us" and "them," as further developed, for example, in the organizational dynamics model by Hatch and Schultz (2002) and by Pratt (2012). This interrelation has sensitized OI research to investigate relations with *others* via perceived images (i.e., how are we perceived by them?), as demonstrated in the classic study by Dutton and Dukerich (1991). Turning within the organization, exploring the relationships among members has prompted a closer look at the links between identity and culture (see also Ravasi, this volume, Ch. 3). Here, identity serves to bridge internal and external notions of the collective, in at least partial service to helping the collective communicate both its similarities and differences with other collectives. OI is also suspended in *time* between who we were and who we are becoming as an organization, and recent contributions have begun to unpack how past, present, and future identities are intertwined (see, for example Anteby and Molnár, 2012, and Schultz and Hernes, 2013, as well as Suddaby et al., Ch. 16).

OI also links different *levels of analysis* (see Ashforth, this volume, Ch. 4). Indeed, the concept of OI links institutional dynamics with those within the organization (e.g., DeJordy and Creed, Ch. 20; Besharov and Brickson, this volume, Ch. 21), as well as between organizations and their members (Petriglieri and Devine, this volume, Ch. 13; Elsbach and Dukerich, this volume, Ch. 14) and other stakeholders (Bartel, Baldi, and Dukerich, this volume, Ch. 25).

Third, and similarly, OI is also appealing as it serves as a *nexus concept*. A nexus can be something that links things together, as well as a central meeting place. Again, OI relates to both uses of the term. In our second point we noted how the relational nature of OI suspends the concept between seemingly antithetical constructs. Here we show how OI also serves as a "place" where other theories can meet and "hang out."

It is amazing how many theories have become associated with and inspired by OI. A very partial list includes sensemaking, institutional logics, theories of power and politics, cultural theories, theories of threat and threat response, theories of strategy and strategizing, mergers and acquisitions, metaphors, materiality, communication, history and memory, leadership, pluralism, innovation, identification, and organizational change. Also, research on OI has attracted scholars with different ontologies and epistemologies (Ravasi and Canato, 2013), as well as those who utilize inductive and deductive, quantitative and qualitative methods (Foreman and Whetten, Ch. 2). This richness in the conceptualization and empirical elaboration of OI is reflected across the sections in the handbook, as we deliberately invited authors who have expanded the identity concept by scrutinizing its connections to other concepts or phenomena, and showed its broad relevance to organization studies. Several chapters develop the associations between identity and significant other concepts from organization studies, such as power and politics (Kenny, Whittle, and Willmott, this volume, Ch. 8), critical theory (Alvesson and Robertson, this volume, Ch. 9), communication and employee identification (Schinoff, Rogers, and Corley, this volume, Ch. 12), theories of threat and response (Petriglieri and Devine, Ch. 13), leadership (van Knippenberg, this volume, Ch. 18), as well as narratives and discourse analysis (Tienari and Vaara, Ch. 24).

Finally, we believe that OI is appealing because it is *inherently useful*. As often stated by practitioners when they turn to identity questions, knowing who you are is the foundation for being able to state what you stand for and what you are promising to others, no matter their relationship with the organization. As such, OI underpins everything from strategic direction to what organizations communicate about themselves and what they consider to be central and distinctive about their products and services, as exemplified by the Apple story in Chapter 17 on materiality and identity by Watkiss and Glynn. In more general terms, OI is powerful because it has a pragmatic function in organizations, as argued by Watson (this volume, Ch. 7) in his elaboration of what makes OI a valuable analytical resource.

Indeed, even in early uses of the concept, OI has been helpful for organizational members in making sense of and responding to a variety of dilemmas they face, such as how managers handled the presence of homeless patrons in Port Authority buildings (Dutton and Dukerich, 1991), or how the managers of Bang & Olufsen on numerous occasions turned to a redefinition of their OI as a source of renewed competitiveness (Ravasi and Schultz, 2006). As we see in the handbook, OI can be useful in navigating a variety of organizational threats, challenges, and dilemmas. Anthony and Tripsas (this volume, Ch. 22) demonstrate the profound importance of OI to innovation, drawing on examples of both failure and success. Other chapters show how managers deliberately seek to influence OI to attain valued goals. Examples include planned efforts to change identity claims (as shown by Bhatt, van Riel, and Baumann, this volume, Ch. 23), often to enhance identification among stakeholders (Bartel, Baldi, and Dukerich Ch. 25), and attempts to reconstruct identity anew following a comprehensive merger and acquisition in order to reduce ambiguity and uncertainty (Tienari and Vaara Ch. 24).

Integrating some of these points, OI has been particularly useful in understanding how different groups, as well as different conceptualizations of "who we are," relate to each other within the same organization. As noted by Kenny et al. (Ch. 8), any sense of a "unified" OI is likely the outcome of power and politics—that is, out of contestation. Thus, many scholars suggest that organizations may be viewed as having multiple identities (Pratt, this volume, Ch. 6). At times, these identities may conflict. Indeed, early work in social identity theory arose to meet the need to understand intergroup conflict (Tajfel and Turner, 1979). In organizations, identity has also been viewed at the heart of group conflict. For example, identity and conflict have been illustrated in disagreements over how nurses dealt with an increase in patient acuity and their interactions with physicians (Pratt and Rafaeli, 1997); how board members dealt with managers over budget issues in a non-profit organization (Golden-Biddle and Rao, 1997); how musicians and managers negotiated a strike in a symphony orchestra (Glynn, 2000); and how members of a food co-operative managed both the idealistic and pragmatic nature of their organization (Ashforth and Reingen, 2014). In particular, research suggests that conflicts over resources, both tangible and abstract, become bound up in identity, making it very difficult to manage the conflict that ensues (Fiol, Pratt, and O'Connor, 2009; Pratt, Fiol, O'Connor, and Panico, 2012).

Even when multiple organizational identities do not directly conflict, they still require attention and effort to manage (Pratt and Foreman, 2000). But no matter the specific circumstances, reading chapters across the handbook will expand our knowledge about how different ways of expressing identity—using narratives, stories, values, and claims—are forceful ways of influencing and engaging both internal and external stakeholders.

A Roadmap to Organizational Identity

Our handbook is meant to raise the major issues and topics that have been associated with OI, as well as point to where OI research may go in the future. In particular, our seven sections mirror the field, writ small: providing a present-day review that is both backward glancing and future facing. We begin by providing a roadmap of our handbook, and then talk about the handbook in light of the field at large.

Mapping the Organizational Identity Field

Section 1, "Mapping," is meant to provide the "big picture" regarding the theoretical and methodological challenges facing the field, as well as to provide a deep-dive on some central themes that undergird the rest of the handbook.

In Chapter 1, Gioia and Hamilton tackle the epistemological and ontological debates that have emerged around OI in the past thirty years. Ontologically, they tackle the issue of whether OI really exists: is it a "thing," a process, both, or none of the above? Epistemologically, these scholars trace the emergence of the social actor versus social construction perspective on OI and add to this mix an institutional one. The authors end with their take on how to resolve these debates. To whet your appetites for one solution, we'll leave you with one word: gerund.

Chapter 2 by Foreman and Whetten complements the preceding one by exploring the variety of methods that have been used to "capture" OI. Through an analysis of 82 OI-related articles culled from ABI Inform and EBSCO, the authors were able to identify clusters of articles that differed on their measurement/methods as well as their conceptual/theoretical lenses. As with the Gioia and Hamilton article, Foreman and Whetten touch upon how OI is conceptualized in these articles—not just how it was measured—and note a strong relationship between the two. They conclude that, unlike many fields in science that move from primarily qualitative research to quantitative, the reverse is happening for OI. They also note that the qualitative research employed tends to focus on OI exclusively (rather than OI and other concepts) and tends to focus only on a single organization. They conclude by discussing what they view as the implications of this trend for the field of OI, as well as their preferred future directions. Is their outlook bright or bleak? We suggest reading this chapter along with those in Section 2 in order to more fully understand the challenges scholars see to the development of research in OI.

This section concludes with four "mini-chapters" written by the handbook editors. Building on what makes OI such an attractive and powerful force in organizational scholarship, these selections each highlight central themes that are often implicit in our chapters.

To begin, Ravasi (Ch. 3) tackles nomological issues inherent in OI—specifically how the concept is similar to and different from organizational culture and organizational image. He underlines a general distinction between OI as an internal set of beliefs and understandings and organizational image as an external set of perceptions and representations, and briefly reviews other types of organizational images (construed, desired, projected) described in previous research. He argues in favor of considering OI and culture as separate constructs (a distinction questioned by Alvesson and Robertson in Ch. 9), and shows how the empirical examination of their interrelations improves our understanding of change and stability in organizations.

While much is known about identity dynamics within levels of analysis (e.g., organization, subunit, individual), far less is known about between-level dynamics, thus impeding the development of a systemic or holistic model of identity in organizations. Chapter 4, by Ashforth, examines how an OI emerges from founder(s)/leaders' initial conceptions of what the organization is or can be, and how this identity in turn both enables and constrains the subunit and individual identities nested within it. The result is a recursive system that experiences dynamic tension between stability (when identity constrains) and change (when identity enables). The ongoing "bottom-up" and "top-down" dynamics reflect a blend of processes that are supplementary (fleshing out an initial or abstract identity), complementary (fostering differentiation to reflect a complex internal and external reality), and conflicted (when actors contest an identity).

The chapter by Schultz (Ch. 5) focuses on identity change: how does identity change and what about identity changes? Since its early conception as "enduring," debates about identity change have been central to the field, and the chapter outlines three views of OI change: 1) Identity as enduring stability; 2) Identity as periodic change and 3) Identity as ongoing change. The chapter argues how recent developments toward temporal- and process-based views return to a focus on the continuity provided by OI, exploring the simultaneous existence of continuity and change.

The first section concludes with Pratt's chapter (Ch. 6), which talks explicitly about the role of plurality of organizational identities. In particular, he distinguishes between two different conceptualizations of such plurality: hybrid organizational identities and multiple organizational identities. He argues that the former deals with two opposing identities that may be structured within or between groups. The latter conceptualization, however, simply argues that organizations can have multiple identities, and that these identities need not be oppositional (e.g., they can be complementary). He compares and contrasts research from these conceptualizations, as well as a central ongoing challenge for work in this area.

Critical Perspectives on Organizational Identity

Whereas Section 1 staked out the foundations of OI research, Section 2 sets out to make those very foundations problematic.

In Chapter 7, Watson suggests that OI is perhaps best viewed as a pragmatic tool for helping scholars understand how individuals relate to their organizations. Going back to Albert and Whetten's (1985) conceptualization, he notes how the concept came from trying to understand how a group of individuals in an organization came to overreact to a relatively minor budget cut. From a pragmatic perspective, he suggests caution in viewing OI in terms of correct "definitions," and caution in how we deploy such terms. For example, personifying an organization by calling attention to its "identity" treats organizations as homogeneous and unitary and thus covers up diversity, power contestation, and conflict. Echoing the process-sentiments of later chapters (e.g., Kreiner and Murphy, Ch. 15), he suggests instead focusing on OI work that considers how organizational identities "arise out of the negotiated order of relationships between the various constituencies inside and outside of the organization upon which the organization is dependent for its long-term existence" (see also DeJordy and Creed, Ch. 20).

The dangers of unitary conceptualizations of OI are further raised by Kenny et al. (Ch. 8). Indeed, these authors insightfully argue that the term "OI" itself may be misleading as it de-emphasizes the differing and sometimes discordant views of "who we are" as an organization. In short, to the degree that organizations claim to have a unified identity, such a claim is the result of an exercise of power within the organization. Drawing on work by renowned social and political theorists such as Foucault, Lukes, Laclau, and Mouffe, these scholars make a strong case for better understanding the political and power dynamics that underlie OI. Illustrating their arguments with the branding of a business school, they show how different practices bound up in the formation of the school depict different dimensions of power as well hegemony.

This section ends with the most broad-based critique of the identity field in our handbook. Here, Alvesson and Robertson (Ch. 9) question fundamental taken-for-granted assumptions inherent in scholars' treatment of OI, and in doing so not only raise issues similar to others in this section (e.g., issues of power and reification of OI), but other concerns such as the nature of the relationship between OI and member identification, and OI and organizational culture. They offer several propositions for advancing research in OI in light of its shortcomings, including advocating for a more process-based view of OI, for greater immersion in organizations when studying OI, for a greater integration of politics, power, and culture in OI studies, as well as for exploring a wider range of organizations in OI research (e.g., non-celebrity and non-tainted organizations).

Integrative Models of Organizational Identity

Section 3 ponders how organizations settle on an overarching OI, given the myriad possibilities that exist. In particular, the two chapters in this section propose models that both incorporate and ultimately transcend different perspectives on how OI works and develops.

Zuckerman (Ch. 10) begins with the intriguing question, why do organizations and individuals alike strive to balance *conformity* to the practices of other actors with *differentiation* from them? While optimal distinctiveness theory argues that actors seek to balance a need for inclusion (conformity) with a need for exclusiveness (differentiation), and different audience theory argues that actors face institutional audiences (who want conformity) and market audiences (who want differentiation), Zuckerman argues for a third approach that is richer and yet more parsimonious than either of the other two, namely two-stage valuation theory. In a nutshell, audiences that ostensibly want differentiation actually want conformity on *most* of an actor's salient characteristics (to show that the actor is a bona fide member of whatever social category is in play, such as a bank or charter school), along with differentiation on select characteristics (to better address the audience's particular desires). Thus, the "two-stage valuation" refers to an initial judgment of conformity (do they exemplify the social category?), followed by a judgment of value-added (do they address my desires better than other members of the category?). Zuckerman concludes that, whether at the organizational or individual level of analysis, the tension between conformity and differentiation is not about the internal needs of the actor but about the external needs of the audience and the resources they can provide.

Reconciling the social constructionist, social identity, and social actor perspectives into a single, parsimonious model of OI formation and change is the ambitious goal of Cornelissen, Haslam, and Werner (Ch. 11). They argue that a root metaphor is associated with each perspective and that, when linked, the three metaphors provide the foundation for a processual model of OI formation. Specifically, social constructionism suggests a framing metaphor wherein individuals jointly, albeit tentatively, define who they are. The result may be a diverse set of loosely coupled frames that jostle for prominence. As consensus emerges, the prevailing frames increasingly shape action and sensemaking. In turn, social identity theory suggests a categorizing metaphor wherein the prevailing frames crystallize into seemingly more objective groupings demarcated with clearer boundaries. Individuals who exemplify a particular category are given license to engage in sense*giving*, reinforcing the categories. Finally, the social actor perspective suggests a personification metaphor wherein human-like characteristics and propensities are attributed to the organization. Over time, one particular category is likely to prevail as "the" OI and become embedded in roles, routines, and rituals. Whereas OI under social constructionism is explicitly subjective, OI under the social actor perspective is more objective and taken-for-granted, suggesting a process of gradual objectification. Nonetheless, an objective OI can be problematized by stakeholders, presumably triggering iterations of the three perspectives. Cornelissen et al. dub their provocative argument the "social interactionist model of organizational identity formation and change."

How Individuals Relate to Organizational Identity

An organization's identity is enacted by members of the organization, and has implications for how members come to see themselves and how members' actions may in turn affect the OI. Section 5 includes three varied perspectives on how individuals relate to the OI.

An assumption in much of the literature is that perceptions of OI are more or less shared by organizational members. Schinoff et al. (Ch. 12) posit the crucial question, how do we actually communicate who we are? Focusing on identity custodians, "individuals seen as communicating identity content on behalf of the organization," Schinoff and her colleagues argue that there are three primary means of communicating OI: (1) *saying*, sending a verbal or written message, as through one-on-one conversations and mass communications (e.g., email, annual reports); (2) *showing*, modeling behaviors or displaying artifacts (e.g., physical setting, company products); and (3) *staging*, choreographing a context in which members can experience or enact the OI (e.g., via roles, rituals, routines). Schinoff et al. then formulate a 2x2 based on identity custodians' understanding of the OI (low versus high) and custodians' intentional communication of the OI (low versus high). The authors argue that there are pros and cons attached to each of the resulting four cells, including—counterintuitively—cons of articulating OI (e.g., overwriting the OI on personal identities, thereby sowing confusion if custodians disagree) and pros of not doing so (e.g., preserving strategic ambiguity, thereby allowing members to buy in via filling in the gaps; enabling identity at other levels to appropriately dominate, as in the occupational identity of stylists in a hair salon).

How do the perceptions and responses of organizational members to an OI threat affect the wider organization's response to the threat? Petriglieri and Devine (Ch. 13) note that threats to the way that members see the organization come from both internal events (e.g., change initiatives, scandals) and external events (e.g., environmental turbulence, negative publicity). They argue that unless a threat to the organization's identity is also a threat to the individual's identity (as when individuals identify with their employer), then the individual is unlikely to be sufficiently motivated to respond. The authors make the important point that not all members see the OI or the "threat" in the same way, necessitating that frontline members mobilize consensus and support for action via bottom-up processes, and that senior managers mobilize via top-down processes. The analysis closes with provocative directions for research, such as: distinguishing between responses that *protect* the threatened OI from those that *change* it; examining how the organization's response to a threat may in itself constitute a threat (as when members disagree with senior managers' actions); and exploring the potentially positive consequences of OI threat.

An OI has implications for how organizational members see themselves. Elsbach and Dukerich (Ch. 14) close this section by pondering what happens when an organization imposes an identity on members that is undesired. Specifically, in pursuing an OI that is legitimate and distinctive, an organization may require individuals to adopt role- or group-based identities that are antithetical to how the individuals see themselves. For example, artistic workers such as designers and architects may be required to enact the role of pragmatic corporate professional. Because individuals are necessarily tethered to their roles and groups, Elsbach and Dukerich argue that the most viable defensive response is to reframe the *meaning* of the imposed identity. This is accomplished through either redefining the meaning of the role or group (e.g., seeing oneself as a rebel) or demonstrating non-investment in the role or group (e.g., signaling that one's role enactment is insincere). The authors highlight intriguing research questions, such as what happens when individuals understand the organizational need for the undesired identity, thus fostering ambivalence.

Sources and Processes of Organizational Identity

How do organizations engage in identity reconstruction? What are the resources deployed by actors when engaging in such processes? These are the questions that have guided the chapters in Section 5, which shows how studies of OI have turned to more process-based and temporally informed views as OI is increasingly conceived as a never ending "work-in-progress."

The notion of "identity work" has had significant impact at the individual level of analysis, but has only more recently been taken to the organizational level—enhancing the relational nature of OI. The chapter by Kreiner and Murphy (Ch. 15) conceptualizes OI work by drawing on both insights from individual-level analysis and relating to other kinds of "agentic work," such as boundary work and institutional work. Acknowledging the multiplicity of definitions at all levels, the authors go to great lengths explaining the conceptual underpinning of their definition of "organizational identity work as comprising discursive, cognitive, and behavioral processes that help individuals and collectives create, sustain, share, and/or change organizational identity." This definition, in turn, suggests how organizational members, by engaging in processes of identity work, transform the content of identity—although the authors also explore how both institutional and boundary work influence the conditions for organizational identity work. In addition, they encourage an exploration of other kinds of "work" in relation to OI, such as the work of remembering and/or forgetting who we were as an organization.

The relationship between language and history in identity work is the focus of the following chapter by Suddaby et al. (Ch. 16), adding narrations of collective history and memory to the conceptualization of identity work. Referring to several empirical studies on how history has been "re-Membered" in organizations across time, the authors argue how grounding OI narratives in organizational history makes them more powerful in persuading stakeholders to identify with the organization. They suggest the term "rhetorical history" to stress managerial agency in the narrative use of history, tapping into the collective memory of the organizations. They argue that the inclusion of historical narratives in identity work not only paves the way for rhetorical identification processes, but also serves as a resource of competitiveness in drawing distinctions from others.

The importance of OI to competitiveness is also a theme of the next chapter by Watkiss and Glynn (this volume, Ch. 17) in that they illustrate the influence of materiality on OI via the success of Apple. The authors argue that identity not only emerges from collective self-definitions about "who we are," but also derive from "what we do." Whereas the preceding chapters emphasize the discursive, cognitive, and rhetorical resources of identity work, this chapter introduces the importance of materiality to OI, as manifested in artifacts, products, and practices. Using illustrations from the development of the identity of Apple, the authors argue how these forms of materiality contribute to the shaping of OI construction via processes defined as categorization, symbolization, and repertoires for performance. In arguing the importance of materiality to OI, the chapter also elaborates the relations with organizational culture and its early interest in symbols and artifacts, among other qualities.

No matter the resources underpinning OI, the above chapters all assume the presence of leadership without making this the topic of their conceptual contribution. In contrast, the chapter by van Knippenberg (Ch. 18) makes how leaders give sense to OI the focus of inquiry. The chapter departs from the assumption that leaders work to communicate a desired understanding of OI and further explores what enables leaders to change organizational members' understanding of OI. The chapter stresses the importance of credibility and legitimacy to identity leadership, but in particular suggests that the ability of a leader to embody the perceived shared identity—or to be group prototypical—serves as an important foundation for a leader's potential to give sense to the ways in which organizational members make sense of their OI. In the conception of group prototypicality the author relies on social identity theory and theories of categorization, showing how theorizing OI leadership comprises multiple levels of analysis, a point also discussed by Ashforth in Chapter 4.

Identity and the Organization's Environment

How do members' understandings of "who we are" as an organization draw on resources from the broader environment? And how do these understandings influence how they interpret and respond to environmental changes? This is what the three chapters in Section 6 examine.

In their chapter, Phillips, Tracey, and Kraatz (Ch. 19) examine how the concept of OI has been used by institutional theorists over time. First, they remind us about the important intellectual legacy of Phillip Selznick and his idea that some organizations acquire a distinctive "character"—Selznick's equivalent of OI—through complex social and political processes and a history of commitments to a core set of values. Second, they point out how organizational identities may draw on socially constructed "collective identities," institutionalized understandings that organizations share similarity in important characteristics and belong to the same type and "category" (an issue also touched by Zuckerman in Ch. 10). Finally, they draw attention to how "institutional entrepreneurs" can forge new organizational identities by combining elements from different institutional logics, understood as different coherent sets of organizational principles characterizing different domains such as commerce, charity, the family, or the arts.

Why do people construct identities for organizations? This is the question that DeJordy and Creed (Ch. 20) address in the second chapter of this section. Organizational identities, they convincingly argue, help us fulfill personal identity projects, as affiliation with organizations that claim particular values help us make sense of our own identity and give sense of it to others, by expressing a "commonality of values." Organizations—they point out—are constantly facing pluralistic demands from their environment, reflecting the different identity projects of their constituents. Members are therefore engaged in an ongoing construction and reconstruction of the OI in order to address these demands. The result of their effort, DeJordy and Creed claim, is a particular organizational "self" (Pratt and Kraatz, 2012) that connects and prioritizes identities, addressing the demands of different constituents. Building on these ideas, they develop a multilevel model linking the individual, organizational, and institutional level of analysis, and use a comparative analysis of OI in three different Christian denominations to illustrate their ideas.

Finally, Besharov and Brickson (Ch. 21) address the apparent contradiction between theories proposing that organizational identities are shaped by institutional forces and those that emphasize members' agency in socially constructing the identity of their organization, possibly drawing on institutional "building blocks." They propose that these two positions correspond to the extreme ends of a continuum, and that the content and structure of both OI and institutional forces will influence the actual nature of their interaction. By content, Besharov and Brickson refer to the particular answers that members give to the self-defining question "who are we as an organization?", and the particular demands imposed by institutional forces; by structure, they refer to the degree of alignment among multiple identities and pluralistic demands. When the content of identities is more aligned with the content of demands, they argue, organizations will be more responsive to these demands, but also less flexible in their interpretation of them, shifting to the more constrained end of the continuum. They conclude their chapter by discussing potential avenues for further research based on the idea of OI acting as an interpretive filter for institutional demands.

Implications of Organizational Identity

The last section of the handbook focuses on the implications of OI, highlighting the relevance of identity to what goes on in and around organizations.

The first chapter by Anthony and Tripsas (Ch. 22) explores the neglected relation between innovation and OI by looking at both how identity influences the direction of innovative activities, and, in turn, how those activities influence the further evolution of OI. However, the authors argue that innovative activities do not have the same influence on OI, which is developed in the distinctions between identity-enhancing, identity-stretching, and identity-challenging activities. Although innovation is rarely pursued with the explicit aspiration to change OI, the authors show how identity and innovation in reality reinforce each other, leading to periodic identity change as the organization sets out to pursue new innovative paths.

The next chapter by Bhatt, van Riel, and Baumann (Ch. 23) takes a more explicit focus on how leaders embark on planned OI change. Drawing on insights from a successful planned change in OI claims in a Dutch funeral services organization, the authors point out how planned change is directed at both internal and external audiences. In particular, they stress how internal identity change implies that employees must be aligned with the new set of identity claims by being informed, motivated, and capable of realizing the new identity. By the same token, creating awareness and attractiveness of the new set of identity claims among external audiences is a condition for the identity change to be embraced and enacted. Although the authors illustrate their arguments with a successful example of planned identity change, they also discuss a number of contextual conditions and challenges to identity change in relation to its practical implementation.

In the following chapter, Tienari and Vaara (Ch. 24) look closer at the implications of OI during mergers and acquisitions, focusing on how organizations and organizational members engage in self-definitions during such extreme organizational change. The authors discuss how organizational members evoke and apply a variety of cultural and discursive resources in order to construct, transform, and on some occasions deconstruct definitions of OI. The authors point to new ways of connecting identity to culture in that they go beyond the dominant focus on power and cultural clashes to explain how mergers develop—and often fail. Instead they suggest how organizational culture provides "language-based means," such as stereotypes and narratives, which are used by organizational members in making sense of who they are, as a merger unfolds. This in turn influences the extent to which organizational members are able and willing to identify with the newly merged organization. Such collective constructions of new self-definitions are conceived as processes of discursive sensemaking, demonstrating how sensemaking—and in particular its discursive foundation—is salient to

OI, not only in its theoretical development, but also in relation to how identity is being practiced in organizations.

While the above chapters mostly address the implications of OI in relation to internal stakeholders, the last chapter (Ch. 25) by Bartel, Baldi, and Dukerich focuses on external stakeholders, elaborating the conceptual relations between OI and organizational image. The chapter explores what makes external stakeholders feel a sense of belonging to the organization, defined as when the organization becomes important to stakeholders' sense of self. Departing from the explosion in social media and online-based mass communication, the authors discuss how organizations translate and communicate their internally held OI into an organizational image attractive enough to create stakeholder identification. They suggest three motivational forces that encourage external stakeholders to identify with the organization: the perceived legitimacy of the OI influencing stakeholder uncertainty; the extent to which the communicated identity fits a continuation of the stakeholders' perception of self; and finally how the esteem and desirability of the OI may or may not enhance the self-esteem among external stakeholders.

Conclusion

While each section of our handbook addresses an important area in OI research, they together may be viewed as questions a growing field asks itself. Indeed, you can view the succession of chapters and sections as addressing the following about OI: "Who are we (as a field)?" "How did we get here?" "What is our place in the larger world?" and "Why does it matter?" If OI tells us anything, it is that while the questions remain, the answers are in flux. Thus, our handbook, like OI itself, should be viewed as a roadmap of what has happened in the last 30 years (post- Albert and Whetten [1985], at least), as well as for what may happen in the next 30 and beyond. This stream of research continues to flow. Join us in mapping where we have been, where we are, and where we might yet go.

References

Akerlof, G. A. and Kranton, R. E. (2000). "Economics and Identity." *Quarterly Journal of Economics* 115(3): 715–53.

Albert, S., Ashforth, B. E., and Dutton, J. E. (2000). "Organizational Identity and Identification: Charting New Waters and Building New Bridges." *Academy of Management Review* 25(1): 13–17.

Albert, S. and Whetten, D. A. (1985). "Organizational Identity." *Research in Organizational Behavior* 7: 263–95.

Alvesson, M. and Robertson, M. (2016). "Organizational Identity: A Critique." In *The Oxford Handbook of Organizational Identity*, edited by M. G. Pratt, M. Schultz, B. E. Ashforth, and D. Ravasi, 160–80. Oxford: Oxford University Press.

Anteby, M. and Molnár, V. (2012). "Collective Memory Meets Organizational Identity: Remembering to Forget in a Firm's Rhetorical History." *Academy of Management Journal* 55(3): 515–40.

Anthony, C. and Tripsas, M. (2016). "Organizational Identity and Innovation." In *The Oxford Handbook of Organizational Identity*, edited by M. G. Pratt, M. Schultz, B. E. Ashforth, and D. Ravasi, 417–35. Oxford: Oxford University Press.

Ashforth, B. E. (2016). "Organizational, Subunit, and Individual Identities." In *The Oxford Handbook of Organizational Identity*, edited by M. G. Pratt, M. Schultz, B. E. Ashforth, and D. Ravasi, 79–92. Oxford: Oxford University Press.

Ashforth, B. E. and Reingen, P. H. (2014). "Functions of Dysfunction: Managing the Dynamics of an Organizational Duality in a Natural Food Cooperative." *Administrative Science Quarterly* 59(3): 474–516.

Bartel, C., Bardi, C., and Dukerich, J. M. (2016). "Fostering Stakeholder Identification through Expressed Organizational Identities." In *The Oxford Handbook of Organizational Identity*, edited by M. G. Pratt, M. Schultz, B. E. Ashforth, and D. Ravasi, 474–93. Oxford: Oxford University Press.

Besharov, M. L. and Brickson, S. L. (2016). "Organizational Identity and Institutional Forces: Toward an Integrative Framework." In *The Oxford Handbook of Organizational Identity*, edited by M. G. Pratt, M. Schultz, B. E. Ashforth, and D. Ravasi, 396–414. Oxford: Oxford University Press.

Bhatt, M., van Riel, C. B. M., and Baumann, M. (2016). "Planned Organizational Identity Change: Insights from Practice." In *The Oxford Handbook of Organizational Identity*, edited by M. G. Pratt, M. Schultz, B. E. Ashforth, and D. Ravasi, 436–54. Oxford: Oxford University Press.

Brewer, M. B. and Gardner, W. (1996). "Who Is This 'We'? Levels of Collective Identity and Self Representations." *Journal of Personality and Social Psychology* 71(1): 83–93.

Clark, B. R. (1972). "The Organizational Saga in Higher Education." *Administrative Science Quarterly* 17(2): 178–84.

Cornelissen, J. P., Haslam, S. A., and Werner, M. D. (2016). "Bridging and Integrating Theories on Organizational Identity: A Social Interactionist Model of Organizational Identity Formation and Change." In *The Oxford Handbook of Organizational Identity*, edited by M. G. Pratt, M. Schultz, B. E. Ashforth, and D. Ravasi, 200–15. Oxford: Oxford University Press.

DeJordy, R. and Creed, W. E. D. (2016). "Institutional Pluralism, Inhabitants, and the Construction of Organizational and Personal Identities." In *The Oxford Handbook of Organizational Identity*, edited by M. G. Pratt, M. Schultz, B. E. Ashforth, and D. Ravasi, 374–95. Oxford: Oxford University Press.

Dutton, J. E. and Dukerich, J. M. (1991). "Keeping an Eye on the Mirror: Image and Identity in Organizational Adaptation." *Academy of Management Journal* 34(3): 517–54.

Elsbach, K. and Dukerich, J. M. (2016). "Organizational Identity and the Undesired Self." In *The Oxford Handbook of Organizational Identity*, edited by M. G. Pratt, M. Schultz, B. E. Ashforth, and D. Ravasi. 257–75. Oxford: Oxford University Press.

Erikson, E. H. (1968). *Identity: Youth and Crisis*. New York: W. W. Norton.

Fiol, C. M., Pratt, M. G., and O'Connor, E. J. (2009). "Managing Intractable Identity Conflicts." *Academy of Management Review* 34(1): 32–55.

Foreman, P. and Whetten, D. (2016). "Measuring Organizational Identity: Taking Stock and Looking Forward." In *The Oxford Handbook of Organizational Identity*, edited by M. G. Pratt, M. Schultz, B. E. Ashforth, and D. Ravasi, 39–64. Oxford: Oxford University Press.

Gioia, D. A. and Hamilton, A. L. (2016). "Great Debates in Organizational Identity Study." In *The Oxford Handbook of Organizational Identity*, edited by M. G. Pratt, M. Schultz, B. E. Ashforth, and D. Ravasi, 21–38. Oxford: Oxford University Press.

Glynn, M. A. (2000). "When Cymbals Become Symbols: Conflict over Organizational Identity within a Symphony Orchestra." *Organization Science* 11: 285–98.

Goffman, E. (1959). *The Presentation of Self in Everyday Life*. Garden City, NY: Doubleday.

Golden-Biddle, K. and Rao, H. (1997). "Breaches in the Boardroom: Organizational Identity and Conflicts of Commitment in a Nonprofit Organization." *Organization Science* 8(6): 593–611.

Hatch, M. J. and Schultz, M. (2002). "The Dynamics of Organizational Identity." *Human Relations* 55(8): 989–1017.

Kenny, K., Whittle, A., and Willmott, H. (2016). "Organizational Identity: The Significance of Power and Politics." In *The Oxford Handbook of Organizational Identity*, edited by M. G. Pratt, M. Schultz, B. E. Ashforth, and D. Ravasi, 140–59. Oxford: Oxford University Press.

Kreiner, G. E. and Murphy, C. (2016). "Organizational Identity Work." In *The Oxford Handbook of Organizational Identity*, edited by M. G. Pratt, M. Schultz, B. E. Ashforth, and D. Ravasi, 276–93. Oxford: Oxford University Press.

Mead, G. H. (1934). *Mind, Self, and Society: From the Standpoint of a Social Behaviorist*. Chicago, IL: University Chicago Press.

Petriglieri, J. and Devine, B. A. (2016). "Mobilizing Organizational Action against Identity Threats: The Role of Organizational Members' Perceptions and Responses." In *The Oxford Handbook of Organizational Identity*, edited by M. G. Pratt, M. Schultz, B. E. Ashforth, and D. Ravasi, 239–56. Oxford: Oxford University Press.

Phillips, N., Tracey, P., and Kraatz, M. (2016). "Organizational Identity in Institutional Theory: Taking Stock and Moving Forward." In *The Oxford Handbook of Organizational Identity*, edited by M. G. Pratt, M. Schultz, B. E. Ashforth, and D. Ravasi, 353–73. Oxford: Oxford University Press.

Pratt, M. (2012). "Rethinking Identity Construction Processes in Organizations: Three Questions to Consider." In *The Construction of Identity in and around Organizations*, edited by M. Schultz, S. McGuire, A. Langley, and H. Tsoukas, 21–50. Oxford: Oxford University Press.

Pratt, M. G. (2016). "Hybrid and Multiple Organizational Identities." In *The Oxford Handbook of Organizational Identity*, edited by M. G. Pratt, M. Schultz, B. E. Ashforth, and D. Ravasi, 106–20. Oxford: Oxford University Press.

Pratt, M. G., Fiol, C. M., O'Connor, E. J., and Panico, P. (2012). "Promoting Positive Change in Physician-Administrator Relationships: Lessons for Managing Intractable Identity Conflicts." In *Using a Positive Lens to Explore Social Change and Organizations: Building a Theoretical and Research Foundation*, edited by K. Golden-Biddle, and J. E. Dutton, 267–88. New York: Routledge, Taylor & Francis Group.

Pratt, M. G. and Foreman, P. O. (2000). "Classifying Managerial Responses to Multiple Organizational Identities." *Academy of Management Review* 25(1): 18–42.

Pratt, M. G. and Kraatz, M. S. (2009). "E Pluribus Unum: Multiple Identities and the Organizational Self." In *Exploring Positive Identities and Organizations: Building a Theoretical and Research Foundation*, edited by J. Dutton and L. Morgan Roberts, 385–410. New York: Routledge.

Pratt, M. G. and Rafaeli, A. (1997). "Organizational Dress as a Symbol of Multilayered Social Identities." *Academy of Management Journal* 40(4): 862–98.

Ravasi, D. (2016). "Organizational Identity, Culture, and Image." In *The Oxford Handbook of Organizational Identity*, edited by M. G. Pratt, M. Schultz, B. E. Ashforth, and D. Ravasi, 65–78. Oxford: Oxford University Press.

Ravasi, D. and Canato, A. (2013). "How Do I Know Who You Think You Are? A Review of Research Methods on Organizational Identity." *International Journal of Management Reviews* 15(2): 185–204.

Ravasi, D. and Schultz, M. (2006). "Responding to Organizational Identity Threats: Exploring the Role of Organizational Culture." *Academy of Management Journal* 49(3): 433–58.

Schinoff, B., Rogers, K., and Corley, K. G. (2016). "How Do We Communicate Who We Are? Examining How Organizational Identity Is Conveyed to Members." In *The Oxford Handbook of Organizational Identity*, edited by M. G. Pratt, M. Schultz, B. E. Ashforth, and D. Ravasi, 219–38. Oxford: Oxford University Press.

Schultz, M. (2016). "Organizational Identity Change and Temporality." In *The Oxford Handbook of Organizational Identity*, edited by M. G. Pratt, M. Schultz, B. E. Ashforth, and D. Ravasi, 93–105. Oxford: Oxford University Press.

Schultz, M., and Hernes, T. (2013). "A Temporal Perspective on Organizational Identity." *Organization Science* 24(1): 1–21.

Selznick, P. (1948). "Foundations of the Theory of Organization." *American Sociological Review*, 13(1): 25–35.

Suddaby, R., Foster, W., and Quinn Trank, C. (2016). "Re-Membering: Rhetorical History as Identity-Work." In *The Oxford Handbook of Organizational Identity*, edited by M. G. Pratt, M. Schultz, B. E. Ashforth, and D. Ravasi, 297–316. Oxford: Oxford University Press.

Tajfel, H. and Turner, J. C. (1979). "An Integrative Theory of Intergroup Conflict." In *The Social Psychology of Group Relations*, edited by W. G. Austin and S. Worchel, 33–47. Monterey, CA: Brooks-Cole.

Tienari, J. and Vaara, E. (2016). "Identity Construction in Mergers and Acquisitions: A Discursive Sensemaking Perspective." In *The Oxford Handbook of Organizational Identity*, edited by M. G. Pratt, M. Schultz, B. E. Ashforth, and D. Ravasi, 455–73. Oxford: Oxford University Press.

van Knippenberg, D. (2016). "Making Sense of Who We Are: Leadership and Organizational Identity." In *The Oxford Handbook of Organizational Identity*, edited by M. G. Pratt, M. Schultz, B. E. Ashforth, and D. Ravasi, 335–49. Oxford: Oxford University Press.

Watkiss, L. and Glynn, M. A. (2016). "Materiality and Identity: How Organizational Products, Artifacts, and Practices Instantiate Organizational Identity." In *The Oxford Handbook of Organizational Identity*, edited by M. G. Pratt, M. Schultz, B. E. Ashforth, and D. Ravasi, 317–34. Oxford: Oxford University Press.

Watson, T. J. (2016). "Organizational Identity and Organizational Identity Work as Valuable Analytical Resources." In *The Oxford Handbook of Organizational Identity*, edited by M. G. Pratt, M. Schultz, B. E. Ashforth, and D. Ravasi, 123–39. Oxford: Oxford University Press.

Zald, M. N. and Denton. P. (1963). "From Evangelism to General Service: The Transformation of the YMCA." *Administrative Science Quarterly* 8(2): 214–34.

Zuckerman, E. (2016). "Optimal Distinctiveness Revisited: An Integrative Framework for Understanding the Balance between Differentiation and Conformity in Individual and Organizational Identities." In *The Oxford Handbook of Organizational Identity*, edited by M. G. Pratt, M. Schultz, B. E. Ashforth, and D. Ravasi, 183–99. Oxford: Oxford University Press.

SECTION I

MAPPING THE ORGANIZATIONAL IDENTITY (OI) FIELD

CHAPTER 1

··

GREAT DEBATES IN ORGANIZATIONAL IDENTITY STUDY

··

DENNIS A. GIOIA AND AIMEE L. HAMILTON

GREAT debates take place over great issues. In academia the greatest issues often come down to basic philosophical considerations—and there are no greater philosophical fundamentals than those involving ontology, epistemology, and methodology. If we treat these imposing terms in their simplest guises, then ontology has to do with our assumptions about the nature of the beast we are studying, epistemology has to do with how we know the beast we are studying, and methodology has to do with the procedures we use to go about studying the beast. Of these grand notions, ontology and epistemology are clearly the weightier notions, because they are more foundational concepts and in many ways govern the methodologies invoked. Organizational identity, as an important and maturing area of organization study, is not immune from debates about these issues (see Foreman and Whetten, Ch. 2, this volume). As a now central domain in our field, perhaps we would only be surprised if there were not some lively debates in the field involving these issues.

Historically speaking, there have been a number of great debates in the organizational identity literature. Undoubtedly the most basic of these debates is, "Is there such a thing as *organizational* identity? Or is the notion just linguistic game playing that presumes the idea of identity is so central to individuals that it can be applied conceptually to collectives of individuals as well" (or even collectives of organizations—see Patvardhan, Gioia, and Hamilton, 2015)? The issue, then, is how we might construe identity as a cross-level or multilevel phenomenon (see Ashforth, Rogers, and Corley, 2011). This debate might best be characterized as an ontological debate. What is the essential nature of the organizational identity phenomenon? Is it mainly an "extended metaphor" or is it something more substantive than that? Obviously, we as authors will argue that, regardless of the specific ontological status of identity, there is such a phenomenon as organizational identity (otherwise, if we presumed that the concept of organizational identity was a fiction, we actually would have nothing further to discuss in this chapter).

A second debate has to do with how we should conceive of organizational identity as a way of knowing the phenomenon. This is essentially an epistemological debate that has manifested itself by pitting various "camps" against each other. Should we treat identity as a set of substantive social constructions made by the collective holders of that identity? Or, should we treat it as a set of claims made by a collective social actor, acting as an entity with person-like attributes (features, roles, and responsibilities) within the larger society? Or is it a set of institutionalized principles and practices that all relevant parties have agreed to treat as legitimate? Are these epistemological questions so disparate that they represent east-is-east-and-west-is-west-and-never-the-twain-shall-meet contradictions? Or, is there some common ground or convergent conceptualization that might enable a reconciliation of conflicting assumptions?

If you, as interested reader, consider both of these initial questions more closely, however, you might also notice that even the manner of stating the questions presumes its own kind of ontological assumptions. Notice that the content of the questions presumes an "entity" status for the notion of identity. Simply put, the questions seem to treat identity as some sort of "thing"—even if that thing is mainly an intangible concept—with facets and attributes that make it somehow "substantive" (see Watson, this volume, Ch. 7). Is it? That question leads to a more recent debate that turns out to be a combination of these first two ontological and epistemological debates: At its essential roots, is organizational identity substantive, such that we study it as some sort of thing? Or, is it more ethereal, and should we therefore instead treat it more as some sort of ongoing process, always dynamic, always changing, fluid-like, and flowing? Are these two questions reconcilable in a fashion that the various "camps" engaged in the debate might find to be workable? Or will we end up with some version of the physicists' debate about the nature of and ways of knowing about light—understandable sometimes as composed of particles and sometimes as waves? Questions. Questions.

THE EPISTEMOLOGICAL DEBATE ABOUT ORGANIZATIONAL IDENTITY

To date, the epistemological debate has received the most attention in the literature. Although not always overtly, issues of epistemology are what distinguish the dividing lines among the three camps noted above. The three primary perspectives on organizational identity—what have been termed the "social actor," social constructionist," and "institutional" views (Gioia, Patvardhan, Hamilton, and Corley, 2013)—make different assumptions about how we know about identity and employ different approaches to obtaining that knowledge.[1] In the next three sections, we briefly review these viewpoints with an emphasis on the epistemological issues. We follow with a consideration of the burgeoning debate about the content versus process nature of organizational identity that we believe will be more prominent in the next wave of theory and research.

The Social Actor Perspective

In the social actor view, organizational identity is considered to be a property of an organization as a "social actor" to whom society has granted legal rights and powers similar to those enjoyed by individuals (Whetten, 2006; Whetten and Mackey, 2002). Albert and Whetten introduced the concept of organizational identity by describing it as the answer organizational members provide to the "self-reflective question," Who are we, as an organization? (1985: 264). They proposed that organizational members will answer this question by describing what is *central*, *enduring*, and *distinctive* about their organization—hence establishing the widely employed "CED" definition of organizational identity (Albert and Whetten, 1985). These authors further asserted that organizations "define who they are by creating or invoking a classification scheme and locating themselves within it" (1985: 267)—e.g., "We are a bank—similar to, but distinguished from other banks—but our identity is most influenced by identifying ourselves, first and foremost, as a bank." This is an important point because it highlights the relational and comparative nature of organizational identity, an underlying theme shared by all three of the major perspectives.

From the social actor perspective, what can be known about an organization's identity is what can be gleaned from the various *claims* made by organizational representatives about "who we are, as an organization" (Whetten, 2006). "Social actors are recognizable because of the way they are perceived and interpreted by other actors" (King, Felin, and Whetten, 2010: 3), an observation that echoes Ashforth and Mael's (1989) articulation of the notion of *social* (rather than personal) identity. Epistemologically, then, organizational identity in the social actor view can be known only by discerning the patterns in an organization's formal commitments, actions, and official claims (Corley et al., 2006). These "identity referents" (Whetten, 2006, 2007) indicate the organization's self-determined, self-defined, and self-proclaimed position in social space.

Research adopting the social actor stance has yielded some important insights into organizational phenomena, notably in cases of external threats as well as internal conflict. For example, Elsbach and Kramer (1996) observed the phenomenon

---

[1] Perhaps another perspective is the "social category" view, adopted in population ecology studies (see Hannan, Polos, and Carroll, 2007) and some sociological research (e.g., Zuckerman, 1999, this volume, Ch. 10). We view this work as using the identity label in a different fashion than the other three camps and do not consider it in this chapter.

of "identity threat" in their investigation of how prestigious business schools dealt with public business school rankings that challenged their core identity referents. The authors found that school leaders shifted their comparison categories in response to rankings that threatened valued dimensions of their schools' organizational identities. In addition to showing how identity threats affect an organization, the study also showed how organizational leaders attempted to actively manage organizational identity. Regarding the role of organizational identity in internal conflict, Glynn (2000) adopted the social actor lens to investigate the impact of a hybrid organizational identity in a symphony orchestra. She found that the symphony orchestra's central/enduring/distinctive features included "artistic excellence" and "fiscal solvency," and that incompatibilities between these core values led to significant conflict within the organization, culminating in a contentious musicians' strike. Further, Foreman and Whetten (2002) investigated the hybrid identities of rural farm cooperatives that had both "business" and "family" identity referents. They found that conflicting social actor identity referents can result in conflict, not only among organizational members but also *within* them as they attempt to reconcile paradoxical expectations and beliefs about the organization.

In sum, the social actor perspective provides insights into organizational phenomena by treating organizational identity as a set of overt claims that conveys consistent expectations to both internal and external stakeholders regarding how the organization should be seen and how it should conduct itself. Ravasi and Schultz (2006) noted that this conception emphasizes the *sensegiving* (Gioia and Chittipeddi, 1991) function of organizational identity, that is, the ways in which organizational identity guides strategic action and signals how other organizations should relate to the organization. In contrast, as discussed in the following section, the social construction view emphasizes "collective beliefs"—a view explicitly rejected by the social actor perspective (Corley et al., 2006).

The Social Construction Perspective

In contrast to the social actor view, the social construction view gives much greater emphasis to the self-reflective nature of organizational identity and the ways in which organization members collectively fashion an identity that they see as fitting for themselves. From this perspective, organizational identity is "an organization's members' collective understanding of the features presumed to be central and continuous, and that distinguish the organization from other organizations" (Gioia, Schultz, and Corley, 2000: 64). As a social construction, organizational identity is subject to periodic revision as members interact with each other and with outsiders, and renegotiate their collective interpretation of organizational experiences—a view that, at minimum, calls into question the degree to which identity is actually "enduring," per se (and which explains why social constructionists tend to prefer the use of the term "continuous," rather than "enduring" to describe one of the key features of identity).

The social construction view holds that organizational identity is a self-referential concept defined by the members of an organization to explain who they are as an organization to themselves as well as outsiders. In the social construction view, organizational identity is the shared or consensual *understandings* of organizational members about what it means to be "who we are, as an organization" (Gioia et al., 2000). This view focuses more intently on the (sometimes changing) meanings associated with the expressed claims made and labels used by organization members and therefore does not necessarily accept claims or labels alone as presenting a bona fide depiction of organizational identity. In the social constructionist view, identity involves the consensual interpretive schemes that members collectively construct to provide meaning to their shared experience. Undoubtedly, the social construction stance problematizes the notions of "collective" and "shared," in defining organizational identity (Corley et al., 2006). Some researchers have directly addressed these problematic issues in their work (Corley, 2004; Humphreys and Brown, 2002). Regardless of how these concepts are defined, however, it is fair to say that epistemologically, the social constructionist view focuses primarily on understanding identity labels and the meanings members associate with them. For example, Corley and Gioia (2004) used a social construction framework to understand the identity consequences of a corporate spin-off. They found that the spin-off led to "identity ambiguity" in members' collective beliefs which made it difficult to function as a new organization. Interestingly, these authors found that by maintaining consistent labels while the meanings associated with these labels changed over time, the members of the spun-off organization found a way out of the identity ambiguity that had inhibited their development as a competitive organization.

In addition, in a study of identity construction at Bang & Olufsen, Ravasi and Schultz (2006) found that organizational identity was revised when members imbued old labels with new meanings or interpretations, thus preserving a sense of continuity with the past while enabling new strategic directions. Relatedly, Clark, Gioia, Ketchen, and Thomas (2010) showed the importance of labels and meanings during a corporate merger. The authors found that a "transitional identity" acceptable to both partners in the merger provided a necessary touchstone during the profound transformation wrought by the merger.

Ravasi and Schultz (2006) suggested that the social construction perspective draws upon the *sensemaking* aspect of organizational identity as a shared interpretive scheme among organizational members. Juxtaposed with the sensegiving emphasis of the social actor view, these authors suggested that the social actor and social construction views are complementary, representing two sides of the same coin. In their study of organizational identity formation at a new iSchool, Gioia, Price, Hamilton, and Thomas (2010) concluded that the two views might better be conceived as mutually recursive and constitutive of each other. In other words, consensual understandings affect identity claims and conversely claims affect understandings. Hence, they suggested that a synthesis of both views is necessary for a complete understanding of organizational identity.

The Institutional Perspective

The third perspective differs somewhat from the social construction and social actor views (although it is arguably more closely related to the social actor view) because of its emphasis on how institutional forces affect organizations and their identities. In the institutional view, organizational identity is still internally determined, but because organizations are embedded in broader social contexts, identity is highly influenced by strong external forces (Glynn and Marquis, 2007). Seen from this point of view, a prominent aspect of an organization's identity is its claims to "membership in a social category or collective identity at the level of the organizational field" (Greenwood, Raynard, Kodeih, Micelotta, and Lounsbury, 2011: 346–347). As a result, in contrast to the social actor and social construction views that tend to focus on the "distinctiveness" aspect of organizational identity, the institutional view has typically emphasized the "sameness" or isomorphic aspect of organizational identity (e.g., Glynn and Abzug, 2002). The institutional perspective with its emphasis on external influences provides valuable insights into organizational identity and its implications. For example, this view brings the relationship between legitimacy (perhaps *the* key issue for organizational survival: see Suchman, 1995) and identity into clearer focus. Several institutionally oriented works have found that new organizations fare better and gain greater legitimacy when their identity claims better reflect the environmental context (e.g., Czarniawska and Wolff, 1998; Suddaby and Greenwood, 2005). Further, research adopting the institutional stance has shown that something as potentially distinctive as an organization's chosen name, which often is a significant identity referent, nonetheless tends to reflect the powerful influence of broader contextual pressures toward conformity (Glynn and Abzug, 2002; Glynn and Marquis, 2005).

Recent institutionalist studies have made greater attempts to explain the "distinctiveness" element of identity as well (e.g., Glynn, 2008; Navis and Glynn, 2010; Rindova, Dalpiaz, and Ravasi, 2011). Glynn (2008) has considered how organizations construct their identities through "institutional bricolage" that blends and refracts logics drawn from the broader institutional context. In addition, in an approach that adopts aspects of both the institutional and social actor perspectives, King et al. (2011) examined how new organizations in emerging industries employ both mimicry and differentiation processes to develop distinct identities when the industry category is "underspecified."

It might be fair to say that our initial framing of the three camps highlights the differences and understates the similarities among the perspectives. Indeed, the more recent studies noted above seem to blur some of the (previously more dramatic) distinctions between the social actor and institutional views. They also provide a point of potential convergence with social construction views, because the actions taken and claims made by such organizations represent what Brewer (1991) has termed an attempt to achieve "optimal distinctiveness" (being similar to, but sufficiently distinctive from a chosen reference group), a process found to be key to Gioia et al.'s (2010) study of organizational identity formation. These more recent lines of inquiry may yet lead to new insights into the connection between identity differentiation and phenomena such as conflicting institutional logics (Purdy and Gray, 2009) and institutional "pluralism" (Kraatz and Block, 2008). Institutional logics are undoubtedly a resource for organizational identity construction (Glynn, 2008; Glynn and Marquis, 2007), yet in addition, Greenwood et al. (2011) surmise that organizational identity serves as an important filter through which organizations can manage conflicting logics and environmental complexity—a view that converges with Gioia and Thomas' (1996) treatment of identity and images as filters for understanding the need for strategic change.

The Ontological Debate about Organizational Identity

The liveliness of the debate noted above notwithstanding, there is actually a more fundamental and theoretically intriguing issue to be considered. To wit: Is the essential nature of organizational identity better construed as *entitative* or *processual* (i.e., more "content-based" or "process-based")?

Identity as Entity versus Identity as Process

Put differently, should we treat identity as something "substantive," in that its essence is appropriately captured via articulating a key set of attributes, or should we treat it as "continuously dynamic"? Put yet differently, do we as theorists and researchers better capture the essential character of organizational identity by treating it as a noun or a verb? If organizational identity is deemed to be a noun, then the presumption is that we can treat it as entitative, that is, as substantive—although most acknowledge that identity is not composed of physical substance, but rather is substantive in the "substantive argument" sense of the term. Even in this "substantive-not-substance" sense, however, the dominant presumption seems to be that identity is best described by articulating key attributes associated with an entity, which also implies that identity is largely static in character (or can be treated as such for purposes of analysis).

If we release such comforting strictures, however, and entertain the idea that identity can also be presumed and described in more vibrant, processual terms, might we be able to capture a better sense of identity as a more fluid concept that emphasizes, not just its mutability, but its essential dynamism? As noted, most scholars recognize that there can be nothing "tangible" about identity. Identity, for instance, is not build-ings, per se. Identity is not even "practices," per se. Buildings might be representa-tions of identity, and practices might be manifestations of identity (and in the case of practices, closely connected to identity), but the character of identity does not reside in these tangibles and observables. Shouldn't we then consider organizational identity in terms that better represent both its ethereality and its dynamism? Such a stance generates a different way of understanding identity.

Considering a processual view of identity begins with William James' (1909/2014: 352) old observation that, "What really exists is not things made but things in the making." Tsoukas and Chia (2002) played off this profound recognition in the context of reconceptualizing organizational change and counseled that we should consider change, not as some special case of stability or routine, but rather in its own right, as an inherently dynamic enterprise (see also Weick and Quinn, 1999). Organizational identity is conceptually similar. As a viable first approximation, identity might be better conceived not as a "thing made," but a "thing in the making" (assuming that we can treat "thing" as a figure of speech for the moment). The difference is not trivial. It echoes Feldman's (2000) argument that we as scholars should focus more intently and appreciatively on the human agency involved in the transformation of routines, for instance. More importantly, perhaps, for our role as theorists, refocusing our attention on identity as process and flow (Gioia and Patvardhan, 2012) highlights what Bergson (1946) so famously termed as attending to what might be seen but not noticed.

To bring this different set of assumptions about identity more front-and-center, consider an exercise that is prevalent in academia, the simple act of defining a concept. As is often noted, Albert and Whetten (1985) asserted the idea that organizations have identities and defined identity in memorable terms as "that which is *central, enduring, and distinctive* about an organization." If you consider this straightforward defini-tion carefully, however, there is a clever act of cognitive misdirection involved in it. Although it is the key CED attributes that stand out prominently in this definition, it is the rather adroit use of the phrase preceding it that is more interesting. The key question is, What does the phrase "that which ..." have as its *referent*? Normal lin-guistic convention usually takes "that which" as referring to some noun. When we are referring to identity, most of us presume that we are referencing some kind of (usually intangible) entity—for example, a consensual constellation of the key elements of, or claims about organizational identity ... but maybe not. "That which" can actually refer to quite a range of possibilities.

For instance, consider Albert and Whetten's (1985) alternative—and more evocative—definition of organizational identity as "Who we are, as an organization." The fascinating feature of this definition is that it also appears to specify some kind of anthropomorphized entity—a living being at some higher, more collective level of analysis and understanding—an extended metaphor of the personal/social notion of identity perhaps? Now this definition, although less precise than the stark cen-tral/enduring/distinctive set of attributes, has *life*. It has *presence*. It has *agency* and maybe even *spirituality*. The clear implication is that the "who" referent connotes that organizational identities mirror individual identities in many essential features.[2] And perhaps well they should, because organizations are the creations of individuals—even if they might quickly take on a quasi-independent life and assume features that distinguish them from individuals. This more ambiguous way of defining and conceiving organizations tends to be more reassuring, because it portrays organizations as more complex extensions of *us*—and concomitantly helps us preserve our "creator" status in producing an entity that mimics us (even if this version of identity is more "embodied" than the "consensual-constellation-of-elements-and-claims" version of identity).

This more comforting definition, however, nonetheless continues to assume that there is an entity in there somewhere. "Whoever" is in there exists and displays features and actions that make it look a lot like its creators. This conceptualization continues to treat identity as yet another version of a substantive entity. The larger point of our musings is not to argue the exact nature of organizational identity but rather to point out the ontological assumption shared by these entity-based conceptualizations. An arguably more interesting ontological question is, Why should we consider identity, whether at the individual or collective level, as either an inanimate or animate, tangible or intangible *thing* (see Watson, this volume, Ch. 7)? Even if we concede that identity is more of a concept than a physical presence, the underlying assumption remains that identity has entitative status. This assumption constrains us from thinking about organizational identity in terms that might better represent its essential character. How might we instead re-conceptualize this notion that is so dear to our personal and organizational hearts?

What if we took seriously the idea that identity can viably be construed as a verb and not a noun? Can we conceive of identity (at both the individual/organizational levels), not merely as the product of genes/founding principles and experiences/events, but as an ongoing process of constructing, negotiating, performing, reconstructing, legitimating, etc.—in other words, not as the product of some collection of experiences, but rather an ongoing stream of experience (see Schutz, 1967; Weick, 1979)? Notice that all the terms in the previous sentence are also gerunds—that is, *verbs acting as nouns*— which is a useful observation that has more than linguistic implications because it also provides an avenue for reconciling the paradox of identity as simultaneously content and process. Such gerunds strongly suggest a view of identity as flux; if it is static in any reasonable sense, it is static momentarily, as a progressing set of ongoing "accomplishments" that are either repeatedly affirmed or incrementally adjusted (or on rare occasion, destroyed). In this depiction, identity is not just dynamic, it is flow, always up for negotiation and adjustment (Gioia and Patvardhan, 2012). Identity then is cast not as a frozen snapshot in time, but as a movie in continuous motion.

Admittedly, it is conceptually disconcerting to envision our subject of study as ontologically *always* in motion. Instability is discomfiting, even to the educated. As

---

[2] Note, however, that Albert and Whetten (1985) made conceptual comparisons between organizational and individual identity, yet explicitly wished to avoid treating organizations *as* individuals.

lay people and even as ostensibly enlightened scholars, it is much easier to conceive of even a dynamic social world as moving from one equilibrium state to another, and much more difficult to construe the equilibrium state as the rarity. We prefer stability, and we consequently build our understandings on that preference. When works like Weick and Quinn (1999) and Tsoukas and Chia (2002) come along that invite us to think about disequilibrium as the "normal" state, these treatments can sometimes be discounted as impracticable fantasizing. But they are not. Opening ourselves to the profound possibility that organizational identity is flow, and better viewed as constantly "becoming" has the kind of gravitas that ought to characterize us learned types.

Of course, even in this identity-as-flow view we are understandably adept at bracketing the ongoing experience of identity (stopping the movie, as it were), examining the frozen image as if it were a still life, and sometimes getting snookered into conceiving of identity as a series of isolated snapshots. And, if we're good at anything, we're good at the "as if" way of framing experience via reification. "As if" is a fundamental individual and collective enterprise. Everyone engages in it all the time, so we get duped into thinking that the fiction is real. And as Thomas and Thomas (1928) so astutely put it so many years ago: If people treat situations as real, they become real in their consequences. Our sense of identity very much gives that impression. But it just ain't so. The real beauty of *understanding* identity at its essence is the inspired recognition that it flows (or perhaps better phrased as, it *is* flow). If any of us needed reminding, we will note that the term Ph.D. translates as "Doctor of Philosophy" and suggests that we holders of that degree should have a deep understanding of ontology and epistemology of the social world—even if we choose to behave *as if* it were like the physical world in some superficial aspects, for the sake of living comfortably with our fellow scholars and lay people who would prefer that we don't sound *too* weird.

Reconciling the Debates

Commentary on the Epistemological Debate

The basic epistemological question in the domain of organizational identity is: Can organizational identity be more effectively viewed as a set of coherent claims made by the organization acting as a collective agent in society? (as the "social actor" view proponents would have it) or as a set of consensual *constructions* by the members of an organization? (as the "social construction" advocates see it), or as a set of legitimized structures and procedures? (as the "institutional" view supporters would prefer it). In your role as interested reader, you might expect us as authors to behave as typical academics who plunge a stake in the ground and declare one of these views as the more useful approach to acquiring knowledge about organizational identity. Both of us authors are, after all, known proponents of the social construction view, and the time-honored tradition of intellectual debate by defending various positions has been quite functional in extending organizational identity theory. The main representatives in the debate (Albert and Whetten, 1985; Gioia et al., 2000; Glynn, 2000; Pratt and Foreman, 2000; Glynn and Abzug, 2002; Whetten and Mackey, 2002; Corley et al. 2006; Ravasi and Schultz, 2006; Whetten, 2006; Glynn, 2008; Gioia et al., 2010, among others) have taken part in some lively discussions of these alternative ways of seeing as if they were fundamentally incompatible.

Ravasi and Schultz (2006) took the first best shot at trying to achieve some sort of détente among the disagreeing parties by arguing that the social actor and social construction views can be viewed as complementary. That stance certainly helped the search for common ground. The next attempt at reconciliation was Gioia et al.'s (2010) study on identity formation (which started life as a social constructionist study). In a sense, that study highlighted the necessity of the identity-as-process ontology. If it showed us anything beyond the several sequential and concurrent processes that attend the formation of identity, it was that using only one (entitative) view of identity leads to an impoverished overall understanding. It also showed that social actor and social construction processes are actually mutually constitutive. Neither is sufficient; both are necessary. And although the authors did not specifically address the institutional view in that study, the reported data appear to implicate institutional processes as well. Yes, there is complementarity, as Ravasi and Schultz (2006) so effectively showed; yet a sole focus on this might emphasize identity's substantive aspects and elide the *processual* aspects, many of which may be intertwined and co-constitutive.

Further, to reveal the bona fide character of recursiveness at the macro level requires going beyond complementarity. For that reason, in the epistemological domain we advocate stepping beyond the easy formulation of saying one needs all three views to grasp the character of identity from its inception. "Either-or" thinking obviously won't do, while "both-and" thinking is far more appropriate, even if that mode of thinking leaves us still a step short. *Structurational* thinking (Giddens, 1984) is perhaps even better because of its explicit attention to the recursiveness involved in so many social processes. Meaning making (via social construction processes), claims making (via social actor processes), and legitimizing forces (via institutionalization processes), all swirl together recursively to produce this phenomenon we treat as the subject of our study.

Commentary on the Ontological Debate

Even more intriguing than the epistemological debate around the various views of identity is the ontological debate around the very character of identity itself. The big question is: Should we continue to treat identity in our default "content/entitative" fashion, or should we accommodate a more dynamic process view, even if it inconveniences not only our conceptual but also our methodological approaches? Once again, even in this ontological domain, a complementary view can help. Cognitively speaking, it is not difficult to entertain the abstract idea that identity can be conceived both as an intangible entity *and* a process continuously in flux (although the latter tends to be treated as more of an academic abstraction). Whatever identity is, it clearly can display characteristics associated with each view. This social science stance parallels the physical scientists' penchant for allowing both wave and particle models of light to co-exist more or less independently as a convenient way of accommodating explanations for light's observed characteristics. Once again, however, we want to emphasize that the nature of physical and social phenomena is profoundly different, despite our bend-over-backward attempts to act as if they are not. So, again both-and framing can help in allowing us a more comprehensive understanding of identity (see Hatch and Schultz, 2002; Clegg et al., 2007; Clark et al., 2010; and Ashforth et al., 2011 for examples). Still, both–and thinking also elides the complexity of what is really going on. Structurational thinking again affords a more nuanced and realistic portrayal of organizational identity as both process and product. As Tsoukas and Chia (2002) noted in the context of conceiving organizational change differently:

> *Organizations* are sites of continuously changing human action, and *organization* is the making of form, the patterned unfolding of human action. Organization in the form of institutionalized categories is an input into human action, while in the form of emerging pattern it is an outcome of it; organization aims at stemming change but in the process of doing so it is generated by it. (p. 577)

Substitute the concept of "identity-as-content" for the concept of "organizations" in this statement and the concept of "identity-as-process" for "organization" (or to be more precise, *organizing*) in this statement, and the benefit of seeing identity in structurational (recursively intertwined) terms becomes more evident.

Furthermore, Tsoukas and Chia (2002) made the useful observation that when we look at change synoptically (i.e., as discontinuous and unusual events), the ongoing reality seems to be more stable than it actually is (see also Weick and Quinn, 1999, and Feldman, 2000 for similar statements). As Bateson (1979: 45) so insightfully noted, we are inclined to say that an acrobat on a high wire maintains his stability, when in fact he does so, paradoxically, by "continual correction of his imbalance." We need both "synoptic" and "performative" (Feldman, 2000) accounts to better understand change—to help us notice features and patterns while also accounting for dynamic progressions over time. A directly parallel notion applies to organizational identity. Attribute-focused descriptions of identity give us a sense of the main features that members consider to be essential to their conception of themselves, while process-focused descriptions give us a sense of the continuous, ongoing development of identity as enactings and accomplishings.

We would be remiss at this point if we did not mention the narrative perspective on organizational identity (see Czarniawska, 1997; Brown, 2006). Like the identity-as-process view, it conceptualizes identity as dynamic. Some research in this area maintains that identity *is* the narrative (e.g., Brown and Humphreys, 2006) or, more precisely, suggests that multiple narratives co-exist, and they are what actually constitutes an organizational identity. These various narratives may complement each other, or conflict and compete, and they are embraced or rejected, and embellished, refined, or abridged over time by organizational members in the course of their activities (e.g., Chreim, 2005; Humphreys and Brown, 2002). To our way of thinking, this perspective brings to the study of identity a valuable consideration of texts, plurality, and change over time. We would like to avoid privileging narratives over other potential symbolic systems in organizations, however. Further, we view organizational narratives as one important aspect of identity-as-process, along with other aspects, for example organizational knowledge and practices (see Nag, Corley, and Gioia, 2007).

To capture the dynamism of identity, it would be beneficial if we as scholars more frequently used terms consistent with a process view, such as becoming, changing, in flux (see Langley and Tsoukas, 2010) as well as doing, acting, interacting, etc. (see Pratt et al., 2006) and claiming, granting, mirroring, expressing, impressing, reflecting (see Hatch and Schultz, 2002). In a larger sense, it is useful to constantly think in terms of *gerunds*—to view identity formation and change as (metaphorically speaking) a kind of dynamic "performing art," rather than a static "fine art." Gerunds are ideally suited for dynamic and structurational thinking because they are hybrid terms, nouns in form and verbs in function.[3] These kinds of terms confer one other advantage, as well—they encourage connectivity. Among its many other virtues, identity is a connector concept; that is, it is connected to many other important notions that have taken root on our academic landscape. And, more often than not, those notions are dynamic notions. As Pratt (2012: 40) has put it recently:

> identity processes are, at minimum, often associated with other processes including sensemaking and sensegiving (Gioia & Chittipeddi, 1991; Pratt, 2000; Ravasi & Schulz, 2006; Gioia et al., 2010), learning and unlearning (Pratt et al., 2006); changing (Fiol, 2002); negotiating (Clegg et al., 2007), communicating (Cheney, 1983), controlling and struggling (Alvesson & Wilmott, 2002; Sveningsson & Alvesson, 2003), comparing/mimicking/legitimizing (Czarniawska & Wolff, 1998; Clegg et al., 2007; Glynn, 2008) and modifying, editing and deleting (Weber & Glynn, 2006). The presence of so many other processes in identity construction begs the question of what role they play in underlying, intertwining, walking beside, or prefacing and following this construction.

We encourage you to read these last passages and note all the "ing" words in them. Using such dynamic language in our conceptualizations can only help in the effort to understand organizational identity in its processual forms.

CONCLUSION

Concerning our first debate, we'll end by asking a facetious question: Can you, as an individual, be adequately described by invoking a single perspective for

---

[3] Many thanks to Michael Pratt for helping us clarify this point.

understanding you? That simplistic question might insult your complex sense of self, and you might rightfully insist on a more comprehensive set of views. All the puzzle pieces together give a better picture. Yet we also know that those puzzle pieces are discrete (the pieced-together picture has lots of lines in it, which creates a strange-looking, artificial portrait), so we need to fuse them somehow into a whole picture. That's what "co-constitutive" or "structurational" thinking does for us when it comes to understanding individual or organizational identity—it gives a synthesized picture of your identity (i.e., by dissolving the puzzle-piece lines), and even your many situated identities, which collectively constitute your *self* (see Mead, 1934; Pratt, 2012). Precisely the same notion extends to understanding organizational identity. All the processes that make up those multiple views synthesize in a fashion that in the words of the old systems theorists give us a whole greater than the sum of its parts (Ashby, 1956).

Concerning our second debate, we'll ask a related question: Does your individual identity change over time? That is, are you better understood as having an identity that is "stable" or one that is "mutable"? A cursory comparison of who you were in younger days with who you are now likely reveals a constellation of similarities and differences. Where did those differences come from? In part they were the outcomes of conscious efforts to change ourselves by trying on possible selves (Markus and Nurius, 1986) and provisional selves (Ibarra, 1999), each dynamic and mutable, a "continually active, shifting array of accessible self-knowledge" (Markus and Wurf, 1987: 306). Changes to self-concept, however, are adaptive responses, not only to images we project into the social environment and have reflected back to us in some altered form (Cooley, 1902), but also to other-generated images that convey strong social expectations. Given the overwhelming power of image to transmute substance (Alvesson, 1990), and perhaps even to transform identity into image and then into an altered identity (Gioia, Hamilton, and Patvardhan, 2014), one's self-concept (and identity) can only be construed as continually changing. It is not a stretch to suggest that organizational identities share this dynamic propensity.

The view of organizational identity as flow opens up intriguing questions for future research. If identity is flow, it is likely to be a non-random flow, thus prompting us to wonder what bounds and shapes it. By affording opportunities to observe patterns that link gerunds—connecting form and action—this ontological perspective allows us to discern the nature of the flow, possibly revealing fundamental yet previously murky organizing processes.

Acknowledgments

We sincerely thank Michael Pratt (our primary editor) and his co-editors (Blake Ashforth, Davide Ravasi, and Majken Schultz) for many insightful comments and suggestions that helped strengthen this chapter.

References

Albert, S. and Whetten, D. A. (1985). "Organizational Identity." In *Research in Organizational Behavior*, vol. 7, edited by L. L. Cummings and B. M. Straw. 263–95. Greenwich, CT: JAI Press.

Alvesson, M. (1990). "Organization: From Substance to Image?" *Organization Studies* 11(3): 373–94.

Ashby, W. R. (1956). *An Introduction to Cybernetics*. New York: John Wiley & Sons.

Ashforth, B. E. and Mael, F. (1989). "Social Identity Theory and the Organization." *Academy of Management Review* 14(1): 20–39.

Ashforth, B. E., Rogers, K. M., and Corley, K. G. (2011). "Identity in Organizations: Exploring Cross-Level Dynamics." *Organization Science* 22(5): 1144–56.

Bateson, G. (1979). *Mind and Nature: A Necessary Unity*. Toronto: Bantam.

Bergson, H. (1946). *The Creative Mind: An Introduction to Metaphysics*. New York: Dover Publications.

Brewer, M. B. (1991). "The Social Self: On Being the Same and Different at the Same Time." *Personality and Social Psychology Bulletin* 17(5): 475–82.

Brown, A. D. (2006). "A Narrative Approach to Collective Identities." *Journal of Management Studies* 43(4): 731–53.

Brown, A. D. and Humphreys, M. (2006). "Organizational Identity and Place: A Discursive Exploration of Hegemony and Resistance." *Journal of Management Studies* 43: 231–57.

Chreim, S. (2005). "The Continuity–Change Duality in Narrative Texts of Organizational Identity." *Journal of Management Studies* 42(3): 567–93.

Clark, S. M., Gioia, D. A., Ketchen, D., Jr., and Thomas, J. B. (2010). "Transitional Identity as a Facilitator of Organizational Identity Change during a Merger." *Administrative Science Quarterly* 55(3): 397–438.

Clegg, S. R., Rhodes, C., and Kornberger, M. (2007). "Desperately Seeking Legitimacy: Organizational Identity and Emerging Industries." *Organization Studies*, 28(4): 495–513.

Cooley, C. H. (1902). *Human Nature and the Social Order*. New York: C. Schribner's Sons.

Corley, K. G. (2004). "Defined by Our Strategy or Our Culture? Hierarchical Differences in Perceptions of Organizational Identity and Change." *Human Relations* 57(9): 1145–77.

Corley, K. G. and Gioia, D. A. (2004). "Identity Ambiguity and Change in the Wake of a Corporate Spin-Off." *Administrative Science Quarterly* 49(2): 173–208.

Corley, K. G., Harquail, C. V., Pratt, M. G., Glynn, M. A., Fiol, C. M., and Hatch, M. J. (2006). "Guiding Organizational Identity through Aged Adolescence." *Journal of Management Inquiry* 15(2): 85–99.

Czarniawska, B. (1997. *Narrating the Organization: Dramas of Institutional Identity*. Chicago: University of Chicago Press.

Czarniawska, B. and Wolff, R. (1998). "Constructing New Identities in Established Organization Fields." *International Studies of Management & Organization* 28(3): 32–56.

Elsbach, K. D. and Kramer, R. M. (1996). "Members' Responses to Organizational Identity Threats: Encountering and Countering the *Business Week* Rankings." *Administrative Science Quarterly* 41(3): 442–76.

Feldman, M. S. (2000). "Organizational Routines as a Source of Continuous Change." *Organization Science* 11(6): 611–29.

Foreman, P. and Whetten, D. A. (2002). "Member's Identification with Multiple-Identity Organizations." *Organization Science* 13(6): 618–35.

Foreman, P. O. and Whetten, D. (2016). "Measuring Organizational Identity: Taking Stock and Looking Forward." In *The Oxford Handbook of Organizational Identity*, edited by M. G. Pratt, M. Schultz, B. E. Ashforth, and D. Ravasi, 39–64. Oxford: Oxford University Press.

Giddens, A. (1984). *The Constitution of Society*. Berkeley: University of California Press.

Gioia, D. A. and Chittipeddi, K. (1991). "Sensemaking and Sensegiving in Strategic Change Initiation." *Strategic Management Journal* 12(6): 433–48.

Gioia, D. A., Hamilton, A. L., and Patvardhan, S. D. (2014). "Image Is Everything: Reflections on the Dominance of Image in Modern Organizational Life." *Research in Organizational Behavior* 34: 129–54.

Gioia, D. A. and Patvardhan, S. (2012). "Identity as Process and Flow." In *Constructing Identity in and around Organizations*, edited by M. Schultz, S. Maguire, A. Langley, and H. Tsoukas, 50–62. New York: Oxford University Press.

Gioia, D. A., Patvardhan, S. D., Hamilton, A. L., and Corley, K. G. (2013). "Organizational Identity Formation and Change." *The Academy of Management Annals* 7(1): 123–93.

Gioia, D. A., Price, K., Hamilton, A. L., and Thomas, J. B. (2010). "Forging an Identity: An Insider-Outsider Study of Processes Involved in the Formation of Organizational Identity." *Administrative Science Quarterly* 55(1): 1–46.

Gioia, D. A., Schultz, M., and Corley, K. G. (2000). "Organizational Identity, Image, and Adaptive Instability. "*Academy of Management Review* 25(1): 63–81.

Gioia, D. A. and Thomas, J. B. (1996). "Identity, Image, and Issue Interpretation: Sensemaking during Strategic Change in Academia." *Administrative Science Quarterly* 41(3): 370–403.

Glynn, M. A. (2000). "When Cymbals Become Symbols: Conflict over Organizational Identity within a Symphony Orchestra." *Organization Science* 11(3): 285–98.

Glynn, M. A. (2008). "Beyond Constraint: How Institutions Enable Identities." In *Handbook of Organizational Institutionalism*, edited by R. Greenwood, C. Oliver, K. Sahlin, and R. Suddaby, 413–30. Los Angeles: SAGE.

Glynn, M. A. and Abzug, R. (2002). "Institutionalizing Identity: Symbolic Isomorphism and Organizational Names." *Academy of Management Journal* 45(1): 267–80.

Glynn, M. A. and Marquis, C. (2005). "Fred's Bank: How Institutional Norms and Individual Preferences Legitimate Organizational Names." In *Artifacts and Organizations: Beyond Mere Symbolism*, edited by A. Rafaeli, and M. G. Pratt, 223–39. Mahwah, NJ: Erlbaum.

Glynn, M. A. and Marquis, C. (2007). "Legitimating Identities: How Institutional Logics Motivate Organizational Name Choices." In *Identity and the Modern Organization*, edited by C. A. Bartel, S. Blader, and A. Wrzesniewski, 17–33. Mahwah, NJ: Lawrence Erlbaum Associates Publishers.

Greenwood, R., Raynard, M., Kodeih, F., Micelotta, E. R., and Lounsbury, M. (2011). "Institutional Complexity and Organizational Responses." *Academy of Management Annals* 5: 317–71.

Hannan, M. T., Polos, L., and Carroll, G. R. (2007). *Logics of Organization Theory: Audiences, Codes, and Ecologies*. Princeton, NJ: Princeton University Press.

Hatch, M. J. and Schultz, M. (2002). "The Dynamics of Organizational Identity." *Human Relations* 55(8): 989–1017.

Humphreys, M. and Brown, A. D. (2002). "Narratives of Organizational Identity and Identification: A Case Study of Hegemony and Resistance." *Organization Studies* 23: 421–47.

Ibarra, H. (1999). "Provisional Selves: Experimenting with Image and Identity in Professional Adaptation." *Administrative Science Quarterly* 44(4): 764–91.

James, W. A. (2014). *Pluralistic Universe.* New York, NY: Sheba Blake Publishing.

King, B. G., Clemens, E. S., and Fry, M. (2011). "Identity Realization and Organizational Forms: Differentiation and Consolidation of Identities among Arizona's Charter Schools." *Organization Science* 22(3): 554–72.

King, B. G., Felin, T., and Whetten, D. A. (2010). "Finding the Organization in Organizational Theory: A Meta-Theory of the Organization as a Social Actor." *Organization Science* 21: 290–305.

Kraatz, M. S. and Block, E. S. (2008). "Organizational Implications of Institutional Pluralism." In *Handbook of Organizational Insitutionalism,* edited by R. Greenwood, C. Oliver, K. Sahlin, and R. Suddaby, 243–75. Los Angeles: SAGE.

Langley, A. and Tsoukas, H. (2010). "Introducing 'Perspectives on Process Organization Studies.'" In *Process, Sensemaking, & Organizing,* vol. 1, edited by T. Hernes and S. Maitlis, 1–26. Oxford: Oxford University Press.

Markus, H. and Nurius, P. (1986). "Possible Selves." *American Psychologist* 41(9): 954–69.

Markus, H. and Wurf, E. (1987). "The Dynamic Self-Concept: A Social Psychological Perspective." *Annual Review of Psychology* 38(1): 299–337.

Mead, G. H. (1934). *Mind, Self and Society.* Chicago: University of Chicago Press.

Nag, R., Corley, K. G., and Gioia, D. A. (2007). "The Intersection of Organizational Identity, Knowledge, and Practice: Attempting Strategic Change via Knowledge Grafting." *Academy of Management Journal* 50(4): 821–47.

Navis, C. and Glynn, M. A. (2010). "How New Market Categories Emerge: Temporal Dynamics of Legitimacy, Identity, and Entrepreneurship in Satellite Radio, 1990–2005." *Administrative Science Quarterly* 55: 439–71.

Patvardhan, S. D., Gioia, D. A., and Hamilton, A. L. (2015). "Weathering a Metalevel Identity Crisis: Forging a Coherent Collective Identity for an Emerging Field." *Academy of Management Journal* 58(2): 405–35.

Pratt, M. G. (2012). "Rethinking Identity Construction Processes in Organizations: Three Questions to Consider." In *Constructing Identity in and around Organizations,* edited by M. Schultz, S. Maguire, A. Langley, and H. Tsoukas, 21–49. New York: Oxford University Press.

Pratt, M. G. and Foreman, P. O. (2000). "The Beauty of and Barriers to Organizational Theories of Identity." *Academy of Management Review* 25(1): 141–3.

Pratt, M. G., Rockmann, K. W., and Kaufmann, J. B. (2006). "Constructing Professional Identity: The Role of Work and Identity Learning Cycles in the Customization of Identity among Medical Residents." *Academy of Management Journal* 49(2): 235–62.

Price, K., Gioia, D. A., and Corley, K. G. (2008). "Reconciling Scattered Images." *Journal of Management Inquiry* 17(3): 173–85.

Purdy, J. M. and Gray, B. (2009). "Conflicting Logics, Mechanisms of Diffusion, and Multilevel Dynamics in Emerging Institutional Fields." *Academy of Management Journal* 52(2): 355–80.

Ravasi, D. and Schultz, M. (2006). "Responding to Organizational Identity Threats: Exploring the Role of Organizational Culture." *Academy of Management Journal* 49(3): 433–58.

Rindova, V., Dalpiaz, E., and Ravasi, D. (2011). "A Cultural Quest: A Study of Organizational Use of New Cultural Resources in Strategy Formation." *Organization Science* 22(2): 413–31.

Schutz, A. (1967). *The Phenomenology of the Social World.* Evanston, IL: Northwestern University Press.

Suchman, M. C. (1995). "Managing Legitimacy: Strategic and Institutional Approaches." *Academy of Management Review* 20(3): 571–610.

Suddaby, R. and Greenwood, R. (2005). "Rhetorical Strategies of Legitimacy." *Administrative Science Quarterly* 50: 35–67.

Thomas, W. I. and Thomas, D. S. (1928). *The Child in America: Behavior Problems and Programs.* New York: Knopf.

Tsoukas, H. and Chia, R. (2002). "On Organizational Becoming: Rethinking Organizational Change." *Organization Science* 13(5): 567.

Watson, T. J. (2016). "Organizational Identity and Organizational Identity Work as Valuable Analytical Resources." In *The Oxford Handbook of Organizational Identity*, edited by M. G. Pratt, M. Schultz, B. E. Ashforth, and D. Ravasi, 123–39. Oxford: Oxford University Press.

Weick, K. E. (1979). *The Social Psychology of Organizing.* New York: Addison-Wesley.

Weick, K. E. and Quinn, R. E. (1999). "Organizational Change and Development." *Annual Review of Psychology* 50(1): 361–86.

Whetten, D. A. (2006). "Albert and Whetten Revisited: Strengthening the Concept of Organizational Identity." *Journal of Management Inquiry* 15(3): 219–34.

Whetten, D. A. (2007). "A Critique of Organizational Identity Scholarship: Challenging the Uncritical Use of Social Identity Theory When Social Identities Are also Social Actors." In *Identity and the Modern Organization*, edited by C. A. Bartel, S. Blader, and A. Wrzesniewski, 253–72. Mahwah, NJ: Lawrence Erlbaum.

Whetten, D. A. and Mackey, A. (2002). "A Social Actor Conception of Organizational Identity and its Implications for the Study of Organizational Reputation." *Business and Society* 41(4): 393–414.

Zuckerman, E. W. (1999). "The Categorical Imperative: Securities Analysts and the Illegitimacy Discount." *American Journal of Sociology* 104(5): 1398–438.

Zuckerman, E. (2016). "Optimal Distinctiveness Revisited: An Integrative Framework for Understanding the Balance between Differentiation and Conformity in Individual and Organizational Identities." In *The Oxford Handbook of Organizational Identity*, edited by M. G. Pratt, M. Schultz, B. E. Ashforth, and D. Ravasi, 183–99. Oxford: Oxford University Press.

CHAPTER 2

....

MEASURING ORGANIZATIONAL IDENTITY

taking stock and looking forward

....

PETER O. FOREMAN AND DAVID A. WHETTEN

Introduction

....

THE concept of organizational identity [OI] was introduced by Albert and Whetten in 1985, and their definition of the construct has since been widely cited: generally held views of an organization that are central, distinctive, and enduring. Interestingly, that essay also contains a proposed means to operationalize and study OI that has gone relatively unnoticed: "extended metaphor analysis." The authors argued that the contemporary research university had a hybrid identity, and the two elements of that identity could be seen as analogous to that of a "church," with deeply rooted normative values and a "business", having equally strong utilitarian principles. Researchers could build on these extended metaphors to operationalize the conflicting identity elements and examine a range of related phenomena. That early work could hardly have envisioned the diversity of approaches for measuring OI that now comprise the nearly 300 empirical studies on the subject. The purpose of this chapter is to survey the means by which scholars have variously operationalized and/or measured the concept.

Several notable reviews of OI scholarship have been published (e.g., Ashforth, Rogers and Corley, 2011; Brown et al., 2006; Corley et al., 2006; Cornelissen, 2006; Cornelissen, Haslam, and Balmer, 2007; Gioia et al., 2013; Glynn, 2008; Ravasi and Canato, 2013; Ravasi and van Rekom, 2003; van Rekom and van Riel, 2000; Whetten, 2006). For the most part, these have examined the subject from a *conceptual* perspective. Scholars have discussed definitional issues and terminology (Brown et al., 2006; Cornelissen et al., 2007; Ravasi, this volume, Ch. 3), outlined the distinctions between the social actor and social constructionist views of OI (Corley et al., 2006; Whetten, 2006; Gioia and Hamilton this volume, Ch. 1), and highlighted differences in theoretical perspectives and research communities (Ravasi and van Rekom, 2003; Cornelissen, 2006; Glynn, 2008).

A few essays have addressed *methodological* issues in OI research. Some have discussed specific means of operationalizing the OI construct and/or conducting an analysis of OI (Brown, 2006; van Rekom and van Riel, 2000). Others have provided a broader assessment of multiple methods, but have typically been limited in their scope and depth (Corley et al., 2006; Ravasi and van Rekom, 2003). In the most rigorous of such efforts, Ravasi and Canato (2013) categorized the research methods employed by OI scholars according to their ontological assumptions, but only included a limited range of work (33 studies). In the end, the OI field lacks a truly comprehensive and systematic review of the various methodologies employed in empirical research.

Our assessment complements previous work in two ways. First, we extend prior conceptual treatments of the subject by examining how different conceptions have actually been operationalized. Clearly, how OI is conceptualized influences how it is measured, and the measures selected by researchers reveal their assumptions about OI's meaning. Second, we extend previous methods-oriented reviews by providing a more comprehensive investigation of various kinds of research designs—we build out from earlier work examining a particular kind of methodology or phenomenon of interest by exploring the entire range of those which are present in more than 80 selected articles.

Our core criterion for inclusion in this review was simple: a study had to attempt to, or propose a means by which one could, "measure" organizational identity. We defined this notion of measurement quite broadly. Although the term implies a quantifiable assessment of a tangible object—the *Oxford English Dictionary* definition is "to ascertain the size, amount, or degree of [something] by using an instrument or device marked in standard units"—we saw measurement as any attempt to operationalize and empirically observe organizational identity, including approaches that were more qualitative or abstract. Two important qualifiers were: 1) the research had to be concerned with the construct of *identity*; and 2) the referent needed to be one or more *organizations*. Thus we did not include studies that only dealt with concepts *related to* OI, like image, reputation, or legitimacy at the organizational level, or organizational identification at the individual level (Brown et al., 2006; Foreman, Whetten, and Mackey, 2012). Nor did we include research which examined issues of collective identities *within* organizations but not *of* organizations, such as professional or social identities (Cornelissen et al., 2007; Pratt, 2003; Whetten, 2007).

Given the phenomenological ambiguity inherent in the OI concept (Corley et al., 2006; Ravasi and Canato, 2013; Whetten, 2006), we accepted that scholars inferred the identity of organizations via information gathered from a variety of sources: for example, internal documents, interviews, and/or observations, as well as ascribed memberships in social categories. Hence, we suspended judgment on whether one type of measure was more valid than another. Furthermore, in keeping with the catholic view of the handbook, we did not invoke a particular conceptualization of OI as a selection mechanism. Thus, for example, we included research that treats OI as an internal subjectively held view, along with that which sees it as an objective organizational feature.

Said differently, we do not view ourselves as the "validity police" described by Hirsch and Levin (1999), in that we do not bring to our review a specified set of standards by which to judge the appropriateness of measures. Instead, we take an "agnostic" view, and our assessment is thus largely inductive and descriptive—classifying different ways of measuring OI and identifying the implications of those differences. We do examine the empirical value of alternate methodologies, using citation counts and journal impact factors as two particular yardsticks. But these and other ex post inferences and conclusions are not based on any a priori assumptions regarding the relative value of each approach.

The consequence of our inclusive scope and agnostic view is that both the rows (number of studies) and the columns (classification categories) are broader than previous methodologically focused reviews of this literature. No assessment of OI research has encompassed a similar expanse of ontological perspectives, types of data, analytical techniques, and phenomena of interest. This greater diversity seems especially important when attempting to identify implications for the future of OI research.

In the next section, we describe the mechanics of our study, including the criteria for selecting articles, the coding scheme for classifying them, and the use of analytic procedures for identifying groups of similar research. This is followed by a summary of the results of our analysis, highlighting the distinguishing features of five research design types. We then identify key patterns and themes in the data, based on the similarities and differences across these groups. Additionally, we make comparisons between groups using certain other data, such as date of publication, authors, citation counts, and impact factors. These combined assessments allow us to make inferences about the relative impact of different types of methodologies, identify implications of using various methods, and speculate on future challenges and opportunities for OI research.

METHODS

The objective of this review is to assess the body of empirical research in OI with respect to how OI is operationalized and measured or observed. Implicit in that objective is that distinct groups of studies would be identified, reflecting major differences in how scholars have conducted OI research. There are many ways by which one can assign cases into groups, based on their relative similarity across a set of characteristics. These various classification mechanisms are of two main forms (Bailey, 1994): a conceptually-driven, deductive *typology* or a numerically derived, inductive *taxonomy*. Prior categorizations of OI research have mostly taken the form of typologies, which in the words of Bailey (1994: 5–6) are conceptual ("representing type concepts rather than empirical cases") and qualitative ("formed without quantification or statistical analyses"). In contrast, and given our objective, a taxonomic approach was warranted.

To execute our intended assessment of OI research methodologies, we needed to: 1) select a suitably inclusive set of studies, guided by some predetermined criteria; 2) categorize those articles along several dimensions, according to a particular coding scheme; and 3) identify groups of studies employing similar methods, using analytical procedures appropriate to the task. In this section, we discuss the mechanics involved in each of these steps.

Selecting the Article Database

First, given the inclusive approach to this review, we cast the net broadly, searching the *ABI Inform* and *EBSCO* databases for all articles with the terms "organization/al" and "identity" in the abstract or keywords. We then scanned the results for the terms "measure/ment" or "analysis," yielding a set of over 300 articles. Given the intended audience of this review, we deliberately focused on management research. Thus, work appearing in marketing, communications, or other fields was excluded, narrowing the set of articles considerably. The initial scan occurred in mid-2012, and a follow-up scan included all work published or forthcoming by the end of that year.

The two co-authors then independently reviewed the abstracts of the remaining articles (approximately 130), determining which should be included. The qualifications for inclusion varied somewhat between authors, but the core criteria were twofold, as explained earlier. First, the research had to be primarily about organizational identity. Second, there must be a specific means and/or attempt to operationalize OI and subsequently identify, measure, and/or study it. The co-authors' assessments were then compared by a research assistant, and a list of discrepancies was compiled and distributed to the authors for further evaluation. After three rounds of this procedure, there was essentially complete agreement, resulting in a set of 82 articles to be coded (see Table 2.1 for a partial list).

Establishing and Applying a Coding Framework

Our coding scheme was informed by previous reviews of OI research (Corley et al., 2006; Cornelissen, 2006; Glynn, 2008; Ravasi and Canato, 2013; Ravasi and van Rekom, 2003), and a comprehensive framework was developed, consisting of six main issues (see Table 2.2). In keeping with the emphasis on conceptualization in prior reviews (Corley et al., 2006; Cornelissen, 2006; Glynn, 2008; Whetten, 2006), the first set of classification categories dealt with the questions of what constitutes OI and how it is defined. The next set of categories identified whether OI was operationalized in terms of the views of insiders or outsiders or both. The third set of categories encompassed the range of analytical approaches (quantitative and qualitative) and the types of data

Table 2.1 Representative list of selected articles

Date	Author(s)	Journal	Citations
1991	Dutton & Dukerich	AMJ	2317
1996	Gioia & Thomas	ASQ	1279
1999	Zuckerman	AJS	1051
2001	Lounsbury & Glynn	SMJ	898
1996	Elsbach & Kramer	ASQ	810
2004	Corley & Gioia	ASQ	580
2006	Ravasi & Schultz	AMJ	533
2002	Dukerich, Golden, & Shortell	ASQ	531
2002	Foreman & Whetten	OSc	482
2000	Glynn	OSc	398
2002	Humphreys & Brown	OSt	391
2000	Zuckerman	ASQ	389
1998	Fox-Wolfgramm, Boal & Hunt	ASQ	365
1997	Golden-Biddle & Rao	OSc	361
2001	Bartel	ASQ	347
2002	Fiol	OSc	336
2010	Battilana & Dorado	AMJ	325
2005	Hsu & Hannan	OSc	312
2006	Dyer & Whetten	ETP	288
2002	Glynn & Abzug	AMJ	287
2007	Nag, Corley & Gioia	AMJ	268
2006	Brown	JMS	247
2000	Rao, Davis & Ward	ASQ	232
2007	Lievens, van Hoye, & Anseel	BJM	198
2005	Brickson	ASQ	196
2009	Tripsas	OSc	187
2010	Gioia, Price, Hamilton, & Thomas	ASQ	165
2006	Brown & Humphreys	JMS	146
2005	Chreim	JMS	137
2010	Navis & Glynn	ASQ	128

Thirty most influential empirically oriented OI papers, based on a combination of impact factor and citations (min. 100), as of Spring 2014.

Table 2.2 Article coding scheme

1. CONCEPTUALIZING OI

How is OI defined? What constitutes OI?

A. *Social categories/forms/types*—industry or market structure to delineate categories and assign OI

B. *Attributes or characteristics*—certain attributes as indicators of self-definitional characteristics of OI

C. *Formal theoretical typology*—a priori theoretical typology to assign OI

D. *Internal claims and understandings*—perceptions or interpretations of org. self-definitions (OI)

E. *Narratives/discourse*—OI reflected in language/rhetoric/metaphors/themes/stories

F. *Schemas/scripts*—OI as cognitive maps or scripts employed

II. PERSPECTIVE

OI as seen from whom—which stakeholders?

A. *Insider*—leaders and/or members of the organization(s)

B. *Outsider*—external stakeholders, including third parties such as media

C. *Both*—a combination of insiders and outsiders

III. MEASURING OI

What kind of data and how is it analyzed?

A. *Qualitative:*

  1. Source of data

    a. Interviews

    b. Focus groups

    c. Non-participant observations

    d. Internal documents

    e. External documents

    f. Symbols

    g. Other

  2. Type of analysis

    a. Ethnographic

    b. Narrative

    c. Discourse

    d. Semiotics

Table 2.2 Continued

    e. Content analysis

    f. Case history

    g. Other

B. *Quantitative:*

  1. Source of data

    a. Surveys

    b. Internal documents

    c. External documents

    d. Secondary data

    e. Other

  2. Type of analysis

    a. Exploratory factor analysis

    b. Confirmatory factor analysis

    c. Path analysis–structural equations modeling

    d. Regression

    e. ANOVA and t-tests

    f. Cluster/scaling analyses

    g. Content analysis

    h. Other

IV. USE OF OI

Is this a study of OI only, or of OI and something else?

A. *OI only*–study of OI dynamics only

    1. Composition

    2. Construction

    3. Change

    4. Conflict

    5. Management

B. *OI and ___*–identity used with another concept

    1. OI as an X antecedent, predicting a Y outcome

    2. OI as a Y outcome, predicted by an X antecedent

    3. OI as a Z moderator/mediator, affecting an X→Y relationship

---

(continued)

Table 2.2 Continued

V. UNIT OF ANALYSIS
What is the referent—OI residing in "what/who"?

A. *Unit*—department/division of a larger organization

B. *Multiple units*—multiple departments of one organization

C. *Brand*—product or service based identity

D. *Organization*—a single organization

E. *Multiple organizations*—multiple organizations, each as a separate entity

F. *Sector/cluster/community*—groups of organizations

G. *Form/type*—organizational forms/institutions

VI. TIME FRAME
Over what time period is OI measured?

A. *Now*—current perceptions or observations

B. *Past*—a recollected past, drawn from current sources

C. *History*—progression over time, but looking backward

D. *Longitudinal*—temporal progression, tracked in real time

involved in "measuring" OI (Corley et al., 2006; Ravasi and Canato, 2013; Ravasi and van Rekom, 2003; van Riel and van Rekom, 2000).

The following section of the coding scheme captured how OI was actually used in the study—that is, was identity examined in conjunction with any other concepts or variables and if so how? Finally, the remaining two sets of coding categories identified the unit or level of analysis and the timeframe or temporal scope of the study. It is important to note that these last three issues (use of OI, unit of analysis, timeframe) have for the most part not been included in prior reviews of OI research. Again, the emphasis in the past has overwhelmingly been on differences in research tradition or paradigm, with the associated ontological or conceptual issues. Much of the actual mechanics of studying OI have largely been unexamined.

This coding scheme differs from prior frameworks in several ways. First, it is more comprehensive in its scope, encompassing both conceptual and mechanical elements of methodologies. Additionally, it includes the full range of analytical approaches, from narrative to ecological research designs. Moreover, the coding framework is considerably more specific and detailed than prior efforts. There are categories within categories within categories—for example, III.A.2.b. = a narrative *type of analysis* as a qualitative *approach* for how OI is *measured* (see Table 2.2). This level of specificity allows for a more fine-grained classification of OI research, leading to increased opportunities for insights and inferences.

Identifying OI Research Clusters

There are several means of conducting a taxonomic classification: for example, cluster analysis, discriminant analysis, factor analysis, or multidimensional scaling. For the purposes of classifying entities on the basis of their relative similarity across a range of specific attributes, cluster analysis is the most commonly used technique (Aldenderfer and Blashfield, 1984; Bailey, 1994). We followed generally established guidelines for performing cluster analyses in social science research (Aldenderfer and Blashfield, 1984; Everitt, 1993; Romesburg, 1984). The mechanics of the process are fairly complex, and a thorough explanation is beyond the scope of this chapter. However, in the following paragraphs we briefly discuss the most critical elements involved, including the choice of a similarity measure, the means employed to cluster the cases, and the determination of the number of clusters to be recognized.

Our data consisted of a population of cases (research studies), each of which was coded according to the presence (1) or absence (0) of a series of attributes (properties of the study), as noted in the coding scheme. Given this type of data, a nonparametric measure of association was necessary—particularly one based on the "matches" of the various attributes within each case. There are a number of such similarity measures available, with differing approaches to the relative inclusion and weighting of matches versus non-matches. Of particular relevance for our data set, some measures completely exclude "joint absences"—that is, where two cases both lack the presence of a particular attribute. Using such measures, any two OI studies would not be judged as relatively similar simply because they both lack some feature. For example, while neither Dutton and Dukerich's (1991) qualitative study of identity and image in the New York Port Authority, nor Zuckermann's (1999) quantitative examination of the role of identity in securities markets contained survey data, they would not be considered similar in their methodologies on the basis of this "joint absence." We thus employed three measures of association which exclude 0-0 joint absences: Jaccard (equal weight given 1-1 matches and 1-0/0-1 non-matches), Sorenson (matches weighted double), and Sokal and Sneath (non-matches weighted double) (Aldenderfer and Blashfield, 1984; Romesburg, 1984). We performed cluster analyses with each of these and found similar solutions.

In terms of the clustering mechanism, there are several different commonly employed algorithms. These can be described as space-contracting, yielding broader, more inclusive, often overlapping clusters, versus space-dilating, yielding tighter, more homogenous, characteristically distinct groups (Everitt, 1993; Romesburg, 1984). Given the objectives of this study, wanting to identify clearly distinctive groups if possible, we preferred the latter type of approach, and specifically employed the complete-linkage (or furthest-neighbor) method of clustering. In addition, because Ward's method—another approach that expands the space between groups—often produces clusters that are easier to discriminate, we used this algorithm as well, with results comparable to the complete-linkage solutions.

Perhaps the most difficult aspect of cluster analysis is determining the appropriate number of groups—that is, that which would accurately capture the patterns of similarities and differences between cases. Although several statistical metrics have been proposed, none of these are without concerns and limitations (Aldenderfer and Blashfield, 1984; Everitt, 1993; Romesburg, 1984). In the end, the most straightforward method is often to simply observe the dendograms, or graphically displayed trees of cluster assignments, and "cut the tree" at a point where there is a clear gap in the "branching." We employed this approach, guided by the dendograms from the use of Ward's algorithm—which generated more visibly distinguishable clusters.

RESULTS

In this section we discuss the results of our analyses, first providing general descriptions of the clusters of OI research that emerged, and then identifying specific patterns and trends across those groups of studies. As noted, we performed several cluster analyses, using three measures of association and two clustering algorithms. These generated very similar solutions. We report the results from the complete-linkage clustering method, using the Sorenson measure of association, which together produced the clearest and seemingly most valid clusters. The solutions suggested that there were between five and six distinct groups of OI research studies. Given the similarity between two of those groups, we present them as five, with two "Grounded Theory" subgroups (see Table 2.3). In addition to having common methodologies, each cluster tended to reflect similar theoretical perspectives, and thus could be characterized in such conceptual terms. However, in keeping with the methodological focus and intent of this chapter, we use the "methods" labels to refer to the groups throughout our subsequent discussion.

Descriptions of Clusters

The first group of studies employs qualitative research methods and a highly interpretivist approach to analyzing the data (e.g., Alvesson, 1994; Brown, 2006; Chreim, 2005; Clegg, Rhodes, and Kornberger, 2007; Humphreys and Brown, 2002). For lack of a better term, and because the methods could be characterized as such, we label this cluster *Narrative and Discourse Analysis*. These 17 studies see OI in the form of stories, themes, language, discourse, etc., residing in oral and written "texts." These narrative themes or discourses are discovered through reading and listening to members' accounts. In general, this research takes a strong constructivist perspective, in the

Table 2.3 Clusters of organizational identity research

	Measurement/ Methods	Conceptual/ Theoretical Lens	No. of Papers	Basic Description	Exemplars
1	Narrative/ Discourse Analysis	Narrative/ Discourse	17	OI as stories, themes, language, discourse, etc. Residing in "texts"—conversations and documents Discovered through reading/listening to members' accounts	Alvesson (1994) Humphreys & Brown (2002) Chreim (2005) Brown (2006)
2a			10	OI as socially constructed claims and understandings Residing in the perceptions and beliefs of members Discovered through ethnographic methods & grounded theory; —using a more structured, systematic approach	Gioia & Thomas (1996) Corley & Gioia (2004) Ravasi & Schultz (2006)
2b	Grounded Theory	Social Construction	12	OI as claims and understandings; also schemas and scripts Residing in the perceptions and beliefs of members Discovered through ethnographic methods & grounded theory	Golden-Biddle & Rao (1997) Glynn (2000) Fiol (2002) Tripsas (2009)
3	Case Study Method	Mixed	10	OI as social claims, attributes, characteristics Residing in member perceptions, org documents, visible characteristics, etc. Discovered through qualitative case-study-like methods	Dutton & Dukerich (1991) Elsbach & Kramer (1996) Lounsbury & Glynn (2001) Battilana & Dorado (2010)
4	Survey Data Analysis	Social Actor/ Essentialist	18	OI as key attributes and characteristics Residing in structures, systems, mission, values, etc.; reflected in members' perceptions Discovered through focus groups, key informants, surveys	Bartel (2001) Foreman & Whetten (2002) Dukerich et al. (2002) Brickson (2005)
5	Secondary Data Analysis	Social Category/ Institutionalist	15	OI as social categories or forms Residing in org form/type, industry group, legal structure, etc. Discovered through external, formal designation or assignment	Zuckerman (1999) Rao, Davis, & Ward (2000) Hsu & Hannan (2005) Navis & Glynn (2010)

vein of naturalistic inquiry (Lincoln and Guba, 1985), wherein things such as "facts" and "truth" are problematized. These characteristics set this approach apart from the other qualitative work in Clusters 2 and 3.

The second group consists of 22 studies using largely *Grounded Theory* methods (e.g., Corley and Gioia, 2004; Fiol, 2002; Gioia and Thomas, 1996; Glynn, 2000; Golden-Biddle and Rao, 1997; Ravasi and Schultz, 2006; Tripsas, 2009). Organizational identity is viewed as socially constructed claims and understandings, residing in the perceptions and beliefs of members. These claims and understandings are discovered through qualitative methods and (most often) a Grounded Theory approach (Strauss and Corbin, 1990). Some cluster solutions split this large set of cases into two subsets. A close inspection of the key characteristics of the two factions indicates that, although they are similar in many respects, one subset employs more structured and systematic research designs.

The third group consists of an eclectic mix of studies, but which are similar in seeing OI as a combination of socially constructed beliefs and key organizational characteristics (e.g., Battilana and Dorado, 2010; Dutton and Dukerich, 1991; Elsbach and Kramer, 1996; Lounsbury and Glynn, 2001). These 10 studies employ a pluralistic (though largely qualitative) methodology, following the classic *Case Study Method* (Eisenhardt, 1989; Yin, 1994). The organization's identity is thus observed through a wide range of sources, including members' perceptions, internal and external documents, nonparticipant observations, symbols and artifacts, and visible organizational attributes. These qualitative data are then analyzed with techniques typical of the case study method; for example, thematic coding, pattern-matching, tabular data displays, etc. (Miles and Huberman, 1994).

The fourth group of research, labeled *Survey Data Analysis*, takes a social actor or essentialist view, seeing OI in the form of self-defining attributes of the organization (e.g., Bartel, 2001; Brickson, 2005; Dukerich et al., 2002; Dyer and Whetten, 2006; Foreman and Whetten, 2002; Glynn and Abzug, 2002). These definitional attributes are understood as real properties of the organization, and as such reside in its structures, systems, mission, values, goals, priorities, etc. This group gathers quantitative data as indicators of the OI, typically in the form of surveys, which are then analyzed via regression or other ANOVA-type methods.

The final group of studies views OI as social categories, using a range of *Secondary Data Analysis* methods (e.g., Hsu and Hannan, 2005; Navis and Glynn, 2010; Rao, Davis, and Ward, 2000; Zuckerman, 1999). This more sociological view of the organization sees identity as residing in the organizational form, industry group, or legal structure of the entity, and these social categorizations of OI are discovered through recognizing formal (typically external) designations, classifications, or assignments of the organization into a particular category or group. Similar to the prior cluster, these studies employ quantitative methodologies, but use secondary rather than primary data, often in the form of large historical data sets. The analyses are conducted using regression or event history techniques.

Key Patterns and Trends

From a methodological point of view, there is a significant difference between the first three and the last two clusters (see Table 2.4). Basically, the 49 articles in the first three groups use qualitative methods, and the 33 articles in the last two use quantitative methods. The 49–33 split reflects the fact that OI research as a whole has been more qualitative than quantitative. Moreover, qualitative studies of organizational identity have increased over time, accounting for a greater proportion of research in recent years: 27 v. 12 in 2007–2013, compared with 22 v. 21 in 1991–2006 (see Figure 2.1). In other words, whereas in the first 15 years of OI research there was a relatively equal qualitative–quantitative balance, in the seven years since there were more than twice as many qualitative as quantitative studies.

In addition to this qualitative–quantitative distinction, there is a considerable skewedness in the type of informants used in OI research. A fraction of the work (17 out of 82) combined insider and outsider perspectives, seven used only an outsider perspective, and the rest relied exclusively on data collected from (internal) organizational members. Moreover, nearly two-thirds of the studies measured only a single construct: organizational identity. That is, a majority of the research (51 v. 31) looked at OI only—in isolation from other concepts. Comparing the clusters on this dimension, only 6 of the 49 articles in groups 1–3 studied OI in conjunction with another construct, whereas 25 of 33 articles in the other two clusters examined OI and one or more concepts. Thus, the lopsided distribution in how the OI concept is employed essentially mirrors the qualitative–quantitative divide.

In terms of the unit of analysis and the timeframe of the study, there were similar patterns of unevenness. First, a majority of the studies (48 of 82) examined a single organization or organizational form. In particular, research in the Narrative/Discourse Analysis and Grounded Theory clusters was overwhelmingly focused on only one organization (33 of 39), while nearly two-thirds of the studies in the other three clusters (28 of 43) studied OI in multiple organizations. Moreover, only a handful of studies were comparative in any fashion. None systematically utilized comparative organizational analysis (King, Felin, and Whetten, 2009) to examine critical OI-related issues—for example, the consequences of organizations selecting different identities or emphasizing different aspects of their identities. With respect to the timeframe of study, there was a lack of diversity in most groups. That is, within a given cluster, the methodological approach had a common timeframe; for example, all cross-sectional in Survey Data, all historical in Secondary Data, and nearly all longitudinal in Grounded Theory. The tendencies for a single-organization unit of analysis and a longitudinal timeframe in Clusters 1 and 2 reflect to a certain degree the emphasis on studying identity processes, or identity "as a process."

In summary, a "big picture" view of the cluster characteristics in Table 2.4 indicates a noticeable trend from groups 1 to 5: from a micro to a macro conceptualization, from using qualitative to quantitative data and analyses, from an insider to an outsider

Table 2.4 Major characteristics of OI research clusters

	N	Conceptualization	Perspective	Data	Analysis	OI Only	OI &___	Unit of Analysis	Time Frame
1	17	*Discourse/ narratives only*	Mostly insider	*Predominantly interviews*	*All narrative/ discourse analysis*	16: conflict, management, change	1	*Mostly single org, or units w/i an org.*	Current or longitudinal
2	22	*Claims and understandings predominantly*	*Insider only*	Interviews, internal documents, some observations	*Grounded theory; ethnographic*	20: change and conflict	2	*Mostly single org.*	Mostly longitudinal
3	10	*Multiple concepts: claims, narratives, attributes, etc.*	Insider or both	External & internal documents, interviews, extensive observations	*Case study method; ethnographic*	7: mostly construction	3	Multiple orgs. or sector/ form	*Past or historical*
4	18	*Attributes; theoretical typology*	Mostly insider	*Mostly surveys*	*Regression, ANOVA, EFA/CFA*	3: composition	15: IV mostly	*Mostly multiple orgs.*	*All current*
5	15	*Social categories; corporate names/ symbols*	*Outsider or both*	*Secondary data*	*Predominantly regression*	5: construction, composition	10: IV and DV	*Mostly sector/ form; some multiple orgs*	*All historical*

Note: particularly distinguishing elements of a cluster are indicated by *italics*

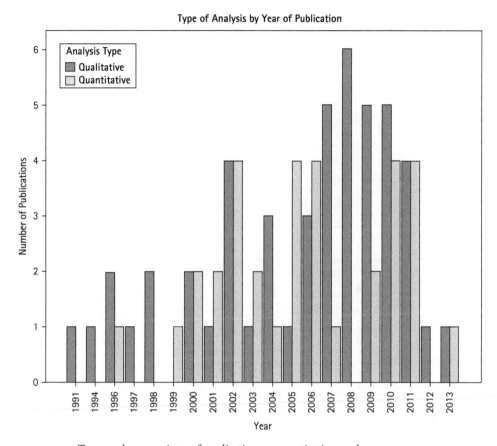

FIGURE 2.1 Temporal comparison of qualitative vs. quantitative analyses

view, from examining OI only to OI in conjunction with other concepts, from studying a single organization to multiple organizations, and from studying organizations
as they go forward to how they are now or have been. Within this broad trend, a general pattern of methodological uniformity and lack of cross-pollination emerges—all
but ten authors (out of almost 130) are found in only one cluster. Moreover, a majority
of the scholars conducting more than one study of OI (15 of 25) tended to favor a single
methodological approach. This suggests that there is very little attempt to use multiple
methodological perspectives and mechanics in OI research.

Further Insights

In addition to the patterns and trends in the major characteristics of the research clusters, key insights emerged from supplementary descriptive statistics of the groups—
data that were not used in the cluster analysis (see Table 2.5). Following from the prior

Table 2.5 Additional descriptive statistics of OI research clusters

Cluster	Papers	Unique Authors	Cites Mean	Cites Median	Cites/Yr Mean	Cites/Yr Median	Ln Cites/Yr Mean	Impact Factor Mean	OI Main Focus	Multiple OIs
1 Narrative/Discourse	17	20	108	90	10.69	9.17	2.01	2.87	6	5
2 Grounded Theory	22	42	219	96	21.46	15.42	2.66	3.48	9	7
3 Case Study Method	10	19	499	211	33.34	21.46	2.91	3.50	4	4
4 Survey Data Analysis	18	41	234	111	19.30	13.35	2.58	3.44	12	10
5 Secondary Data Analysis	15	27	209	134	18.37	14.00	2.66	3.97	12	2

comment regarding the location of authors in particular clusters, there were key differences in the number of "unique" (i.e., non-duplicate) authors within a given cluster and the associated ratio of authors to papers. While most clusters have approximately a 2:1 ratio of authors to papers, the Narrative/Discourse Analysis group is essentially 1:1, suggesting that the same set of scholars are producing the majority of the research in that area, and that this conversation is not attracting new entrants.

We also examined the relative influence of research in each cluster, based on the metrics of citation counts and journal impact factor. Given the relatively small numbers of cases in each group, and the possibility for one or two papers to highly skew the statistics, these data and the insights gleaned should be taken with some caution. Due to the potential for skewedness, we report both the mean and median number of total citations and citations per year. Additionally, to compensate for the effect of time of publication on citations (i.e., articles in press longer will naturally accrue more citations), we note the number of citations per year, along with a natural log transformation of these data. The citation count and impact factor statistics are one area where the two subsets of the Grounded Theory cluster differed. Specifically, the subgroup employing very structured and more systematic Grounded Theory methods had higher citation counts and impact factors than the subgroup employing a less methodical and more pluralistic approach. The overall pattern of numbers in Table 2.5 suggests that the use of well-established, "systematic" methods produced the most cited articles. On the other hand, it appears that the more unconventional, or more interpretivist the methodology employed, the lower the impact of the research.

On a different note, the two rightmost columns in Table 2.5 provide insight into how OI research has progressed from its earliest foundations. In their seminal essay, Albert and Whetten originally set out to understand resistance to change, but their discovery of the role of OI in the process had an epiphany-like effect, causing them to reverse the figure and ground, such that identity became the focus of their research. In the 30-plus years since, research on OI has tended to reverse the figure and ground again. Just over half (43 of 82) of the articles we examined placed OI as the main focus of the research, with the two quantitative clusters having a greater percentage of such work (24 of 33 studies). Interestingly, in Clusters 1–3 the concept of OI tended to be used in one of two ways: 1) as a lens or perspective to examine other phenomena, such as managing change or gaining legitimacy; or 2) as an opportunity to demonstrate the merits of a particular epistemology, such as discourse analysis.

In a similar fashion, whereas Albert and Whetten framed the OI construct within the context of hybrid identities, very little work has subsequently examined the phenomenon of multiple organizational identities. Although the notion of multiple identities is generally recognized as central to the conceptualization of OI (Corley et al., 2006; Pratt and Foreman, 2000a; Whetten, Foreman, and Dyer, 2013; Pratt, this volume, Ch. 6), most empirical work has not incorporated it. In fact, less than a third (28 of 82) of the studies specifically operationalized the OI construct in terms of multiple/hybrid identities (e.g., Batillana and Dorado, 2010; Brickson, 2005; Foreman and Whetten, 2002; Glynn, 2000; Gioia and Thomas, 1996; Golden-Biddle and Rao, 1997).

Interestingly, ten of the 28 that did so are in the Survey Data group—not surprising given the cluster's relative adherence to the original Albert and Whetten formulation of OI.

DISCUSSION AND IMPLICATIONS

The study of organizational identity appears to be a microcosm of the field of organizational studies. Almost every kind of research topic, theoretical lens, and methodological approach is represented. It shouldn't be surprising that a subject that is so central to our field's conceptions of organizing and organizations would attract a diverse set of interests and perspectives. While this observation suggests that the study of OI has achieved a major milestone in terms of academic legitimacy, this achievement has not come without cost or concern.

Our assessment of methodologies used in OI research indicates a highly compartmentalized field, with little methodological pluralism or cross-fertilization, resulting in five very different conversations. Compounding the concern over these "methods silos" is that scholars' choices of methods appear to be tightly aligned with and shaped by their view of OI, with the ensuing conceptual fragmentation threatening an erosion of OI as a defined concept. Moreover, much of OI research is conducted in a way that limits its ability to inform and contribute to the larger organizational studies community, endangering the relevance and legitimacy of the OI construct. We discuss these three related concerns of methodological compartmentalization, conceptual dilution, and academic legitimation below.

The fact that five distinct groups emerged from our classification process is not altogether surprising—it is to a degree a natural consequence of the cluster analysis procedure. However, what we found especially striking is how predictable the measurement approaches in the five clusters have become. In most cases, knowing which cluster a study is in (per Table 2.4) allows potential readers to extrapolate and make fairly accurate statements about the research questions being asked, the types and sources of data collected, the analytical techniques used, and broadly speaking, the conclusions drawn regarding the nature of organizations and their identities. As a result, rather than OI research being phenomenologically driven, work in the field is essentially methodologically driven. This perception is supported by our finding that authors of multiple OI studies tend to use the same methodology.

While this observation of methodological compartmentalization is certainly not peculiar to the study of OI, it appears to contradict the age-old advice given to doctoral students to match their method to their research focus and question, rather than shaping their topic to match their preferred method. Moreover, it is inconsistent with the view offered by Edmonson and McManus (2007) and Colquitt and Zapata-Phelan (2007), that qualitative methods are most appropriate early in the life cycle of a research topic, due to their capacity for building theory (introducing new concepts, proposing X–Y predictions), which can be subsequently tested using quantitative methods. In contrast, what we observe in organizational identity research is qualitative and quantitative studies largely examining different questions or facets of OI altogether—which, in most cases, reinforce long-standing conceptual divides in the OI literature. For example, the issue of the relative continuity or stability of OI—what Albert and Whetten termed enduringness—has been the topic of much debate and inquiry (Corley et al., 2006; Gioia et al., 2013; Whetten, 2006). Interestingly, all of the research attempting to examine this question has been of the qualitative sort (e.g., Chreim, 2005; Corley and Gioia, 2004; Gioia et al., 2010; Tripsas, 2009; Ravasi and Schultz, 2006), with an emphasis on studying "OI as a process." To date there are no quantitative assessments of the enduringness of OI.

Such methodological parochialism is a concern in itself. But potentially more disconcerting is that these methodological bents appear to some degree to be a reflection of strong assumptions and biases regarding the conceptualization of the OI construct. Previous reviews of the OI literature have identified conceptual fault lines and urged scholars to adopt synthetic (both-and) treatments of the subject over fractious (either-or) ones (e.g., Brown et al., 2006; Corley et al., 2006; Cornelissen et al., 2007; Ravasi and Canato, 2013). Our review highlights a critical obstacle to both-and research becoming the norm: the simple observation that scholars' preferences for how OI is conceptualized are typically closely aligned with their methodological predilections and that this alignment is self-reinforcing.

What we observe in the data is a general theme: that studies built upon a particular set of assumptions regarding the nature of social reality use their findings to "define" the properties of OI, typically in a manner that is consistent with those a priori assumptions. As such, there is the danger that methods are driving the conclusions in OI research. For example, referring to the aforementioned issue of enduringness, there is growing consensus that OI is unstable, but this is in large part due to the fact that most studies look at it in flux (e.g., during organizational change) and examine an "extreme case"—there is a lack of comparisons with other contexts where the organization and its identity might be perfectly stable. Unfortunately, inasmuch as such data-based conceptualizations of OI typically fail to add the all-important qualifier, "a view of OI from the X perspective," it might appear, especially to newcomers, that the OI literature has little in common other than the name itself (Brubaker and Cooper, 2001; Cornelissen et al., 2007; Pratt and Foreman, 2000b). The combined methodological and ontological provincialism of OI research leads to a degree of fragmentation that threatens to erode the notion of OI as a clearly defined concept. The concern is that organizational identity may end up being seen less as a construct and more as a lens—a perspective for studying organizations—or become subsumed under a related construct, such as "logic" or "rhetoric."

These concerns of methodological compartmentalization and conceptual fragmentation have significant ramifications for the place of the OI construct in the organizational studies field. It can be argued that the process of legitimating a new concept contains two equally important requirements. First, interest in studying the concept must expand beyond a handful of devotees—attracting the attention of a wide array of scholars seeking a better understanding of what it is. As has been noted, from our results we can safely conclude that OI research has satisfied this requirement. Having succeeded in attracting scholars to the study of OI, the second "academic legitimacy" hurdle for a new concept to clear is being included in research on other topics and concepts. Whereas the first hurdle entails creating a critical mass of interest, the second hurdle involves a shift from predominantly internal conversations ("OI only" research) to demonstrating the utility of OI when paired with concepts that are central to other conversations ("OI and ___"). Scholars studying other concepts must recognize the merits of the new concept, either as a predictor or an outcome of their central interest. Taking existing studies "of" the new concept and adding subsequent studies "with" the new concept signal its emergence as a central theoretical construct within the broader field.

If we take the overall trends we have noted—particularly the increasing proportion of qualitative research and the emphasis on OI only—and combine them with the fact that the majority of qualitative studies are looking at only one organization, there is a growing amount of work being done in a manner which potentially limits the ability of OI scholarship to inform the broader organizational studies literature and managerial practice. We can imagine several harmful consequences if OI research fails to become relevant to scholars studying other organizational concepts. First, the novelty of OI research will eventually wear off, as the study of OI eventually runs its course, having exhausted any remaining interesting questions or issues pertaining to how OI is constituted, managed, and changed. Second, parallel to a loss of novelty, scholars who were once attracted to a new conversation will increasingly conclude that research on OI is no longer germane to their respective core research interests—leaving behind a relatively small set of scholars writing papers for a diminishing internal audience.

DIRECTIONS FOR FUTURE RESEARCH

As a methodological countermove to the observed trend toward greater compartmentalization, fragmentation, and isolation, we propose replacing "simple" approaches to studying OI, exemplified by Clusters 1–5, with more complex research designs. Such studies would feature, among other things, multiple methods, multiple levels of analysis, multiple organizations, and multiple concepts. Said differently, we propose removing the methodological barriers to studying a more complex, holistic conception of OI. More specifically, among other things, we feel that the field needs to move beyond an N of 1: where identity is being studied in depth but within one organization, or studied across multiple organizations but within one form or type. Furthermore, there is a need to move beyond studying OI only—in isolation from other concepts. And in general, while recognizing the challenges in conducting mixed-method research (Creswell and Plano Clark, 2011), scholars should consider how to incorporate multiple types of data and analyses into their research designs.

The use of complex research designs opens the door to systematic investigations of how organizations manage to achieve "optimal distinctiveness"—balancing their twin needs for similarity and uniqueness (Gioia et al., 2010; Navis and Glynn, 2010; Whetten, 2007). This dual focus, in turn, highlights the merits of combining in the same study organizational identity, organizational legitimacy (similarity), and organizational reputation (uniqueness) (Foreman et al., 2012). Findings from such studies might offer promising insights for combining the sociological focus on explaining surprising similarities between organizations and the economic focus on using surprising organizational differences to explain outcomes important to organizations.

Complex research designs would also allow for the simultaneous study of both the internal (shared understandings) and external (social category memberships) perspectives for conceptualizing and measuring OI (Clegg et al., 2007; Navis and Glynn, 2010). This, in turn, would invite systematic comparisons of the identity tensions involved in being true to an organization's past and adapting to changing circumstances (Ravasi and Schultz, 2006; Tripsas, 2009; Schultz, this volume, Ch. 5). Coupled with research on strategic change, this line of inquiry could offer a counterpoint to strategy's single-minded focus on adaptation as a prerequisite for effective competition.

More complex designs, including multiple levels of analysis and multiple organizations, would highlight the cross-level nature and utility of the OI construct (Ashforth et al., 2011; Ashforth, this volume, Ch. 4), and provide opportunities for comparative organizational research (King et al., 2009). The combined effect would also bring to the foreground the *organizational* level of analysis. It seems ironic that organizational identity, a concept capable of supporting the premise—lying at the core of organizational studies—that the organizational level is a source of significant variability, has frequently been operationalized at the level of either individuals or institutions.

One particular and practical means of achieving complex research designs is for researchers to work with colleagues from different traditions. Currently, OI studies that include scholars from multiple theoretical perspectives and/or different methodological approaches are extremely rare. What would we learn if more research took such a combined team approach?

Finally, in the absence of such collaboration and more complex research designs, OI researchers should be more circumspect about drawing conclusions from their work, given that such findings are likely based on a limited range of organizational contexts, types of data, and analytical techniques. Scholars should "recognize their silo" and be more aware of the potential limitations and constraints that follow (Pratt and Foreman, 2000b).

CONCLUSION

The study of organizational identity has attracted a large number of scholars bringing with them a wide range of methodological approaches. Indeed, our study suggests that this body of research could serve as an informative case study for an organizational studies methods course, illustrating how the major methodological approaches in our field have been applied to a single topic. That being said, it is not at all clear that the collective understanding of organizational identity has benefited from such a diverse set of research methods. While we are heartened by promising interest in utilizing both-and conceptions of OI to inform OI research, our results suggest that sustained, consequential progress toward that goal is being hindered by researchers' personal preferences for methodologies that foster either-or conclusions about OI. It appears from our analysis that OI research is becoming increasingly bifurcated—polarized by two centers of gravity—rather than moving in the opposite direction as many have implored. One side employs qualitative methods, using primarily internal perceptions to study OI-as-a-process (or OI-related processes). The other side employs quantitative methods, using external observations to study OI-as-a-social-form.

In addition, it appears that long-standing conceptual disagreements over the nature of an organization's identity are being reinforced by scholars' choice of methods for studying OI that are congruent with their preferred view of OI. This has the effect of research findings being used to characterize the concept of OI in a manner that is consistent with, and thereby simply reinforcing, the authors' a priori assumptions. The absence of a generally accepted definition of OI, combined with the use of parochial research designs, results in authors shaping the concept of OI to fit their ontological and epistemological suppositions about the nature of organizations and organizing. Indeed, especially given the pattern of methods silos we have identified, it appears that the prevailing conception of OI has devolved to "how this study and others using this method have measured it." In our view, a body of literature that has to be indexed by method is highly problematic. Unless fundamental changes are made in the design and execution of individual research studies, the prevalence of a strong alignment between OI conceptualization and measurement is likely to promote greater balkanization in OI scholarship, and thereby endanger the relevance and impact of such work.

We suggest that the most promising path for advancing the study of organizational identity involves more complex research designs, with multiple methods and measures, systematic comparisons between organizations, and the study of OI in combination with other concepts, either as a predictor or outcome. The resulting body of scholarship would likely offer more robust, valid, empirically based conclusions regarding the distinctive meaning of this concept and its role in organizational design and processes, and would enhance the relevance of OI scholarship for the broader field of organizational studies. This direction necessitates a fundamental shift in how OI is studied: from seeing the concept as an opportunity "to advance the way I think and conduct research as a scholar" to examining what we know about OI as both a construct and a causal mechanism, and designing research that addresses unanswered questions about OI's properties and capabilities.

Acknowledgments

The authors would like to express their appreciation to their action editor, Mike Pratt, for his valuable guidance and advice, shepherding us through the process of writing this chapter. We are also grateful to him and the rest of the editorial team for providing their reactions, insights, and suggestions on several previous drafts. We would also like to thank David Hunsacker for his help in the initial stages of selecting and coding articles.

References

Albert, S. A. and Whetten, D. A. (1985). "Organizational Identity." In *Research in Organizational Behavior*, vol. 7, edited by L. L. Cummings, and B. M. Staw, 263–95. Greenwich, CT: JAI.

Aldenderfer, M. S. and Blashfield, R. K. (1984). *Cluster Analysis*, Quantitative Applications in the Social Sciences, vol. 44. Newbury Park, CA: SAGE.

Alvesson, M. (1994). "Talking in Organizations: Managing Identity and Impressions." *Organization Studies* 15(4): 535–63.

Ashforth, B. E. (2016). "Organizational, Subunit, and Individual Identities." In *The Oxford Handbook of Organizational Identity*, edited by M. G. Pratt, M. Schultz, B. E. Ashforth, and D. Ravasi, 70–92. Oxford: Oxford University Press.

Ashforth, B. E., Rogers, K. M., and Corley, K. G. (2011). "Identity in Organizations: Exploring Cross-level Dynamics." *Organization Science* 22(5): 1144–56.

Bailey, K. D. (1994). *Typologies and Taxonomies: An Introduction to Classification Techniques*, Quantitative Applications in the Social Sciences, vol. 102. Newbury Park, CA: SAGE.

Bartel, C. A. (2001). "Social Comparisons in Boundary-Spanning Work: Effects of Community Outreach on Members' Organizational Identity and Identification." *Administrative Science Quarterly* 46: 379–413.

Battilana, J. and Dorado, S. (2010). "Building Sustainable Hybrid Organizations: The Case of Commercial Microfinance Organizations." *Academy of Management Journal* 53: 1419–40.

Brickson, S. L. (2005). "Organizational Identity Orientation: Forging a Link between Organizational Identity and Organization's Relations with Stakeholders." *Administrative Science Quarterly* 50: 576–609.

Brown, A. D. (2006). "A Narrative Approach to Collective Identities." *Journal of Management Studies* 43: 731–753.

Brown, T. J., Dacin, P. A., Pratt, M. G., and Whetten, D. A. (2006). "Identity, Intended Image, Construed Image, and Reputation: An Interdisciplinary Framework and Suggested Terminology." *Journal of the Academy of Marketing Science* 34(2): 99–106.

Brubaker, R. and Cooper, C. (2001). "Beyond 'Identity.'" *Theory and Society* 29: 1–47.

Chreim, S. (2005). "The Continuity–Change Duality in Narrative Texts of Organizational Identity." *Journal of Management Studies* 42: 567–93.

Clegg, S. R., Rhodes, C., and Kornberger, M. (2007). "Desperately Seeking Legitimacy: Organizational Identity and Emerging Industries." *Organization Studies* 28: 495–513.

Colquitt, J. A. and Zapata-Phelan, C. P. (2007). "Trends in Theory Building and Theory Testing: A Five-Decade Study of the *Academy of Management Journal.*" *Academy of Management Journal* 50: 1281–303.

Corley, K. G. and Gioia, D. A. (2004). "Identity Ambiguity and Change in the Wake of a Corporate Spin-Off." *Administrative Science Quarterly* 49: 173–208.

Corley, K. G., Harquail, C. V., Pratt, M. G., Glynn, M. A., Fiol, C. M., and Hatch, M. J. (2006). "Guiding Organizational Identity through Aged Adolescence." *Journal of Management Inquiry* 15: 85–99.

Cornelissen, J. P. (2006). "Metaphor and the Dynamics of Knowledge in Organization Theory: A Case Study of the Organizational Identity Metaphor." *Journal of Management Studies* 43(4): 683–709.

Cornelissen, J. P., Haslam, S. A., and Balmer, J. M. T. (2007). "Social Identity, Organizational Identity, and Corporate Identity: Towards an Integrated Understanding of Processes, Patternings and Products." *British Journal of Management* 18: S1–S16.

Creswell, J. W. and Plano Clark, V. L. (2011). *Designing and Conducting Mixed Method Research.* Thousand Oaks, CA: SAGE.

Dukerich, J. M., Golden, B. R., and Shortell, S. M. (2002). "Beauty Is in the Eye of the Beholder: The Impact of Organizational Identification, Identity, and Image on the Cooperative Behavior of Physicians." *Administrative Science Quarterly* 47: 507–33.

Dutton, J. E. and Dukerich, J. M. (1991). "Keeping an Eye on the Mirror: Image and Identity in Organizational Adaptation." *Academy of Management Journal* 34(3): 517–54.

Dyer, W. G. and Whetten, D. A. (2006). "Family Firms and Social Responsibility: Preliminary Evidence from the S&P 500." *Entrepreneurship Theory and Practice* 30(6): 785–802.

Edmonson, A. C. and McManus, S. E. (2007). "Methodological Fit in Field Research." *Academy of Management Review* 32: 1155–79.

Eisenhardt, K. M. (1989). "Building Theories from Case Study Research." *Academy of Management Review* 14: 532–50.

Elsbach, K. D. and Kramer, R. M. (1996). "Members' Responses to Organizational Identity Threats: Encountering and Countering the *Business Week* Rankings." *Administrative Science Quarterly* 41(3): 442–76.

Everitt, B. S. (1993). *Cluster Analysis*, 3rd edn. London: Arnold.

Fiol, C. M. (2002). "Capitalizing on Paradox: The Role of Language in Transforming Organizational Identities." *Organization Science* 13(6): 653–66.

Foreman, P. O. and Whetten, D. A. (2002). "Members' Identification with Multiple-Identity Organizations." *Organization Science* 13: 618–35.

Foreman, P. O., Whetten, D. A., and Mackey, A. (2012). "An Identity-Based View of Reputation, Image, and Legitimacy: Clarifications and Distinctions among Related Constructs." In *The Oxford Handbook of Corporate Reputation*, edited by M. Barnett, and T. G. Pollock, 179–200. Oxford: Oxford University Press.

Gioia, D. A. and Hamilton, A. L. (2016). "Great Debates in Organizational Identity Study." In *The Oxford Handbook of Organizational Identity*, edited by M. G. Pratt, M. Schultz, B. E. Ashforth, and D. Ravasi, 21–38. Oxford: Oxford University Press.

Gioia, D. A., Patvardhan, S. D., Hamilton, A. L., and Corley, K. G. (2013). "Organizational Identity Formation and Change." *The Academy of Management Annals* 7(1): 123–92.

Gioia, D. A., Price, K. N., Hamilton, A. L., and Thomas, J. B. (2010). "Forging an Identity: An Insider-Outsider Study of Processes Involved in the Formation of Organizational Identity." *Administrative Science Quarterly* 55(1): 1–46.

Gioia, D. A. and Thomas, J. B. (1996). "Identity, Image, and Issue Interpretation: Sense-making during Strategic Change in Academia." *Administrative Science Quarterly* 41(3): 370–403.

Glynn, M. A. (2000). "When Cymbals become Symbols: Conflict over Organizational Identity within a Symphony Orchestra." *Organization Science* 11(3): 285–98.

Glynn, M. A. (2008). "Beyond Constraint: How Institutions Enable Identities." In *The SAGE Handbook of Organizational Institutionalism*, edited by R. Greenwood, C. Oliver, R. Suddaby, and K. Sahlin-Andersson, 413–30. London: SAGE.

Glynn, M. A. and Abzug, R. (2002). "Institutionalizing Identity: Symbolic Isomorphism and Organizational Names." *Academy of Management Journal* 45: 267–80.

Golden-Biddle, K. and Rao, H. (1997). "Breaches in the Boardroom: Organizational Identity and Conflicts of Commitment in a Nonprofit Organization." *Organization Science* 8(6): 593–611.

Hirsch, P. M. and Levin, D. Z. (1999). "Umbrella Advocates versus Validity Police: A Life-Cycle Model." *Organization Science* 10(2): 199–212.

Hsu, G. and Hannan, M. T. (2005). "Identities, Genres, and Organizational Forms." *Organization Science* 16: 474–90.

Humphreys, M. and Brown, A. D. (2002). "Narratives of Organizational Identity and Identification: A Case Study of Hegemony and Resistance." *Organization Studies* 23: 421–47.

King, B. G., Felin, T. and Whetten, D. A. (eds.). (2009). *Studying Differences between Organizations: Comparative Approaches to Organizational Research*. Bingley, UK: JAI Press.

Lincoln, Y. S. and Guba, E. G. (1985). *Naturalistic Inquiry*. Thousand Oaks, CA: SAGE Publications.

Lounsbury, M. and Glynn, M. A. (2001). "Cultural Entrepreneurship: Stories, Legitimacy, and the Acquisition of Resources." *Strategic Management Journal* 22: 545–64.

Miles, M. and Huberman, M. (1994). *Qualitative Data Analysis: A Source Book of New Methods*, 2nd edn. Thousand Oaks, CA: SAGE.

Navis, C. and Glynn, M. A. (2010). "How New Market Categories Emerge: Temporal Dynamics of Legitimacy, Identity, and Entrepreneurship in Satellite Radio, 1990–2005." *Administrative Science Quarterly* 55(3): 439–71.

Pratt, M. G. (2003). "Disentangling Collective Identities." In *Identity Issues in Groups: Research on Managing Groups and Teams*, vol. 5, edited by J. T. Polzer 161–88. Boston: Elsevier Science.

Pratt, M. G. (2016). "Hybrid and Multiple Organizational Identities." In *The Oxford Handbook of Organizational Identity*, edited by M. G. Pratt, M. Schultz, B. E. Ashforth, and D. Ravasi, 106–20. Oxford: Oxford University Press.

Pratt, M. G. and Foreman, P. O. (2000a). "Classifying Managerial Responses to Multiple Organizational Identities." *Academy of Management Review* 25: 18–42.

Pratt, M. G. and Foreman, P. O. (2000b). "The Beauty of and Barriers to Organizational Theories of Identity." *Academy of Management Review* 25(1): 141–3.

Rao, H., Davis, G. F., and Ward, A. (2000). "Embeddedness, Social Identity and Mobility: Why Firms Leave the NASDAQ and Join the New York Stock Exchange." *Administrative Science Quarterly* 45: 268–92.

Ravasi, D. (2016). "Organizational Identity, Culture, and Image." In *The Oxford Handbook of Organizational Identity*, edited by M. G. Pratt, M. Schultz, B. E. Ashforth, and D. Ravasi, 65–78. Oxford: Oxford University Press.

Ravasi, D. and Canato, A. (2013). "How Do I Know Who You Think You Are? A Review of Research Methods on Organizational Identity." *International Journal of Management Reviews* 15(2): 185–204.

Ravasi, D. and Schultz, M. J. (2006). "Responding to Organizational Identity Threats: Exploring the Role of Organizational Culture." *Academy of Management Journal* 49: 433–58.

Ravasi, D. and van Rekom, J. (2003). "Key Issues in Organizational Identity and Identification Theory." *Corporate Reputation Review* 6(2): 118–32.

Romesburg, H. C. (1984). *Cluster Analysis for Researchers.* Malabar, FL: Krieger.

Schultz, M. (2016). "Organizational Identity Change and Temporality." In *The Oxford Handbook of Organizational Identity*, edited by M. G. Pratt, M. Schultz, B. E. Ashforth, and D. Ravasi, 93–105. Oxford: Oxford University Press.

Strauss, A. and Corbin, J. (1990). *Basics of Qualitative Research: Grounded Theory Procedures and Techniques.* Newbury Park, CA: SAGE.

Tripsas, M. (2009). "Technology, Identity, and Inertia through the Lens of 'The Digital Photography Company.'" *Organization Science* 20(2): 441–60.

Van Rekom, J. and van Riel, C. B. M. (2000). "Operational Measures of Organizational Identity: A Review of Existing Methods." *Corporate Reputation Review* 3(4): 334–50.

Whetten, D. A. (2006). "Albert and Whetten Revisited: Strengthening the Concept of Organizational Identity." *Journal of Management Inquiry* 15(3): 219–34.

Whetten, D. A. (2007). "A Critique of Organizational Identity Scholarship: Challenging the Uncritical Use of Social Identity Theory When Social Identities Are also Social Actors." In *Identity and the Modern Organization*, edited by C. A. Bartel, S. Blader, and A. Wrzesniewski, 253–72. Mahwah, NJ: Lawrence Erlbaum.

Whetten, D. A., Foreman, P. O., and Dyer, W. G., Jr. (2013). "Organizational Identity and Family Business." In *The SAGE Handbook of Family Business*, edited by L. Melin, M. Nordqvist, and P. Sharma, 480–97. London, UK: SAGE.

Yin, R. K. (1994). *Case Study Research: Design and Methods*, 2nd edn. Beverly Hills, CA: SAGE.

Zuckerman, E. W. (1999). "The Categorical Imperative: Securities Analysts and the Illegitimacy Discount." *American Journal of Sociology* 104(5): 1398–438.

....

CHAPTER 3

ORGANIZATIONAL IDENTITY, CULTURE, AND IMAGE

....

DAVIDE RAVASI

WHEN presenting one's research to colleagues or introducing organizational identity to students or executives, it is not uncommon to be asked about whether and
how this concept really differs from more familiar and established ones, such as
image or culture. In this chapter, I first briefly discuss the prevailing view among
organizational identity scholars about how organizational identity differs from organizational image. I then focus on the more debated issue of whether and how
organizational identity and culture differ, and review past work investigating the
dynamic relationships between these two constructs. I conclude by highlighting
how interrelations among the three constructs affect dynamism in organizational
identities.

ORGANIZATIONAL IDENTITY AND IMAGE

....

Organizational identity scholars generally agree to use the term "organizational identity" to refer to (internal) members' perceptions, and to use the term "organizational
image" or "reputation" to refer to (external) stakeholders' perceptions (see Brown,
Dacin, Pratt, and Whetten, 2006; Corley et al., 2006; Whetten, 2006; Price and Gioia,
2008; Gioia, Hamilton, and Patvardhan, 2014). Gioia, Schultz, and Corley (2000) further propose to distinguish between the "transient impressions" of an organization
that a specific action or event leave on stakeholders, and the "reputation" of an organization, understood as the "relatively stable, long-term, collective judgements by outsiders" (p. 67). This distinction, however, is not universally accepted, and some scholars use either the term "image" (e.g., Hatch and Schultz, 1997, 2002) or "reputation"

(e.g., Whetten and Mackey, 2002; Brown et al., 2006) to label external perceptions, with no further distinction.

Scholars also use the term "construed external image" to refer to members' beliefs about the perception of external audiences (Dutton, Dukerich and Harquail; 1994). They use the term "intended image" (Brown et al., 2006) or "desired future image" (Gioia and Thomas, 1996) to refer to members' aspirations about how their organizations is perceived externally, and the term "projected images" to refer to the content of communicative actions aimed at achieving these aspirations (Rindova, 1997).

Occasionally, organization scholars use the term "corporate identity," borrowed from the field of corporate communication (Olins, 1989), to refer to a relatively coordinated set of visible and tangible representations of an organization (logos, products, visual communication materials, building features, design of uniforms, etc.) (Rindova and Schultz, 1998); these representations influence how an organization is perceived externally—that is, its image—and should therefore be carefully orchestrated (Olins, 1989).

Recent developments in organizational sociology threaten to blur the conceptual distinction between identity and image as an internal versus external issue. As exemplified by Zuckerman (this volume, Ch. 10), macro-organizational sociologists have adopted the term "identity" to refer to socially constructed categories used by stakeholders to "classify" organizations (Hsu and Hannan, 2005) and to decide whether they are worthy of their attention and support (Zuckerman, 1999). These developments may be reflected in the occasional distinction between "internal identity" and "external identity" (e.g., Tripsas, 2009).

Gioia and colleagues, however, argue that this use of the term is "a mis-labeling of the concept of image" (Gioia, Patvardhan, Hamilton, and Corley, 2013: 127) and it is incompatible with current theories of organizational identity. While macro-level research now widely uses the term "identity" to examine how audiences categorize organizations, recently published studies investigating organizational identity at meso- and micro-level (organization, group, individual) still tend to conform to the traditional terminology, and use "identity" to refer to internal perceptions, and "image" to refer to external ones (e.g., Ravasi and Phillips, 2011; Drori, Wrzesniewski, and Ellis, 2013; Hoon and Jacobs, 2014).

Several studies explored the dynamic interrelations between different types of image and identity. Dutton and Dukerich (1991) first observed that construed images reflecting media coverage of organizational actions may induce members to reassess the appropriateness of these actions in light of a re-examination of the identity of the organization ("Is this who we really are?"). Elsbach and Kramer (1996) revealed different cognitive tactics that members use to preserve a sense of who they are in the face of images that question their self perceptions. Later work argued that a discrepancy between current and desired images may drive changes in strategy (Gioia and Thomas, 1996; Ravasi and Phillips, 2011) and identity (Gioia et al., 2000). Research also shows how external images tend to be sticky and inertial (Tripsas, 2009), and that members may be "captivated" by particularly attractive images and unable to adapt identity to changing internal and external circumstances (Kjærgaard, Morsing, and Ravasi, 2011).

ORGANIZATIONAL IDENTITY AND CULTURE

Clarifying the difference between organizational identity and culture has been a recurrent preoccupation of identity scholars (e.g., Fiol, 1991; Hatch and Schultz, 1997, 2002; Fiol, Hatch, and Golden-Biddle, 1998; Corley et al., 2006; Whetten, 2006) and culture scholars alike (e.g., Martin, 2002; Alvesson, 2013). In fact, as Alvesson and Robertson (this volume, Ch. 9) illustrate, some scholars wonder whether, after all, organizational identity scholars are simply using a different terminology to describe what previous work investigated as "culture." This confusion is understandable, because organizational culture, as I discuss later in more depth, is an important referent for the self-referential claims and understandings that constitute what we commonly refer to as "organizational identity."

In the last two decades, scholarly understanding of organizational identity and culture has evolved, as identity scholars have gradually disentangled the various facets of the phenomenon (Ravasi and Canato, 2013), and culture scholars explored alternative views of culture (Weber and Dacin, 2011). At the same time, empirical research has gradually illuminated, not only the distinction, but also the dynamic interrelations between these two constructs (e.g., Ravasi and Schultz, 2006; Rindova, Dalpiaz, and Ravasi, 2011; Canato, Ravasi, and Phillips, 2013; Hatch, Schultz, and Skov, 2015). This line of inquiry sharpened our understanding of the theoretical differences between these constructs, and showed the importance of this theoretical distinction for our capacity to understand organizational phenomena.

Organizational scholars generally view organizational culture as composed of ideational and material elements (e.g., Smircich, 1983; Martin, 2002). Ideational elements are embodied in the knowledge structures that members use to interpret their organizational reality (variously referred to as beliefs, assumptions, frames, categories, schematas, etc.) and define "the correct way to perceive, think, and feel" about this reality (Schein, 1985). These ideational elements are in turn manifested in various cultural forms (symbols and artefacts, stories, language, rituals, etc.), formal practices (policies, structures, and systems), and informal practices (unwritten norms and conventions) (Trice and Beyer, 1984; Martin, 2002) that shape behavior within an organization.[1]

---

[1] Over the years, as the study of culture gained popularity, different interpretations of this concept proliferated (see Giorgi, Lockwood, and Glynn, 2015 for a recent review). Two perspectives, in particular, offer contraposed views of culture as a "constraint on action versus a resource for action" (Weber and Dacin, 2011: 289). Early conceptualizations of organizational culture described it as a relatively stable set of taken-for-granted elements that shape members' thoughts and actions in a coherent and predictable way, and provide the structural stability fundamental for the everyday functioning of an organization (Geertz, 1973; Schein, 1985). Later research drew attention to the possible co-existence of multiple sub-cultures associated, for instance, with different professional

Attempts to establish a theoretical difference between identity and culture observed that, compared to the broader notion of culture, organizational identity refers to a narrower set of meaning structures focused on "how members develop, express, and project their organizational sense of self" (Hatch and Schultz, 2000: 23). These structures are inherently comparative and self-reflective (Pratt, 2003; Corley et al., 2006), in that they shape members' understanding of how their organization differs from comparable ones. It has also been argued that the more explicit nature of identity claims distinguishes them from the largely tacit nature of cultural meaning structures (Hatch and Schultz, 2000).

Based on these ideas, empirical research has investigated the dynamic interrelations between the two constructs. Some studies built on Albert and Whetten's (1985) early idea that culture serves as an important referent for organizational identity, and investigated how culture affects members' understandings of "who we are as an organization," and helps them preserve a sense of continuity amid changes (Corley, 2004; Ravasi and Schultz, 2006). Other studies built instead on the idea that organizational identity contextualizes members' understanding of cultural norms (Fiol, 1991), and examined how new organizational identities may foster organizational and cultural changes (e.g., Gioia and Thomas, 1996; Rindova et al., 2011; Hatch, Schultz, and Skov, 2015).

Organizational Culture as an Identity Referent

Establishing the theoretical distinction and empirical relations between organizational identity and culture was central to early efforts to theorize the former. When first introducing the concept of organizational identity as members' claims about central, distinctive, and enduring features of their organization, Stuart Albert and David Whetten (1985) acknowledged that culture could be an important referent for these claims. In other words, Albert and Whetten observed that, when members try to answer the "identity question" ("Who are we?"), culture—or, more appropriately, some elements of the organizational culture—could be part of the answer, and that whether or not members use culture as an identity referent is an "empirical question."

This observation echoed findings from early research on organizational culture, indicating that "cultural manifestations such as stories and rituals serve as vehicles

communities or organizational units (Meyerson and Martin, 1987; Sackmann, 1992), but did not question the fundamental idea of culture as a set of relatively shared beliefs and norms prescribing or proscribing behavior within a particular group (*culture-as-values*).

Building on an increasingly influential perspective in cultural sociology (Swidler, 1986; DiMaggio, 1997), more recent developments have begun to question the idea of organizational culture as a system of norms and beliefs constraining action. While not denying the idea that culture resides in relatively shared knowledge structures (DiMaggio, 1997) that influence how people make sense of their organization and environment, and structure relationships inside the organization (Schein, 1985), this rising perspective assumes that individuals may flexibly use culture as a repertoire of resources (ideas, symbols, stories, words, rituals, etc.) to pursue their own strategies of action (Swidler, 1986; Weber, 2005) (*culture-as-toolkit*).

for claims of uniqueness" (Martin, Feldman, Hatch, and Sitkin, 1983: 49), and that "shared values define the fundamental character of the organization, the attitude that distinguishes it from all others. In this way, they create a sense of identity for those in the organization" (Deal and Kennedy, 1982: 23) (see also Collins and Porras, 1994). Collectively, these studies proposed that a subset of cultural values—celebrated in organizational folklore and corporate narrative—shape how members think about "who we are as an organization" or "what makes us different from our competitors."

Some disagreement, however, remains between leading scholars in the fields of culture and identity. Whereas Schein proposes that organizational identity is rooted in the deeper, tacit layer of cultural assumptions that "provides members with a basic sense of identity and defines the values that provide self-esteem" (Schein, 2010: 29), David Whetten argues that culture and identity do not completely overlap, and may do so only temporarily:

> When member agents invoke elements of their organization's culture in ways, for purposes and at times that are consistent with the specified uses of legitimate identity claims, then these cultural elements are functioning as part of the organization's identity.
>
> (2006: 228)

Corley and colleagues concur with Whetten, observing that "when organizational identities do contain some of the organization's values, these values are part of what is believed to be central, distinctive and continuous about the organization" (Corley et al., 2006: 88). In fact, research shows that, while important, organizational culture is not the only referent for identity, as members' claims and beliefs may also be influenced by organizational images (Dutton and Dukerich, 1991), social categories (Glynn, 2008), status (Elsbach and Kramer, 1996), or any other feature members perceive as central, enduring, and distinctive. Also, not all the beliefs and norms that constitute an organization's culture are equally likely to become identity referents; some will be common to other organizations in the same industry (Porac, Thomas, and Baden-Fuller, 1989; Phillips, 1994) or in the same country (Hofstede, 1980).

A study of how Bang & Olufsen, a Danish producer of audio-video equipment, responded to what members perceived as identity threats substantiated and extended the idea that culture serves as a referent for identity (Ravasi and Schultz, 2006). It did so, by showing how, when current claims and understandings about central and distinctive features are threatened by changes that question their validity and/or their prospective viability, members look at established cultural practices and artifacts as a source of stability, to provide an answer to the question "Who are we, really?" or "Who do we want to be?" that maintains a sense of continuity with the past. This study foreshadowed later proposals to view culture as a "toolkit" for the construction of organizational identity (Weber and Dacin, 2011), by observing how members "find in these visible and tangible elements of their organization's culture a reservoir of cues supporting and mediating interorganizational comparisons" (Ravasi and Schultz, 2006: 451).

Research also shows that the tendency to turn to the organization's culture to answer identity questions seems to be stronger for employees at lower levels in the hierarchy than for top managers, who instead tend to see the identity of the organization as "an outgrowth of the organization's strategy" (Corley, 2004: 1157). The idea that—especially in times of change (see Gioia and Thomas, 1996)—top managers' decisions may be driven by a prospective, aspirational understanding of the organization is exemplified well in a recent study of Carlsberg, a large Danish producer of beer. This study illustrates the difficulties initially encountered by the CEO as he tried to encourage the organization to be "more like a FMCG [fast-moving consumer goods] company" (Hatch et al., 2015: 7), as part of a strategy of global expansion. These difficulties partly reflected the resistance of members—whose understanding of the organization was more firmly rooted in its history and culture—to a "new" identity that they perceived as betraying traditional values associated with passion, craftsmanship, and local roots.

Not all scholars, however, agree with this idea, and Ashforth and Mael (1996) remind us that "self-definition and strategic choice are intertwined such that an organization may enact and express a valued identity through strategy and may infer, modify, or affirm an identity from strategy and the responses it evokes (p. 33, italics in the original)."

Organizational Identity and the Contextual Understanding of Cultural Norms

Marlena Fiol introduced a parallel take on the interrelation between organizational culture and identity, arguing that new identities may facilitate changes in organizational culture, understood as a system of "rules," to the extent that managers "decouple new behaviour patterns and their related identities sufficiently from traditional organizational values" (1991: 206). Her theoretical arguments shift attention from the assumptions and values that shape how members think, to the collective norms that guide how they act (Cooke and Rousseau, 1988), understood as "behavioural expressions of those values" (Fiol, 1991: 193).

Rindova, Dalpiaz, and Ravasi (2011) elaborate these ideas by showing how new organizational identities shape members' "contextual understanding" (Fiol, 1991) of established or emerging rules by suggesting a categorization of the organization that justifies and legitimizes the enforcement of these rules. Their longitudinal study of Alessi, an Italian producer of kitchenware, shows how this categorization may be interpreted literally (as in, "This organization IS an industrial manufacturer, so we should behave like one") or analogically (as in, "This organization should also ACT LIKE a publisher, in the way we relate to renowned designers"). Organizational leaders, then, can use new identity claims that draw analogical connections with other types of organizations to give sense to desired changes in cultural norms and beliefs (Rindova et al., 2011). As the case of Carlsberg mentioned earlier suggests, however, these efforts may need to be supported by specific mechanisms for cultural change (see Hatch et al., 2015), to the extent that members perceive new identities as clashing with values that are a source of personal or organizational pride.

Categories and Features, and the Dynamic Interrelation between Identity and Culture

It could be argued that the two perspectives on the interrelations between organizational identity and culture outlined in the previous paragraphs appear contradictory: Does culture help members make sense of identity, as Albert and Whetten (1985) initially claimed? Or, as Fiol (1991) argued, does identity help members make sense of culture? In fact, this contradiction is only apparent, and can be resolved by acknowledging the dual nature of organizational identity as being constituted by social categories (invoked to substantiate claims of similarity) and organization-specific features (claimed as distinctive), and the temporal dynamism that characterizes the relationship between culture and identity (Hatch et al., 2015).

Organizational identities "classify" organizations by specifying "what kind of organization this is" and "how this organization differs" from other comparable organizations (Gioia, 1998). Using terminology borrowed from cultural sociologists, we can see organizational identity as composed of the different categories—or types of organizations—that an organization is believed or claimed to belong to (Glynn, 2008; Pratt and Kraatz, 2009), and a number of organization-specific features that members see as distinguishing them from other organizations belonging to the same category. Categorical membership requires organizations to conform to institutionalized expectations about appropriate goals, structures, policies, practices, etc. (Zuckerman, 1999). Distinguishing features pressure organizations to "act in character" or "honor the past" to preserve a distinctive and valuable social position and satisfy members' needs for continuity and self-enhancement (Whetten, 2006).

Acknowledging the dual nature of organizational identity as being simultaneously about similarity and difference (Whetten, 2006) helps us bring together different perspectives on the dynamic relationship between culture and identity. On the one hand, idiosyncratic patterns of thought and behavior that characterize an organization's culture may help members make sense of foundational, distinguishing, and enduring features that contribute to define "who we are as an organization." When pressured by competitors' moves that threatened their perceived distinctiveness, for instance, Bang & Olufsen turned to its cultural practices and artifacts to articulate the unique way in which they approached the design of audio-video equipment, and redefined their claimed uniqueness in terms of what they referred to as "corporate identity components" (e.g., "Essentiality," "Domesticity," "Inventiveness," etc.), and later "fundamental values" ("Excellence, Synthesis, and Poetry") (Ravasi and Schultz, 2006).

On the other hand, "categorical self-descriptors" (Whetten and Mackey, 2002) may help members make sense of appropriate norms and practices—and related assumptions—by linking these norms to institutionalized understandings of how a certain kind of organization should (or should not) be structured and operate. In this respect, the incorporation of new categorical claims in organizational self-referential discourse may encourage members to change deeply ingrained (cultural) patterns of thought and action because they are no longer appropriate for the kind of organization that it now is (as, for instance, in the case of privatization or listing on the stock exchange), or that members want it to be (Gioia and Thomas, 1996). New claims can be used literally by top managers—for example, Penn State becoming "a Top Ten University" (Gioia and Thomas, 1996) or Carlsberg becoming a "FMCG company" (Hatch et al., 2015)—to encourage modification in goals, structure, and policies to conform to different categorical requirements. They could also be used analogically— for example, kitchenware manufacturer Alessi acting like a "publisher," or motorcycle producer Ducati being an "entertainment company"—to justify the introduction of new hybrid practices combining elements from multiple organizational forms.

These examples show that while culture, as a set of values perceived as core and unique by organizational members, may act as an "anchor" and a source of stability for claims and beliefs about central, enduring, and distinctive features (Albert and Whetten, 1985; Ravasi and Schultz, 2006), new categorical identities could be used instrumentally to encourage cultural changes. New categorical claims can be used to facilitate the acceptance and assimilation of new beliefs and practices associated with a different type of organization—for example, a publisher or an FMCG company—as a new "way we do things around here," by drawing on consolidated expectations and assumptions about what is appropriate for this type.

As the case described by Kenny and colleagues in this handbook indicates, however, (Kenny, Whittle, and Willmott, Ch. 8, this volume), members—at least some of them—may resist a proposed "re-categorization" of an organization that implies a redistribution of power, status, or resources, and/or that threatens their personal or occupational identity (see also Humphreys and Brown, 2002; Nag, Corley, and Gioia, 2007). In these circumstances, "identity struggles"—internal conflicts between different groups over the categorization of the organization—may reflect more profound conflicts over the distribution of material and symbolic resources in organizations (see Glynn, 2000 for an example).

Recent research on the implementation of Six Sigma at 3M between 2002 and 2007 also points to the difficulty of changing deeply ingrained and emotionally laden "core values"—reflected in celebrated and enduring organizational features that infuse members with pride—and shows that these values define the boundaries of acceptable change in organizations (Canato et al., 2013). This study suggests that the culture of an organization may be more malleable than currently assumed (e.g., Ogbonna and Harris, 1998). However, resistance will intensify if the displayed effects of organizational changes begin to threaten a deeper layer of cultural beliefs that, in members' eyes, define what the organization is and stands for—that is the organizational identity—as well as their own identity within the organization (Canato et al., 2013). Schein locates these identity-defining cultural beliefs at the most tacit and taken-for-granted level of basic assumptions (Schein, 2010). In contrast, this study indicates that identity-defining beliefs may also be quite explicit, corresponding to what Schein refers to as the level of "espoused values." It suggests also that the identity-relevance of cultural norms and beliefs, rather than their degree of tacitness and taken-for-grantedness, may really explain whether and how members will resist managerial attempts to alter them (Canato et al., 2013).

Collectively, the studies reviewed in these paragraphs begin to unpack the mutual interrelation between identity and culture first theorized by Hatch and Shultz (2002). On the one hand, they do so by showing how, at any point in time, organizational identities may express elements of the organizational culture, embodied in an organization's products, structures, practices, and symbols. On the other hand, they show how the suggested introduction of new identities, in addition to or in the place of current ones, triggers a reflection on the prospective viability of cultural beliefs and practices, and may ultimately result in their modification. These findings suggest that future studies may investigate the tension between identity and culture, not only as a potential problem for organizations, but also as a fundamental driver of change.

These studies also suggest, more generally, that a reconceptualization of both organizational culture and identity may be in order to account for the different degrees of malleability that elements of both constructs seem to exhibit. Both constructs seem to be characterized by a deeper layer, whereby members make sense of a set of enduring cultural norms and practices—celebrated as foundational and distinguishing—as "core values." These core values, in their eyes, define what the organization "is" and "stands for," and how it differs from other comparable organizations, and they are highly resistant to change.

Similarly, both constructs may be characterized by an outer layer, which, in the case of culture may take the form of a "repertoire" of ideas, symbols, rituals, and patterns of interaction that members draw upon flexibly as they perform their tasks or pursue their interests (Swidler, 1986). At the same time, multiple categorical identities may be available to members to make (or give) sense of what they do, in ordinary or specific circumstances. These categories may be less emotionally charged than identity features, and their use more situational and fluid (Brown, 2006), as they are invoked to envision and justify the use of particular cultural resources—engagement in particular practices—to support a particular course of action. Future research could incorporate these ideas in further investigation of the conditions under which organizational identities facilitate or oppose cultural changes, and vice versa.

CONCLUSION

In this chapter, I have reviewed available theoretical and empirical work addressing the distinction and interrelations between organizational identity and image, and organizational identity and culture respectively. These interrelations, however, are often dynamically related, as first observed by Hatch and Schultz (2002). Their insightful model applied Mead's theory of the dynamic interaction between the "I" and the "me"

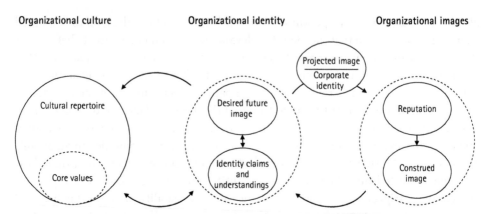

FIGURE 3.1 Interrelations between organizational identity, image, and culture in past research (a simplified visual representation)

to understand interrelations between identity, image, and culture. Figure 3.1 offers a simplified representation of these interrelations, reflecting the multiple facets of these constructs highlighted by later studies and presented in this chapter. In line with theoretical (Giorgi et al., 2015; Patterson, 2014) and empirical work (Canato et al., 2013) suggesting reconciliation between the notions of culture-as-values and culture-as-toolkit, it highlights a general distinction between a broader set of cultural resources (artifacts, rituals, language, ideas, etc.) available to members, and a more deeply held and affectively laden set of core values, serving as identity referent, and shaping members' use of the organizational cultural repertoire.

Collectively, the studies reviewed in this chapter suggest an understanding of organizational identity as the result of the interaction between the destabilizing influence of external images (Gioia et al., 2000) and the stabilizing influence of culture (Ravasi and Schultz, 2006), the former encouraging members to reconsider their identity in the face of their deteriorating image (Dutton and Dukerich, 1991) or in search of a more attractive one (Gioia and Thomas, 1996), the latter offering them a cognitive (and, perhaps, affective) anchor to cling to when the organizational identity is threatened or called into question (Canato et al., 2013). Current theories, however, cannot explain yet whether the result of this interaction will be a reaffirmation of the current identity (and culture) or the beginning of more profound cultural changes triggered by an image-identity gap. Both outcomes have been observed in past studies. Producing a more fine-grained understanding of how organizations address and resolve these tensions offers an interesting theoretical challenge for future research.

References

Albert, S. and Whetten, D. A. (1985). "Organizational Identity." In *Research in Organizational Behavior*, vol. 7, edited by L. L. Cummings, and B. M. Staw, 263–95. Greenwich, CT: JAI.

Alvesson, M. (2013). Understanding Organizational *Culture*, 2nd edn. London, SAGE.

Alvesson, M. and Robertson, M. (2016). "Organizational Identity: A Critique." In *The Oxford Handbook of Organizational Identity*, edited by M. G. Pratt, M. Schultz, B. E. Ashforth, and D. Ravasi, 160–80. Oxford: Oxford University Press.

Ashforth, B. E. and Mael, F. (1996). "Organizational Identity and Strategy as a Context for the Individual." *Advances in Strategic Management* 13: 19–64.

Brown, A. D. (2006). "A Narrative Approach to Collective Identities." *Journal of Management Studies* 43: 731–53.

Brown, T. J., Dacin, P. A., Pratt, M. G., and Whetten, D. A. (2006). "Identity, Intended Image, Construed Image, and Reputation: An Interdisciplinary Framework and Suggested Terminology." *Journal of the Academy of Marketing Science* 34(2): 99–106.

Canato, A., Ravasi, D., and Phillips, N. (2013). "Coerced Practice Implementation in Cases of Low Cultural Fit: Cultural Change and Practice Adaptation during the Implementation of Six Sigma at 3M." *Academy of Management Journal* 56(6): 1724–53.

Collins, J. C. and Porras, J. I. (1994). *Built to Last: Successful Habits of Visionary Companies.* New York: Harper Business.

Cooke, R. A. and Rousseau, D. M. (1988). "Behavioral Norms and Expectations: A Quantitative Approach to the Assessment of Organizational Culture." *Group & Organization Studies* 13: 245–73.

Corley, K. G. (2004). "Defined by our Strategy or our Culture? Hierarchical Differences in Perceptions of Organizational Identity and Change." *Human Relations* 57: 1145–77.

Corley, K. G., Harquail, C. V., Pratt, M. G., Glynn, M. A., Fiol, C. M., and Hatch, M. J. (2006). "Guiding Organizational Identity through Aged Adolescence." *Journal of Management Inquiry* 15: 85–99.

Deal T. E. and Kennedy, A. A. (1982). *Corporate Cultures: The Rites and Rituals of Corporate Life.* Harmondsworth: Penguin Books.

DiMaggio, P. J. (1997). "Culture and Cognition." *Annual Review of Sociology* 23(1): 263–87.

Drori, I., Wrzesniewski, A., and Ellis, S. (2013). "One out of Many? Boundary Negotiation and Identity Formation in Postmerger Integration." *Organization Science* 24(6): 1717–41.

Dutton, J. and Dukerich, J. (1991). "Keeping an Eye on the Mirror: Image and Identity in Organizational Adaptation." *Academy of Management Journal* 34: 517–54.

Dutton, J., Dukerich, J., and Harquail C. V. (1994). "Organizational Images and Membership Commitment." *Administrative Science Quarterly* 39: 239–63.

Elsbach, K. D. and Kramer, R. M. (1996). "Members' Responses to Organizational Identity Threats: Encountering and Countering the *Business Week* Rankings." *Administrative Science Quarterly* 41: 442–76.

Fiol, M. C. (1991). "Managing Culture as a Competitive Resource: An Identity-Based View of Sustainable Competitive Advantage." *Journal of Management* 17(1): 191–211.

Fiol, M., Hatch, M. J., and Golden-Biddle, K. (1998). "Organizational Culture and Identity: What's the Difference Anyway?" In *Identity in Organizations*, edited by D. Whetten and P. Godfrey, 56–9. Thousand Oaks, CA: SAGE.

Geertz, C. (1973). *The Interpretation of Cultures: Selected Essays.* New York: Basic Books.

Gioia, D. A. (1998). "From Individual to Organizational Identity." In *Identity in Organizations: Developing Theory through Conversations*, edited by D. A. Whetten and P. C. Godfrey, 17–31. Thousand Oaks, CA: SAGE.

Gioia, D. A., Hamilton, A. L., and Patvardhan, S. D. (2014). "Image Is Everything." *Research in Organizational Behavior* 34: 129–54.

Gioia, D. A., Patvardhan, S. D, Hamilton, A. L., and Corley, K. G. (2013). "Organizational Identity Formation and Change: Review and Reflection on Three Decades of Research." *Academy of Management Annals* 7(1): 123–92.

Gioia, D. A, Schultz, M., and Corley, K. (2000). "Organizational Identity, Image, and Adaptive Instability." *Academy of Management Review* 25: 63–82.

Gioia, D. A. and Thomas, J. B. (1996). "Identity, Image and Issue Interpretation: Sensemaking during Strategic Change in Academia." *Administrative Science Quarterly* 41: 370–403.

Giorgi, S., Lockwood, C. and Glynn, M. A. (2015). "The Many Faces of Culture: Making Sense of 30 Years of Research on Culture in Organization Studies." *Academy of Management Annals* 9: 1–54.

Glynn, M.A. (2000). "When Cymbals Become Symbols: Conflict over Organizational Identity within a Symphony Orchestra." *Organization Science* 11: 285–98.

Glynn, M. A. (2008). "Beyond Constraint—How Institutions Enable Identities." In *The SAGE Handbook of Organizational Institutionalism*, edited by R. Greenwood, C. Oliver, R. Suddaby, and K. Sahlin-Andersson, 413–30. London: SAGE.

Harrison, S. H. and Corley, K. G. (2011). "Clean Climbing, Carabineers and Cultural Cultivation: Developing an Open-Systems Perspective of Culture." *Organization Science* 22(2): 391–412.

Hatch, M. J. and Schultz, M. (1997). "Relations between Organizational Culture, Identity and Image." *European Journal of Marketing* 31(5): 356–65.

Hatch, M. J. and Schultz, M. (2000). "Scaling the Tower of Babel: Relational Differences between Identity, Image and Culture in Organizations." In *The Expressive Organization*, edited by M. Schultz, M. J. Hatch, and M. H. Larsen, 11–36. Oxford: Oxford University Press.

Hatch, M. J. and Schultz, M. (2002). "The Dynamics of Organizational Identity." *Human Relations* 55: 989–1018.

Hatch, M. J., Schultz, M., and Skov, A. M. (2015). "Organizational Identity and Culture in the Context of Managed Change: Transformation in the Carlsberg Group, 2009–2013." *Academy of Management Discoveries* 1(1): 56–88.

Hofstede, G. (1980). *Culture's Consequences: International Differences in Work-Related Values*. Beverly Hills CA: SAGE.

Hoon, C. and Jacobs, C. D. (2014). "Beyond Belief: Strategic Taboos and Organizational Identity in Strategic Agenda Setting." *Strategic Organization* 12(4): 244–73.

Hsu, G. and Hannan, M. T. (2005). "Identities, Genres, and Organizational Forms." *Organization Science* 16(5): 474–90.

Humphreys, M. and Brown, A. D. (2002). "Narratives of Organizational Identity and Identification: A Case Study of Hegemony and Resistance." *Organization Studies* 23(3): 421–47.

Kenny, K., Whittle, A., and Willmott, H. (2016). "Organizational Identity: The Significance of Power and Politics." In *The Oxford Handbook of Organizational Identity*, edited by M. G. Pratt, M. Schultz, B. E. Ashforth, and D. Ravasi, 140–59. Oxford: Oxford University Press.

Kjærgaard, A., Morsing, M., and Ravasi, D. (2011). "Mediating Identity: A Study of Media Influence on Organizational Identity Construction in a Celebrity Firm." *Journal of Management Studies* 48: 514–43.

Martin, J. (2002). *Organizational Culture: Mapping the Terrain*. Thousand Oaks, CA: SAGE.

Martin, J., Feldman, M. S., Hatch, M. J., and Simkin, S. B. (1983). "The Uniqueness Paradox in Organizational Stories." *Administrative Science Quarterly* 28: 438–53.

Meyerson, D. and Martin, J. (1987). "Culture Change: An Integration of Three Different Views." *Journal of Management Studies* 24: 623–47.

Nag, R., Corley, K. G., and Gioia, D. A. (2007). "The Intersection of Organizational Identity, Knowledge, and Practice: Attempting Strategic Change via Knowledge Grafting." *Academy of Management Journal* 50: 821–47.

Ogbonna, E. and Harris, L. (1998). "Managing Organizational Culture: Compliance or Genuine Change?" *British Journal of Management* 9: 273–88.

Olins, W. (1989). *Corporate Identity: Making Business Strategy Visible through Design*, London: Thames and Hudson.

Patterson, O. (2014). "Making Sense of Culture." *Annual Review of Sociology* 40: 1–30.

Phillips, M. (1994). "Industry Mindsets: Exploring the Cultures of Two Macro-Organizational Settings." *Organization Science* 5(3): 384–402.

Porac, J. F., Thomas, H. and Baden-Fuller, C. (1989). "Competitive Groups as Cognitive Communities: The Case of Scottish Knitwear Manufacturers." *Journal of Management Studies* 26: 397–416.

Pratt, M. G. (2003). "Disentangling Collective Identity." In *Identity Issues in Groups: Research in Managing Groups and Teams*, edited by J. Polzer, E. Mannix, and M. Neale, 161–88. Stamford, CT: Elsevier Science.

Pratt, M. G. and Kraatz, M. S. (2009). "E Pluribus Unum: Multiple Identities and the Organizational Self." In *Exploring Positive Identities and Organizations. Building a Theoretical and Research Foundation*, edited by L. M. Roberts and J. E. Dutton. New York, NJ: Psychology Press.

Price, K. and Gioia, D. A. (2008). "The Self-Monitoring Organization: Minimizing Discrepancies among Differing Images of Organizational Identity." *Corporate Reputation Review* 11(4): 208–21.

Ravasi, D. and Canato, A. (2013). "How Do I Know Who You Think You Are? A Review of Research Methods on Organizational Identity." *International Journal of Management Reviews* 15(2): 185–204.

Ravasi, D. and Schultz, M. (2006). "Responding to Organizational Identity Threats: Exploring the Role of Organizational Culture." *Academy of Management Journal* 49: 433–58.

Ravasi, D. and Phillips, N. (2011). "Strategies of Alignment: Organizational Identity Management and Strategic Change at Bang & Olufsen." *Strategic Organization* 9(2): 103–35.

Rindova, V. P. (1997). "The Image Cascade and the Formation of Corporate Reputations." *Corporate Reputation Review* 1: 188–94.

Rindova, V. Dalpiaz, E., and Ravasi D. (2011) "A Cultural Quest: A Study of Organizational Use of New Cultural Resources in Strategy Formation." *Organizational Science* 22: 413–31.

Rindova, V. P. and Schultz, M. (1998). "Identity within and Identity without: Lessons from Corporate and Organizational Identity." In *Identity in Organizations: Developing Theory through Conversations*, edited by D. A. Whetten and P. C. Godfrey, 46–51. Thousand Oaks, CA: SAGE.

Sackmann, S. (1992). "Culture and Subculture: An Analysis of Organizational Knowledge." *Administrative Science Quarterly* 37: 140–61.

Schein, E. H. (1985). *Organizational Culture and Leadership*, 1st edn. San Francisco, CA: Jossey-Bass.

Schein, E. H. (2010). *Organizational Culture and Leadership*, 4th edn. San Francisco, CA: Jossey-Bass.

Smircich, L. (1983). "Concepts of Culture and Organizational Analysis." *Administrative Science Quarterly* 28: 339–58.

Swidler, A. (1986). "Culture in Action: Symbols and Strategies." *American Sociological Review* 51: 273–86.

Trice, H. M. and Beyer, J. M. (1984). "Studying Organizational Cultures through Rites and Ceremonials." *Academy of Management Review* 9: 653–69.

Tripsas, M. (2009). "Technology, Identity, and Inertia through the Lens of 'The Digital Photography Company.'" *Organization Science* 20: 441–60.

Weber, K. (2005). "A Toolkit for Analyzing Corporate Cultural Toolkits." *Poetics* 33: 227–52.

Weber, K. and Dacin, M. T. (2011). "The Cultural Construction of Organizational Life: Introduction to the Special Issue." *Organization Science* 22: 287–98.

Whetten, D. A. (2006). "Albert and Whetten Revisited: Strengthening the Concept of Organizational Identity." *Journal of Management Inquiry* 15: 219–34.

Whetten, D. A. and Mackey, A. (2002). "A Social Actor Conception of Organizational Identity and its Implications for the Study of Organizational Reputation." *Business and Society* 41(4): 393–414.

Zuckerman, E. W. (1999). "The Categorical Imperative: Securities Analysts and the Illegitimacy Discount." *American Sociological Review* 104: 1398–438.

Zuckerman, E. (2016). "Optimal Distinctiveness Revisited: An Integrative Framework for Understanding the Balance between Differentiation and Conformity in Individual and Organizational Identities." In *The Oxford Handbook of Organizational Identity*, edited by M. G. Pratt, M. Schultz, B. E. Ashforth, and D. Ravasi, 183–99. Oxford: Oxford University Press.

CHAPTER 4

··

ORGANIZATIONAL, SUBUNIT, AND INDIVIDUAL IDENTITIES

multilevel linkages

··

BLAKE E. ASHFORTH

... identity does not refer to a particular level of analysis. It refers to a perspective. It describes the way that parts of a ... system, at any level of analysis, define themselves in relation to the system.

(Fiol, 1991)

INTRODUCTION

··

ORGANIZATIONS are dynamic systems of interacting individuals and groups. Thus, our theorizing about organizations must consider how levels of analysis—particularly individuals, subunits, and the organization itself—interact over time (Kozlowski and Klein, 2000; Mathieu and Chen, 2011). This is particularly true of the "root construct" of identity (Albert, Ashforth, and Dutton, 2000: 13), because how an individual, subunit, and organization define themselves affects an incredible array of organizational phenomena, from motivation to performance to corporate reputation.[1]

We know a great deal about identity *within* each level of analysis. This is because separate literatures have emerged regarding individual identity (e.g., identity theory,

---

[1] For the sake of parsimony, I'm focusing on the most widely studied levels of analysis. Other levels with much theoretical potential include dyads, occupations, careers, strategic groups, industries, institutions, nations, and geographic regions.

focusing on one's network of roles; Stryker and Burke, 2000), collective identity, in-cluding subunits (e.g., social identity theory, focusing on how in-groups seek to define themselves via contrasts with out-groups; Tajfel and Turner, 1986), and organizational identity (e.g., the social actor perspective, focusing on the organization as a unitary entity concerned with its legitimacy among stakeholders; Whetten and Mackey, 2002). However, we know surprisingly little about how identity at a given level of analysis affects identities at other levels—and thus, how identities may cohere (or not) in the organization to constitute a dynamic system.

Accordingly, rather than offer a traditional literature review, this introductory mini-chapter offers a conceptual framework that synthesizes research that at least pertains to the multilevel linkages among individual, subunit, and organizational identities (see Figure 4.1). The framework is adapted from Ashforth, Rogers, and Corley (2011). I will bypass the ontological and epistemological debates about the various meanings of identity (e.g., Cornelissen, Haslam, and Balmer, 2007; Gioia, Schultz, and Corley, 2002), and apply Albert and Whetten's (1985) seminal defini-tion of identity to all nested levels of analysis. That is, identity is the central, distinc-tive, and more or less enduring character of an entity. Identity, in short, answers the question, "Who am I in this organization and how am I different from others?" or "Who are we as a subunit/organization and how are we different from others?" (By individual identity, I mean the role or function that the individual plays in the

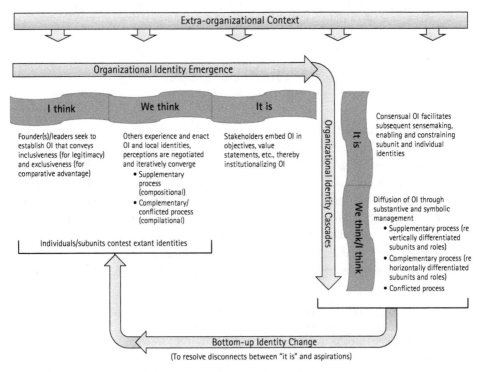

FIGURE 4.1 Organizational identity emergence and cascades

organization rather than the personal attributes, such as traits, that make an individual unique.)

Morgeson and Hofmann (1999) argue that while the structure of organizational constructs may vary across levels of analysis, the function is generally the same. However, in the case of identity, both structure and function appear to be relatively isomorphic across levels (Ashforth et al., 2011). Regarding structure, because individuals serve their subunits, and subunits serve their organization, the content of individual and subunit identities tends to reinforce organizational identity (and vice versa), fostering similarity across levels. Regarding function, despite the different literatures attached to each level of analysis, they appear to agree that identity essentially defines (usually in a positive manner) and situates an actor in a network of related actors, thereby providing a foundation for commitment and concerted action. That said, in the pages that follow I note how considering multilevel linkages sheds light on the differentiation and conflict that may impair isomorphism across levels.

Crucial to any discussion of how individual, subunit, and organizational identities are linked is the role of *time* (e.g., Schultz and Hernes, 2013). I will argue in this chapter that collective identities tend to emerge from individual identities, or at least individual conceptions of what the collective is or can be, and collective identities in turn both enable and constrain identities nested within them, including individual identities. The result is a dynamic and recursive set of linkages between levels of analysis (cf. structuration theory, Giddens, 1984).

Multilevel Linkages over Time

Emergence of Identity

Identity is "emergent" in the sense meant by Kozlowski and Klein (2000: 55): "A phenomenon is emergent when it originates in the cognition, affect, behaviors, or other characteristics of individuals, is amplified by their interactions, and manifests as a higher-level, collective phenomenon." Following Ashforth et al. (2011; cf. Wiley, 1988), collective identities emerge from a process of "I think" → "we think" → "it is." It's important to note that this process by which the subjective (I think/we think) becomes more objective (it is) can occur within any newly forming collective level, from a new organization to a new project team to a new industry. Further, although I focus on initial identity formation, this process likely also applies to changes in an extant identity, albeit in a more politicized form (e.g., Kreiner et al., 2015). Finally, because the nuances vary between given instances of identity formation (or identity change), the description below is meant to apply to the modal or typical case.

"I think." An organization's founder(s) and leaders typically play a major role in the initial formation of organizational identity as they espouse and enact their entrepreneurial vision and values (Fauchart and Gruber, 2011; Scott and Lane, 2000). At this

point, the identity is *intrasubjective* (Wiley, 1988) in the sense that it is not yet widely understood, endorsed, or co-enacted by others. In enacting the incipient organizational identity, the founder(s)/leaders seek to both legitimate the organization as a bona fide member of its chosen institutional field (e.g., "We are a family restaurant"), and simultaneously establish a more or less distinctive niche (e.g., "We specialize in high-end Japanese food"; Pedersen and Dobbin, 2006). In short, just as individuals have been argued to pursue "optimal distinctiveness" in their identities (e.g., Brewer, 2012; Kreiner, Hollensbe, and Sheep, 2006)—a balance between competing desires for inclusiveness and exclusiveness—so the founder(s)/leaders are concerned with the organizational identity being both the same as others (to gain legitimacy) and yet different from others (to establish comparative advantage; Gioia, Price, Hamilton, and Thomas, 2010; see Zuckerman, this volume, Ch. 10). That said, Alvesson and Empson (2008) found, in a comparative analysis of management consulting firms, that founders/leaders differ widely in how explicit, coherent, and complex their initial identity formulations are—and even in their recognition of the importance of a coherent identity. Additionally, espoused identities tend not to be literal descriptions of the organization's essence, but somewhat idealized and aspirational depictions so as to win the hearts and minds of stakeholders (Ashforth and Mael, 1996; Ran and Duimering, 2007).

"We think." If the embryonic organization begins to gain traction among stakeholders, new members are likely to be added. As members and other stakeholders follow the lead of the founder(s)/leaders, they experience and enact the initial organizational identity for themselves. Their own role-specific contributions, perspectives, preferences, and dialogues with one another tend to add breadth and depth to the initial identity, possibly pushing it in directions the founder(s)/leaders had not anticipated. In the multilevel terminology of Kozlowski and Klein (2000), identity emergence is generally "compositional," as individuals implicitly share and converge in their perceptions. However, to the extent that individuals' views are complementary or conflicted rather than supplementary, the process can be characterized as "compilational"—"the combination of related but different lower-level properties" (p. 16; cf. locus of collective identity, Pratt, 2003). In such cases, agreement represents a synergistic or dialectical combination of diverse views or, if highly contested, a political resolution (cf. Watson, this volume, Ch. 7; Kenny, Whittle, and Willmott, this volume, Ch. 8; Alvesson and Robertson, this volume, Ch. 9.

In short, the initial "I think" identity claim is negotiated—whether explicitly or implicitly—among stakeholders. As the dean of a new college put it, "Debating among ourselves who we were going to be was necessary because of tensions that existed among the different perspectives. The whole process of trying to reconcile differences led people to discover that they could talk to each other and find common ground" (Gioia et al., 2010: 25). As interpretations iteratively converge, the resulting consensus fosters a sense of "we think"—an *intersubjective* (Wiley, 1988) sense of what defines the organization (Weick, 1995). The sense of sharedness adds confidence and momentum to the identity claim and its enactment. Further, sharedness may further enhance the idealized tinge as members rally around the flag they are hoisting.

"*It is.*" Finally, as stakeholders embed the organization's identity in objectives, value statements, job descriptions, hiring criteria, recurring tasks, information flows, brand names, reward systems, and so on, it becomes increasingly institutionalized. Thus, the identity comes to seem less like a subjective understanding held by individuals ("we think") and more like an objective—albeit somewhat idealized—description of the work environment, external to any individual or subunit and relatively stable ("it is," what Wiley [1988] refers to as *generic subjective*). The more institutionalized the identity, the more difficult and even unthinkable major identity change becomes. Indeed, the identity may become taken for granted, analogous to the air that stakeholders breathe, and only become salient when it's threatened or some major change is considered (Albert and Whetten, 1985). The founder(s) and initial leadership cadre may eventually move on, but elements of the "imprinted" identity are likely to persist (Hoang and Gimeno, 2010; Kroezen and Heugens, 2012). The power of an institutionalized identity, then, is that it becomes "the" reality that shapes identities nested within it, especially the individual identities of newcomers who have only experienced "it is." The driving dynamic of "I think" → "we think" becomes subordinate to the top-down effects under "it is." That said, "organizational identity is continually reproduced and reinforced through myriad micro-level interactions among organizational stakeholders" (Gioia, Patvardhan, Hamilton, and Corley, 2013: 166).

The extra-organizational context. Organizations are, of course, embedded in broader institutional, historical, national, and industrial contexts that both enable and constrain identities. Indeed, perceived legitimacy is key to institutionalization, as stakeholders and the wider society act as if the organization's identity is bona fide and more or less stable (Gioia et al., 2013). As an example of the institutional context, Chreim, Williams, and Hinings (2007) describe how physicians at a Canadian health clinic initiated a major change from an independent-practitioner model focused on narrow medical treatments to a more team-oriented focus on patient wellness. However, "Physician role reconstruction is embedded in a web of relationships involving a multitude of institutional level governing and funding bodies" (p. 1525). Thus, the physicians had to consider what was likely to be construed as legitimate and feasible within their institutional context. Their cause was assisted by an emerging institutional discourse on alternative forms of medical treatment. Ultimately, the change would not have been possible without the active collaboration of the regional health authority, government, and professional association, which led to a cascading series of actions, from institutional approvals, to an organizational redesign of the physical structure and information flows, to altered relationships with allied professions such as nursing. Finally, consistent with the "we think" dynamic above, the change was validated by the appreciative responses from patients and other practitioners. In sum, while "I think" occurred within the clinic, it was only conceivable—and could only morph into "we think" and "it is"—with an enabling context.

Social construction versus social actor perspectives. Scholars have drawn clear distinctions between a social constructionist view of organizational identity and a social actor view (e.g., Gioia and Hamilton, this volume, Ch. 1; Cornelissen, Haslam, and Werner, this volume, Ch. 11; King, Felin, and Whetten, 2010; Whetten and Mackey, 2002). However, following Gioia et al. (2010: 35, see also Ravasi and Schultz, 2006), these two views can be seen not as alternative formulations but as "mutually constitutive processes that are recursively implicated in generating an identity." Social constructionist processes are most evident in the discussion of "I think" and "we think," as stakeholders negotiate a shared understanding of "who we are" as an organization. Processes associated with the social actor view—which holds that identity is a property of the organization itself as a distinct social and legal entity—are most evident in the initial identity claims of the founder(s)/leaders as the head of the organization and in the discussion of "it is" as an objectified institutional status. As Ravasi and Schultz (2006) argue, if *sensemaking* is the domain of the social constructionist view, then *sensegiving* is the domain of the social actor view. It is not a case of which camp is more correct, but under which circumstances each or both help explain identity dynamics.

Enabling and Constraining Nested Identities

The emergence of identity via "I think" → "we think" → "it is" fosters a consensual sense of what defines the organization. As the organization grows, members tend to become increasingly specialized and grouped into common-cause subunits, fostering both horizontal (functional/product) differentiation and vertical (hierarchical) differentiation. As noted, the identity of the organization provides a sensegiving foundation for the identity of the resulting subunits and individual roles (King et al., 2010; Ravasi and Schultz, 2006). That is, as subunits and roles are created to operationalize the vision of the growing organization, the organization's identity serves to both enable their identities ("this is who we are") and constrain them ("this is who we are not"). "It is" now shapes "I think" and "we think."

Identity cascades. The top-down diffusion of identity occurs through substantive and symbolic management (Alvesson and Willmott, 2002; Ashforth and Mael, 1996; Pratt, 2003; cf. van Knippenberg, this volume, Ch. 18). Substantive management involves material change in organizational practices so as to align the parts of the organization into a means–end chain that supports the whole. This involves further elaborating strategy, structure, and so on, such that the identity is more firmly and consistently embedded throughout the levels of analysis. Of particular importance are human resource management practices, including recruiting individuals who "get" the identity, socializing them to live the identity, and rewarding those who exemplify the identity (cf. Werbel and DeMarie, 2005). Further, if the identity is somewhat inchoate, it may become crystallized through substantive management or even retro-spectively imputed. That is, there is a recursive loop between action (what we do) and self-definition (who we are).

Symbolic management refers to how "identity custodians" (Howard-Grenville, Metzger, and Meyer, 2013: 119)—typically formal and informal leaders—portray the organization. Schinoff, Rogers, and Corley (this volume, Ch. 12; see also Schultz and Hernes, 2013) argue that this occurs through three mechanisms. First, "saying" in-volves verbal or written communications, including conversations, mass communica-tions such as emails and annual reports, and stories and narratives. Narratives have been particularly well studied and are noteworthy as they enable actors to reframe the past (as necessary) in the service of the present and a desired future, emphasizing high points and glossing over missteps and tangents (Brown, 2006; Czarniawska, 1997). A strength of saying is that it enables identity custodians to couch organizational machinations in terms of an overarching identity (whether valid or not). Second, "showing" involves modeling behaviors and displaying artifacts, including mentoring programs, arrangement of the physical setting, employee dress, and company prod-ucts. Schinoff et al. note that, of the three mechanisms for portraying identity, showing is most likely to unintentionally convey "who we are," as when a mentor's dismissive demeanor toward subordinates conveys the importance of hierarchy. Third, "stag-ing" involves enabling members to actually experience the organizational identity, as through training programs, traditions and rituals, and operating routines—and as such blurs somewhat with substantive management. The immersive and visceral reality of experience is a very potent tutor, and can have a much greater impact than simply being told (saying) or shown an identity. Staging is particularly potent when conducted in groups, as the shared experience enables members to converge on and reinforce the imputed meaning (Schinoff et al., 2016; Van Maanen and Schein, 1979).

Much like the shift from "I think" to "we think," identity cascades typically reflect a meld of supplementary, complementary, and conflicted processes. Supplementary processes occur when the macro identity is fleshed out to reflect the specific goals of vertically differentiated subunits and roles. For instance, Google's motto of "don't be evil" may be elaborated into "don't exploit customers" and "avoid conflicts of interest" for front-line service agents. Complementary processes occur largely within a given level as functional/product differentiation leads to subunits and roles that fulfill differ-ent tasks. For IT engineers, Google's espoused value of "fast is better than slow" may mean shaving time off internet searches, whereas for customer relations it may mean resolving customer complaints in a timely manner.

Conflicted processes occur when subunits or individuals contest the identity cas-cade, at least as it pertains to them. There are various causes of such "nested identity conflicts" (Horton, Bayerl, and Jacobs, 2014: S9). First, a hybrid identity—that is, "two organizational identities that are 'not expected to go together' (Albert and Whetten, 1985: 270)" (Pratt, this volume, Ch. 6), such as "for-profit" and "health-care"—may give rise to actors who gravitate toward one identity or the other, and stakeholders are likely to differ in which aspects of a higher-order identity are most salient and meaningful to them (Corley, 2004). Hsu and Elsbach (2013) found that, while students and employees perceived their university to be collaborative, small, supportive, and friendly, the students tended to further emphasize learning, career-focused, and demanding, whereas the employees tended to further emphasize innovative, respected, and resource-poor. Second, identities may be destabilized by environmental turbulence, managerial incompetence, ambivalence toward a given identity, and political struggles. Destabilization in turn may foster ambiguous, mixed, or dubious messages from identity custodians and, thus, confusion and opportunistic gamesmanship. Senior managers of an aerospace firm espoused the need for greater efficiency while continuing to reward employees for displaying technical excellence, thereby sowing confusion among employees about the prevailing identity (Larson and Tompkins, 2005). Third, identities that are not affirmed and renewed by senior management on a regular basis may lose their motivational force, fostering "identity drift" (cf. Albert and Whetten, 1985)—as when strategic changes at Bang & Olufsen fostered a gradual loss of consensus and clarity regarding its identity (Ravasi and Phillips, 2011). Ironically, institutionalization ("it is") may cause the means by which the identity is realized—objectives, operating routines, and so on—to become more salient than the identity itself, as members go on "autopilot." Identity drift encourages and may reflect opportunism. Finally, a higher-order identity may be seen as intrusive or inappropriate, causing lower-level actors to resist the identity and perhaps extol a counter-identity or "identity foil" (Ashforth and Johnson, 2001; see Elsbach and Dukerich, this volume, Ch. 14). Corley and Gioia (2004) describe how a soon-to-be-spun-off subunit, as part of its process of developing a new identity, defined itself in opposition to its parent organization. Indeed, a burgeoning critical management and postmodernist literature focuses on how individuals and subunits often resist the identities bequeathed to them by senior management and attempt to forge, via identity work, a more desirable sense of self (Bardon, Clegg, and Josserand, 2012; Thomas, 2009). Note that in all of these causes the resulting conflict need not be dysfunctional; indeed, it may rejuvenate the organization, enable lower-order identities to compensate for the deficiencies in higher-order identities, or simply enable actors to carve out more gratifying particularized identities.

Bottom-up processes. A "bottom" only exists if there is a "top," so bottom-up change refers to a lower-level identity affecting an extant—"it is"—higher-level identity. A bottom-up impetus for change occurs not only during the institutionalization process—that is, the conflicted processes I have described regarding the identity cascade—but after institutionalization has ostensibly settled conflicts. Disconnects between "it is" and "what we wish it could be" occur in many forms and within or between each level of analysis. For example, an extant identity may no longer be in step with the times or with what individuals want, the promise of an espoused identity may not have been realized in practice, or external threats may cause a disconnect between the external image and internal identity (e.g., Brickson, 2013; Dutton and Dukerich, 1991). As noted, the more institutionalized the identity, the more difficult change becomes—particularly bottom-up change. However, bottom-up identity change can and does indeed occur, as suggested by diverse chapters in this volume (see Schultz, Ch. 5; Cornelissen et al., Ch. 11; Petriglieri and Devine, Ch. 13; Kreiner and Murphy, Ch. 15; DeJordy and Creed, Ch. 20).

Diverse literatures ranging from upward influence to tempered radicals, and from voice to organizational change, indicate that a host of factors are likely to enhance the probability of successful bottom-up identity change efforts. Examples include if the individual is powerful or of high status, has political skill, and conceives of him/herself as a change agent (thereby emboldening effort), if the need for change is legitimated (e.g., by external events), if the change can be expressed through extant identity narratives, if small wins can be leveraged to build momentum for more systemic change, and so on (e.g., Barley and Tolbert, 1997; Meyerson and Scully, 1995; Reay, Golden-Biddle, and Germann, 2006). Regardless, the impact of bottom-up processes is most likely to be strongest on the adjacent level of analysis (individual → subunit → organization).

Future Research

This thumbnail sketch of linkages among individual, subunit, and organizational identities suggests at least three promising areas for future research. The first is temporal issues. What factors at each level of analysis affect the speed with which "I think" → "we think" → "it is" occurs? Is the transition generally paced by linear "clock time" or by "event time" (Ancona, Okhuysen, and Perlow, 2001), such as tipping effects, backsliding, interruptions, delayed effects, feedback loops, and so on? Which aspects of identity are most speedily transmitted and deeply internalized, and how much does it matter if certain aspects are at least temporarily out of sync? Is it more effective for founders/leaders to move slowly and steadily or to hasten the process?

The second promising area is supplementary, complementary, and—especially—conflicted processes. It was argued that identity emergence is generally compositional (suggesting a supplementary process) rather than compilational (suggesting a complementary or conflicted process). What are the pros and cons of each? For example, while compilation is more likely to involve nasty politics, it may also result in a more multifaceted (albeit divided) identity. Similarly, it was argued that conflicted processes may actually prove functional for the organization; what factors influence whether nested identity conflicts are dysfunctional or functional? To what extent should organizations prize rather than pillory their deviants, naysayers, and gadflies?

The third area is, not surprisingly, levels of analysis. While the discussion in this chapter implied relatively tight coupling between levels, how might looser coupling affect the dynamics? For instance, the notion of identity cascades suggests a relatively smooth flow from organization to subunit to individual: under what conditions might the subunit serve to buffer or filter the impact of the organization on the individual—and vice versa? How prevalent are "skip-level" dynamics, as when an individual engages in whistle-blowing and directly challenges the organization's identity? To what extent do the dynamics described earlier hold if we add additional levels of analysis to the mix, such as dyads, strategic groups, and geographic regions? Individuals have been found to have various identity motives beyond a situated sense of self (e.g., self-enhancement, self-expression, self-coherence, optimal distinctiveness, self-continuity; Ashforth, Harrison, and Sluss, 2014). While optimal distinctiveness was mentioned earlier, to what extent do other levels of analysis have similar—or different—identity motives?

In closing, research has revealed a great deal about within-level identity dynamics, but it is the between-level dynamics that hold the most promise for developing a truly systemic understanding of identity in organizations.

References

Albert, S., Ashforth, B. E., and Dutton, J. E. (2000). "Organizational Identity and Identification: Charting New Waters and Building New Bridges." *Academy of Management Review* 25(1): 13–17.

Albert, S. and Whetten, D. A. (1985). "Organizational Identity." *Research in Organizational Behavior* 7: 263–95.

Alvesson, M. and Empson, L. (2008). "The Construction of Organizational Identity: Comparative Case Studies of Consulting Firms." *Scandinavian Journal of Management* 24(1): 1–16.

Alvesson, M. and Robertson, M. (2016). "Organizational Identity: A Critique." In *The Oxford Handbook of Organizational Identity*, edited by M. G. Pratt, M. Schultz, B. E. Ashforth, and D. Ravasi, 160–80. Oxford: Oxford University Press.

Alvesson, M. and Willmott, H. (2002). "Identity Regulation as Organizational Control: Producing the Appropriate Individual." *Journal of Management Studies* 39(5): 619–44.

Ancona, D. G., Okhuysen, G. A., and Perlow, L. A. (2001). "Taking Time to Integrate Temporal Research." *Academy of Management Review* 26(4): 512–29.

Ashforth, B. E., Harrison, S. H., and Sluss, D. M. (2014). "Becoming: The Interaction of Socialization and Identity in Organizations over Time." In *Time and Work*, vol. 1: *How Time Impacts Individuals*, edited by A. J. Shipp and Y. Fried, 11–39. London: Psychology Press.

Ashforth, B. E. and Johnson, S. A. (2001). "Which Hat to Wear? The Relative Salience of Multiple Identities in Organizational Contexts." In *Social Identity Processes in Organizational Contexts*, edited by M. A. Hogg and D. J. Terry, 31–48. Philadelphia: Psychology Press.

Ashforth, B. E. and Mael, F. A. (1996). "Organizational Identity and Strategy as a Context for the Individual." *Advances in Strategic Management* 13: 19–64.

Ashforth, B. E., Rogers, K. M., and Corley, K. G. (2011). "Identity in Organizations: Exploring Cross-level Dynamics." *Organization Science* 22(5): 1144–56.

Bardon, T., Clegg, S., and Josserand, E. (2012). "Exploring Identity Construction from a Critical Management Perspective: A Research Agenda." *M@n@gement* 15(4): 350–66.

Barley, S. R. and Tolbert, P. S. (1997). "Institutionalization and Structuration: Studying the Links between Action and Institution." *Organization Studies* 18(1): 93–117.

Brewer, M. B. (2012). "Optimal Distinctiveness Theory: Its History and Development." In *The Handbook of Theories of Social Psychology*, vol. 2, edited by P. A. M. Van Lange, A. W. Kruglanski, and E. T. Higgins, 81–98. London: SAGE.

Brickson, S. L. (2013). "Athletes, Best Friends, and Social Activists: An Integrative Model Accounting for the Role of Identity in Organizational Identification." *Organization Science* 24(1): 226–45.

Brown, A. D. (2006). "A Narrative Approach to Collective Identities." *Journal of Management Studies* 43(4): 731–53.

Chreim, S., Williams, B. E., and Hinings, C. R. (2007). "Interlevel Influences on the Reconstruction of Professional Role Identity." *Academy of Management Journal* 50(6): 1515–39.

Corley, K. G. (2004). "Defined by Our Strategy or Our Culture? Hierarchical Differences in Perceptions of Organizational Identity and Change." *Human Relations* 57(9): 1145–77.

Corley, K. G. and Gioia, D. A. (2004). "Identity Ambiguity and Change in the Wake of a Corporate Spin-off." *Administrative Science Quarterly* 49(2): 173–208.

Cornelissen, J. P., Haslam, S. A., and Balmer, J. M. T. (2007). "Social Identity, Organizational Identity and Corporate Identity: Towards an Integrated Understanding of Processes, Patternings and Products." *British Journal of Management* 18(S1): S1–S16.

Cornelissen, J. P., Haslam, S. A., and Werner, M. D. (2016). "Bridging and Integrating Theories on Organizational Identity: A Social Interactionist Model of Organizational Identity Formation and Change." In *The Oxford Handbook of Organizational Identity*, edited by M. G. Pratt, M. Schultz, B. E. Ashforth, and D. Ravasi, 200–15. Oxford: Oxford University Press.

Czarniawska, B. (1997). *Narrating the Organization: Dramas of Institutional Identity*. Chicago: University of Chicago Press.

DeJordy, R. and Creed, W. E. D. (2016). "Institutional Pluralism, Inhabitants, and the Construction of Organizational and Personal Identities." In *The Oxford Handbook of Organizational Identity*, edited by M. G. Pratt, M. Schultz, B. E. Ashforth, and D. Ravasi, 374–95. Oxford: Oxford University Press.

Dutton, J. E. and Dukerich, J. M. (1991). "Keeping an Eye on the Mirror: Image and Identity in Organizational Adaptation." *Academy of Management Journal* 34(3): 517–54.

Elsbach, K. and Dukerich, J. M. (2016). "Organizational Identity and the Undesired Self." In The Oxford Handbook of Organizational Identity, edited by M. G. Pratt, M. Schultz, B. E. Ashforth, and D. Ravasi. 257–75. Oxford: Oxford University Press.

Fauchart, E. and Gruber, M. (2011). "Darwinians, Communitarians, and Missionaries: The Role of Founder Identity in Entrepreneurship." *Academy of Management Journal* 54(5): 935–57.

Fiol, C. M. (1991). "Managing Culture as a Competitive Resource: An Identity-Based View of Sustainable Competitive Advantage." *Journal of Management* 17(1): 191–211.

Giddens, A. (1984). *The Constitution of Society: Outline of the Theory of Structuration*. Berkeley, CA: University of California Press.

Gioia, D. A. and Hamilton, A. L. (2016). "Great Debates in Organizational Identity Study." In *The Oxford Handbook of Organizational Identity*, edited by M. G. Pratt, M. Schultz, B. E. Ashforth, and D. Ravasi, 21–38. Oxford: Oxford University Press.

Gioia, D. A., Patvardhan, S. D., Hamilton, A. L., and Corley, K. G. (2013). "Organizational Identity Formation and Change." *Academy of Management Annals* 7: 123–93.

Gioia, D. A., Price, K. N., Hamilton, A. L., and Thomas, J. B. (2010). "Forging an Identity: An Insider-Outsider Study of Processes Involved in the Formation of Organizational Identity." *Administrative Science Quarterly* 55(1): 1–46.

Gioia, D. A., Schultz, M., and Corley, K. G. (2002). "On Celebrating the Organizational Identity Metaphor: A Rejoinder to Cornellisen." *British Journal of Management* 13(3): 269–75.

Hoang, H. and Gimeno, J. (2010). "Becoming a Founder: How Founder Role Identity Affects Entrepreneurial Transitions and Persistence in Founding." *Journal of Business Venturing* 25(1): 41–53.

Horton, K. E., Bayerl, P. S., and Jacobs, G. (2014). "Identity Conflicts at Work: An Integrative Framework." *Journal of Organizational Behavior* 35(S1): S6–S22.

Howard-Grenville, J., Metzger, M. L., and Meyer, A.D. (2013). "Rekindling the Flame: Processes of Identity Resurrection." *Academy of Management Journal* 56(1): 113–36.

Hsu, G. and Elsbach, K. D. (2013). "Explaining Variation in Organizational Identity Categorization." *Organization Science* 24(4): 996–1013.

Kenny, K., Whittle, A., and Willmott, H. (2016). "Organizational Identity: The Significance of Power and Politics." In *The Oxford Handbook of Organizational Identity*, edited by M. G. Pratt, M. Schultz, B. E. Ashforth, and D. Ravasi, 140–59. Oxford: Oxford University Press.

King, B. G., Felin, T., and Whetten, D. A. (2010). "Finding the Organization in Organizational Theory: A Meta-theory of the Organization as a Social Actor." *Organization Science* 21(1): 290–305.

Kozlowski, S. W. J. and Klein, K. J. (2000). "A Multilevel Approach to Theory and Research in Organizations: Contextual, Temporal, and Emergent Processes." In *Multilevel Theory, Research, and Methods in Organizations: Foundations, Extensions, and New Directions*, edited by K. J. Klein and S. W. J. Kozlowski, 3–90. San Francisco: Jossey-Bass.

Kreiner, G. E., Hollensbe, E. C., and Sheep, M. L. (2006). "On the Edge of Identity: Boundary Dynamics at the Interface of Individual and Organizational Identities." *Human Relations* 59(10): 1315–41.

Kreiner, G. E., Hollensbe, E., Sheep, M. L., Smith, B. R., and Kataria, N. (2015). "Elasticity and the Dialectic Tensions of Organizational Identity: How Can We Hold together while We Are Pulling apart?" *Academy of Management Journal* 58(4): 981–1011.

Kreiner, G. E. and Murphy, C. (2016). "Organizational Identity Work." In *The Oxford Handbook of Organizational Identity*, edited by M. G. Pratt, M. Schultz, B. E. Ashforth, and D. Ravasi, 276–93. Oxford: Oxford University Press.

Kroezen, J. J. and Heugens, P. P. M. A. R. (2012). "Organizational Identity Formation: Processes of Identity Imprinting and Enactment in the Dutch Microbrewing Landscape." In *Constructing Identity in and around Organizations*, edited by M. Schultz, S. Maguire, A. Langley, and H. Tsoukas, H., 89–127. Oxford: Oxford University Press.

Larson, G. S. and Tompkins, P. K. (2005). "Ambivalence and Resistance: A Study of Management in a Concertive Control System." *Communication Monographs* 72(1): 1–21.

Mathieu, J. E. and Chen, G. (2011). "The Etiology of the Multilevel Paradigm in Management Research." *Journal of Management* 37(2): 610–41.

Meyerson, D. E. and Scully, M. A. (1995). "Tempered Radicalism and the Politics of Ambivalence and Change." *Organization Science* 6(5): 585–600.

Morgeson, F. P. and Hofmann, D. A. (1999). "The Structure and Function of Collective Constructs: Implications for Multilevel Research and Theory Development." *Academy of Management Review* 24(2): 249–65.

Pedersen, J. S. and Dobbin, F. (2006). "In Search of Identity and Legitimation: Bridging Organizational Culture and Neoinstitutionalism." *American Behavioral Scientist* 49(7): 897–907.

Petriglieri, J. and Devine, B. A. (2016). "Mobilizing Organizational Action against Identity Threats: The Role of Organizational Members' Perceptions and Responses." In *The Oxford Handbook of Organizational Identity*, edited by M. G. Pratt, M. Schultz, B. E. Ashforth, and D. Ravasi, 239–56. Oxford: Oxford University Press.

Pratt, M. G. (2003). "Disentangling Collective Identities." *Research on Managing Groups and Teams* 5: 161–88.

Pratt, M. G. (2016). "Hybrid and Multiple Organizational Identities." In *The Oxford Handbook of Organizational Identity*, edited by M. G. Pratt, M. Schultz, B. E. Ashforth, and D. Ravasi, 106–20. Oxford: Oxford University Press.

Ran, B. and Duimering, P. R. (2007). "Imaging the Organization: Language Use in Organizational Identity Claims." *Journal of Business and Technical Communication* 21(2): 155–87.

Ravasi, D. and Phillips, N. (2011). "Strategies of Alignment: Organizational Identity Management and Strategic Change at Bang & Olufsen." *Strategic Organization* 9(2): 103–35.

Ravasi, D. and Schultz, M. (2006). "Responding to Organizational Identity Threats: Exploring the Role of Organizational Culture." *Academy of Management Journal* 49(3): 433–58.

Reay, T., Golden-Biddle, K., and Germann, K. (2006). "Legitimizing a New Role: Small Wins and Microprocesses of Change." *Academy of Management Journal* 49(5): 977–98.

Schinoff, B., Rogers, K., and Corley, K. G. (2016). "How Do We Communicate Who We Are? Examining How Organizational Identity Is Conveyed to Members." In *The Oxford Handbook of Organizational Identity*, edited by M. G. Pratt, M. Schultz, B. E. Ashforth, and D. Ravasi, 219–38. Oxford: Oxford University Press.

Schultz, M. (2016). "Organizational Identity Change and Temporality." In *The Oxford Handbook of Organizational Identity*, edited by M. G. Pratt, M. Schultz, B. E. Ashforth, and D. Ravasi, 93–105. Oxford: Oxford University Press.

Schultz, M. and Hernes, T. (2013). "A Temporal Perspective on Organizational Identity." *Organization Science* 24(1): 1–21.

Scott, S. G. and Lane, V. R. (2000). "A Stakeholder Approach to Organizational Identity." *Academy of Management Review* 25(1): 43–62.

Stryker, S. and Burke, P. J. (2000). "The Past, Present, and Future of an Identity Theory." *Social Psychology Quarterly* 63(4): 284–97.

Tajfel, H. and Turner, J. C. (1986). "The Social Identity Theory of Intergroup Behavior." In *Psychology of Intergroup Relations*, 2nd edn., edited by S. Worchel and W. G. Austin, 7–24. Chicago: Nelson-Hall.

Thomas, R. (2009). "Critical Management Studies on Identity: Mapping the Terrain." In *The Oxford Handbook of Critical Management Studies*, edited by M. Alvesson, T. Bridgman, and H. Willmott, 166–85. Oxford: Oxford University Press.

van Knippenberg, D. (2016). "Making Sense of Who We Are: Leadership and Organizational Identity." In *The Oxford Handbook of Organizational Identity*, edited by M. G. Pratt, M. Schultz, B. E. Ashforth, and D. Ravasi, 335–49. Oxford: Oxford University Press.

Van Maanen, J. and Schein, E. H. (1979). "Toward a Theory of Organizational Socialization." *Research in Organizational Behavior* 1: 209–64.

Watson, T. J. (2016). "Organizational Identity and Organizational Identity Work as Valuable Analytical Resources." In *The Oxford Handbook of Organizational Identity*, edited by M. G. Pratt, M. Schultz, B. E. Ashforth, and D. Ravasi, 123–39. Oxford: Oxford University Press.

Weick, K. E. (1995). *Sensemaking in Organizations.* Thousand Oaks, CA: SAGE.

Werbel, J. D. and DeMarie, S. M. (2005). "Aligning Strategic Human Resource Management and Person–Environment Fit." *Human Resource Management Review* 15(4): 247–62.

Whetten, D. A. and Mackey, A. (2002). "A Social Actor Conception of Organizational Identity and its Implications for the Study of Organizational Reputation." *Business and Society* 41(4): 393–414.

Wiley, N. (1988). "The Micro–Macro Problem in Social Theory." *Sociological Theory* 6(2): 254–61.

Zuckerman, E. (2016). "Optimal Distinctiveness Revisited: An Integrative Framework for Understanding the Balance between Differentiation and Conformity in Individual and Organizational Identities." In *The Oxford Handbook of Organizational Identity*, edited by M. G. Pratt, M. Schultz, B. E. Ashforth, and D. Ravasi, 183–99. Oxford: Oxford University Press.

....

CHAPTER 5

ORGANIZATIONAL IDENTITY CHANGE AND TEMPORALITY

....

MAJKEN SCHULTZ

THE discussion of what constitutes "sameness" and "change" of a phenomenon has puzzled philosophers for centuries and extends well beyond the area of organizational identity. However, the classic discussion pinpoints a fundamental paradox also of profound relevance to organizational identity, as it questions whether an object that has all of its elements replaced remains fundamentally the same object or whether replacement of one of more elements implies that the object has changed. The paradox was first articulated by Plutarch in his tale about the Ship of Theseus:

> The ship wherein Theseus and the youth of Athens returned from Crete had thirty oars, and was preserved by the Athenians down even to the time of Demetrius Phalereus, for they took away the old planks as they decayed, putting in new and stronger timber in their place, in so much that this ship became a standing example among the philosophers, for the logical question of things that grow; one side holding that the ship remained the same, and the other contending that it was not the same.
>
> (Plutarch, *Theseus*)

The paradox has been further refined, speculating what if the original planks were picked up after they had been replaced, and used to build a second ship: would that be the Ship of Theseus? The paradox has been "resolved" in different ways by philosophers through time, but has never been settled as it raises fundamental questions of both what constitutes a "thing" (in this case a ship) and what the criteria are that define "sameness" (how do we know the thing is the same)?

In a similar vein, scholars of organizational identity have questioned if and how it changes. Does identity change when identity claims and/or interpretations of their meaning are replaced over time? Do such replacements imply a fundamental change in identity? Does the organizational identity need to change in order to stay the same, reflecting the effort it involves to remain the same. And finally, what are the implications for identity, if there is no deliberate change effort, but the evolving of time? Will the organization cease to exist, as indicated in the Ship of Theseus, where the decay of the planks eventually will sink the ship? In spite of whether organizational identity changes fundamentally or not, what are the dynamics underpinning the ongoing development of identity over time?

The discussion of organizational identity change has been intrinsic to the definition of the organizational identity construct itself in organization studies, since the "degree of sameness and continuity over time" was suggested by Albert and Whetten as one of the three definitional pillars in "the criterion of claimed temporal continuity" defining "who we are" as an organization (Albert and Whetten, 1985: 266). The discussion of identity change has to a large extent derived from elaborations, criticisms, or counter views to this claim for endurance. The ambition of this chapter is to provide an overview of some key positions in the ongoing debate on identity change, as well as to highlight some of the current discussions.

The first view, articulated by Albert and Whetten (1985), assumes that organizational identity derives from the stable and enduring characteristics of organizational self-definition based in the organization as a social actor. The debates in the following decades were often based in the dichotomy that identity—or specific dimensions of identity—were conceived as either stable or changing, as scholars demonstrated how identity shifts between periods of stability and change. As argued by Gioia, Schultz, and Corley: "we reconceptualize organizational identity as a potentially precarious and unstable notion, frequently up for redefinition and revision by organization members" (Gioia, Schultz, and Corley, 2000: 64). This paved the way for a second view on identity change as periodic, often taking a social constructivist perspective on the organization (e.g., Elsbach and Kramer, 1996; Gioia, Schultz, and Corley, 2000; Glynn and Marquis, 2004; Ravasi and Schultz, 2006; Clark, Gioia, Ketchen, and Thomas, 2010). Finally, a third view has emerged which argues that identity is continuously being reconstructed, challenging the dichotomy between stability and change in the search for new ways of theorizing identity as a dynamic construct across time (e.g., Gioia and Patvardhan, 2012; Pratt, 2012; Schultz and Hernes, 2013). Continuing the narrative of the ship of Theseus, scholars may argue that the original design of the ship provides stability amidst the ongoing replacement of the elements of the ship, while others may say that it is the authenticity of the remaining old planks that constitutes the core of the identity. The chapter outlines some of these questions regarding identity change and suggests directions for future research on organizational identity.

DIFFERENT VIEWS ON ORGANIZATIONAL IDENTITY CHANGE

The three views are summarized in Table 5.1. The first column provides examples of how the three views have been used and further elaborated in organization studies,

Table 5.1 Dominant views on identity change

View on identity change	Examples of view	Examples of mechanisms of identity change or stability	Examples of authors
1. Identity as enduring stability	a) Identity is enduring and changes very slowly over time. b) Identity endures through selection and forgetting of memories. c) Identity shows inertia.	a) Identity claims are stable commitments that exhibit some degree of sameness and continuity over time. b) Selective forgetting of identity by omitting or neutralizing contradicting identity elements from the past. c) Identity inertia is enforced by enduring images and/or established knowledge.	a) Albert & Whetten, 1985; Whetten & McKay; Whetten 2006. b) Anteby & Molnár, 2012; Nissley & Casey, 2002. c) Tripsas, 2009; Nag, Corley, & Gioia, 2007.
2. Identity as periodic or partial change	a) Identity claims and their meanings change as they adapt to external changes, shifts in strategies, and/or respond to identity threats. b) Identity labels/claims change, conforming to shifting environments and new requirements for legitimacy. c) Some identity elements may change, while others remain stable; e.g., identity labels or claims are stable, while their meanings are malleable.	a) Identity change in response to shifting images and renewed sensemaking: e.g., as cognitive tactics, relationship sensemaking–sensegiving; sensemaking through discursive resources; identity change facilitated by identity ambiguity or transitional identity; or strategic formation processes. b) Identity change via institutional forces and relations between institutional and organizational levels. c) Partial identity change via processes of adaptive instability, institutional isomorphism or loss of corporate reputation.	a) Gagliardi, 1986; Elsbach & Kramer, 1996; Gioia & Thomas, 1996; Corley & Gioia, 2004; Brickson, 2005; Ravasi & Schultz, 2006; Clark, Gioia, Ketchen, & Thomas, 2010; Rindova, Dalpiaz, & Ravasi, 2011; Kjaergaard, Morsig & Ravasi, 2011; Bhatt, van Riel, & Bauman (this volume, Ch. 23); Tienari & Vaara (this volume, Ch. 24). b) Fox-Wolgramm, Boal & Hunt, 1998; Greenwood et al., 2011; Besharow & Brickson; Philips, Tracey, & Kraatz; DeJordy & Creed (this volume, Chs 21, 19, & 20). c) Gioia, Schultz, & Corley, 2000; Glynn & Abzug, 2002; Glynn & Marquis, 2004.

(*continued*)

Table 5.1 Continued

View on identity change	Examples of view	Examples of mechanisms of identity change or stability	Examples of authors
3. Identity as ongoing change	a) Identity as process and flow. b) Identity is constituted by dynamic relations with other constructs, such as culture, image, and/or innovation. c) Identity is continuously reconstructed in time as ongoing relations between past, present, and future.	a) Identity is by definition always in the making and never settles. Identity formation distinguished from "self-processes" across time. b) Identity dynamics as relations between culture, identity, and images; unfolding through identity activation; mutually constitutive dynamics between innovation and identity. c) The past is continuously connected to future identities in on ongoing present using members' lived experiences, various memory forms or narratives, and rhetorical resources based in history.	a) Gioia, Price, Hamilton, & Thomas, 2010; Gioia & Patvardhan, 2012; Pratt, 2012; Gioia & Hamilton (this volume, Ch. 1). b) Hatch & Schultz, 2002; Pratt, 2012; Hatch, Schultz, & Skov, 2015; Anthony & Tripsas (this volume, Ch. 22). c) Chreim, 2005; Ybema, 2010; Schultz & Hernes, 2013; Howard-Grenville, Metzger, & Meyer, 2013; Kreiner & Murphy (this volume, Ch. 15); Suddaby, Foster, & Trank (this volume, Ch. 16).

while the second column comments on which mechanisms initiated and/or supported identity change. In the third column selected authors are mentioned, including authors from this volume. The table shows that the same scholars have contributed to different views on organizational identity change, illustrating that identity is in itself a highly dynamic field.

Identity as Enduring Stability

The first view is called the central–enduring–distinctive definition (CED) and is rooted in the claim that endurance, along with centrality and distinctiveness, constitute organizational identity (Albert and Whetten, 1985). Although Whetten (2006) in a later reflection acknowledges that changes underpin life in organizations, he argues that such fluctuating shifts in organizations are not constitutive of its identity: "if something isn't a central and enduring feature of an organization, then practically speaking, it isn't likely to be invoked as a distinguishing feature, and thus it falls outside the domain specified for this concept (Whetten, 2006: 225). Thus, Albert and Whetten (1985) refer to identity claims as a fundamental extension of past developments that holds commitments for future actions, thereby turning identity into a sort of temporal glue in organizations that maintains stability in spite of changing circumstances.

In the early years of organizational identity studies, scholars often took the enduringness of identity for granted by applying the overall CED definition of identity as the point of departure for their empirical work. However, the concern with how enduringness is constructed has gotten a revival after a decade of criticism and focus on identity change. In their recent study of how companies are narrating their rhetorical history through annual reports, Anteby and Molnár (2012) show how the selection and forgetting of memories help sustain organizational identity over decades. Their study shows how the endurance of identity is a result of continuous managerial intervention rather than an inherent characteristic per se. In a similar vein, scholars have suggested identity inertia as another form of identity endurance. Identity inertia emerges from organizational inertia, such as failed market adaptation—as in Tripsas's (2009) study of the digital photography business—or lack of adaptation between knowledge, practice, and identity (Nag, Corley, and Gioia, 2007). Thus, although the notion of endurance has been constitutive for the definition of identity, later studies have shown that identity may remain stable for a number of reasons not implied by its definition.

Identity as Periodic or Partial Change

Scholars have challenged the enduring dimension of the CED, arguing that identity *does* change and that change can be prompted by a variety of different circumstances. In addition, scholars expanded the identity construct from its original focus on claims (the social actor perspective) to include the self-defining beliefs, understandings, and narratives (the social constructivist perspective), which enabled distinctions about *which* elements of identity are changing. However, these contributions all share the assumption that organizational identity changes occasionally or periodically and remains more stable between the periods of change. Such perceptions of change are similar to perceptions of organizational change as punctuated equilibrium, as suggested by Gersick (1991) and Romanelli and Tushman (1994), although identity studies point to a mixed set of circumstances initiating identity change.

One set of scholars conceives identity change as reactions to or implications of changes in the organizational context, whether these changes are derived from perceived threats to the existing identity, changing external environments, or a new strategic context. A significant amount of empirical work has studied such identity change in terms of the relationships between identity and images, showing how identity claims change as they adapt to shifting images (and/or reputation) or desired future images (e.g., Elsbach and Kramer, 1996; Gioia and Thomas, 1996; Ravasi and Schultz, 2006; Bhatt, van Riel, and Baumann, this volume, Ch. 23). Drawing on Weick (1995), some studies suggest how changes in the competitive landscape, new competitors, or changes in ownership pose threats to established self-perceptions, encouraging actors to engage in renewed sensemaking about who they are as an organization. For example, the study of three periods of identity change in Bang & Olufsen shows how the interplay between sensemaking and sensegiving initiated a redefinition of identity claims as reactions to identity threats, suggesting how cultural resources were mobilized in identity change (Ravasi and Schultz, 2006). The chapter by Tienari and Vaara (this volume, Ch. 24) enhances the importance of sensemaking to identity reconstruction in situations of mergers and acquisitions, arguing how organizational members draw upon and mobilize cultural and discursive resources when making sense of who they are becoming as the new organization. Stressing the impact of changes in the organizational context, Corley and Gioia (2004) demonstrate how identity change was accompanied by identity ambiguity during a corporate spin-off, whereas the study of the identity transformation at Oticon points to the importance of the media for identity change enhancing the influences from external perceptions (Kjaergaard, Morsing, and Ravasi, 2011).

Drawing on institutional theory, another group of identity scholars focuses on how institutional forces or changes in the institutional environment create pressure for organizational identity change, while they also explore how organizational identity may serve as a filter in how organizations respond to institutional change, as argued in Chapter 21 of this volume (for an early contribution see Fox-Wolgrann, Boal, and Hunt, 1998; for a recent extensive review, see Greenwood et al., 2011). Based in the works of Selznick (1949, 1957) the chapter by Philips, Tracey, and Kraatz (this volume, Ch. 19) argues how organizational identity has been conceived within institutional theory, suggesting how recent developments in institutional theory are taking a more dynamic view, both of institutional and organizational identity change—advocating the need to further develop their mutual relationship with respect to change.

Finally, several studies suggest that while some identity elements may remain stable, others are changing. For example, as a counterpoint to the endurance of identity claims, Gioia, Schultz, and Corley (2000) introduced the idea of "adaptive instability" for periods when identity claims or labels appear stable, while their associated meanings and beliefs are changing (see also Gagliardi, 1986). Thus, the meaning of identity claims shift as reactions to changing times, such as how the meaning of an identity of high-tech has changed dramatically in the last decade. By the same token, Glynn and Marquis (2004), drawing on institutional theory, demonstrate how perceptions of a central identity element—the corporate name—may change with the implication that the organization loses its legitimacy. In another study of organizational names, Glynn and Abzug (2002) point to a different mechanism, as they illustrate how companies are changing their names as they respond to shifts in their institutional environments, thereby showing how institutional conformity shapes and changes organizational names over time.

The examples we have cited substantiate how organizational identity or specific elements of identity change as reactions, responses, or adaptations to changes happening in or around the organization. Depending on the theoretical position, scholars highlight different mechanisms in their analysis of how identity changes, that is, whether actors are engaged in reconstructing who they are through collective sensemaking or are subject to isomorphic pressure from their organizational environments. However, while all of these contributions point to the changing nature of identity, few question the underpinning definition of identity as "who we are" as an organization.

Identity as Ongoing Change

In contrast, the third view argues that identity change is ongoing and inherent to the construction and thus the definition of identity itself. Rather than searching for external reasons for identity change, the changing nature of identity is inherent in the intertwined claims and perceptions constituting organizational identity, implying that identity studies should be concerned with the ongoing making of identity embedded in time. Also, the theoretical underpinning of identity studies shifted and became more clearly inspired by pragmatists (such as G. H. Mead, 1932, 1934, and Bergson 1946/2007), more recent contributions to process studies (such as Tsoukas and Chia, 2002; Langley and Tsoukas, 2010; Hernes, 2014), and the notion developed by Weick (1995) of identity as an ongoing accomplishment that is continuously redefined through interaction. As a result, the central analytical question with respect to identity change itself transforms from asking what generates identity change to questioning how identity changes and what creates stability in the making of identity constantly on the move. Similar to the other main views, there are important nuances in how identity is conceived as ongoing change.

Drawing on distinctions from process thinking (e.g., Hernes, 2014; Schultz, McGuire, Langley, and Tsoukas, 2012) between identity as an "entity" in a state of being *versus* identity as "process" in a state of becoming, scholars have suggested replacing the conception of identity as a "noun" with a "verb." As argued by Gioia and Hamiltonin Chapter 1 in this volume (see also Gioia and Patvardhan, 2012), identity has no fixed referent, as assumed in the CED definition, but can instead be conceived as a "flow" replacing the conceptualizing of identity as a manifestation of self-defining claims with a conceptualization of identity as continuous flows of expressions and reinterpretations of identity. Without making claims about "flow," an earlier study by some of the same authors suggests how the unfolding of an identity flow may occur, as shown in eight related processes of identity formation in a new college (Gioia et al., 2010). In a deeper scrutiny of how we usually talk about identity and process, Pratt (2012: 32) explores alternative ways of articulating identity as process based in G. H. Mead's notion of "self-process," suggesting how self-processes may develop across different moments in time. The view of identity as fluid and inherently fragmented is also found in critical and postmodern perspectives on individual identity (e.g., Bardon, Clegg, and Josserand, 2012; Thomas, 2009), as discussed by Ashforth in Chapter 4, this volume.

Other scholars have pointed to an organizational identity dynamic emerging from the ongoing relations between identity, culture, and images (e.g., an early conceptualization was suggested by Hatch and Schultz in 2002; see also Hatch, Schultz, and Larsen, 2000). These works draw on several early contributions (e.g., Dutton and Dukerich, 1991; Gioia and Thomas, 1996), but go beyond identity change as periodic processes. In a recent study of a complex transformational change in Carlsberg Group, Hatch, Schultz, and Skov (2015) coin the concept of "identity activation," showing how a program of planned identity change (i.e., introduction of new identity claims) over a five-year period was both resisted and supported by constant company-wide processes of reflecting, questioning, and debating among organizational actors. Such identity activation emerges from tensions in the ongoing organizational cultural change, which in turn influences the unfolding inclusion of alternative identity claims. Thus, the ongoing identity change is intertwined with changes in the organizational culture. In addition, the chapter by Anthony and Tripsas (this volume, Ch. 22) suggests an overlooked dynamic between innovation and organizational identity in that they are mutually constitutive, albeit innovation activities may influence organizational identity in different ways, ranging from identity-enhancing to identity-stretching and to identity-challenging activities.

A last group of studies focuses more explicitly on the duality between continuity and change and a further conceptualization of the role of time. An early study by Chreim (2005) addresses the simultaneous references to continuity and change in identity narratives in a merger, whereas later works expand the duality between continuity and change in time by asking how memories of past identities in LEGO Group are brought into what Schultz and Hernes (2013) label the "ongoing present." Here, the management team evoked past identities through combinations of different forms of textual, oral, and material memories, which in turn influenced the time horizon of the envisioned future in that going far back in time inspired actors to look far into the future. Hence the redefinition of what the organization is becoming takes place, while actors are constructing their own trajectory of time. A related finding is offered in the study of the resurrection of the past identity of Eugene as an iconic "Track-Town" (referring to the track for runners, such as Steve Fontaine;

Howard-Grenville, Metzger, and Meier, 2013). The authors show how the emotional experience of tapping into the past motivated actors to engage in the identity resurrection process and enabled them to attract additional resources to the re-establishment of Track Town. The importance of the past for identity and identification directed at the future is also stressed by the chapter on identity work as "re-membering" by Suddaby, Foster, and Trank (Ch. 16, this volume), suggesting how history is a resource for identity reconstruction, that is, by the concept of rhetorical history. The importance of temporality to identity work is also discussed in the chapter by Kreiner and Murphy (Ch. 15, this volume) arguing how the temporality of identity work addresses issues of the intentionality of identity work, that is, are past identities deliberately manipulated and forgotten, or is identity also constructed more unconsciously in the flow of time?

FUTURE RESEARCH

The views on identity change have come full circle in the sense that the criticism of the initial insistence of identity endurance and continuity now is challenged by studies enhancing how threads of continuity across time enable and motivate organizational actors to embrace the ongoing identity dynamic and become active co-creators in the making of identities. Organizational identities will pass through shifting ebbs and flows of engagement and organization-wide implications, but identity is always constructed in time, and the notion of identity as a stable reservoir of resources across time is contested. This, in turn, opens a new set of questions with respect to how the making of identity in time unfolds in organizations. How do we study the relations between the organization as an actor tapping into evocative memories from its past of "who we were," when constructing identity claims for "who we are becoming" in the future? How do we address the relations between identity claims for the future articulated by headquarters and dispersed organizational actors having their localized perceptions of what constitutes past and future? What constitutes credible and authentic threads of identity continuity in the midst of ongoing identity change?

These questions also have profound implications for the role of management, as most studies have stressed the proactive role of management as "change agents" enhancing and directing identity change. If identity is ever-changing and always in the making, the role of management becomes to be "maintenance-agents" providing the threads of sameness and continuity that stabilize the organization in the midst of ongoing change. Thus, in addition to setting the direction for the ship of Theseus, the captain on board should remind himself and others that it is the ongoing process of changing the planks that maintains the ship and its ability to sail.

References

Albert, S. and Whetten, D. A. (1985). "Organizational Identity." In *Research in Organizational Behavior*, vol. 7, edited by L. L. Cummings, and B. M. Staw, 263–95. Greenwich, CT: JAI Press.

Anteby, M. and Molnár, V. (2012). "Collective Memory Meets Organizational Identity: Remembering to Forget in a Firm's Rhetorical History." *Academy of Management Journal* 55: 515–40.

Anthony, C. and Tripsas, M. (2016). "Organizational Identity and Innovation." In *The Oxford Handbook of Organizational Identity*, edited by M. G. Pratt, M. Schultz, B. E. Ashforth, and D. Ravasi, 417–35. Oxford: Oxford University Press.

Ashforth, B. E. (2016). "Organizational, Subunit, and Individual Identities." In *The Oxford Handbook of Organizational Identity*, edited by M. G. Pratt, M. Schultz, B. E. Ashforth, and D. Ravasi, 79–92. Oxford: Oxford University Press.

Bardon, T., Clegg, S., and Josserand, E. (2012). "Exploring Identity Construction from a Critical Management Perspective: A Research Agenda." *M@n@gement* 15(4): 350–66.

Bergson, H. (2007). *The Creative Mind*. New York: Dover.

Besharov, M. L. and Brickson, S. L. (2016). "Organizational Identity and Institutional Forces: Toward an Integrative Framework." In *The Oxford Handbook of Organizational Identity*, edited by M. G. Pratt, M. Schultz, B. E. Ashforth, and D. Ravasi, 396–414. Oxford: Oxford University Press.

Bhatt, M., van Riel, C. B. M., and Baumann, M. (2016). "Planned Organizational Identity Change: Insights from Practice." In *The Oxford Handbook of Organizational Identity*, edited by M. G. Pratt, M. Schultz, B. E. Ashforth, and D. Ravasi, 436–54. Oxford: Oxford University Press.

Brickson, S. L. (2005). "Organizational Identity Orientation: Forging a Link between Organizational Identity and Organizations' Relations with Stakeholders." *Administrative Science Quarterly* 50(4): 576–609.

Chreim, S. (2005). "The Continuity–Change Duality in Narrative Texts of Organizational Identity." *Journal of Management Studies* 42(3): 567–93.

Clark, S. M., Gioia, D. A., Ketchen, D., Jr., and Thomas, J. B. (2010). "Transitional Identity as a Facilitator of Organizational Identity Change during a Merger." *Administrative Science Quarterly* 55(3): 397–438.

Corley, K. G. and Gioia, D. A. (2004). "Identity Ambiguity and Change in the Wake of a Corporate Spin-Off. "*Administrative Science Quarterly* 49(2): 173–208.

DeJordy, R. and Creed, W. E. D. (2016). "Institutional Pluralism, Inhabitants, and the Construction of Organizational and Personal Identities." In *The Oxford Handbook of Organizational Identity*, edited by M. G. Pratt, M. Schultz, B. E. Ashforth, and D. Ravasi, 374–95. Oxford: Oxford University Press.

Dutton, J. E. and Dukerich, J. M. (1991). "Keeping an Eye on the Mirror: Image and Identity in Organizational Adaptation." *The Academy of Management Journal* 34(3): 517–54.

Elsbach, K. D. and Kramer, R. M. (1996). "Members' Responses to Organizational Identity Threats: Encountering and Countering the *Business Week* Rankings." *Administrative Science Quarterly* 41(3): 442.

Fox-Wolfgramm, S. J., Boal, K. B., and Hunt, J. G. (1998). "Organizational Adaptation to Institutional Change: A Comparative Study of First-Order Change in Prospector and Defender Banks." *Administrative Science Quarterly*, 43: 87–126.

Gagliardi, P. (1986). "The Creation and Change of Organizational Cultures: A Conceptual Framework." *Organization Studies* 7(2): 117–34.

Gersick, C. (1991). "Revolutionary Change Theories: A Multilevel Exploration of the Punctuated Equilibrium Paradigm." *Academy of Management Review* 16(1): 10–36.

Gioia, D. A. and Hamilton, A. L. (2016). "Great Debates in Organizational Identity Study." In *The Oxford Handbook of Organizational Identity*, edited by M. G. Pratt, M. Schultz, B. E. Ashforth, and D. Ravasi, 21–38. Oxford: Oxford University Press.

Gioia, D. A. and Patvardhan, S. (2012). "Identity as Process and Flow." In *Constructing Identity in and around Organizations*, edited by M. Schultz, S. Maguire, A. Langley, and H. Tsoukas, 50–62. New York: Oxford University Press.

Gioia, D. A., Patvardhan, S. D., Hamilton, A. L., and Corley, K. G. (2013). "Organizational Identity Formation and Change." *The Academy of Management Annals* 7(1): 123–92.

Gioia, D. A., Price, K. N., Hamilton, A. L., and Thomas, J. B. (2010). "Forging an Identity: An Insider-Outsider Study of Processes Involved in the Formation of Organizational Identity." *Administrative Science Quarterly* 55(1): 1–46.

Gioia, D. A., Schultz, M., and Corley, K. G. (2000). "Organizational Identity, Image, and Adaptive Instability." *Academy of Management Review* 25(1): 63–81.

Gioia, D. A. and Thomas, J. B. (1996). "Identity, Image, and Issue Interpretation: Sensemaking during Strategic Change in Academia." *Administrative Science Quarterly* 41(3): 370.

Glynn, M. A. and Abzug, R. (2002). "Institutionalizing Identity: Symbolic Isomorphism and Organizational Names." *Academy of Management Journal* 45(1): 267–280.

Glynn, M. A. and Marquis, C. (2004). "When Good Names Go Bad: Symbolic Illegitimacy in Organizations." In *Research in the Sociology of Organizations*, vol. 22, edited by C. Johnson, 147–70. Bradford, UK: Emerald Group Publishing.

Greenwood, R., Raynard, M., Kodeih, F., Micelotta, E. R., and Lounsbury, M. (2011). "Institutional Complexity and Organizational Responses." *Academy of Management Annals* 5: 317–71.

Hatch, M. J. and Schultz, M. (2002). "The Dynamics of Organizational Identity." *Human Relations* 55(8): 989–1017.

Hatch, M. J., Schultz, M., and Skov, A. M. (2015). "Organizational Identity and Culture in the Context of Managed Change: Transformation in the Carlsberg Group, 2009–2013." *Academy of Management Discoveries* 1(1): 58–90.

Hernes, T. (2014). *A Process Theory of Organization*. Oxford: Oxford University Press.

Howard-Grenville, J., Metzger, M., and Meyer, A. D. (2013). "Rekindling the Flame: Processes of Identity Resurrection." *Academy of Management Journal* 56(1): 113–36.

Kjaergaard, A., Morsing, M., and Ravasi, D. (2011). "Mediating Identity: A Study of Media Influence on Organizational Identity Construction in a Celebrity Firm." *Journal of Management Studies* 48: 514–43.

Kreiner, G. E. and Murphy, C. (2016). "Organizational Identity Work." In *The Oxford Handbook of Organizational Identity*, edited by M. G. Pratt, M. Schultz, B. E. Ashforth, and D. Ravasi, 276–93. Oxford: Oxford University Press.

Langley, A. and Tsoukas, H. (2010). "Introducing 'Perspectives on Process Organization Studies.'" In *Perspectives on Process Organization Studies*, edited by A. Langley, and H. Tsoukas, 1–25. Oxford, UK: Oxford University Press.

Mead, G. H. (1934). *Mind, Self, and Society: From the Stand-Point of a Social Behaviorist*. Chicago, IL: University Chicago Press.

Mead, G. H. (1932). *The Philosophy of the Present*. Chicago: Open Court Publishing Company.

Nag, R., Corley, K. G., and Gioia, D. A. (2007). "The Intersection of Organizational Identity, Knowledge, and Practice: Attempting Strategic Change via Knowledge Grafting." *Academy of Management Journal* 50(4): 821–47.

Nissley, N. and Casey, A. (2002). "The Politics of the Exhibition: Viewing Corporate Museums Through the Paradigmatic Lens of Organizational Memory." *British Journal of Management* 13: 35–46.

Phillips, N., Tracey, P., and Kraatz, M. (2016). "Organizational Identity in Institutional Theory: Taking Stock and Moving Forward." In *The Oxford Handbook of Organizational Identity*, edited by M. G. Pratt, M. Schultz, B. E. Ashforth, and D. Ravasi, 353–73. Oxford: Oxford University Press.

Pratt, M. (2012). "Rethinking Identity Construction Processes in Organizations: Three Questions to Consider." In *The Construction of Identity in and around Organizations*, edited by M. Schultz, S. McGuire, A. Langley, H. Tsoukas, 21–50. Oxford: Oxford University Press:

Ravasi, D. and Schultz, M. (2006). "Responding to Organizational Identity Threats: Exploring the Role of Organizational Culture." *Academy of Management Journal* 49(3): 433–58.

Rindova, V., Dalpiaz, E., and Ravasi, D. (2011). "A Cultural Quest: A Study of Organizational Use of New Cultural Resources in Strategy Formation." *Organization Science* 22(2): 413–31.

Romanelli, E. and Tushman, M. (1994). "Organizational Transformation as Punctuated Equilibrium: An Empirical Test." *Academy of Management Journal* 37(5): 1141–666.

Schultz, M. and Hernes, T. (2013). "A Temporal Perspective on Organizational Identity." *Organization Science* 24:1–21.

Schultz, M., McGuire, S., Langley, A., and Tsoukas, H. (eds.) (2012). *The Construction of Identity in and around Organizations*. Oxford: Oxford University Press.

Schultz, M., Hatch, M.J. , and Larsen, M. H. (eds.) (2000). *The Expressive Organization: Linking Identity, Reputation and the Corporate Brand*, Oxford: Oxford University Press.

Selznick, P. (1949). *TVA and the Grass Roots: A Study of Politics and Organization*, vol. 3. Berkeley, CA: University of California Press.

Selznick, P. (1957). *Leadership in Administration: A Sociological Interpretation*. Evanston, IL: Row, Peterson.

Suddaby, R., Foster, W., and Quinn Trank, C. (2016). "Re-Membering: Rhetorical History as Identity-Work." In *The Oxford Handbook of Organizational Identity*, edited by M. G. Pratt, M. Schultz, B. E. Ashforth, and D. Ravasi, 297–316. Oxford: Oxford University Press.

Thomas, R. (2009). "Critical Management Studies on Identity: Mapping the Terrain." In *The Oxford Handbook of Critical Management Studies*, edited by M. Alvesson, T. Bridgman, and H. Willmott, 166–85. Oxford: Oxford University Press.

Tienari, J. and Vaara, E. (2016). "Identity Construction in Mergers and Acquisitions: A Discursive Sensemaking Perspective." In *The Oxford Handbook of Organizational Identity*, edited by M. G. Pratt, M. Schultz, B. E. Ashforth, and D. Ravasi, 455–73. Oxford: Oxford University Press.

Tripsas, M. (2009). "Technology, Identity and Inertia through the Lens of 'The Digital Photography Company.'" *Organization Science* 20: 440–61.

Tsoukas, H. and Chia, R. (2002). "On Organizational Becoming: Rethinking Organizational Change." *Organization Science* 13(5): 567.

Weick, Karl E. (1995). *Sensemaking in Organizations.* Thousand Oaks, CA: SAGE.

Whetten, D. A. (2006). "Albert and Whetten Revisited: Strengthening the Concept of Organizational Identity." *Journal of Management Inquiry* 15(3): 219–34.

Whetten, D. A. and Mackey, A. (2002). "A Social Actor Conception of Organizational Identity and its Implications for the Study of Organizational Reputation." *Business and Society* 41(4): 393–414.

Ybema, S. (2010). "Talk of Change: Temporal Contrasts and Collective Identities." *Organization Studies* 31(4), 481–503.

CHAPTER 6

....

HYBRID AND MULTIPLE ORGANIZATIONAL IDENTITIES

....

MICHAEL G. PRATT

ALTHOUGH this is the Handbook of Organizational *Identity*, most chapters in our volume at least entertain the notion that organizations can have more than one identity or draw upon research in this area (see Chs. 1, 2, 7–9, 11–13, 15–21, 24). The notion that organizations can have more than one identity has been around at least as long as Albert and Whetten's (1985) foundational work on the topic. Conceptualizing an organization as having identit*ies* is not surprising given that Albert and Whetten, and many who have followed, have used theories of identity pertaining to individuals as the starting point for theorizing about organizational-level ones. These foundational theories for organizational identity, such as those in psychology (social identity theory) and sociology (identity theory), view entities as having more than one conceptualization of "who I am," and thus view the concept as plural (identities) rather than singular (an identity). In drawing upon these foundational theories and applying them to the organizational level of analysis, scholars have viewed organizations as having multiple identities as well.[1]

In organizational research, there tends to be two main conceptualizations of organizational identity "plurality": hybrid organizational identities and multiple organizational identities. While the two are sometimes used synonymously (see Albert and

[1] Depending on what theories one uses to conceptualize identity, what *multiple* organizational identities means may vary. For some, it may mean that organizations may have multiple categories—possibly influenced by residing in pluralistic institutional environments or being influenced by multiple institutional logics. For others, organizational identities may be more akin to a role, thus multiple organizational identities may refer to multiple conceptualizations of what organizations do, and for whom they do it. Still others may view multiple organizational identities as residing in different groups in the organization—each of whom have a different view of "who we are" as an organization.

Whetten, 1985; Foreman and Whetten, 2002), there are some subtle and important differences between the two (see Corley et al., 2006). In particular, assumptions underlying (a) the number of possible identities, and (b) the range of relationships between or among the identities, differ depending on which conceptualization you take. Below, I give a very brief overview of each research stream, drawing heavily on Albert and Whetten (1985) and Pratt and Foreman (2000) as these articles lay out some of the major tenets of each conceptualization. I append each discussion with ideas about future research directions. I conclude the mini-chapter by noting what appears to be the biggest issue still facing research in this area: how do organizations with multiple identities deal with unity and holism?

HYBRID ORGANIZATIONAL IDENTITIES: A BRIEF OVERVIEW

Hybrid identities refer to two organizational identities that are "not expected to go together" (Albert and Whetten, 1985: 270). Albert and Adams (2002: 36) further refine the term by noting that these identities are "defended as inviolate, experienced as incompatible, and yet found to be indispensable." That is, hybrid identities are essential to "who the organization is," are perceived to be unalterable, yet are viewed as being at odds.[2] In their original conceptualization of organizational identities, Albert and Whetten (1985) argue that these identities can theoretically vary along a number of dimensions (an issue I will return to later). However, they strongly argue that a central dimension that characterizes hybrids is the normative–utilitarian dimension, a distinction that pre-dates the conceptualization of organizational identity (e.g., Barnard, 1938; Etzioni, 1975; Selznick, 1957). Utilitarian identities represent a "for-profit," "monetary," or "economic" focused self-definition. Normative identities, by contrast, are non-economic and can represent a variety of religious, cultural, aesthetic, and similarly non-monetary focused identities. When Selznick (1957) refers to organizations as "infused with meaning," and when leaders propose a higher organizational "purpose," they are referring to an organization's normative identity (see Philips, Kraatz, and Tracey, Ch. 19). Examples of organizations with hybrid identities would be universities, for-profit hospitals, and social enterprises. Hybrid organizational identities can be structured in two primary ways: ideographic and holographic.[3] Ideographic

---

[2] Hybrid organizational identities should not be confused with hybrid organizations or hybrid organizing, which are broader concepts referring to organizations that combine identities, forms, and/or or institutional logics to create a new type of organization (see Battilana and Lee, 2014 for review).

[3] To continue the parallel with hybrid organizing, this literature similarly differentiates among "blended" and "structurally differentiated" hybrids, with blended being similar to holographic, and structurally differentiated being similar to ideographic (see Greenwood et al., 2011: 352).

hybrid identities are structured such that each organizational unit or group has only one identity, and opposing identities are housed in or embodied by different units or groups. For example, in Glynn's (2000) study of the Atlantic Symphony Orchestra, the normative aspect of this organization's identity was embodied by the musicians, while the utilitarian was embodied by the professional administrators. More recently, in a natural food-cooperative, either "idealist" or "pragmatic" identities were strongly advocated by competing subgroups (Ashforth and Reingen, 2014). Holographic identities, by contrast, occur when competing organizational identities are housed in the same unit or group. Golden-Biddle and Rao's (1997) study of the board of directors at Medlay illustrates this type of identity. Here the board of directors reflected the identity of the organization as both "an advisor" to volunteers and a "family of friends."

Empirical research in the area of hybrid organizational identities has been relatively sparse (see Foreman and Whetten, Ch. 2). Perhaps not surprising, given the nature of these identities, many empirical treatments deal with the reactions of individuals or groups within these organizations to the organization's hybrid organizational identities. For example, such research has explored the impact of these hybrid identities on members' cooperation and conflict (Ashforth and Reingen, 2014; Glynn, 2000; Golden-Biddle and Rao, 1997; Pratt and Rafaeli, 1997), and/or on how members identify with their organizations (Foreman and Whetten, 2002; MacLean and Webber, 2015). However, I did not find empirical papers in top journal outlets that explored how organizational identity hybridity influenced the organization's relationship with external stakeholders, even though organizational hybrids are thought to form, at least in response, to environmental demands (Albert and Whetten, 1985).

There are other areas of inquiry regarding hybrid organizational identities that also remain relatively unexplored. To begin, existing treatments of hybrid identities—either holographic or ideographic—have largely, if not exclusively, been in not-for-profit organizations (e.g., Golden-Biddle and Rao, 1997; Glynn, 2000; see also Battilana and Dorado, 2010). However, future research may wish to adopt this conceptualization as a way of capturing for-profit organizations, especially in the wake of an increased emphasis on corporate social responsibility and "triple bottom lines." In a similar vein, while Albert and Whetten (1985) suggest that over their life cycle, organizations can move from single-identity organizations to hybrids, there has been little, if any, empirical research that has examined this development. Again, organizations adopting more normative identities, especially in the wake of public pressure to do so, would appear to be an ideal case for such development (Lepisto, 2015).

Moreover, it is not clear whether holographic and ideographic hybrids might develop differently, or whether organizations might shift from ideographic to holographic (and vice versa). One could imagine, however, that the addition of a new unit within the organization could lead to an ideographic organizational identity. For example, in response to public pressure, a primarily utilitarian organization could create a corporate social responsibility (CSR) department (or foundation) that houses a normative identity. Over time, however, the functions of this CSR department could be internalized into the entire organization, such that people are selected and trained with the expectation that the organization is about both "making money" and "doing good" (Battilana and Dorado, 2010) Hence, over time, organizations might shift from an ideographic hybrid identity to a holographic one.[4] Similarly, as an organization with a holographic hybrid identity grows, organizational elites may decide that having units embody both identities is inefficient and may instead come to structurally represent the normative and utilitarian identities in different departments—thus shifting from hybrid to ideographic. More generally, researchers may wish to explore more fully the origins of hybridity. At present, some recent research suggests a few intriguing possibilities. While not focusing on hybrid organizational identities per se, Battilana and Dorado (2010), for example, suggest that an organization's "hybridity" may be due, at least in part, to competing institutional demands. Thus, organizations that lie at the intersection of different institutions (see DeJordy and Creed, Ch. 20), or that incorporate competing institutional logics (see Besharov and Brickson, Ch. 21), may become hybrid "at birth" or may develop a hybrid identity when they find themselves in a contested or pluralistic institutional field(s). Similarly, one might expect that organizations with two powerful, but conflicting groups of stakeholders (e.g., the government and student families for publicly funded universities) might be better served by, and thus might be more likely to form, hybrid organizational identities.

Implicit in the very conceptualization of normative-utilitarian hybrid organizational identities is the idea that the opposing identities differ—at least in part—by their content. However, research on the actual content of organizational identities remains sparse. As I have noted, Albert and Whetten (1985) seemed to indicate that normative–utilitarian might only be one of several "dimensions" along which a hybrid identity is organized. In making a case for an extended metaphor analysis, a way to examine hybrid organizations, they note that "there is no comprehensive theory to predict how many identities an organization has, or how the dimensions of each are to be defined" (pp. 280–1). Thus, research on organizational identity may want to examine other types of hybrid-identity "dimensions" beyond normative–utilitarian. More generally, scholars may wish to examine how the content of organizational identities might influence both the identity dynamics within an organization as well as those between an organization and other organizations and institutions.

Interestingly, in one of the first empirical examples of a hybrid identity, the ideographic split did not fall cleanly along the normative and utilitarian dimension. In Pratt and Rafaeli's (1997) study of a nursing rehabilitation unit, they found that one shift of nurses tended toward an acute care identity while another, a rehabilitation identity. These two identities of "who they were" had diametrically opposed views of the mission of the unit, the types of patients they had, and the roles nurses performed. The core difference between the units, however, was about how the nurse related to patient care (e.g., distant/acute care versus close/rehabilitation), both of which could be considered normative. Similarly, Ashforth and Reingen (2014) posit a pragmatic

[4] Alternatively, it is possible that the organization as a whole never really internalizes the normative identity of the CSR. This may be the case in organizations which engage in "green

versus idealistic difference in organizational identities. While idealistic may be more normative than pragmatic, neither group would claim to be strongly utilitarian. In sum, the issue of multiple "dimensions" of organizational identity, and the importance of the content of identities more generally, seems to have fallen by the wayside since Albert and Whetten (1985). Might a re-emphasis on the actual content of organizational identities be useful for conceptualizing a broader range of hybridity (or multiplicity), or would a focus on OI content weaken the hybrid identity concept, allowing most any or all organizations to be considered hybrid in some fashion?

MULTIPLE ORGANIZATIONAL IDENTITIES: A BRIEF OVERVIEW

While the idea that organizations can have many identities is hinted at by Albert and Whetten (1985), Pratt and Foreman's (2000) paper on managing multiple organizational identities more fully articulates a multiple organizational identity conceptualization. Unlike Albert and Whetten (1985), who draw upon a wide range of identity theories, ranging from developmental psychology to the writing of William James, the conceptual foundation of a multiple organizational identity approach by Pratt and Foreman is decidedly micro-sociological, borrowing heavily from identity theory. This theory suggests that individuals can have a large number of identities, arranged in some form of dynamic hierarchy, which may or may not conflict. Drawing parallels from this literature to the organization level, they begin from a different conceptual starting point than a hybrid organizational identity conceptualization that limits the number of organizational identities to two (e.g., normative and utilitarian), and limits the relationship between those identities to being oppositional. Specifically, multiple organizational identity conceptualization relaxes these constraints—suggesting that organizations can have more than two identities, and that these identities may be related in a variety of ways, namely oppositional or complementary, or more "relationally neutral" – simply different, neither clearly complementary nor oppositional (Corley et al., 2006).

Building from these relaxed assumptions, Pratt and Foreman (2000) argue that the key issues in managing multiple organizational identities are their amount or numbers (i.e., identity plurality) and the relationship between or among them (i.e., identity synergy). With regard to plurality, the number of identities that an organization can hold is largely an issue of resources—human, financial, physical, political, and otherwise. The general premise is that multiple identities are "expensive" and thus organizational agents need to consider whether they can "afford" them. Synergy refers to the degree to which organizational identities are complementary. Pratt and Foreman (2000) suggest that the more complementary two or more identities are, the more likely that they can be managed in an integrative fashion.

Combining these two dimensions leads to four "ideal" ways of managing multiple organizational identities (see Figure 6.1). If organizations have enough resources, they can keep complementary organizational identities via the creation of a meta-/superordinate identity or other bridging device that allows the identities to be connected yet still function relatively independently (see also Gaertner, Dovidio, and Bachman's (1996) conceptualization of dual identities). When Time Inc. and Warner Communications merged in 1990, they attempted this type of *aggregation* strategy. Whereas Time Inc. had been historically strong in print, such as magazines, and Warner's historical strengths had been in movies and records, their aggregated identity revolved around "media." If well-resourced organizations have multiple neutral or even conflicting identities, such as may be the case with a conglomerate or a university, they may manage these identities via *compartmentalization*—that is, the physical, temporal, or symbolic separation of identities. Organizations with synergistic identities but few resources may *integrate* the identities by combining them to make a new identity. While true integrations are rare, the merging of the disparate "Baby Bells" back into the "new" AT&T could be considered a type of integration. Finally, organizations with few resources and competing or neutral identities may have to delete one or more of their identities (see "identify divestiture" in Albert

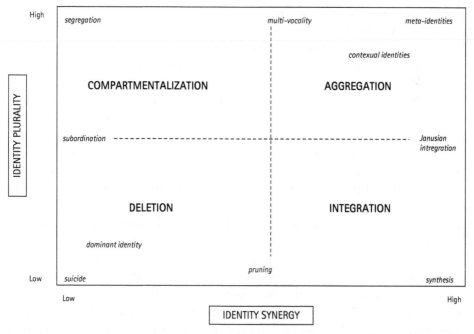

FIGURE 6.1 A classification scheme for multiple organizational identity management responses[a, b]

[a] The placement of specific responses (e.g., multi-vocality) is for illustrative purposes only. Further research is needed before we can more exactly map these responses.

[b] This figure is re-printed with permission from Pratt and Foreman (2000: 27).

and Whetten, 1985). This may happen via a spin-off (e.g., removing the name Chrysler from Daimler-Chrysler) or by eliminating an identity entirely (e.g., firing all of the Chrysler workers). As noted by Albert (1992) in his algebra of change, subtraction is exceedingly difficult. Taken together, this ACID (aggregation, compartmentalization, integration, and deletion) model represents "pure" types of responses to issues raised by plurality and synergy, however, Pratt and Foreman also note responses that fall between these pure types.

While the primary differences between a hybrid and a multiple organizational identity conceptualization are largely in identity number and relationships, it is important to note some more subtle differences between the conceptualizations. For example, research does not appear to view multiple organizational identities as having different "structures" such as holographic or ideographic. That said, while it is plausible that multiple organizational identities could be of either type, empirical research (e.g., Corley, 2004) and empirical examples (Pratt and Foreman, 2000) have tended to be ideographic in nature. In addition, Foreman and Whetten (2002) view hybrid organizational identities from a social actor perspective. More generally, research on hybrids has tended to focus on professions and other institutions that are hybrid in nature (Battilana and Dorado, 2010; Pratt and Dutton, 2000). Thus one might expect this perspective to be more institutional in nature. Empirical research on multiple organizational identities, by contrast, ranges from the explicitly social constructivist (Sillince and Brown, 2009) to the undeclared (Corley, 2004; Larson and Pepper, 2003). However, a neat parceling of conceptualizations may be premature.

Indeed, there is evidence that a multiple organizational identity conceptualization may fit well with institutional perspectives. To illustrate, Kraatz and Block (2008) suggest that some organizations are embedded in multiple institutions at the same time, thus it is possible that such organizations will come to manifest multiple identities (see also Pratt and Kraatz, 2009). It is also interesting to note that recent work on multiple institutional logics bears a striking resemblance to work on multiple organizational identities, even sharing some of the same dimensions along which to examine them. For example, Besharov and Smith (2014: 371) suggest a "degree of compatibility" among logics as a critical dimension for assessing the type of logic multiplicity within an organization which directly parallels Pratt and Foreman's (2000) "identity synergy" dimension for assessing multiple organizational identities. Their dimension of "centrality" similarly echoes Pratt and Foreman's (2000) concern about the presence or absence of powerful stakeholders in advocating a particular identity.

Beyond the different views of organizational identity used to examine them, another important distinction is that some of the initial articulations of these two approaches began from different starting points. Whereas the Albert and Whetten (1985) conceptualization spends more time on the evolution of hybrids, Pratt and Foreman's (2000) more overtly managerial focus begins with organizations already having multiple organizational identities, and thus focuses on how they are managed. In this way, the conceptualizations may complement each other, with hybrids providing insights into the genesis of multiple organizational identities, and research on managing multiple organizational identities providing insights into how hybrid organizational identities can be managed.

A final difference is the focus of the empirical research. While both conceptualizations do share some areas of concern, such as issues regarding employee identification (Larson and Pepper, 2003) and conflicting perspectives among groups in the organization (Corley, 2004), research on multiple organizational identities has also looked outside the organization. Indeed, Pratt and Kraatz (2009) argue that it is the presence of multiple external stakeholders that necessitates multiple identities in the first place. On the face of it, the internal focus of hybrid identity research seems odd given the initial focus on social actor views of hybrids. It may be, however, that this focus will change as empirical research in this area grows. From a multiple organizational identity conceptualization, multiple organizational identity claims have already been posited to garner legitimacy from a variety of external stakeholders (Sillince and Brown, 2009); and legitimacy is a core concern of a social actor perspective. Table 6.1 summarizes some of the differences between the hybrid and multiple organizational identities conceptualizations.

With regard to future research in the area of multiple organizational identities, I have already suggested that scholars may wish to focus on how organizations come to have them. In addition to institutional forces, researchers may want to pay particular attention to conditions where different organizations join together or split apart. To illustrate, organizational mergers and acquisitions would appear to be ideal for examining the genesis of multiple organizational identities, since the newly merged organization is likely to retain, at least for a while, the identities of their "host" organizations.

Table 6.1. Hybrid vs. multiple organizational identity conceptualizations

	Hybrid Organizational Identities	Multiple Organizational Identities
Number of Identities	Two	Two or more
Relationship among Identities	Oppositional	Oppositional, complementary, or simply different (and relationships among identities may potentially change over time)
Structure	Holographic and ideographic	None proposed
Initial Focus	Development of OIs	Management of OIs
Common (but not Exclusive) OI Perspective	Social actor	Social Construction Institutional
Initial Empirical Focus	Identification, conflict	Identification, conflict, legitimacy with external stakeholders

Moreover, there is little reason to suggest that these identities would always be low in synergy (thus creating a hybrid), unless perhaps the acquisition was a hostile one (and one would have to question the wisdom of merging with an organization that had an identity antithetical to one's own). Multiple organizational identities may even be at play when merged organizations split or when organizations spin off a new company (e.g., Corley and Gioia, 2004). In particular, "legacy" or "phantom limb" identities may persist even as the newly spun-off organization is attempting to find its own identity. The field also needs more empirical work that inductively examines and more directly tests how organizations manage their multiple self-conceptualizations.

A multiple organizational identity approach that views organizational identities as complementary, oppositional, or simply different also raises broader issues about how organizational identities relate to each other. For example, research often treats opposition between identities as essentially fixed: "baked in" due to their content (as seems to be the case of hybrid identities). But is it possible that the relationship among identities might shift over time? This would be more consonant with the emerging process-oriented approach to viewing identity. One could imagine that an organizational identity about being philanthropic and one about making money could be seen historically as antagonistic, but today might be viewed as more complementary. Part of the issue may lie with one's view of organizational identities. For example, if the multiple organizational identities are seen as a reflection of deeply embedded institutional logics, then it would be difficult to shift the relationship among identities without a corresponding shift in logics. But if organizational identities are socially constructed, and more fluid, might their relationships be as well? What are the implications of viewing the relationship of organizational identities as situationally or momentarily oppositional (or complementary, or simply different) rather than inherently so?

In addition, in their original conceptualization, Pratt and Foreman (2000) suggest that some organizational identities may be latent and not consciously articulated until a crisis or some other triggering event. This raises the intriguing possibility of whether and how latent identities can exist in organizations. The notion of latent identities would appear quite different from research in organizational identity that has viewed identity dynamics as largely conscious (see, for example, Hatch and Schultz's (2000) depiction of organizational identity as "explicit"). In particular, the notion of latent organizational identities raises the issue of whether some collective level understandings of "who we are" might influence member behavior on an unconscious level, thus provoking some unconscious responses (Ashforth and Reingen, 2014; Petriglieri and Petriglieri, 2010).

Finally, just as social constructivist and social actor views are increasingly viewed as complementary (Gioia and Hamilton, Ch. 1; Ravasi and Schultz, 2006) it may be that hybrid and multiple organizational conceptualizations may be combined in some fashion. Indeed, a re-reading of some empirical and theoretical work suggests that organizations may be viewed in terms of multiple hybrid identities. As noted above, Albert and Whetten (1985) seem to imply that organizations can have other dimensions beyond normative–utilitarian. If so, it may be that organizations can have hybrid identities along multiple dimensions (see research on identity "fault lines" for a parallel in groups). Such a structure seems consistent with the findings of Pratt and Rafaeli (1997). While they noted that the unit identity was hybrid (acute care versus rehabilitation), another hybrid identity active in the unit was tied to their profession: nursing. In particular, nurses struggled with whether they should be subservient or more autonomous with regard to other medical professionals, such as physicians. While we did not link these professional issues to the unit's identity, other research suggests that the identity of organizations comprising a specific profession often comes to take on those professional characteristics—even their hybrid characteristics (Pratt and Dutton, 2000). Thus, we could view that rehabilitation unit as having identities about "relationships with patients" and "relationships with physicians," and that within each of these identities, there are oppositional sub-identities (i.e., multiple hybrids). Returning to an earlier example, organizations with both a normative CSR identity and a utilitarian could find that their CSR identity is divided between "pragmatists" and "idealists." Thus, it seems at least possible that organizations can have multiple, hybrid identities (or multiple and hybrid identities). Future research may wish to more carefully examine these possibilities and whether and how such "multiple hybrids" play out in organizations.

Hybrid and Multiple Identities: What about Unity?

While hybrid and multiple organizational identities continue to provide a fruitful area for theorizing, and offer several promising avenues for future empirical research, the very notion that organizations can have more than one identity begs the question of in what ways, if any, do members (or other stakeholders) want, need, or expect there to be some integrated sense of "who we are" as an organization. As I noted at the start of this chapter, research on organizational identity has its roots in theories about the identity of individuals; and the desire for a unifying or holistic sense of "who I am," while at the same time allowing for identity "plurality," is a fundamental tension in identity theorizing at this level. I would argue that this tension exists at the organizational level as well. [5] Further, I believe this tension is as fundamental to collective

---

washing."

[5] This tension is also evident in research on organizational culture. Meyerson and Martin (1987), for example, view organizational culture from three perspectives: integration, differentiation, and fragmentation. The integration perspective views organizational cultures as monolithic, the differentiation perspective focuses on conflicts, not unlike the hybrid perspective, and the fragmentation perspective focuses on the inherent ambiguity in cultural understandings. While the fragmentation perspectives goes farther than even a multiple identity conceptualization in that

identity as the one about being similar to and distinct from others (see issues of "optimal distinctiveness" in Zukerman, Ch. 10) and the tension between internal and external determinants of identity (a tension captured in social construction and social actor perspectives). At present, research seems to be largely capturing either end of this tension: that is, viewing organizations as either having multiple identities or a single identity. This chapter has largely been about the former. With regard to the latter, however, some identity theorists follow an "essentialist" perspective, finding it difficult to conceive of an organizational identity as anything but a unified sense of "who we are" (see Corley et al., 2006 for a review).[6]

Scholars exploring hybrid and multiple identities have touched upon this tension. Recent work by Ashforth and Reingen (2014: 485), for example, notes that despite the hybrid nature of the identity of the food cooperative, Natura, there nonetheless existed a common identity, a "shared belief that Natura's identity was right [and] good." This parallels the work of Battilana and Dorado (2010) on hybrid organizing that argues that a common identity was able to manage the demands of competing institutional logics in a commercial finance organization. It is also interesting to note that an early and foundational empirical piece on organizational identity, the Port Authority paper by Dutton and Dukerich (1991), viewed the identity of this organization as having multiple characteristics, yet nonetheless conceptualized the organization as having a single identity. Fast forward over twenty years later and Hsu and Elsbach (2013) suggest that organizational identities are comprised of multiple categories, but that some categories are consistently salient across groups, thus providing a sense of unity. The latter may be viewed as one way to conceptualize an organization as having some identity plurality as well some unity.

To date, explicit treatment of what philosophers might consider the "parts versus wholes" tension in organizational identity is rare. My own work with Matt Kraatz (Pratt and Kraatz, 2009), however, takes Mead's (1934) conceptualization of the distinction between identity and self and uses it to explain how an organization can have multiple identities, yet also have some sort of holistic sense of "who we are" in the form of an organizational self (see also Pratt, 2012). In particular, we suggest that just as individuals come to internalize the expectations of others in their community (as role identities) and then create a unique sense of who they are across those identities (i.e., a self), so too might organizations internalize the expectations of some stakeholders (i.e., in the form of organizational identities) and ultimately create a gestalt of these identities (i.e., an organizational self). While we suggest some mechanisms (e.g., the creation of an "externalized other" or a holistic sense of others' expectations) that may be involved in its creation, the process through which an organizational self might develop remains under-examined and under-explained. It may be that other

collective consensus does not coalesce even within a subculture (Martin, 1992), the articulation of these perspectives echoes the tension around how to depict unity and multiplicity of understandings.

[6] It is important to remember, however, the critical management response to an essentialist perspective: if an organization expresses only a single identity, it is likely to be due to the exercise

conceptualizations of identity that have attempted to address this tension may be useful fodder for organizational theorizing (e.g., Markus and Wurf's (1987) working self-concept). However, as our field matures, perhaps we might be able to create our own theories of how organizations manage the tension between a unified self and the divided identities that comprise it[7]—and even contribute back to the very rich identity theorizing from which we draw.

CONCLUSION

The purpose of this chapter is to remind us that the question of "who are we?" as an organization may have more than one answer. Indeed, as noted by many scholars in this handbook, we may conceptualize organizations as having more than one identity. While we currently view such identity plurality in terms of hybrid or multiple organizational identities (see Table 6.1), research (especially empirical) in this area remains under-explored and underdeveloped. At the same time, the notion of how organizations can have a united sense of "who we are" while at the same time allowing for diverse views on the topic is a fundamental question inherent to social organizing. It is my hope that organizational identity scholars can both draw upon and richly contribute to these classic conversations about the very nature of organizations.

REFERENCES

Albert, S. (1992). "The Algebra of Change." *Research in Organizational Behavior* 14: 179–229.
Albert, S. and Adams, E. (2002). "The Hybrid Identity of Law Firms." In *Corporate and Organizational Identities: Integrating Strategy, Marketing, Communication, and Organizational Perspective*, edited by G. Soenen and B. Moingeon, 35–50. New York: Routledge.
Albert, S. and Whetten, D. A. (1985). "Organizational Identity." In *Research in Organizational Behavior*, vol. 7, edited by L. L. Cummings and B. M. Staw, 263–95. Greenwich, CT: JAI Press.
Alvesson, M. and Robertson, M. (2016). "Organizational Identity: A Critique." In *The Oxford Handbook of Organizational Identity*, edited by M. G. Pratt, M. Schultz, B. E. Ashforth, and D. Ravasi, 160–80. Oxford: Oxford University Press.
Ashforth, B. E. and Reingen, P. H. (2014). "Functions of Dysfunction: Managing the Dynamics of an Organizational Duality in a Natural Food Cooperative." *Administrative Science Quarterly* 59(3): 474–516.

of top-down power, and the suppression of disparate voices in the organization (see Section 2 of this book).

[7] Another interesting avenue would be to explore whether there is such a thing as an organization that has multiple identities, but not an integrated sense of self. How much do organizations with a "fragmented self" (or perhaps better put, a lack of a self) function?

Barnard, C. I. (1938). *The Functions of the Executive*. Cambridge, MA: Harvard University Press.

Battilana, J., and Dorado, S. (2010). "Building Sustainable Hybrid Organizations: The Case of Commercial Microfinance Organizations." *Academy of Management Journal* 53(6): 1419–40.

Battilana, J. and Lee, M. (2014). "Advancing Research on Hybrid Organizing: Insights from the Study of Social Enterprises." *The Academy of Management Annals* 8(1): 397–441.

Besharov, M. L. and Brickson, S. L. (2016). "Organizational Identity and Institutional Forces: Toward an Integrative Framework." In *The Oxford Handbook of Organizational Identity*, edited by M. G. Pratt, M. Schultz, B. E. Ashforth, and D. Ravasi, 396–414. Oxford: Oxford University Press.

Besharov, M. L. and Smith, W. K. (2014). "Multiple Institutional Logics in Organizations: Explaining their Varied Nature and Implications." *Academy of Management Review* 39(3): 364–81.

Corley, K. G. (2004). "Defined by our Strategy or our Culture? Hierarchical Differences in Perceptions of Organizational Identity and Change." *Human Relations* 57(9): 1145–77.

Corley, K. G. and Gioia, D. A. (2004). "Identity Ambiguity and Change in the Wake of a Corporate Spin-Off." *Administrative Science Quarterly* 49(2): 173–208.

Corley, K. G., Harquail, C. V., Pratt, M. G., Glynn, M. A., Fiol, C. M., and Hatch, M. J. (2006). "Guiding Organizational Identity through Aged Adolescence." *Journal of Management Inquiry* 15(2): 85–99.

Cornelissen, J. P., Haslam, S. A., and Werner, M. D. (2016). "Bridging and Integrating Theories on Organizational Identity: A Social Interactionist Model of Organizational Identity Formation and Change." In *The Oxford Handbook of Organizational Identity*, edited by M. G. Pratt, M. Schultz, B. E. Ashforth, and D. Ravasi, 200–15. Oxford: Oxford University Press.

DeJordy, R. and Creed, W. E. D. (2016). "Institutional Pluralism, Inhabitants, and the Construction of Organizational and Personal Identities." In *The Oxford Handbook of Organizational Identity*, edited by M. G. Pratt, M. Schultz, B. E. Ashforth, and D. Ravasi, 374–95. Oxford: Oxford University Press.

Dutton, J. E. and Dukerich, J. M. (1991). "Keeping an Eye on the Mirror: Image and Identity in Organizational Adaptation." *Academy of Management Journal* 34(3): 517–54.

Etzioni, A. (1975). *A Comparative Analysis of Complex Organizations*. New York: Free Press.

Foreman, P. and Whetten, D. A. (2002). "Members' Identification with Multiple-Identity Organizations." *Organization Science* 13(6): 618–35.

Foreman, P. and Whetten, D. (2016). "Measuring Organizational Identity: Taking Stock and Looking Forward." In *The Oxford Handbook of Organizational Identity*, edited by M. G. Pratt, M. Schultz, B. E. Ashforth, and D. Ravasi, 39–64. Oxford: Oxford University Press.

Gaertner, S. L., Dovidio, J. F., and Bachman, B. A. (1996). "Revisiting the Contact Hypothesis: The Induction of a Common Ingroup Identity." *International Journal of Intercultural Relations* 20(3): 271–90.

Gioia, D. A. and Hamilton, A. L. (2016). "Great Debates in Organizational Identity Study." In *The Oxford Handbook of Organizational Identity*, edited by M. G. Pratt, M. Schultz, B. E. Ashforth, and D. Ravasi, 21–38. Oxford: Oxford University Press.

Glynn, M. A. (2000). "When Cymbals Become Symbols: Conflict over Organizational Identity within a Symphony Orchestra." *Organization Science* 11(3), 285–98.

Golden-Biddle, K. and Rao, H. (1997). "Breaches in the Boardroom: Organizational Identity and Conflicts of Commitment in a Nonprofit Organization." *Organization Science* 8(6): 593–611.

Greenwood, R., Raynard, M., Kodeih, F., Micelotta, E. R., and Lounsbury, M. (2011). "Institutional Complexity and Organizational Responses." *The Academy of Management Annals* 5(1): 317–71.

Hatch, M. J. and Schultz, M. S. (2000). "Scaling the Tower of Babel: Relational Differences between Identity, Image and Culture in Organizations." In *The Expressive Organization: Linking Identity, Reputation and the Corporate Brand*, edited by M. Schultz, M. J. Hatch, and M. H. Larsen, 11–36. Oxford: Oxford University Press.

Hsu, G. and Elsbach, K. D. (2013). "Explaining Variation in Organizational Identity Categorization." *Organization Science* 24(4): 996–1013.

Kenny, K., Whittle, A., and Willmott, H. (2016). "Organizational Identity: The Significance of Power and Politics." In *The Oxford Handbook of Organizational Identity*, edited by M. G. Pratt, M. Schultz, B. E. Ashforth, and D. Ravasi, 140–59. Oxford: Oxford University Press.

Kraatz, M. and Block, E. (2008). "Organizational Implications of Institutional Pluralism." In *The SAGE Handbook of Organizational Institutionalism*, edited by R. Greenwood, C. Oliver, R. Suddaby, and K. Sahlin-Andersson, 243–75. Thousand Oaks, CA: SAGE.

Kreiner, G. E. and Murphy, C. (2016). "Organizational Identity Work." In *The Oxford Handbook of Organizational Identity*, edited by M. G. Pratt, M. Schultz, B. E. Ashforth, and D. Ravasi, 276–93. Oxford: Oxford University Press.

Larson, G. S. and Pepper, G. L. (2003). "Strategies for Managing Multiple Organizational Identifications: A Case of Competing Identities." *Management Communication Quarterly* 16(4): 528–57.

Lepisto, D. (2015). "Reason for Being: Exploring the Emergence and Members' Responses to Organizational Purpose in an Athletic Footwear and Apparel Company." Published dissertation. Boston College. http://gradworks.umi.com/37/45/3745584.html.

Maclean, T. and Webber, S. (2015) "Navigating Multiple Identities across Multiple Boundaries: A Cross-Level Model of Organizational Identification." *Journal of Management Inquiry* 24(2): 156–73.

Markus, H. and Wurf, E. (1987). "The Dynamic Self-Concept: A Social Psychological Perspective." *Annual Review of Psychology* 38(1): 299–337.

Martin, J. (1992). *Cultures in Organizations: Three Perspectives.* New York: Oxford University Press.

Mead, G. H. (1934). *Mind, Self, and Society.* Chicago: University of Chicago Press.

Meyerson, D. and Martin, J. (1987). "Cultural Change: An Integration of Three Different Views." *Journal of Management Studies* 24(6): 623–47.

Petriglieri, J. and Devine, B. A. (2016). "Mobilizing Organizational Action against Identity Threats: The Role of Organizational Members' Perceptions and Responses." In *The Oxford Handbook of Organizational Identity*, edited by M. G. Pratt, M. Schultz, B. E. Ashforth, and D. Ravasi, 239–56. Oxford: Oxford University Press.

Petriglieri, G. and Petriglieri, J. L. (2010). "Identity Workspaces: The Case of Business Schools." *Academy of Management Learning and Education* 9(1): 44–60.

Phillips, N., Tracey, P., and Kraatz, M. (2016). "Organizational Identity in Institutional Theory: Taking Stock and Moving Forward." In *The Oxford Handbook of Organizational Identity*, edited by M. G. Pratt, M. Schultz, B. E. Ashforth, and D. Ravasi, 353–73. Oxford: Oxford University Press.

Pratt, M. G. (2012). "Rethinking Identity Construction Processes in Organizations: Three Questions to Consider." In *Perspectives on Process Organization Studies: Constructing Identity in and around Organizations*, edited by M. Schultz, S. Maguire, A. Langley, and H. Tsoukas, 21–49. Oxford: Oxford University Press.

Pratt, M. G. and Dutton, J. E. (2000). "Owning up or Opting out: The Role of Emotions and Identities in Issue Ownership." In *Emotions in the Workplace: Research, Theory, and Practice*, edited by N. M. Ashkanasy, C. Hartel, and W. Zerbe, 103–129. Westport, CT: Quorum Books.

Pratt, M. G. and Foreman, P. O. (2000). "Classifying Managerial Responses to Multiple Organizational Identities." *Academy of Management Review* 25(1): 18–42.

Pratt, M. G. and Kraatz, M. S. (2009). "E Pluribus Unum: Multiple Identities and the Organizational Self." In *Exploring Positive Identities and Organizations: Building a Theoretical and Research Foundation*, edited by J. Dutton and L. M. Roberts, 385–410. New York: Psychology Press.

Pratt, M. G. and Rafaeli, A. (1997). "Organizational Dress as a Symbol of Multilayered Social Identities." *Academy of Management Journal* 40(4): 862–898.

Ravasi, D. and Schultz, M. (2006). "Responding to Organizational Identity Threats: Exploring the Role of Organizational Culture." *Academy of Management Journal* 49(3): 433–58.

Schinoff, B., Rogers, K., and Corley, K. G. (2016). "How Do We Communicate Who We Are? Examining How Organizational Identity Is Conveyed to Members." In *The Oxford Handbook of Organizational Identity*, edited by M. G. Pratt, M. Schultz, B. E. Ashforth, and D. Ravasi, 219–38. Oxford: Oxford University Press.

Selznick, P. (1957). *Leadership in Administration: A Sociological Interpretation*. London: Harper and Row.

Sillince, J. A. and Brown, A. D. (2009). "Multiple Organizational Identities and Legitimacy: The Rhetoric of Police Websites." *Human Relations* 62(12): 1829–56.

Suddaby, R., Foster, W., and Quinn Trank, C. (2016). "Re-Membering: Rhetorical History as Identity-Work." In *The Oxford Handbook of Organizational Identity*, edited by M. G. Pratt, M. Schultz, B. E. Ashforth, and D. Ravasi, 297–316. Oxford: Oxford University Press.

Tienari, J. and Vaara, E. (2016). "Identity Construction in Mergers and Acquisitions: A Discursive Sensemaking Perspective." In *The Oxford Handbook of Organizational Identity*, edited by M. G. Pratt, M. Schultz, B. E. Ashforth, and D. Ravasi, 455–73. Oxford: Oxford University Press.

van Knippenberg, D. (2016). "Making Sense of Who We Are: Leadership and Organizational Identity." In *The Oxford Handbook of Organizational Identity*, edited by M. G. Pratt, M. Schultz, B. E. Ashforth, and D. Ravasi, 335–49. Oxford: Oxford University Press.

Watkiss, L. and Glynn, M. A. (2016). "Materiality and Identity: How Organizational Products, Artifacts, and Practices Instantiate Organizational Identity." In *The Oxford Handbook of Organizational Identity*, edited by M. G. Pratt, M. Schultz, B. E. Ashforth, and D. Ravasi, 317–34. Oxford: Oxford University Press.

Watson, T. J. (2016). "Organizational Identity and Organizational Identity Work as Valuable Analytical Resources." In *The Oxford Handbook of Organizational Identity*, edited by M. G. Pratt, M. Schultz, B. E. Ashforth, and D. Ravasi, 123–39. Oxford: Oxford University Press.

Zuckerman, E. (2016). "Optimal Distinctiveness Revisited: An Integrative Framework for Understanding the Balance between Differentiation and Conformity in Individual and Organizational Identities." In *The Oxford Handbook of Organizational Identity*, edited by M. G. Pratt, M. Schultz, B. E. Ashforth, and D. Ravasi, 183–99. Oxford: Oxford University Press.

SECTION II

CRITICAL PERSPECTIVES ON OI

....

ORGANIZATIONAL IDENTITY AND ORGANIZATIONAL IDENTITY WORK AS VALUABLE ANALYTICAL RESOURCES

....

TONY J. WATSON

CONCEPT CHOICE AND APPLICATION IN TWO UNIVERSITY BUSINESS SCHOOLS

....

THE notion of organizational identity is widely recognized as coming upon the scene with the appearance of an article entitled "Organizational Identity" (Albert and Whetten, 1985). Such conceptual innovations do not occur "out of the blue," so to speak. Something must stimulate researchers and theorists to move in a certain conceptual direction. Something must trigger their new interest. Fortunately, we have available to us invaluable insights into how an interest in organizational identities was triggered. These are to be found in the form of what Gioia calls "Dave Whetten's memorable little anecdote" (1998: 30). Whetten explains that "Stuart Albert and I began using the concept 'organizational identity' out of necessity—we needed an interpretive framework to make sense out of our experience as faculty members at the University of Illinois during a period of financial turbulence" (1998: vii).

Whetten and Albert observed and took part in focus group discussions set up to explore the options facing their organization. What they observed was an "incredibly animated organization response" to the issues being examined, and they were particularly puzzled by the intensity of these debates given the "relatively benign environmental stimulus" (1998: 30). The challenge was one of explaining why there was such an overreaction to what were rather minor difficulties, compared, that is, to the scale of the cuts and the extent of downsizing occurring in the business world more generally. The two colleagues concluded that they were observing "the anguished personal and collective examination of members' taken-for-granted assumptions about what was core, enduring, and distinctive about an American research university in general," and about their own university in particular (1998: viii). Organizational members were worried that the smallest shift in the university's configuration might uncontrollably erode both the organizational identities and individuals' personal identities. Here are the origins of the widely used concept of organizational identity as that which is central, distinctive, and enduring about an organization.

At about the same as this development occurred, the dean of a UK business school with which I was closely involved was becoming worried about certain aspects of the school's activities. He became particularly exercised by the almost total failure of staff to attend the series of academic seminars to which he had invited leading scholars and organizational practitioners to speak. Did the staff resent him personally, he asked me, or did the staff feel too overloaded with teaching to attend research-oriented events? Or was it a matter of the school employing too many people of "low caliber"? When I said to the dean that all of this was either wrong or too simplistic, he invited me—"as an organizational expert"—to think about "what is going on" and to write a confidential paper for him and his senior colleagues. I was to provide an analysis of the school, and he and his departmental heads would consider what actions to take if they found the analysis convincing.

In my report, I described the school as having a "confused culture." The school had been created from departments in a public-sector advanced technical education establishment in which, until fairly recently, there had been a mix of executive short courses and professional qualification programs. But the organization had been promoted by the state to a higher status, which meant a move into university-style degree programs, with a commitment to further development into masters and doctoral programs. The culture of the school was muddled in that nobody could determine whether it was a big "further education technical college" department or a university school. I clearly made central analytical use of the concept of "culture," and most readers of the report found this rather novel. The great burst of interest among management and organization in notions of organizational/corporate cultures which followed the publication of Peters' and Waterman's *In Search of Excellence* (1982) had not yet occurred. This latter point is important because it indicates that I was not simply jumping onto to a popular conceptual bandwagon by talking about cultures. Instead, I was striving to find a concept from what, pre-1982, were non-organizational sources to help make sense of organization phenomena, exactly as Albert and Whetten were doing before they alighted on the notion of organizational identity.

Why did I not turn to a notion of organizational identity? The answer to this is simple. As a sociologist—and an anthropologically inclined one at that—I would not at any cost risk an implication that organizations are "like people," with identities, personalities, motives, or whatever. But the question needs to be raised of what my analysis might be missing by my not deploying a concept like "organizational identity." I would respond to this question by saying that I missed the opportunity to make the link in organizational behavior between features of the organization and features of the people working in it—something that Albert and Whetten did very successfully. In follow-up work I did for the school dean, it became very clear that a significant and influential proportion of the staff had central to their self-identities a notion of themselves as primarily marketing managers, production managers, accountants, or personnel specialists who were now "passing on managerial and professional wisdom" to a younger generation of marketing managers, personnel managers, and so on. A handful of staff was more interested in combining their teaching work with formal academic research and scholarly publishing. And I observed a disturbing pattern whereby this latter group were ostracized by the majority. This group of younger lecturers, with rather different self and occupational identities, were seen as a threat by their older more business-experienced colleagues. The tensions created by the relationship between people's self-identities and what I might now call a (confused) organizational identity were at the centre of what the dean called the "significant dysfunctionalities" of the school. Albert and Whetten's (published) analysis of their school gives a much stronger focus on the relationships between "the organization" and "the organizational member" than my (unpublished) one did.

RESEARCH, PRAGMATISM, AND REALITY

My comparison of these two business school cases leads, then, to the conclusion that one way of conceptualizing certain aspects of organizational life is somehow better than the other. This superiority of the Albert and Whetten conceptualization is expressed above in terms of its providing a stronger "focus" on certain issues than the alternative would. To leave it at that would be to beg the question of to what ends one seeks a "stronger focus." An answer to this question is provided by the tradition of American pragmatic philosophy (Mills, 1966; Mounce 1997; Keleman and Rumens, 2013) and its emphasis on judging the value of knowledge in terms of the potential of one piece of knowledge, theory, or research, relative to other pieces, for informing human action (Urmson, 2005; Watson, 2011). I judge the type of analysis offered by Albert and Whetten to have greater potential for enabling people involved with organizational situations (whether they be managerial figures, frontline workers, or educational dissidents) to be better informed in choosing how to act than they would be if informed by adopting an alternative frame of reference like my own.

Pragmatism requires us to drop standard scientistic views of (social) science research as a process of cautious and cumulative data collection and analysis which slowly but surely takes scientists toward the final goal of complete or "true" explanations of (social) phenomena. Instead, pragmatism, alongside the great philosopher of science, Karl Popper, recognizes that science can never reach ultimate truths but proceeds by challenging existing understandings to produce knowledge which can stand as valid, for the time being. This, then, encourages us to treat our endeavors as attempts to make sense of the dilemmas which confront human beings in their lives in a way which enables members of society to deal more effectively than otherwise with situations which arise in their personal lives, in their work roles (whether in university business schools or elsewhere), and in their roles as social citizens. Implicit in this thinking is the idea of concepts as "tools" which are judged not by their "truth" or "correctness" but by how useful they are in producing knowledge which enhances human beings' ability to cope with the world in which they are located.

Pragmatism's notion of research and theorizing as a way of informing human practices, in organizations or elsewhere, together with its notion of concepts as means toward such ends, locates it clearly as a realist enterprise. In saying this, however, one must turn away from the general tendency to treat realism as if it were a single ontological position that can be contrasted with social constructionism. Various writers bring this dual distinction into discussions of organization identity. Kenny et al. (2011), for example, identify "realist" conceptions of organization identity as ones which treat an organizational identity as a "property" or "asset." "Constructionists," like these authors themselves and like Goia et al. (2000), regard the organizational identity very differently: as "a set of representations" which articulate "beliefs." Realists are said to study "organization identity," analyzing empirical phenomena which they regard as "measurable through scientific investigation," whereas constructionists "analyze sensemaking processes whereby meanings are constructed in context-contingent ways by different actors."

The position adopted and recommended here is quite different. It can be characterized as "pragmatic realism" (Watson, 2011, 2012), whereby one treats reality, not in terms of properties and underlying mechanisms, but in the broader pragmatist tradition of treating reality as the circumstances with which people have to come to terms in order to cope in the world. The approach followed in the present chapter is a realist one which makes central use of the *concept* of social construction without being "social constructionist" as such. Concepts are the building blocks of theories, as more or less helpful devices for the production of action-relevant theories or "research accounts." This suggests a position one might label "pragmatic instrumentalism." To help us make sense of the human, social, or organizational dilemmas which we come across (within and beyond the business school cases we have considered) we take concepts from existing literature or we develop our own concepts which are as helpful or useful as possible, given our particular research project. In analyzing the contemporary social and organization world, social scientists are increasingly deploying concepts such as process, social construction, narrative, discourse, and relationality. This trend is often interpreted in terms of the emergence of new paradigms, perspectives, "approaches," or "lenses." The danger in this is that *means* tend to become *ends*, and attention given to developing process theories, discursive approaches, social constructionism, and all the rest. In contrast, the trend would be understood by the pragmatism-informed social scientist as a matter of researchers deploying concepts, and the bundles of concepts which we call conceptual or theoretical frameworks, to produce social scientific accounts or theories (notions of "the way the social world works" we might say) in terms of how well they inform the people who read them as they pursue their projects with regard to the aspect of life covered by those accounts (Watson, 2011).

CONCEPTS AS USEFUL BUT SOMETIMES DANGEROUS "INSTRUMENTS"

The concepts we deploy in social science are not "definitions" of the kind we see in dictionaries. We do not seek the correct definition of organizational identity, for example. Rather, we borrow or develop the most useful working definition given the project in which we are engaged. Thus a psychologist will work with a concept ("working definition") of, say, "personality" that is the most helpful to the research they are doing. Or an economist will choose whichever concept of "money" is the most helpful in analyzing the aspect of the economy with which they are concerned. Indeed, they might choose a different working definition of "money" when they move onto a project looking at a different aspect of economic behavior. Although one would not wish to push this too far, we might see this as analogous to the surgeon putting down one surgical instrument and picking up another as they moved from operating on one part of a human body to dealing with another. There is an insight here but we must recognize that whilst we can say that "a surgical knife is a surgical knife is a surgical knife," we cannot say "an organizational identity is an organizational identity is an organizational identity." Unlike surgeons with their precision steel operating instruments, organizational researchers must shape anew their conceptual apparatus each time they engage in a new research project. But where do we find the words that we must use to articulate our concepts? Here metaphors come onto the scene.

Part of many discussions of organizational identities is a concern with the extent to which the organizational identity concept is or is not a metaphor. The position unfolding here is that it is most helpful in research terms to avoid the idea that there is a direct equivalence between organizational identities and human identities. Instead, there are some analytically fruitful but limited *parallels* between human and organizational identities. This is perhaps similar to Cornelissen's notion of metaphors having "heuristic value for aiding our understanding of the world of organizations" (2002: 261). Such a statement is helpful, as far as it goes. But there are two problems with Cornelissen's further arguments. First, he sees metaphors being used "to contribute to our mapping and understanding of real mechanisms and identities." This type of realism is highly vulnerable to the criticism made by Goia et al. (2002) that it is predicated on an implicit faith that social phenomena are "ontologically similar to physical phenomena and, therefore, ought to be describable with physical science assumptions, models and methods" (2002: 272). But, say these critics of Cornelissen, "They are not. Social phenomena are different." And this difference, it is argued, precludes the use of notions such as "real mechanisms and identities."

The second problem with the Cornelissen critique is that attention is given to metaphors and their role in social analysis, without giving sufficient attention to the role of concepts. Although metaphors have a degree of relevance to social science as heuristic devices, they are much more significant as stimulants to concept development. And this is something that is rarely acknowledged. The problem for the social scientist trying to develop concepts is that the phenomena which make up social institutions and shape social processes are generally abstract and intangible. Hence the social scientist is forced to turn to metaphors. "Management," "strategy," and "organization" are ones which come quickly to mind. Perhaps most interestingly, we have the metaphors of "structure" and "culture," whether applied at the societal or the organizational level. We tend to take these two central concepts for granted as analytical devices. What we forget is that the first of these concepts is using language borrowed from the realms of engineering and biology (machines, bodies, and plants having a substance which social arrangements do not). The second concept has its roots (sic!) in agriculture and processes of growing crops. And these origins carry powerful connotations on into the social and organizational world into which they have been carried by social scientists.

The problem is that we too easily ignore or forget just what baggage is being carried by these concepts and their connotive power. Let me illustrate this notion of hidden implications of concept-use from personal fieldwork. In an interview with a "senior operations manager," carried out within an ethnographic study of managerial work in a large engineering organization (Watson, 2001), I was told that a major problem with the company was that its "structure" was "too bureaucratic." An argument along these general lines was quite popular with a number of the managers at this level in the firm. I did not think too much about the detail of this man's wording. But I was prompted to return to it when reading the transcript of the interview with his marketing manager colleague. This individual talked about the organization's "bureaucratic culture." It would be so easy to infer that these managers were talking about the same thing. And, indeed, to a considerable extent they were. But I could not help reflecting on why the first man talked of "bureaucracy" as a structural matter and the second man spoke of it in cultural terms. This could, of course, simply be a matter of the words that come into these two people's heads in the course of a busy day. However, as I examined the transcripts more closely, it became apparent that there were different connotations in the term "bureaucratic structure" on the one hand and "bureaucratic culture" on the other. The implication of the structure metaphor is that the phenomenon under discussion is something "made," something "built," and hence something that can be re-made, or rebuilt. Hence, perhaps, his talking to me in later parts of the interview of the sort of "restructuring" he felt the organization should undergo. On the other hand, the marketing manager spoke of how "deep-rooted" the problems were and that he welcomed the senior management's "commitment to a big culture change pro-gram." One must not exaggerate here the power of "hidden metaphors" or see what was happening here as solely a matter of metaphors. It may or may not be relevant, for example, to note that part of the self-identity of the first man was his pride in being a "chartered engineer," whilst the second manager referred on several occasions to the obviously identity-relevant fact of his "education as a historian."

ORGANIZATIONAL IDENTITY AND THE PROBLEM OF THE DOUBLE-EDGED SWORD

The key point emerging here is that the concepts we use have connotations and "prompts to action" that might not be immediately obvious to us. And this brings us back to the need to take enormous care when deploying any concept of organizational identity. There are important advantages in using the concept as an analytical device or instrument. But, we might say by cheekily turning to a further analogy, the instru-ment or weapon that we take into battle is something of a double-edged sword—one which might help us in our struggle to make sense of the organizational world but which might equally slip in our hand and cruelly decapacitate us as researchers. The advantages of using a concept of organization identity centre upon the recognition of a parallel between corporate efforts and individual human efforts to handle similarities to and differences from other corporations and individuals. Connected to this is the potential for empirically relating personal issues in the lives of organizational mem-bers, investors, and clients to issues for those shaping organizational activities. It is not possible to understand organizational structures and processes without identifying the ways in which these are both influenced by personal identity issues of individu-als and the ways in which these organizational phenomena bear upon the lives of the individuals who have some relationship with the organization. But we have to proceed with great care to avoid the considerable risks that we take when we talk of organiza-tional identities. There is the significant risk of treating organizations as if they were like people—the risk of the reification or personification of organizations.

To speak of organizations as if, like human beings, they had agency or possessed decision-making powers is often a matter of simplification for the sake of convenience. In everyday conversation, we are not likely to be troubled by friends and neighbors saying things like, "It is a pity that BigRetail are closing both of their branches in the town. I wish the council would get its act together and do something about this sort of thing." But researchers surely should not think or speak in this way. It begs the ques-tion of just which individual or which managerial faction in BigRetail decided upon the current branch-reduction strategy; it begs the question of what personal or group interests were at work within the business's management; it begs the question of what alternatives might have been considered, ones that could have brought about a differ-ent set of winners and losers. These are matters about which the citizens of the town might well wish to be informed—by journalists following rigorous investigative tech-niques if not by professional academic researchers. The social relevance of research here is perhaps even greater when it comes to the case of "the council," an organization actually constituted with a notion of accountability to the public. Such relevance is not likely to be achieved if each of the two organizations involved in these events are con-ceptualized as solid thinking-and-acting unitary entities. Human agency and choice are pushed out of the picture. This is something which happens not only in casual everyday conversations such as the overheard one described above. It appears to be standard amongst economists and business-school students influenced by economics to talk, for example, about "when firms choose to diversify" or "how small businesses often fail to come to terms with the problems brought about by significant growth" (both of these overheard by the present author the day before writing this paragraph!).

This sidelining of vital questions of human agency, power, and democratic choice can too readily result from the choice of metaphors which treat organizations as if they were human individuals. The choice of metaphor is not an innocent one. At a societal level, government spokespersons frequently use notions such as "what so-ciety wants" to bolster their power and discourage the questioning of state policies. And in the sphere of organizations and management, academic writers and teach-ers have, wittingly or not, provided the dominant coalitions within organizational managements with the comforting unitarist notion of organizational goals. Such a concept rules out consideration of the part played by sectional interests in managerial processes, as well as all the associated issues of choice and legitimacy. This danger is equally present with the notion of organizational identity, with its potential to imply the existence of what Goia and Hamilton (in Ch. 1 of the present volume) refer to as "some kind of anthropomorphized entity." Individuals have goals; individuals have identities. We take a dangerous leap into potentially apolitical unitarist corporate ideologies if we carelessly allow goals, purposes, beliefs, and identities to be lifted out of the hands of people into the hands of corporations (and do notice that "corpora-tion" is a unitarizing metaphor too; treating the business, the university, the church, as a body).

With regard to organizational identities, Cornelissen highlights the manipulative potential of such metaphorical devices: "managers might reduce this metaphor to the single extension of 'a monolithic structure of feeling and thought,' which, when con-ceived in that way, can then be used as a rhetorical and political device, as a matter of managerial manipulation, venturing delicately to put people together in a bundle" (2002: 266). Managerial use of a concept of organizational identity, Cornelissen con-tinues, implies the existence of "an overarching set of values and beliefs [which] is presumed to exist and to transcend individual members of the organization," helping managerial groups to fulfill an aim of "giving them some sense of purpose and direct-ing their creative energies towards the realization of corporate objectives" (2002: 264). To some extent, Cornelissen is hoist with his own petard here, letting himself slip into the language of "corporate goals," a usage which implies a unity among senior managers. His main argument is, nevertheless, well made.

At this point it is useful to return to the two university business school cases we considered earlier. Comparing the two accounts, one can identify a degree of unitarism in the US case. Albert and Whetten conceptualize "organizational identity" as that which is "central, distinctive, and enduring" about an organization. There is undoubtedly value in this and, in the UK case, we could possibly say that the dean of the school was seeking to establish an identity for the school which would be distinctive and would endure into the long term. This would be a reasonable aspiration for a university manager to hold. But if we bring to the analysis of what was going on in the school a concept of "organizational identity" which incorporates this level of coherence and potential unity of purpose, our attention is drawn away from the degree of conflict and contestation which may be present. If I were to utilize *a concept* of organizational identity which would do justice to what was occurring it would have to be one which incorporated a much more "conflict aware" element. I would say that the organizational identity of the school at the time of the investigation was confused and in flux, if not in complete turmoil. Hence, as we move now to actually developing an alternative notion of "organizational identity," it is important that we ensure that the concept does not underplay fluidity, conflict, and contestation in organizational life.

ORGANIZATIONAL IDENTITIES, POWER, CONFLICT, AND CONTESTATION

At this point, as we come to terms with the serious unitarist dangers in the use of concepts like organizational identity, it might seem reasonable to throw out the notion altogether. But, in the light of the considerable advantages of using some kind of "organizational identity" concept, we should be wary of what might be called throwing out the conceptual baby with the methodological bathwater (I use the term "methodological" here in the philosophy-of-science sense of ontological and epistemological underpinning of social science, and not in the sense of investigative "methods"). To retain a notion of organizational identity we need, first, to recognize that no concept exists on its own. It must take its part within a broader theoretical scheme or conceptual framework. And, second, we need to develop both a particular organizational identity concept and a broader conceptual scheme which avoids the dangers of organizational personification/reification. A primary danger of organizational personification is that of treating the organization as a unified entity. A set of concepts is required which gives full recognition of power and conflict within organizations and of the negotiated nature of social realities.

Before departing on this journey we can prepare ourselves for it by reflecting a little more on the necessary avoidance of treating organizational managements as unified.

In presenting thoughts about this matter a little earlier, I used the term "dominant coalition" to refer to what we might call "the group of managers in charge" of an organization. The concept of dominant coalition in organization theory was developed by Cyert and March (2003), precisely to deal with the pluralistic nature of "top" managerial groups. Contest, conflict, and challenge are often as significant in "top teams" as they are across organizations generally. Such teams would not be able to function, however, any more than would organizations themselves, if this plurality and conflict led to utter chaos and confusion. Hence, there is the need to recognize the significance of power as a force shaping and directing human activities within organizations. With the emergence of one or two dominant figures at a particular time "the management" or "the bosses" become an operating "coalition," rather than a unified team. And this is important for any notion of organizational identity, as field research within managements shows us.

As part of an ethnographic study of managerial life (2001) I observed a series of board meetings, situating what I observed and experienced in these meetings with conversations with individual board members. The managing director of the business, having just arrived from a two-day conference led by a new group of managing directors, announced to his fellow directors that "the business was facing a fundamental change." "We have all," he went on, "felt ourselves to be part of a business which for the past seventy to eighty years has been a designer and manufacturer of telephones and telephone systems." Many around the table nodded in agreement. "And our customers and our competitors have seen it the same way." More nods followed, but faces were showing growing discomfort, presumably about what was to come. "That's all got to change," he said. "We have got to think of ourselves from now on as a service industry." It was then explained that the "new direction" for the business was to be one of "managing the telecoms of our customer businesses." Instead of selling "switches (organizations' telephone exchanges), we will do here for customers with our own technology what they did themselves with our equipment." One might have expected a lively debate to follow this statement of "the way forward." But the discussion was very subdued and I left it a day or so before I started my round of conversations with board members. I did this to allow time for them to think through their views and feelings about what one could well conceptualize as the company's dominant coalition having decided, not only to change the essential nature of the work done in the organization, but also to give the firm a new identity.

Each director that I spoke to had clearly been looking at what these changes would mean for themselves and their departments. They talked a lot about changing "core competencies" (a term often used in the company's management and organizational development activities), but much of this was connected by them to their own self-identities: "I am a manufacturing person through and through"; "I'm not the sort who has got close to all the computing side of our business, and that's now going to be the big thing"; "I am one of those who welcomes a challenge and this sounds like a good one to me." One individual concentrated more on the matters of strategy and told me that "the business made a big mistake in the past when it was decided not to take the wireless approach to telephony (this refers to mobile or "cell" phones). We had only a few wireless types and they were got rid of. And look at what has happened to the telephones market now—it's wireless, wireless, wireless." When asked how this "disaster," as the director called it, came about, he gave an explanation which we can readily analyze in terms of personal identities. The company was dominated by "dyed-in-the-wool electrical engineers and manufacturing types." He believed that the "people in charge" now were not going to allow such a mistake to occur again. Not only, it seemed, was the business's identity going to change, so were the occupational and hence self-identities of employees. We can make a similar reading, in organizational and personal identity terms, of Schoenberger's (1995) study of a period in the strategic management history of the US Lockheed Corporation. The self-identities of members of the dominant coalition contained a powerful notion of themselves as "aircraft makers," rather than "aerospace" people. They retained, and expressed both internally and externally, an "aircraft manufacturing" organizational identity for Lockheed, in effect. The consequence of what we are here interpreting as a mutually supporting aircraft-centered organizational identity and similarly aircraft-focused managerial self-identities of dominant decision-makers, was that no interest was taken in the growing and lucrative market for missiles. Again, we see corporate strategic directions being influenced by the relationship between organizational identities and individual self-identities.

ORGANIZATIONAL IDENTITY, NEGOTIATED ORDERS AND RESOURCE-DEPENDENT CONSTITUENCIES (OR "MULTIPLE STAKEHOLDERS")

The crucial requirement for a framework for studying identity aspects of organizations and their relationship to the self-identities of people involved with organizations, is a conceptual frame of reference which avoids the danger of unitary or person-like assumptions of what organizations are. We have already moved some way in this direction in the present chapter by utilizing Cyert and March's (2003) concept of "dominant coalition" to give recognition to pluralism at the "top" of organizations. But we need to build upon this. We need to broaden our focus to produce one that brings in the organization as a whole as well as the various external people and organizations with which it deals. To do this, use will now be made of, first, the notion of the organization as a negotiated order and, second, the notion of the organization as involving multiple internal and external strategic constituencies (or stakeholders). Once this has been done, we can provide a formal concept of organizational identity (and its relationship to self-identities and social identities) which avoids some of the difficulties which have been discussed so far and which can take forward organizational identity research.

The treatment of organizations as relatively unitary entities—as large organisms or, more typically, "systems"—has been a dominant tendency over the history of organization and management studies, in spite of the dangers which we have identified as inherent in such an approach. There have, however, been less metaphor-bound alternatives available and a particularly useful frame of reference first emerged as part of a hospital study (Strauss et al., 1963). This was later refined, especially in the light of ethnographic research on managerial activity (Dalton, 1959), by Strauss (1978). This research demonstrated that the "order" of the hospital was not primarily achieved by following the blueprint, the rule book, or the "organization chart" set down by the organization's designers. Rather, it was an outcome of a continual process of adjustment and negotiation between doctors, nurses, patients, social workers, administrators, patients' families, and so on. Each grouping involved with the organization, internally and externally, has its own interests and understandings and it exerts its interests with the degree of success of its initiatives varying with its relative power within what is to a large extent a political arena. Organizations are essentially resource-dependent bodies (Watson, 2012; Hillman et al., 2009; Pfeffer and Salancik, 1978). They could not survive without making exchanges in various ways with resource-dependent constituencies ranging from managers, customers, employees, and suppliers to investors, local authorities, and state agencies. Such parties are often referred to as "stakeholders," but the perhaps less appealing but analytically more sophisticated concept of resource-dependent constituency is preferred here to the, rather metaphor-bound, notion of "stakeholder," with the implication that each party involved with the organization is more or less equal in influence to the others.

In spite of these reservations, we can note that the stakeholder metaphor has been used to bring out certain aspects of organizational processes that are being emphasized here. Scott and Lane offer a "manager–stakeholder view" which views organizational identity as "emerging from the complex interactions among managers, organizational members, and other stakeholders" (2000: 44). These authors argue that organizational identity is "best understood as contested and negotiated through iterative interactions between managers and stakeholders" (p. 44). Contest and negotiation are thus brought to the center of organizational analysis. In spite of this significant progress in thinking, Scott and Lane can be seen to over-privilege "managers" conceptually, by treating them from the start as people who "deal with" stakeholders rather than viewing them as one type of stakeholder among others. They write, for example, of managers "being sensitive to their obligations to stakeholders," and they discuss examining "the extent to which managers consider stakeholder needs." It is perhaps surprising that they do not treat managers as one (or, more realistically, several) constituencies or stakeholder groups among others, given that they make reference to managers' "own needs for self-definition." Empirically, we cannot deny that managers are often the most active people attempting to shape organizational identities. But this is no reason to close off conceptually the empirical possibility that an organizational identity might emerge in certain circumstances regardless of managerial preferences. One such circumstance would be that in which managers lose control of their organization's identity. Post-financial-crisis banks provide an example of this. Another circumstance would be that in which one group of managers wished to see their organization being identified by all other stakeholder/constituencies in a different way from another group of managers.

An illustration of this latter possibility arises in the case of a medical business, one which had been set up by a group of doctors and medical ancillaries who had previously been employed in the UK's National Health Service. Several members of this management team retained at the core of the work aspect of their self-identities a conception of themselves as doctors who were now serving the publicly owned NHS in a different way, as a result of changes to health provision imposed by the UK government. Their preferred organizational identity for the business was as part of NHS provision, which simply had different funding arrangements from other parts—arrangements that did not need to be understood by the patients they served. Other members of the directorate, however, had shifted the occupational dimension of their self-identities. They had not abandoned their attachment to the medical profession, but they modified it to regard themselves as "medical business people," in the words of one of the directors. Their preference was for their organization to make publicly and "in house" its "sensitivity to the market," and the opportunities which the organization provided to potential patients and general practitioner doctors to exercise "choice" in the treatments they used. We can conceptualize what was occurring, at least as a starting point, by suggesting that we have a case of two managerial constituencies in one organization, made up of people with different work-related self-identities which were clashing with each other over the organizational identity of the organization. The ongoing negotiation of order in the organization between the two groups included debates over some of the specific means by which organizational identities can be managerially manipulated. These included, internally, issues such as staff uniforms, employee recruitment, and training practices, and a "reward structure" and, externally, issues of press release policy, visual expression of organizational image, and documentation provided to client practitioners and potential patients. Discussions of "branding" had become so heated that the notion of "brand" was dropped from all managerial and policy discussions.

ORGANIZATIONAL AND PERSONAL IDENTITY WORK

As Kreiner and Murphy observe, in the course of presenting their own notion of "organizational identity work" in Chapter 15 of the present volume, researchers on organizational identity have "rarely invoked the term 'identity work.'" However, in the account we have presented, we can see the individuals who set up a business engaging in what is often conceptualized as identity work (Sveningson and Alvesson, 2003; Watson, 2008)—efforts which human beings make "internally" through self-reflection and "externally" in the way they present themselves to others to maintain a relatively coherent notion of personal self-identity. Closely connected to this is the work (in the more formal sense of "work") that individuals in "senior" positions do in organizations to build or maintain an organizational identity. We can call this organizational identity work and note that it is likely to form a significant part of the work role of organizational "leadership" figureheads and spokespersons in activities ranging from talks at shareholder meetings and interviews with press, radio, and television, to addresses to the workforce. But it is equally a dimension of the work done by human resource, public/corporate relations, and marketing departments, as well as activities undertaken by those who design the liveries of the organization's transport vehicles or speak to customers from organizational call centres.

In setting alongside each other the concepts of "personal identity work" and "organizational identity work," we must once again take care to balance the value of the insights we gain by noting a *parallel* between the two concepts with caution about treating them as too similar or too equivalent to each other. This takes us back to the present chapter's key theme of avoiding treating organizations as person-like unified entities. Organizations in which organizational identity work occurs are quite different from the human individuals who engage in personal identity work. The person who fails to achieve a relatively coherent and consistent sense of self-identity goes mad, both in the medical sense of becoming schizophrenic and in the social sense of becoming an unpredictable person to whom others cannot relate. And it is the person themselves, in "dialogue" with the culture around them, who works on their self-identity. But the organization cannot do organizational identity work in the way that individuals do personal identity work. Organizational identity work is performed by a range of organizational workers, people who are extremely unlikely to share the same priorities, preferences, and interests. To study organizational identity work is to study organizational interactions, "micropolitics," and negotiations between the various constituencies that make up the organization (see Kenny, Whittle, and Willmott, Ch. 8 in the present volume). Where there is failure in an organization to develop an effective organizational identity—as we saw earlier in the two business school cases—this has to be understood in terms of social, political, and economic relationships between the various parties involved with the organization.

Having now introduced a new concept of "organizational identity work," and noted both the parallels and the differences between this notion and that of personal identity work, we can move toward presenting a broad theoretical framework that could be utilized in future study and research.

We now need to pull together the arguments presented so far about how we can most helpfully apply a notion of organizational identity in our research. To do this we can present a broad conceptual framework to give formal definition to the focal organizational identity concept and to locate it in a broader set of concepts without which it would have little value. Organizational identities are understandings of what any given organization "is" or "is like" among members of the variety of resource-dependent constituencies, inside and outside the organization, with which the organization has dealings. They arise out of the negotiated order of relationships between the various constituencies inside and outside the organization upon which the organization is dependent for its long-term existence. Organizational identities are always in flux and are subject to conflicts of interest, contest, ambiguity, and confusion. Any particular organization may have an organizational identity which is clear, shared, and is relatively consistent across various constituencies. Equally, an organization may be subject to a variety of different identities in the eyes of the different constituencies with which that organization is concerned—some of these identities being relatively clear and some being relatively vague. Organizational identities are not the properties of organizations. They are elements of the socially constructed dimension of reality that exists in the cultural realm of social life. Individuals in the identity work which they necessarily do throughout their lives, in order to maintain a coherent sense of who and what they are, engage with the these organizational identities, utilizing them as resources for general social sensemaking, personal self-identity maintenance, and prompts to action. Managers within organizations will, to varying degrees in different circumstances, engage in organizational identity work, this including a range of staff engagement practices, public relations efforts, and image-creating and reputation-building activities (aimed sometimes at a limited range of constituencies and sometimes at a wider range) such as advertising and branding.

CONCLUSION

The above conceptual framework, which has the notions of organizational identity and organizational self-identity at its centre, is, in a sense, the conclusion of the present chapter. It is being offered as an "instrument" which researchers might wish to make use of. Alternatively, it is offered as something which, especially in its wariness about metaphors and about "unitary" styles of organizational analysis, will allow fellow scholars to avoid some of the traps into which it is so easy to fall if we are not careful about how we utilize the organizational identity conceptual instrument.

The conceptual scheme has come about, first, through reading the valuable work which has already been produced on organizational identity issues, second, through critical reflection on the author's own research work over the years and, third, through the application of ontological and epistemological principles derived from American (or "philosophical") pragmatism and Popperian fallibilism (Popper, 1963). Organizational identities are not properties of organizations which research has discovered or "uncovered." They are not phenomena "out there" in an unambiguous social world which, eventually, organizational researchers will come fully and finally to explain. Instead, a concept of "organizational identity," defined this way or that, is simply an analytical tool which can only be effective in research and theorizing if it is treated as a component of a broader conceptual framework, one which can only be judged in terms of how helpful it proves to be as a way of informing human projects.

REFERENCES

Albert, S. and Whetten, D. (1985). "Organizational Identity." In *Research in Organizational Behavior*, edited by L. L. Cummings and B. M. Staw, 263–95. Greenwich, CT: JAI Press.

Cornelissen, J. P. (2002). "On the 'Organizational Identity' Metaphor." *British Journal of Management* 13: 259–68.

Cyert, R. M. and March J. G. (2003). *A Behavioural Theory of the Firm*. Englewood Cliffs, NJ: Prentice-Hall.

Dalton, M. (1959). *Men Who Manage*. New York: Wiley.

Gioia, D. A. (1998). "From Individual to Organizational Identity." In *Identity in Organizations: Developing Theory through Conversations*, edited by D. A. Whetten and P. Godfrey, 17–31. Thousand Oaks, CA: SAGE.

Gioia, D. A. and Hamilton, A. L. (2016). "Great Debates in Organizational Identity Study." In *The Oxford Handbook of Organizational Identity*, edited by M. G. Pratt, M. Schultz, B. E. Ashforth, and D. Ravasi, 21–38. Oxford: Oxford University Press.

Gioia, D. A., Schultz, M., and Corley K. G. (2000)."Where Do We Go From Here?", *Academy of Management Review* 25: 145–7.

Gioia, D. A., Schultz, M., and Corley K. G. (2002)."On Celebrating the Organizational Identity Metaphor: A Rejoinder to Cornelissen." *British Journal of Management* 13: 269–75.

Hillman, A. J., Withers, M. C., and Collins B. J. (2009)."Resource Dependence Theory: A Review." *Journal of Management* 35: 1404–27.

Keleman, M. and Rumens, N. (eds.) (2013). *American Pragmatism and Organization*. Farnham: Gower.

Kenny, K., Whittle, A., and Willmott, H. (2011). *Understanding Identity and Organizations*. London: SAGE.

Kenny, K., Whittle, A., and Willmott, H. (2016). "Organizational Identity: The Significance of Power and Politics." In *The Oxford Handbook of Organizational Identity*, edited by M. G. Pratt, M. Schultz, B. E. Ashforth, and D. Ravasi, 140–59. Oxford: Oxford University Press.

Kreiner. G. E. and Murphy, C. (2016)."Organizational Identity Work." In *The Oxford Handbook of Organizational Identity*, edited by M. G. Pratt, M. Schultz, B. E. Ashforth, and D. Ravasi, 276–93. Oxford: Oxford University Press.

Mills, C. W. (1966) *Sociology and Pragmatism*. New York: Oxford University Press.

Mounce, H. O. (1997). *The Two Pragmatisms*. London: Routledge.

Peters T. J. and Waterman, R. H. (1982). *In Search of Excellence*. New York: Harper and Row.

Pfeffer, J. and Salancik. G. R. (1978). *The External Control of Organizations: A Resource Dependence Perspective*. Stanford, CA: Stanford University Press.

Popper, K. (1963). *Conjectures and Refutations*. London: Routledge, Kegan and Paul.

Schoenberger, E. (1995). *The Cultural Crisis of the Firm*. Oxford: Blackwell.

Scott, S. G. and Lane V. R. (2000). "A Stakeholder Approach to Organizational Identity." *Academy of Management Review* 25: 43–62.

Strauss, A. (1978). *Negotiations*. New York: Wiley.

Strauss, A., Schatzman, L., Erlich, D., Bucher, R., and Sabsin, M. (1963). "The Hospital and its Negotiated Order." In *The Hospital in Modern Society*, edited by E. Friedson, 147–69. New York: Macmillan.

Sveningsson S. and Alvesson, M. (2003)."Managing Managerial Identities: Organizational Fragmentation, Discourse and Identity Struggle." *Human Relations* 56: 1163–94.

Urmson, J. O. (2005). "Truth." In *The Concise Encyclopedia of Western Philosophy and Philosophers*, 3rd edn., edited by J. O. Urmson and J. Rée. London: Routledge.

Watson, T. J. *In Search of Management*. (2001). London: South Western Cengage, 2001.

Watson, T. J. (2008). "Managing Identity: Identity Work, Personal Predicaments and Structural Circumstances." *Organization* 15: 121–43.

Watson T. J. (2011)."Ethnography, Reality and Truth: The Vital Need for Studies of 'How Things Work' in Organisations and Management." Journal of *Management Studies* 48(1): 202–17.

Watson T. J. (2012). *Sociology, Work and Organisation*. London: Routledge.

Whetten, D. A. (1998)."Preface: Why Organizational Identity, and Why Conversations?" In *Identity in Organizations: Developing Theory through Conversations*, edited by D. A. Whetten and P. Godfrey, vii–xi. Thousand Oaks, CA: SAGE.

....

CHAPTER 8

ORGANIZATIONAL IDENTITY

the significance of power and politics

....

KATE KENNY, ANDREA WHITTLE,
AND HUGH WILLMOTT

INTRODUCTION

....

WHAT is conveyed by the idea of organizational identity? Are most organizations unified entities to which a single identity can be ascribed? If an "organization" comprises many groups and individuals with diverse orientations, purposes, and objectives, how does diversity come to be represented as uniformity?

Perhaps "organizational identity" (OI) is an innocent term, no more than a convenient shorthand. When, for example, there are changes in a firm, these are conveniently characterized as "organizational." As a consequence of the changes, a different "identity" may be attributed to the organization. That attribution is analytically defensible when it is well established that the changes are universally desired and supported by its diverse membership, and indeed other stakeholders outside the firm as well. However, in many situations, any such agreement is at best partial, conditional, or instrumental. Commonly, changes involve some measure of skepticism or compliance that is reluctant or grudging. Thus, referring to "organizational identity," with its assumptions about shared and consensual representation, may be misleading or even disingenuous.

The term "OI" is perhaps more credibly understood to involve a (more or less intentional) "sleight of hand," not a "shorthand." In effect, it is often invoked to make a "normalizing" rhetorical move which, by disregarding contestation, obscures or suppresses some degree of diversity or dissensus. When they mystify the exercise of power by naturalizing certain representations of an organization, appeals to OI deftly facilitate forms of domination and exploitation in the name of uniformity and normality. OI, in short, "tends to pave over ... diversity embedded within its boundaries, particularly that predicated on social categories of race, gender, religion, class, or age" (Glynn, Barr, and Dacin, 2000: 731).

To de-mystify OI, it is necessary to appreciate how politics and power are integral to, and deeply embedded in, processes of its (re)production.[1] If the "we" that is attributed to an organization is diverse—in terms of allegiances, priorities, and values—then it is presumptuous to believe that any representation of "who we are," whether generated and promulgated inside or outside an organization, is impartial or neutral. So, when a particular definition of OI "sticks," it should not be presumed that it is simply a consequence of its reflection of what the organization "is." Rather, analysis is needed to investigate the (power-invested) processes that have been effective in naturalizing and legitimizing that definition.

OI scholarship has recently begun to consider how power-invested representations of OI contribute to the re/production of forms of domination and exploitation (see e.g., Brown and Humphreys, 2006; Gioia et al., 2010; Glynn, 2000; Humphreys and Brown, 2002; Lok and Willmott, 2014; Nag et al., 2007; Pratt and Rafaeli, 1997). Our purpose in this chapter is to explore how power is central to OI processes, and to advance this focus of study by illuminating the more "invisible" and constitutive operation of power. The chapter begins with a necessarily selective review of literature on organizational identity in which power and politics have been directly addressed. Next, we consider the contribution of perspectives on power that appreciate its constitutive aspects, drawing upon the analysis of Lukes and supplemented by the insights of Foucault and Laclau and Mouffe. We then demonstrate the contribution of these perspectives by reference to a study of OI conducted by one of the authors. We conclude by discussing our proposition that attentiveness to the more "unobtrusive" and constitutive aspects of power has considerable potential for guiding the future development of the field.

Perspectives on Organizational Identity: A Critical Review

Organizational identity (OI) has been used to describe how people generate meaning about events (Gioia and Thomas, 1996), communicate knowledge (Empson, 2001), interpret their core competencies (Glynn, 2000), make decisions (Fombrun, 1996), carry out corporate governance activities (Golden-Biddle and Rao, 1997), and so on. Given this wide range of contexts and interpretations, it is important to clarify what is meant by "organizational identity."

---

[1] Given the contested nature of the term "power," we recognize the diversity of scholarly perspectives and approaches to the topic. As we do not have space here to offer a comprehensive review of these, or to outline the distinction between "power" and "politics," interested readers may wish to consult texts such as Buchanan and Badham (2008), Clegg (1989), Clegg, Courpasson, and Phillips (2006), Dyberg (1997), and Willmott (2013).

The notion of OI conveys a sense of *unity* and *distinctiveness* with regard to a set of activities. For example, a set of activities involving selling consumer goods might be characterized as a "retail organization" or, more economically, as a "retailer." Beyond that, the deliberate branding of a particular retailer is intended to convey its distinctiveness: that which is unique about its offer—for instance its "low cost" or "high quality." The variant of a *constructionist* position taken here brackets the question of what an organization "essentially" or "really" is. OI is then conceived as the articulation of particular *sensemaking* processes (see the exchange between Cornelissen, 2002, and Gioia, Schulz, and Corley, 2002 on this point).[2] OI refers to the *claims* of distinctiveness (Glynn, 2000); it does not, and cannot, reflect directly the properties of the organization. Constructionist analyses of OI typically explore the meaning-making and narratives told by actors about "who we are," while suspending consideration of the accuracy or veracity of such claims (Czarniawska-Joerges, 2004; Glynn, 2000; see also Hatch and Schultz, 1997; Gioia et al., 2010) on the grounds that there is no independent benchmark, or "God's eye view," for making such evaluations that is not invested in power, politics, and interests. Rather, there are only different frames of reference through which diverse actors, including scholars and researchers, render their worlds meaningful.

The particular variant of the constructionist approach engaged here attends to OI as the outcome of politics and power in which *all* forms of sensemaking and sensegiving are seen to be *politically charged and significant*. It is not just that when people "define situations as real, they are real in their consequences" (Thomas and Thomas, 1928: 572). There are also political conditions governing how things are defined as "real" in the first place, as well as political consequences following from how these definitions impede or facilitate access to scarce and valued symbolic and material resources. In turn, this means appreciating how OI processes are embedded in social, historical, and cultural structures of domination and exploitation that pre-exist and condition the (re)production of the attribution of identity to organization(s).

The Construction, Preservation, and Transformation of OI

The construction, preservation, and transformation of OI can be studied, we propose, as a process of contestation and struggle to establish and control its meaning. Claims and indicators of unity and accord are interpreted as possible outcomes of co-optation or "manufactured consent" (Burawoy, 1979; Herman and Chomsky, 1988) rather than the product of deliberation, informed consent, or spontaneous consensus. It is within relations of power, institutionalized as forms of domination and exploitation, that a particular OI comes to be regarded as "neutral," or perhaps even "natural."

---

[2] For further discussion on the "objective" property versus "constructivist" sensemaking distinction within OI research, see Ravasi and van Rekom (2003).

Many individuals and groups are engaged, and become materially and symboli-cally invested, in the formation and shaping of OI. In the case of corporations, they include executives and employees as well as consumers, employees, image consultants, journalists, suppliers, shareholders, and regulators. Much may "ride" on how OI is formulated, especially in contexts where it is an important aspect of attracting invest-ment (see Fiol, 2001; Willmott, 2011) or gaining the support of a variety of stakeholders (Pratt and Foreman, 2000). Internally, OI can be a potent means of developing and managing the motivation and "engagement" of staff, thereby extracting "discretionary effort"—that is, labor performed beyond the contractual obligation of employees—at no extra cost.[3] All of these effects can be interpreted as a product of the operation of so-called "soft" forms of power (Clegg, Courpasson, and Phillips, 2006; Nye, 2011).

Kärreman and Rylander's (2008) study of corporate branding in a Swedish IT con-sultancy firm demonstrates the "systematic efforts from top management to influence and shape frames of references, norms and values among organizational members" (p. 108). The managerially sanctioned OI defined its members in terms of high perfor-mance in the delivery of services, and it incorporated everything from dress, manner, and demeanor, to reliability, quality, and dedication, through the use of images of celebrity sports stars. One employee remarked that working for the company was like joining a "sect" (p. 114). Those who did not successfully emulate the "sports star" image were "managed out" of the organization, if they had not jumped ship already before they were "volunteered." That said, for those who remain, the operation of power may of course be experienced as positive for self-identity, as Garbett's (1988) study of sales-people at 3M has shown, and as we will illustrate later in our study of the branding of a UK business school.

During periods of contestation and change, an established OI may bring unintended consequences for management. Turbulent events, such as strike action, can serve as focal points for the articulation of competing identities attributed to organizations—as Glynn's (2000) study of the musicians' strike by the Atlanta Symphony Orchestra shows. Bouchikhi and Kimberley's (2003) study of workers in a steel company not only highlights the relationship between self-identity and OI, but also illuminates the power inherent in attempts to break down and change this relationship:

> By clinging to a definition of their organization as a steel company instead of learn-ing to regard it as, say, a manufacturing-services company, [employees] preserve their personal identity and their emotional equilibrium. At the same time, they reinforce the steel-company identity of their employing organization. Add up all such employees and other stakeholders and you have a major potential roadblock to transformation.
>
> (p. 21)

---

[3] This can manifest in voluntary overtime, the forgoing of breaks for the sake of getting work done, extra effort in serving customers well, and other activities that involve employees "going the extra mile."

To secure such "transformation" of OI, various power stratagems and political tactics may be engaged that include efforts to induce, coerce, manipulate, and persuade workers to abandon their attachment to the earlier OI, and so weaken their resistance to its replacement (see e.g., Fiol, 2002; Kjaergaard, Morsing, and Ravasi, 2011). This process of dis-identification and re-identification may be facilitated by the veiled threat, or anticipation, of adverse material consequences. Those who are assessed to be "unfit" for the new OI are passed over or may be made redundant, while those who exemplify or "fit" it remain to reap material and symbolic rewards. Attention is hereby focused upon how versions of "who we are" can have a wide range of effects on different people and groups. Some are marginalized and devalued by what emerges as the dominant "version," while others are privileged and advantaged by it.

Humphreys and Brown's (2002) account of a further education college in the UK offers a particularly rich example of the power and politics implicated in OI change processes. At "Westville Institute" (a pseudonym), a radical change occurred when management decided to pursue a new OI that was "research-active," with the objective of obtaining university status. However, the managerial OI existed in some tension with well-established narratives at Westville about "who we are," which emphasized excellent teaching rather than research, and particularly educational opportunities for local students that would enrich the local region. Many of the practices supported and legitimized by the established OI would have to be devalued, if not dismantled, if the new OI was to be implemented. Within such struggles, access to resources is rarely symmetrical. Indeed, not everyone occupies a position that enables them to articulate and disseminate their preferred OI.

Triggers for the political processes associated with change do not only come from internal sources, such as attempts by management to change OI. Studies have shown how external symbols of OI, such as media reports (Kjaergaard, Morsing, and Ravasi, 2011) or rankings (Elsbach and Kramer, 1996), can also spark political battles and power struggles around "who we are," triggered by the representations of external agents. Dutton and Dukerich's (1991) study of the Port Authority of New York and New Jersey traces how wider community politics were implicated in OI when the number of homeless people taking shelter in the bus and train stations operated by the authority steadily increased. Their presence was initially regarded by management as "tainting" the Port Authority's OI, particularly its reputation as a "safe" and "clean" place for customers. A decision was therefore taken to remove homeless people from its stations. Some of the authority's employees, however, had a different view of the Port Authority's OI, considering it to have a moral responsibility to the wider community, more akin to a social service agency. They demanded that the authority rethink its policy on the exclusion of homeless people from its stations. Negative coverage of the authority in the local press, and changes in legislation concerning loitering, led to further reflection about "who we are." As a consequence, the authority developed a new OI that emphasized its social responsibility, and new homeless drop-in centers were introduced. Here we see that negotiations over OI do not only affect employees and customers but also wider communities and civil society.

Having outlined a number of studies that illustrate the relevance of power and poli-tics for the analysis of OI, we now consider the relevance of an influential framework by the power theorist Steven Lukes for studying the different ways in which power shapes the (re)-formation of OI.

Perspectives on Power and Organizational Identity

As our selective review has shown, existing research that addresses politics, power, and OI has tended to focus on forms of conflict, negotiation, and domination in OI processes that are more or less explicit and visible—such as how various groups engage in struggles to define OI. Comparatively little attention has been given to the less "vis-ible" and "constitutive" forms of power operating within processes of OI construction and reproduction. This insidious form of power operates to constitute the very way people come to think about, talk about, and act upon, an organization's identity in ways that make it difficult to view particular versions as "questionable," "oppressive," or "interest-laden." Our analysis is indebted to Lukes' identification of three "dimen-sions of power," which we revise and extend by drawing upon the post-structuralist thought of Foucault, and Laclau and Mouffe (see also Clegg, 1989). Our framework is summarized in Table 8.1.

Lukes: Power as Domination over Interests

Power: A Radical View, written by political and social theorist Steven Lukes, is one of the most influential books on power (at the time of writing it has amassed over 9,000 citations according to Google Scholar). Lukes' theory has also exerted consider-able influence on organization scholars interested in power.[4] Lukes presents a "three dimensional" model of power. The *first* dimension refers to manifest exercises that result in one party complying with the demands of the other. Here, one party gets most of what they demand, and the demands of the other party are either unrealized or, at best, only partially fulfilled. Conflict is "out in the open," and it is not difficult to grasp that a "power struggle" is going on. Instances of this first dimension of power are evident in the examples of the further education college, the symphony orchestra and the port authority already discussed, where there was overt contestation over the OI between different groups.

---

[4] In comparison, in the field of management and organization studies, Jeffrey Pfeffer's *Power in Organizations* (1981) has 5,440 Google citations and Stewart Clegg's *The Frameworks of Power* (1989), has 2,797 Google citations (information accessed on March 10, 2015).

Table 8.1 Framework for analyzing power and organizational identity

Theoretical framework	Focus of analysis	Empirical concerns
Lukes: power and *interests*	Whose interests are furthered in the promotion of a particular perspective on OI?	Study the interests at play: whose interests have been advanced and realized, and whose have been denied, in the construction of OI, regardless of overt resistance?
Foucault: power and *discourse* and *subjectivity*	How do definitions of OI produce discourses and subject positions that are experienced as productive and positive?	Study how subjects internalize and mobilize power/knowledge discourses within particular OI constructions.
Laclau and Mouffe: power and *hegemony*	How do particular versions of OI become dominant?	Study how, in the absence of any foundations, a status quo is established and maintained through political processes and strategies.

The *second* dimension is less overt. It refers to how demands are excluded or out-flanked. It includes, for instance, the ways in which agendas of meetings are deliberately constructed to avoid, or at least minimize, the possibility of certain demands being voiced or supported. Lukes (2005: 103) gives an example drawn from Flyvbjerg's (1998) study of the location of a new bus terminal in Aalborg, Denmark. Flyvbjerg shows how members of an "elite" within the city—namely members of the chamber of industry and commerce, the police department, and the main city newspaper—contrived to frame issues, to present information, and to devise arguments that successfully circumvented the demands of opponents of the scheme so that overt conflicts were minimized. For example, in Golden-Biddle and Rao's (1977) study of an organization in which the notion of "family and friends" prevailed, certain issues and demands were effectively excluded or suppressed.

The first and second dimensions of power refer to actually or potentially observable behavior. They each relate to how the demands of one party are overtly faced down or circumvented. For Lukes, the operation of power is not confined to these dimensions. For him, power is most potent and insidious when it is least visible or obtrusive: "Power is at its most effective when least observed" (Lukes, 2005: 1). What he terms the "third dimension" of power refers to *how actors' preferences are shaped or conditioned* within relations of domination—relations that seem to be harmless or innocuous only because they are taken for granted as "how things are" or "how things should be." The third dimension is in operation when, for instance, a group is able to establish its claims about OI as "natural"—just "who we are"—thereby obscuring how what is ostensibly "natural" or "given" articulates the preferences of an advantaged group, and so serves to reproduce their advantage over others.

Studies that attend only to the first and second dimensions of power, Lukes argues, overlook how its third dimension operates to *condition our very beliefs and desires,* such that certain demands are never felt, and so cannot be voiced:

> is it not the supreme exercise of power to get another or others to have the desires— that is, to secure their compliance by controlling their thoughts and desires.

> (1974: 23)

If interests and preferences and their associated demands are not even recognized, they cannot be expressed, thereby eliminating the need to exercise more overt forms of power to obstruct or overcome them. This third dimension of power is understood to ensure that marginalized, disenfranchised, and subordinated groups come to accept—or perhaps even support—their (subordinate) "place" in society as "natural" and "right." The effectiveness of such ideological conditioning is seen to result in oppressed groups suffering from what Marx termed "false consciousness" as they are unable to develop an awareness of their "real interests." In effect, they are prevented from forming conscious preferences or desires other than those ascribed to them by the dominant ideology.

Consider once again the port authority example discussed earlier. The overt conflict over management's decision to remove homeless people from its stations might have remained suppressed or unexpressed if all employees of the authority had been inculcated to accept a conservative neo-liberal ideology in which personal economic responsibility is unquestioned. The question of whether the port authority should help the homeless would then never have arisen. Similarly, at Westville Institute, if the staff had been indoctrinated into the aspiration to be a research-oriented institution, dissent about the idea of becoming such a place would not have been voiced. In each case, compliance could have been secured by "controlling their thoughts and desires" (Lukes 1974: 23).

Foucault: Power as Operating through the Subject

While Lukes's *Power: A Radical View* has been influential across the social sciences, it has not escaped criticism. Notably, critics have challenged his assumption that subordinated groups have "real interests" that, seemingly, are recognizable only by social scientific observers (Clegg, 1989; Knights and Willmott, 1982). As Lukes (2005: 88 et seq.) himself observes when reflecting on his work some thirty years later, the insights of French philosopher Michel Foucault have much to contribute to this issue.

Foucault conceives of power as *relational* and also as having *positive* and "productive" as well as negative and "repressive" qualities. He rejects the conception of power as only a property or instrument which, in binary fashion, some individuals or groups have and others lack; and which some actors may therefore mobilize to generate "false consciousness" in others. For Foucault, power is relational and systemic, and not just possessed and episodic. It takes the form of "strategies and techniques" that operate *through* individuals not just *over* them. In the case of OI, these strategies and techniques could include mission or vision statements designed to articulate the preferred OI, marketing, and branding activities targeted at customers or clients, and culture management programs designed to inculcate the preferred OI into the value-systems of employees (Willmott, 1993). Notably, Foucault appreciates how power "is tolerable only on condition that it masks a substantial part of itself. Its success is proportional to its ability to hide its own mechanisms" (Foucault, 1980: 86, cited in Lukes, 2005: 90).

In this regard, Foucault affirms Lukes' basic proposition that power operates most effectively in insidious and invisible ways. However, Foucault does not rely upon an appeal to "real interests" or "false consciousness" in order to account for this. Instead, he associates the "masking" of power with its *productive* appeal for actors who are constituted by it. For Foucault, power is enabling as well as constraining: it induces pleasure as well as defining the limits of pleasure. Power operates to produce (normal-ized) subjects (actors)—that is to say, in Lukes' terms, it "render(s) them capable and willing to adhere to norms of sanity, health, sexuality and other forms of propriety" (Lukes, 2005: 91). For example, the power invested in the identity of an organization—such as in the examples discussed earlier—can induce "pleasure" in its recruits, cus-tomers/clients, suppliers, etc. This, in turn, can lead them to "choose" to participate in practices that shape and condition their preferences, resulting in the unacknowledged reinforcement of their investment.

In other words, power is most effective, not when "real interests" are obscured and mystified but rather when, taking a positive form, power is not recognized as such: when its subjects believe that they are self-determining and that they have actively "chosen" to constitute and discipline themselves according to the values and priorities provided by the OI—such as being "innovative," or producing "excellent research," or providing "good customer service." For Foucault, such "choice" is not itself freely ex-ercised. Rather, it is articulated through media of governmentality: the way the state, or another authority, exercises control over the population. The media of governmen-tality include (a) styles of reasoning—or "rationalities of rule"—that are embodied in governing practices; (b) conceptions of the person that these rationalities serve to in-culcate; and (c) "technologies of the self" that subjects incorporate within themselves in order to acquire certain habits and disciplines (see also Rose, 1989). This approach abandons the apparent ontological and epistemological bedrock of "real interests," even if it is conceived, as Lukes does, as "a function of one's explanatory purpose," rather than as something that "will resolve moral conflicts and set the seal of prof-fered explanations, confirming them as true" (Lukes, 1995: 148). This approach also, and relatedly, abandons the attribution of "false consciousness," even when it is con-ceived as a placeholder for "the power to mislead" rather than an expression of "the arrogant assertion of a privileged access to truths presumed unavailable to others" (Lukes, 1995: 149).

Laclau and Mouffe: Power as the Organization of Hegemony

Insights from Foucault have proved valuable for organization scholars interested in power and politics (for early contributions, see Hoskin and Macve, 1986; Knights and Morgan, 1991; Knights and Willmott, 1989), but they have not yet found their way into analyses of OI. In what follows, we draw upon an inflection of Foucauldian thinking developed in the work of political theorists Ernesto Laclau and Chantal Mouffe (1985). Approaching the question of power from a different, postfoundationalist direction, *Hegemony and Socialist Strategy* (1985) bears the influence of Foucauldian thinking as it advances a post-Marxist analysis that, according to Clegg (1989: 182), provides a useful counterpoint to Lukes' theorization. Laclau and Mouffe's focus is upon how, for example, intersubjectively formed preferences become politically articulated and instituted as reflections, or deflections, of actors' ostensibly "real interests."[5] In recent years, their thinking has become increasingly influential among organizational scholars interested in power (Kenny and Scriver, 2012; Spicer and Bohm, 2007; Willmott, 2005).

Within Laclau and Mouffe's framework, social realities, such as OI, are understood, postfoundationally, to be "fully dependent on political articulations and not on entities constituted outside the particular field—such as class 'interests'" (Laclau and Mouffe, 2001: xi). Laclau and Mouffe here echo Foucault's conception of freedom as a condition of possibility of the exercise of power—"power is exercised only over free subjects" (Foucault, 1982: 221)—as it would make no sense to exercise it over subjects whose actions are already determined. Furthermore, because social realities are inherently open, they are continually being renegotiated (Laclau and Mouffe, 2001: 105). This is not because they suppress, deny, or invert "real interests" but, rather, because social realities defy closure and so invite or provoke disruption. Practices of hegemonic closure are imperfect and contingent, and so contain within themselves the seeds of their own undoing. A particular OI, even something as simple as the notion of a "steel company" (Bouchikhi and Kimberley, 2003), is stable only insofar as there is hegemonic closure around the claims made about the organization, and this is inherently open to contestation.

For Laclau and Mouffe, hegemony persists only by being upheld by actors; it "continues to produce its effects insofar as social agents define their basic identity in relation to it" (Laclau and Mouffe, 1985: 53). For instance, in the hospital rehabilitation unit studied by Pratt and Rafaeli (1997), nurses identified with two distinct senses of "who we are." Generally speaking, there are multiple alternative signifiers with which subjects might identify, and so identification is necessarily "overdetermined": it is

---

[5] As Laclau and Mouffe (2001: xi) put it, "politico-hegemonic articulations retroactively create the interests they claim to represent."

irreducible to a single, stable identity. In the case of OI, the "signifiers" could be a particular word or symbol associated with the organization, such as a mission statement or set of organizational values promoted by the corporate culture, or a visual signifier like a logo or image, such as the "sports stars" images and terminology used in Alvesson and Empson's (2008) study. Laclau and Mouffe (1985: 128) note how "every social identity becomes the meeting point for a multiplicity of articulatory practices," so that hegemony is never finally complete. Identification—such as with OI—is multiple, often paradoxical and inescapably incomplete. To the extent that it "holds," its paradoxical in/completeness is secured through the operation of the different dimensions of power.

In what follows, we illustrate the operation of different forms of power outlined by Lukes, Foucault, and Laclau and Mouffe with reference to an empirical study of branding in a UK business school, in order to illustrate how future research could take up the framework we propose in this chapter.

CASE ILLUSTRATION: BRANDING
THE BUSINESS SCHOOL

This section draws on data from a qualitative study conducted by one of the authors into processes of organizational identity formation at a business school—which we refer to here as "B-School," in a British university we call "B-Uni."[6] Specifically, we consider the diverse signifiers invoked in practices of (re)forming the "brand" of B-School. The study involved semi-structured interviews with key actors engaged in, or affected by, this branding process.

The idea of deliberately and strategically engaging in "branding" was a new endeavor for B-School. Across the UK, and indeed in many other parts of the world, increasing emphasis was being placed on universities becoming more commercial and business-like, especially in their marketing activities. The adoption of the language and practices of "branding," developed primarily in the private sector, is well documented within the literature on the marketization of higher education (see e.g., Lowrie and Willmott, 2006; Molesworth, Scullion, and Nixon, 2011). At B-School, manifestations of marketization included the introduction of merchandizing, brand logos, brochures, marketing plans, mission statements, the pursuit of accreditations and professional associations, and the use of new "customer relationship management" systems for monitoring and scoring aspects of the "customer interface" with students, employers, and alumni. Indeed, the term "customer" had increasingly been used to describe the students and other stakeholders with whom the university engaged.

---

[6] We have anonymized persons and organizations in this case example.

B-School Branding and Lukes' Three Dimensions

Following the appointment of a new dean at B-School, a committee dedicated to external engagement activities was established. Prior to this, according to one informant, B-School had made few, if any, *systematic* attempts to create or promote its OI to prospective students, alumni, staff, and sponsors. Instead, its reputation had been based primarily upon word of mouth and the occasional ad hoc attempt to refresh its image through changed letterheads or new signs for buildings, in addition to the usual promotional activities such as course brochures. The creation of an external engagement committee was described by one senior academic staff member interviewed as indicative of a "significant shift in a more brand-oriented direction."

One of the first tasks of the external engagement committee (EEC) was the commissioning of a brand identity review. The recommendations of the review specified three main "elements" of B-School's organizational identity: to be internationally recognized and "world-leading" in the following areas: 1) teaching and learning; 2) research; and 3) external engagement with businesses, industry, and other stakeholders. Of those, B-School's reputation in one of these areas—research—was considered to be of particular importance to the "distinctiveness" of its established identity, as noted by most of our interviewees:

> So, what are we known for? We are known for, more than ever, for being very good at research. [pause] Nationally and to some extent internationally. And I think we're also known for having very high quantity postgrad and undergrad programmes.
>
> (Academic senior manager)

The brand identity review recommended that B-School should further strengthen its strong reputation around research excellence and promote itself as a world-leading place for teaching and learning. How, then, were power and politics implicated in B-School's identity-building activities? And what were the consequences, unintended as well as intended, of this effort to consolidate and develop its identity? By emphasizing a very specific set of claims about what constituted the organization's preferred or desired identity, the branding exercise—and OI practices that flowed from it—simultaneously devalued certain types of people and activities. This power effect, which we assess to be largely unintended but not necessarily unwelcome to most members of the top management team (TMT) or the EEC, was evident in the interview with "Steven." Steven was a senior manager (and professor). During the interview, he talked about the discussions about OI that had taken place during a series of top management team (TMT) meetings:

> STEVEN: We [the TMT] often reflect on: "If we do this, what will that imply for our image and reputation?" And in fact we often use that argument to prevent bad things happening.

Intrigued by what these "bad things" might be, the interviewer asked Steven if he could elaborate:

> STEVEN: So if someone comes to us with a proposal, which is inappropriate for a [top-ranked] School in the UK, in a Russell Group University,[7] then we can use the argument: "that would be negative for our image and reputation." So it's used to stop bad things, but not often used to shape the development of better things.
>
> INTERVIEWER: What sort of things are you talking about?
>
> STEVEN: We may get proposals for, say, short courses or e-learning modules, which are not award-bearing courses. They're not masters, they're not diplomas. They are just: "B-School is offering a short course on how to set up your own business"… And we say: "That would be bad for our image and reputation. That's not what we do."

This example illustrates the *first dimension of power,* as described by Lukes (1974), wherein some actors are able to refuse the demands of others. Specifically, some staff members were not permitted to offer short courses that they wanted to teach. The prescribed OI was explicitly mobilized to enforce their exclusion. Notice how notions of "construed external image" (Gioia, Schultz, and Corley, 2000)—ideas about what outsiders think about the organization—are grounded in existing definitions of "who we are" and "what we do" (and by definition "who we are *not*" and "what we do *not* do"), which also in turn informs policies about what work activities members are permitted to undertake.

Aspects of Lukes' *second dimension of power* are evident in the *process* whereby the EEC was formed and populated. This committee had been awarded a strategic role within the TMT, along with substantial resources, new professional support staff (PSS) posts and senior management support. As a consequence, the tone and content of TMT meetings were likely to have tilted in support of this new committee by virtue of its presence and its managerial support (see Bachrach and Baratz, 1962). Likewise, the recommendation of the brand identity review was reflective of the composition of the group recruited to undertake it: it was led by external brand consultants and involved marketing specialists and businesses, alongside representatives from the school. The composition of this group, endorsed by TMT, made it highly likely, although not inevitable, that its deliberations would produce a distinctly business-oriented *framing* of the brand, which infiltrated into versions of "who we are" and "what we represent" as articulated by the TMT. This example illustrates how the seemingly innocent and impartial selection of committee members possessing "relevant expertise" can substantially influence the agenda, process, direction, and outcomes of its decision-making.

To push our analysis further and attend to the less "obtrusive" third dimension of power, this can be detected in how preferences and desires relating to doing "excellent

---

[7] The Russell Group comprises 24 British public research universities, which currently receive approximately two-thirds of all university research grants and contract income in the United Kingdom. See <http://en.wikipedia.org/wiki/Russell_Group#cite_note-Russell-1>. Accessed December 3, 2013.

research" were articulated. Indeed, a particular conception of what was meant by being "good at research" (senior manager—academic staff quoted earlier), was being subtly shaped and embraced. In the following reflection, Steven elaborates on how the claim to be "excellent in research" related to actual activities of staff within the school, day to day:

> STEVEN: I expect there's a fairly widespread and shared understanding that research means publishing outputs which are recognisable to our academic peers as high quality. And I would guess that 80-90% of the School recognise that's what we mean by research. That's research which is published in the leading journals in whatever field we happen to be working in.

This "widespread and shared" understanding was strongly endorsed by senior figures such as the associated dean for external relations, as described by another interviewee, "Karen":

> KAREN: There are some groups in the school, they just don't do research.
> INTERVIEWER: I guess it depends on your definition of research? [...]
> KAREN: Absolutely. And it's interesting actually, because some accreditation bodies, like AACSB, want to know all about applied research. I think they call it active research or live research. [...] But like [the associate dean of external relations] was saying to people at the engagement meeting we had last week, who were talking about "In our research this and that", he said, "With all due respect, I don't think many people [here] would think *that* was research."

We interpret these observations as attempts by senior managers to shape and/or reinforce the beliefs, preferences, and desires of employees—what Lukes refers to as the *third dimension* of power. Importantly, this "shared" OI comprises quite specific understandings about "research" (which we deliberately place in "scare quotes" to underscore their contingent and contested meaning). Steven's version of "research" involves written outputs that appear in "leading" academic journals, presumably those that are assigned a high ranking by an agency to which authority is attributed (Willmott, 2011; Willmott and Mingers, 2013; Willmott and Tourish, 2015). "Who we are" as researchers then becomes intertwined with this categorization. Action research, policy work, consultancy, and research outputs that do not appear in "leading journals" (e.g., books, trade journals, practitioner magazines, web-based media, or policy briefings), is degraded and de-legitimated. This categorization is presented as if it is self-evident. It is presented as simply what "real research" or "good research" is.

Further to this, Karen's observation that others had articulated an incongruent conception of "research" is also reflected in Steven's reference to staff who do not share his definition:

> STEVEN: There is a small minority of people who see research in a different way... And they need to be persuaded, or enlightened [interviewee and interviewee both laugh], that there is another world of research and that's the game we're trying to play.

Steven's suggestion that staff "need to be persuaded or enlightened" to share his definition illustrates how, as in Lukes' third dimension, preferences and desires are actively shaped so that staff would freely choose to engage in activities preferred by the managerially sanctioned definition of OI.

Our example of B-School has therefore illustrated how Lukes' third dimension of power may operate to undermine oppositional demands (first dimension) and render "institutionalized bias" (second dimension) unnecessary by moving to the point where academic staff become so "enlightened" as to believe that they are "freely choosing" what type of research to do and how to disseminate it. It is a mundane example of domination: a certain kind of research activity and output is targeted for "cleansing" by the determination to brand B-School with a particular OI.

Understanding Power at B-School: Beyond Lukes

Whereas within Lukes' (1974) initial formulation of the third dimension of power, it is assumed that subjects' "real interests" are obscured by power but identifiable by social scientists aware of this dimension, for Foucault and Laclau and Mouffe, such "interests" are attributed and contingent rather than foundational or essential (see also Clegg, 1989). Branding activities, such as those we have described, have taken place against a backdrop of broader discourses and technologies that lend legitimacy to, and have served to normalize, emphasis upon a particular kind of research (for relevant analyses, see Bell and Taylor, 2005; Clarke, Knights, and Jarvis, 2012; Keenoy, 2005; Knights and Clarke, forthcoming; Willmott, 1995; Lowrie and Willmott, 2009; Willmott, 2011; Willmott and Mingers, 2013; Willmott and Tourish, 2015; Worthington and Hodgson, 2005). As Steven himself observed:

> STEVEN: The [last government research assessment] made us push even more
> strongly on the research reputation as the defining characteristic of the brand.
> I think that's the most significant event.... And I think that the brand message
> of "we're very good at research" is successfully communicated.

B-School was, at the time of our research, embroiled in a wider (and relatively recent) discourse of "research excellence" that was circulating in the UK, and beyond. Institutionalization of particular definitions of "research," as articulated and legitimized through systems of classification and inspection (Foucault, 1970), such as research audits and journal rankings, can exercise a "normalizing" effect on organizational members. As a consequence, academic staff may design their research activities in order to affirm their identification as "a researcher" with B-School's preferred OI. When read in this way, Karen and Steven's observations indicate that they are reproducing the dominant discourse of what "research" is, as defined and classified by authoritative sources such as governmental bodies, associations, and accreditation bodies. To return to Lukes' third dimension, this is not just, or simply, an exercise in domination from "outside," but rather a process of subjectification which operates on and through those who are caught up in, and constituted by, particular discourses of OI. It is difficult to regard those embroiled in the discourse as passive, hoodwinked victims of a deception. More plausibly, they are participants in its reproduction who, at some indeterminate point, may shift in the direction of opposition instead of accommodation.

Hegemony and Discourses of Excellence: Insights from Laclau and Mouffe

Laclau and Mouffe's concept of hegemony offers some further insight into how such regimes of power/knowledge, as Foucault terms them, become established and reproduced. We have focused upon contestation around the meaning of "research"—a struggle through which managers at B-School were attempting to gain closure in relation to a preferred OI. Crucially, for Laclau and Mouffe, every hegemonic closure around a particular meaning is inherently unstable. In the B-School example, closure is dependent upon staff identifying, whether fervently or cynically, with a hegemonic signifier, such as the meaning attributed to "good research." In B-School, "who we are" comprises researchers who are, according to Steven, "very good at research": as defined by the branding exercise, amongst other OI practices. Power effects flowed from this "closure" around what research meant: in particular, the production of outputs in journals highly ranked by the Association of Business Schools (ABS). Forms of status and prestige, career advancement, salary rises, and lighter teaching and administrative duties, could accrue to those who affirmed the OI by delivering research that fitted this "articulation." Those deemed by the dominant discourse to be "non-research active" could find their careers blocked, their research funding reduced, and even have their (non-excellent) research groups shut down.

Many staff at B-School had already embraced a version of "research" privileged by the senior management team. Nonetheless, hegemonic closure was by no means guaranteed. Different chains of equivalence were assembled by different actors, including those who comfortably affirmed the "very good at research" identity; and competing definitions of "research" were circulating, which included those of accreditation bodies which valorize "live" or "applied" research. In the UK, this emphasis upon application and relevance has been boosted in recent years, by governmental evaluation regimes that incorporate consideration of the "impact" of research in addition to notions of "scholarly quality." Such developments offer some basis for counter-hegemonic arguments that anticipate a future in which other priorities—such as "applied" or "impactful" research—may be more strongly valorized.

CONCLUSION

In this chapter, we have sought to extend existing approaches to studying power and politics in relation to OI. Inspiration has been drawn from Lukes' three dimensions

of power and the poststructuralist ideas of Foucault and Laclau and Mouffe. To show
how each approach to power has relevance for the study of OI, we examined practices
involved in the (re)formation of OI in a study of branding in a UK business school.

By scrutinizing a branding exercise at B-School, we have endeavored to illuminate
the power-laden activities that comprise the (re)construction of OI. Furthermore, by
developing a framework that includes consideration of the more insidious and unobtrusive dimensions of power, we have shown how the development of OI involves the
engagement of wider hegemonic discourses. We have also shown how organizational
identities are defined and invoked—productively as well as offensively—through processes of contestation and de/institutionalization. It is through such processes that relations of domination become naturalized, and it is through critical analysis that their
contingency is appreciated, and their necessity or inevitability is challenged. We hope
that future research in this field will attend to how, in its multiple forms, power is implicated in the practices through which OI is established, developed, and transformed,
especially where more "visible" forms of conflict and struggle are absent.

REFERENCES

Alvesson, M. and Empson, L. (2008). "The Construction of Organizational Identity:
Comparative Case Studies of Consulting Firms." *Scandinavian Journal of Management*
24: 1–16.
Bachrach, P. and Baratz, M. (1962). "Two Faces of Power." *American Political Science Review*
56: 947–52.
Bell, E. and Taylor, S. (2005). "Living with Accreditation: Business School Badging and
Academic Identity." *Studies in Higher Education* 30(3): 239–55.
Bouchikhi, H. and Kimberley, J. R. (2003). "Escaping the Identity Trap." *Sloan Management
Review* Spring: 20–6.
Brown, A. D. and Humphreys, M. (2006). "Organizational Identity and Place: A Discursive
Exploration of Hegemony and Resistance." *Journal of Management Studies* 43(2): 231–57.
Buchanan D. and Badham R. (2008). *Power, Politics and Organizational Change: Winning
the Turf Game*. London: SAGE.
Burawoy, M. (1979). *Manufacturing Consent*. Chicago: University of Chicago Press.
Clarke, C., Knights, D., and Jarvis, C. (2012). "A Labour of Love? Academics in Business
Schools." *Scandinavian Journal of Management* 28(1): 5–15.
Clegg, S. R. (1989). *Frameworks of Power*. London: SAGE.
Clegg, S. R., Courpasson, D., and Phillips, N. (2006). *Power in Organizations*. London: SAGE.
Cornelissen, J. P. (2002). "On the 'Organizational Identity' Metaphor." *British Journal of
Management* 13: 259–68.
Czarniawska-Joerges, B. (2004). *Narratives in Social Science Research*. Thousand Oaks,
CA: SAGE.
Dutton, J. and Dukerich, J. (1991). "Keeping an Eye on the Mirror: Image and Identity in
Organizational Adaptation." *Academy of Management Review* 34: 517–54.
Dyberg, T. B. (1997). *The Circular Structure of Power: Politics, Identity, Community*.
London: Verso.

Empson, L. (2001). "Fear of Exploitation and Fear of Contamination: Impediments to Knowledge Transfer in Mergers between Professional Services Firms." *Human Relations* 54(7): 839–62.

Fiol, C. M. (2001). "Revisiting an Identity-Based View of Sustainable Competitive Advantage." *Journal of Management* 27: 691–9.

Fiol, C. M. (2002). "Capitalizing on Paradox: The Role of Language in Transforming Organizational Identities." *Organization Science* 13(6): 653–66.

Flyvbjerg, B. (1998). *Rationality and Power: Democracy in Practice.* Chicago: Chicago University Press.

Fombrun, C. (1996). *Reputation: Realizing Value from the Corporate Image.* Cambridge, MA: Harvard University Press.

Foucault, M. (1970). *The Order of Things.* London: Tavistock.

Foucault, M. (1980). *The History of Sexuality, Volume 1*, trans. Robert Hurley. New York: Random House.

Foucault, M. (1982). "The Subject and Power," published as the Afterword to H. L. Dreyfus and P. Rabinow, *Michel Foucault: Beyond Structuralism and Hermeneutics*, Brighton: Harvester.

Garbett, T. (1988). *How to Build a Corporation's Identity and Project its Image.* Levington, MA: D.C. Smith.

Gioia, D. A., Price, K. N., Hamilton, A. L., and Thomas, J. B. (2010). "Forging an Identity: An Insider-Outsider Study of Processes Involved in the Formation of Organizational Identity." *Administrative Science Quarterly* 55: 1–46.

Gioia, D. A., Schultz, M., and Corley, K. G. (2000). "Organizational Identity, Image, and Adaptive Instability." *Academy of Management Review* 25(1): 63–81.

Gioia, D. A., Schultz, M., and Corley, K. G. (2002). "On Celebrating the Organizational Identity Metaphor: A Rejoinder to Cornelissen." *British Journal of Management* 13: 269–75.

Gioia, D. A. and Thomas, J. (1996). "Identity, Image and Issue Interpretation: Sensemaking during Strategic Change in Academia." *Administrative Science Quarterly* 41: 370–403.

Glynn, M. (2000). "When Cymbals Become Symbols: Conflict over Organizational Identity within a Symphony Orchestra" *Organization Science* 8(6): 593–611.

Glynn, M. A., Barr, P., and Dacin, M. T. (2000). "Pluralism and the Problem of Variety." *Academy of Management Review* 25(4): 726–34.

Golden-Biddle K., and Rao H., (1997). "Breaches in the Boardroom: Organisational Identity and Conflicts of Commitment in a Nonprofit Organisation." *Organization Science* 8(6): 593–611.

Hatch, M. J. and Schultz, M. (1997). "Relations between Organizational Culture, Identity and Image." *European Journal of Marketing* 31(5/6): 356–65.

Herman, E. S. and Chomsky, N. (1988). *Manufacturing Consent.* London: Pantheon.

Hoskin K. and Macve R. (1986). "Accounting and the Examination: A Genealogy of Disciplinary Power." *Accounting, Organization and Society* 11(2): 105–36.

Humphreys, M. and Brown, A. D. (2002). "Narratives of Organizational Identity and Identification: A Case Study of Hegemony and Resistance." *Organization Studies* 23: 421–47.

Kärreman, D. and Rylander, A (2008). "Managing Meaning through Branding: The Case of a Consulting Firm." *Organization Studies* 29(1): 103–25.

Keenoy, T. (2005). "Facing Inwards and Outwards at Once: The Liminal Temporalities of Academic Performativity." *Time and Society* 14(2/3): 304–21.

Kenny, K. and Scriver, S. (2012). "Dangerously Empty? Hegemony and the Construction of the Irish Entrepreneur." *Organization* 19(5): 615–33.

Kjaergaard A., Morsing, M., and Ravasi, D. (2011). "Mediating Identity: A Study of Media Influence on Organizational Identity Construction in a Celebrity Firm." *Journal of Management Studies* 48(3): 514–43.

Knights, D. and Clarke, C. (2014) "It's a Bittersweet Symphony, This Life: Fragile Academic Selves and Insecure Identities at Work." *Organization Studies* 35(3): 335–57.

Knights, D. and Willmott, H. C. (1982). "Power, Values and Relations." *Sociology* 16(4): 578–85.

Knights, D. and Morgan, G. (1991). "Corporate Strategy, Organizations and Subjectivity: a Critique." *Organization Studies* 12(9): 251–73.

Knights, D. and Willmott, H. (1989). "Power and Subjectivity at Work." *Sociology* 23(4): 535–58.

Laclau, E. and Mouffe, C. (1985). *Hegemony and Socialist Strategy: Toward a Radical Democratic Politics*. London: Verso.

Laclau, E. and Mouffe, C. (2001) *Hegemony and Socialist Strategy*, 2nd edn. London: Verso.

Lok, J. and Willmott, H. C. (2014). "Identities and Identifications in Organizations: Dynamics of Antipathy, Deadlock, and Alliance." *Journal of Management Inquiry* 23(3): 215–30.

Lowrie, A. and Willmott, H. (2006). "Marketing Higher Education: The Promotion of Relevance and the Relevance Promotion." *Social Epistemology* 20(3–4): 221–40.

Lowrie, A. and Willmott, H. (2009). "Accreditation Sickness in the Consumption of Business Education: The Vacuum in AACSB Standard Setting." *Management Learning* 40(4): 411–20.

Lukes, S. (1974). *Power: A Radical View*. London: Macmillan.

Lukes, S. (2005). *Power: A Radical View*, 2nd edn. London: Macmillan.

Molesworth, M., Scullion, R., and Nixon, E. (2011). *The Marketization of Higher Education and the Student as Consumer*. London: Routledge.

Nag, R, Corley, K. G., and Gioia, D. A. (2007). "The Intersection of Organizational Identity, Knowledge, and Practice: Attempting Strategic Change via Knowledge Grafting." *Academy of Management Journal* 50(4): 821–47.

Nye, Joseph S. (2011). *The Future of Power*. New York: Public Affairs.

Pfeffer, J. (1981) *Power in Organizations*. Marshfield, MA: Pitman.

Pratt, M. G. and Foreman, P. O. (2000). "Classifying Managerial Responses to Multiple Organizational Identities." *Academy of Management Review* 25(1): 18–42.

Pratt, M. G. and Rafaeli, A. (1997). "Organizational Dress as a Symbol of Multilayered Social Identities." *Academy of Management Journal* 40(4): 862–98.

Ravasi, D. and van Rekom, J. (2003). "Key Issues in Organizational Identity and Identification Theory." *Corporate Reputation Review* 6(2): 118–32.

Rose, N. (1989). *Governing the Soul*. London: Routledge.

Spicer, A. and Böhm, S. (2007). "Moving Management: Theorizing Struggles against the Hegemony of Management." *Organization Studies* 28(11): 1667–98.

Thomas, W. I., and Thomas, D. S. (1928). *The Child in America: Behavior Problems and Programs*. New York: Knopf.

Willmott, H. (1993). "Strength Is Ignorance; Slavery Is Freedom: Managing Culture in Modern Organizations." *Journal of Management Studies* 30: 515–52.

Willmott, H. (1995). "Managing the Academics: Commodification and Control in the Development of University Education in the UK." *Human Relations* 48(9): 993–1027.

Willmott, H. (2005). "Theorizing Contemporary Control: Some Post-Structuralist Responses to Some Critical Realist Questions." *Organization* 12(5): 747–80.

Willmott, H. C. (2011). "Back to the Future: What Does Studying Bureaucracy Tell Us?" In *Managing Modernity: Beyond Bureaucracy?*", edited by S. Clegg, M. Harris, and H. Höpfl, 257–94. Oxford: Oxford University Press.

Willmott, H. (2013). "OT and Power: The Significance of Value-Orientations and a Plea for Pluralism." *Tamara* 11(2): 51–64.

Willmott, H. and Mingers, J. (2013). "Taylorizing Business School Research: On the 'One Best Way' Performative Effects of Journal Ranking Lists." *Human Relations* 66(8): 1051–73.

Willmott, H. and Tourish, D. (2015). "In Defiance of Folly: Journal Rankings, Mindless Measures and the ABS Guide." *Critical Perspectives on Accounting* 26: 37–46.

Worthington F. and Hodgson J. (2005). "Academic Labour and the Politics of Quality in Higher Education: A Critical Evaluation of the Conditions of Possibility of Resistance." *Critical Quarterly* 47(1–2): 96–110.

CHAPTER 9

ORGANIZATIONAL IDENTITY

a critique

MATS ALVESSON AND MAXINE ROBERTSON

INTRODUCTION

IN this chapter we offer a critique of the concept of organizational identity (OI), challenging some basic assumptions and knowledge claims in this field from a Critical Management Studies (CMS) perspective (cf. Alvesson and Willmott 2012; Alvesson et al., 2009; Fournier and Grey, 2000). Here "critical" is understood as promoting more extensive reflection upon established ideas, ideologies, institutions, and practices in order to reduce repression and self-constraints, especially from subtle forms of domination, which may not necessarily be recognized as exercising social constraints. From this perspective, academic and other ideas which construct "reality" in certain ways can, and should be challenged. Socially relevant knowledge interferes with, is part of, and creates reality in specific and not always neutral or innocent ways (Foucault, 1980). CMS aims to challenge dominant understandings, if and when these are seen as problematic, with the aim of creating critical awareness of the exercise of power and the grip of ideologies in order to support resistance and liberation from a social world increasingly managed and controlled by social technologies and domination through specific definitions of reality.

CMS have always questioned the legitimacy of managers to maintain a strong grip on working life and their attempts to regulate employees' identities (Alvesson and Willmott 2002). We believe that OI plays a role in this and, as such, motivates critical scrutiny around key assumptions that have steered developments in this field. Our approach in the chapter is to identify and challenge some common, dominant assumptions that exist across OI studies (Alvesson and Sandberg, 2013).

Firstly, we consider how OI researchers take for granted the idea that OI is pregiven. We then address the assumptions surrounding the inter-relationship between OI, employee identification, and organizational image in OI research and what issues this throws up. In the third section we extend this argument and challenge the reifi-cation of OI. We suggest that whilst treating OI as a property or characteristic of an organization may make it easier to study, it does not offer a realistic and sensitive un-derstanding of how employees may address issues around direction, priorities, mean-ing, and distinctiveness. In the final section we discuss OI in relationship to earlier work on organizational culture (OC). There is a tendency to view OI as a novel and distinct subject matter and area of study; however, we identify remarkable similarities across these two areas. We suggest that some key insights from OC studies, particu-larly those that have demonstrated the need to account for the complexity, ambiguity, and variation of cultural meanings that typically exist in organizations, should also be (re)considered by researchers interested in OI.

Throughout the chapter we advocate the adoption of more sensitivity to process, and local and varied meanings, as well as the use of power associated with various claims of what is distinctive and unique about an organization. In this way, OI re-search will be better able to capture the complexity that exists in organizations. Gioia and Hamilton this volume, Chapter 1, have advocated viewing identity as both "an intangible entity *and* as a dynamic process continuously in flux" (p. 19) but we believe that viewing identity as an entity simply offers a way of placing boundaries around this area of inquiry, making it more amenable to research and the use of traditional research methods, and ultimately over-simplifying what is naturally a complex or-ganizational phenomenon.

The Taken-for-Granted Nature of OI and Related Assumptions

The majority of OI studies, regardless of whether they adopt a positivist or social con-structionist perspective tend to view OI as robust, consisting of central features. As Kenny, Whittle, and Willmott (2011) emphasize, even social constructionists view OI as anchored in firm beliefs and meanings, and not just as stories or language use ex-pressing a variety of versions of how to represent the organization. A recent review of the field by Gioia, Patvardhan, Hamilton, and Thomas (2013) argue that central features are pre-given, saying that they have

> emerged as perhaps the most essential feature (sic), simply because if there are no perceived central or core features, it is difficult to conceive of the idea of identity.
>
> (p. 126)

The reasoning here is somewhat tautological as it seems that in order to avoid prob-lems of conceptualization, there must be central features, that is, characteristics which can readily be articulated. But the assumption of an "essence" of "perceived central or core features" is questionable. Why could it not be the case that "identity" may be understood in far more varied or ambiguous ways? This is not to deny that ideas or claims about central features may exist and may be relevant but, as we will argue, this is not an obvious characteristic of all organizations. The idea that studying OI calls for identification of central features—that they exist in the views held by employees or as characteristics of organizations is far from unproblematic. Alternatively, perhaps central features are "produced" by researchers motivated as a way of understanding particular organizational phenomena. Gioia et al., and many others in the OI field, appear to conveniently order reality so that studying it becomes bounded and therefore an easier matter. In so doing "identity" is pre-packaged in a particular way.

Gioia et al. (2013) define central features *as* "key values, labels, products, services or practices etc." (p. 125). This definition includes just about everything that could or might be considered to be characteristic of an organization. It is not clear what the difference is between organization and organizational identity, that is, what does the latter term add? Issues about identity arguably appear in specific situations where identity is relevant to consider, for example in complex decision-making around change or conflicts. OI then becomes invoked in thinking and communication, but this is often probably quite different from a general, abstract view of what constitutes the "central features" of the organization, which are often viewed as given.

Numerous OI studies (Ravasi and Schultz, 2006; Gioia, Price, Hamilton, and Thomas, 2010) have offered a variety of central features. However typically, even in longitudinal studies that have analyzed changes to OI over time, these are determined via interviews with a relatively small section of the workforce, often fairly senior management. This data is typically supplemented with analysis of archival material, where again senior management will have considerable control over content. Ravasi and Canato (2013) do point to the need to be sensitive to alternative views and narratives in OI research, but we go further and question whether it is typical that the majority of employees would characterize central features in the same way. There is naturally going to be some widely shared agreement around superficial characteristics such as "this is a fast-food company," or "this a very large and old firm," or "this university is research-led," but this does not offer much insight. For Gioia et al. (2013) centrality is so self-evident that it is beyond doubt:

> because there must be some sort of perceived anchors to even talk about identity—
> we do not view the notion of "central" features as particularly controversial unless
> scholars want to pick a fight on arcane philosophical grounds.
>
> (p. 168)

This view reflects a wish for an ordered, clear, and integrated corporate world. Implicitly this echoes a managerial perspective, camouflaged as a self-evident, objective view of how organizations actually function. According to Gioia et al. it would be stupid to even question this idea and only conflict-seeking or esoteric people would "want to pick a fight" about this.

Recently however, some OI researchers have begun to challenge notions of centrality and distinctiveness (Kreiner, Hollensbe, Sheep, Smith, and Kataria, 2014). It is also worth noting that, somewhat paradoxically, even Gioia et al. (2013) do reflect upon the difficulties in defining what is central, because it can be assessed in many ways. We believe that the field would benefit from a more open, emergent approach to OI which is less committed to a set of assumptions that have steered the direction of OI research to date, the key assumption here being that in most organizations there is a shared view of what is central and it is precise enough to have some guiding role in terms of meaning.

The Inter-Relationship between OI, Employee Identification, and Organizational Image

Another assumption (often implicit) is that workers' sense of membership in the organization constitutes some sort of social group that shapes their self-concept and that this is, in part, driven by the identity of the organization. This assumption is rarely considered debatable. The assumption draws upon social identity theory and the original work of Dutton, Dukerich, and Harquail (1994). However, few of the ideas and assumptions which they offered and which are embedded in arguments in more recent studies (e.g., Elsbach and Battacharrya, 2001; Kreiner, Hollensbe, and Sheep, 2006a, 2006b) are labeled as such. Instead, the impression that is created is that argument and logic are grounded in specific factors reflecting self-evident truth. Firstly, there is an organizational identity in the sense of an employee having beliefs about the distinctive, central, and (relatively) enduring attributes of the organization; secondly, employees *sometimes* define themselves via, or at least draw upon, some of the same attributes that they believe define the organization and, thirdly, there is a construed and shared view of the external organizational image, which also contributes to these beliefs.

This logic assumes that employees have a) fairly fixed beliefs (at least in the short and medium time perspective or until something drastic happens) about attributes and, b) that these are distinctive, central, and enduring. But is this actually the case? Alternatively, perhaps employees do not have fixed beliefs, not even at a specific time, but take temporary positions on attributes and, on occasion, express uncertainty and doubt about these attributes (see Kreiner et al. 2006b for such an example); secondly, they relate to these attributes dynamically in terms of events and processes, rather than statically (which has not yet been researched); and thirdly, they are often unsure whether these attributes are distinctive, central, or enduring (again not yet researched).

Some researchers who have adopted a "weak" process perspective (one that methodologically defines process as having a start and end point, for example, Hatch and

Schultz (2002), Ravasi and Schultz (2006), Gioia et al. (2013), have argued that OI construction is less enduring and changes over time. Whilst this does begin to address the idea that OI is more dynamic and contingent, our point goes much further in questioning the beliefs that are assumed to be held by the majority of employees, a point made almost 30 years ago by Pratt (1998). We suggest that these (counter) assumptions, and the research that addressed them would lead to a different account of the relationship between organizational identification and OI.

OI studies also focus upon the relationship and interaction between image and OI, typically assuming that the former affects the latter (Hatch and Schultz 2002; Kjaergaard, Morsing, and Ravasi, 2011). This is assumed to influence organizational identification, a positive image being a key driver behind the latter (Dutton et al., 1994). This is framed as insiders having a homogenous view of the views of outsiders, including the media. Here we note an assumption that a homogenous image affects homogenous insiders. However, perhaps insiders do not hold particularly firm views about the organization possessing an external image? Apart from the relatively few cases of global brands such as Coca Cola, Harvard, Apple etc., could it not be the case that insiders may be unconcerned, uncertain, or confused about what outsiders believe or think? Insiders may, for example, believe that outsiders' perceptions are fickle, vague, and/or fluid, contingent upon the latest media report. Gendron and Spira's (2010) study of the demise of Arthur Andersen in response to the Enron scandal would support this idea.

Further, are all "outsiders" also homogenous? It is likely that a variety of "outsider" groups may have different ideas, and some (many?) may have little or no perception at all of lesser known organizations. It is perhaps different and fluctuating signifiers that are the objects of attention/communication/perception to outsiders. The multitude of images and also how they may change and reflect back on identity within an organization is definitely worthy of more consideration (Gioia, Schultz, and Corley, 2000), but again we argue for a more open approach in OI studies, sensitive to context. Recent research by Kjaergaard et al. (2011) reported the case of Oticon, where insiders felt that media representations of the firm, although celebrating the originality and progressive nature of the firm, were actually quite misleading, but did not warrant correction. Employees recognized that what was being reported was fake and misleading, and this generated some internal ambivalence and uncertainty about OI. This study generally supports the argument that we are making about the need to take nuances, complexities, and ambiguities seriously. The identity aspect here became quite complicated. This is perhaps one of the few studies that has begun to address how complex organizational life can be in identity terms, particularly in the face of the media. OI, identification, and their inter-relationship are far from straightforward.

Much OI research, therefore, takes for granted ideas that employees hold fairly unitary and stable beliefs and perceptions that are clear, distinct, coherent, and measurable about their organizations, themselves, and what outsiders think (Dutton et al., 1994). These can be identified and compared. A need to create an ordered world, devoid of uncertainty, ambivalence, or incoherence is quite apparent in much OI research. Many emphasize the changing nature of images of organizations, and the instabilities and variation of identities (Gioia et al., 2000; Gioia et al., 2013; Humphreys and Brown, 2002), but nevertheless there is an assumption that these are perceived by employees as forming and changing in fairly consistent and similar ways (cf. Gioia et al., 2010). Even when the term "hybrid" identities is invoked for example, this still tends to mean rather distinct and clear categories, "internally" characterized by key traits. Again, we believe that these are debatable assumptions, but unfortunately, in terms of academic publishing, it is usually crucial to demonstrate clear patterns, which often tends to lead to research reaffirming the points of departure of existing OI studies.

Finally, whilst OI researchers recognize that they have to rely to a great extent on employee accounts of their "true" beliefs, perceptions, etc., and methodologically they look for multiple sources for confirmation; nevertheless they maintain that they are "real" in that "they produce effects on behaviour ... and can be studied through *knowledgeable informants*" (Ravasi and Canato, 2013: 191). Here, research skill is needed in helping informants articulate what is often rarely reflected upon and implicit, in order to produce new concepts. However, we believe that there are good reasons to try to make sense of perceptions, or lack of perceptions, in a more open-minded way. For example, do the majority of employees express a clear and strong set of coherent beliefs about attributes, or do they express uncertainty or a variety of beliefs (cf. Kreiner et al., 2014)? Some OI studies have considered multiple identities (e.g., Pratt and Foreman, 2000; Corley and Gioia, 2004; He and Baruch, 2009), but not ambiguous identities or the absence of identity. Why not consider the possibility that the majority of employees might express strong beliefs about the organization being unremarkable? Many organizations may be characterized by isomorphism (DiMaggio and Powell 1983) and not be perceived as distinct by employees. If this were the case, what would the implications be in terms of OI and organizational identification?

These two OI themes of *central characteristics* and *distinctiveness* are associated with a belief in the "thing-like" nature of OI. Next, therefore, we turn to what we see as the reification of OI and the issues that this generates.

THE ESSENCE/REIFICATION PROBLEM SURROUNDING IDENTITY

A closely related issue to the question of the assumptions embedded in OI research, concerns reification. Whilst most OI researchers refer loosely to "constructions," this often conceals an inclination toward essentialism, that is, that there is a core substance behind all surface manifestation of OI, which is central and which impacts a wide range of other phenomena. Gioia et al. (2013) are perhaps most explicit in their review stating:

> If there is any concept that is essential to any member of society, it is the concept of identity. Whether considering an individual (the first epigram), an organization (the second epigram), or even a nation (third epigram) identity is a core concept invoked to make sense and explain action. Indeed identity now has become one of the core concepts in organizational study itself.
>
> (p. 125)

This implies that without OI there is nothing to give meaning to employees or direct action. We have already suggested that this might not be the case, but this is largely screened out because of the reification of OI in existing studies. Even those studies that have focussed upon multiple organizational identities (Humphreys and Brown, 2002; Corley, 2004) suggest that each identity can be characterized. Pratt and Foreman (2000) also give the impression that multiple identities can be dis-aggregated and managed via compartmentalization, aggregation, deletion, and integration.

Despite what we have argued is the inherent slipperiness and unknowability of what is central or core, Gioia et al. (2013) also emphasize:

> Identity at all levels, taps into the apparently fundamental need for all social actors to see themselves as having a sense of "self", to articulate core values, and to act accordingly to deeply rooted assumptions about "who we are as individuals, or-ganizations and, societies", etc.
>
> (p. 127)

This tendency to draw analogies between organizations and individuals is typical of many OI studies and exacerbates the reification problem. Whetten (2006) also notes the tendency in existing sociological classification to rely heavily on an anthropomor-phized treatment of organizations as the basis for conceptual clarification within the OI field arguing that "modern society treats organizations in many respects as if they were individuals" and "the identity of individuals and organizations is an observable subjective state" (p. 221).

From a CMS perspective there are two problems with adopting an anthropomor-phic view. Firstly, it assumes an overly integrated, coherent, and essentialist under-standing of the individual. In a fluid, fragmented, customer/market-oriented society, researchers have argued that people may not be inclined to cling on to an essential sense of self. Instead they may be more engaged in situational, contingent identity work, adapting, revising, and expanding multiple selves, or at least process-sensitive and shifting identity constructions (Alvesson 2010; Gubrium and Holstein 2001; Shotter and Gergen 1989; Weedon 1987). They may also be less concerned about iden-tity issues at work (Alvesson and Robertson, 2016). Secondly, irrespective of appropri-ate ways to describe individuals, organizations operate differently. People enter and exit organizations; organizations form, merge, and split. Although some organizations have long histories, far from all are like individuals in terms of life history: they are typically pluralistic, and seldom monolithic. Most organizations organize around sub-units or have their share of divisions, with multiple logics (Meyer and Rowan, 1977), which may operate only as loosely coupled systems (Weick, 1976) and/or as organized hypocrisies (Brunsson, 2003). Drawing analogies between organizations and individuals is fairly common in organizational theory. Czarniawska-Joerges (1994), for example, states it is common to view an organization as a "superperson." However, we see this treatment exacerbating the reification of OI. In so doing, it is naturally more likely that we are able to identify, label, and measure *it*, but is this appropriate?

If we adopt a processual perspective that views OI as an ongoing accomplishment, we could potentially avoid reification and challenge the idea that all organizations "have" an identity. Without going so far as to claim that process is everything (Chia and Tsoukas 2002), doing OI research could be addressed in a multitude of context-sensitive ways. Gioia et al., (2010) and others (Ravasi and Schultz, 2006), have provided a number of process models and/or longitudinal analyses to capture the formation and changing nature of OI over time. Nevertheless, these studies do not conceptualize OI as an ongoing accomplishment. The process model that Gioia et al. (2010) offer, for example, provides an end-point at which an "optimally distinctive identity" emerges. In Ravasi and Schultz's historical analysis of Bang & Olufsen they identify discrete and different OIs emerging over time. Whilst Gioia et al. (2013) encourage future researchers to consider what they refer to as the "deep processes" around OI formation, they view these as building upon their earlier model, and refer to these as *common* processes across organizations and time. Their suggestions, with an emphasis again on identifying patterns, reinforces the notion of common characteristics etc.

Perhaps, instead, OI could be characterized across two dimensions, such as "implicit" versus "espoused," and homogenous versus heterogeneous beliefs which, when combined, provide four versions of, or possibilities to research? "Implicit" would refer to more or less taken-for-granted, (possibly) difficult-to-articulate beliefs of enduring central, distinctive features, which might be homogenous (shared) or heterogeneous (vary across sub units or even different employees). "Espoused" would refer to common discourses—talk and text—about identity claims, which are again shared more or less across different organizations. These ideas are largely screened out by the reification and entity-like treatment currently afforded in OI studies. However it is important to carefully consider all of these options both theoretically and empirically, to allow for the likelihood that other versions of OI can and do exist.

MANAGERIAL POWER AND OI

From a critical perspective, constructions of OI, whether they vary, endure, or fluctuate, bear strong imprints of power. The issues here are: who is making identity claims about distinctiveness, coherence, and endurance that have consequences for others and for the organizations as a whole (or parts of it)? How are they doing this, and with what effects? As Kenny et al. (2011) write, the interesting question is what:

> claims about the central enduring and distinctive properties of the organization do—that is, what power effects they have?
>
> (p.139)

It is unlikely that a broad consensus inevitably and spontaneously emerges of organizations' possible central features, or even that a synthesis of the views of everyone in an organization might emerge. Management often tries to control what meanings are derived by organizational members, not least in terms of how they want the organization to be understood. Alvesson and Willmott (2002) see identity regulation as a key element of contemporary management, targeting people both directly and also indirectly through OI. Moreover when people express a belief, it may simply be an outcome of the effects of strongly asymmetrical relations that have persisted over time, leading to employees following the "party-line" when talking about the organization's characteristics.

Often employees view the organization quite differently from top management. Non-identification and dis-identification have been addressed (Elsbach 1999), and few people would claim that all organizations are largely populated by workers who view "membership" as key in their work life. But still there is a romantic notion in OI studies that the majority of employees are, if not exactly "happy," then at least content "members" in a large organizational community—a part of a great "we." Issues around exploitation, lay-offs, organizational differentiation, meaningless work, instrumental attitudes, etc. tend to be largely marginalized in the OI literature, and yet we know that today, cynicism appears to be a fairly common attitude in contemporary working life (Naus, van Iterson, and Roe, 2007; Paulsen, 2014).

It is important, therefore, to consider the idea that OI is potentially contested terrain. Formulations and successful imprinting of OI claims tend to serve and reinforce sectional (typically managerial) interests and contribute to the construction of the organizational world in quite specific ways, whilst simultaneously denying other constructions. An actor or a group's claim of "who we are" (i.e., the organization is), may only reflect the actor or group's desire to see the organization in a particular way and strive accordingly. This often involves, if not the wielding of overt power, at least a form of normative control. A few OI studies consider resistance to OI change (cf. Humphreys and Brown, 2002), but they are the exception. Further, even when OI concerns do not surface, there may be forms of domination preventing the airing of issues, due to certain taken-for-granted notions which control employees and create discursive closure by constraining communication which exposes or produces dissent (Deetz, 1992). Power and politics, whether explicit or not, are marginal phenomena in most OI research. It has largely adopted a consensual perspective, often with a fairly strong senior management orientation, which may or may not be made explicit (Ravasi and Schultz, 2006). To some extent this reflects the core assumptions we highlighted at the outset, where common beliefs about the organization are the taken-for-granted starting point and definition of OI studies.

An alternative approach would be to investigate claims made about OI and look at their effects. Not only claims made in public by senior management, but also in other communication, perhaps implicit or even in more covert situations (informal interactions), and across different sections of the workforce. In this way, a potential range of claims about, or around OI could be considered, and the responses (acceptance, open or hidden resistance, cynicism, etc.) and their differing effects could be investigated. This demands a genuine interest in the plurality of managers and workers and ideally, longitudinal, ethnographic research in order to explore situations where OI claims are made, as well as focusing upon the meanings beyond the surface of discourse (talk and text), for example, a form of critical hermeneutics (Alvesson and Sköldberg, 2009). It is also crucial from this perspective to listen carefully to the recipients of OI messages.

In our final section, we step away from the alternative perspectives we have offered for the study of OI and consider the remarkable parallels and overlaps across OI and OC research.

ORGANIZATIONAL CULTURE DRESSED UP AS OI?

Frequently, studies of organizational identity (OI) come very close to themes already covered extensively in organizational culture (OC) without referring to the wealth of work here. For example, Albert, Ashforth, and Dutton (2000) state as organizations become ever more organic:

> In the absence of an externalized bureaucratic structure, it becomes more important to have an internalized cognitive structure of what the organization stands for and where it intends to go—in short, a clear sense of the organization's ...
>
> (p. 13)

Here the reader may expect the missing word to be "*culture*" and a few years earlier this would probably have been the case. But what follows is:

> ... a sense of *identity* [our emphasis] which serves as a rudder for navigating difficult waters.
>
> (Albert et al., 2000: 13)

Gioia et al. (2013) suggest that conceptual and empirical work on OI has been ongoing for the last thirty years but there is almost no evidence in their review that this is the case, other than reference to the original work of Albert and Whetten (1985).

There has, however, been considerable academic interest in organizational culture (OC) since the late 1970s (e.g., Pettigrew, 1979; Smircich, 1983). This work continues today, for example Alvesson (2013), Canato, Ravasi, and Philips (2013). The majority of OI researchers have tended to overlook this. Is this a case of conceptual amnesia? Or is this an academic language game and a re-labeling of OC as OI? Increasingly, there seems to be a tendency in contemporary research generally to attach labels somewhat superficially and place artificial boundaries around areas of study. Hence OI studies will refer to other "OI" studies, that is, ones that are labeled as such and disregard perhaps more relevant studies from other areas of enquiry. There are many similarities between common views on OI and OC.

For example Gioia et al. state that:

> Identity is imputed from expressed values, but the interpretation of those values is not necessarily fixed or stable. Interpretations change, so invocations like "We stand for service!" or "We are an innovating company" mean different things to different groups at different times.
>
> (Gioia et al., 2000: 65)

Yet, Meyerson and Martin made almost the same point about culture 13 years earlier stating:

> "Paradigm" researchers pay attention to inconsistencies, lack of consensus, and non-leader centred sources of cultural content. This approach emphasizes the importance of various subunits ... organizations are not simply a single, monolithic dominant culture. Instead, a culture is composed of a collection of values and manifestations, some of which may be contradictory.
>
> (Meyerson and Martin 1987: 630)

Despite many similarities, numerous OI researchers have aimed to demonstrate that OI and OC are conceptually different and typically neglected the large OC literature. Work by Hatch (1993) and Hatch and Schultz's (1998, 2000, 2002) expressly set out to do this, though always maintaining that OI and OC are inextricably linked and can only be understood when the two concepts are considered in comparison, and relative to one another. Not all OI researchers have agreed with this idea, however. Some argue that OC might be considered an aspect of OI. For example, in their original article on OI, Albert and Whetten (1985) asked the question:

> Is culture part of organizational identity? The relation of culture or any other aspect of an organization to the concept of identity is both an empirical question (does the organization include it among those things that are central, distinctive and enduring?) and a theoretical one (does the theoretical characterization of the organization in question predict that culture will be a central, distinctive, and an enduring aspect of the organization?).
>
> (p. 265–6)

This argument has been clarified more recently by Whetten (2006), viewing culture as "a particularly distinguishing property (e.g., IBM's "culture" ... and "as part of the organization's identity" (p. 228). Albert and Whetten only see organizational culture as a potential part of what members consider to be central, distinctive, and enduring. This reflects a rather impoverished view of culture, reducing it to a thing-like variable; an organizational property, tangential to other aspects of organizations. However, it could be argued that any common understanding of an organization's central, distinctive, and enduring characteristics *is a cultural matter*, that is, a counter-point to what is proposed by Whetten. If the focus is not about trying to provide some objective "measure" of centrality, etc., but instead, an analysis of organizational members' meanings and beliefs, these *are* cultural meanings and can never be considered "external" to culture (cf. Smircich 1983; Alvesson 2013). The various conceptual distinctions that OI researchers have offered do suggest that there is disparity of opinions and also a lack of clarity and coherence in the OI field as to what the inter-relationship is.

The overlap/similarities across OI and OC highlighted in Table 9.1 and the ambiguity that exists around the distinctions that have been made, have created problems for OI researchers. Some researchers "solve" the problem by simply omitting or disregarding the less fashionable OC terminology, that is, they favor identity but simultaneously argue that considerable parallels can be drawn between the two. For example Corley (2004) states:

> it is not surprising that individuals located in different levels of an organization's hierarchy might have different perceptions about what is central and distinctive about the organization. A similar finding is well accepted among researchers interested in organizational culture, another organizational phenomenon based in the social construction of shared beliefs about the organization. Although research has conceptually and empirically distinguished organizational culture from organizational identity (*see Hatch and Schultz, 1998, 2000, and 2002 for detailed discussions of these differences*—emphasis added), drawing parallels between the two helps clarify and support this study's purpose and contributions.

> (p. 1150)

This approach seems to neatly sidestep any academic angst that might be generated by the problems of conceptual overlap, but overestimates the clarity of available distinctions.

More recently Gioia et al. (2013) have offered a specific interpretation of the conceptual distinction between OI and OC stating, with reference to Schein's (1985) levels of culture and state that the *deepest level of culture "is actually better construed as the identity level,"* leading them to:

> prefer to view identity as the generative basis of culture, which is especially evident when one considers that identity formation likely precedes and provides a foundation for the formation of culture.

> (p.176)

Table 9.1 Is OI conceptually different from OC?

Broad similarities between OI and OC	OI	OC
Definition	"OI provides a guide for what an organization's members do and how other organizations should relate to it ... in these dual roles identity serves purposes of both internal coordination as well as external interaction" (Gioia et al., 2013: 161).	"The pattern of basic assumptions— invented, discovered or developed by a given group as it learns to cope with the problems of external adaptation and internal integration—that has worked well enough to be considered valuable and, therefore, to be taught to new members" (Schein, 1982: 9).
Leadership role	"the symbolic construction of corporate identity is communicated to organizational members by top management, but is interpreted and enacted by organizational members based on cultural patterns of the organization" (Hatch & Schultz, 1997: 358).	"the only important thing that leaders do is create and manage culture" (Schein, 2006: 11).
Textual representation	Culture is "relatively more easily placed in the conceptual domains of the contextual, tacit and emergent than is identity which, when compared with culture, appears to be more textual, explicit and instrumental" (Hatch & Schultz 2002: 997).	"a dominant and coherent set of shared values conveyed by such symbolic means as stories, myths, legends, slogans, anecdotes and fairy tales" (Peters & Waterman, 1982: 103)
Multiple interpretations	"Identity is imputed from expressed values, but the interpretation of those values is not necessarily fixed or stable. Interpretations change, so invocations like 'We stand for service!' or 'We are an innovating company' mean different things to different groups at different times (Gioia et al., 2000: 65).	Paradigm2 researchers pay attention to inconsistencies, lack of consensus, and non-leader centred sources of cultural content. This approach emphasizes the importance of various subunits, ... organizations are not simply a single, monolithic dominant culture. Instead, a culture is composed of a collection of values and manifestations, some of which may be contradictory (Martin & Meyerson 1987: 630).
Levels	"Members clearly differentiated between those aspects they believed were the central essence that defined its very nature—core attributes—from those attributes that supported the essence" (Margolis & Hansen, 2002: 2983).	To really understand a culture and to ascertain more completely the group's values and overt behaviour, it is imperative to delve into the underlying assumptions which are typically unconscious but which actually determine how members perceive, think and feel (Schein, 1983: 3).

Here then they argue that identity is actually the foundation or "root" of culture. They appear so confident of their position that several times within their review they refer to previous studies of organizational culture as misrepresentations because, in their opinion, they are identity studies, citing the work of Cook and Yanow (1993), Fiol (1991), and Gagliardi (1986) as evidence of this!

This seems to be a rather misleading claim in the face of the considerable research that has been published within the OC field, which has extensively explored the dynamics, processes, symbols, etc. that lead to the emergence and development of cultural assumptions, values, and norms, without ever mentioning OI (see Kunda, 1992; Meyerson and Martin, 1987; Olie, 1994; Watson, 1994). However in re-labeling Schein's deepest level of OC as OI, a rationale is offered for drawing distinctions between OI and OC research and, perhaps to some extent it also offers self-referential legitimacy for OI research? Their distinction is also soundly contradicted by Hatch and Schultz who view OI as a largely instrumental, discursive (management) tool which is drawn upon to influence internal and external perceptions of the organization.

If we were to "accept" that OI is the foundation for OC, it is notable that very few OI studies rely on anything other than interviews and/or text-based analysis, often taken at face value and targeted for codification, in order to study the ways in which OI forms, changes, is resisted, etc. They are far removed from what Schein (1985) means by basic assumptions. What OI researchers are actually studying tends to be identity *claims* (Ravasi and Canato, 2013), but how does what is claimed in single interviews reveal the foundations of culture? Can interviews so easily reveal basic assumptions, which are partly non-conscious? While some OC research in the past has relied upon interviews and surveys, others (cf. Geertz, 1973; Van Maanen, 1991; Kunda, 1992; Alvesson; 1995; Robertson and Swan, 2003) have adopted varieties of ethnography and interpretivism/social constructionism in order to gather and analyze an array of data (observations, symbols, narrative accounts of working life, stories, gossip, fantasies, etc.) to study the complex interplay between the deepest levels of culture(s) and the organizational norms and symbolic mechanisms through which it might be observed (Alvesson and Berg, 1992). These OC researchers are more interested in the lived experiences of organizational members within organizational cultures, than measuring the strength of it. Rather than looking to identify a unitary, dominant culture, they focus upon the deeper meaning that OC may or may not have for workers. However, this is not easy: it demands extensive participation in the field and in-depth, often recursive analysis of multiple and complex data sources—visual, discursive, and textual—gathered across an organization. Perhaps now is the time for OI researchers to embrace the ethnographic and strong, process-sensitive methods that have been extensively adopted in OC research, if they wish to analyze the foundations of OC. As some in-depth OI studies have shown, identity claims are often multiple, contested, emergent, and fluctuating (Humphreys and Brown, 2002), and future ambitious studies are likely to reveal more of these qualities.

Finally, it could be argued that OI is a step back compared to the in-depth-studies and deeper insights offered by some OC studies. Early OC studies began with a unitary, managerial view of "unique" corporate cultures which was fairly easy to grasp. Subsequent studies moved on to emphasize pluralism, fragmentation, and ambiguity, considering the fine-grained aspects of symbolism and the need to explore the implicit meaning of cultural manifestations (Alvesson, 2013; Martin, 2002). With OI, other than a few notable exceptions, we are therefore in a sense back to where we started in our efforts to explore organizations, their meanings for and effects on employees and managers.

Some Possible Developments

We do then have some fundamental objections to much OI research, based on its assumptions; empirical focus; methodologies commonly deployed, as well as the way in which influential authors have positioned the field, vis. à vis. OC. However, this suggests that it is timely to consider new and interesting research questions within the study of OI. Based on our critique we propose the following:

1. Rather than assuming that there are shared, clear beliefs about OI, researchers should perhaps consider the possibility of beliefs and perceptions being fluid, varying, processual, contingent on issue or theme, open and often poorly expressed. Perhaps there are ambiguities, uncertainties, and ambivalence? We are not suggesting a postmodernist privileging of counter assumptions here, but we believe that more open-ended, careful interpretive work is required, if we are going to advance the study of OI and identification. Such work would neither a priori prescribe unity of meaning, nor fragmented, local meanings. Whether a distinct/unitary or a multitude of contingent views of OI prevail should be investigated, not assumed. Similarly, whether people ascribe to organizations a set of attributes or produce varied, incoherent talk about how the organization is conceived is a valid empirical question.

2. Rather than taking claims as objective properties, instead recognize them for what they are. We can seldom access people's true beliefs simply through using interviews or surveys, but we can study claims and counter-claims—text and talk—preferably in "natural" settings. Immersion in organizations offers opportunities which could yield statements about OI "beyond the level of representations," that is, how talk about the organization may (or may not) reflect beliefs and/or "objective properties." The study of how employees actively attempt to construct versions of OI (if that is what it appears as if they are doing) and how constructions are negotiated, resisted, de-constructed, etc. is also a worthwhile endeavor in order to further develop the field.

3. Rather than focusing upon how employees construct, identify with (or against) organizations, instead study how employees relate to them more openly. This approach may identify social categories in operation in quite unanticipated ways (e.g., Van Maanen and Barley, 1984). Methodologies and key insights from OC studies would be helpful here. How, for example do people respond to claims of OI?

4. Rather than overlooking the fact that OI representations of who "we" are, and what is appropriate for "us" to do (and not do) are made with an often political purpose, instead focus upon the power struggles that these might generate and the effects of such representations on different groups of workers. Acknowledge the organization as a political system, an arena with a diversity of groups and individuals with worldviews, affiliations, loyalties, and sectional interests, all perhaps aiming to (re)produce versions of OI that are aligned with their own convictions and interests. The politics and power associated with OI, may not lead to explicit conflict, but nevertheless may constitute an important aspect of organizational hegemony, and is worth exploring in depth.

5. Rather than elevating OI studies to be a more comprehensive approach to the study of organizations, take cultural analysis seriously and view identity issues in a cultural context. Instead of repressing, sidestepping, or marginalizing OC as being a possible property of OI, view OC as fundamental to any study of OI; seeing OI manifestations as cultural expressions, and positioning the OC context as central. The study of OI manifestations in terms of key cultural aspects—taken-for-granted assumptions, myths, shared (or contested) meanings, key symbols, etc.—through ethnographic work would be a demanding but potentially also a very productive way of taking OI ideas seriously, counteracting the packaging of them in (problematic) definitions which insist that they are central, distinctive, and enduring.

6. Rather than focus on high media profile cases of celebrity or tainted firms that offer ample opportunities to construct particular images of organizations and then consider the effects, instead study organizations that are not subject to intense media interest and consider the variety of member claims that this generates and their effects. This would be challenging as often little is known about some organizations outside of their sectors and/or there are often only vague or varying images. Nevertheless, this could extend theorizing around the relationship between image, brand, and identity.

CONCLUSION

In our task as critical reviewers we have emphasized problems and shortcomings, rather than addressed the positive developments in OI studies. This is done in other chapters. We have contributed to this field (e.g., Alvesson, Ashcraft, and Thomas,

2008; Alvesson and Robertson, 2006) and we do recognize the value of the study of OI and identity in organizations. However, we are concerned about the boundaries that have been constructed around the scope of OI research. These we see as having been largely driven by the original definition of OI and the dominant and what are now considered to be "legitimate" methodologies that are used to study OI. We have also highlighted that we do not see the move from OC to OI studies as a sign of progress, but to cite Hatch and Schultz "a move from the contextual, tacit and emergent to a focus on the more textual, explicit and instrumental." This we see as over-simplifying the complexity of organizational life.

We have pointed to four major problems, recognizing that for all the critiques there are of course, exceptions and exceptional studies:

- Dominant assumptions about the self-evident nature of OI. When for example Gioia et al. (2013) refer to "the fact that insiders *believe* that they have distinctive identities is one of the keys enabling the sense of identity itself" (p. 169) they take the "fact" about what people believe for granted.
- The tendency to reify OI. It is often treated as a thing or a thing-like phenomenon. Even when researchers refer to constructions, these tend to be defined in robust terms, rather than processual, discursive, and interpretation-sensitive constructions. This seems to occur as a result of the methods used.
- A rather top management-centric view of OI. Organizational differentiation, fragmentation, and conflict of possible beliefs/claims (or disbeliefs) around organization's central, distinctive, and enduring attributes may be as, or even more common than senior managements' and consultants' (and some management researchers') desires for well-integrated and homogenous organizations.

Theorizing around OI exhibits a degree of opportunism and fashion-following, particularly with respect to organizational culture (OC) studies. It seems as if sometimes OI is invoked as a way to disregard or marginalize the significant work and developments in OC studies. Many of the core insights and the methodological depth of (some) OC research should not be overlooked by OI researchers.

OI as a field appears to be characterized by a tension between objectivist ideas about the fundamental nature of organizations and the strong possibility that organizational life today is far more complex, characterized by varied and contested identity claims. The latter can perhaps be understood discursively, that is, with a focus on language use, or in relationship to meanings, understandings, and (largely positive) effects. One option is here to consider their interplay, but in a world celebrating branding, images, and mass media representations, we have highlighted that espoused manifestations of OI and meanings related to organizations may, in practice, be quite disconnected (Kjaergaard et al., 2011). OI studies could benefit, then, from taking a more process, situational, and practice-centered as well power-sensitive view of identity statements and how they relate to other themes in organizations. This we believe calls for a much more skeptical and empirically ambitious approach than that favored by the great majority of OI researchers to date.

References

Albert, S., Ashforth, B., and Dutton, J. (2000). "Organizational Identity and Identification." *Academy of Management Review* 25(1): 13–17.

Albert, S. and Whetten, D. (1985). "Organizational Identity." In *Research in Organizational Behaviour*, vol. 7, edited by L. L. Cummings and B. M. Staw, 263–95. Greenwich, CT: JAI Press.

Alvesson, M. (1995). *Management of Knowledge-Intensive Companies*. Berlin/New York: de Gruyter.

Alvesson, M. (2010). "Self-Doubters, Strugglers, Story-Tellers, Surfers and Others: Images of Self-Identity in Organization Studies." *Human Relations* 63(2): 193–217.

Alvesson, M. (2013). *Understanding Organizational Culture*. London: SAGE.

Alvesson, M., Ashcraft, K. L., and Thomas, R. (2008) "Identity Matters: Reflections on the Construction of Identity Scholarship in Organization Studies." *Organization* 15(1): 5–28.

Alvesson, M. and Berg, P. O. (1992) *Corporate Culture and Organizational Symbolism*. Berlin/New York: de Gruyter.

Alvesson, M., Bridgman, T., and Willmott, H. (eds.) (2009). *The Oxford Handbook of Critical Management Studies*. Oxford: Oxford University Press.

Alvesson, M. and Robertson, M. (2006). "The Brightest and the Best: The Role of Elite Identity in Knowledge Intensive Companies." *Organization* 13(2): 195–224.

Alvesson, M. and Robertson, M. (2016). "Money Matters: Teflonic Identity Manoeuvring in the Investment Banking Sector." *Organization Studies* 37: 7–34.

Alvesson, M. and Sandberg, J. (2013). "Has Management Studies Lost its Way? Ideas for More Imaginative and Innovative Research." *Journal of Management Studies* 50(1): 128–52.

Alvesson, M. and Sköldberg, K. (2009) *Reflexive Methodology*, 2nd edn. London: SAGE.

Alvesson, M. and Willmott, H. (2002). "Producing the Appropriate Individual: Identity Regulation as Organizational Control." *Journal of Management Studies* 39(5): 619–44.

Alvesson, M. and Willmott, H. (2012). *Making Sense of Management: A Critical Introduction*. London: SAGE.

Brunsson, N. (2003). "Organized Hypocrisy." In *The Northern Lights: Organization Theory in Scandinavia*, edited by B. Czarniawska and G. Sevón, 201–22. Oslo: Copenhagen Business School Press.

Canato, A., Ravasi, D., and Phillips, N. (2013). "Coerced Practice in Cases of Low Cultural Fit." *Academy of Management Journal* 56: 1724–53.

Chia, R. and Tsoukas, H. (2002). "On Organizational Becoming: Rethinking Organizational Change." *Organization Science* 13(5): 280–97.

Cook, S., and Yanow, D. (1993). "Culture and Organizational Learning." *Journal of Management Inquiry* 2: 373–90.

Corley, K. (2004). "Defined by Our Strategy or Our Culture? Hierarchical Differences in Perceptions of Organizational Identity and Change." *Human Relations* 57(9): 1145–77.

Corley, K. G., and Gioia, D. A. (2004). "Identity Ambiguity and Change in the Wake of a Corporate Spin-Off." *Administrative Science Quarterly* 49(2): 173–208.

Czarniawska-Joerges, B. (1994). "Narratives of Individual and Organizational Identities." In *Communication Yearbook 17*, edited by S. Deetz, 193–221. Thousand Oaks, CA: SAGE.

Deetz, S. (1992). *Democracy in an Age of Corporate Colonization*. Albany: State University of New York Press.

DiMaggio, P. and Powell, W. (1983). "The Iron Cage Revisited: Institutional Isomorphism and Collective Rationality in Organizational Fields." *American Sociological Review* 48: 147–60.

Dutton, J., Dukerich, J. and Harquail, C. (1994). "Organizational Images and Member Identification." *Administrative Science Quarterly* 39: 239–63.

Elsbach, K. (1999). "An Expanded Model of Organizational Identification." *Research in Organizational Behaviour* 21: 163–200.

Elsbach, K. D., and Bhattacharya, C. B. (2001). "Defining Who You Are by What You're Not: Organizational Disidentification and the National Rifle Association." *Organization Science* 12(4): 393–413.

Fiol, C. M. (1991). "Managing Culture as a Competitive Resource: An Identity-Based View of Sustainable Competitive Advantage." *Journal of Management* 17: 191–211.

Foucault, M. (1980). *Power/Knowledge*. New York: Pantheon.

Fournier, V. and Grey, C. (2000). "At the Critical Moment: Conditions and Prospects for Critical Management Studies." *Human Relations* 53(1): 7–32.

Gagliardi, P. (1986). "The Creation and Change of Organizational Cultures: A Conceptual Framework." *Organization Studies* 7: 117–34.

Geertz, C. (1973). *The Interpretation of Culture*. New York: Basic Books.

Gendron, Y. and Spira, L. (2010). "Identity Narratives under Threat: A Study of Former Members of Arthur Andersen." *Accounting, Organizations and Society* 35(3): 275–300.

Gioia, D. A. and Hamilton, A. L. (2016). "Great Debates in Organizational Identity Study." In *The Oxford Handbook of Organizational Identity*, edited by M. G. Pratt, M. Schultz, B. E. Ashforth, and D. Ravasi, 21–38. Oxford: Oxford University Press.

Gioia, D., Patvardhan, S., Hamilton, A., and Corley, K. (2013). "Organizational Identity Formation and Change." *The Academy of Management Annals* 7(1): 123–93.

Gioia, D.A., Price, K. N., Hamilton, A. L., and Thomas, J. B. (2010). "Forging an Identity: An Insider-Outsider Study of Processes Involved in the Formation of Organizational Identity." *Administrative Science Quarterly* 55(1): 1–46.

Gioia, D., Schulz, M., and Corley, K. (2000). "Organizational Identity, Image, and Adaptive Instability." *Academy of Management Review* 25(1): 63–81.

Gubrium, J. and Holstein, J. (2001). "Introduction: Trying Times, Troubled Selves." In *Institutional Selves*, edited by J Gubrium and J. Holstein, 1–20. New York: Oxford University Press.

Hatch, M. J. (1993). "The Dynamics of Organizational Culture." *Academy of Management Review* 18(4): 657–93.

Hatch, M. J. and Schultz, M. (1998). "The Identity of Organizations." In *Identity in Organizations: Developing Theory through Conversations*, edited by D. A. Whetten and P. C. Godfrey, 33–82. Thousand Oaks, CA: SAGE.

Hatch, M. J. and Schultz, M. S. (2000). "Scaling the Tower of Babel: Relational Differences between Identity, Image and Culture in Organizations." In *The Expressive Organization: Linking Identity, Reputation, and the Corporate Brand*, edited by M. Schultz, M. J. Hatch and M. H. Larsen, 13–35. Oxford: Oxford University Press.

Hatch, M. J. and Schulz, M. (2002). "The Dynamics of Organizational Identity." *Human Relations* 55(8): 989–1018.

He, H. and Baruch, Y. (2010). "Organizational Identity and Legitimacy under Major Environmental Changes: Tales of Two UK Building Societies." *British Journal of Management* 21:44–62.

Humphreys, M. and Brown, A. (2002). "Narratives of Organizational Identity and Identification: A Case Study of Hegemony and Resistance." *Organization Studies* 23(3): 421–47.

Kenny, K., Whittle, A., and Willmott, H. (2011). *Understanding Identity and Organizations*. London: SAGE.

Kjærgaard, A., Morsing, M., and Ravasi, D. (2011). "Mediating Identity: A Study of Media Influence on Organizational Identity Construction in a Celebrity Firm." *Journal of Management Studies* 48(3): 514–43.

Kreiner, G, Hollensbe, E., and Sheep, M. (2006a). "On the Edge of Identity: Boundary Dynamics at the Interface of Individual and Organizational Identities." *Human Relations* 59(10): 1315–41.

Kreiner, G. Hollensbe, E., and Sheep, M. (2006b). "Where Is the 'Me' among the 'We'? Identity Work and the Search for Optimal Balance." *Academy of Management Journal* 49(5): 1031–57.

Kreiner, G., Hollensbe, E., Sheep, M., Smith, B., and Kataria, N. (2015). "Elasticity and the Dialectic Tensions of Organizational Identity: How Can We Hold together while We're Pulling apart?" *Academy of Management Journal* 58: 981–1011.

Kunda, G. (1992). *Engineering Culture: Control and Commitment in a High-Tech Corporation*. Philadelphia, PA: Temple University Press.

Martin, J. (2002). *Organizational Culture: Mapping the Terrain*. Thousand Oaks, CA: SAGE.

Meyer, J. and Rowan, B. (1977). "Institutionalized Organizations: Formal Structure as Myth and Ceremony." *American Journal of Sociology* 83: 340–63.

Meyerson, D. and Martin, J. (1987). "Cultural Change: An Integration of Three Different Views." *Journal of Management Studies* 24: 623–48.

Naus, F., van Iterson, A., and Roe, R. (2007). "Organizational Cynicism: Extending the Exit, Voice, Loyalty, and Neglect Model." *Human Relations* 60(5): 683–718.

Olie, R. (1994). "Shades of Culture and Institutions in International Mergers." *Organization Studies* 15: 381–405.

Paulsen, R. (2014). *Empty Labour*. Cambridge: Cambridge University Press.

Pettigrew, A. (1979). "On Studying Organizational Cultures." *Administrative Science Quarterly* 24(4): 570–81.

Pratt, M. (1998). "To Be or Not to Be? The Question of Organizational Identification." In *Identity in Organizations: Developing Theory through Conversations*, edited by D. A. Whetten and P. C. Godfrey, 171–98. Thousand Oaks, CA: SAGE.

Pratt, M. and Foreman, P. (2000). "Classifying Managerial Responses to Multiple Organizational Identities." *Academy of Management Review* 25(1): 18–42.

Ravasi D. and Canato, A. (2013). "How Do I Know Who You Think You Are? A Review of Research Methods on Organizational Identity." *International Journal of Management Reviews* 15: 185–204.

Ravasi, D. and Schultz, M. (2006). "Responding to Organizational Identity Threats: Exploring the Role of Organizational Culture." *Academy of Management Journal* 49: 433–58.

Robertson, M. and Swan, J. (2003). "Control—What Control? Culture and Ambiguity Within a Knowledge Intensive Firm." *Journal of Management Studies* 40(4): 831–58.

Schein, E. (1985). *Organizational Culture and Leadership*. San Francisco: Jossey-Bass.

Shotter, J. and Gergen K. (1989). *Texts of Identity*. London: SAGE.

Smirchich, L. (1983). "Concepts of Culture and Organizational Analysis." *Administrative Science Quarterly* 28: 339–58.

Van Maanen, J. (1991). "The Smile Factory." In *Reframing Organizational Culture,* edited by P. J. Frost, L. F. Moore, M. R. Louis, C. C. Lundberg, and J. Martin, 58–76. Newbury Park, CA: SAGE.

Van Maanen, J. and Barley, S. (1984). "Occupational Communities: Culture and Control in Organizations." In *Research in Organizational Behaviour,* vol. 7, edited by B. M. Staw and L. L. Cummings. Greenwich, CT: JAI Press.

Watson, T. (1994). *In Search of Management.* London: Routledge.

Weick, K. (1976). "Educational Organizations as Loosely Coupled Systems." *Administrative Science Quarterly* 21(1):1–19.

Weedon, C. (1987). *Feminist Practice and Poststructuralist Theory.* Oxford: Basil Blackwell.

Whetten, D. A. (2006). "Albert and Whetten Revisited: Strengthening the Concept of Organizational Identity." *Journal of Management Inquiry* 15(3): 219–34.

SECTION III

INTEGRATIVE MODELS OF OI

CHAPTER 10

OPTIMAL DISTINCTIVENESS REVISITED

an integrative framework for understanding the balance between differentiation and conformity in individual and organizational identities

EZRA ZUCKERMAN

INTRODUCTION

As is true for individual identities, every organizational identity reflects the confluence of two seemingly contradictory tendencies: to *conform* to the practices that other organizations have adopted and to *differentiate* its identity from other organizations. How and why must this challenge be met? And how do the issues at the individual level relate to the organizational level?

The existing literature has advanced three notable approaches that speak to these questions, but they have not been integrated in a productive manner.[1] Perhaps the most influential approach is "optimal distinctiveness" theory (Brewer 1991; Leonardelli, Pickett, and Brewer 2010; Chan, Berger, and van Boven 2012), which argues that human beings have two competing needs: (a) for "assimilation" or "inclusion" in a collectivity; and (b) for "uniqueness" or "differentiation" from other individuals. In general, the theory supposes that these needs are optimally balanced in a small-to-moderate sized group of similar others. The problem with a very small group (e.g., size 1) is that members' needs for inclusion are unsatisfied; conversely, the problem with large groups (as they approach majority status) is that they cannot satisfy a member's need for differentiation.

---

[1] Simmel's (1957) classic analysis of fashion prefigures each of these three contemporary approaches.

The second and third approaches in the literature—what we might call "different audience" theory (Deephouse 1999) and "two-stage valuation" theory[2]—are similar in several respects. First, they were developed to explain identity at the *organizational* level (including products and services of organizations) rather than the individual level. Second, as organizations are emergent social actors that cannot be reduced to their individual members' attributes (thus making it problematic to apply "optimal distinctiveness" approach to the organizational level), these approaches do not derive conformity and differentiation from human needs. Third, while these approaches recognize that organizations are placed into *categories* that distinguish like from unlike, these approaches do not ascribe the pursuit of conformity to collective or *group* membership (but see Porac et al. 2011). Fourth, they see the pursuit of differentiation as driven, not by the internal needs of the organization, but by the external need to compete for the favor of "audiences" of resourceholders. In particular, since customers are willing to pay more for products and services that satisfy them, firms must gain recognition as holding an identity that signals a distinctive capability and commitment to deliver attractive offerings to those customers.

Yet while agreeing on why organizations pursue differentiation, these two externally oriented approaches differ as to why identities generally balance differentiation with conformity. On the one hand, the "different audiences" approach argues that organizations pursue conformity because firms face "institutional" audiences—that is, regulators and other non-market resource providers—as well as a market audience, and the former demand conformity with conventional practices. Note further that by locating pressures for conformity in environmental factors that are particular to organizations, the implication is that insofar as individual identities also reflect a balance between conformity and differentiation, this must be for different reasons. By contrast, the "two-stage valuation" approach sees pressures for both conformity and differentiation as stemming from a single audience. In short, since valuation necessarily involves two stages—categorization of the offerings to be considered and selection from among them—it elicits a response that balances conformity (to demonstrate membership in the category being considered) with differentiation (from other members of that category).

The foregoing raises two questions. First, do we need two sets of theories, one for the organizational level and one for the individual level? Second, insofar as the two externally oriented approaches agree regarding the origins of differentiation but disagree as to the impetus for conformity, can this divergence be reconciled so as to integrate these theories?

---

[2] This approach emerged first in marketing (Urban, Weinberg, and Hauser, 1993), draws on work in cognitive psychology (Payne, 1976), and has been extended and applied in economic sociology (Zuckerman, 1999; Phillips and Zuckerman, 2001; Zuckerman et al., 2003; Phillips et al., 2013). A closely related approach (see the section entitled 'From Human Needs to Identity' where I note a difference) is that of Porac, Thomas, and Baden-Fuller (1989; 2011).

The main argument of this chapter is that the answer to the first question is no and the answer to the second question is yes. In particular, I show how the "two-stage valuation" approach can (a) account for patterns at the individual level, including a key pattern that cannot be understood by "optimal distinctiveness" theory; (b) be extended to incorporate the distinctive observations of the other two approaches; and (c) be extended to illuminate related puzzles.

A Model: How (Not) to Be Cool

In laying out the issues involved, I have found from my doctoral teaching that it is productive (and fun) to turn to an unorthodox "social theorist." In particular, I will now make use of a sketch called "Dragon Man" from the television show *Important Things with Demetri Martin* in an episode entitled "Coolness." Like all very good comedy, it is based on astute observation of the logic implicit in prevalent social patterns (cf. Turco and Zuckerman, forthcoming); and in this case, it successfully captures our intuition for how and why actors balance differentiation and conformity, and the larger social processes involved. I will now proceed to summarize this comedy sketch and then draw lessons from it. It is highly recommended, however, that readers view the sketch themselves.[3]

The sketch begins with a scene-setting shot of the underside of the Manhattan Bridge, with a view of the Brooklyn Bridge and lower Manhattan against the night sky. We are therefore made to understand that the subsequent events take place in the hip, DUMBO ("Down Under the Manhattan Bridge") section of Brooklyn. The next shot is of the inside of a metallic, exterior door, surrounded by unpainted brick walls; presently, we see that this door leads to a rooftop party of hip young men and women. We then hear the voice of a man who is steeling himself to a difficult task. He tells himself in a low, determined voice: "Ok, just be confident. C'mon! It was a good decision. You look great.... Go for it!" At this point in the story, we do not see the protagonist who is giving this internal monologue; instead, the camera acts as his eyes.

The next stage of the story is the protagonist's initial encounter with the partygoers. It begins as we see the door opened by a man who looks startled by the protagonist; the man's look suggests something between disbelief and disgust, and he issues a barely audible, "whoa ..." But this man's reaction is apparently unimportant since he recedes from view and the camera—representing the protagonist's eyes—proceeds toward the center of the action, which most immediately includes three attractive young women chatting over drinks. We also see that the rooftop scene has a gritty feel to it, as evidenced by the graffiti on the concrete walls. An instrumental rock-an-roll

---

[3] In the US the sketch can be accessed here: http://www.cc.com/video-clips/3nhjfp/important-things-with-demetri-martin-the-dragon-man. (Please forgive the advertisement.)

soundtrack begins softly at this point, and the interior monologue continues: "You look cool now. People will notice you. You are cool! You're cool!" The camera then pans across various groups of partygoers: the first set of attractive women offer glances that recall the mix of disbelief and disgust of the first man, but the glances of the next set of partygoers suggest that they are impressed and amazed by the protagonist. The internal monologue continues: "Hello, ladies ... Take a look at this!" At this point, the camera lingers for a moment on a pretty young woman wearing a sleeveless dress (her long hair covers her front in such a way that we see her upper torso with no clothing visible) and we see her reaction as she looks up with a coquettish smile and then—when she presumably catches sight of the protagonist—her look transforms into one of awe. "Now everybody, look at me," the protagonist then says to himself. At this point, the camera pulls back (so that it becomes a third-party, objective observer rather than the protagonist) and we see the pony-tailed back of the protagonist's head with partygoers in the distance looking upon him. The music in the background builds toward a climax as the protagonist exclaims to himself: "Behold! I am ... the dragon man!!" At this point, we finally see what the partygoers see: the face of a young man (played by Demetri Martin) with the image of a red dragon tattooed over his entire face. Martin wears a smirk of self-content on his face as he gazes upon the partygoers with self-satisfaction.

The next stage of the story reinforces the previous stage—that is, the protagonist has achieved his goal of being recognized as cool. The subsequent few seconds show Martin posturing as if he is surveying an adoring public. His expressions suggest someone who knows that he is the center of attention, and deservedly so. Again, the camera lingers on the pretty young woman who acts out an exaggerated look of beguiled astonishment and she is accompanied by a hip-looking handsome young man (in a "hoodie" sweatshirt with the hood over his head) who is entranced by Martin's daring. Martin's interior monologue concludes: "Best eight thousand dollars I ever spent." Then, with the pretty young woman and the hip young man standing before him, Martin speaks out loud for the first time as he challenges an unseen partygoer in the distance: "Yeah, it's real! And it hurt like a [bleeped-out expletive]!" The scene continues some unknown moments later with Martin seated and holding forth as he is surrounded by admiring onlookers. He is holding court, and those surrounding him are paying court. At center stage are the pretty young woman and the hip young man. Martin speaks first, continuing his mock bravado: "It felt *good* though too because it was like yeah! [said with an expression suggesting pain as pleasure] ... like I'm doing this y'know! Like forever!" As he says this, the camera shows the admiring look of the hip young man and then the enraptured look of the pretty young woman. She speaks for the first time, in a soft, admiring voice, *"It's so hard core!"* Their dialogue continues, as the camera continues to show a wide array of partygoers gathered around and listening, paying homage:

MARTIN   It's just nice to make a decision and be like—yes! (with a raised fist)—
   that's me!—You know. Especially on the forehead ... it's all bone you know.
YOUNG WOMAN   You're so brave!
MARTIN [with exaggerated cool]   Yeah, I guess so. Guilty as charged!

Martin then says, "Check this out," as he shows the assembled partygoers that when he sticks his tongue out of the side of his mouth, it appears as if it is the dragon's tongue. The young woman responds with the exaggerated giggle of a toady who is trying to ingratiate herself with a superior. She has become the quintessential "groupie." Their dialogue reaches its climax, as the young woman exclaims adoringly, "I've never met anyone who would do something like that!" Martin responds with a detached look of cool and in a soft voice, "I guess you haven't. Yeah."

But then the scene changes abruptly. The partygoers who are surrounding Martin look up and begin to show evidence of shock in their faces as we hear the squeak of the rooftop door and the dramatic exclamation of a man's voice from the direction of the door: "The dragon has arrived!" We then see the young woman's reaction, as she observes the man who has entered; her expression transforms from one of adoration to one of bewilderment and disappointment. Martin wheels around to see who has entered, and the camera then reveals what he observes—a man played by H. Jon Benjamin with exactly the same dragon tattoo on his face! As the background music reaches another climax, Benjamin's face morphs quickly from one of self-satisfaction to horrified disbelief as he sees Martin looking at him; and Martin's face goes through a similar transformation. We then see the faces of the pretty young woman and then that of the hip young man, as they—and then other partygoers—turn away from Martin with faces that suggest feelings of disbelief, horror, betrayal, and disgust. Martin then looks down in dismay and declares in anguish, "Shit!"

The sketch concludes with a final scene. Martin and Benjamin are now by themselves, at the beer keg, with the other partygoers far from them. One gets the sense that they are being avoided by the others. They try to make small talk.

MARTIN Hey!
BENJAMIN Hey!
MARTIN So ... , uh ... how do you know Dan?
BENJAMIN Oh ... uh. we work at the same temp agency.

Martin responds with an expression that suggests a mixture of indifference and resignation. Benjamin's look is one of shock at his predicament. The scene then ends with the two men "hiding" in their beers; the only thing visible is their twin dragon tattoos and the red cups in their mouths.

KEY IMPLICATIONS FROM MARTIN'S SKETCH

Martin's sketch is highly entertaining. And it also helps set the stage for integrating the three approaches as to why individuals and organizations balance conformity and differentiation as they develop their identities. In particular, let us note several key points.

First, even though the context is individual rather than organizational, the sketch illustrates the basis for differentiation described by both the "two-stage valuation" and the "different audiences" approaches. In short, social exchange among partygoers (and more generally) can be likened to a market for many intents and purposes (e.g., Coleman, 1990). Rather than prices in currency, the terms of exchange may be sex (with the attractive young woman) or esteem (from the hip young man), but the logic is the same. Those who distinguish themselves as "cooler" than others in the eyes of the audience stand to "profit" whereas those who fail to distinguish themselves are in lower demand (e.g., Gould, 2002). The key implication is that *one does not need to assume a need for uniqueness*—as does "optimal distinctiveness" theory—in order to explain why individuals pursue differentiation. Rather, just as firms must stand out from their competitors so they may gain access to resources on favorable terms, the same imperative applies to individuals.

To be sure, the fact that the same, externally driven basis for pursuing differentiation is relevant both for organizations and for individuals does not rule out the possibility that human beings have distinctive drives for uniqueness and assimilation. But now consider a second implication from the sketch—that is, that the optimal group seems to be of size 1.[4] Martin's character is happy when he is the only partygoer with a dragon tattoo and he is miserable when there are two dragon men. He is not seeking membership in a moderately sized group; he wants to stand *alone*. Moreover, Martin is capturing a very general phenomenon here; we are all familiar with the horror of discovering that another person is wearing one's outfit—or hairstyle, etc.—to a party. But this feeling of horror cannot be explained by optimal distinctiveness theory. Indeed, while Chan and colleagues (2012) rework the theory to argue (with supporting evidence) that the need for uniqueness is better satisfied via within-group than between-group differentiation, their version (and that by Brewer and colleagues; see Leonardelli et al., 2010 for review) of the theory still assumes that the *optimal group size* is well above 1. The reason is that as group size declines toward 1, the need for assimilation should become particularly insistent. But this is precisely the driving goal of Martin's protagonist—that is, *to be unrivaled in his coolness*. Thus not only does optimal distinctiveness theory's focus on individual needs render it unhelpful for explaining organizational identity, it also cannot explain a key puzzle of individual identity—why individuals often seek to stand apart.

But can this be explained by the other two approaches? At first blush, the "different audiences" approach would seem better able to address this puzzle. It holds that actors seek uniqueness when they are in a context that is outside the "institutional" domain—that is, a state of (market) competition. And perhaps the rooftop party in Martin's sketch is such a context. But in fact, it is crucial to recognize that Martin's sketch is a story of conformity as much as it is a story of differentiation. Elaboration

---

[4] Here, I am defining "group" as Brewer (1991) does—i.e., the number of people who act in the same way.

on this point clarifies how the *very same audience* can demand a balance between conformity and differentiation, as argued by the "two-stage valuation" approach.

To see why the dragon tattoo involves conformity as well as differentiation, we must see it in the larger context—the time and place when it is depicted and the other actions that could have been taken. Consider first that the use of tattoos to impress upper-middle-class Americans (the larger culture within which these hipsters are a subculture) would have little chance of working ten years earlier (i.e., before the recent vogue in tattoos) or at any other point in American history. Thus Martin's protagonist is very much "conforming" to current styles. And the more this event recedes into history, the more will this sketch seem quaint or perhaps even bizarre. Second, if it is perhaps possible to impress a contemporary audience with a dragon tattoo (obviously, the sketch is a "caricature" of what would in fact impress contemporary hipsters), there are many other tattoos that could provide even greater distinction, but which would less plausibly help to achieve Martin's goal. For example, suppose Martin had tattooed his face with the image of a swastika or a pencil sharpener or a penis. The first image might strike the audience as politically offensive, the second as odd or idiosyncratic, and the third as socially offensive. The choice of a dragon is thus ironically a "safe" choice—one that has a much greater chance of being understood and accepted.

In this respect, Martin captures an important pattern: *what we call acts of differentiation are properly regarded as acts of conformity on most dimensions of difference* used by an audience, with an adjustment on one or two dimensions. This observation is critical and it clarifies why labeling something as conformity or differentiation is a matter of perspective (and also why what appears to be differentiation at a given moment tends to look like conformity when viewed in retrospect). In the case of given names (Lieberson, 2000), we find that whereas new names are created all the time, they tend to follow very standard formats (e.g., all American names are written in Latin letters and they rarely are names strongly associated with pets such as "Fido" or "Spot") and to be part of popular themes (e.g., biblical names, names that start with the letter 'K'; see also Berger et al., 2012). Similarly, new product innovations are typically introduced, not by emphasizing their differences but their similarities to existing products (see Kahl and Yates, 2006; Hargadon and Douglas, 2001; Navis and Glynn, 2011). And Uzzi et al. (2013: 468) find that scientific articles are most impactful when they are highly conventional with an "intrusion of unusual combinations."

The key implication of the foregoing is that *we need a theory that can explain why reception by the very same audience* (for either organizations or individuals) might create incentives for conformity (on most dimensions) together with incentives for differentiation (on a few), as well as why these incentives shift depending on context. I now argue that the "two-stage valuation" approach represents this needed theory. Moreover, it successfully integrates the key insights of the other approaches.

Two-Stage Valuation as Basis
for Theoretical Integration

The foundation of this approach is the two-stage process of selection by audiences and what this implies for those who might wish to impress an audience. To be precise, let us generally assume a social context where there are two types of actors, with potential for exchange between members of each type. What distinguishes each type is that it has the ability to offer a distinctive array of goods and/or services (including social interactions of all kinds) to the other type and/or it has a distinctive set of interests in the goods and services that the other type has to offer. Thus for example, in the typical product or labor market, the exchange is asymmetric, in that one type can be thought of as "candidates" who offer goods and services to attract the interest of an "audience"; audience members, in turn, pay for offerings using a general medium of exchange such as money. And this implies that while audience members are generally judicious in their selection of candidates, candidates are generally indifferent as to audience members, and seek those who will pay them the highest price (but see Ranganathan, 2014; Zuckerman, 2016). Note finally that while it is analytically convenient to consider such cases where candidates and audiences are distinct, the basic logic applies to situations where they are not. In particular, in competing for membership and status (with associated benefits) in a bounded group, the actors are both candidates and audience for one another (e.g., Gould, 2002).

We have already discussed how a demand for differentiation emerges from such a candidate–audience interface. In short, insofar as an audience selects candidates on the basis of their relative performance, this creates an incentive for candidates to distinguish themselves from others as higher performers. To be precise, a "differentiation" strategy involves some kind of modification to a standard offering, with the goal of making the new and improved offering more attractive either to the audience generally (based on shared performance standards)—"vertical differentiation"—or to a particular segment of the audience (based on its particular standards)—"horizontal differentiation" (see e.g., Saloner, Shepard, and Podolny, 2001).[5]

But as discussed in the previous section, differentiation is generally limited to a small set of relevant dimensions of difference. The reason is that even when the ultimate goal of valuation is to select a single candidate, this *selection stage* is necessarily preceded by a *categorization stage*, where the audience defines the set of candidates that it will consider for selection and eliminates all others. At its core, the reason that categorization necessarily precedes selection has to do with the basic computational problem that it takes time and effort to consider various offerings and select the best

---

[5] Thanks to Cat Turco for emphasizing the need to clarify the role of horizontal differentiation.

one.[6] For any given good or service, there are typically numerous alternatives that are used in *extremis*. But in normal situations, they are not "worth" considering. Even if some of them could do just as well or better than alternatives, the time and effort it takes to figure this out is often very large (even for a computer). And so, audiences will economize on such effort by first categorizing on the basis of *indirect indicators that they meet minimal requirements* ("Which offerings look like they can do the job for a reasonable price?") and then selecting their preferred candidate based on further investigation. This in turn implies that even though selection may be made on the basis of a candidate's ability to distinguish her offerings on the audience's performance standards, the candidate's primary, "categorical" imperative (Zuckerman, 1999) is to demonstrate that the audience should consider it a member of the relevant category. And this induces *conformity* with the audience's definition of that category's boundaries.

To recap, the "two-stage valuation" approach predicts that identities will reflect a balance of conformity and differentiation whenever the actors that "own" such identities (be they individuals or organizations) compete with one another for valued resources. Such competition induces differentiation because competition implies selection. Such competition induces conformity because selection requires categorization.

DIFFERENT TYPES OF AUDIENCES AND CONTEXTS

If the two-stage valuation model provides a general framework, it should be able to accommodate empirical patterns that have heretofore been understood in terms of the other two approaches. Or, to put it differently, it should be clear what additional assumptions must be made in order to regard these approaches as special cases of the general framework. To that end, let us now consider the "different audiences" approach and then turn back to "optimal distinctiveness."

The "different audiences" approach hinges on (a) the general observation that some audiences demand conformity and some demand differentiation; and (b) the specific observation that market audiences are examples of the former and institutional audiences are examples of the latter. Our earlier discussion and the larger literature provide strong reasons to doubt this formulation of the specific observation. On the one hand, we have seen that (market) competition generates its own pressures for conformity (as well as differentiation). Indeed, there is by now a large literature on

---

[6] Note that the issue here is not that human beings have a need to categorize, as has been interpreted by some organization theorists (see especially Hannan, Carroll, and Polos, 2007). Rather, categorization is a means for addressing our cognitive/computational limitations and thereby achieving more efficient selection.

categorization in markets that depicts market audiences as inducing substantial conformity.[7] And on the other hand, two of the three types of institutional isomorphism identified by DiMaggio and Powell (1983)—that is, *normative* and *mimetic*—can be readily understood in terms of the two-stage model of valuation (see Zuckerman 1997, Ch. 2). Normative judgment is inextricably intertwined with performance assessment. Audiences use norms to define categories of legitimate/acceptable candidates for consideration on the basis of their performance. And candidates mimic each other in a bid to ensure that their behavior is regarded as normative (i.e., at a minimum level of acceptance) by the audience.

At the same time, it is possible to restate both the general and the specific observations underpinning the "different audiences" approach in a way that can capture what we in fact observe within the "two-stage valuation" framework. The general observation is that some audiences *effectively* emphasize categorization over selection, and thereby induce greater conformity relative to differentiation. The specific observation is that "regulatory" audiences engage solely in categorization; and insofar as they control key resources, they induce conformity with their standards. In particular, let us consider DiMaggio and Powell's (1983) third type of institutional isomorphism—*regulative isomorphism*. The goal of a regulator—whether governmental or nongovernmental—is not to select the most attractive candidate, but rather to qualify or certify candidates for exchange with others. In that sense, a regulator is an agent for other audiences (e.g., consumers), helping them to engage in the categorization stage of valuation. They exist solely as part of a larger selection process, in which they specialize in the categorization stage.

More generally, audiences vary in the extent to which they privilege conformity or differentiation. Consider evidence from two recent studies: (a) Berger and Heath's (2007, 2008) finding that individuals exhibit greater tendency to consume low-popularity products (and to avoid those popular in out-groups) when those products are understood to signal "identity"; and (b) Obukhova, Zuckerman, and Zhang's (2014) observation that in authoritarian societies, a premium is placed on conformity over differentiation, even on seemingly apolitical forms of cultural expression (i.e., given names). The distinction between "identity" products versus more mundane products reflects the fact that audiences in liberal societies generally use a subset of cultural expressions and consumer products (e.g., music players but not toothbrushes) to distinguish more preferred from less preferred exchange partners (in short, for their "coolness"). The distinction between authoritarian and more liberal societies reflects the fact that some audiences are "greedier" than others (Coser, 1974; cf. Phillips et al., 2013) in that they regard virtually all expressions of difference—other than those that demonstrate superior service to them—as indicating *deviance* (i.e., lack of

---

[7] In fact, while much of this literature—what Durand and Paolella (2013) discuss as the "prototype" approach (see especially Hannan et al., 2007)—does not account for why market audiences reward differentiation, this is explicitly captured by the two-stage valuation approach. See Zuckerman (2016) for general review.

commitment to the audience and/or its standards; see Phillips et al., 2013). When such greedy audiences are powerful, they drive differentiation out of a system.

The general implication is that there are indeed different types of audiences and such variation can be productively understood in terms of the two-stage valuation model.[8] More specifically, to understand how and why conformity and differentiation are balanced in a given context, we must know: (a) whether resource-holders tend to focus on regulation (i.e., qualifying some candidates on behalf of audiences that engage in selection) or on selection among qualified candidates (in which case, categorization is important in setting the stage for selection); (b) which resources candidates depend on most; and (c) whether powerful resource-holders are "greedy" in regarding difference as deviance.

FROM HUMAN NEEDS TO IDENTITY

But what about the empirical patterns upon which the "optimal distinctiveness" approach is based? In particular, are there general human needs for assimilation in collectivities and for distinctiveness from others? If so, this would seem to be outside the two-stage valuation framework, as it derives its predictions from audience demands, not the internal features of candidates.

In fact, it is difficult to find results from this literature (see Leonardelli et al., 2010; Chan et al., 2012 for review) that require the positing of such needs. As far as I am aware, such needs are observed only indirectly, via their "activation" by contextual conditions that are manipulated. Accordingly, one can interpret such results in terms of a general need for resources controlled by others, with the contextual manipulations determining whether such resource holders (typically, real or imagined people who collectively control access to group membership and status) focus more on categorization or on selection. To return to the example of authoritarian regimes (see Obukhova et al., 2014), this context induces conformity, not because it activates needs for assimilation but because a regime with no legitimacy rules by force and is therefore fearful of dissent. Conformity is the rule in such a context because citizens depend on a "greedy" audience for life-giving resources.

---

[8] Pontikes (2012) has recently proposed a distinction between two different types of market audiences—"market-takers", represented by consumers, which demand conformity; and "market-makers," represented by venture capitalists, which reward innovation. Two observations allow us to integrate this observation into the current discussion. First, these two audiences are not independent of one another; just as regulators qualify sellers on behalf of consumers, venture capitalists must be understood as working on behalf of consumers, funding the exploration of new ways of creating value for consumers (albeit in ways that allow funded producers to capture significant value for themselves). Second, we have noted how consumers do in fact reward differentiation (on a few dimensions) and it is well known that investors exhibit much conformity in their investment

Thus the contextual effects demonstrated by "optimal distinctiveness" scholars can be interpreted without positing human needs for uniqueness and assimilation. In addition, insofar as there seems to be cross-contextual stability in how individuals respond to the "need for uniqueness" scale (e.g., Timmor and Katz-Navon, 2008), this can be incorporated into the two-stage valuation model once we recognize how the incentives for differentiation vary depending on the individual or organization's position or *established identity*.

To appreciate this point, observe first that attempts at differentiation are always subject to what we might call "valuation risk." Such risk is dramatized by the reactions to Martin when he first enters the party: he ends up being regarded as cool (before Benjamin enters the scene), but the reactions of the partygoers suggest a struggle to decide whether his attempt at differentiation should instead be regarded as an act of *incompetence* (i.e., failure to meet the audience's performance standards) or of *deviance*. In general, aversion to valuation risk greatly reinforces the tendency to limit attempts at differentiation. Accordingly, Porac et al., (2011) argue that there will be no differentiation when it comes to "diagnostic attributes" for a category. In fact however, any differentiation that is truly innovative *necessarily* involves what are sometimes termed descriptive or membership norms.. As Phillips et al. (2013) discuss, there are typically some unconventional practices that have the potential to generate higher performance; such practices violate membership norms only because they have not yet been proven to enhance performance and one must reject conventional practices in order to adopt them. Thus if one can tolerate the valuation risk, unconventional practices hold the promise of eventually earning the highest returns (see Zuckerman, 1999: 1402–3; Reagans and Zuckerman, 2008; cf. Sgourev and Althuizen, 2014).

Moreover, as the literature on "middle-status conformity" (see Phillips and Zuckerman, 2001 for review; cf. Phillips et al., 2013) demonstrates, valuation risk is less salient for the incumbents of two types of social positions: (a) those whose categorical membership is well established and thus "unquestioned" (Hughes, 1946); and (b) those whom the audience already regards as incompetent or deviant. In many systems, these positions are identifiable as the top and bottom rungs of the status hierarchy, as reflected in the public ranking of identities used by the audience. Since a high status identity implies that the actor has exceeded minimal performance standards, the audience does not use membership norms to engage in categorization. And insofar as the lowest status actors are already outside the category, they are essentially forced to pursue alternative audiences (who employ alternative performance standards).

The implication then should be clear. Evidence that an individual's "need for uniqueness" (actually the balance of the purported needs for assimilation and uniqueness) is stable across contexts can be understood as reflecting the individual's occupancy of a fairly stable identity across such contexts (with the identity having meaning in a larger, societal context). To be sure, behavioral proclivities toward more or less differentiation (versus conformity) might not be *directly responsive* to changes in identity (i.e., there might be lag between a sharp increase or decrease in social status and such proclivities). But at the same time, our recognition of a link between social status and such behavioral patterns suggests why they might be relatively stable (no other explanation of this has been proposed to my knowledge), and it suggests how a broader theoretical integration is possible.

Conclusion: Incorporating the Paradoxical Demand for Authenticity

In the foregoing, I have demonstrated how the three approaches to the balance of conformity and differentiation may be integrated to form a more general, robust framework. Of course, many questions remain, and space (and intelligence!) constraints prevent a comprehensive treatment of them. But it seems important to touch briefly on one question that has not been adequately addressed in the past literature, and which seems to be a promising area for future research. In particular, why is it that one dragon man is cool, but two dragon men are pariahs?

To recall, this seems to be a very general issue; we are all familiar with the fear that someone else will be wearing what we are wearing at a party—as well as the shame when that fear is realized. But while we have pointed out the "two-stage valuation" model can account for why the optimal number is 1 (and why differentiation is in fact so limited), it remains unclear why there is such a dramatic difference between 1 and 2. Moreover, especially in the case of organizations (but see Reagans, 2005 at the individual level), past research suggests that the arrival of new members of the same category has a *legitimizing* effect on that category, whereby their unconventional practices (or attributes) are more apt to be recognized as meeting the audience's performance standards (Carroll and Hannan, 1995). As such, we must understand why in some contexts, competition serves to delegitimize instead.

Recent research (see Hahl, Zuckerman, and Kim, 2016) suggests an answer that is fraught with irony. In particular, while the motivation for balancing conformity and differentiation lies in the need to compete for the audience's favor, this *does not mean that the audience wants this motivation to be evident*. To the contrary, many modern audiences prize "moral authenticity," which we may define as obtaining when action appears to be driven by internal rather than external motives. To illustrate, let us again return to Martin's sketch and note what he says to whom. When talking to himself, his narrative focuses on becoming *recognized* as cool, he addresses the primary audience he cares about ("Hello, ladies!"), and he justifies his action in terms of costs and benefits ("Best eight thousand dollars I ever spent"). He is highly instrumental and focused on managing impressions. But when he speaks out loud, he presents himself as motivated by an inner vision. In particular, he begins by combatting the implicit accusation that there is something inauthentic about what he did and justifies his claim to authenticity by citing the costs he undertook without apparent expectation of gain ("Yeah, it's real!

And it hurt like a [bleeped-out expletive]!") And when he holds court, he continues in this vein, suggesting in various ways that he acted out of an internal rather than an external or objective sense of cost and benefit ("It felt good!"), without regard to his future self and his audiences (Like forever!"), and based on a heedless commitment to an ideal ("It's so hard core," sighs the pretty young woman). But then Benjamin arrives, and this narrative is fundamentally undermined. What are the chances that two people would each be so heedless of others, guided solely by an internal compass, but end up with exactly the same result?

The sketch thus reflects a key paradox at the heart of modern Western culture, or to put it more prosaically, in a key premise underlying audience selection of individuals for their cultural expression. In particular, the overriding myth to which audience members subscribe is that what makes us individuals are *inner* differences. To be a "cool" individual according to this myth is to be someone who not only performs well according to the audience's performance criteria (such that others will then follow her lead), but somehow does so without regard to what other people think. The very word "cool" reflects this ideal, in that it suggests that the actor is emotionally indifferent to audience reception. Accordingly, it is problematic when two individuals—who present themselves to the world according to the myth that their external (cultural) expression reflects a distinctive inner vision—present themselves in the same way. What is thereby revealed is that the myth of individualism is indeed myth. The similarity in their behavior signals that they are in fact acting as *candidates* who are highly attuned, and largely conforming, to the performance standards used by the audience.[9]

It is a great paradox that many contemporary audiences evaluate candidates in part on the basis of their capability and commitment to appearing indifferent to audience response. And insofar as this is true, it puts strong pressure on all of us who are beholden to such audiences. Somehow, we must master the ever-shifting challenge of presenting ourselves in a manner that is conventional enough to demonstrate capability and commitment to the audience but different (and indifferent) enough to demonstrate an internal compass. We may prefer such pressures to the pressures for conformity associated with authoritarian regimes (Obukhova et al., 2014). But ours is no less of an iron cage.

Two final notes are in order. First, insofar as moral authenticity is expected of individuals rather than organizations, this would explain why competition is generally more legitimizing in the latter case. In general, organizations are *expected*, and expressly designed, to serve audiences. At the same time, recent research demonstrates that organizations are also prized for their moral authenticity in certain contemporary markets (see e.g., Carroll and Wheaton, 2009; Hahl, forthcoming), a fact that seems driven (at least in part) by individuals' desire to attain "moral authenticity by association,"

---

patterns (see e.g., Navis and Glynn, 2011), if on different dimensions than that exhibited by consumers.

[9] There is also a second-order effect, in that suppliers of cultural material cater to the demand for marginal differentiation, such that insofar as one acquires one's means of cultural expression via the market, one's choices will necessarily be limited.

via consumption of products (Hahl et al., 2016). But much more research is needed on these questions.

Second, consider the following irony: While the "optimal distinctiveness" approach posits that individuals generally seek practices of moderate popularity so as to strike a balance between their inner need for uniqueness versus their inner need for assimilation, we have concluded that audiences (in modern, liberal societies) are often suspicious of people who seem driven by external demands rather than internal needs and desires. So it is not that inner needs are irrelevant in determining the balance between differentiation and conformity. It is that they play a different role than has been posited: such needs are central to *myths* used by audiences to evaluate candidates. The implication is that our attempts to balance conformity and differentiation are motivated by audience pressure to enact myths about internal needs, rather than by true internal needs.

ACKNOWLEDGMENTS

Thanks to Mike Pratt and the other *Handbook* editors for graciously inviting me to contribute to this volume and for their excellent feedback. I am also grateful for the feedback provided by Gino Cattani, Stefan Jonsson, Minjae Kim, Ming Leung, Cat Turco, and Christophe van den Bulte.

REFERENCES

Berger, J., Bradlow, E., Braunstein, A., and Zhang, Y. (2012). "From Karen to Katie: Using Baby Names to Understand Cultural Evolution." *Psychological Science* 20: 1–7.

Berger, J. and Heath, C. (2007). "Where Consumers Diverge from Others: Identity Signaling and Product Domains." *Journal of Consumer Research* 34: 121–34.

Berger, J. and Heath, C. (2008). "Who Drives Divergence? Identity Signaling, Outgroup Dissimilarity, and the Abandonment of Cultural Tastes." *Journal of Personality and Social Psychology* 95: 593–607.

Brewer, M. (1991). "The Social Self: On Being the Same and Being Different at the Same Time." *Personality and Social Psychology Bulletin* 17: 475–82.

Carroll, G. R. and Hannan, M. T. (1995). "Theory Building and Cheap Talk about Legitimation: Reply to Baum and Powell." *American Sociological Review* 60: 539–44.

Carroll, G. R. and Wheaton, D. R. (2009). "The Organizational Construction of Authenticity: An Examination of Contemporary Food and Dining in the U.S." *Research in Organizational Behavior* 29: 255–82.

Chan, C., Berger, J., and van Boven, L. (2012). "Identifiable but Not Identical: Combining Social Identity and Uniqueness Motives in Choice." *Journal of Consumer Research* 39: 561–73.

Coleman, J. S. (1990). *Foundations of Social Theory*. Cambridge, MA: Harvard University Press.

Coser, L. A. (1974). *Greedy Institutions: Patterns of Undivided Commitment*. New York: Free Press.

Deephouse, D. L. 1999. "To Be Different, or to Be the Same? It's a Question (and Theory) of Strategic Balance." *Strategic Management Journal* 20: 147–66.

DiMaggio, P. M. and Powell, W. W. (1983). "The Iron Cage Revisited: Institutional Isomorphism and Collective Rationality in Organizational Fields." *American Sociological Review* 48: 147–60.

Durand, R. and Paolella, L. (2013). "Category Stretching: Reorienting Research on Categories in Strategy, Entrepreneurship, and Organization Theory." *Journal of Management Studies* 50(6): 1100–23.

Gould, R. V. (2002). "The Origins of Status Hierarchies: A Formal Theory and Empirical Test." *American Journal of Sociology* 107: 1143–78.

Hahl, O. "Turning Back the Clock in Baseball: The Increased Prominence of Extrinsic Rewards and Demand for Authenticity." *Organization Science* (forthcoming).

Hahl, O., Zuckerman, E. W., and Kim, T.-Y. (2016). "Why Authenticity Is in Demand: Overcoming High-Status Denigration with Outsider Art." Unpublished manuscript, Carnegie Mellon University Tepper School of Business.

Hannan, M. T., Pólos L., and Carroll, G. R. (2007). *Social Codes and Ecologies: Logics of Organization Theory*. Princeton, NJ: Princeton University Press.

Hargadon, A. and Douglas, Y. (2001). "When Innovations Meet Institutions: Edison and the Design of the Electric Light." *Administrative Science Quarterly* 46: 476–501.

Hughes, E. C. (1946). "The Knitting of Racial Groups in Industry." *American Sociological Review* 11: 512–19.

Kahl, S. and Yates, J. A. (2006). "Radical Incrementalism: Factoring Customer Use into Technological Change." *Academy of Management Proceedings* 1: G1–G6.

Leonardelli, G. J., Pickett, C. L., and Brewer, M. B. (2010). "Optimal Distinctiveness Theory: A Framework for Social Identity, Social Cognition, and Intergroup Relations." In *Advances in Experimental Social Psychology* 43, edited by M. P. Zanna and J. M. Olson, 63–113. Amsterdam: Elsevier.

Lieberson, S. (2000). *A Matter of Taste: How Names, Fashions, and Culture Change*. New Haven, CT: Yale University Press.

Navis, C. and Glynn, M. A. (2011). "Legitimate Distinctiveness and the Entrepreneurial Identity: Influence on Investor Judgments of New Venture Plausibility." *Academy of Management Review* 36: 479–99.

Obukhova, E., Zuckerman, E. W., and Zhang, J. (2014). "When Politics Froze Fashion: The Effect of the Cultural Revolution on Naming in Beijing." *American Journal of Sociology* 120: 555–83.

Payne, J. W. (1976). "Task Complexity and Contingent Processing in Decision Making: An Information Search and Protocol Analysis." *Organizational Behavior and Performance* 16: 166–87.

Phillips, D. J., Turco, C. J., and Zuckerman, E. W. (2013). "Betrayal as Market Boundary: Identity-Based Limits to Diversification among High-Status Corporate Law Firms." *American Journal of Sociology* 118: 1–32.

Phillips, D. J. and Zuckerman, E. W. (2001). "Middle-Status Conformity: Theoretical Restatement and Empirical Demonstration in Two Markets." *American Journal of Sociology* 107: 379–429.

Pontikes, E. G. (2012). "Two Sides of the Same Coin: How Ambiguous Classification Affects Multiple Audience Evaluations." *Administrative Science Quarterly* 57: 81–118.

Porac, J. F., Thomas, H., and Baden-Fuller, C. (1989). "Competitive Groups as Cognitive Communities: The Case of Scottish Knitwear Manufacturers." *Journal of Management Studies* 26: 397–416.

Porac, J. F., Thomas, H., and Baden-Fuller, C. (2011). "Competitive Groups as Cognitive Communities: The Case of Scottish Knitwear Manufacturers Revisited." *Journal of Management Studies* 48: 646–64.

Ranganathan, A. (2014). "The Price is Right? Product Attachment and Price-Setting in the Sale of Handicraft Products in Southern India." Unpublished manuscript, MIT Sloan School of Management.

Reagans, R. (2005). "Preferences, Identity, and Competition: Predicting Tie Strength from Demographic Data." *Management Science* 51: 1374–83.

Reagans, R. E. and Zuckerman., E. W. (2008). "All in the Family: Reply to Burt, Podolny, and van den Rijt, Ban, and Sarkar." *Industrial and Corporate Change* 17: 979–99.

Saloner, G., Shepard, A., and Podolny, J. M. (2001). *Strategic Management.* New York: Wiley.

Sgourev, S. V. and Althuizen, N. (2014). "'Notable' or 'Not Able': When Are Acts of Inconsistency Rewarded?" *American Sociological Review* 79: 282–302.

Simmel, G. (1957). "Fashion." *American Journal of Sociology* 62: 541–58.

Timmor, Y. and Katz-Navon, T. (2008). "Being the Same and Being Different: A Model Explaining New Product Adoption." *Journal of Consumer Behaviour* 7: 249–62.

Turco, C. J. and Zuckerman, E. W. "*Verstehen* for Sociology: Comment on Watts." *American Journal of Sociology* (forthcoming).

Urban, G. L., Weinberg, B. D., and Hauser, J. R. (1993). "Premarket Forecasting of Really-New Products." *Journal of Marketing* 60: 47–60.

Uzzi, B., Mukherjee, S., Stringer, M., and Jones, B. (2013). "Atypical Combinations and Scientific Impact." *Science* 342: 468–72.

Zuckerman, E. W. (1997). "Mediating the Corporate Product: Securities Analysts and the Scope of the Firm." Doctoral Dissertation, University of Chicago.

Zuckerman, E. W. (1999). "The Categorical Imperative: Securities Analysts and the Illegitimacy Discount." *American Journal of Sociology* 104: 1398–438.

Zuckerman, E. W. (2016). "The Categorical Imperative Revisited." *Research in the Sociology of Organizations* (forthcoming).

Zuckerman, E. W., Kim, T.-Y., Ukanwa, K., and von Rittmann, J. (2003). "Robust Identities or Non-Entities? Typecasting in the Feature Film Labor Market." *American Journal of Sociology* 108: 1018–75.

CHAPTER 11

....

BRIDGING AND INTEGRATING THEORIES ON ORGANIZATIONAL IDENTITY

a social interactionist model of organizational identity formation and change

....

JOEP P. CORNELISSEN, S. ALEXANDER HASLAM, AND MIRJAM D. WERNER

THE literature on organizational identity is characterized by a diversity of theoretical traditions. This reflects the broad array of disciplinary domains in which there is interest in the subject—encompassing (but not restricted to) fields of corporate communication, management, marketing, organizational behavior, social and organizational psychology, personnel psychology, human resources, strategy, and institutional theory (e.g., Ashforth and Mael, 1989; Cornelissen et al., 2007; Haslam and Ellemers, 2005). Surveying this broad and varied literature, we observe that three dominant theoretical, or rather meta-theoretical, perspectives on this topic have taken hold: a social constructionist, a social identity, and a social actor conception of organizational identity. Our overall goal in this chapter is to unpack and discuss these three different meta-theoretical perspectives—seeking to identify their different assumptions, premises, and concerns. Furthermore, we argue that individuals in organizations themselves alternate between these three different perspectives as ways of thinking, in the context of their day-to-day sensemaking about organizational life—as they reflect both on issues of an organization's identity and on their own position in relation to a given organizational identity.

More specifically, we aim to do two things. First, we summarize the prior literature on organizational identity and systematically deconstruct the main meta-theoretical perspectives that dominate scholarship in the field. One particular way in which we deconstruct, analyze, and compare these meta-theoretical perspectives is by teasing out and elaborating foundational or root metaphors that are (at least to some extent) implicit in each—a framing metaphor in social constructionist accounts, a categorization metaphor within social identity and ecology scholarship, and a personification metaphor that is at the heart of a social actor conception. We demonstrate how these different root metaphors each come with certain assumptions, drive particular conjectures and inferences, and direct lines of research on organizational identity. Second, we compare and contrast these meta-theories to draw out differences and commonalities and to highlight the potential for closer links and more productive conversations in the future. We also build directly on the commonalities and intersections between the three meta-theories to formulate a parsimonious process model that connects and integrates different strands of organizational identity scholarship. This process model describes the key processes and outcomes of organizational identity formation and change from a social interactionist perspective and provides a viable theoretical framework for future empirical research. Our hope is that this model is a catalyst for theoretical innovation that pushes the boundaries of existing theories and identifies possibilities for greater cross-fertilization and integration in future research.

METAPHORS OF ORGANIZATIONAL IDENTITY

The literature on organizational identity is vast, as evidenced both by this handbook and by previous surveys (e.g., Corley et al., 2006; Cornelissen et al., 2007; Gioia et al., 2013; Haslam and Ellemers, 2005). As a starting point for our survey of organizational identity theory, we first searched through electronic databases (SSCI and EBSCO) for articles in business and management journals that directly mention organizational identity (in the title, abstract, or keywords) and read through the listed papers. We then coded and clustered papers based on theoretical traditions (such as institutional theory, organizational cognition/sensemaking, and social identity) and cross-citation patterns. To structure our thinking, this clustering was also informed by influential recent reviews of the literature (e.g., Corley et al., 2006; Gioia et al., 2013; Haslam and Ellemers, 2005; King et al., 2010; Ravasi and Schultz, 2006; Whetten, 2006). This process led us to settle on three broad codes; *social constructionism, social identity,* and *social actor* theories of organizational identity. We then reread the articles with these broad codes in mind, and coherently assigned articles to each category. This also meant that certain articles were excluded from our review (e.g., those adopting a more critical or discursive psychological perspective).

After settling on these three categories we reread the articles to tease out the broader meta-theories, including key assumptions, focal constructs, and patterns of argumentation. As mentioned, one methodological step here involved identifying the root metaphors associated with each meta-theory. We iteratively went back and forth before we agreed on three root metaphors (along lines suggested by guidelines for thematic analysis; e.g., Braun and Clarke, 2006; Haslam and McGarty, 2014). As we have noted, these are the framing, categorization, and personification metaphors that are each associated with a particular theoretical perspective on organizational identity. We briefly explain each metaphor in turn—as our way of interrogating and capturing different theoretical perspectives on organizational identity—although we refer the reader to alternative articles and publications for more extensive reviews of each metatheory (e.g., Cornelissen et al., 2007; Ravasi and Schultz, 2006; Gioia et al., 2013; Gioia and Hamilton, this volume, Ch. 1).

Organizational Identity as a Frame of Reference

The frame of reference, or framing, notion sees organizational identity as the outcome of an ongoing shared construction of meaning, which in turn creates a collective frame of reference or cognitive orientation that guides individual and collective sensemaking in context (e.g., Dutton and Dukerich, 1991). Research in this tradition defines organizational identity as a jointly constructed cognitive frame (Dutton and Dukerich, 1991; Elsbach and Kramer, 1996), orientation (Brickson, 2005, 2007), or perceptual lens (Dukerich et al., 2002; Gioia and Thomas, 1996; Gioia et al., 2000) for individual and collective sensemaking activities.

Defined in this way, the root metaphor serves to emphasize the way in which individuals cognitively operate from commonly established frames of reference pertaining to "who they are" (which then leads them to *mirror, filter,* and *scan* the organizational environment in certain ways). It points to ways in which their perceptions and behaviors become guided by such frames (as lenses through which to define, see, and interpret the organization in relation to the environment and other organizations). It also addresses the question of why and how individuals detect and understand regularities in their experience of the organization and see such experiences as relatively central, distinctive, and enduring "*givens*" (Albert and Whetten, 1985; Brickson, 2005, 2007; Gioia et al., 2013; cf. March and Simon, 1958).

In this theoretical tradition, researchers are often concerned with the cognitive *products* of social construction—the inter-subjectively defined and objectified frames associated with an organization's identity, which then shape and guide people's subsequent sensemaking (Gioia et al., 2013). There is also a related focus on the *process* of construction; seeking to understand how particular types of social interactions and the symbols and language used within them produce joint cognitive frames (Corley and Gioia, 2004). And whilst the concept of frame may or may not be directly mentioned in this tradition of organizational identity scholarship, it is central to the main focus on understanding the labels and meanings that individuals use to describe themselves and their organization's core attributes (Gioia et al., 2000; Gioia et al., 2013).

Organizational Identity as a Categorization

The categorization perspective considers organizational identity (after Tajfel et al., 1971; Turner, 1982) to be an internalized knowledge structure which develops and can be activated and made salient within a given organizational context. The basic assumption is that individuals categorize themselves and others in terms of their membership of an organization (or a particular organizational unit; e.g., a department or team), and that this categorization is cognitively internalized in such a way that it contributes to a person's sense of self (Turner, 1982).

The focus here is on the way in which organizational members, individually and collectively, activate existing knowledge representations of organizational and group categories (e.g., departments, teams, professions) and develop new ones, in the process coming to define themselves and others in terms of their category membership (Haslam, 2001; Hogg and Terry, 2000; Ashforth and Mael, 1992; Turner and Haslam, 2001). It is understood that this in turn then serves to structure their perceptions and behavior (Haslam, 2004).

The underlying root metaphor is that of a categorization. Individuals are understood to organize themselves and others with reference to a specific grouping, akin to the way in which they would sort natural objects into types (Rosch, 1978; Medin, 1988). Accordingly, organizational members also identify boundaries and contours between these categories that then serve to structure organizational life (e.g., Lau and Murnighan, 1998). The categorization metaphor is most prominent in research on social identity (Haslam, 2001), although more recently ecology and institutional researchers interested in categorization and category dynamics have in effect joined in this research effort (e.g., Hannan et al., 2007). What this accumulating body of research suggests is that questions of identity are often premised on categorizations, and on salient categories, which may furthermore stretch from an individual to group and organizational level of analysis (Haslam et al., 2003), such that the categorized identity becomes a property of a group or of the entire organization, rather than being limited or restricted to the cognitions of an individual (Pratt, 2003).

Organizational Identity as a Personification

The social actor meta-theory has its roots in early institutional work by Selznick (1949, 1957) and Stinchcombe (1965), who emphasized the unique nature of organizations as individual actors with emergent, path-dependent personalities and enduring qualities. Whilst the social actor conception, as a general perspective, can be traced back to earlier writings, it is only recently that the perspective has been formalized and defined as a meta-theory in relation to organizational identity (Whetten, 2006; King et al., 2010; Navis and Glynn, 2010). In particular, Whetten (2006) defined the social actor perspective on organizational identity as referring to a set of external legitimizing claims and behavioral commitments which are path-dependent and binding, and in this way provide the organization with central, enduring, and distinctive characteristics.

The root metaphor underlying social actor theories is one of a personification, whereby an organizational identity involves the attribution of a human-like personality or character to an organization, and which provides organizations with the intentionality, image, and status of being a "social actor" (e.g., Hatch and Schultz, 2002; King et al., 2010; Whetten and Mackey, 2002). The focus here is on *an objectified and externalized sense of a collective self*, such that individuals within and outside the organization automatically refer to and construe the organization as a single actor. Such a personification metaphor compresses the collective nature of an organization (and also all the various individuals working for it) into that of a single actor, who operates (and is seen to operate) in a particular institutional environment where it attempts to differentiate itself from rival firms to gain status, reputation, and legitimacy (Hatch and Schultz, 2002; King et al., 2010; Glynn and Abzug, 2002; Steele and King, 2011).

The root metaphor also gives rise to the objectification and reification of the collective as a single unitary actor in the minds of people both within and outside the organization. For example, individuals will refer to a particular bank or retailer as having taken a particular stance on a given issue, as having expressed certain opinions, or as having done certain things, and so on (Cornelissen, 2008). As such, "the organization is an actor that is, every day, practically, legally, and linguistically granted intentionality and agency" (Steele and King, 2011: 62). The associated argument here is that in modern societies organizations are by law and in common parlance treated as if they are individuals—granting them analogous powers to act and assigning them analogous responsibilities and rights (Christensen and Cornelissen, 2011; Steele and King, 2011; Whetten, 2006).

Taking Stock: Points of Divergence and Contact

Having looked at each of the three root metaphors that are drawn upon in work on organizational identity, in this section we focus on comparing and contrasting them in more detail. Based on what we think are important connections between existing theoretical perspectives, we then go on to elaborate a number of opportunities for progress in the study of organizational identity. Indeed, we believe that the difference in their scope and level of analysis suggests that there are real benefits to be gained from activities that seek, not to drive a wedge between different perspectives, but rather to build on their distinctive strengths in order to advance and enrich scholarship in this area.

Key Differences between the Root Metaphors

Table 11.1 summarizes the key tenets of the root metaphors associated with different theories of organizational identity. Reading across the table, it is apparent that there are a number or more or less important differences between them. In particular, the table highlights the differences in terms of disciplinary roots, primary scope and level of analysis, preferred methodologies for furthering analysis, and the broader set of constructs with which scholars engage.

One significant dimension on which the approaches differ—if only in emphasis—concerns the subjective or objective nature of organizational identity. From a framing perspective, organizational identity involves a jointly constructed frame of reference between individuals within an organization. This joint frame provides meaning to individuals, on an individual (subjective) and collective (inter-subjective) basis, and thereby provides a platform for identification. Researchers operating at this level of analysis tend to conceptualize organizational identity as a "bottom-up" process of meaning construction. Here, researchers generally follow the tenets of social constructionism in which collective thoughts and feelings are seen to result from

Table 11.1 Metaphors of organizational identity

Root metaphor	Frame	Categorization	Personification
Theoretical foundations	Managerial and organizational cognition	Social and cognitive psychology	Institutional theory and cultural sociology
Definition	The jointly constructed shared meanings about the organization which, as a frame of reference, guides individuals' perceptions, thoughts, and behaviors	Individuals' knowledge that they belong to certain groups, together with the emotional and value significance of that group membership	The objective and externalized attribution of an actor status to an organization with a distinct profile and legitimacy
Primary level of analysis	Individual and group (within groups)	Individual and group (inter- and intra-group processes)	Organization
Preferred methodology	Qualitative, Case studies	Quantitative, Experimental	Mixed methods, large-scale archival and content analyses
Associated constructs	Sensemaking/giving, Discourse, Symbols, Meaning, Schema	Categorization, Permeability, Stability, Identification, Salience, Prototypicality, Influence	Image, Reputation, Legitimacy, Status, Visibility

the way in which people interact, and use language and other symbols to create meaning.

A categorization metaphor, in contrast, suggests that organizational identity is a cognitive structure that is internalized in the minds of individuals and shared within groups. As a result, it is not constructed anew or built up in every interaction, but has the capacity to become a relatively persistent feature of the way in which groups think about themselves and others in certain contexts. In this way, even though categorization is understood to be an inherently subjective process, organizational identities nevertheless come to assume the status of objective, stable, and essentialized categories that are internalized by members of the organization and fed forward into future interactions (Haslam et al., 2003).

A personification metaphor goes even one step further in externalizing the very category of the organization, so as to cast it as an objective entity that exists outside and independent of members of the organization (King et al., 2010). Consistent with institutional theory, the result is an assumption that organizational identity is not consciously *invoked* by members of the organization in their thoughts and feelings, but rather is habitually *evoked* by them in their actions and behaviors.

Points of Contact between the Metaphors

When one looks across the three metaphors, it is apparent that, as well as their obvious differences, there are a number of important commonalities and connections between them. In particular, we see that they all focus on ways in which organizational identities are (or come to be seen as) positive and distinctive, and on the consequences of this at individual, group, and organizational levels. Moreover, each metaphor counterposes differentiation and distinctiveness on the one hand with similarity and familiarity on the other. This is perhaps not that surprising given that all perspectives on organizational identity share a root understanding of the *comparative* nature of identity. In addition, Albert and Whetten's (1985) original definition of organizational identity as involving central, enduring, and distinctive features has influenced each strand of theorizing, albeit that these features have been operationalized in different ways—as emergent outcomes of shared meaning construction, as properties of in- and out-group categories, or as relatively stable features of identity claims and commitments. Another point worth noting is that whilst these different metaphors are oftentimes applied to a particular level of analysis, they nonetheless all assume that organizational identities involve joint cognition and behavior that is qualitatively different from that associated with lower-level individual or group identities (Cornelissen et al., 2007; Pratt, 2003).

Drawing on these commonalities, some recent work is also starting to pull together distinct theories of organizational identity with a view to developing richer theorizing that has broader explanatory scope (Gioia et al., 2013; Gioia and Hamilton, this volume, Ch. 1). For example, Gioia et al. (2013: 170) argue for stronger connections between the constructionist and social actor traditions, based on what are seen to be complementary vantage points. Similarly, Ravasi and Schultz (2006: 436) argue that social actor and constructionist perspectives "focus on complementary aspects of the same phenomenon." Where social actor work focuses on identity claims, and presumes that these guide how members of an organization construct a sense of a collective self, the constructionist perspective reflects a more bottom-up, emergent assumption that emphasizes agency and choice in how members (re)negotiate shared interpretations about what their organization is about and what its official identity claims really mean to them (see also Gioia et al., 2013: 160). Accordingly, Ravasi and Schultz (2006: 436) argue for the "juxtaposition of these perspectives" as producing "a more accurate representation of organizational identities as dynamically arising from the interplay between identity claims and understandings."

Toward an Integrative Framework: A Social Interactionist Model of Organizational Identity Formation and Change

Taking this line of thinking one step further, there are, we believe, possibilities for actively seeking to integrate the three metaphors of organizational identity within an integrated framework. Indeed, in the context of organizational identity, one recent approach that has attempted to do just this is presented by Ashforth and colleagues (2011). The process their model describes is one in which individuals have their own intra-subjective identity and dispositions, but then in social settings construct an inter-subjective shared understanding of their social group, which over time may further evolve and transcend individuals and become an institutionalized fiction at the organizational level. In other words, the first part of their model focuses on individuals' sensemaking moving from defining identity in personal terms to defining it in social terms (in terms of "we" rather than "I"), consistent with constructionist and social identity theorizing. The second part of their model focuses on this sensemaking moving from a constructed inter-subjective understanding to an objectified "generic subjective" through repetitive behaviors and the codifying of a common identity through goals, routines, and so on, such that over time an identity becomes "seen as a reified, taken-for-granted reality that is not tied to any particular individual" (Ashforth et al., 2011: 1146).

By elaborating these sub-processes, Ashforth et al. (2013) in effect bridge between the levels of analysis associated with different meta-theories of identity and in a way that offers important direction to the field. For example, their process model is attentive to the way in which in entrepreneurial firms, identities may gradually evolve over time so as to become established and institutionalized (Drori et al., 2009). In addition, they highlight the possible influences and interactions across levels, such as the influence of institutional labels and claims in a particular setting on individual sensemaking and group definitions. They also conceptualize such interactions as recursive:

> Just as the intra-subjective initially enabled and constrained the inter-subjective, which in turn enabled and constrained the generic subjective, so the generic subjective in turn enables and constrains the other subjectivities, thus completing the recursive loop.
>
> (Ashforth et al., 2011: 1147)

Ashforth et al.'s (2011) model highlights a number of outcomes such as the inter-subjective or generic subjective, but it does not yet directly theorize about the associated processes through which organizational identities are constructed and changed. The questions that they leave unanswered relate primarily to how and when a particular bottom-up framing and labeling of the organization's identity acquires institutional status such that this scales up to the organizational level and becomes fully naturalized and taken for granted by members of the organization as well as by stakeholders and other audiences.

Approaching this question requires, we believe, an integrative perspective that combines assumptions and processes associated with all three of the root metaphors that we have been considering. In what follows, we sketch out our own attempt to integrate these within a unified framework that we refer to as a *social interactionist model of organizational identity formation and change* (SIMOI). We label this a social interactionist model because its grounding assumption (shared across all three of the metaphors discussed above) is that identity is the product of recursive interaction between self and society such that each shapes, and is shaped by, the other (Stryker, 1994; Turner and Oakes, 1997). This model is represented schematically in Figure 11.1, and in what follows we discuss its key features. We can here only provide a brief and schematic overview of the model, and we refer the interested reader to a more comprehensive and detailed treatment of the model elsewhere (Haslam et al., 2015).

The key feature of the SIMOI model is that it describes the processes through which an initial socially constructed framing of an inter-subjective group or social identity may eventually scale up to become a property of the organization as a whole. These processes, as we hope to demonstrate, not only cut across but also connect the different meta-theories of organizational identity (social construction, social identity, and social actor). As we have already suggested, one way of connecting these meta-theories is by connecting the root metaphors at the base of each theory so as to provide a more integrative process model of organizational identity formation and change.

Starting with the process of social construction on the ground (see Figure 11.1), the frames that individuals by themselves and in interaction with others produce are in the first instance tentative comparisons. That is, when a particular framing is first produced by individual actors in an organization, the words that are used to describe the organization's identity as well as the original source of these terms refer to specific concepts from different cultural domains. Indeed, from a constructionist standpoint, members of an organization may alternate between a wide range of loosely coupled

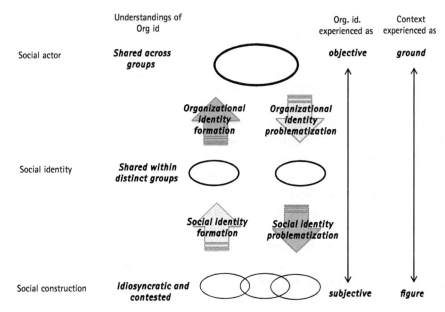

FIGURE 11.1 A social interactionist model of organizational identity formation and change (SIMOI)

and alternative metaphors that they use to describe various aspects of the organization and what they consider as its main attributes (Ashforth et al., 2011). For example, when managers of Bang & Olufsen compared the company's design heritage to the Bauhaus tradition or to poetry (Ravasi and Schultz, 2006), they drew on alternative metaphors to frame the identity of the company.

A particular outcome of these kinds of metaphorical framings and their alignment with the company in question is that the common relational structure (in words and cognitive associations) that forms the interpretation may increase in salience relative to non-aligned or even contrasting aspects of the metaphorical source and target domains (Gentner et al., 2001). Continuing with the example of Bang & Olufsen, Ravasi and Schultz (2006) demonstrate as part of their analysis that the sensemaking of members of the organization became centered on an emerging relational structure that cast Bang & Olufsen as a creative designer of audiovisual equipment and that at the same time, also increasingly served to contrast them from other "producers" in the same industry. The salience of such emerging interpretations in turn tightens the contiguous causal or relational links between parts of a framing (in part, by increasing normative and comparative fit; Oakes et al., 1994), which can furthermore be reinforced through the repeated mention of the framing that serves to communicate and consensualize the emerging identity (Postmes et al., 2005).

In other words, if the source terminology around architecture, poetry, and design is repeatedly aligned with the targeted context of consumer electronics, then the highlighted relational structure (around design operations, outcomes, and markets) may become conventionally associated with the target as an abstracted metaphorical category. The result of this process is that the abstracted category may become "cognitively embedded" as a new collective schema that collectively informs group members' perceptions and behavior (e.g., as a basis for discursive and interactive norms)—in line with social identity and ecological theorizing. This in turn would mean that, over time, Bang & Olufsen and its employees would come to consider themselves, as well as be considered by others, creative designers.

The shift in the overall process is thus a move from tentative and changing comparisons, as an act of social construction, to the abstraction of a collective category, which becomes inter-subjectively recognized and salient at the group and organizational levels (through a process of *social identity formation*; Postmes et al., 2005). Initially, members of the organization will recognize the provisional nature of the framing and often as only one among many others (see Ravasi and Schultz, 2006). Here too, individual organizational members (i.e., opinion leaders) will typically champion particular models of social identity and seek to influence other group members through "sensegiving" to do the same (Ravasi and Schultz, 2006)—with their success being partly a function of their capacity to be seen as people who both represent that identity and who are in a position to take it forward in ways that are seen as (likely to be) positive, distinct, and enduring (Haslam et al., 2011).

As a result of these processes of group-based communication and influence (e.g., Turner, 1991), over time, one particular version of a social or collective identity is likely to become ascendant and to be embedded in the activities, practices, and rituals of the organization (and the broader society in which it is located), such that there is repeated, taken-for-granted, usage of the same labels and metaphors. Within Bang & Olufsen, the various metaphors that had been coined became reduced to common statements and identity frameworks, winnowing the breadth of alternative frames into a number of categorical statements and claims (Ravasi and Schultz, 2006). In this way what was once provisional discourse evolves into common cognitive categories that conventionally and seemingly naturally and automatically describe the collective (Glucksberg et al., 1997). At this stage, such abstracted categories will also have become "objective" and internalized by individuals within (and outside) the organization as organizing principles of thought and experience (i.e., as "given" categories; Haslam et al., 1998) so that, for example, Bang & Olufsen employees consider themselves simply *as* designers. When this happens, such category prototypes lay a strong claim on the social constructions of group members (especially those who identify with the group in question), in effect directing and guiding, not only their personal sensemaking but also their sensegiving for others (cf. Ravasi and Schultz, 2006). In this way, the conventional words and structures of experience associated with the in-group category prime and constrain sensemaking on the ground.

However, the overall process may not end here, as the evolution from frames to categories may continue until the derived category has become fully naturalized, is considered as taken for granted or "given," and loses its connection with the original source domain in the process (Zucker, 1983). This is more likely to occur to the extent that the models of organizational identity that a particular group embraces are seen as legitimate and secure (i.e., so that a given understanding of organizational identity is not politically contested by groups with alternative models) (see Watson, 2008). For this to happen it also requires repeated instantiations of the category, such that it becomes naturalized, and so that employees and other stakeholders of the organization "forget" that it was originally a socially constructed label or frame. This kind of "forgetting" and the subsequent reification of the category may take a significant period of time and the efforts of managers or leaders, as "entrepreneurs of identity," to advance and embed the identity in question (Reicher et al., 2005). When a category is furthermore incorporated into roles, routines, procedures, and so on, this in turn may also facilitate the institutionalization process. Yet the overall outcome of such processes is a dead and taken-for-granted categorization of an organization that is simply considered an "objective" external reality, and where the initially contextual groundings of that categorization have become more or less invisible (Ashforth et al., 2011; Whetten, 2006).

Ashforth et al. (2011: 1146) describe this objectified reality as one of moving from "we think" about our organization in these terms to one where members and stakeholders simply say that the identity of the organization is simply how "it is" (see also Haslam, 2001: 54). The process in other words involves a shift from a conditional and self-referential statement to an objectified and externalized institutional fiction of the organization as a social actor. In both cases, individuals make a categorical statement as to what their organization is (and is not), yet the difference is the objective validity with which it is made and the degree to which the statement has been externalized and grounded in facts and behaviors. In the latter instance, the psychological reality of an in-group category is transformed into the default category for the entire organization, so that everything associated with that organization is personified as exemplary of that category and is attributed with a status and structure that is somewhat independent of the social collective. In other words, it has become a generic subjective—that is, an institutionalized fiction of the organization as an independent social actor.

Nevertheless, speaking to the political dynamics of this process (see also Watson, 2008), it is always possible for this process to operate in reverse. In particular, those who do not buy into the consensual forms of understanding and associated action that have emerged through the above processes are able to interrogate and unpack this historical process in ways that serve to subvert and destabilize it (e.g., by documenting practices of corporate myth-making). At one level, then, organizational identity can be problematized by members of different groups (e.g., workers, shareholders) who have different collective experiences of organizational identity and who are motivated to contest them (in particular, because they are seen as illegitimate and insecure). At another level, particular group-based models of organizational identity can be problematized when—and by those for whom—a particular social identity is seen as unfitting (e.g., because they do not identify with the group in question, or because a high degree of apparent contextual variation makes the categorization too loose).

In summary then, the SIMOI model that we have outlined above lends processual detail to the Ashforth et al. (2011) model by linking the social construction of labels and frames to abstracted collective categories based on the repeated use and group-based alignment of those frames. Future research may help to elaborate the detail of the processes that we have just described. Such research may explore processes of framing, categorization, and institutional reification within various empirical settings, and the degree to which such processes within organizations at any one point constrain sensemaking or leave room for individual agency and the ability to reflect on, and possibly deviate from, a given organizational identity. Such research may also be attentive to further nuances regarding situations where hybrid or multiple identities (Pratt and Foreman, 2000) may emerge through processes of framing, categorization, and personification.

CONCLUDING COMMENTS

In this chapter, we reviewed the metaphorical underpinnings of different theories of organizational identity and the ways in which these metaphors direct and guide theorizing and research on organizational identity. In doing this, we also showed how the emphasis of each of these root metaphors serves to direct thought in a particular direction and along a particular path, and in ways that are often quarantined from research that follows a different line of thinking. This account also goes some way toward explaining the existence of separate research paradigms on organizational identity, rooted in very different sets of (metaphorical) assumptions.

However, in the process of delineating these distinct metaphors, we have also sought to encourage greater reflexivity among researchers within and across disparate research paradigms. In particular, by laying bare the root foundations of different theories, we hope to have signaled ways in which researchers might draw them more closely together. Through our presentation of a SIMOI model, we have also tried to give a concrete form to what might otherwise be only vague and rather uncompelling urgings for dialogue. As it stands, this model provides the broad contours of an integrated research program on organizational identity, and is as such largely untested (at least in its entirety). Nevertheless, it is indicative of what we see as very real prospects for integration and alignment of the key constituent processes of framing, categorization, and personification associated with different theories of organizational identity. We hope that future research will continue in this direction, and thereby afford greater opportunities for productive conversation and collaboration between researchers who from various disciplinary backgrounds share the same interest in studying organizational identity.

REFERENCES

Albert, S. and Whetten, D. A. (1985). "Organizational Identity." In *Research in Organizational Behavior*, vol. 7, edited by L. L. Cummings, and B. M. Staw, 263–95. Greenwich, CT: JAI Press.

Ashforth, B. E. and Mael, F. (1989). "Social Identity Theory and the Organization." *Academy of Management Review* 14: 20–39.

Ashforth, B. E., Rogers, K. M., and Corley, K. G. (2011). "Identity in Organizations: Exploring Cross-Level Dynamics." *Organization Science* 22(5): 1144–56.

Braun, V. and Clarke, V. (2006). "Using Thematic Analysis in Psychology." *Qualitative Research in Psychology* 3: 77–101.

Brickson, S. L. (2005). "Organizational Identity Orientation: Forging a Link between Organizational Identity and Organizations' Relations with Stakeholders." *Administrative Science Quarterly* 50: 576–609.

Brickson, S. L. (2007). "Organizational Identity Orientation: The Genesis of the Role of the Firm and Distinct Forms of Social Value." *Academy of Management Review* 32: 864–88.

Christensen, L. T. and Cornelissen, J. P. (2011). "Corporate and Organizational Communication in Conversation." *Management Communication Quarterly* 25(3): 383–414.

Corley, K. G. and Gioia, D. A. (2004). "Identity Ambiguity and Change in the Wake of a Corporate Spin-Off." *Administrative Science Quarterly* 49(2): 173–208.

Corley, K. G., Harquail, C. V., Pratt, M. G., Glynn, M. A., Fiol, C. M., and Hatch, M. J. (2006). "Guiding Organizational Identity through Aged Adolescence." *Journal of Management Inquiry* 15: 85–99.

Cornelissen, J. P. (2008). "Metonymy in Language about Organizations: A Corpus-Based Study of Company Names." *Journal of Management Studies* 45(1): 79–99.

Cornelissen, J. P., Haslam, S. A., and Balmer, J. M. T. (2007). "Social Identity, Organizational Identity, and Corporate Identity: Towards an Integrated Understanding of Processes, Patternings and Products." *British Journal of Management* 18: S1–S16.

Drori, I., Honig, B., and Sheaffer, Z. (2009). "The Life Cycle of an Internet Firm: Scripts, Legitimacy, and Identity." *Entrepreneurship Theory and Practice* 33: 715–38.

Dukerich, J. M., Golden, B. R., and Shortell, S. M. (2002). "Beauty Is in the Eye of the Beholder: The Impact of Organizational Identification, Identity, and Image on the Cooperative Behavior of Physicians." *Administrative Science Quarterly* 47: 507–33.

Dutton, J. E. and Dukerich, J. M. (1991). "Keeping an Eye on the Mirror: Image and Identity in Organizational Adaptation." *Academy of Management Journal* 34: 517–54.

Elsbach, K. D. and Kramer, R. M. (1996). "Members' Responses to Organizational Identity Threats: Encountering and Countering the *Business Week* Rankings." *Administrative Science Quarterly* 41(3): 442–76.

Gentner, D., Bowdle, B., Wolff, P., and Boronat, C. (2001). "Metaphor Is Like Analogy." In *The Analogical Mind: Perspectives from Cognitive Science*, edited by D. Gentner, K. J. Holyoak and B. N. Kokinov, 199–233. Cambridge, MA: MIT Press.

Gioia, D. A. and Hamilton, A. L. (2016). "Great Debates in Organizational Identity Study." In *The Oxford Handbook of Organizational Identity*, edited by M. G. Pratt, M. Schultz, B. E. Ashforth, and D. Ravasi, 21–38. Oxford: Oxford University Press.

Gioia, D. A., Patvardhan, S. D., Hamilton, A. L., and Corley, K. G. (2013). "Organizational Identity Formation and Change." *The Academy of Management* 7(1): 123–192.

Gioia, D. A., Schultz, M., and Corley, K. G. (2000). "Organizational Identity, Image, and Adaptive Instability." *Academy of Management Review* 25(1): 63–81.

Gioia, D. A., M. Schultz, and K. G. Corley (2002). "On Celebrating the Organizational Identity Metaphor: A Rejoinder to Cornelissen." *British Journal of Management* 13: 269–75.

Glucksberg, S., McGlone, M. S., and Manfredi, D. A. (1997). "Property Attribution in Metaphor Comprehension." *Journal of Memory and Language* 36: 50–67.

Glynn, M. A. (2000). "When Cymbals Become Symbols: Conflict over Organizational Identity within a Symphony Orchestra." *Organization Science*, 11(3): 285–98.

Glynn, M. A. and Abzug, R. (2002). "Institutionalizing Identity: Symbolic Isomorphism and Organizational Names." *Academy of Management Journal* 45: 267–80.

Hannan, M. T., Polos, L., and Carroll, G. R. (2007) *Logics of Organization Theory: Audiences, Code, and Ecologies*. Princeton, NJ: Princeton University.

Haslam, S. A. (2001). *Psychology in Organizations: The Social Identity Approach*. London: SAGE.

Haslam, S. A. (2004). *Psychology in Organisations: The Social Identity Approach*, 2nd edn. London: SAGE.

Haslam, S. A., Cornelissen, J. P., and Werner, M. D. (2015). "A Closer Look at Theories and Metaphors of Organizational Identity: The Detailed Case for a Social Interactionist Model of Organizational Identity Formation and Change." Unpublished manuscript, University of Queensland and Erasmus University.

Haslam, S. A. and Ellemers, N. (2005). "Social Identity in Industrial and Organizational Psychology: Concepts, Controversies and Contributions." In *International Review of Industrial and Organizational Psychology*, vol. 20, edited by G. P. Hodgkinson and J. K. Ford, 39–118. Chichester: Wiley.

Haslam, S. A. and McGarty, C. (2014). *Research Methods and Statistics in Psychology* 2nd edn. London: SAGE.

Haslam, S. A., Postmes, T., and Ellemers, N. (2003). "More than a Metaphor: Organizational Identity Makes Organizational Life Possible." *British Journal of Management* 14: 357–69.

Haslam, S. A., Reicher, S. D., and Platow, M. J. (2011). *The New Psychology of Leadership: Identity, Influence and Power*. Hove: Psychology Press.

Hatch, M. J. and Schultz, M. (2002). "The Dynamics of Organizational Identity." *Human Relations* 55: 989–1018.

Hesse H. (1966). *Models and Analogies in Science*. Notre Dame, IN: Notre Dame University Press.

Hogg M. A. and Terry, D. J. (2000). "Social Identity and Self-Categorization Processes in Organizational Contexts." *Academy of Management Review* 25: 121–40.

King, B. G., Felin, T., and Whetten, D. A. (2010). "Finding the Organization in Organizational Theory: A Meta-Theory of the Organization as a Social Actor." *Organization Science* 21: 290–305.

Lau, D. C. and Murnighan, J. K. (1998). "Demographic Diversity and Faultlines: The Compositional Dynamics of Organizational Groups." *Academy of Management Review* 23: 325–40.

March, J. C. and Simon, H. A. (1958). *Organizations*. New York: Wiley.

Medin, D. L. (1988). "Social Categorization: Structures, Processes, and Purposes." In *Advances in Social Cognition*, vol. 1, edited by T. K. Srull and R. S. Wyer, 119–26. Hillsdale, NJ: Erlbaum.

Navis, C. and Glynn, M. A. (2010). "How New Market Categories Emerge: Temporal Dynamics of Legitimacy, Identity, and Entrepreneurship in Satellite Radio, 1990–2005." *Administrative Science Quarterly* 55(3): 439–71.

Oakes, P. J., Haslam, S. A., and Turner, J. C. (1994). *Stereotyping and Social Reality*. Oxford: Blackwell.

Postmes, T. and Haslam, S. A, and Swaab, R. (2005). "Social Influence in Small Groups: An Interactive Model of Identity Formation." *European Review of Social Psychology* 16: 1–42.

Pratt, M. G. (2003). "Disentangling Collective Identity." In *Identity Issues in Groups: Research in Managing Groups and Teams*, vol. 5, edited by J. Polzer, E. Mannix, and M. Neale, 161–88. Stamford, CT: Elsevier Science.

Pratt, M. and Foreman, P. (2000). "Classifying Managerial Responses to Multiple Organizational Identities." *Academy of Management Review* 25: 18–42.

Ravasi, D. and Schultz, M. J. (2006). "Responding to Organizational Identity Threats: Exploring the Role of Organizational Culture." *Academy of Management Journal* 49: 433–58.

Reicher, S. D., Haslam, S. A., and Hopkins, N. (2005). "Social Identity and the Dynamics of Leadership: Leaders and Followers as Collaborative Agents in the Transformation of Social Reality." *Leadership Quarterly* 16: 547–68.

Rosch, E. (1978). "Principles of Categorization." In *Cognition and Categorization*, edited by E. Rosch and B. B. Lloyd, 27–48. Hillsdale, NJ: Erlbaum.

Selznick, P. (1949). *TVA and the Grass Roots: A Study in the Sociology of Formal Organization*. New York: Harper and Row.

Selznick, P. (1957). *Leadership in Administration*. New York: Harper and Row.

Steele, C. and King, B. G. (2011). "Collective Intentionality in Organizations: A Meta-Ethnography of Identity and Strategizing." *Advances in Group Processes* 28: 59–95.

Stinchcombe, A. L. (1965). "Social Structure and Organizations." In *Handbook of Organizations*, edited by J. G. March, 142–193. Chicago: Rand McNally and Company.

Stryker, S. (1994). "Identity Theory: Its Development, Research Base, and Prospects." *Studies in Symbolic Interaction* 16: 9–20.

Tajfel, H., Flament, C., Billig, M. G., and Bundy, R. F. (1971). "Social Categorization and Intergroup Behaviour." *European Journal of Social Psychology* 1: 149–77.

Turner, J. C. (1982). "Towards a Cognitive Redefinition of the Social Group." In *Social Identity and Intergroup Relations*, edited by H. Tajfel, 15–40. Cambridge: Cambridge University Press.

Turner, J. C. (1991). *Social Influence*. Milton Keynes: Open University Press.

Turner, J. C. and Haslam, S. A. (2001). "Social Identity, Organizations and Leadership." In *Groups at Work: Advances in Theory and Research*, edited by M. E. Turner, 25–65. Hillsdale, NJ: Erlbaum.

Turner, J. C. and Oakes, P. J. (1997). "The Socially Structured Mind." In *The Message of Social Psychology: Perspectives on Mind in Society*, edited by C. McGarty and S. A. Haslam, 355–73. Oxford: Blackwell.

Watson, T. J. (2008). "Managing Identity: Identity Work, Personal Predicaments and Structural Circumstances." *Organization* 15: 121–43.

Whetten, D. A. (2006). "Albert and Whetten Revisited: Strengthening the Concept of Organizational Identity." *Journal of Management Inquiry* 15: 219–34.

Whetten, D. A. and Mackey, A. (2002). "A Social Actor Conception of Organizational Identity and its Implications for the Study of Organizational Reputation." *Business and Society* 41(4): 393–414.

Zucker, L. G. (1983). "Organizations as Institutions." In *Research in the Sociology of Organizations*, edited by S. Bacharach, 1–47. Greenwich, CN: JAI Press.

SECTION IV

HOW INDIVIDUALS RELATE TO OI

CHAPTER 12

··

HOW DO WE COMMUNICATE WHO WE ARE?

examining how organizational identity is conveyed to members

··

BETH S. SCHINOFF, KRISTIE M. ROGERS, AND KEVIN G. CORLEY

IMAGINE a CEO sending an email with a meaningful message to all members of the organization; a trainer proudly displaying a product that best captures the essence of the company in a new employee orientation; a manager providing an opportunity for subordinates to perform a task that represents the core of "who we are." Organizational identity (OI)—"those features of an organization that in the eyes of its members are central to the organization's character ... make the organization distinctive from other similar organizations, and are viewed as having continuity over time" (Gioia, Patvardhan, Hamilton, and Corley, 2013: 125)—is an essential part of organizational life (Albert and Whetten, 1985; Haslam, Postmes, and Ellemers, 2003). While varying perspectives exist on the nature of OI (reviewed in the next section), a rarely discussed assumption across perspectives is that perceptions of organizational identity are more or less shared by members.[1] Despite this widely held notion that individuals, to some degree, share a common sense of "who we are as an organization," the dynamics of how this shared understanding develops is not well understood. This is particularly surprising given the everyday scenarios, like those described in the opening paragraph, indicating that organizational identity is conveyed all around us.

Convergence of identity-related perceptions among members suggests that identity content may be communicated in ways that facilitate such shared understandings.

---

[1] Brickson (2005) empirically demonstrated that members hold consistent views of internal and external organizational identity orientation. Recent work has also shown that, in addition to a common understanding, individuals may also hold divergent perspectives of organizational identity depending on members' attributes, such as the groups to which they belong (Hsu and Elsbach, 2013).

Though scholars have begun to acknowledge that we must further appreciate how collective identity is transmitted (e.g., Ashforth, Rogers, and Corley, 2011), we currently lack a unified understanding of the various ways in which organizational identity is communicated. In particular, we don't fully understand who conveys identity content, and when, why, and how such communication occurs. This chapter is accordingly guided by two primary research questions: "how is organizational identity content communicated to members?" and "what determines the nature of that communication?" To begin answering these questions, we develop a framework of organizational identity communication. We theorize that identity custodians (individuals seen as communicating identity content on behalf of the organization, Howard-Grenville, Metzger, and Meyer, 2013) convey "who we are" through three primary means: saying (i.e., telling members who we are), showing (i.e., modeling behaviors that communicate who we are), and staging (i.e., providing opportunities for members to enact who we are).

We first discuss prototypical forms of saying, showing, and staging in organizational life. Building on this framework, we then present a typology of how the nature of this communication is shaped by two dimensions: the clarity of custodian perceptions of organizational identity content, and the extent to which custodians intentionally communicate identity content to members. This typology reveals four archetypal scenarios that emerge from these two dimensions, ranging from the absence of intentionally saying, showing, or staging to a heavy reliance on intentional communication through all three modes. Finally, we discuss our contributions to the organizational identity literature and implications for future research. To set the stage for the rest of the chapter, we begin with a set of boundary conditions and conceptual clarifications.

Assumptions and Points of Clarification

Scholars with various philosophical beliefs have conceptualized organizational identity differently (see Gioia, 1998). While some view it as a set of claims that belong to the collective and represent who the organization is as a social actor (e.g., King, Felin, and Whetten, 2010; Whetten and Mackey, 2002; Whetten, 2006), others see it as a socially constructed, collectively shared schema that resides within individuals' understandings of the central, distinctive, and more or less enduring aspects of the organization (e.g., Gioia, Schultz, and Corley, 2000). Though traditionally viewed as contradictory, recent scholarship has begun to acknowledge that these two perspectives—social actor and social constructionist, respectively—are indeed complementary, if not mutually recursive (e.g., Ashforth et al., 2011; Gioia, Price, Hamilton, and Thomas, 2010; Howard-Grenville et al., 2013; Ravasi and Schultz, 2006). We agree with these scholars that members see organizations as social actors capable of intentional and self-reflective behavior, but that these same members simultaneously construct their own understandings of organizational identity. As a result, we view organizational identity as a set of institutionalized identity claims that have achieved continuity over time (i.e., statements of what the organization represents; Ashforth and Mael, 1996) and reside in individuals' beliefs, understandings, and enactments of those claims. Indeed, as Ravasi and Schultz (2006) argued, "the juxtaposition of these perspectives will produce a more accurate representation of organizational identities" (p. 436).

Although scholars make these fine-grained distinctions between perspectives, examples from the organizational communications literature and popular press suggest that practitioners may not. Rather, individuals in organizations take as a given that organizational members craft and deliver identity messages on behalf of the organization (e.g., Cheney and Christensen, 2001; Heyman and Lieberman, 2014). We thus see identity claims as constructed at an individual level and interpreted at an individual level, but often released as if they were a statement made by the collective itself, and regularly perceived as representative of "who we are" (Scott and Lane, 2000). For example, as Bosch migrated its Indian brand, MICO, to the Bosch brand, leaders rolled out a two-phase initiative to intentionally communicate Bosch's identity to MICO employees. The company held a meeting with senior executives of MICO, displayed posters with statements such as "I am Bosch," and encouraged team leaders to verbally communicate to employees about the merged identity (Gupta, 2013). In this case, the identity claims espoused by leaders were perceived as "owned" by Bosch as an organization.

But who are the people conveying organizational identity content? Scholars have proposed various terms for those acting on behalf of the organization, such as "stewards" (Davis, Schoorman, and Donaldson, 1997), "agents" (Brickson and Akinlade, 2016), "member-agents" (King et al., 2010; Whetten and Mackey, 2002), and the term we adopt, "identity custodians" (Howard-Grenville et al., 2013). An identity custodian is perceived by other members of an organization as "an actor who focuses attention, invests time, and exerts energy in an effort to sustain a collective identity" (Howard-Grenville et al., 2013: 119).[2] We apply this concept to individuals occupying any level of the organization, though leaders have access to various communication channels via financial, human, and physical resources that other members do not (Fiol, 2002; Howard-Grenville et al., 2013). Identity custodians are seen as speaking and acting on behalf of the organization (King et al., 2010), as organizational identity infuses their behavior with purpose and meaning (Brickson, 2013). Thus, because organizations are themselves not capable of communicating (Shepherd and Sutcliffe, 2015), identity custodians are a crucial conduit for the propagation of organizational identity.

What exactly do identity custodians convey to organizational members? Like Gioia and colleagues (2000), we believe that the content of organizational identity messages consists of labels used to describe identity (i.e., that which is core and distinctive)

---

[2] Our conceptualization of the term "identity custodian" differs slightly from Howard-Grenville et al. (2013) in that they applied the term to individuals actively engaging in extra-role efforts to sustain collective identity, whereas we use the term to refer to anyone *perceived* as communicating organizational identity content through in-role and/or extra-role efforts.

and the meanings underlying those labels (i.e., "what it means to be [that label]"—Petriglieri, 2011: 646). As a boundary condition of this chapter, however, our discussion of identity communication, defined as conveying both organizational identity labels and their respective meanings to organizational members, does not directly examine the nature of the content communicated (e.g., whether the labels and meanings are widely accepted institutionalized messages, or reflective of identity custodians' personal beliefs about the organizational identity content). Relatedly, though scholars have argued that an organization's internally focused identity and externally focused image are intertwined (e.g., Cheney and Christensen, 2001; Dutton and Dukerich, 1991; Price, Gioia, and Corley, 2008), we focus only on communicating identity to organizational members (i.e., employees). We see concerns of image likely influencing the content of individuals' understandings of identity messages, rather than the way that content is conveyed (cf. Gioia et al., 2000; Hatch and Schultz, 1997).

With these clarifications and boundary conditions in mind, we articulate our framework for understanding identity communication. We first examine the primary modes of communicating organizational identity to members: saying, showing, and staging. Following this, we present our typology of when organizational identity custodians employ these particular modes of communicating.

COMMUNICATING ORGANIZATIONAL IDENTITY: SAYING, SHOWING, AND STAGING IDENTITY CONTENT

The literature on organizational identity presents many paths through which identity content is transmitted, such as organizational dress (Pratt and Rafaeli, 1997) and forms of value (Brickson and Akinlade, 2016). Scholars have also examined broader categories like identity media and symbols (Pratt, 2003), and textual, material, and oral forms (Schultz and Hernes, 2013). Our goal is to build on this work by presenting an organizing framework for thinking about how identity custodians communicate all types of identity content: by *saying, showing*, and *staging* "who we are." Each of these three ways provides the wherewithal for individuals to self-reflexively and publicly communicate "'who-am-I-as-an-individual?'/'who-are-we-as-an-organization?'" (Gioia et al., 2013: 127), and, when undertaken intentionally, signal a collective investment in organizational identity as an "irreversible commitment" (Selznick, 1957; Whetten, 2006).

SAYING WHO WE ARE

The first type of identity communication in our framework is "saying" who we are. By saying, we mean sending a verbal or written message containing identity content to one or more members of the organization. This may happen through a variety of means, such as one-on-one exchanges or messages that are mass-communicated to members. Identity custodians likely engage in "saying" because it is a direct form of communicating labels and meanings that is low-cost, easy for custodians to control, and provides the potential to deliver an unambiguous message that requires little effortful interpretation.

We believe that saying primarily occurs through conversations, including narratives and stories (Kärreman and Alvesson, 2001). Indeed, Pratt (2003) observed that, "verbal language is the most obvious means of transmitting identity throughout a collective" (p. 176). For example, in a study of how organizational character was regenerated each year at a summer camp, Birnholtz, Cohen, and Hoch (2007) described how members of Camp Poplar Grove met around the flagpole before each meal for announcements, which became occasions to build a shared sense of "who we are" by "providing everyone with identical information" (p. 325). Additionally, scholars argue that collective identities are comprised of a string of narratives that are told and retold over time (e.g., Brown, 2006; Dailey and Browning, 2014). Narratives indicate not only the present, but also the future and past notions of organizational identity (Czarniawski, 1997; Schultz and Hernes, 2013). Narratives may also reflect individuals' interpretations and/or crafting of the identity content (Kärreman and Alvesson, 2001). Thus, they represent real, idealized, or fantastical representations of who the organization was, currently is, or may become, and serve an integral function in maintaining collective self-esteem and a sense of continuity in identity (Brown and Starkey, 2000).

In addition to narratives, stories, and conversations, identity content communicated by saying also includes widely disseminated information (i.e., mass communications) relevant to "who we are" as an organization. Mass communications are formal espousals of identity that provide members with general exposure to an organization's identity-related content (Alessandri, 2001). Likely forms include emails or letters, white papers, press releases, media articles (e.g., newspapers or magazines), the company's website, and formal corporate espousals of mission or vision statements (such as in annual reports). Most mass communications are spread via identity custodians (e.g., an email on behalf of the CEO to all employees of a company), who lend credence to perceptions of validity and authenticity of the identity content being conveyed (Tyler, 1997). Additionally, unlike conversations, mass communications are often retained in an organization's archives, thus allowing past or desired identity-related information to inform the transmission of current identity-related content. To be sure, Schultz and Hernes (2013) found that corporate (i.e., mass) communications serve as a way of linking an organization's historical memory to its current identity.

SHOWING WHO WE ARE

The second key type of identity communication is "showing" who we are. By showing, we refer to modeled behaviors or displayed artifacts that communicate identity content to one or more members of the organization. Similar to saying, showing may occur through one-on-one interactions and displays of identity-related behaviors or artifacts that identity custodians expect members will observe. We posit that custodians engage in "showing" because it provides grounded examples of identity enactment that convey meaning when identity content is difficult to verbalize.

One primary way that identity content is "shown" is through organizationally sanctioned mentoring programs and informal mentoring relationships, as these are scenarios where members deliberately model identity-related behaviors. A mentoring relationship is traditionally conceptualized as a developmental bond between a more senior individual and a less experienced individual (Higgins and Kram, 2001). This type of connection has been found to be an important source of identity information for organizational members. For example, in a case study of accounting firms, Covaleski, Dirsmith, Heian, and Samuel (1998) described how mentors conveyed appropriate language, professional appearance, and information about organizational politics, among other organizational values.

We see another fundamental way of showing "who we are" as displays of the visible physical objects that serve as symbols of organizational identity content. Displays are likely to take a number of forms that organizational members confront on a daily basis. Exemplar forms include the physical setting of the organization (e.g., Berg and Kreiner, 1990), how individuals dress (Pratt and Raffaeli, 1997; Raffaeli and Pratt, 1993), the images that represent the organization (e.g., corporate logo: Harquail, 2006), and the company's products (e.g., Cappetta and Gioia, 2006). For example, in Apple's internal training program "What Makes Apple, Apple," facilitators show a slide of the highly complicated Google TV remote (Apple's competitor) and contrast it to the Apple TV remote with only three buttons. The remote example communicates what members perceive to be central, distinctive, and more or less enduring attributes of Apple: its commitment to simplicity, functionality, and working collaboratively (Chen, 2014).

Showing may also be the form through which identity custodians are most likely to communicate identity content without realizing it (i.e., unintentionally convey to others "who we are"). Just because individuals are *perceived* by others as being custodians does not mean that they are necessarily aware of their role in conveying organizational identity content. Indeed, members of the organization may observe custodians' day-to-day role enactment, and infer identity-related information. We see this being particularly true for those in highly visible roles (e.g., top management), but also likely for individuals who are especially proximal. As a result, "showing" done by members of one's "tribe"(e.g., one's immediate supervisor, fellow members of one's department, or workgroup) may be particularly impactful in shaping members' perceptions of the organization as a whole (Ashforth and Rogers, 2012).

STAGING WHO WE ARE

The third type of identity communication in our framework is "staging" who we are. Through staging, identity custodians provide a context in which one or more members of the organization can experience or enact organizational identity. Illustratively, when the top management of Japanese pharmaceutical company Eisai wanted employees to understand that the company was adopting "human health care (hhc)"—a focus on patients and their families—as a core value and belief of the firm, they selectively chose 100 managers to participate in a training program. As described by the authors of the case study, "The core of the training was the hands-on experience gained in the geriatric hospital ward, which actualized hhc ... by working on the ward, Eisai employees ... could thereby not merely rationally understand but actually 'feel' the meaning of hhc" (Takeuchi, Nonaka, and Yamazaki, 2011: 5). Another example of staging is provided by hearing aid manufacturer, Oticon. During the reconstruction of Oticon's identity as the "Spaghetti Organization," the CEO invited media into the organization to interview members. Through these interviews, members shaped how the media saw Oticon while also furthering their own understanding of Oticon's organizational identity (Kjaergaard, Morsing, and Ravasi, 2011; Morsing, 1999).

We speculate that custodians engage in staging because enactment provides a visceral experience that being shown or told "who we are" cannot, and might therefore communicate identity content in more memorable and self-referential ways. Also, when done in groups, staging allows members to experience the identity content in similar ways, which may promote a high level of agreement among members' perceptions of the identity content. Staging thus gives custodians an opportunity to provide a common experience whereby members interact with the identity in a controlled way.

Established organizational practices or structures also play a critical function in staging as they likely reflect identity content embedded in an organization's way of operating. Prototypical forms of staging include rituals or routines that are enabled or supported by organizational structures. As Pratt (2003) articulated, "the *content* of [these forms] ... can each convey the central and enduring qualities of a collective" (p. 176). Routines, or "stable patterns of behavior that characterize organizational reactions to variegated, internal or external stimuli" (Zollo and Winter, 2002: 341), are a crucial mechanism for staging identity content. Routines have been posited to both maintain and change an organization's self-concept (Brown and Starkey, 2000), and generate value that transmits organizational identity information to members (Brickson and Akinlade, 2016). For example, in their study of the NY/NJ Port Authority, Dutton and Dukerich (1991) found that members' sense of organizational identity was associated with the enactment of Port Authority's standard ways of dealing with the issue of homelessness. Routines are often connected to rituals, or standardized ways of behaving that communicate meaning (Friedland and Alford, 1991; Islam and Zyphur, 2009). At the University of Cambridge, for instance, members learned the college's implicit hierarchies as they participated in its dining rituals (Dacin, Munir, and Tracey, 2010).

Additionally, the organization's structure itself, or "the formal allocation of work roles and administrative mechanisms to control and integrate work activities" (Child, 1972: 2) plays an important part in identity staging. By setting and reinforcing the organizational structure, custodians provide members opportunities to gain a sense of organizational identity through enacting certain roles or interacting with other members (e.g., sharing new ideas with multiple supervisors from different departments in a matrix-structure organization).

A TYPOLOGY OF ORGANIZATIONAL IDENTITY COMMUNICATION

While our discussion of saying, showing, and staging identity labels and their associated meanings provides a solid basis for understanding the concrete ways that organizational identity is communicated to members, the lack of a coherent understanding of when, why, and how such communication tools are utilized leaves us with an incomplete picture of the phenomenon. Figure 12.1 captures a parsimonious yet holistic typology of two determining factors that help us understand the nature of identity communication: the extent to which identity custodians clearly understand the content of organizational identity and the extent to which these custodians deliberately communicate this content. When organizational identity content is clear to custodians (the vertical axis), they "seem quite sure of the meanings associated with their identity labels and what those meanings mean" (Corley and Gioia, 2004: 186). The horizontal axis, or custodians' intentional communication of organizational identity

	Custodians' Intentional Communication of OI Content	
Custodians' Clarity of OI Content High	"We don't need to communicate who we are" *Characteristics of organizations:* • Mature organizations in stable environments • Organizational identity is deeply embedded *How identity is communicated:* • Identity content is primarily "shown" *Example: Cook & Yanow, 1993*	"This is who we are" *Characteristics of organizations:* • Hold organizational identity and identification in high regard • Have a particularly strong or ideologically driven identity *How identity is communicated:* • Identity content is "said," "shown," and "staged" *Example: Pratt, 2000*
Low	"We don't know who we are" *Characteristics of organizations:* • Changing/new organizations • Organizations in which strategic ambiguity is desirable • Organizations in which the organizational identity is *not* central to completing work *How identity is communicated:* • Identity content is not "said," "shown," nor "staged" *Example: McGinn, 2007*	"We don't know who we are, but will communicate who we might be" *Characteristics of organizations:* • New organizations • Organizations undergoing change • Organizations in which the organizational identity *is* central to completing work *How identity is communicated:* • Identity content is primarily "said" *Example: Corley & Gioia, 2004*
	Low Custodians' Intentional Communication of OI Content High	

FIGURE 12.1 A typology of organizational identity communication

content, denotes deliberate efforts to communicate that identity content to organizational members (Fiol, 2002).

Each axis of the figure represents a continuum; identity custodians may have low (i.e., ambiguous) to high (i.e., unambiguous) clarity of organizational identity content, and the intention behind communicating that identity content may also be low (i.e., unintentional) to high (i.e., deliberate). The four sections of the figure illustrate how organizational identity communication will likely occur (i.e., whether the identity is said, shown, staged, or none of the above) depending on where the identity custodian falls on the axes. We discuss each quadrant below, including the probable characteristics of organizations that fall into each, as well as the benefits and drawbacks of each quadrant.

Low Clarity—Low Intent: "We Don't Know Who We Are"

The bottom left quadrant represents organizations with identity custodians who are low on clarity of identity content and low on intentionally communicating that content to members. Organizations that fall into this quadrant include those with identity custodians who do not devote time and attention to "who we are," and are therefore unlikely to intentionally communicate identity content to members through saying, showing, or staging. At the same time, identity custodians in this quadrant may purposely invoke a strategy of low-clarity–low-deliberateness in order to achieve strategic ambiguity, or the practice of orienting individuals toward conflicting or multiple goals (Eisenberg, 1984). Given the extensive research on the importance of a common set of identity understandings in organizations, it's difficult to imagine why organizations would occupy this quadrant for long without either failing or moving to another quadrant. Considering examples that illustrate "low" on both axes, however, helps clarify the types of organizations that may fall into the low–low quadrant.

First, as noted, being low on the Y-axis (clarity of identity content) suggests that custodians' perceptions of organizational identity are unclear. There are many reasons why this could be the case. The organization may be very new (Gioia et al., 2010) or in the midst of change, making the content ambiguous, fluid, or unsettled (Corley and Gioia, 2004). Identity custodians in these situations may choose not to deliberately communicate identity content, given that there isn't a clear message to communicate. Another reason for a lack of clarity about organizational identity content may be that the most salient or important identity for members is not at the organizational level, but rather the occupational, workgroup, or relational levels. One example is an organization that operates as a collection of independent contractors who are highly identified with their occupation and the relationships through which they complete their work (e.g., a salon where stylists rent their stations and independently build their own client bases through relationships). In these cases, identity custodians might recognize that the strong identity of the occupation supersedes or substitutes for identity at the organizational level. For instance, in a study of longshoremen in California, McGinn (2007) found that longshoremen's sense of identity was derived from their community of longshoremen peers, rather than the different organizations that employed them on a daily basis.

There are both pros and cons when identity custodians don't fully understand the identity and also don't intentionally communicate it. On the pro side, there are circumstances when communicating organizational identity could be an unwise allocation of time and resources, such as when identity at other levels (e.g., workgroup, occupational, relational) is more central to completing work than organizational identity. Additionally, strategic ambiguity is posited to be useful in times of change because it allows members to "fill in" the gaps of any identity-related communication received (Eisenberg, 1984; Eisenberg and Witten, 1987). Furthermore, it is possible that not paying attention to identity communication may generate short-term gains, for example when members are focused on the work at hand and maximizing efficiency, rather than attempting to understand and live the identity content espoused by custodians. On the other hand, because identity communication has been empirically found to strengthen organizational identification (e.g., Smidts, Pruyn, and van Riel, 2001; see also Scott and Lane, 2000), not communicating a clear organizational identity might confuse members about "who we are." Thus, in the absence of identity custodians knowing and communicating "who we are," it is less likely that organizational members will find meaning in their work toward collective goals. In such cases, the lack of identity information might lead members to focus their efforts on other, less organizationally beneficial identities.

High Clarity—Low Intent: "We Don't Need to Communicate Who We Are"

The top left quadrant represents organizations with identity custodians who have a clear sense of organizational identity but do not intentionally communicate identity content to members. In these organizations, members are largely left to their own devices to pick up on implicit identity cues in order to reach their own understandings of "who we are." Because organizational identity content is unambiguous and likely well understood, the most prominent mode of identity communication will be showing, as custodians will not take explicit measures to communicate identity, but will instead (1) behave in ways consistent with the identity, and (2) embed the identity in the symbols and physical space of the organization.

Organizations in this quadrant are likely mature firms with established organizational identity content operating in a stable environment. The expectation that identity content will be clearly perceived without explicit communication suggests that identity has become deeply embedded in daily organizational life. Custodians, by showing organizational identity, promulgate natural convergence around identity content without the need for formal espousals. Unlike those organizations with custodians who explicitly communicate identity content, members of organizations (particularly newcomers) in this quadrant are not expected to understand "who we are" immediately. For example, in their case study of a global leader in flute making, Cook and Yanow (1993) highlighted the implicit ways new members of the Powell flute company came to understand what distinguishes Powell from its closest competitors (in essence, its identity). No formal identity statements were communicated nor was formal training provided; instead, new members had to "learn a new 'feel', a different way of 'handling the pieces'" by watching others perform "the collective activity of the workshop as a whole" (p. 381).

The intersection of having a clear idea of 'who we are' yet not explicitly communicating it has both pros and cons. On the one hand, custodians have a coherent sense of the identity, suggesting that the identity messages that are conveyed will be relatively consistent. On the other hand, implicit understanding of organizational beliefs and values takes time (Ashforth, Harrison, and Sluss, 2014). This implies that members will have to work through ambiguity to gain a sense of the collectively held identity. Additionally, because identity content is primarily conveyed through showing, the inability to triangulate the identity content being communicated may reduce members' shared understanding of identity content, as custodians have no other formal statements of the identity to compare behavior to, and members have no formally espoused messages through which to understand the identity content being shown. However, the clarity of the identity suggests that once implicit communication efforts are successful (likely through showing), the unitary identity will be quite sustainable.

Low Clarity—High Intent: "We Don't Know Who We Are, but Will Communicate Who We Might Be"

The bottom right quadrant represents organizations with custodians who don't have a clear understanding of "who we are" but who still engage in efforts to intentionally communicate organizational identity. In these cases, formally espoused statements of identity are highly common, though the messages themselves are likely conflicting or unclear. To be sure, research suggests that organizations recognizing the potential benefits of an ambiguous identity will continue to send identity-related messages to employees (e.g., Clark, Gioia, Ketchen, and Thomas, 2010). As a result, organizational members may perceive inconsistencies between the espoused identity and the identity actually "in-use" (Argyris and Schon, 1974). Due to the lack of clarity around the identity, enacting and creating contexts for members to reach a shared understanding of "who we are" becomes challenging for custodians. We thus expect that verbal and written modes of communication (i.e., saying) will be most prevalent for organizations in this quadrant.

There are many possible types of organizations in this quadrant. Certain forms of political arenas, or organizations rife with politics and conflict, potentially fall into this quadrant, as individuals may illegitimately abuse their role as identity custodians to build power (Mintzberg, 1985). We may also expect to see organizations in this quadrant with multiple or conflicting identities (e.g., Pratt and Foreman, 2000), those undergoing a major change such as an acquisition or spin-off (e.g., Corley and Gioia, 2004), or those still forming their identity (e.g., Gioia et al., 2010). For instance, when "Bozkinetic" spun off from Fortune 100 parent company, "Bozco," the executive team of Bozkinetic communicated a new vision, mission, strategy, and "commitment statements" in an attempt to help allay the identity ambiguity (Corley and Gioia, 2004).

Like other combinations of identity clarity and intentional communication, this quadrant also breeds both pros and cons. In terms of opportunities, because the identity content itself is somewhat ambiguous even to identity custodians, the lack of clarity may provide the opportunity to customize the identity content being communicated. This, in turn, may further facilitate custodian and member identification with the organization as they have the opportunity to shape how they themselves see the organization. In this way, individuals may perceive a greater overlap between who they are and the organizational narratives they are constructing (Cheney, 1983; Scott and Lane, 2000). At the same time, existing literature has empirically found that organizations with leaders who do not agree on organizational identity content perform poorer than those with leaders who do (Voss, Cable, and Voss, 2006). Ambiguous communication may confuse and frustrate custodians and members alike, who look to organizational identity as a way of gaining their bearings in the organizational context and as a lens for interpreting organizational life (Ashforth, 2001; Corley and Gioia, 2004). Thus, when custodians espouse unclear messages about "who we are," it may lead to sustained disjointed understandings of organizational identity. Furthermore, depending on the intensity and pervasiveness of the political arena mentioned above, organizations "captured by conflict" are thought to be unsustainable (Mintzberg, 1985: 133).

High Clarity—High Intent: "This Is Who We Are"

The top right quadrant represents organizations with custodians who have a clear perception of organizational identity and intentionally communicate that understanding. Organizations that fall into this quadrant likely have custodians who hold organizational identity in high regard because they value communicating a cohesive message. In this quadrant, custodians are most likely to engage in all three modes of communicating identity: saying, showing, and staging. Utilizing all three communication approaches maximizes the likelihood that identity content is effectively and accurately conveyed and facilitates triangulation that fosters a cohesive message to members.

There are noteworthy characteristics of organizations that fall into this quadrant. First, identity custodians in these organizations likely value member identification and the positive outcomes that tend to follow (Ashforth, Harrison, and Corley, 2008),

and are motivated to communicate identity content in hopes of "cueing" member identification (Scott and Lane, 2000). For example, Pratt (2000) describes how Amway, a
network marketing organization, fostered identification among new Amway distributors through "dream building." In dream building, individuals are exposed to dreams
through written, visual, and audio means. Dreams are also staged in "dream-building
sessions" and reinforced through strong mentoring relationships. A second type of
organization that may fall into this quadrant is one with identity custodians who are
motivated to maintain a strong distinctive or ideologically driven identity. For instance, Greil and Rudy (1984) provide examples such as Alcoholics Anonymous or
new religious movements, referred to as identity transformation organizations (ITOs),
where communicating identity is especially crucial to the organization's success. In
extreme cases, ITOs facilitate "encapsulation" where "the organization attempts to
create a situation in which the reality it proffers is the only game in town" (Greil and
Rudy, 1984: 263). ITOs surround newcomers with individuals who can "lend credence
to their new world view" (Greil and Rudy, 1984: 264), likely through saying, showing,
and staging identity content.

The major advantage of intentionally communicating a clear identity is the resulting consensus achieved—all members are ostensibly "on the same page." On the other
hand, organizations with custodians who deliberately communicate clear content (especially in a fervent manner) potentially emphasize organizational identity to such
an extreme that members' personal identities are divested, creating angst and resent-
ment, or possibly over-identification with the organization (Ashforth, 2001). Cable,
Gino, and Staats (2013) suggest that more positive organizational outcomes (i.e.,
greater customer satisfaction and employee retention) occur when personal identities are also emphasized during the socialization process, which, given the emphasis
on communicating organizational identity, may be challenging for members in this
quadrant to do.

DISCUSSION

How are answers to the question "who are we?" conveyed to organizational members? In this chapter, we suggest that there are identity custodians in organizations
who are seen as capable and legitimate communicators of the organization's deepest
held meanings and beliefs. These custodians convey organizational identity in three
primary ways: by saying "who we are," showing "who we are," and staging contexts
for members to embody "who we are." We theorize that there are some organizations
where identity custodians do not understand identity content well and also have little
intention of communicating it. In these contexts, organizational identity is neither
said, shown, nor staged. At the other end of the spectrum, we paint a picture of organizations with custodians who have a very clear sense of organizational identity and
who are highly intentional in communicating that identity content, indicating that

identity content is so solidly embedded in the organization that custodians can create contexts (i.e., staging) in which members enact the identity. In between these two extremes, custodians likely engage in saying or showing, as the lack of clarity or lack of intentional communication of organizational identity content suggests that they only have the tools to do one or the other.

Implications for Theory and Future Research

We see our implications for theory as twofold, and highlight the ways that each implication may shape future research on organizational identity. First, our framework stresses the important role of individual custodians to better elucidate the cross-level processes inherent in organizational identity. While more research is needed to understand these custodians and their role in the organization, we believe our theorizing on custodians' role in identity communication serves as an important theoretical foray into the cross-level dynamics of organizational identity and how individuals "interact" with identity content. That is, our typology of saying, showing, and staging provides insight into how individuals interface with and present their interpretation of organizational identity content to other members.

We thus see great potential for future research to better understand the custodians of organizational identity. Though we argued, in line with previous research (e.g., King et al., 2010; Whetten and Mackey, 2002), that anyone can be a custodian, examining what makes certain individuals legitimate communicators of identity content in the eyes of members is an important area for future scholarship. Further, as the primary communicators of identity content, custodians likely have tremendous opportunity to shape the shared sense of "who we are." It is therefore critical that we better understand how identity custodians, in addition to simply maintaining identity content, actually change perceptions of organizational identity. Perhaps it is inevitable, given the interaction of a custodian's social and personal identities, that a custodian's idiosyncrasies would shape the saying, showing, and staging of identity content in ways that impact organizational identity content over time. Indeed, members' individualized enactment of the identity content may allow them to personalize an organizational identity, and possibly even imprint their uniqueness on the organization by serving as a custodian to other members. This is yet another way that a deeper appreciation for the role of identity custodians enables us to better understand the cross-level dynamics of organizational identity.

A second implication of our chapter is emphasizing just how critical cross-level and dynamic approaches are to further advancing our knowledge of organizational identity processes. Our theorizing about identity custodians and members' perceptions of identity communication further articulates Ashforth and colleagues' (2011) notion that much of the identity transmission process happens at the interpersonal (or "intersubjective") level. As we have noted, individuals within the organization are the ones actually *doing* the saying, showing, and staging. Thus, even though organizational identity is a collective phenomenon, individuals enact many of the processes involved in its maintenance and change (Brickson and Akinlade, 2016; cf. Kreiner, Hollensbe, Sheep, Smith, and Kataria, forthcoming). We suggest that scholars studying organizational identity at just one level of analysis are likely missing much of the story, and challenge future research to account for multiple levels, as well as dynamism across levels. To illustrate, we consider the example of identity communication: scholars exploring this topic could simultaneously examine the bottom-up component of the largely top-down communication process discussed throughout this chapter. As Ravasi and Schultz (2006) noted, "organizational identities arise from sensemaking and sensegiving processes ... one needs, therefore, to account for both perspectives" (p. 436). Taking a multi-level approach, could reveal, for example, that identity content transmitted by custodians (top-down) becomes believable to members through first-hand experiences of organizational life that confirm what is said, shown, or staged (bottom-up). Further, both current theorizing (Ashforth et al., 2011) and popular press accounts (e.g., Baer, 2014) note that members of the organization are not just passive receivers of identity content, but can also impact the content of a collective identity; unfortunately, we have little insight into this process.

Additionally, Figure 12,1 painted a static picture of how identity custodians communicate "who we are." However, organizational identity is seen by many as a dynamic phenomenon (Gioia et al., 2013; Hatch and Schultz, 2002). Future research might benefit from an exploration of organizations' movement from one quadrant of Figure 12.1 to another, likely in response to a change or event (e.g., replacing a CEO, engaging in a merger or acquisition, entering a high-risk product market). Such a shift in the organization may prompt identity custodians to gain and/or lose clarity of organizational identity content or increase/decrease the intent with which they communicate that identity content. For instance, current theorizing would suggest that it is unlikely an organization could survive (or employ strategic ambiguity) for long in the low clarity/low intentional communication quadrant. Yet we don't understand the processes or outcomes, collectively and/or individually, that may induce identity custodians' marked increase (or decrease) in identity communication. For example, what processes are involved as an organization's custodians gain clarity about organizational identity content, increase their intentional communication of identity content, and move toward that upper right quadrant?

CONCLUSION

Though the communication of organizational identity has been highlighted as crucial, how identity content is conveyed to members has remained underexplored. In this chapter, we began to resolve this disparity by examining the various ways that identity custodians convey organizational identity content, and the conditions under which such communication occurs. It is our hope that future research will continue to explore the nature of organizational identity communication, including how, by whom, and when identity content is communicated, as well as the ways in which these messages are received and interpreted by organizational members.

References

Argyris, C., and Schon, D. A. (1974). *Theory in Practice: Increasing Professional Effectiveness.* San Francisco, CA: Jossey-Bass.

Albert, S. and Whetten, D. A. (1985). "Organizational Identity." *Research in Organizational Behavior* 7: 263–95.

Alessandri, S. W. (2001). "Modeling Corporate Identity: A Concept Explication and Theoretical Explanation." *Corporate Communications: An International Journal* 6(4): 173–82.

Ashforth, B. E. (2001). *Role Transitions in Organizational Life: An Identity-Based Perspective.* Mahwah, NJ: Lawrence Erlbaum.

Ashforth, B. E., Harrison, S. H., and Corley, K. G. (2008). "Identification in Organizations: An Examination of Four Fundamental Questions." *Journal of Management* 34(3): 325–74.

Ashforth, B. E., Harrison, S. H., and Sluss, D. M. (2014). "Becoming: The Interaction of Socialization and Identity in Organizations over Time." In *Time and Work*, vol. 1: *How Time Impacts Individuals*, edited by A. J. Shipp and Y. Fried, 11–39. Philadelphia, PA: Psychology Press.

Ashforth, B. E. and Mael, F. A. (1996). "Organizational Identity and Strategy as a Context for the Individual." *Advances in Strategic Management* 13: 19–64.

Ashforth, B. E. and Rogers, K. M. (2012). "Is the Employee-Organization Relationship Misspecified? The Centrality of Tribes in Experiencing the Organization." In *The Employee-Organization Relationship: Applications for the 21st Century*, edited by L. M. Shore, J. A.-M. Shapiro, and L. E. Tetrick, 23–53. New York: Routledge.

Ashforth, B. E., Rogers, K. M., and Corley, K. G. (2011). "Identity in Organizations: Exploring Cross-Level Dynamics." *Organization Science* 22(5): 1144–56.

Baer, D. (2014). "Here's What Google Teaches Employees in its 'Search Inside Yourself' Course." Retrieved from http://www.businessinsider.com/search-inside-yourself-googles-life-changing-mindfulness-course-2014-8.

Berg, P. O. and Kreiner, K. (1990). "Corporate Architecture: Turning Physical Settings into Symbolic Resources." In *Symbols and Artifacts: Views of the Corporate Landscape*, edited by P. Gagliardi, 41–65. Berlin: Walter de Gruyter.

Birnholtz, J. P., Cohen, M. D., and Hoch, S. V. (2007). "Organizational Character: On the Regeneration of Camp Poplar Grove." *Organization Science* 18(2): 315–32.

Brickson, S. L. (2005). "Organizational Identity Orientation: Forging a Link Between Organizational Identity and Organizations' Relations with Stakeholders." *Administrative Science Quarterly* 50(4): 576–609.

Brickson, S. L. (2013). "Athletes, Best Friends, and Social Activists: An Integrative Model Accounting for the Role of Identity in Organizational Identification." *Organization Science* 24(1): 226–45.

Brickson, S. L. and Akinlade, D. (2016). "Organizations as Internal Value Creators: Toward a Typology of Value within Organizations and a Process Model of its Creation." Unpublished Manuscript, Department of Managerial Studies, University of Illinois at Chicago.

Brown, A. D. (2006). "A Narrative Approach to Collective Identities." *Journal of Management Studies* 43(4): 731–53.

Brown, A. D. and Starkey, K. (2000). "Organizational Identity and Learning: A Psychodynamic Perspective." *Academy of Management Review* 25(1): 102–20.

Cable, D. M., Gino, F., and Staats, B. R. (2013). "Breaking Them in or Eliciting Their Best? Reframing Socialization around Newcomers' Authentic Self-expression." *Administrative Science Quarterly* 58(1): 1–36.

Cappetta, R. and Gioia, D. A. (2006). "Fine Fashion: Using Symbolic Artifacts, Sensemaking, and Sensegiving to Construct Identity and Image." In *Artifacts and Organizations: Beyond Mere Symbolism*, edited by M. G. Pratt and A. Rafaeli, 199–219. Mahwah, NJ: Lawrence Erlbaum.

Chen, B. X. (2014). "Simplifying the Bull: How Picasso Helps to Teach Apple's Style." Retrieved from http://www.nytimes.com/2014/08/11/technology/-inside-apples-internal-training-program-.html?_r=1.

Cheney, G. (1983). "The Rhetoric of Identification and the Study of Organizational Communication." *Quarterly Journal of Speech* 69(2): 143–58.

Cheney, G. and Christensen, L. T. (2001). "Organizational Identity: Linkages between Internal and External Communication." In *The New Handbook of Organizational Communication: Advancing Theory, Research, and Methods*, edited by F. M. Jablin and L. L. Putnam, 231–69. Thousand Oaks, CA: SAGE.

Child, J. (1972). "Organizational Structure, Environment and Performance: The Role of Strategic Choice." *Sociology* 6(1): 1–22.

Clark, S. M., Gioia, D. A., Ketchen, D. J., and Thomas, J. B. (2010). "Transitional Identity as a Facilitator of Organizational Identity Change during a Merger." *Administrative Science Quarterly* 55(3): 397–438.

Cook, S. D. N. and Yanow, D. 1993. "Culture and Organizational Learning." *Journal of Management Inquiry* 2(4): 373–90.

Corley, K. G. and Gioia, D. A. (2004). "Identity Ambiguity and Change in the Wake of a Corporate Spin-off." *Administrative Science Quarterly* 49(2): 173–208.

Covaleski, M. A., Dirsmith, M. W., Heian, J. B., and Samuel, S. (1998). "The Calculated and the Avowed: Techniques of Discipline and Struggles over Identity in Big Six Public Accounting Firms." *Administrative Science Quarterly* 43(2): 293–327.

Czarniawska, B. (1997). *Narrating the Organization: Dramas of Institutional Identity*. London: University of Chicago Press.

Dacin, M. T., Munir, K., and Tracey, P. (2010). "Formal Dining at Cambridge Colleges: Linking Ritual Performance and Institutional Maintenance." *Academy of Management Journal* 53(6): 1393–418.

Dailey, S. L. and Browning, L. (2014). "Retelling Stories in Organizations: Understanding the Functions of Narrative Repetition." *Academy of Management Journal* 39(1): 22–43.

Davis, J. H., Schoorman, F. D., and Donaldson, L. (1997). "Toward a Stewardship Theory of Management." *Academy of Management Review* 22(1): 20–47.

Dutton, J. E. and Dukerich, J. M. (1991). "Keeping an Eye on the Mirror: Image and Identity in Organizational Adaptation." *Academy of Management Journal* 34(3): 517–54.

Eisenberg, E. M. (1984). "Ambiguity as Strategy in Organizational Communication." *Communication Monographs* 51: 227–42.

Eisenberg, E. M. and Witten, M. G. (1987). "Reconsidering Openness in Organizational Communication." *Academy of Management Review* 12(3): 418–26.

Fiol, C. M. (2002). "Capitalizing on Paradox: The Role of Language in Transforming Organizational Identities." *Organization Science* 13(6): 653–66.

Friedland, R. and Alford, R. (1991). "Bringing Society back in: Symbols, Practices, and Institutional Contradictions." In *The New Institutionalism in Organizational Analysis*, edited by W. W. Powell and P. J. DiMaggio, 232–63. Chicago: University of Chicago Press.

Gioia, D. (1998). "From Individual to Organizational Identity" In *Identity in Organizations: Building Theory through Conversations*, edited by D. Whetten, and P. Godfrey, 17–31. Thousand Oaks, CA: SAGE.

Gioia, D. A., Patvardhan, S. D., Hamilton, A. L., and Corley, K. G. (2013). "Organizational Identity Formation and Change." *Academy of Management Annals* 7(1): 123–93.

Gioia, D. A., Price, K. N., Hamilton, A. L., and Thomas, J. B. (2010). "Forging an Identity: An Insider-Outsider Study of Processes Involved in the Formation of Organizational Identity." *Administrative Science Quarterly* 55(1): 1–46.

Gioia, D. A., Schultz, M., and Corley, K. G. (2000). "Organizational Identity, Image, and Adaptive Instability." *Academy of Management Review* 25(1): 63–81.

Greil, A. L. and Rudy, D. R. (1984). "Social Cocoons: Encapsulation and Identity Transformation Organizations." *Sociological Inquiry* 54(3): 260–78.

Gupta, S. (2013). "Bosch in India." *HBS No. IMB 409*. Bangalore: Indian Institute of Management.

Harquail, C. V. (2006). "Symbolizing Identity: When Brand Icons Become Organizational Icons." *Academy of Management Proceedings* H1–6.

Haslam, S. A., Postmes, T., and Ellemers, N. (2003). "More than a Metaphor: Organizational Identity Makes Organizational Life Possible." *British Journal of Management* 14(4): 357–69.

Hatch, M. J. and Schultz, M. (1997). "Relations between Organizational Culture, Identity and Image." *European Journal of Marketing* 31(5): 356–65.

Hatch, M. J. and Schultz, M. (2002). "The Dynamics of Organizational Identity." *Human Relations* 55(8): 989–1018.

Heyman, J. and Lieberman, C. (2014). "'Own it' as an Organization." *Huffpost Business*. Retrieved from http://www.huffingtonpost.com/joanne-heyman/own-it-as-an-organization_b_5133891.html

Higgins, M. C. and Kram, K. E. (2001). "Reconceptualizing Mentoring at Work: A Developmental Network Perspective." *Academy of Management Review* 26(2): 264–88.

Howard-Grenville, J., Metzger, M. L., and Meyer, A. D. (2013). "Rekindling the Flame: Processes of Identity Resurrection." *Academy of Management Journal* 56(1): 113–36.

Hsu, G. and Elsbach, K. D. (2013). "Explaining Variation in Organizational Identity Categorization." *Organization Science* 24(4): 996–1013.

Islam, G. and Zyphur, M. J. (2009). "Rituals in Organizations: A Review and Expansion of Current Theory." *Group and Organization Management*, 34(1): 114–39.

Kärreman, D. and Alvesson, M. (2001). "Making Newsmakers: Conversational Identity at Work." *Organization Studies* 22(1): 59–89.

King, B. G., Felin, T., and Whetten, D. A. (2010). "Finding the Organization in Organizational Theory: A Meta-Theory of the Organization as a Social Actor." *Organization Science* 21(1): 290–305.

Kjaergaard, A., Morsing, M., and Ravasi, D. (2011). "Mediating Identity: A Study of Media Influence on Organizational Identity Construction in a Celebrity Firm." *Journal of Management Studies* 48(3): 514–43.

Kreiner, G., Hollensbe, E., Sheep, M., Smith, B., and Kataria, N. (2015). "Elasticity and the Dialectic Tensions of Organizational Identity: How Can We Hold together while We're Pulling apart?" *Academy of Management Journal* 58(4): 981–1011.

McGinn, K. L. (2007). "History, Structure, and Practices: San Pedro Longshoremen in the Face of Change." In *Exploring Positive Relationships at Work: Building a Theoretical and Research Foundation*, edited by J. E. Dutton and B. R. Ragins, 265–75. Mahwah, NJ: Lawrence Erlbaum Associates.

Mintzberg, H. (1985). "The Organization as Political Arena." *Journal of Management Studies* 22(2): 133–54.

Morsing, M. (1999). "The Media Boomerang: The Media's Role in Changing Identity by Changing Image." *Corporate Reputation Review* 2(2): 116–35.

Petriglieri, J. L. (2011). "Under Threat: Responses to and the Consequences of Threats to Individuals' Identities." *Academy of Management Review* 36(4): 641–62.

Postmes, T., Tanis, M., and de Wit, B. (2001). "Communication and Commitment in Organizations: A Social Identity Approach." *Group Processes and Intergroup Relations* 4(3): 227–46.

Pratt, M. G. (2000). "The Good, the Bad, and the Ambivalent: Managing Identification among Amway Distributors." *Administrative Science Quarterly* 45(3): 456–93.

Pratt, M. G. (2003). "Disentangling Collective Identities." In *Identity Issues in Groups: Research on Managing Groups and Teams*, vol. 5, edited by J. T. Polzer and M. Neale, 161–88. Stamford, CT: Elsevier Science.

Pratt, M. G. and Foreman, P. O. (2000). "Classifying Managerial Responses to Multiple Organizational Identities." *Academy of Management Journal* 25(1): 18–42.

Pratt, M. G. and Rafaeli, A. (1997). "Organizational Dress as a Symbol of Multilayered Social Identities." *Academy of Management Journal* 40(4): 862–98.

Price, K., Gioia, D. A., and Corley, K. G. (2008). "Reconciling Scattered Images: Managing Disparate Organizational Expressions and Impressions." *Journal of Management Inquiry* 17(3): 173–85.

Rafaeli, A. and Pratt, M. G. (1993). "Tailored Meanings: On the Meaning and Impact of Organizational Dress." *Academy of Management Review* 18(1): 32–55.

Ravasi, D. and Schultz, M. (2006). "Responding to Organizational Identity Threats: Exploring the Role of Organizational Culture." *Academy of Management Journal* 49(3): 433–58.

Schultz, M. and Hernes, T. (2013). "A Temporal Perspective on Organizational Identity." *Organization Science* 24(1): 1–21.

Scott, S. G. and Lane, V. R. (2000). "A Stakeholder Approach to Organizational Identity." *Academy of Management Review* 25(1): 43–62.

Selznick, P. (1957). *Leadership in Administration: A Sociological Interpretation* Berkeley, CA: University of California Press.

Shepherd, D. A. and Sutcliffe, K. M. (2015). "The Use of Anthropomorphizing as a Tool for Generating Organizational Theories." *Academy of Management Annals*, 9(1): 97–142.

Smidts, A., Pruyn, A. T., and van Riel, C. B. M. (2001). "The Impact of Employee Communication and Perceived External Prestige on Organizational Identification." *Academy of Management Journal* 44(5): 1051–62.

Takeuchi, H., Nonaka, I., and Yamazaki, M. (2011). "Knowledge Creation at Eisai Co., Ltd." *HBS. No. 9-711-492*. Boston, MA: Harvard Business School Publishing.

Tyler, T. R. (1997). "The Psychology of Legitimacy: A Relational Perspective on Voluntary Deference to Authorities." *Personality and Social Psychology Review* 1(4): 323–45.

Voss, Z. G., Cable, D. M., and Voss, G. B. (2006). "Organizational Identity and Firm Performance: What Happens when Leaders Disagree about 'Who We Are?'" *Organization Science* 17(6): 741–55.

Whetten, D. A. (2006). "Albert and Whetten Revisited: Strengthening the Concept of Organizational Identity." *Journal of Management Inquiry* 15(3): 219–34.

Whetten, D. A. and Mackey, A. (2002). "A Social Actor Conception of Organizational Identity and its Implications for the Study of Organizational Reputation." *Business and Society* 41(4): 393–414.

Zollo, M. and Winter, S. G. (2002). "Deliberate Learning and the Evolution of Dynamic Capabilities." *Organization Science* 13(3): 339–51.

CHAPTER 13

MOBILIZING ORGANIZATIONAL ACTION AGAINST IDENTITY THREATS

the role of organizational members' perceptions and responses

JENNIFER L. PETRIGLIERI AND BETH A. DEVINE

INTRODUCTION

THIS chapter examines why and how organizational members perceive and respond to threats to their organization's identity and how these individual efforts coalesce (or not) into an organizational response.

Organizational identity threats are events that refute or cause members to question their beliefs about their organization's central and distinctive attributes (Ravasi and Schultz, 2006). These events—for example organizational crises and environmental changes—usually harm organizational functioning by disrupting processes such as corporate strategy (Ravasi and Schultz, 2006), organizational governance (Golden-Biddle and Rao, 1997), and efforts to uphold a sound external reputation and image (Dutton and Dukerich, 1991). For example, the successful merger of two rival health-care organizations required both to abandon their former identities for a joint, transitional identity that supported massive structural and strategic change (Clark, Gioia, Ketchen, and Thomas, 2010). Technological innovation, economic recession, and increased competition threatened Bang & Olufsen's identity, prompting them to reinvent it three times over three decades (Ravasi and Schultz, 2006). More recently, the BP Gulf of Mexico oil spill threatened the company's identity as an environmentally conscious and technologically competent firm (Petriglieri, 2015). The pervasiveness of threats to organizational identity, coupled with the potential impact they have on operational effectiveness, has made them an important domain of study for scholars in the organizational field.

Research on organizational identity threat has focused on understanding how organizations respond to threats and what the consequences of these threat responses are (Dutton and Dukerich, 1991; Gioia and Thomas, 1996; Gioia, Schultz, and Corley, 2000; Golden-Biddle and Rao, 1997; Phillips and Kim, 2009). Less work has been done on how organizations come to recognize an event as threatening, or whether and how individual organizational members who perceive events as threatening can mobilize organizational action. This is a significant gap, given how often and consequentially organizations have failed to recognize threats to their identities and to formulate adequate responses. To understand why some threats provoke responses while others do not, it is crucial that organizational scholars develop a better theoretical understanding of how organizations come to recognize an event or change in their environment as threatening.

In this chapter, we examine how individual members' perceptions and responses to organizational identity threats drive (or not) an organizational threat response. We suggest that for an organizational identity threat to be recognized as such and to provoke a response in an individual member, the threat must put the member's own identity at stake. Our central contention is that an organizational identity threat must translate into a threat to the members' own identity for a member to respond to it.

We also propose that individual members who perceive an organizational identity threat can only mobilize organizational action when there is a consensus—in other words, broad support—about the presence and significance of the threat. When there is no consensus, organizations do not form an adequate threat response. We identify two ways that this consensus can be built: (1) bottom-up processes via a critical mass of organizational members and (2) top-down processes via senior management initiatives. In addition, we explore the role of political mechanisms that underpin and determine whether the two processes of consensus building are successful. We conclude by outlining an agenda for future cross-level research in the domain of identity threat.

Defining the Field

Organizational identity is often treated as a single answer to the question, "Who are we as an organization?" All members of an organization are assumed to share one answer, or more precisely, have shared elements in their different answers. This common view conveys what members believe distinguishes their organization from others, and members use it to craft and communicate images of the organization to outsiders (Gioia, Schultz, and Corley, 2000; Hatch and Schultz, 2002). While the idea that members share a single unified identity is common, empirical research has demonstrated that such a uniformly agreed-on perception is rare. Instead, members hold different, albeit related and overlapping, perceptions of their organization's identity (Barney et al., 1998; Hsu and Elsbach, 2013).

Variations in members' perceptions of their organization's identity are evident in disagreements about higher-order categorizations that describe the general form of the organization (King and Whetten, 2008). Such variations often occur between distinct groups within an organization. Studying a symphony orchestra, for example, Glynn (2000) observed that musicians viewed the organization's identity as an artistic enterprise, whereas the administrators viewed it as a business. Different perceptions of organizational identity are also evident in within-form categorizations that describe the way an organization is distinctive vis-à-vis other similar organizations (King and Whetten, 2008). Take universities: although both students and faculty will likely agree that they are providers of education, students perceive their university's identity as demanding, emphasizing learning, and career focused, whereas faculty at the same university view it as resource deprived, research focused, and high quality (Hsu and Elsbach, 2013).

Building on this research we work from a definition that recognizes variation in how members view organizational identity. Specifically, we are interested in the *perceived* organizational identity, defined as "what the member believes is central, enduring, and distinctive about the organization" (Dutton, Dukerich, and Harquail, 1994: 239). Importantly, this definition locates organizational identity in the perceptions of individual members and allows for variances between them. Any consensus beyond the individual is therefore an accomplishment, requires maintenance, and can be undone.

We extend this definition of organizational identity to organizational identity threat, which we define as *an event or occurrence that a member perceives as calling into question what he or she believes is distinctive, central, and enduring about his or her organization* (Ravasi and Schultz, 2006). Because members have different perceptions of their organization's identity, an event is unlikely to be perceived by all members as threatening. Some may view it as threatening whereas others may not. Basing the definition of organizational identity threat on the perceptions of individual members is important, because although the event threatens the collective, it is members who recognize the event as threatening and mobilize an organizational response against it.

Before exploring the mechanisms by which this happens, we provide a classification of organizational identity threats that forms the basis of our discussion.

Classifying Organizational Identity Threats

A vast array of experiences can cause members to question their beliefs about their organization's identity. To build a conceptual foundation for theorizing about the spread of organizational identity threat among an organization's members, we reviewed the literature and classified threats into two broad categories based on their origin and what aspect of the organizational identity they target.

Internal Events or Changes That Are Inconsistent with Organizational Identity Perception

The first type of organizational identity threat stems from events or changes inside the organization that are perceived as inconsistent with the organization's identity. These cause members to question whether what they perceived the organization to be is really what the organization is. One common way for these internal threats to arise is when organizational change initiatives, more or less intentionally, target domains related to the organization's identity. For example, in the mid-2000s, the German police force tried to implement changes aimed at modernizing its managerial practices. The planned changes, such as more formal paperwork and processes to support promotion decisions, brought an administrative organizational logic to the police force that threatened the perception many police officers held of the organization's identity as a group of street-savvy crime fighters (Jacobs, Christie-Zeyse, Keegan, and Pólos, 2008).

In addition to planned organizational change, unexpected actions by organizational members can also threaten an organization's identity. The nonprofit foundation Medlay, the members of which held a strong consensus that its distinguishing feature was its identity as a "family of friends," provides a good example. When some board members questioned the foundation's expense budget, others perceived that to be highly inconsistent with, and thus threatening to, the organization's cherished identity (Golden-Biddle and Rao, 1997). Unexpected organizational actions, such as crises, industrial accidents, or scandals, can also threaten an organization's identity. For example, General Motor's failure to fix a deadly ignition switch flaw, blamed for the death of 13 motorists in 2013, threatened the organization's postbankruptcy identity as an organization focused on customer safety.

These internal changes or events are threatening because they are discrepant with members' perception of their organization's identity, a threat that can be summarized as the emergence in members' minds of the reaction, "This is not who we are!"

External Events that Question the Validity of Organizational Identity Perceptions

The second type of organizational identity threat stems from external events that raise questions about the validity of an organization's identity. These events cause members to question whether their organization can continue to claim its central and distinctive identity attributes. They can be environmental changes that, while not direct attacks on the organization's identity, still threaten it. For instance, the identity of Bang & Olufsen—a producer of high-end audio and visual consumer goods—came under threat following three changes: the market entry of low-end competitors, consumer preferences in a recession, and copycat competitors. These developments challenged the organization's ability to sustain its identity as a design-driven maker of artistic goods and to survive in the marketplace (Ravasi and Schultz, 2006).

Alternatively, external events can directly challenge and thus threaten an organization's identity. These include negative media coverage and public rankings that portray the organization in a fashion that negates its claimed identity (Corley and Gioia, 2000; Martins, 2005). Threats can target the central and distinctive identity attributes of the organization or its status. For example, the vast number of homeless people taking refuge in the buildings of the New York-New Jersey Port Authority in the late 1980s made outsiders, and particularly the media, label the Port Authority as "out-of-control" and "callous" (Dutton and Dukerich, 1991). These labels were discrepant with, and thus threatened, how the Port Authority's own members perceived its identity as a high-quality, first-class organization. Similarly, *Business Week* magazine's ranking of US business schools threatened many institutions whose position in the ranking was discrepant with how they perceived their identity and status (Elsbach and Kramer, 1996). When the University of Texas, for example, was excluded from the top 20, it created a significant threat, captured in the words of a student who said, "I applied to a top 20 school and this is not a top 20 school" (p. 454).

These external events, whether they directly or indirectly target the organization, threaten the validity of the organization's identity and can be captured in the overarching question posed by organizational members: "Is this really who we are?"

Threat Strength

An important feature of an identity threat is its strength. A strong threat either confers a great degree of potential harm to the organization's identity or is continuous and thus encountered frequently (Burke, 1991). In theory, threats can vary in strength, but there exists a tipping point at which they become highly salient to organizational members and outsiders and can no longer be ignored. One example of a tipping point is when threats become public discourse through press coverage. This can occur with both internally and externally derived threats. For example, in 2011 newspapers broke the story that Joe Sandusky, a football coach at Penn State University, had sexually abused children in his role as coach. Although the incidents had been known to university administrators for some time, they were not viewed as a strong threat until they became public (Grandey, Krannitz, and Slezak, 2013). While these identity-threatening events took many years to become part of the public discourse and thus a strong threat, others, such as the scandal of British Members of Parliament (MPs) overclaiming personal expenses and thus threatening their identities as "Right Honourable Gentlemen," was immediately a strong threat because of timely press reporting (Graffin, Bundy, Porac, Wade, and Quinn, 2013). Typically, externally derived threats are stronger than those that are internally derived because the former are more likely to be immediately reported in the press. Nevertheless, an internally derived threat may become a very strong threat if it enters the public discourse.

The Spread of Organizational Identity Threat to Organizational Members

We suggest that in order for any of the organizational identity threats just detailed to be relevant to, and hence provoke a response in, an individual member, the threat must transfer to the member's own identity. This means that something is personally at stake for the organizational member that will motivate him or her to respond to the threat (Staw, Sandelands, and Dutton, 1981). To understand how threats to an organization's identity can penetrate to its members, we first explore why an organization's identity matters to its members, and thus what is at stake for them when their organization's identity is threatened. We propose that organizational identity matters for two reasons: (1) to provide the content and structure of a valued self-identity and (2) to satisfy fundamental self-motives.

People have multiple identities that are derived from three bases: membership in groups (e.g., organizations), holding a specific role (e.g., being a parent), and idiosyncratic traits and characteristics (e.g., being musically talented) (Ramarajan, 2014). With a societal culture that valorizes a focus on work, the identity derived from organizational membership is increasingly salient and important to people (Gini, 2001; Kanter, 2010). In fact, many invest in their organizations as *identity workspaces* in which they clarify, affirm, and revise their personal identities with others (Petriglieri and Petriglieri, 2010). The identity derived from membership is both a self-categorization (e.g., "I am a member of Twitter") and a set of attributes contained in this categorization (e.g., "As a member of Twitter I am a dynamic and entrepreneurial person"). These attributes derive from what the person perceives to be the identity attributes of his or her organization.

The alignment between individuals' perceptions of their own identity and their organization's identity occurs through the process of identification, by which members come to experience a sense of oneness with their organization (Pratt, 1998). Thus, the first reason that an organization's identity matters to its members is because it provides the content and structure of an identity that is prized by society. When something threatens the validity of the organization's identity, therefore, it can subsequently threaten the validity of the identity members derive from it. For example, the 2010 BP rig explosion and subsequent oil spill threatened the organization's identity as environmentally conscious and technologically adept, which, in turn, threatened its members' identities as environmentally conscious, technologically adept people (Petriglieri, 2015).

People have a need for self-coherence, that is, a consistent, integrated sense of self across contexts (Swann, Rentfrow, and Guinn, 2002). Closely related to this need is a drive for self-continuity, that is, a desire to have self-coherence over time (Atchley, 1989). People are thus attracted to and identify with organizations when their perceptions of the organization's identity are consistent with their own self-perceptions

(Dutton, Dukerich, and Harquail, 1994; Swann, Johnson, and Bosson, 2009). People are also invested in preserving their organization's identity in a stable, continuous form over time because this, in turn, provides them with a personal sense of self-continuity. This means that an event that threatens the consistency of an organization's identity can threaten the sense of self-coherence and self-continuity members derive from it.

As a source of self-definition, organizational identity is also tied to members' self-esteem. The need for self-enhancement—to positively evaluate oneself—strongly motivates people to identify with their organization as long as the organizational identity is broadly valued (Dutton, Dukerich, and Harquail, 1994; Pratt, 1998). When identified members believe that their organization is highly regarded by outsiders, their self-esteem is enhanced and they feel proud (Cialdini, Borden, Thorne, Walker, Freeman, and Sloan, 1976). When the converse is true, their self-esteem is eroded and they experience feelings of shame, embarrassment, and even disgrace (Dutton, Dukerich, and Harquail, 1994). This means that when an identity threat derogates the status or value of an organization, the self-esteem of identified members is at stake, making the organizational-level threat directly relevant to them.

The content and structure of a person's identity as derived from his or her organization's identity and the importance of this organizational identity in fulfilling self-motives for coherence, continuity, and affirmation thus form an umbilical cord that attaches identified members to their organization and serves as a conduit through which threat can be transmitted from the organization to the individual. Because members may have different perceptions of their organization's identity, they will not uniformly perceive any given event as threatening to that identity. In the next section we highlight two points of variation, one based on hierarchy and one on organizational group membership.

Hierarchy

A member's role and position in the organization's hierarchy determine his or her everyday experience. This experience, in turn, makes certain dimensions of the organizational identity salient to the person as a result of repeated exposure (Bodenhausen and Macrae, 1998; Stangor, 1988). For example, senior managers' everyday experiences concern organizational strategy and interfaces with external stakeholders and organizational outsiders. As a result, they tend to view organizational identity in terms of strategic purpose and differentiation from their competitors (Corley, 2004). This strategic, external focus makes them more sensitive to identity threats stemming from external events that threaten the validity of the organizational identity. In contrast, employees who occupy lower levels of the organizational hierarchy and whose everyday experiences revolve around the internal processes and procedures of the organization are more likely to view organizational identity in terms of organizational culture (Corley, 2004). This internal, cultural focus makes them more sensitive to identity threats that stem from internal events that are inconsistent with their current identity beliefs.

Organizational Groups

Independent of their position in the hierarchy, members often belong to different organizational groups that may, particularly in large organizations, align strongly with
different high-order identity categorizations (Pratt and Foreman, 2000). For example,
medics in a hospital are likely to identify with and hence be more sensitive to threats to
the organizational identity of caregivers to the sick, whereas hospital administrators
are likely to identify with and hence be more sensitive to threats to the organizational
identity of a well-run business (Fiol, Pratt, and O'Connor, 2009). Equally, when the
founder and CEO of environmental NGO Friends of the Earth, a grass-roots activist,
resigned, organizational members who were grass-roots activists felt threatened by
the potential evolution of the organization into a lobbying group, whereas members
who were lobbyists welcomed the change (Balser and Carmin, 2009).

These two points of variation can help to explain why some organizational members perceive an event as threatening and others do not. In addition, the stronger any
given threat is, the more likely organizational members will generally recognize it as
threatening.

From Individual Threat Perception
to the Mobilization of Organizational
Responses to Threat

There is no guarantee that individuals or organizational groups who perceive an
organizational identity threat will be able to mobilize an organizational response.
Threats to organizational identity are often overlooked or responded to slowly, both
of which reactions can significantly damage the organization. For example, Shell's
proposal in the early 1990s to dump its decommissioned oil storage buoy (Brent Spar)
in deep Atlantic waters created a severe threat to its organizational identity as a safety-
conscious firm (Livesey, 2001). This threat was exacerbated by the company's inability
to mobilize action against it. By the time the company reversed its proposal and towed
the buoy to the Norwegian coast, petrol stations across Europe were being boycotted,
and the company's reputation was already damaged.

The question is when and how a perception of organizational identity threat among
individuals or groups leads to organizational mobilization. Mobilizing organizational
action requires that people overcome inertia that stabilizes organizational systems
and prevents change (Gould, 2001; Jacques, 1955; Long, 2006; Menzies, 1960). We argue
that to overcome this organizational inertia, the perception of threat must coalesce
into a powerful voice (Hirschman, 1970). We propose two processes by which this can
occur: (1) a bottom-up process by which a critical mass of members simultaneously
perceive the threat and can mobilize a response through the power of numbers and

(2) a top-down process by which the threat is perceived by very senior members of the organization who have the authority to mobilize the organization's resources themselves through the organizational hierarchy. In the next sections we describe each of these processes and then explore the role of political mechanisms that underpin and determine whether the two processes of consensus building are successful.

Bottom-Up: A Critical Mass of Members Simultaneously Perceives a Threat

If organizational members en masse perceive a threat to their organization's identity, their collective voice can be powerful enough to trigger the organization into responding, regardless of whether senior management initially perceives the threat. This bottom-up path to organizational mobilization is most likely to be triggered by internal events that are highly discrepant with the organization's identity. When such a large discrepancy exists, even if members have somewhat different perceptions of their organization's identity, they are likely to see the event as threatening. Such internal events are likely to involve crises, major scandals, or industrial accidents. Although originating internally, these events often generate negative media coverage that can amplify the identity threat by projecting it into the public discourse. The 2009 scandal of UK MPs overclaiming expenses threatened other parliamentarians who saw their identity as principled and moral. This threat was exacerbated by negative media coverage. Because MPs across all parties perceived this threat, they were able to rapidly pass a new law about expense disclosures that was designed to defend the integrity of Parliament (Graffin, Bundy, Porac, Wade, and Quinn, 2013).

Although organizational mobilization in cases of mass perception of threat can be relatively quick, it is not always straightforward. The potential involvement of company leadership in either causing or covering up the triggering event, or its unwillingness to accept that the organization's identity is under severe threat, may create resistance to, slow down, or extinguish a response altogether. This can lead senior managers consciously or unconsciously to act to deny the threat and block efforts to mobilize a response against it (Anteby and Molnár, 2012; Long, 2006). The child abuse scandal in the Roman Catholic Church provides a sobering example. Although most members of the Church found the revelations abhorrent and perceived them as a strong threat to the Church's identity, its leaders were slow to mobilize an appropriate response. In that case, members themselves mobilized a response outside of the formal Church structure by forming internal groups, such as Voice of the Faithful, that pushed the Vatican to finally make changes (Gutierrez, Howard-Grenville, and Scully, 2010). While this mobilization did not immediately change leaders' demeanor in handling the scandal, it had long-term influence as evidenced by the stance of Pope Francis toward sexual abuse within the Church. En masse efforts of members to mobilize an organization against identity threat, however, may not succeed at all. Consider Market Basket, the Massachusetts supermarket chain targeting low-income consumers that fired its CEO because he had focused too much on keeping prices low to benefit customers. The firing created a significant threat to the organization's identity of being customer focused. Employees staged a mass walk out and organized rallies (joined by many customers). Nevertheless, they were not able to make the organization reverse its decision. In fact, the company executives took the opposite action and pursued an even more profit- and shareholder-driven strategy that led to huge financial losses (Newsham and Ross, 2014).

Top-Down: Hierarchical Power Drives Mobilization

Members higher up in the organizational hierarchy, especially those at the executive level, typically have more power and control over resources than other organizational members and thus greater ability to instigate and direct action. They have more authority to mobilize the organization without having to form a broad coalition or critical mass of supporters first. Thus, when they perceive an identity threat, they can quickly and relatively independently trigger an organizational response (Magee and Galinsky, 2008). For example, pharmaceutical giant Johnson & Johnson defines itself via a credo that prioritizes, above all, being responsible to "the doctors, nurses and patients, to mothers and fathers and all others who use our products and services" (Johnson & Johnson, 2015). When poisoned Tylenol capsules caused seven consumer deaths in 1982, J&J failed the expectations of themselves and their consumers to uphold their self-definition. This discrepancy threatened their identity as a safety-conscious organization, and the leadership team acted quickly to protect the firm's identity. Beyond their public relations response of compensation and victim empathy, they rallied employee effort toward development of more secure packaging and revised inspection procedures (Berge, 1990). The internal changes assured employees that the organization was committed to upholding their identity, rather than merely protecting their reputation. Those efforts are regularly hailed as a model response to such a crisis (Benson, 1988; Greyser, 1992).

Although this may appear to be the quickest and most efficient way for an organization to respond to an identity threat, there are two potential hurdles to this mechanism. First, people at the top of the hierarchy attend to certain pieces of information more readily than others and thus may not readily pick up on all organizational identity threats. Specifically, individuals at the top of an organization's hierarchy tend to be attentive to strategic threats to organizational identity rather than cultural ones (Corley, 2004). Therefore, this mechanism cannot account for how all threats are responded to. Second, although the leadership may be able to sanction organizational action unilaterally, without mass support the response may stall or even be mobilized against by members lower in the organizational hierarchy. For example, an organization known as "*the* digital photography firm" in the mid-1990s was threatened by external technological innovation, prompting the leadership to abandon photography completely as an aspect of the organization's identity. In response, employees experienced a sense of "identity ambiguity" (Tripsas, 2009: 444) about who they were as an organization. Struggling to rally against such drastic changes in strategic direction, the company was ultimately acquired by another firm in the mid-2000s.

Underlying Mechanism: Political Mobilization by Organizational Groups

Regardless of whether the process is bottom up or top down, organizational members who perceive a threat need to build broad consensus and support to mobilize an organizational response (Davis, McAdam, Scott, and Zald, 2005; Rao, Monin, and Durand, 2003). This consensus building is done through political processes—those that groups or individuals use to influence others to take desired actions. It requires people to form alliances with others from different groups or positions and influence them to support their cause (Kellogg, 2009; Zald and Berger, 1978).

People use their networks to build alliances with others and to influence and mobilize them into action (Tichy, 1981). The networks of members or groups in an organization, however, differ in their breadth (how many other people and groups in the organization they are connected to) and their power (how powerful, and therefore able to drive change, the others are they are connected to). This means that some organizational groups are better placed to mobilize organizational action than others. For example, groups with members who reflect the majority demographic characteristics of the organization at leadership levels (typically white males) tend to reap greater benefit from identity group homophily (i.e., network ties to similar others) and are therefore better positioned to form powerful alliances (Ibarra, 1993, 1992).

Because political mobilization is difficult, groups may not always be able to mobilize organizational responses to threats that they perceive. For example, two hospitals that Kellogg (2009) studied had different levels of success in implementing reduced work hours for their surgical residents (from 120 to 80 per week). This change threatened some employees' views of the identity of a surgical residency and of a surgeon, and these threatened employees worked to defend the status quo. The successful group in each case was the one able to mobilize the most support for its point of view—the reformers at one hospital and the defenders at the other. In another example, the efforts by leaders of a higher education institute to achieve university status induced threat in the faculty, for bringing into question their prioritization of teaching over research. However, the staff responded in different and sometimes opposing ways, through identification, disidentification, a combination of both, or general ambivalence. Their conflicting responses amplified an existing sense of fragmentation, and while this slowed the process it did not enable them to mobilize actively against the change effort (Humphreys and Brown, 2002).

In other cases, political mobilization may be relatively straightforward once the members of an organizational group have spoken out about their perception of threat. For example, resistance at 3M against the CEO-led implementation of "six sigma," a management process aimed at eliminating errors, was rapid once organizational members witnessed respected managers working around the new system (Canato, Ravasi, and Phillips, 2013).

Groups can be helped or hindered in their attempts to build consensus around a threat by external validation (i.e., publicizing) of it. In particular, external validation can aid a bottom-up political process because the public diagnosis of the threat forces the leadership to acknowledge and respond. In the case of the Catholic Church, news coverage of the scandal helped the employee movements gain public support, thus spurring Church leadership to respond with larger and more direct action than previously observed (Gutierrez, Howard-Grenville, and Scully, 2010). However, external validation can complicate a top-down lobbying process because the leadership loses control of the situation to the public and is forced to simultaneously seek support within the company as well as deal with its public relations image via implementation of impression management strategies. For example, when the University of California (the governing body for the ten UC campuses) tried to augment its visual identity by the addition of a modern logo to its historic seal, the media coverage erroneously suggested that the seal was being *replaced* by the logo. This invoked a sense of identity threat within UC employees and students alike, who protested and created multiple petitions to stop the change. Leadership attempts at clarifying the motivation for the new logo were drowned out by organizational members' fear and the continued misuse of the new logo by the press. As a result, the organization was forced to cancel the use of the additional emblem completely (Vega, 2012).

These examples illustrate political processes that are observable behaviors, whether as open confrontation between interest groups or by quieter organization of subversive members. However, other political processes may be invisible or even occur unconsciously (Lukes, 1974). Chapter 10 in this handbook provides a more detailed overview of the different types of political processes and their associated forms of power, giving particular attention to those processes that are less visible and how they manifest in organizational identity formation and change.

CONCLUDING THOUGHTS AND FUTURE DIRECTIONS FOR RESEARCH

In this chapter, we explored why and how organizational members perceive and respond to threats to their organization's identity and how these individual efforts coalesce (or not) into an organizational response. We argued that members must feel that their own identity is threatened before they will attempt to mobilize organizational action. This spread of threat from the organization to the individual occurs via members' bond of identification with their organization, when the identity derived from organizational membership satisfies fundamental self-motives. We highlighted two processes organizational members can use to mobilize organizational action against threats to their organization's identity—top-down hierarchical power and a bottom-up critical mass of members perceiving threat—and discussed the importance of political processes to the success of each.

It is likely that other mechanisms beyond political mobilization exist. This chapter focused on dynamics within organizations, but people outside organizations also have stakes in them. Shareholders, customers, joint venture partners, and similar organizations in a given industry, all may detect a threat to an organization and lobby its leaders to respond in order to prevent the threat spreading to them as well. Scholars interested in pursuing these questions might seek to investigate the rich body of work on social activism and organizations, which has explored how shareholders and social activist groups shape organizational actions (e.g. Baron, 2003; Proffitt and Spicer, 2006; Reid and Toffel, 2009). Applying an identity lens to these problems might help unpack the mechanisms that underlie these efforts.

In empirically tackling the question of how organizational identity threats spread to organizational members, it would be interesting to seek out and explain differences between individuals. This might help predict who attends to what kind of organizational identity threats. To whom organizational identity threat is most likely to spread and the variations by which threatened members respond are two important questions to be addressed. In this chapter we suggested that position in the hierarchy and organizational group memberships are two factors that influence the spread of threat. Additional individual-level factors are also worth exploring, including the level of importance individuals place on their organizational membership (Ashforth and Johnson, 2001) and the strength of their organizational identification (Pratt, 1998). Because a number of personal factors—such as levels of social support, the presence of alternative identities, and identity importance (Petriglieri, 2011)—impact how people respond to threat, it is unlikely that organizational members will respond uniformly to threats. Parsing out variations in members' responses will also help to elucidate the organizational consequences of identity threat.

Beyond individual factors, organizational structure is likely to play a role in influencing the way threats spread and how quickly that occurs. How organizational structure—that is, flat versus hierarchical—affects the spread of threat is another potential avenue for future research. Addressing this question may be most interesting in relation to circumstances in which the threat is internally generated, as in the case of the German police force (Jacobs, Christie-Zeyse, Keegan, and Pólos, 2008), or the internal tension between hospital staff and administration (Fiol, Pratt, and O'Connor, 2009). In such situations, the initial awareness of a threatening event may be located in a particular organizational level or area as opposed to a general awareness of some public event.

Future research could investigate how threat spreads, not only within, but also between similar firms. For example, could the threat assessment and response by Bang & Olufsen (Ravasi and Schultz, 2006) influence a similar process in a firm such as Bose? Could a stand-off between hospital administrators and medical staff spread to neighboring hospitals (Fiol, Pratt, and O'Connor, 2009)? Finally, in the case of a corporate spin-off (Corley and Gioia, 2004), would the historically highly identified parent organization experience a degree of threat as well? Since this spread can carry particularly large consequences, understanding the potential for such organizational identity threat contagion between firms could be an important direction for future research.

Because organizations often fail to respond adequately to identity threats, future research on threat response would be of great significance. Assuming that members and groups who perceive an organizational identity threat can mobilize the leadership to drive an organizational response, there is still the question of what that response might be. The ways in which groups and their members defend themselves against threat are linked (Brown and Starkey, 2000; Janis, 1982). We suspect that the initial responses of individuals and groups who perceived the threat will influence the organizational responses. Therefore, a future line of research should examine two distinct types of responses: protecting the threatened identity, which we believe is the default response to threat (Brown and Starkey, 2000; Petriglieri, 2011), and changing the threatened identity. A particularly generative avenue of focus would be to investigate the impact of time on the threat responses of an organization and its members, an subject that has rarely been explored (a notable exception is Dutton and Dukerich's (1991) study of the evolution of organizational responses to threat by the New York-New Jersey Port Authority). Such longitudinal research is particularly interesting when considering cross-level dynamics, such as how the responses of an organization and its members shape each other.

Future research could also explore the aftereffects of threat, that is, the organizational consequences of threat response. When the threat response of individual members is aligned with the organization's threat response, beneficial consequences may result, because the individual responses enhance the organizational response. For example, when the threat to the Medlay Group's organizational identity attribute of "family of friends" spread to its members' identities, they responded by engaging in face-saving tactics that restored social norms and the organizational identity attribute (Golden-Biddle and Rao, 1997). Conversely, when the individual and organizational responses are misaligned, problematic consequences usually follow. This occurs most often when the threat to members' identities is caused by the organizational threat response (i.e., it is a secondary threat), as opposed to the original threat itself. This was the case when top-tier consulting firm McKinsey's organizational identity attribute of "trusted confidential advisor" was threatened after its ex-CEO was jailed for insider trading. The organization's initial response was defensive and an attempt to distance itself from the incident. This response, however, threatened the identities of both current members and alumni of the firm. Their actions in response to the threat shaped a secondary response from the organization's leaders, who changed some of the firm's practices to realign its image to its desired identity.

In conclusion, we offer one final suggestion to scholars interested in organizational identity threat. The focus of much previous work, and of this chapter, has been on the recognition and mobilization of organizations *against* identity threat. However, threat is not necessarily negative; in fact, it can provoke changes to an organization's identity that enable it to adapt to environmental changes and to evolve with an industry or market. Understanding when organizational identity threat can be harnessed in a generative way is another exciting area for future research.

REFERENCES

Anteby, M. and Molnár, V. (2012). "Collective Memory Meets Organizational Identity: Remembering to Forget in a Firm's Rhetorical History." *Academy of Management Journal* 55(3): 515–40.

Ashforth, B. E. and Johnson, S. A. (2001). "Which Hat to Wear? The Relative Salience of Multiple Identities in Organizational Contexts." In *Social Identity Processes in Organizational Contexts*, edited by M. A. Hogg and D. J. Terry, 31–48. Philadelphia: Psychological Press.

Atchley, R. C. (1989). "A Continuity Theory of Normal Aging." *The Gerontologist* 29(2): 183–90.

Balser, D. B. and Carmin, J. (2009). "Leadership Succession and the Emergence of an Organizational Identity Threat." *Nonprofit Management and Leadership* 20(2): 185–201.

Barney, J. B., Bunderson, J. S., Foreman, P., Gustafson, L. T., Huff, A. S., Martins, L. L., Reger, R. K., Sarason, Y., and Stimpert, J. L. (1998). "A Strategy Conversation on the Topic of Organization Identity." In *Identity in Organizations: Building Theory through Conversations*, edited by D. A. Whetten and P. C. Godfrey, 99–168. Thousand Oaks, CA: SAGE.

Baron, D. P. (2003). "Private Politics." *Journal of Economics and Management Strategy*, 12(1): 31–66.

Benson, J. A. (1988). "Crisis Revisited: An Analysis of Strategies Used by Tylenol in the Second Tampering Episode." *Communication Studies* 39(1): 49–66.

Berge, D. T. (1990). *The First 24 Hours: A Comprehensive Guide to Successful Crisis Management*. Cambridge, MA: Basil Blackwell.

Bodenhausen, G. V. and Macrae, C. N. (1998). "Stereotype Activation and Inhibition." In *Advances in Social Cognition*, vol. 11, edited by R. S. Wyer, 1–52. Hillsdale, NJ: Lawrence Erlbaum Associates.

Brown, A. D. and Starkey, K. (2000). "Organizational Identity and Learning: A Psychodynamic Perspective." *Academy of Management Review* 25(1): 102–20.

Burke, P. J. (1991). "Identity Processes and Social Stress." *American Sociological Review* 56(6): 836–49.

Canato, A., Ravasi, D., and Phillips, N. (2013). "Coerced Practice Implementation in Cases of Low Cultural Fit: Cultural Change and Practice Adaptation during the Implementation of Six Sigma at 3M." *Academy of Management Journal* 56(6): 1724–53.

Cialdini, R. B., Borden, R. J., Thorne, A., Walker, M. R., Freeman, S., and Sloan, L. R. (1976). "Basking in Reflected Glory: Three (Football) Field Studies." *Journal of Personality and Social Psychology* 34: 366–75.

Clark, S. M., Gioia, D. A., Ketchen, D. J., and Thomas, J. B. (2010). "Transitional Identity as a Facilitator of Organizational Identity Change during a Merger." *Administrative Science Quarterly* 55(3): 397–438.

Corley, K. G. (2004). "Defined by our Strategy or our Culture? Hierarchical Differences in Perceptions of Organizational Identity and Change." *Human Relations*, 57(9): 1145–77.

Corley, K. G. and Gioia, D. A. (2000). "The Rankings Game: Managing Business School Reputation." *Corporate Reputation Review* 3(4): 319–33.

Corley, K. G. and Gioia, D. A. (2004). "Identity Ambiguity and Change in the Wake of a Corporate Spin-Off." *Administrative Science Quarterly* 49(2): 173–208.

Davis, G., Mcadam, D., Scott, W., and Zald, M. (2005). *Social Movements and Organization Theory*. Cambridge: Cambridge University Press.

Dutton, J. E. and Dukerich, J. M. (1991). "Keeping an Eye on the Mirror: Image and Identity in Organizational Adaptation." *Academy of Management Journal* 34(3): 517–54.

Dutton, J. E., Dukerich, J. M., and Harquail, C. V. (1994). "Organizational Images and Member Identification." *Administrative Science Quarterly* 39(2): 239–63.

Elsbach, K. D. and Kramer, R. M. (1996). "Members' Responses to Organizational Identity Threats: Encountering and Countering the *Business Week* Rankings." *Administrative Science Quarterly* 41(3): 442–76.

Fiol, C. M., Pratt, M. G., and O'Connor, E. J. (2009). "Managing Intractable Identity Conflicts." *Academy of Management Review* 34(1): 32–55.

Gini, A. (2001). *My Job, My Self*. London: Routledge.

Gioia, D. A., Schultz, M., and Corley, K. G. (2000). "Organizational Identity, Image, and Adaptive Instability." *The Academy of Management Review* 25(1): 63–81.

Gioia, D. A. and Thomas, J. B. (1996). "Identity, Image, and Issue Interpretation: Sensemaking during Strategic Change in Academia." *Administrative Science Quarterly* 41(3): 370–403.

Glynn, M. A. (2000). "When Cymbals Become Symbols: Conflict over Organizational Identity within a Symphony Orchestra." *Organization Science* 11(3): 285–98.

Golden-Biddle, K. and Rao, H. (1997). "Breaches in the Boardroom: Organizational Identity and Conflicts of Commitment in a Nonprofit Organization." *Organization Science* 8(6): 593–611.

Gould, L. J. (2001). "Introduction." In *The Systems Psychodynamics of Organizations*, edited by L. J. Gould, L. F. Stapley, and M. Stein, 1–15. London: Karnac.

Graffin, S. D., Bundy, J., Porac, J. F., Wade, J. B., and Quinn, D. P. (2013). "Falls from Grace and the Hazards of High Status: The 2009 British MP Expense Scandal and its Impact on Parliamentary Elites." *Administrative Science Quarterly* 58(3): 313–45.

Grandey, A. A., Krannitz, M. A., and Slezak, T. (2013). "We are … more than Football: Three Stories of Identity Threat by Penn State Insiders." *Industrial and Organizational Psychology* 6: 134–55.

Greyser, S. A. (1992). "Johnson & Johnson: The Tylenol Tragedy." *Harvard Business School Case*, 583043.

Gutierrez, B., Howard-Grenville, J., and Scully, M. A. (2010). "The Faithful Rise up: Split Identification and an Unlikely Change Effort." *Academy of Management Journal* 53(4): 673–99.

Hatch, M. J. and Schultz, M. (2002). "The Dynamics of Organizational Identity." *Human Relations* 55(8): 989–1018.

Hirschman, A. O. (1970). *Exit, Voice and Loyalty: Responses to Decline in Firms, Organizations, and States*. Cambridge, MA: Harvard University Press.

Hsu, G. and Elsbach, K. D. (2013). "Explaining Variation in Organizational Identity Categorization." *Organization Science*, 24(4): 996–1013.

Humphreys, M. and Brown, A. D. (2002). "Narratives of Organizational Identity and Identification: A Case Study of Hegemony and Resistance." *Organization Studies* 23: 421–47.

Ibarra, H. (1993). "Personal Networks of Women and Minorities in Management: A Conceptual Framework." *Academy of Management Review* 18(1): 56–87.

Ibarra, H. (1992). Homophily and Differential Returns: Sex Differences in Network Structure and Access in an Advertising Firm." *Administrative Science Quarterly* 37(3): 422–47.

Jacobs, G., Christie-Zeyse, J., Keegan, A., and Pólos, L. (2008). "Reactions to Organizational Identity Threats in Times of Change: Illustrations from the German Police." *Corporate Reputation Review* 11(3): 245–61.

Jacques, E. (1955). "Social Systems as a Defence against Persecutory and Depressive Anxiety." In *New Directions in Psychoanalysis*, edited by M. Klein, 478–98. London: Tavistock.

Janis, I. L. (1982). *Groupthink*, 2nd edn. Boston: Houghton Mifflin.

Johnson & Johnson. (2015). "Our Credo." Retrieved from http://Www.Jnj.Com/About-Jnj/Jnj-Credo on February 13, 2015.

Kanter, R. M. (2010). "Leadership in a Globalizing World." In *Handbook of Leadership Theory and Practice*, edited by N. Noria and R. Khurana, 569–610. Boston, MA: Harvard Business Press.

Kellogg, K. C. (2009). "Operating Room: Relational Spaces and Microinstitutional Change in Surgery." *American Journal of Sociology* 115(3): 657–711.

King, B. G. and Whetten, D. A. (2008). "Rethinking the Relationship between Reputation and Legitimacy: A Social Actor Conceptualization." *Corporate Reputation Review*, 11(3): 192–207.

Livesey, S. M. (2001). "Eco-Identity as Discursive Struggle: Royal Dutch/Shell, Brent Spar, and Nigeria." *Journal of Business Communication* 38(1): 58–91.

Long, S. (2006). "Organizational Defenses against Anxiety: What Has Happened since the 1955 Jaques Paper?" *International Journal of Applied Psychoanalytic Studies* 3(4): 279–95.

Lukes, S. (1974). *Power: A Radical View*. London: Macmillan.

Magee, J. C. and Galinsky, A. D. (2008). "Chapter 8: Social Hierarchy: The Self-Reinforcing Nature of Power and Status." *Academy of Management Annals* 2(1): 351–98.

Martins, L. L. (2005). "A Model of the Effects of Reputational Rankings on Organizational Change." *Organization Science* 16(6): 701–20.

Menzies, I. E. P. (1960). "A Case-Study in the Functioning of Social Systems as a Defence against Anxiety." *Human Relations* 13: 95–121.

Newsham, J. and Ross, C. (2014). "More Vendors Say They Cut Ties to Market Basket." *Boston Globe*, August 19.

Petriglieri, G. and Petriglieri, J. L. (2010). "Identity Workspaces: The Case of Business Schools." *Academy of Management Learning and Education*, 9(1): 44–60.

Petriglieri, J. L. (2011). "Under Threat: Responses to and the Consequences of Threats to Individuals' Identities." *Academy of Management Review* 36(4): 641–62.

Petriglieri, J. L. (2015). "Co-creating Relationship Repair Pathways to Reconstructing Destabilized Organizational Identification." *Administrative Science Quarterly* 60(3): 518–57.

Phillips, D. J. and Kim, Y. (2009). "Why Pseudonyms? Deception as Identity Preservation among Jazz Record Companies, 1920-1929." *Organization Science* 20(3): 481–99.

Pratt, M. G. (1998). "To Be or Not to Be? Central Questions in Organizational Identification." In *Identity In Organizations: Building Theory Through Conversations*, edited by D. A. Whetten and P. C. Godfrey, 171–207. Thousand Oaks, CA: SAGE.

Pratt, M. G. and Foreman, P. O. (2000). "Classifying Managerial Responses to Multiple Organizational Identities." *Academy of Management Review* 25(1): 18–42.

Proffitt Jr., W. T. and Spicer, A. (2006). "Shaping the Shareholder Activism Agenda: Institutional Investors and Global Social Issues." *Strategic Organization* 4(2): 165–90.

Ramarajan, L. (2014). "Past, Present, and Future Research on Multiple Identities: Toward an Intrapersonal Network Approach." *Academy of Management Annals* 8(1): 589–659.

Rao, H., Monin, P., and Durand, R. (2003). "Institutional Change in Toque Ville: Nouvelle Cuisine as an Identity Movement in French Gastronomy." *American Journal of Sociology* 108(4): 795–843.

Ravasi, D. and Schultz, M. (2006). "Responding to Organizational Identity Threats: Exploring the Role of Organizational Culture." *Academy of Management Journal* 49(3): 433–58.

Reid, E. M. and Toffel, M. W. (2009). "Responding to Public and Private Politics: Corporate Disclosure of Climate Change Strategies." *Strategic Management Journal*, 30(11): 1157–78.

Stangor, C. (1988). "Stereotype Accessibility and Information Processing." *Personality and Social Psychology Bulletin* 14: 694–708.

Staw, B. M., Sandelands, L. E., and Dutton, J. E. (1981). "Threat-Rigidity Effects in Organizational Behavior: A Multilevel Analysis." *Administrative Science Quarterly* 26(4): 501.

Swann Jr, W. B., Rentfrow, P. J., and Guinn, J. S. (2002). "Self-Verification: The Search for Coherence." In *Handbook of Self and Identity*, edited by M. R. Leary and J. J. P. Tangney, 367–83. New York: Guilford Press.

Swann, Jr, W. B., William B., Johnson, R. E., and Bosson, J. K. (2009). "Identity Negotiation at Work." *Research in Organizational Behavior* 29: 81–109.

Tichy, N. M. (1981). "Networks in Organizations." In *Handbook of Organization Design*, vol. 2, edited by P. C. Nystrom and W. H. Starbuck, 225–48. New York: Oxford University Press.

Tripsas, M. (2009). "Technology, Identity, and Inertia through the Lens of 'The Digital Photography Company.'" *Organization Science* 20(2): 440–61.

Vega, T. (2012). "Campus Protests Return, but over Rebranding." *New York Times*, December 26.

Zald, M. N. and Berger, M. A. (1978). "Social Movements in Organizations: Coup D'état, Insurgency, and Mass Movements." *American Journal of Sociology* 83(4): 823–61.

Zuckerman, E. (2016). "Optimal Distinctiveness Revisited: An Integrative Framework for Understanding the Balance between Differentiation and Conformity in Individual and Organizational Identities." In *The Oxford Handbook of Organizational Identity*, edited by M. G. Pratt, M. Schultz, B. E. Ashforth, and D. Ravasi, 183–99. Oxford: Oxford University Press.

CHAPTER 14

ORGANIZATIONAL IDENTITY AND THE UNDESIRED SELF

KIMBERLY D. ELSBACH AND JANET M. DUKERICH

INTRODUCTION

IN this chapter we focus on the relationship between an organization's identity and its members' self-concepts. Organizational identity has been defined as "the central, distinctive, and continuous characteristic of an [organization] ... [that is related to] a more or less clear mission or role, along with certain values, goals, beliefs" (Ashforth, Rogers, and Corley, 2011: 1145). The individual self-concept may be defined as the conception an individual has of him or herself as a physical, social, and spiritual being (Gecas, 1982).

Organizations often engage in attempts to form and affirm desired organizational identities in order to gain institutional legitimacy or attain some level of distinctiveness that differentiates the organization from similar others (Elsbach and Kramer, 1996). If successful, such endeavors often lead to financial and reputational rewards for both the organizations (Millward and Postmes, 2010), and their members (Dutton and Dukerich, 1991). In particular, positive or distinctive organizational identities are likely to benefit members who *identify* with the organization (i.e., perceive a sense of overlap between their self-concepts and the identity of the organization (Ashforth and Mael, 1989)). For example, empirical studies indicate that organizations with prestigious or positively distinct identities are likely to provide individual identifiers (e.g., employees who identify with the organization) with enhanced self-esteem (van Dick et al., 2004; van Knippenberg and van Schie, 2000), positive distinctiveness (Clegg, Rhodes, and Kornberger, 2007; Gioia et al., 2010), and improved learning (Walumbwa, Cropanzano, and Hartnell, 2009). In turn, research indicates that organizations may gain a number of benefits from identifiers, including greater cooperation and work effort (Bartel, 2001), affective commitment (Carmeli, Gilat, and Weisberg, 2006; Kim et al., 2010), citizenship behaviors (Dukerich, Golden, and Shortell, 2002), and lower turnover (Olkkonen and Lipponen, 2006).

What we know much less about is *how the affirmation of desired organizational identities might pose threats to the self-concepts of organizational members*, that is, we know little about how leaders' efforts to form and/or affirm desired organizational identities may threaten the self-concepts of organizational members by compelling them to take on roles or personas that run counter to who they want to be. In other words, these identities may impose on organizational members *undesired selves*. Ogilvie (1987) defines the *undesired self* as the self-perception: "how I hope never to be," which contrasts with self-perceptions of the idealized self (i.e., "who I would like to be").

In the following sections we explore the relationship between organizational identity and the undesired self. We examine how efforts to attain desired organizational identities may compel organizational members to enact undesired selves through their roles and group memberships—which may also align members with unwanted values and ideologies. For example, in attempting to attain an organizational identity of "high status," leaders may (inadvertently) compel their workers to engage in activities or assume roles important to that identity (e.g., being highly competitive), that also require them to enact undesired selves (e.g., being a cut-throat competitor, being a corporate spy). We examine how such outcomes may occur in the pursuit of a number of different organizational identities. In addition, we explore how organizational members may cope with the imposition of such undesired selves in their organizational lives. Through an explication of these coping strategies, we begin to explain how individuals may remain closely identified with an organization, despite their enactment of undesired selves. Before covering these issues, however, we provide a brief theoretical review of the undesired self and related constructs.

Understanding the Undesired Self: A Theoretical Overview

The concept of the undesired self is grounded in psychological research on different domains of the self (Higgins, 1987). According to this research, individuals have three basic domains of the self: (1) the *actual self*, which is their representation of how they are, most of the time, (2) the *ideal self*, which is their representation of how they wish to be, and (3) the *ought self*, which is their representation of how they should be. Much of the research on these self-domains has examined the effects of *discrepancies* between actual self-states and ideal or ought self-states from both the individual's standpoint as well as their beliefs as to how a significant other would assess them (Higgins, 1987).

Self-discrepancy research. In general, research on self-discrepancies has shown that experiencing incongruity between one's perceptions of desired and actual selves leads to distinct perceptual and emotional states. Thus, experiencing discrepancies between actual and ideal selves is shown to lead to perceptions that desired outcomes are unattainable (individuals' hopes and wishes or the hopes and wishes of others have not been fulfilled), and result in dejection-related emotions (i.e., disappointment, sadness, dissatisfaction). By contrast, experiencing discrepancies between actual and ought selves is shown to lead to perceptions that undesired outcomes are likely (such as punishment from the self or others because one has not attained the state that he or she is obligated to achieve), and result in agitation-related emotions (i.e., fear, threat, restlessness).

These findings—which comprise *a self-discrepancy theory* (Higgins, 1987; Higgins, Klein, and Strauman, 1985)—are useful because they help to explain why and how individuals may engage in different kinds of self-protective behaviors in the face of self-discrepancies. For example, discrepancies between actual and ideal selves (that result in disappointment) are predicted to lead to a "promotion focus" (i.e., a desire to seek and attain positive outcomes), and may motivate individuals to redouble their efforts to achieve their idealized selves (Higgins, 1987). By contrast, discrepancies between actual and ought selves (that result in fear) are predicted to lead to a "prevention focus" (i.e., pursuit of safety and avoidance of unwanted outcomes), and may motivate individuals to avoid future tasks that may highlight their shortcomings (Higgins, 1987).

Empirical research provides strong support for these predictions and for self-discrepancy theories in general (Higgins, 1987; 1999; Higgins et al., 1986; Shah, Higgins, and Friedman, 1998; Higgins et al., 1994). Despite these virtues, self-discrepancy theories largely ignore an important self-domain: *the undesired self.* As noted earlier, the undesired self is defined as "how I hope never to be" (Olgilvie, 1987: 381), and is viewed as the logical rival to the ideal self (i.e., "how I wish to be"). That is, the undesired self, not the actual self, may be the primary antagonist to the ideal self.

Research on the undesired self. The undesired self is predicted to contain, not only abstracted images of undesired possible selves ("there but for the grace of God go I"), but also memories of "dreaded experiences, embarrassing situations, fearsome events, and unwanted emotions that actually occurred sometime in the individual's past" (Ogilvie, 1987: 380).[1] In this manner, the undesired self is seen as more concrete and less abstract than the ideal self, which is hypothesized to contain more idealized and fictional images (Ogilvie, 1987). For example, an undesired self might be defined as "the angry, out of control person that surfaced once when I was cut-off on the freeway by another driver." As a result of such concrete images, the undesired self is more firmly embedded in a person's self-concept than is the ideal self, and thus, is harder to ignore when making comparisons to one's actual self. Thus, the undesired self is

---

[1] Carver, Lawrence, and Scheier (1999) discuss a similar concept, the "feared self," which consists of "a set of qualities the person wants not to become but is concerned about possibly becoming" (p. 785).

predicted to be the preferred reference point for judging life satisfaction. Laboratory research has supported these predictions (Phillips, Silvia, and Paradise, 2007), and shown that, compared to the ideal self, enacting an undesired self is more strongly predictive of increased depressive mood (Heppen and Olgivie, 2003), access to implicit death thoughts (Ogilvie, Cohen, and Solomon, 2008), and reports of fatigue and lack of energy (Mora et al., 2012).

Despite these laboratory findings, we know little about how the undesired self operates in organizational contexts. For example, while extant laboratory research suggests that the undesired self is related to personal characteristics and traits (e.g., being characterized as "untrustworthy," "arrogant," or "greedy"), we know less about how it might relate to enactment of occupations or roles in organizations (e.g., being a "manager" or "salesperson"). In addition, we don't know if the undesired self has a range of "levels" or degrees that may vary by organizational role. That is, can an undesired self comprise a set of characteristics and/or traits that one wishes merely to avoid expressing (e.g., portraying a very formal, "professional" appearance and demeanor), as well as characteristics and traits one finds completely unthinkable and abhorrent (e.g., being an aggressive salesperson)? Such variations in enacted selves may be aligned with different organizational roles that individuals are compelled to take on at work. Finally, it is unclear how the undesired self relates to organizational identities. Organizational scholars have long held that individual self-concepts are related to organizational identities (Ashforth and Mael, 1989). For example, a positive and desirable organizational identity has been shown to enhance the self-concepts of individuals who are affiliated and identified with that organization (Dutton and Dukerich, 1991), while a negative or undesired organizational identity may pose a threat to those same self-concepts (Elsbach and Kramer, 1996). Yet, we know little about how an organizational identity might relate to the undesired selves of organizational members.

In the remainder of this chapter, we examine how organizations that are attempting to affirm desired organizational identities may, unwittingly, foist undesired selves onto their members. We examine how this might occur through the imposition and definition of organizational roles and group memberships, and how the level of undesiredness of selves may vary across these roles and group memberships. We also examine how organizational members cope with the requirement to enact undesired selves in their organizations. We perform these examinations through a review of illustrative case study research where undesired selves appeared to be imposed on organizational members as a consequence of organizational identity affirmation.

How Organizational Identity Affirmations Impose Undesired Selves

Research on organizational identity affirmation (Elsbach, 2006) suggests that two of the most common identities that are desired by organizations are: (1) legitimacy, and (2) distinctiveness. In the following sections, we review extant research on affirmation of these two organizational identities that illustrates how such affirmations may impose onto members' undesired selves.

Legitimate organizational identities and undesired selves. Organizational legitimacy has been defined as a "generalized perception or assumption that the actions of an entity are desirable, proper, or appropriate within some socially constructed system of norms, values, beliefs, and definitions" (Suchman, 1995: 574). As this definition indicates, legitimacy requires conformance with social and institutional norms (Deephouse, 1996). Thus, organizations that wish to portray legitimating identities are often found to engage in actions so as to conform to these norms (Glynn and Watkiss, 2012). As Glynn and Watkiss (2012: 78) note:

> By appropriating sanctioned and institutionalized templates, norms, values, or standards, organizational identities signal their social fitness, increasing their comprehensibility and acceptance.

Such normative conformance is typically displayed by the adoption of well-established and frequently encountered structures or "blueprints" for organizing (Heugens and Lander, 2009). For example, organizations may adopt names that are considered typical for their industry (Glynn and Abzug, 2002). Thus, rather than using the name "Fred's Bank," a financial institution would be more likely to go by "First National Bank" (Glynn and Marquis, 2004). Similarly, organizations are likely to include normative roles, such as a chief financial officer, in their self-descriptions as a means of displaying conformance and attaining legitimacy.

This latter practice, however, may impose undesired selves on employees if the roles required cause these employees to see themselves as "how they hope never to be." For example, in a recent study of professional artistic workers, Elsbach and Caldwell-Wenman (2015) argued that these types of workers—who do creative work like design, writing, or architecture—often view themselves as "artists" and not as "corporate professionals." That is, the role of "corporate professional"—which was imposed on these workers by their titles and roles in their firms—appeared to be an undesired self for many of these workers. As one architect noted:

> I do not know how to put it, but it is a strenuous fight to all the time defend the aesthetic and architectural values and the details, and so forth. And then you know that in the end, the contractor comes with a solution that is uglier and half as expensive and promotes the idea successfully for the client, and then the whole concept is gone and things become, we think, uglier.
>
> (Styhre and Gluch, 2009: 229)

In another case, an advertising agency designer noted: "How can I be creative if I start to think like an MBA?" (Hackley and Kover, 2007: 70). This is a classic problem, as demonstrated by the numerous accounts of the struggles that professionals have in bureaucratic organizations (Beyer, 1981; Freidson, 1975; Goode, 1957; Scott, 1982; Sorensen and

Sorensen, 1974). Thus, Elsbach and Caldwell-Wenman (2015) suggest that many of these workers perceived antagonism between their true identities and those imposed upon them by their corporate positions. As Hackley and Kover (2007: 69) summarize:

> It is not merely out of perverseness that creatives resist many aspects of the organizational discipline to which most workers are subject. They feel that this resistance is fundamentally necessary to the integrity of their professional practice.

In these cases, the presence of an "undesired self" for artists (i.e., occupying a role that is aligned with the identity of a "corporate professional") is clearly evident, but appears relatively moderate compared to an imagined undesired self that would be avoided at all costs (e.g., taking on the role of a criminal "hit man"—who is paid to murder others). In this manner, the strength of the undesired self that is embodied in the role of "corporate professional" might be comparable to the strength of the undesired self that is embodied in the characteristics of being "dishonest and unauthentic". These are self-concepts that individuals are motivated to avoid, but could live with enacting, at least for short periods of time.

A similar type of undesired self may be enacted when employees transition into new roles that are required for organizational legitimacy (Ashforth, 2001). For example, in Ibarra's (1999) discussion of "provisional selves," she describes how rookie employees in investment banking and consulting "tried on" their new roles by attempting to match the role prototypes displayed by seasoned veterans in their fields. While some felt comfortable with these new roles, others felt that matching the prototypes was "not me," and in some cases, "the opposite of me." As one young investment banker noted,

> X is the best banker I have ever seen. He understands both the theory and the people, knows how to sell and how to get paid for it. He doesn't hesitate to ask for outrageous fees and get them. But I can't be like him when he says, 'Screw you, you're the client but you're wrong.'(Ibarra, 1999: 774)

Similarly, another new banker remarked:

> X is excellent with clients, one of the best. I worked with him trying to emulate his style, but it didn't help me. I react negatively to him as a person. Although it's successful, I find it insincere and manipulative. I have to like my role models as individuals.
>
> (Ibarra, 1999: 775)

In these cases, as in the case of the artists occupying roles of corporate professionals, it appears that taking on the norms that accompanied a new organizational role required employees to enact undesired selves that were undesirable, but not necessarily unthinkable.

Together, then, the above examples illustrate how pursuing legitimate and normative organizational identities might impose undesired selves onto employees. But this is not the only way that organizational identities may relate to undesired selves. As we discuss below, pursuing distinctive organizational identities may also impose undesired selves onto organizational members.

Distinctive organizational identities and undesired selves. Organizations typically want their identities to be more than legitimate, they also want them to be distinctive—a reflection of the unique character of the organization and its members (Glynn and Watkiss, 2012). Thus, organizations come to possess identities defined by distinctive traits such as innovation (Apple Computers), integrity (Berkshire Hathaway Investments), and fun (Southwest Airlines). Such identities are often important for attracting loyal constituents (Elsbach and Cable, 2015), and, as a result, are carefully managed over time (Elsbach and Kramer, 1996).

In some situations, however, an organization's adoption of new and distinctive identities that are aligned with new values and ideologies, may change what it means to be affiliated with the organization. For example, Elsbach (2006) described how the automaker Porsche caused discontent among many of its auto club members when the venerable sports car company began producing a Sports Utility Vehicle (SUV) in 2002. Porsche's leadership sold the new SUV as important to the firm's growth potential and desired identity as "complete" automaker, rather than a maker of sports cars only (Elsbach, 2006). Further, it was widely perceived as a move that would enhance the company's product diversity and appeal to the ever-growing SUV market. As an analyst for an automotive industry consulting firm noted, "SUV's have become the new fashion statement in this business" (Tanz, 2002: 2).

Yet, members of the Porsche Club of America were less than thrilled by the identity change, which made them members of a club that could be occupied by "soccer moms," and aligned them with values and ideologies associated with this demographic. As Tanz (2002: 1) notes in his article, adding the Cayenne to Porsche's lineup changed what it meant to be a Porsche owner:

> there can be no vision more heretical to a testosterone-poisoned 911 owner than that of a suburban mother loading groceries into the back of her Porsche after dropping her children off a soccer practice.... *people who have no interest in driving sports cars will be able to describe themselves as Porsche owners.* [emphasis added]

Another Porsche owner echoed this sentiment, saying:

> People will buy these Porche SUV's because they're a fad, and they'll embarrass the *real* Porsche crowd. [emphasis added].

> (Tanz, 2002: 1)

These quotes illustrate just how an organization's attempts to develop and maintain a new and distinctive identity can impose undesired selves onto those who closely identified with the organization's pre-existing identity. Further, they indicate that, in the case of Porsche, the undesired self that was created as a consequence of this identity was a relatively strong motivator of member behavior because it associated members with values and ideologies that were contrary to their self-concepts. As one Porsche driver, Mike Dini, noted in a *New York Times* story:

> Every SUV I've seen is driven by some soccer mom on her cellphone.... *I hate these people*, and that Porsche would *throw me into that category* made me speechless.... Just speechless. [emphasis added].

> (Tanz, 2002: 1)

Summary. Based on the above findings, we suggest that the affirmation of legitimate and/or distinctive organizational identities may impose role or membership requirements on to members that compel them to enact undesired selves. Further, we suggest that these undesired selves—that may be associated with undesired identities, values, or ideologies—may vary in their strength as motivators of behavior. In some cases, undesired selves are viewed as self-concepts to avoid, but not as extreme threats to one's identity (as in the examples of the architects described earlier). In other cases (as in the examples of the Porsche drivers), undesired selves may be negative enough to be viewed as severe threats to one's self-concept and never acceptable to enact.

In a similar vein, Petriglieri and Devine (see Ch. 13 in this handbook) discuss two types of identity threats, one that questions the validity of claimed identity ("you are not what you claim to be"), and one that involves the inconsistency with beliefs about a claimed identity ("you are not who we thought you were"). These two types of identity threats may correspond to the different levels of threat that we observed in the cases we have described. For example, in order to affirm a legitimate organizational identity, members may think of themselves enacting a role that is embarrassing or demeaning, which is akin to demonstrating that one is "not who we thought you were." In other cases, to affirm a new and distinctive organizational identity, members may think of themselves as being associated with an ideology that is opposite to their moral or aesthetic standards, which is akin to demonstrating that one is "not who you claim to be." In the following sections, we explore how individuals respond to both of these types of threats.

How Organizational Members Respond to the Imposition of Undesired Selves

While the studies and examples we have described suggest that, in their attempts to affirm legitimate and/or distinctive identities, organizations may impose undesired selves onto their constituents, this does not mean these constituents are helpless to respond. Along these lines, Petriglieri (2011: 647) describes a number of "identity threat coping responses" that individuals may use in response to identity threats, such as the imposition of undesired selves. She labels these responses as either "identity protection" (i.e., responses aimed at affecting the source of the threat, such as derogating the source of the threat, concealing the threat, or reframing the threat as unthreatening) or "identity restructuring" (i.e., responses aimed at affecting the threatened identity itself, such as reducing the importance of the identity, changing the meaning of the identity, or disengaging from the identity).

In the same manner, researchers of "identity work" examine how individuals attempt to manage perceptions of the various roles that make up their identities, and prevent conflicts between them (Snow and Anderson, 1987; Ibarra, 1999; Kreiner, Hollensbe, and Sheep, 2006; Ashforth, et al., 2007, Kreiner and Murphy (Ch. 15 in this handbook). For example, Kreiner et al. (2006) describe how Episcopal priests used identity work tactics to maintain perceptions of their professional roles (i.e., their roles as priest) that were congruent with, or at least not in conflict with, their personal roles (e.g., their roles as parents, coaches, or friends). Thus, some priests discussed how they maintained other personal roles, such as coaching a softball team, to remind themselves that their professional roles were not all-encompassing. In other cases, priests talked about using their dress (i.e., their priestly robes and collar) as a means of "flipping the switch" between their roles as priests and their other personal roles. Finally, Snow and Anderson (1987) note that "passing" or withholding/concealing information about a particular role or identity that is stigmatized (Goffman, 1963) may be another tactic.

In the case of imposed undesired selves, however, many of these types of responses and tactics may not be viable. This is because, in responding to undesired selves, individuals may wish to separate themselves completely from these identities (which makes most identity protection responses unviable), while at the same time, they remain tethered to these identities through their formal affiliations with the organization (which makes most identity restructuring responses less viable, unless one wishes to leave the organization altogether).

We suggest, then, that "changing the meaning" of their undesired selves is the most viable coping response (Petriglieri, 2011). Petriglieri (2011) uses the case of surgery interns in a study by Pratt, Rockman, and Kaufman (2006) to describe how individuals may change the meaning of identities. In this case, she describes how surgeons-in-training found their identities threatened when they discovered that their job involved large amounts of menial patient care, instead of the super-hero-like acts that they envisioned they would be performing. In response, these surgery interns revised what it meant to be a surgeon by redefining their identity as "the most complete doctors in the hospital" (Pratt et al., 2006: 247). Such a response seems viable for those compelled to enact undesired selves as a result of their organization's attempts to affirm desired identities.

In support of this notion, we found evidence in the case studies we have described and in other research, showing that individuals attempted to change the meaning of undesired selves when they found themselves enacting these self-concepts. They did this by either redefining the meaning of roles or demonstrating non-investment in roles. We discuss these two responses next.

Redefining the meaning of roles. In some cases, we found that organizational members attempted to change the meaning of their roles by taking actions that constrained who could occupy that role. For example, in the case of Porsche and its new, SUV-related identity, we found evidence that some prior owners attempted to define the role of "Porsche Club of American" member as excluding Cayenne (i.e., SUV) owners. In this way, these auto club members took the relatively extreme action of excluding some individuals from their organization as a way to protect their self-concepts. As Tanz (2002: 2) noted in his report on the introduction of Porsche's new SUV:

> At least one member [of the Porsche Club of America] has posted a demand on the organization's Internet bulletin board for a vote on whether Cayenne owners should be included in club events.

In other cases, organizational members may decide to embrace the role that they feel the organization has forced upon them, but to change what the role means to them. For example, in a study of a university faculty who were compelled to take on the role of "teaching faculty" when they did not receive tenure, Vannini (2006) found that this faculty appeared to alter the meaning of this role by defining it as "rebellious" and authentic. As Vannini reports:

> Many professors in the humanities and social sciences feel that what they value— knowledge and education, social emancipation, political responsibility, democratic pedagogy, etc.—is not valued by the university. This difference in personal and institutional values translates into a variety of behaviors and dispositions. At times, professors "rebel" against institutional forces and authentically dedicate themselves to teaching, taking great pride in "being against" the institution that employs them.
>
> (Vannini, 2006: 247)

Demonstrating non-investment in roles. A second coping response that organizational members may use to change the meaning of undesired selves is to signal that they are not fully invested in their enactment of an imposed role. That is, if they are unable to redefine imposed roles (as in the tactic above), organizational members may attempt to change the meaning of their *enactment* of those roles. Specifically, they may attempt to signal that their enactment of an imposed role (and undesired self) is not sincere nor is a reflection of their true selves.

For example, if members are required to enact undesired selves related to roles required for organizational legitimacy, they may claim that they are only enacting those roles to help the organization to look good, but not because they believe the roles reflect their true selves. Thus, in their study of artistic workers in an advertising agency, Hackley and Kover (2007: 68) noted how creative workers signaled their non-investment in engaging in commercial aspects of advertising by ".... distancing themselves ... from the commercial ethos, speaking repeatedly of advertising as 'bullshit', and of their preference for the superior values of art and literature." These types of remarks showed that their enactment of the role of "commercial artist" was merely *surface-acting*, and not a true representation of self and their values of aestheticism over commercialism.

In cases where enacting an undesired self is more difficult to distance from oneself (e.g., when a person becomes identified with a role), more drastic actions might be taken. In these cases, role-occupants might engage in *role-inconsistent behavior*. That is, they may actually flaunt their roles by engaging in behaviors that are explicitly inconsistent with those roles. For example, in their study of commercial architects, Brown et al. (2010: 531) related how some architects pursued aesthetic goals in their work that were clearly not commercially viable, despite their employment by a commercial firm. As one architect noted about one such project:

> I mean at the end of the day ... we can't be making any money off that project, it's a beautiful design and the only reason I'm pushing for it is because it's a beautiful design, like we absolutely, you love the architecture so you push for it. But from a pure commercial sense it just doesn't make sense.

In this case, it appears that the role-inconsistency may not have been obvious to others. Thus, it was possible to engage in such behaviors, on a limited basis, without fear of losing one's job. Such role flaunting does not appear, however, to be a viable defense tactic in situations where one's actions would be obvious to one's employer.

FRAMEWORK AND DISCUSSION

In the preceding sections we have discussed the concept of the undesired self, linked it to organizations' affirmations of desired identities, and examined how individuals compelled to enact it might respond. These ideas comprise a framework (illustrated in Figure 14. 1) relating organizational identity affirmation to the undesired self.

This framework suggests that the undesired self may be a common, yet under-appreciated self-conception that arises in organizational members as a result of organizational identity affirmation by organizational leaders. As a result, the framework has several theoretical implications for understanding links between organizational identities and member self-concepts. Further, this framework suggests a number of directions for future research. We discuss these issues next.

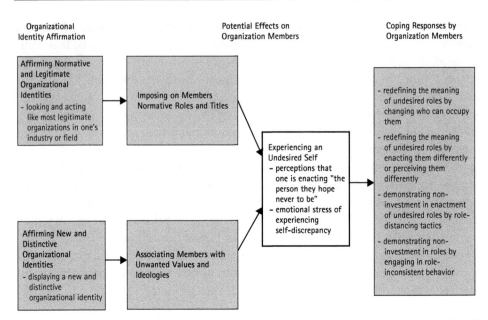

FIGURE 14.1 A framework relating organizational identity affirmation and the undesired self

Theoretical Implications: Organizational Identities and Member Self-Concepts

Organizational theorists have widely established that the identities of organizations have implications for the self-concepts of their members (Glynn, 2000; Corley, 2004). Most of the empirical research in this area has supported the general notion that organizational identities that are viewed positively by organizational members will have positive implications for those members' self-concepts, while organizational identities viewed negatively by members will have negative implications for those members' self-concepts (Dutton and Dukerich, 1991; Elsbach and Kramer, 1996, Dukerich et al., 2002; Humphreys and Brown, 2002).

In contrast to these findings, we suggest that, organizational identities that are viewed positively by *most* members may have negative implications for *some* members' self-concepts. In particular, positive organizational identities that compel some members to enact undesired selves, via their occupation of organizational roles, may threaten those members' self-concepts. This notion highlights the linkage between organizational identities and organizational roles, and suggests that identity theorists pay more attention to this linkage. Extant research on organizational roles has, to date, focused on the importance of organizational leaders, organizational culture, and industry norms as antecedents defining the form and function of organizational roles (Turner, 1986; Bechky, 2006). By contrast, research in organizational identity has had much less to say about organizational role definitions and requirements (Ashforth, 2001).

Our framework suggests that, in particular, organizational identity management tactics (Elsbach, 2006)—that highlight and emphasize specific identity dimensions (e.g., legitimacy or distinctiveness)—may help to define employee roles. Further, it suggests that organizational identity management that imposes undesired roles onto members may have particularly strong effects on role enactment by those members. One interesting implication of this suggestion is the notion of fit or congruence between organizational identities and member roles (i.e., "identity-role fit") as a consideration for organizational leaders engaged in organizational identity management. While extant research has begun to examine the notion of identity synergy (i.e., a state where involvement in an organization affirms important social identities of members (Fombelle, Jarvis, Ward, and Ostrom, 2012), the idea that organizational identities must also fit with the roles they require of members has not been studied to date.

This notion has important implications for the definition of organizational roles. For example, if organizational identities need to fit with the roles that the organization maintains, then defining very flexible and mutable roles that may be adapted to evolving organizational identities, may be an especially desirable strategy for organization leaders. In other words, identities that are connected to broad values (e.g., promoting health) versus narrow stances (e.g., being politically conservative) may be associated with broad role definitions that may be flexibly enacted. In turn, roles that may be flexibly enacted can be more easily modified to fit with these members' self-concepts and thus, may be less likely to impose undesired selves onto members. These ideas fit with research on flexible role enactment which has shown that such flexibility is conducive in working in temporary organizations populated by employees from diverse backgrounds (Bechky, 2006).

In addition, our framework suggests that the effects of organizational identity affirmations on role definitions may be central to defining undesired selves for an organization's members. That is, without the imposition of roles that result from organizational identity affirmation, some organizational members may not know what their undesired selves look like. This perspective reflects the notion of "social antagonism" that suggests that we understand who we are both by identifying practices we engage in and those in which we don't engage (Trent and Gao, 2009). As Elsbach and Caldwell-Wenman (2015: 5) note, "identity construction at work proceeds through a framework of 'structured antagonisms' (Delbridge, 1998: 108) (e.g., being in control versus complying with management) that confront workers on a daily basis." While individuals may have pre-existing ideas about their undesired selves, they may not truly understand the strength of these self-concepts until they are forced to enact them. Thus, it may be important for members to have their self-concepts challenged, occasionally, as a stimulus for re-affirming and maintaining a sense of self in the organization (Delbridge, 1998). In this way, organizational identities and identity management practices may play an important role in the refinement and maintenance of member self-concepts.

DIRECTIONS FOR FUTURE RESEARCH

While our framework provides some new insights about organizational identity and its relation to organizational roles, it also uncovers additional questions that need to be answered. These questions provide at least two directions for future research.

First, our discussion suggests that the relationship between identity management and the roles that members may have to assume in order for those identities to be realized is an area of research that has not been fully explored. When organizational identity management involves purposeful change in the distinctive characteristics of a firm, for example, some organizational members may be required to assume roles to help create the change and in doing so, may find themselves acting in ways that encompass a self-concept that is undesirable. Thus, a sales manager at Porsche may have been charged with pushing the company's new SUV as part of the cool and sophisticated image of what it means to be a Porsche owner, even while believing that the new vehicle diluted the identity of the company and feeling that the company was now catering to "soccer moms." While these findings suggest that many organizational members at many levels may be strongly influenced by changes in organizational identity, most extant research has tended to focus on organizational leaders who envision the creation or change in identity (Ravasi and Schultz, 2006; Rodrigues and Child, 2008; Scott and Lane, 2000). Not as much attention has been paid to those in the middle who have to *enact* the change by virtue of their roles in the organization (Alvesson and Empson, 2008; Alvesson and Willmott, 2002), and while going along with the organizational mandate, find themselves engaging in activities that may run counter to what they would like to believe about themselves.

Second, our insights suggest that further research is needed to understand the link between organizational identities and organizational roles. Being in a role can bring out all the worst parts of the self. As noted earlier, the feared self contains a set of qualities that the person doesn't want but is concerned about becoming (Markus and Nurius, 1986). Ashforth has defined role disidentification as when the role "challenges or contradicts valued aspects of the self" (2001: 76). He argues that strong role disidentification is not a sustainable state, since it would likely result in active resistance to the role and/or the organization, thus leading to turnover. However, at times one may feel compelled to take on a feared role in the organization in order to help the organization attain or maintain desired organizational identities, such as sales people promoted to managers or directors, physicians becoming chief medical officers, lawyers assuming partnership positions, or faculty moving into administrative roles. Through this promotion process, these individuals may find themselves becoming what they most feared to be.

In this vein, it would be interesting to study the processes by which people come to understand their "new selves" in their new role and how, or if, they come to terms with their new identity as they take on very different roles in the organization. As Ashforth

(2001) noted, anyone can feel ambivalence about their role, believing that some parts fit well with their identity while other aspects are antithetical with who they believe they are. In the situations we studied, however, the ambivalence is more complex: individuals feel tension because the role brings out aspects of their undesired selves; however, they believe the roles are necessary for the organization in order to realize the desired organizational identity. How this tension is resolved and the self-concept of the individual maintained is an important area to pursue.

Conclusion

Organizational identity has long been connected to the self-concepts of organizational members. Yet, researchers have neglected an important self-conception in making this connection: the undersired self. In this chapter we have introduced the undesired self as an important self-conception that may be strongly affected by organizational identities. Given the well-known motivating effects of negative self-perceptions, we feel that the undesired self should be considered more centrally in organizational identity research. We hope our introductory framework provides a starting point for this research.

References

Alvesson, M. and Empson, L. (2008). "The Construction of Organizational Identity: Comparative Case Studies of Consulting Firms." *Scandinavian Journal of Management* 24: 1–16.

Alvesson, M. and Willmott, H. (2002). "Identity Regulation as Organizational Control: Producing the Appropriate Individual." *Journal of Management Studies*, 39: 619–44.

Ashforth, B. E. (2001). *Role Transitions in Organizational Life*. Mahwah, NJ: Lawrence Erlbaum Associates.

Ashforth, B. E., Kreiner, G. E., Clark, M. A., and Fugate, M. (2007). "Normalizing Dirty Work: Managerial Tactics for Countering Occupational Taint." *Academy of Management Journal* 50: 149–74.

Ashforth, B. E. and Mael, F. (1989). "Social Identity Theory and the Organization." *Academy of Management Review* 14: 20–39.

Ashforth, B. E., Rogers, K. M. and Corley, K. (2011). "Identity in Organizations: Exploring Cross-Level Dynamics." *Organization Science* 22: 1144–56.

Bartel, C. A. (2001). "Social Comparisons in Boundary-Spanning Work: Effects of Community Outreach on Members' Organizational Identity and Identification." *Administrative Science Quarterly* 46: 379–413.

Bechky, B. A. (2006). "Gaffers, Gofers, and Grips: Role-Based Coordination in Temporary Organizations." *Organization Science* 17: 3–21.

Beyer, J. M. (1981). "Ideologies, Values, and Decision Making in Organizations." In *Handbook of Organizational Design*, vol. 2, edited by P. C. Nystrom and W. H. Starbuck, 166–202. Oxford: Oxford University Press.

Brown, A. D., Kornberger, M., Clegg, S. R., and Carter, C. (2010). "'Invisible Walls' and 'Silent Hierarchies': A Case Study of Power Relations in an Architecture Firm." *Human Relations* 63: 525–49.

Carmeli, A., Gilat, G., and Weisberg, J. (2006). "Perceived External Prestige, Organizational Identification, and Affective Commitment: A Stakeholder Approach." *Corporate Reputation Review* 9: 92–104.

Carver, C. S., Lawrence, J. W., and Scheier, M. F. (1999). "Self-Discrepancies and Affect: Incorporating the Role of Feared Selves." *Personality and Social Psychology Bulletin* 25: 783–92.

Chreim, S. (2005). "The Continuity-Change Duality in Narrative Texts of Organizational Identity." *Journal of Management Studies* 42: 567–93.

Clegg, S. R., Rhodes, C., and Kornberger, M. (2007). "Desperately Seeking Legitimacy: Organizational Identity and Emerging Industries." *Organization Studies* 28: 495–513.

Corley, K. G. (2004). "Defined by our Strategy or our Culture? Hierarchical Differences in Perceptions of Organizational Identity and Change." *Human Relations* 57: 1145–77.

Deephouse, D. L. (1996.) "Does Isomorphism Legitimate?" *Academy of Management Journal* 39: 1024–39.

Delbridge, R. (1998). *Life on the Line in Contemporary Manufacturing: The Workplace Experiences of Lean Production and the "Japanese" Model*. Oxford: Oxford University Press.

Dukerich, J. M., Golden, B. R., and Shortell, S. M. (2002). "Beauty Is in the Eye of the Beholder: The Impact of Organizational Identification, Identity, and Image on the Cooperative Behaviors of Physicians." *Administrative Science Quarterly* 47: 507–33.

Dutton, J. E. and Dukerich, J. M. (1991). "Keeping an Eye on the Mirror: Image and Identity in Organizational Adaptation." *Academy of Management Journal* 34: 517–54.

Elsbach, K. D. (2006). *Organizational Perception Management*. Mahwah, NJ: Lawrence Erlbaum Associates.

Elsbach, K. D. and Cable, D. M. (2015). "The Role of Authentic Self-Expression in Motivating Collective Identification: A Study of NASCAR Fans." Working Paper.

Elsbach, K. D. and Caldwell-Wenman, A. (2015). "The Role of Antagonism in the Identities of Professional Artistic Workers." In *The Oxford Handbook of Creativity, Innovation, and Entrepreneurship*, edited by J. Zhou, C. Shalley, and M. Hitt, 103–20. Oxford: Oxford University Press.

Elsbach, K. D. and Kramer, R. M. (1996). "Members' Responses to Organizational Identity Threats: Encountering and Countering the *Business Week* Rankings." *Administrative Science Quarterly* 41: 442–76.

Fombelle, P. W., Jarvis, C. B., Ward, J., and Ostrom, L. (2012). "Leveraging Customers' Multiple Identities: Identity Synergy as a Driver of Organizational Identification." *Journal of the Academy of Marketing Science* 40: 587–604.

Gecas, V. (1982). "The Self-Concept." *Annual Review of Psychology* 8: 1–33.

Gioia, D. A., Price, K. N., Hamilton, A. L., and Thomas, J. B. (2010). "Forging an Identity: An Insider-Outsider Study of Processes Involved in the Formation of Organizational Identity." *Administrative Science Quarterly* 55: 1–46.

Gioia, D. A., Schultz, M., and Corley, K. G. (2000). "Organizational Identity, Image, and Adaptive Instability." *Academy of Management Review* 25: 63–81.

Glynn, M. (2000). "When Cymbals Become Symbols: Conflict over Organizational Identity within a Symphony Orchestra." *Organization Science* 11: 285–98.

Glynn, M. and Abzug, R. (2002). "Institutional Identity: Symbolic Isomorphism and Organizational Names." *Academy of Management Journal* 45(1): 267–80.

Glynn, M. A. and Marquis, C. (2004). "When Good Names Go Bad: Symbolic Illegitimacy in Organizations." In *Research in the Sociology of Organizations*, vol. 22, edited by C. Johnson, 147–70. Bingley: Emerald Group Publishing.

Glynn, M. A. and Watkiss, L. (2012). "Exploring Cultural Mechanisms of Organizational Identity Construction." In *Constructing Identity in and around Organizations*, edited by M. Schultz, S. Maguire, A. Langley, and H. Tsoukas, 63–88. Oxford: Oxford University Press.

Goffman, E. (1963). *Stigma: Notes on the Management of Spoiled Identity*. Englewood Cliffs, NJ: Prentice-Hall.

Goode, W. J. (1957). "Community within a Community: The Professions." *American Sociological Review* 22: 194–200.

Hackley, C. and Kover, A. J. (2007). "The Trouble with Creatives: Negotiating Creative Identity in Advertising Agencies." *International Journal of Advertising* 26: 63–78.

Heppen, J. B. and Olgivie, D. M. (2003). "Predicting Affect from Global Self-Discrepancies: The Dual Role of the Undesired Self." *Journal of Social and Clinical Psychology* 22: 347–68.

Heugens, P. P. M. A. R. and Lander, M. W. (2009). "Structure! Agency! (and Other Quarrels): A Meta-Analysis of Institutional Theories of Organization." *Academy of Management Journal* 52: 61–85.

Higgins, E. T. (1987). "Self-Discrepancy: A Theory Relating Self and Affect." *Psychological Review* 94: 319–40.

Higgins, E. T. (1999). "When Do Self-Discrepancies Have Specific Relations to Emotions? The Second Generation Questions of Tengney, Niedenthal, Covert, and Barlow (1998)." *Journal of Personality and Social Psychology* 77: 1313–17.

Higgins, E. T., Bond, R. N., Klein, R., and Strauman, T. (1986). "Self-Discrepancies and Emotional Vulnerability: How Magnitude, Accessibility, and Type of Discrepancy Influence Affect." *Journal of Personality and Social Psychology* 51: 5–15.

Higgins, E. T., Klein, R., and Strauman, T. (1985). "Self-Concept Discrepancy Theory: A Psychological Model for Distinguishing among Different Aspects of Depression and Anxiety." *Social Cognition* 3: 51–76.

Higgins, E. T., Roney, C. J. R., Crowe, E., and Hymes, C. (1994). "Ideal versus Ought Predilections for Approach and Avoidance: Distinct Self-Regulatory Systems." *Journal of Personality and Social Psychology* 66: 276–86.

Humphreys, M. and Brown, A. D. (2002). "Narratives of Organizational Identity and Identification: A Case Study of Hegemony and Resistance." *Organization Studies* 23: 421–47.

Ibarra, H. (1999). "Provisional Selves: Experimenting with Image and Identity in Professional Adaptation." *Administrative Science Quarterly* 44: 764–91.

Kim, H., Lee, M., Lee, H., and Kim, N. (2010). "Corporate Social Responsibility and Employee-Company Identification." *Journal Of Business Ethics* 95: 557–69.

Kreiner, G. E., Hollensbe, E. C., and Sheep, M. L. (2006). "Where Is the 'Me' among the 'We'? Identity Work and the Search for Optimal Balance." *Academy of Management Journal* 49: 1031–57.

Kreiner, G. E. and Murphy, C. (2016). "Organizational Identity Work." In *The Oxford Handbook of Organizational Identity*, edited by M. G. Pratt, M. Schultz, B. E. Ashforth, and D. Ravasi, 276–93. Oxford: Oxford University Press.

Markus, H. and Nurius, P. (1986). "Possible Selves." *American Psychologist* 41: 954–69.

Millward, L. J. and Postmes, T. (2010). "Who We Are Affects How We Do: Financial Benefits of Organizational Identification." *British Journal of Management* 21: 327–39.

Mora, P. A., Musumeci-Szabo, T., Popan, J., Beamon, T., and Leventhal, H. (2012). "Exploring the Relationship among the Undesired Self, Health, and Mood in Older Adults." *Journal of Applied Social Psychology* 42: 2041–63.

Ogilvie, D. M. (1987). "The Undesired Self: A Neglected Variable in Personality Research." *Journal of Personality and Social Psychology* 52: 379–85.

Ogilvie, D. M., Cohen, F., and Solomon, S. (2008). "The Undesired Self: Deadly Connotations." *Journal of Research in Personality*, 42: 564–76.

Olkkonen, M. and Lipponen, J. (2006). "Relationships between Organizational Justice, Identification with Organization and Work Unit, and Group-Related Outcomes." *Organizational Behavior and Human Decision Process* 100: 202–15.

Petriglieri, J. L. (2011). "Under Threat: Responses to and the Consequences of Threats to Individuals' Identities." *Academy of Management Review* 36: 641–62.

Petriglieri, J. L. and Devine, B. A. (2016). "Mobilizing Organizational Action against Identity Threats: The Role of Organizational Members' Perceptions and Responses." In *The Oxford Handbook of Organizational Identity*, edited by M. Pratt, M. Schultz, B. Ashforth and D. Ravasi, 239–56. Oxford: Oxford University Press.

Phillips, A. G., Silvia, P. J., and Paradise, M. J. (2007). "The Undesired Self and Emotional Experience: A Latent Variable Analysis." *Journal of Social and Clinical Psychology* 26: 1035–47.

Pratt, M. G., Rockman, K. W., and Kaufman, J. B. (2006). "Constructing Professional Identity: The Role of Work and Identity Learning Cycles in the Customization of Identity among Medical Residents." *Academy of Management Journal* 49: 235–62.

Ravasi, D. and Schultz, M. (2006). "Responding to Organizational Identity Threats: Exploring the Role of Organizational Culture." *Academy of Management Journal* 49: 433–58.

Rodrigues, S. and Child, J. (2008). "The Development of Corporate Identity: A Political Perspective." *Journal of Management Studies* 45: 885–911.

Scott, S. G. and Lane, V. R. (2000). "A Stakeholder Approach to Organizational Identity." *Academy of Management Review* 25(1): 43–62.

Scott, W. R. (1982). "Managing Professional Work: Three Models of Control for Health Organizations." *Health Services Research* 17: 213–40.

Shah, J., Higgins, T., and Friedman, R. S. (1998). "Performance Incentives and Means: How Regulatory Focus Influences Goal Attainment." *Journal of Personality and Social Psychology* 74: 285–293.

Snow, D. A. and Anderson, L. (1987). "Identity Work among the Homeless: The Verbal Construction and Avowal of Personal Identities." *American Journal of Sociology* 92(6): 1336–71.

Sorensen, J. E. and Sorensen, T. L. (1974). "The Conflict of Professionals in Bureaucratic Organizations." *Administrative Science Quarterly* 19: 98–106.

Styhre, A. and Gluch, P. (2009). "Creativity and its Discontents: Professional Ideology and Creativity in Architect Work." *Creativity and Innovation Management* 18: 224–33.

Suchman, M. C. (1995). "Managing Legitimacy: Strategic and Institutional Approaches." *Academy of Management Review* 20: 571–610.

Tanz, J. (2002). "Driving: Wounded to the Quick by an Affair Gone astray." http:www. Newyorktimes.com, December 13.

Trent, J., and Gao, X. (2009). "'At Least I'm the Type of Teacher I Want to be': Second-Career English Language Teachers' Identity Formation in Hong Kong Secondary Schools." *Asia-Pacific Journal of Teacher Education* 37: 253–70.

Turner, J. C. (1986). *Redefining the Social Group. A Self-Categorization Theory.* New York: Basil Blackwell.

van Dick, R., Christ, O., Stellmacher, J., Wagner, U., and Ahlswede, O. (2004). "Should I Stay or Should I Go? Explaining Turnover Intentions with Organizational Identification and Job Satisfaction." *British Journal of Management* 15: 351–60.

van Knippenberg, D., and van Schie, E. C. M. (2000). "Foci and Correlates of Organizational Identification." *Journal of Occupational and Organizational Psychology* 73: 137–47.

Vannini, P. (2006). "Dead Poets' Society: Teaching, Publish-or-Perish, and Professors' Experiences of Authenticity." *Symbolic Interaction* 29: 235–57.

Vannini, P. and Franzese, A. (2008). "The Authenticity of Self: Conceptualization, Personal Experience, and Practice." *Sociology Compass* 2(5): 1621–37.

CHAPTER 15

....

ORGANIZATIONAL IDENTITY WORK

....

GLEN E. KREINER AND CHAD MURPHY

INTRODUCTION

IN this chapter we explore the notion of organizational identity work as well as other forms of agentic "work" that are related to—and inform—organizational identity. From the origins of "identity work" in Snow and Anderson's (1987) seminal ethnographic work on the homeless has sprung a diversity of approaches (and labels) to understanding how individuals work to shape a sense of self vis-à-vis their environments (Phillips and Lawrence, 2012). Indeed, organizations are places of such work, and scholars in multiple disciplines have in recent years studied the work being done to create, sustain, and adapt different forms of identity—individual, professional, and organizational. Here we focus on two major issues. First, to better understand the notion of *organizational* identity work, we apply research on identity work at the individual level to the organizational level. Second, we show how research on other forms of agentic "work" might inform future investigations of organizational identity work. In addition to the more clearly identity-centric "identity work" research, several other manifestations of "work" processes that relate to identity have emerged in recent years. The most prominent of these—"institutional work"—examines what actions are taken to build, disrupt, and/or sustain institutions. But a virtual wellspring of related "works" is also emerging, with each, we argue, somehow illuminating underexplored aspects of identity work, particularly at the organizational level. We review two of these various forms of work undertaken by organizational members (institutional work and boundary work), and offer suggestions on how they might apply to organizational identity. This dynamic approach will be designed to stimulate future research on different forms of "work," organizational identity, and the rich linkages between them.

IDENTITY WORK: A BRIEF REVIEW

We begin with an overview of work to date on *individual*-level identity work and then explore the transposition of such work to the *organizational* level. *Work* implies attempted change from something to something else. These changes might include moving from one identity to another, emphasizing one identity over another, and/or moving toward positive identity growth (Gioia et al., 2010; Glynn; 2000; Kreiner and Sheep, 2009). Identities are not accomplished merely by short bursts of clarity or insight. Rather, they "require repeated work to be sustained" (Anteby, 2008: 203). Indeed, identity work involves attempts to fashion a sense of self in both the short and long term. Identity work can have many triggers, including identity threats, transitions, surprises, events, and interactions (Alvesson and Wilmott, 2002; Petriglieri, 2011).

As is true with the larger "turn to work" in which scholars have recently emphasized forms of agentic work in organizations (Phillips and Lawrence, 2012), identity work can be situated as a hub of activity between the broader social structure and individual agency. This stance is congruent with the philosophies of Giddens (1984), Reed (2003), and Berger and Luckmann (1966), who all emphasize recursive connections between individual action and social context. Specifically, this approach argues the need to recognize the duality inherent in human endeavor—on the one hand, social structures impose norms, opportunities, and constraints, whereas on the other hand, individuals engage in feelings, thoughts, and behaviors that conform to build, change, and/or transcend those structures. The two sides are connected by what we might call "trickle-down" and "bubble-up" processes—influences of the social structure trickling down to individuals, *and* individual feelings, thoughts, and behaviors also bubbling up to collectively affect that social structure. Giddens (1991) theorized how these reciprocal processes would work in regard to identity. Alvesson and Wilmott (2002) then drew on Giddens' framework to argue that individuals try to create and sustain self-concepts that are distinct from other individuals through "identity work," whereas organizations try to control self-construction via discourses and narratives through "identity regulation." From these perspectives, the pivotal role of identity work in organizational life becomes clear, as it bridges the structural context and agentic processes. It is interesting to note, however, that this bridge can enable either identity construction *or* resistance to it. Critical theorists, for example, emphasize that identity work can center on opposition to the normative order and/or the organization's prescribed identity for the individual (Alvesson and Wilmott, 2002). Hence, identity work can facilitate organizational identity—when parties are aligned in purpose—or it can serve as a bulwark against it—when parties are in opposition.

Individual-Level Identity Work

So, what *is* identity work? There has been a virtual explosion of research on individual, occupational, and professional identity work during the past decade (e.g., Beech, 2008; Kreiner, Hollensbe, and Sheep, 2006a; Pratt, Rockmann, and Kaufmann, 2006). But just as research regarding the "turn to work" has developed in a fragmented way, research on "identity work" has also evolved somewhat disjointedly despite authors invoking the same term. Although the term might be shared, definitions and interpretations of it are not. Snow and Anderson's pioneering work (1987: 1348) defined identity work as the "range of activities that individuals engage in to create, present, and sustain personal identities that are congruent with and supportive of the self-concept." Sveningsson and Alvesson (2003: 1165) elaborated on this definition, noting that identity work involves "people being engaged in forming, repairing, maintaining, strengthening or revising the constructions that are productive of a sense of coherence and distinctiveness." At the individual level, both personal and social identities are implicated in identity work. Indeed, Watson (2008) described identity work as a set of mutually constitutive processes in which individuals try to create a relatively coherent personal identity while also coming to terms with their multiple social identities. A social identity of particular interest to organizational scholars is that of professional identity, and an emerging stream of research has shown how identity work is undertaken in that context (e.g., Pratt et al., 2006; Kreiner et al., 2006a; Vough, Cardador, Bednar, Dane, and Pratt, 2013).

How might we translate some of the work on individual identity work to the organizational identity work level? A key consideration here is that researchers overtly incorporate social elements in their definitions of identity work—it is not merely an intra-psychic activity. These social elements can include socially embedded processes such as social construction, social comparison, and drawing on culturally available discourses. This recognition of the inward and outward duality of identity work will be particularly important as we consider *organizational* identity work, as these cognitions can become shared or contested among organizational members. Indeed, these social elements may be the metaphorical sinews through which constructions of identity move from individual to higher levels (Ashforth, Rogers, and Corley, 2011).

Moreover, in considering how research on individual-level identity work can shed light on organizational identity work, the discursive approach (e.g., "discursive work," "discursive identity work," "narrative identity work"—Ibarra and Barbulescu, 2010; Lawrence, Suddaby, and Leca, 2009) merits particular attention. Although there is a great deal of methodological plurality within the discursive arena, these scholars consider how identity is constituted through situated practices of writing and talking. "Narrative identity work," for example, reflects the "social efforts to craft self-narratives that meet a person's identity aims" (Ibarra and Barbalescu (2010:137). Norms, ethics, values, and deeply held beliefs are often transmitted via narratives and other forms of talk and text. For organizations, that transmission may occur through morals of often-told stories about organizational triumphs and failures, themes emphasized in retelling about an organization's founding or key events, or in principles articulated by leaders (Oliver, Statler, and Roos, 2010).

The unique advantages of a discursive approach to organizational identity work are articulated well by Ybema et al (2009: 303), who note:

> taking language seriously enables researchers to begin to unravel the complexities of the processes of identity formation and construction: it can offer insight into how identities are constituted and, over time, reconstituted in everyday organizational talk and texts, it may reveal how dominant organizational discourses play out in members' identifications, it can illustrate how discourses inscribe particular subject positions, or be deconstructed to demonstrate how discursive strategies may encourage or marginalize the adoption of certain meanings.

In short, discursive scholars argue that focusing on the "action" of discursive constructions is often more important than focusing on the "set" of cognitively held beliefs about identity. The discursive approach also acknowledges the agency–structure tension we have discussed. Specifically, discourse scholars argue that identity reflects both "being 'subject' to" social constraints and "an active process of discursive 'work'" targeted at shaping other people and social structures (Benwell and Stokoe, 2006: 18). Indeed, with a more macro lens, Clegg, Rhodes, and Kornberger (2007) demonstrated how organizations developed discursive frameworks to make sense of the "self" and the "other." And Tienari and Vaara (Ch. 24, this volume) examine how organizational identity construction is accomplished via discursive narratives in mergers and acquisitions.

Organizational Identity Work

Although the vast majority of research on identity work has been conducted on individual identity, Schwalbe and Mason-Schrock extended identity work to the collective level, describing it as "anything people do, individually or collectively, to give meaning to themselves and others" (1996: 115). Yet, despite this roomier definition and the proliferation of studies using identity work at the individual level of identity, researchers on *organizational* identity have rarely invoked the term "identity work." When they do (e.g., Anteby and Molnar, 2012; Knapp et al., 2013; Oliver, Statler, and Roos, 2010), it has been somewhat informally, rather than systematically or formally. Adding to the confusion, researchers have also used the terms *identity construction* and *identity management* to refer to forms of identity work at both the individual and collective levels. Hence, to be clear about our use of the term, and consistent with Kreiner et al. (2015), we consider *organizational identity work* as comprising discursive, cognitive, and behavioral processes that help individuals and collectives create, sustain, share, and/or change organizational identity. This approach accentuates agency as a key component of organizational identity work, recognizing that "members are active participants in the shaping of themselves and others" (Kunda, 1992: 21). We consider now two themes in the literature that capture the tensions of organizational identity work's dynamism: identity as "enduring versus fluid" and as "content versus process."

Enduring versus fluid. Indeed, the "work" of organizational identity work clearly indicates that change to identity is possible—lest the purpose of identity work be fully futile. A tension in organizational identity research, however, has existed regarding the degree to which organizational identity should be considered as "enduring" (as proposed by Albert and Whetten, 1985) or fluid and dynamic (as argued by Gioia et al. (2000, 2010), among others). At this point in the debate, the question has evolved more into an emphasis or relative weight on endurance versus dynamism rather than a bifurcated either–or approach. A natural question resulting from this debate involves the role of temporal dynamics in identity. As Brown (2006: 741) noted, "less attention has been paid to how temporality is socially constructed, and deployed hegemonically, in the authorship of collective identities." Since Brown's lament, a few studies have overtly examined organizational identity change using a lens of temporality, which focuses on how an entity defines itself through a comparison of self at different periods of time. These include Ybema's (2010) work, which showed how leaders can construct organizational identity in temporal "discontinuity talk" by contrasting old and new, and Anteby and Molnar's (2012) work showing how purposeful "forgetting" of the past identity enabled change. These actions, we believe, represent an important form of organizational identity work that holds promise for further investigation.

Content versus process. Another current debate in the organizational identity literature involves the degree to which identity should be considered as *content* or *process*. Our treatment of organizational identity work will help address this debate, as we argue that identity work represents the *process* component as individuals and collectives interpret, shape, and reify the *content* of identity. Most scholars have treated identity as "thing-like" rather than studying it as a process (Alvesson and Sandberg, 2011: 262). Recent calls, however, have argued for treating identity as a process—a stance that "prioritizes activity over outcome, change over persistence, novelty over continuity, expression over determination, and becoming over being" (Schultz, Maguire, Langley, and Tsoukas, 2012: 1). A process perspective on organizational identity emphasizes actions such as tranformation, creativity, and flow. As Schultz et al. (2012) note, however, a process lens does not deny the existence of "things" such as events, states, and entities; rather, it focuses on how those "things" can be unpacked to better understand the processes involved in creating, sustaining, and/or dismantling them. Pratt (2012) outlined several examples of identity-related processes—and we note here their direct relevance to identity work—including, "self processes" that refine the identity of an entity vis-à-vis others; "expecting and accepting" involving the suggesting, demanding, or relinquishing of facets of one's or another's identity; "expressing and reflecting," in which entities share and reflect on requests that affect how others see them (Hatch and Schultz, 2002); "integrative processes" in which entities derive a holistic meaning of self that transcends the discrete, fragmented parts; and "claiming and granting" in which entities both seek and give confirmation of desired identities (Glynn, 2000; DeRue and Ashford, 2010).

Continuing with the process lens, organizational identity work has also been examined as a set of dialectic tensions that members wrestle with in understanding their social constructions of identity (Kreiner et al., 2015). Specifically, identity work can comprise how organizational members engage in competing claims regarding (1) what is essential versus negotiable (the *centrality* component), (2) what is consistent versus changeable (the *endurance* component), and (3) what links or separates the "who we are" issues relative to other organizations (the *distinctiveness* component). With a dialectic lens, organizational identity work is undertaken as organizational members and leaders wrestle with each of these three core components to identity. We see considerable promise in further investigating the dialectic nature of identity work—for individual, professional, and organizational identity.

Other Forms of "Work" and How They Inform Organizational Identity Work

As noted, there has been a virtual explosion in the forms of work being studied by management scholars. Having now examined the state of the identity work literature, we consider two other forms of work that can directly inform our current understanding of, and future research on, organizational identity work. Given that it would be impossible to discuss in this chapter each of the many forms of work, we chose two forms of work with ample research (institutional work and boundary work) and that seemed to us to hold the most promise for understanding organizational identity work. What can we learn from these forms of work that has implications for organizational identity work? We are specifically interested in future work that can examine the overlaps, synergies, and conflicts across types of work.

Institutional Work

Institutional work (Lawrence and Suddaby, 2006) has attracted considerable attention in institutional studies. Institutions, as defined by Lawrence and colleagues (2011: 53), are those relatively "enduring aspects of social life that affect the behavior and beliefs of individuals and collective actors by providing templates for action, cognition, and emotion." Any "social processes, obligations, or actualities" become "institutions" when they assume "a rulelike status in social thought and action" (Meyer and Rowan, 1977: 341) and thereby bound the realm of possible thought, action, and feeling for individuals subject to them (Zucker, 1977). This top-down view of the world has inevitably given rise to questions about the role of *individuals* in institutional change (DiMaggio, 1988). More specifically, if institutions constrain individual action, is it possible for individuals to alter the institutions in which they are embedded? If so, what are the conditions and mechanisms that facilitate such bottom-up change efforts?

In response to these issues, scholars have proposed *institutional work*, defined as "the purposive action of individuals and organizations aimed at creating, maintaining and disrupting institutions" (Lawrence and Suddaby, 2006: 215). Broadly speaking, then, institutional work can either be oriented toward change ("creative" or "disruptive" institutional work) or toward resisting that change ("maintaining" or "defensive" institutional work) (Maguire and Hardy, 2009). Scholars have debated the characteristics of institutional work, arguing that it is intentional (goal-oriented), effortful, cognitive, emotional, physical, sometimes conscious and sometimes non-conscious, all without necessarily being rational (Voronov and Vince, 2012; Lawrence, Suddaby, and Leca, 2011). Importantly, institutional work research prioritizes the "experience and motivation" of the path-breaking individual or group of individuals, rather than the institutional change itself, the latter being a focus of the closely related concept of "institutional entrepreneurship" (Lawrence et al., 2009; Garud et al., 2002). In other words, the key interest in institutional work research is the "'why' and 'how' rather than 'what' and 'when'" (Lawrence et al., 2011: 57). Given this background, we suggest that identity scholars follow the lead of such researchers as Creed, DeJordy, and Lok (2010) and Lok (2010), and overtly incorporate institutional work into organizational identity work research.

Research on institutional work suggests interesting possibilities for organizational identity work. To begin, institutions and organizational identities share certain conceptual features. This statement is perhaps surprising given recent scholarly interest in the fluidity of organizational identity, its malleability at the hands of capable leaders (Gioia and Patvardhan, 2012; Corley and Gioia, 2004; Barr, Stimpert, and Huff, 1992). Yet a large body of research has also indicated that, like the "institutions" of institutional theory, organizational identities can provide rather rigid behavioral and cognitive templates for organizations and their leaders (e.g., strong identity organizations such as the military, or so-called "strict" churches; Iannaccone, 1991). An organization's identity influences how its decision-makers perceive, for example, the salience of particular environmental stimuli (Dutton and Dukerich, 1991), the competitive landscape (Porac, Thomas, and Baden-Fuller, 1989), appropriate resource allocation, and organizational routines (Stimpert, Gustafson, and Sarason, 1998). Indeed, organizations and their leaders tend to act and think in ways that are "identity-consistent" (e.g., Hobby Lobby's recent refusal to cover employee insurance costs for contraception, on account of the organization's identity as a Christian business), which further suggests that, like institutions, organizational identity is not simply a product of—but also a constraint on—individual action and perception (Dutton and Penner, 1993; Giddens, 1984).

Given these conceptual linkages, studies of institutional work may offer specific insights of use to identity scholars. Recall that institutional work refers to effort directed at "creating, maintaining and disrupting institutions" (Lawrence and Suddaby, 2006: 215). The first and last of these types of institutional work are especially relevant to the concept of organizational identity work. Lawrence and Suddaby (2006: 222) point out, for example, that institutional work can take the form of "defining," or the construction of field- or industry-level "rule systems that confer status or identity." Such formalized systems—such as certification or accreditation standards—establish requirements for membership, which can provide member organizations with a coherent identity (Patvardhan, Gioia, Hamilton, 2013). Zietsma and Lawrence (2010) extended this view by finding that the revision of industry boundaries and practices (i.e., collective-specific routines) were a key mechanism in the disruption and redefinition of the British Columbia forest industry and its member organizations. Such studies not only demonstrate that an organization's identity may be directly shaped by institutional work, but they also suggest how such organizational identity work might occur, namely, through altering the boundaries, practices, and routines that define an organization.

There are other relevant mechanisms to consider as well. In a study that focuses on "outsider-driven" institutional change, Maguire and Hardy (2009) found that various individual actors together deinstitutionalized an institutionalized practice (the widespread use of the insecticide DDT in the United States) through a form of institutional work known as "translation," or the creative reimagining of the *meaning* of an institution (recorded in various texts), which spread to other actors in the field and thereby drove institutional change. This concept of "translation" suggests that organizational identities may be constructed in part through the analogous spread of identity signifiers among organizational members, either through conversation or more formalized discursive channels (e.g., company newsletters). In addition, the triggers of institutional work are likewise interesting to consider. For example, Voronov and Vince (2012) developed a theoretical framework describing the cognitive and emotional conditions under which different forms of institutional work are likely to occur. They argue, in part, that a person with high cognitive investment but low emotional investment in an institutional order will be likely to work (perhaps unconsciously) toward disrupting that order, because the emotional disconnection will generate dissatisfaction with institutionalized behaviors and attitudes. On the other hand, high cognitive and high emotional investment will encourage maintenance of the order, because one's rational (and emotional) needs are presumably being met. Such a theoretical framework could potentially shed new light on organizational identity work as well, specifically the cognitive and emotional antecedents of individual members' efforts—whether disruptive or maintaining—toward the organization's identity.

In sum, research on institutional work provides tools for thinking about key unresolved issues in our understanding of organizational identity work, specifically the *how* (e.g., through the revision of routines and/or shared translation processes), the *when* (e.g., individual members' cognitive/emotional investment versus disinvestment) and the *types* (e.g., "creative" versus "maintaining" versus "disruptive") of such work.

Boundary Work

Boundary work—the agentic component of boundary theory—offers another form of work that directly informs our understanding of organizational identity work. Boundary theory deals with how people create, change, or maintain boundaries and borders in order to simplify and classify components of their world (Ashforth,

Kreiner, and Fugate, 2000). Boundaries are said to demarcate and delimit the scope and perimeter of any given domain (e.g., home, work, self, group, geographic region) (Zerubavel, 1991). So-called "thick" boundaries are characterized as strong and relatively impermeable and closed to outside influences, whereas "thin" boundaries are said to be weak, relatively permeable, and open to outside influences (Nippert-Eng, 1996). How entities relate to each other regarding boundaries is conceptualized through segmentation and integration; these are characterized in boundary theory as two poles on a continuum, each representing a different way to use boundaries (Ashforth et al., 2000). Segmentation-integration, then, refers to the degree that aspects of a given domain (e.g., various multiple identities, work and home) are kept separate from one another, cognitively, behaviorally, emotionally, and/or physically (Nippert-Eng, 1996).

Boundary theory has been studied in a variety of disciplines and contexts, including psychology, art, work–home balance, political science, organizational theory, anthropology, and architecture. Some research on applying boundaries to identity has also been fruitful. For example, Katherine (1991) examined how boundaries should be established between people for healthy self-concepts, and Kreiner, Hollensbe, and Sheep (2006b) examined the connections between organizational and individual identity boundaries. Boundary theory posits that boundaries are co-constructed accomplishments; individuals and groups do not construct perceptions of the organization's identity in a vacuum. As members of collectives wrestle with the boundaries around and within their collective's identity, shared norms and values can emerge about the content and permeability of the identity (Kreiner et al., 2006b). As boundaries become socially shared and mutually constituted, they can be quite difficult to change or dismantle (Zerubavel, 1991). Indeed, the result of boundary work can be clear and strong expectations about rules, attitudes, and behaviors (Clark, 2000).

That said, identity boundaries are, of course, not entitative "things" but rather are cognitively constructed. As such, it is important to allow for the dynamism inherent in their ongoing accomplishment—or their change. As noted by Okhuysen et al. (2013), previous boundary-related research has too often focused on the stability of the boundary. But simply conceptualizing the boundary as a taken-for-granted thing or "wall" can overemphasize structure and underemphasize agency. A focus on boundary *work*, by contrast, explicitly focuses our attention on the agency side of the equation—what individuals, groups, and organizations can *do* to fashion identity boundaries. Boundary work refers to how people overtly try to build, tear down, or maintain borders between domains. For example, empirical studies have shown how people can negotiate the boundaries between home and work domains through physical objects (e.g., doors, key rings, calendars), communicative strategies (e.g., setting expectations, confronting boundary violators), temporal tactics (e.g., "banking" time, carving out time for respite), and cognitive manipulations (e.g., treating work like an "on/off" switch) (Kreiner, Hollensbe, and Sheep, 2009). Indeed, Nippert-Eng (1996: 152) emphasized that boundary work takes place "within greater or lesser margins of discretionary territory, which are set by the people and situations" of the entities interacting.

Hence, boundary work focuses on the negotiable elements within that "discretionary territory"—in short, the agency within the structure.

How might boundary work be directly applied to organizational identity work—both with existing work and in the future? Identity-related boundary work can focus on the "external" identity boundaries of the organization—dealing with how the organization is unique from others—or on the "internal" identity boundaries—dealing with the co-mingling multiple identities of the organization (Kreiner et al., 2006b). The first perspective, then, would be to consider how organizations conduct boundary work to clarify organizational identity *as it relates to other organizations*. With this lens, the distinctiveness of an organization's identity is at stake, as members determine and lobby for which categories of organization they belong to (e.g., institutional fields, industries). Kreiner et al. (2015), for instance, found that members and leaders of the Episcopal Church engaged in organizational identity work to lobby for their organization to be distinctive as compared either to other churches ("we are different from other Christian denominations") or to organizations in other institutional fields ("we are different from secular organizations"). Hence, "who we are" is partly a function of how we have constructed our position vis-à-vis the relevant boundaries of other organizations.

The second perspective would be to consider how individuals conduct boundary work *between multiple organizational identities*. This lens emphasizes the potential multiplicity of organizational identity and directly asks, to what degree do members segment or integrate these multiple organizational identities? Despite the research done on multiple organizational identities (e.g., Glynn, 2000; Pratt and Foreman, 2000), the logic of boundary work has rarely been directly applied to organizational identity. In one exception, and following Sundaramurthy and Kreiner's (2008) conceptual work, Knapp et al. (2013) applied boundary theory to organizational identity work to study family businesses—a context riddled with multiple identity strife. They found that organizational members and leaders would engage in "social boundary management," which they defined as tactics that can be enacted independent of the formal and structural operating systems. Of particular note here is that they found that these tactics could be invoked at *both* the individual and organizational levels. Organizational tactics emphasized (a) adapting a governance style that leveraged the synergies between multiple organizational identities, and (b) adopting inclusive practices that allowed both identities to flourish. Individual tactics emphasized how to manage identity-laden encounters by (a) adapting conversations through word choices, (b) choosing strategically when to integrate versus segment the identities in different interactions, and (c) selectively disassociating from either the family or the business in certain encounters. These tactics helped to navigate the complexities of both complementary and competing multiple organizational identities.

We believe that future organizational identity work research would greatly benefit from incorporating the insights from boundary work research, as it provides not merely a complementary theoretical lens, but also provides specific processes through which organizational identity is constructed, maintained, and changed. Specifically, we encourage scholars to examine how boundary work affects the "external" identity boundaries (e.g., how are we similar to/different from other organizations?), the "internal" identity boundaries (e.g., how are our multiple identities blended or separated, and with what consequences?), and the interplay between external and internal boundaries (e.g., how are our changing relationships with other organizations fusing or separating our multiple identities?) (Kreiner et al., 2006b).

LOOKING FORWARD

Although within the chapter we have been sporadically speculating about where identity work research might head, we now more fully consider some additional specific issues that future research might take on. First, we strongly suggest that future research incorporate *and* look beyond institutional and boundary work to address the *many* other forms of work that are encompassed in the "turn to work." Phillips and Lawrence (2012) listed fifteen such areas of research (e.g., emotion work, meaning work, values work), each of which can be tied directly to identity work. Such linkages hold potential to contribute to our understanding of how other forms of work both affect and are affected by identity work. To illustrate this potential, we briefly consider two other specific avenues for future organizational identity work research—consciousness and emotions.

Consciousness and Intentionality in Organizational Identity Work

As we have hinted, institutional work research raises intriguing questions about the degree to which organizational identity work can be considered a conscious or intentional process. Indeed, institutional agents may not be fully conscious of the motivation behind their actions (Suddaby, 2010), not least because these motivations may be rooted in emotional needs (Voronov and Vince, 2013). As yet, however, identity scholars have broached, but not fully addressed, this duality. Rather, a typical approach is to study identity work in the context of a scenario that induces people to consciously reflect on questions of identity. Alvesson and Willmott (2002: 626) suggested, for instance, that "specific events, encounters, transitions experiences, surprises, as well as more constant strains" can serve as triggers that "heighten awareness of the constructed quality of self-identity and compel more concentrated identity work." Such triggers may include career transitions (Ibarra and Barbulescu, 2010) or particularly strong organizational/institutional cultures (Kreiner et al., 2006a). Perhaps not surprisingly, then, research on identity work—and its closely-related phrase, identity *construction*—has acquired "functionalist overtones ... [since] both constructing and working are purposeful" (Pratt, 2012). Identity work is thus assumed to be intentional, oriented toward achieving a particular end. By implication, identity work would appear to be a mostly conscious cognitive or behavioral process.

However, in one example of organizational identity work noted earlier, Anteby and Molnar (2012) found that organizations can create a sense of "who they are" in the present by repeatedly and deliberately "forgetting" certain aspects of their past (e.g., through systematic omissions of historical details in public and private documents). The implication, then, is that, in the absence of such strategic "forgetting," organizational identity may simply accrue over time via a complex interplay of events and actions—informed by a kind of historical residue beyond the awareness of any one individual or group. Yet such non-conscious organizational identity "work" may still be intentional, even though the *objective* is not cognitively available. Indeed, as institutional studies suggest, an activity may be intentional yet still operate outside conscious awareness, particularly when emotions are involved (Voronov and Vince, 2012). Moreover, non-conscious yet intentional identity work might stem from the person or organization "losing themselves" by thorough engagement with the work. Gioia and Patvardhan (2012), for example, draw on Csikszentmihalyi's (1990) work to discuss identity as "flow"—an optimal experience in which people experience such a deep involvement with the task at hand that they detach from regular cognitive processing; in the context of identity work, such a flow state can be experienced as individuals become thoroughly engaged (and yet not necessarily consciously so) in constructing individual and/or collective identity.

Future research might more carefully explore the relationships between these concepts and their application to organizational identity work. Intriguing topics might include the conditions under which organizational identity work is consciously pursued versus non-consciously maintained, and the intra- and interpersonal mechanisms that promote such maintenance. Or, since identity work can be enacted in resistance to prescribed organizational identities, how is this done consciously versus non-consciously? It is also provocative to consider the methodological implications of non-conscious identity work. How, for example, might we accurately and thoroughly document these processes when they are—by definition—not overtly thought about by the people we interview? And, what methodological tools are most appropriate for capturing these non-conscious processes?

Emotions in Organizational Identity Work

Building on insights from institutional work research, identity scholars might also further explore the role of emotion in organizational identity work. Of course, the link between emotion and identity is not in itself a new research topic. For instance, Markus and Kitayama (1991) posited that particular kinds of self-construal (i.e., independent versus interdependent) have direct implications for one's emotional life (e.g., tendency to show anger versus sympathy toward others). Further, theory on emotional labor—or organizationally mandated "rules" requiring employees to engage in "surface acting, deep acting, and the expression of spontaneous and genuine emotion" (Ashforth and Humphrey, 1993: 89)—suggests that such emotional expectations create pressure to identify with one's work role. These expectations can trigger identity work, especially to the degree the individual experiences a disconnect between the expected display and their own identity and values. For example, employees of Chick-fil-A are required to say "my pleasure" instead of "you're welcome" to customers. This wording centers on the employee's vantage point and can either reinforce a tie between role identity and positive emotion or lead to cynicism and disidentification (especially when uttered countless times daily).

However, few studies have considered if, and how, emotion influences (or is influenced by) identity work at the collective level. And indeed, just as individual identity work is facilitated by practices that regulate (sometimes unwanted) emotions (Ashforth and Kreiner, 1999), so too might organizational identities be shaped by the implementation of these same structures of emotional regulation. For example, Ashforth and Kreiner (2002: 227; see also Greil and Rudy, 1984) noted that "identity transformation organizations," such as cults, develop processes to neutralize members' emotional responses: for example, "newcomers are temporarily isolated from outsiders and subjected to a powerful and consistent informational context designed to overpower doubts." As a result, "values, beliefs, and practices that may seem bizarre to outsiders are reframed as normal." In this case, the cult's sense of "who we are" as an organization—comprising shared values, beliefs, and practices—emerges and becomes validated as members' negative emotions are reoriented in positive ways, thus supporting the essence of the collective. Specific topics of future consideration, then, might include how organization-level emotional regulation tactics (e.g., socialization processes, collective rituals, etc.) serve as a subset or subsidiary of organizational identity work. Other topics could begin at the individual level and work "upward," addressing, for instance, the mechanisms that allow individual emotional responses to travel from individual to dyad to collective, thereby contributing to a collective emotional status quo that encourages individuals either to sustain—or push to change—the organization's identity.

Final Thoughts

We end the chapter with some final ruminations and questions for the future. First, how do various types of both individual and organizational identity work work together? Typically, any given study focuses on just one type of identity work, leaving this question blatantly unanswered in empirical studies. In what ways are these forms of identity work complementary, supplementary, or competing? How do organizational members accomplish these multiple types of identity work? Are they sequential, parallel, or both? Second, we ask similar questions of the various forms of work (e.g., institutional, boundary, identity work). How do they work together or in opposition with one another? Again, most studies only invoke one form of work, leaving a considerable void. (See Zietsma and Lawrence's [2010] study on boundary work and practice work for a rare exception.) We suspect that to properly answer these questions, researchers will need to draw on multiple methodological tools in their toolkits—interviews, surveys, observations, or archival methods alone will not be able to sufficiently capture the complex and nuanced relationships among these forms of work.

Our final question is—where should identity work be situated with respect to institutional, boundary, and other forms of work (e.g., legitimacy work, values work)? Are each of these forms of work fundamentally about identity, and thus should identity work be placed at the center of them? Does identity shape these other forms of work, or vice versa, or both? Our chapter has demonstrated linkages from these forms of work to the understudied notion of organizational identity work. We can envision future work continuing this path, showing how other forms of work link to identity. Is identity work the foundational process that binds all these forms of work together? Does identity adequately explain the driving forces behind the turn to work? Future research can and should explore this question and strive to develop an integrated model. Identity *work*, indeed.

ACKNOWLEDGMENTS:

We thank the editors of this volume as well as the participants at the handbook conference for their valuable insights into a previous version of this chapter.

REFERENCES

Albert, S. and Whetten, D. A. (1985). "Organizational Identity." In *Research in Organizational Behavior*, vol. 7, edited by L. L. Cummings and M. M. Staw, 263–95. Greenwich, CT: JAI.

Alvesson, M. and Sandberg, J. (2011). "Generating Research Questions through Problematization." *Academy of Management Review* 36(2): 247–71.

Alvesson, M. and Willmott, H. (2002). "Identity Regulation as Organizational Control: Producing the Appropriate Individual." *Journal of Management Studies* 39(5): 619–44.

Anteby, M. (2008). "Identity Incentives as an Engaging Form of Control: Revisiting Leniencies in an Aeronautic Plant." *Organization Science* 19(2): 202–20.

Anteby, M. and Molnar, V. (2012). "Collective Memory Meets Organizational Identity: Remembering to Forget in a Firm's Rhetorical History." *Academy of Management Journal* 55(3): 515–40.

Ashforth, B. E. and Humphrey, R. H. (1993). "Emotional Labor in Service Roles: The Influence of Identity." *Academy of Management Review* 18(1): 88–115.

Ashforth, B. E. and Kreiner, G. E. (1999). "How Can You Do It?": Dirty Work and the Challenge of Constructing a Positive Identity." *Academy of Management Review* 24(3): 413–34.

Ashforth, B. E. and Kreiner, G. E. (2002). "Normalizing Emotion in Organizations: Making the Extraordinary Seem Ordinary." *Human Resource Management Review* 12: 215–35.

Ashforth, B. E., Kreiner, G. E., and Fugate, M. (2000.) "All in a Day's Work: Boundaries and Micro Role Transitions." *Academy of Management Review* 25(3): 472–91.

Ashforth, B. E., Rogers, K. M., and Corley, K. G. (2011). "Identity in Organizations: Exploring Cross-Level Dynamics." *Organization Science* 22(5): 1144–56.

Barr, P. S., Stimpert, J. L. and Huff, A. S. (1992). "Cognitive Change, Strategic Action, and Organizational Renewal." *Strategic Management Journal* 13(S1): 15–36.

Beech, N. (2008). "On the Nature of Dialogic Identity Work." *Organization* 15(1): 51–74.

Benwell, B., and Stokoe, E. (2006). *Discourse and Identity*. Edinburgh: Edinburgh University Press.

Berger, P. L. and Luckmann, T. (1966). *The Social Construction of Reality: A Treatise in the Sociology of Knowledge*. Garden City, NY: Anchor.

Brown, A. D. (2006). "A Narrative Approach to Collective Identities." *Journal of Management Studies* 43(4): 731–53.

Clark, S. C. (2000). "Work/Family Border Theory: A New Theory of Work/Family Balance." *Human Relations* 53(6): 747–70.

Clegg, S. R., Rhodes, C., and Kornberger, M. (2007). "Desperately Seeking Legitimacy: Organizational Identity and Emerging Industries." *Organization Studies* 28(4): 495–513.

Corley, K. G., and Gioia, D. A. (2004). "Identity Ambiguity and Change in the Wake of a Corporate Spin-Off." *Administrative Science Quarterly* 49(2): 173–208.

Creed, W. E. D., DeJordy, R., and Lok, J. (2010). "Being the Change: Resolving Institutional Contradiction through Identity Work." *Academy of Management Journal*, 53(6): 1336–64.

Csikszentmihalyi, M. (1990). *Flow: The Psychology of Optimal Experience*. New York: Harper Row.

DeRue, D. S., and Ashford, S. J. (2010). "Who Will Lead and Who Will Follow? A Social Process of Leadership Identity Construction in Organizations." *Academy of Management Review* 35(4): 627–47.

DiMaggio, P. J. (1988). "Interest and Agency in Institutional Theory." In *Institutional Patterns and Organizations: Culture and Environment*, edited by L. G. Zucker, 3–22. Cambridge: Ballinger.

Dutton, J. E., and Dukerich, J. M. (1991). "Keeping an Eye on the Mirror: Image and Identity in Organizational Adaptation." *Academy of Management Journal* 34(3): 517–54.

Dutton, J. E. and Penner, W. J. (1993). "The Importance of Organizational Identity for Strategic Agenda Building." In *Strategic Thinking: Leadership in the Management of Change*, edited by J. Hendry and G. Johnson, 89–113. New York: Strategic Management Society, Wiley.

Garud, R., Jain, S., and Kumaraswamy, A. (2002). "Institutional Entrepreneurship in the Sponsorship of Common Technological Standards: The Case of Sun Microsystems and Java." *Academy of Management Journal* 45(1): 196–214.

Giddens, A. (1984). *The Constitution of Society*. Berkeley, CA: University of California Press.

Giddens, A. (1991). *Modernity and Self-Identity: Self and Society in the Late Modern Age*. Stanford, CA: Stanford University Press.

Gioia, D. A., and Patvardhan, S. (2012). "Identity as Process and Flow." In *Constructing Identity in and around Organizations*, edited by M. Schultz, S. Maguire, A. Langley, and H. Tsoukas, 50–62. Oxford: Oxford University Press.

Gioia, D. A., Price, K. N., Hamilton, A. L., and Thomas, J. B. (2010). "Forging an Identity: An Insider-Outsider Study of Processes Involved in the Formation of Organizational Identity." *Administrative Science Quarterly*, 55: 1–46.

Gioia, D. A., Schultz, M., and Corley, K. G. (2000). "Organizational Identity, Image, and Adaptive Instability." *Academy of Management Review* 25(1): 63–81.

Glynn, M. A. (2000). "When Cymbals Become Symbols: Conflict over Organizational Identity within a Symphony Orchestra." *Organization Science* 11(3): 285–98.

Greil, A. L. and Rudy, D. R. (1984). "Social Cocoons: Encapsulation and Identity Transformation Organizations." *Sociological Inquiry* 54(3): 260–78.

Hatch, M. J. and Schultz, M. (2002). "The Dynamics of Organizational Identity." *Human Relations* 55(8): 989–1018.

Iannaccone, L. R. (1991). "Why Strict Churches Are Strong." *American Journal of Sociology* 99(5): 1180–211.

Ibarra, H., and Barbulescu, R. (2010). "Identity as Narrative: Prevalence, Effectiveness, and Consequences of Narrative Identity Work in Macro Role Transitions." *Academy of Management Review* 35(1): 135–54.

Katherine, A. (1991). *Boundaries: Where You End and I Begin.* New York: MJF Books.

Knapp, J. R., Smith, B. R., Kreiner, G. E., Sundaramurthy, C., and Barton, S. L. (2013). "Managing Boundaries through Identity Work: The Role of Individual and Organizational Identity Tactics." *Family Business Review* 26: 333–55.

Kreiner, G. E., Hollensbe, E. C., and Sheep, M. L. (2006a). "Where Is the 'Me' among the 'We'? Identity Work and the Search for Optimal Balance." *Academy of Management Journal* 49(5): 1031–57.

Kreiner, G. E., Hollensbe, E. C., and Sheep, M. L. (2006b). "On the Edge of Identity: Boundary Dynamics at the Interface of Individual and Organizational Identities." *Human Relations* 59(10): 1315–41.

Kreiner, G. E., Hollensbe, E. C., and Sheep, M. L. (2009). "Balancing Borders and Bridges: Negotiating the Work–Home Interface via Boundary Work Tactics." *Academy of Management Journal* 52(4): 704–30.

Kreiner, G. E., and Sheep, M. L. (2009). "Growing Pains and Gains: Framing Identity Dynamics as Opportunities for Identity Growth." In L. M. Roberts and J. E. Dutton, *Exploring Positive Identities and Organizations: Building a Theoretical and Research Foundation,* 23–46. Mahwah, NJ: Lawrence Erlbaum and Associates.

Kreiner, G. E., Sheep, M. L., Hollensbe, E. C., Smith, B. R., and Kataria, N. (2015). "Identity Elasticity and its Dialectic Tensions: How Can We Hold together while We're Pulling apart?" *Academy of Management Journal* 58(4): 981–1011.

Kunda, G. (1992). *Engineering Culture: Control and Commitment in a High-Tech Corporation.* Philadelphia, PA: Temple University Press.

Lawrence, T. B., and Suddaby, R. (2006). "Institutions and Institutional Work." In *Handbook of Organization Studies,* 2nd edn., edited by S. R. Clegg, C. Hardy, T. B. Lawrence, and W. R. Nord, 215–54. London: SAGE.

Lawrence, T. B., Suddaby, R., and Leca, B. (eds.) (2009). *Institutional Work: Actors and Agency in Institutional Studies of Organizations.* Cambridge: Cambridge University Press.

Lawrence, T., Suddaby, R., and Leca, B. (2011). "Institutional Work: Refocusing Institutional Studies of Organization." *Journal of Management Inquiry* 20(1): 52–8.

Lok, J. (2010). "Institutional Logics as Identity Projects." *Academy of Management Journal,* 53(6): 1305–35.

Maguire, S., and Hardy, C. (2009). "Discourse and Deinstitutionalization: The Decline of DDT." *Academy of Management Journal* 52(1): 148–78.

Markus, H. R., and Kitayama, S. (1991). "Culture and the Self: Implications for Cognition, Emotion, and Motivation." *Psychological Review* 98(2): 224–53.

Meyer, J. W., and Rowan, B. (1977). "Institutionalized Organizations: Formal Structure as Myth and Ceremony." *American Journal of Sociology* 83(2): 440–63.

Nippert-Eng, C. E. (1996). *Home and Work: Negotiating Boundaries through Everyday Life.* Chicago: University of Chicago Press.

Okhuysen, G. A., Lepak, D., Ashcraft, K. L., Labianca, G., Smith, V., and Steensma, H. K. (2013). "Theories of Work and Working Today." *Academy of Management Review* 38(4): 491–502.

Oliver, D., Statler, M., and Roos, J. (2010). "A Meta-Ethical Perspective on Organizational Identity." *Journal of Business Ethics* 94(3): 427–40.

Patvardhan, S. D., Gioia, D. A., and Hamilton, A. L. (2015). "Weathering a Meta-Level Identity Crisis: Forging a Coherent Collective Identity Formation for an Emerging Field." *Academy of Management Journal* 58(2): 405–35.

Petriglieri, J. L. (2011). "Under Threat: Responses to and the Consequences of Threats to Individuals' Identities." *Academy of Management Review* 36(4): 641–62.

Phillips, N. and Lawrence, T. B. (2012). "The Turn to Work in Organization and Management Theory: Some Implications for Strategic Organization." *Strategic Organization* 10(3): 223–30.

Porac, J. F., Thomas, H., and Baden-Fuller, C. (1989). "Competitive Groups as Cognitive Communities: The Case of Scottish Knitwear Manufacturers." *Journal of Management Studies* 26(4): 397–416.

Pratt, M. (2012). "Rethinking Identity Construction Processes in Organizations: Three Questions to Consider." In *Constructing Identity in and around Organizations,* edited by M. Schultz, S. Maguire, A. Langley, and H. Tsoukas, 21–50. Oxford: Oxford University Press.

Pratt, M. G., and Foreman, P. O. (2000). "Classifying Managerial Responses to Multiple Organizational Identities." *Academy of Management Review* 25(1): 18–42.

Pratt, M. G., Rockman, K. W., and Kaufmann, J. B. (2006). "Constructing Professional Identity: The Role of Work and Identity Learning Cycles in the Customization of Identity among Medical Residents." *Academy of Management Journal* 49(2): 235–62.

Reed, M. I. (2003). "The Agency/Structure Dilemma in Organization Theory: Open Doors and Brick Walls." In *The Oxford Handbook of Organization Theory: Meta-Theoretical Perspectives,* edited by H. Tsoukas and C. Knudsen, 289–309. Oxford: Oxford University Press.

Schultz, M., Maguire, S., Langley, A., and Tsoukas, H. (eds.) (2012). *Constructing Identity in and around Organizations.* Oxford: Oxford University Press.

Schwalbe, M. L., and Mason-Schrock, D. (1996). "Identity Work as Group Process." In *Advances in Group Processes,* vol. 13, edited by B. Markovsky, M. J. Lovaglia, and R. Simon, 113–147. Greenwich, CT: JAI Press.

Snow, D. A., and Anderson, L. (1987). "Identity Work among the Homeless: The Verbal Construction and Avowal of Personal Identities." *American Journal of Sociology* 92(6): 1336–71.

Stimpert, J. L., Gustafson, L. T., and Sarason, Y. (1998). "Organizational Identity within the Strategic Management Conversation: Contributions and Assumptions." In *Identity in Organizations: Building Theory through Conversations,* edited by D. A. Whetten and P. C. Godfrey, 83–98. Thousand Oaks, CA: SAGE Publications.

Suddaby, R. (2010). "Challenges for Institutional Theory." *Journal of Management Inquiry* 19(1): 14–20.

Sundaramurthy, C. and Kreiner, G. E. (2008). "Governing by Managing Identity Boundaries: The Case of Family Businesses." *Entrepreneurship Theory and Practice* 32(3): 415–36.

Svenningsson, S. and Alvesson, M. (2003). "Managing Managerial Identities: Organizational Fragmentation, Discourse and Identity Struggle." *Human Relations* 56(10): 1163–93.

Tienari, J. and Vaara, E. (2016). "Identity Construction in Mergers and Acquisitions: A Discursive Sensemaking Perspective." In *The Oxford Handbook of Organizational Identity*, edited by M. G. Pratt, M. Schultz, B. E. Ashforth, and D. Ravasi, 455–73. Oxford: Oxford University Press.

Voronov, M., and Vince, R. (2012). "Integrating Emotions into the Analysis of Institutional Work." *Academy of Management Review* 37(1): 58–81.

Vough, H., Cardador, T., Bednar, J., Dane, E., and Pratt, M. (2013). "What Clients Don't Get about my Profession: A Model of Perceived Role-Based Image Discrepancies." *Academy of Management Journal* 56(4): 1050–80.

Watson, T. J. (2008). "Managing Identity: Identity Work, Personal Predicaments and Structural Circumstances." *Organization* 15(1): 121–43.

Ybema, S., Keenoy, T., Oswick, C., Beverungen, A., Ellis, N., and Cebelis, I. (2009). "Articulating Identities." *Human Relations* 62(3): 299–322.

Ybema, S. (2010). "Talk of Change: Temporal Contrasts and Collective Identities." *Organization Studies* 31(4): 481–503.

Zerubavel, E. (1991). *The Fine Line: Making Distinctions in Everyday Life.* New York: Free Press.

Zietsma, C., and Lawrence, T. B. (2010). "Institutional Work in the Transformation of an Organizational Field: The Interplay of Boundary Work and Practice Work." *Administrative Science Quarterly* 55(2): 189–221.

Zucker, L. G. (1977). "The Role of Institutionalization in Cultural Persistence." *American Sociological Review* 42: 726–43.

SECTION V

SOURCES AND PROCESSES OF OI

CHAPTER 16

RE-MEMBERING

rhetorical history as identity work

ROY SUDDABY, WILLIAM M. FOSTER, AND CHRISTINE QUINN TRANK

INTRODUCTION

RECENT research demonstrates the critical importance of identification in organizations (e.g., Albert and Whetten, 1985; Ashforth, Harrison, and Corley, 2008; Ashforth, Joshi, Anand, and O'Leary-Kelly, 2013; Brickson, 2000; Brickson, 2013; Elsbach, 1999; Gioia, Patvardhan, Hamilton, and Corley, 2013; He and Brown, 2013; Vadera and Pratt, 2013). Defined broadly as the "perceived oneness with or belongingness to an organization" (Battacharya, Rao, and Glynn, 1995), identification has been shown to positively enhance an organization's relationship with key stakeholders, including employees (Ashforth and Mael, 1989, Dutton, Dukerich, and Harquail, 1994), customers (Battacharya et al., 1995), fans (Foster and Hyatt, 2007), distributors (Pratt, 2000), board members (Golden-Biddle and Rao, 1997) and other actors (Scott and Lane, 2000). Much of this research has been devoted to elaborating the constituent elements of organizational identification.

A further elaboration has theorized identification as a *process* (Pratt, 1998). Theorists use the term *identity work* to refocus the notion of organizational identity as a negotiated process (Kreiner, Hollensbe, and Sheep, 2006), and to devote more attention to understanding how groups and individuals negotiate the boundaries between their multiple and often conflicting identities (Pratt and Foreman, 2000). A number of studies catalogue the various strategies used in identity work (Beech, MacIntosh, and McInnes, 2008; Snow and Anderson, 1987; Snow and McAdam, 2000; Sveningsson and Alvesson, 2003; Watson, 2008).

Our interest, however, is in understanding processes of *collective* identity work. While early research on identity work has been very promising, it overlooks two essential mechanisms through which collective identity work occurs. First, this research overlooks the essential role of *language* as the fundamental symbolic activity upon which processes of identity work rest. Rhetoricians have long understood the important role that language plays in identification. In *A Rhetoric of Motives*, Burke (1969) observed that rhetoric could only be successful when it created a sense of oneness (co-presence or consubstantiation) between speaker and audience. Cheney (1983), leaning on Burke, describes a range of rhetorical tactics used by an organization to create stakeholder identification with the organization. Fiol (2002), more recently, proposed a model of organizational change based, largely, on the strategic use of language to shift patterns of identification by key stakeholders with the organization. These latter two papers can be seen as early attempts to explore the role of persuasive language in organizational identity work.

The second mechanism of identity work missing from current studies of identification is the critical role of history. Affiliation between an individual and a collective is constructed over time. Recent work has started to recognize that the construct of identity implicitly incorporates an element of coherent endurance over time, and that the process of identification requires ongoing management of perceptions of identity in the past, present, and future. So, for example, an emerging stream of research on the dynamics of identification acknowledges the need for dynamic identity reconstructions over time (Anteby and Molnar, 2012; Dutton and Dukerich, 1991; Gioia, Corley, and Fabbri, 2002). The importance of historicity in identity work is captured empirically in Schultz and Hernes' (2013: 12) compelling study of how the past was used by executives of the LEGO group to articulate claims of a future identity that managed to strategically shift the company from a mass-market manufacturer of toys to an "idea company" whose core competence was "systematic creativity."

We extend these two emerging theoretical threads in this essay by focusing on a specific, but overlooked, use of historical language that seems particularly appropriate for identity work—*rhetorical history*. Defined as the "strategic use of the past as a persuasive strategy to manage key stakeholders of the firm" (Suddaby, Foster, and Quinn-Trank, 2010: 157), the construct of rhetorical history has emerged as an important element in managing processes of both organizational (Anteby and Molnar, 2012) and institutional (McGaughey, 2012) change.

Attending to history in the process of organizational identification emphasizes the importance of past events. However, history lacks significance unless it is given meaning by exerting influence on the present constitution and construction of the bond individuals have with their organizations. An organization's history is made relevant to a group by contextualizing past events in the present through memory and recollection, which crystallizes the identification that group members have with their organization. We term the process by which actors use both rhetoric and history to socially construct membership with an organization, *organizational remembering*. By separating the prefix (re) from the root (member), we reinforce the observation that *memory and membership are common social constructions* and that *identification, or the creation of a sense of commonality and belonging, is inherently connected to and dependent upon the strategic and creative narrative reconstruction of history in a given community.*

We present this argument in four stages. First we review the literature on rhetoric and identification to demonstrate that organizational identity work is, at its core, based on the strategic use of persuasive language (rhetoric). In the second part we review literature in sociology that demonstrates how rhetorical history has been used to create identification through shared cultural memory. In part three we argue that rhetorical history is a key mechanism for organizational identity work. We develop this argument by drawing from emerging strands of empirical work in organization theory that demonstrate how history is used strategically to construct the organization as a common community. We conclude with a research agenda based on understanding how organizations use history and various forms of rhetoric to manage identification.

IDENTIFICATION THROUGH RHETORIC

Although the term "rhetoric" is typically used to express the strategic use of language in order to persuade, the American literary theorist Kenneth Burke offered an alternative view. Rhetoric, in his view, was intended to create a strong bond between a speaker and audience. Burke (1969) described this bond as one of identification, and argued that identification was a fundamental component of human existence. Isolation was an ontological "given" of human existence, Burke observed. We are born and die alone. Separateness, and the guilt and anxiety that results from our separateness, is a core motivation for human communication.

We communicate, thus, in order to overcome our inherent isolation. We communicate to construct a foundational element of our shared existence, he argued, and to identify points of similarity, shared experience, and commonality, a process and objective that Burke termed *consubstantiation*. Language is the core symbolic instrument used to establish our identification with the family, the group, the community, or the clan.

Communication scholars have extended Burke's notion of rhetoric to organizations. Cheney (1983) for example, analyzed how organizations use structured forms of communication such as corporate newsletters to foster employee identification. He analyzed different rhetorical strategies used by corporations to create identification among individuals including "antithesis," in which the corporation constructs a common enemy, and the "assumed we" in which the author of the newsletter subtly inserts the "royal we" into the text in an effort to create a sense of unity.

Orlikowski and Yates (1994; Yates and Orlikowski, 1992) draw on rhetoric as they demonstrate how different genres of communication (i.e., memos, meetings, electronic mail) are used to linguistically underpin the commonality of the organization as a shared institution. Genres, they argue are "social institutions that are produced, reproduced, or modified when human agents draw on genre rules to engage in organizational communication" (Yates and Orlikowski, 1992: 305).

Genres have an important temporal component, the authors observe. Genres are recurrent rhetorical situations that create commonality through repetition. They offer a common identity to participants because they emerge and evolve in a particular socio-historical context. Through repetition over time, genres create a series of reciprocal typifications for social action that provide participants with both a reassuring sense of structure (i.e., a set of rules for interacting) and a sense of endurance over time—that is, an identity.

Rhetoricians, thus, offer the core insight that individuals have an abiding need to connect to larger social structures, and that both individuals and collectives (organizations) accomplish this primarily through communicative practices conducted repetitively over time. Identification, thus, is a basic human need that is accomplished, largely, through rhetoric.

HISTORY IS A SPECIFIC FORM
OF RHETORICAL IDENTIFICATION

An implicit element of the rhetorical model of identification is that the history of an organization provides the raw material through which organizational identity is constructed. Indeed Burke viewed history and historical symbolism as a unique subset of rhetoric that was particularly useful in creating identification (Burke, 1984). Monuments, statues, and related shared symbols of the past are uniquely effective in creating a sense of commonality in a given social group. Thus, the communicative practices through which the consubstantiation of the individual and the collective is created requires, not only repeated interaction, but also an shared *memory* of that interaction.

Memory has typically been understood as a psychological construct that operates primarily at the *individual* level of analysis (Weschler, 1945; Squire, 1987; Tulving, 1985; Freud, 1938). An alternative view of memory, however, first advanced by Maurice Halbwachs (1950/1992) is that memory can only occur in a collective or group. Halbwachs argued that without a social context within which memories are constructed, individual memory simply would not exist. Social groups provide a critical context within which memories are created, stored, and recalled. No individual memory could be reconstructed without first situating it in a specific social milieu: "It is in society that people normally acquire their memories. It is also in society that they recall, recognize, and localize their memories" (Halbwachs, 1950/1992: 38). To demonstrate the validity of this notion, Halbwachs observed how individuals who share kinship groups remember events similarly, while individuals in different kinship groups have different memories of the same historical event.

The collective memory of a given group, Halbwachs (1950/1992) argued, provides the foundation of their identity as a group. Social groups he observed define what memories are collectively referential and thus relevant and determine how these memories should be maintained and reproduced to construct a collective identity. The idea that collective memory and collective identity are related underpins an emerging stream of scholarship, termed *social memory studies* (Olick and Robbins, 1998) that examines the processes through which group identity and historical identity are co-constructed. Much of this research occurs at the level of the nation-state, and focuses on how history is reconstructed to create a sense of communal identity in the present. Lowenthal (1985) thus demonstrates how national monuments, museums, and other state-controlled institutions are used to shape the past to serve the interests of the present. Others have also shown how history, memory, and identity are tied to hidden imbalances in power (Hobsbawm and Ranger, 1983), and still others have shown that practices and routines are essential to the reproduction and reinforcement of national identities (Mosse, 1975).

Zerubavel (1996; 2003) uses the concept of *mnemonic communities* to extend our understanding of the relationship between memory and identity. Mnemonic communities are any social group (family, workplace, nation-state) that is constructed on common understandings of the past. The identity of the group is the result of an incredible amount of memory work that includes memorializing past wars, commemorating significant group achievements, mythologizing heroes, re-enacting traditions, and formal documentation of common events in history texts.

While communities may be based on shared values, Zerubavel (2003) argues that those shared values are socially constructed out of shared memories. Moreover, often those shared memories are not necessarily historically accurate, but are the result of incredibly detailed practices of historical socialization that include "invented traditions" (Hobsbawm and Ranger, 1983), manufactured histories (Rowlinson and Hassard, 1993), and selective forgetting (Anteby and Molnar, 2012). That is, an incredible amount of institutional work (Lawrence and Suddaby, 2006) must be expended in order to create a common identity based upon a socially constructed common past. As Olick (1999: 342) observes, this act of reconstructing history or "the act of remembering collective history is thus a mutual production of the individual and the collective and, by participating in the rituals, retelling of myths, ceremonies, etc., the individual reaffirms his or her membership in the collective." It is this process of using history to define the scope of memory and cement membership in a group that we term *re-membering*.

While the social memory studies literature has firmly established a connection between historical memory and member identity, most of this research has occurred at the level of ethnic groups, social classes, and the nation-state. There is very little management scholarship that tries to understand how history, memory, and identity are co-constructed at the organizational level of analysis. In the following section we review the brief literature available on the subject within management before presenting our conceptual model of organizational re-membering.

Using History to Rhetorically
Construct Identification
in Organizations

A growing stream of research on organizational identification practices demonstrates how organizations have used history rhetorically to construct identification of key stakeholders with the organization. In some cases, history is used deliberately and strategically, but more often history is invoked incidentally, as part of a broader program of organizational management. Notably, the role of history in managing identification practices is seriously under-theorized in much of this work.

More significantly, our analysis of the various ways in which the past is used to manage identification in organizations reveals an intimate but largely unarticulated relationship between continuity and change in processes of organizational identification (Pratt, 2012). Although we tend to think of the rhetoric of the past as an obvious means of constructing organizational identity as an enduring element of "central and enduring character" (Kuhn, 1997: 199) or as the "core, distinctive and enduring features of an institution" (Aust, 2004: 516), what we see in our analysis is a tremendous degree of rhetorical flexibility in how actors use the past to manage the process of identification. That is, not only is the past used to construct identification by creating a sense of organizational endurance, it is also used to initiate a change in organizational identity, to repair breaches in identity, or to resurrect an atrophied identity buried over years of neglect. The rhetorical use of the past to create identification, thus, is a remarkably flexible managerial resource that, at least implicitly, offers a nuanced understanding of organizational identity as a process of skillfully and selectively managing change, disruption, and chaos in order to create the perception of continuity, repair, and order.

Invoking history to promote continuity in identity. There is, perhaps, an intuitive understanding of history as a rhetorical strategy used primarily to resist change. So, for example, Suddaby and Greenwood (2005) observed that the American Bar Association drew extensively on the rich and long history of the legal profession as an independent entity to successfully resist the introduction of multidisciplinary professional partnerships as a new organizational form. Similarly, Anteby and Molnar (2012) analyze the use of collective memory in maintaining the organizational identity of France's largest aeronautics manufacturer as a French corporation, despite the increasing presence of foreign technology and expertise. Through an analysis of roughly fifty years of internal bulletins, the authors show how the firm strategically omitted references to foreign (i.e., American) material parts and expertise in an effort to preserve a core identity of the firm as an exemplar of French manufacturing and technological prowess.

History can be so effective in maintaining identification with an organization that, in some cases, the identification endures even when the organization does not. Walsh

and Glynn (2008) illustrate the power of collective memory in organizational identification in their analysis of the role of "legacy" in employees' identification with the
Digital Equipment Corporation (DEC). Although a competitor acquired DEC in 1998,
ending a company of forty years, its organizational identity persisted long after this
as a result of the active recreation of the collective memory of the organization by
former employees who continued to produce company websites and newsletters, and
even hold corporate meetings. Walsh and Glynn (2008: 262) explain how the former
employees rhetorically constructed the firm's history and use the term "organizational
legacy" to describe how organizational members actively drew from "central and
valued organizational identity elements from the past" to maintain their affiliation
with the organization after it ceased to exist.

These are but two of many studies that elaborate how rhetorical accounts of the
past are used to create a sense of endurance of practices, values, and emotions that
constitute the core character of an organization. This view represents the traditional
understanding of both history and organizational identity as constructs of continuity and similarity. As we demonstrate below, however, history has also been used to
legitimate change in identification.

Invoking history to promote change in identity. A number of studies have examined
the important role of history in prompting change in organizational identification.
Ravasi and Phillips (2011), for example, demonstrate how the venerable Danish design
firm, Bang & Olufsen, employed history to realign the core identity of the corporation
in order to better fit with changes in the firm's competitive environment. The authors
explain how the company strategically revised the history of the organization in order
to promote change by masking it as continuity (Ravasi and Phillips, 2011). Similarly,
Ybema (2010 481) shows how newspaper employees' engaged in "temporal discontinuity talk" to construct a distinction between the "missionary" identity of the old
organization and the "open and newsy" identity of the new one.

Another exemplary illustration of how an organization's history is used strategically to motivate change by presenting it as continuity with a firm's core character
is offered by Schultz and Hernes' (2013) account of the process by which the LEGO
group strategically invoked its past as they transformed the company from a building block manufacturer to a promoter of childhood development and creativity. The
authors describe two distinct historical strategies used by the company in its change
efforts. The first strategy encouraged team members to analyze "lessons of the past"
and focused on short-term time horizons. That is, they studied failed attempts at organizational identity change from a few decades in the past, and encouraged team
members to use those findings to develop identity claims in the near future, that is,
nine months ahead.

The second strategy involved much longer time horizons in which team members
reached back 75 years to the early founding of the firm, to identify the essence of the
firm, a time period that extended well beyond the invention of the core product of
the firm (the building block). The team, ultimately, identified the promotion of child

development and creativity as its enduring essence and helped stimulate a renaissance of new products for the firm.

History, thus, proves to be a very elastic rhetorical resource in processes of identity construction. As we see in the cases discussed, history can be used to mask change as continuity by presenting the change as a reaffirmation of enduring values and character. As we note below, however, history can also be used overtly and openly to legitimate a change in identity by calling for a return to the firm's once glorious past.

Invoking history to resurrect identity. A number of empirical studies have documented how appeals to history can be used to resurrect a collective identity after a long period of erosion and decay. In contrast to the cases discussed above, however, instead of using the discourse of historical continuity of identity to mask change, in these cases history is invoked openly to motivate change that returns an organization to its idealized past. Fournier and Lee (2009), for example, describe how the iconic motorcycle manufacturer Harley Davidson's core identity and strategy gradually eroded over several decades and motivated change by using history to champion a return to its past values.

A much more sophisticated illustration of the use of history to resurrect an atrophied collective identity is presented by Howard-Grenville, Metzger, and Meyer's (2013) analysis of the resurrection of the community identity of Eugene, Oregon, as "Track Town." While the authors identify a range of practices and behaviors employed to reconstruct the municipality's collective identity, a key component of their theoretical model is based on the observation that actors used "orchestrated experiences" based on recreating elements of the city's historical "golden age" in an effort to reconnect stakeholders with the city's storied past. These activities involved strategically drawing from "Eugene's history, saluting athletes, rhapsodizing about heroic performances and celebrating Hayward Field itself" (Howard Grenville et al., 2013: 128). History, thus, offers a critical but somewhat invisible or intangible resource that was effectively mobilized by select rhetorical strategies designed to resurrect a communal identity sedimented by years of neglect.

Invoking history to repair a breach of identity. A fourth way in which history has been used to construct identification is to repair rare breaches or ruptures in communal identity. Christianson, Farkas, Sutcliffe, and Weick (2009) offer an illustrative account of the identity disruption that resulted from the collapse of the Baltimore and Ohio Railroad Museum in 2003. The authors observe that the organizational identity was reestablished (and embellished) in large part through the ritual re-creation of the firm's history. The case study demonstrates that the breach in identity that occurred as a result of the extreme event provided an opportunity for the organizational members to reinterpret and reaffirm the organization's identity, in part through a formal reflection on the history of the firm. Actors engaged in a systematic reinterpretation of the firm's mission statements in an effort to rhetorically construct a degree of continuity and familiarity against the backdrop of profound and inevitable change. Under the pretext of historical continuity, the authors observe that the organization successfully translated its core identity from a museum to an attraction.

Although identity studies have always had an implicit understanding of the relationship between history, memory, and identity, these studies are theoretically distinct in three important respects. First, they offer a clear understanding that the past is more than just time. That is, most prior studies of identification have tended to treat the temporality of collective identity in a theoretically essentialist manner in which time is a measured and objective event. Each of these studies, however, adopts a more nuanced view of the past as a truly historical phenomenon in which the narrative reconstruction of the past is subjective and interpretive.

Secondly, each of the studies implicitly recognizes the high degree of agency involved in reconstructing the past to create a collective identity in the present. Prior research in identity has, perhaps, been overly influenced by the importance of organizational imprinting in which the central and enduring characteristics of the organization that comprise identity are formed at a critical phase when the organization is particularly vulnerable to powerful environmental influence (Stinchcombe, 1965; Marquis and Tilcsik, 2013). This view of identity, however, grants too much agency to past actors, that is, founders or previous champions. The insight of these three studies, however, is that they deconstruct the mythology of imprinting by demonstrating that the significance of the past is merely an interpretation or a reconstruction of the past, offered by powerful interpretive agents in the present.

Finally, these studies each reinforce the importance of language and narrative in constructing both the past and collective identity. In the Anteby and Molnar (2012) study, the critical mechanisms of historical identity work involved formal texts, internal bulletins of the corporation. In the Schultz and Hernes (2013) study, the key mechanisms of historical identity work used by the top management team included corporate archives and internal and external reports, all of which were subject to intensive reinterpretation at a variety of workshops and meetings. For Walsh and Glynn, organizational legacy was constructed through electronic bulletin boards, websites and, most importantly, reconstructed narratives produced at communal gatherings. All three studies offer critical insight into the way in which the past of the company is rhetorically reconstructed in a historical narrative and adapted through reminiscence and recollection to suit the interests of the present.

ORGANIZATIONAL RE-MEMBERING

Based on this emerging stream of research we conclude that an organization's identity is embedded in its history. More importantly, an organization's history provides valuable raw material for identity work, and firms strategically use history, or the collective memory of the firm, to create identification and affiliation, that is, membership, between an organization and its key stakeholders. In prior work we refer to the strategic reconstruction of the past by organizations for a competitive advantage in the present as *rhetorical history* (Suddaby, Foster, and Quinn-Trank, 2010).

What we see in the studies described above is a specific variant of rhetorical history in which organizational memory is used to create membership. That is, each act of remembering offers the narrator an opportunity to reconstruct their affiliation to the organization. When the narrator is the organization, it creates an opportunity for the organization to recreate membership with (i.e. re-member) its stakeholders. Organizations actively work their history through organizational (Linde, 2009) and institutional (Douglas, 1986) memory to fuse the memory and identity of the individual and the community in a process that serves the ultimate goal of reproducing the organization as an institution. Yet apart from a smattering of studies, we do not have a comprehensive understanding of how rhetorical history shapes organizational memory and how organizational memory is then used to create organizational membership amongst stakeholders. In the balance of this section we elaborate a model of organizational re-membering.

What Is Organizational Re-Membering?

An excellent example of the strategic use of history to foster identification with an organization is offered by the History Factory, a US-based company that offers "heritage management services." In addition to traditional archival work, heritage management, according to the firm's website, means "the practice of taking the collective memory of an organization and systematically telling a story that is compelling, authentic, and relevant in order to ensure that the organization's past remains a vital element in the collective identity of the future." They go on to describe the critical role that oral history narratives play in aligning employees with a "common vision":

> As stewards of organizational memory and experts in storytelling, we provide the right content for specific needs ... The right stories told the right way help people internalize and remember ... A temporary display at your corporate retreat can remind staff members they are an important part of the team. And a history exhibit that moves among multiple offices helps everyone feel like they're a part of a shared heritage, even if they work on the other side of the country.

In this brief description, the History Factory captures the essential elements of the use of rhetorical history in strategic identification—a compelling historical narrative, crafted and retold with the intent of creating a sense of collective memory and organizational identity. The History Factory acknowledges an impressive client list of Fortune 500 corporations who appear to share an interest in deploying rhetorical history to create a strong corporate identity.

A similar empirical description of organizational re-membering is offered by Ries Roowaan, the corporate historian of ARN AMRO, the Dutch bank, and author of *A Business Case for Business History*. Roowan (2009) observes that while the traditional role of corporate historians has focused on preserving corporate history in an objective and relatively passive manner, contemporary corporate historians are actively engaged in using the past strategically to engage with customers, manage the corporate brand, and assist top management teams in managing processes of organizational change. History is particularly important in banks and other financial services companies, he observes, because their product is relatively undifferentiated, and a bank's history offers both a defining legitimacy based on endurance and a basis for differentiation. Roowan (2009: 60) quotes the head of Wells Fargo's corporate history department, Harold Anderson:

> In a relatively undifferentiated market like financial services, in which most institutions have similar products and services, marketing and advertising are key competitive elements. When a vast majority of an institution's customers are retail, with a strong notion of loyalty to a stable and reliable repository for their money, then history is an important corporate asset.

Perhaps the best empirical illustration of the use of organizational re-membering to crystallize corporate identity is offered in Charlotte Linde's (2009) book *Working the Past*. Her ethnography examines the use of narrative history in a large Midwestern US insurance company facing massive institutional change. Linde analyzes the critical role of narrative history in defining the organization as an institution. These narratives, told by top-management teams as well as individual employees, helped reconstruct the objective past of the organization into a series of subjective accounts—that is, rhetorically constructed memories—that helped participants understand what elements of the organization could be allowed to change without disrupting the institutional essence or core of the hundred-year-old company.

Her analysis focuses explicitly on identity and memory, not as objective fact, but rather as subjective interpretations and collective sensemaking. Linde presents an analysis of three different rhetorical histories of the founding of the firm and observes that the position of the speaker, the audience, and the purpose of the story all determine which constellation of events and emphasis of certain detail will be remembered when a particular version of the founding story is retold. A critical component of this organization's incredible ability to "work the past" was its ability to institutionalize occasions for re-narrating the corporate history, which involved a creative combination of formal (i.e., written or codified) and informal (i.e., oral or narrative) history.

Organizational re-membering, thus, is a complex interaction of organizational identity, rhetorical history, and collective memory. It describes a process by which we understand both an organization's history and an actor's membership in, or identification with, that organization is mutually co-constructed. The organization's history is not an objective fact, but is available for ongoing interpretation or reinterpretation and, as such, provides the raw material for organizational memory and identity work. This identity work is largely rhetorical or narrative in nature and can be used strategically to construct affiliation with a broad range of actors, both individual and organizational. Every act of re-telling an element of the firm's history invariably positions the narrator in some degree of relation to the organization and thereby reaffirms their membership in it. The rhetorical construction of membership through narratives of memory is the essence of re-membering.

In the following section we examine different strategies of organizational re-membering used by different categories of actors.

Who Are the Actors Who in Engage in Organizational Re-Membering?

Organizational re-membering occurs with all stakeholders of the firm. Employees are perhaps the most obvious actor group to be engaged with organizational re-membering strategies. As Roowan (2009: 64) observes, firms can use their past to attract top employees who are often "seeking to identify with a prestigious employer. A long, successful history can play a critical role in this regard." In their study of corporate identification strategies, Melewar and Karaosmanoglu (2007) identified firm history as one of seven critical dimensions of corporate identification, noting that employee perceptions of an organization are formed as a result of interactions over long periods of time. The way in which a firm's history is communicated to employees, thus offers a useful proxy or heuristic for repeated interaction at a collective level, and can be a useful substitute for actual interaction (see also Moingeon and Ramanantsoa, 1997).

Corporations also use in-house museums as sites for using history to create membership and affiliation of their employees (Nissley and Casey, 2002; Stigliani and Ravasi, 2007; Rowlinson, 2002). A review of US corporate museums in *The Economist* (Schumpeter, 2012: 24) describes the broad range of employee engagement activities such sites create:

> Hershey uses its Chocolate World museum to teach its employees about corporate culture. Harley-Davidson uses its collection of old bikes to inspire its designers. Coca-Cola ends its display with a taste of the future: a small machine, named the Freestyle, that can dispense 100 different Coca-Cola products. Mercedes ends it with a look at the road to emission-free mobility.

Each of these activities are oriented specifically toward inspiring employees and encouraging them to orient themselves, as individual workers, within the historical continuity of the firm—a process that Gioia, Corley, and Fabbri (2002) describe as revising the past, while thinking in the future perfect tense.

Customers are also obvious objects of organizational re-membering. The corporate museums, identified above, are most common in organizations that produce retail products, and serve a powerful role in strengthening the customer's engagement with the product and the corporate brand. Thus Coca Cola, Harley Davidson, John Deere, Kohler, SPAM, Wells Fargo, Cadbury, BMW, Mercedes Benz, Carlsberg, and a host of other large corporations have extensive museums open to the public and designed to foster brand identification through extensive education about the evolution of the product.

Government is perhaps a less obvious target of using history to create stakeholder membership. However, a number of researchers have observed a distinct effort to strategically present the history of the corporation unfolding in parallel to, and in support of, the history of the nation-state. So, for example, Foster, Suddaby, Minkus, and Weibe (2011) describe how a Canadian coffee retailer used historical narratives of both the corporation and the nation-state in an advertising campaign designed to fuse consumer and national identity. Roowan (2009) similarly describes how the Dutch airplane company Fokker, used its long history as a dominant part of the Dutch economy and an innovator in the aeronautics industry to lobby both the government and the public to maintain financial subsidies as its market share diminished through the 1960s.

The process of re-membering is directed at all the stakeholders of the firm. Employees, customers, and governments are all targets of organizational identity work. The construction of compelling historical narrative and the strategic recollection of these stories allow organizations to further and/or heighten their member's organizational identification.

How Is Organizational Re-Membering Accomplished?

Although it is relatively clear who it is that organizational re-membering targets, it is not as clear *how* the process occurs. We identify two basic categories of historical identity work in organizations, formal and emergent re-membering.

Formal re-membering involves overt techniques deliberately designed to shape organizational memory toward strategic ends. Commissioned corporate histories and biographies of founders are, perhaps, the most common means of rhetorically reinforcing stakeholder membership. Most firms also employ internal media such as newsletters and elaborate history displays. HSBC, for example, has a large "history wall" in its Canary Wharf offices. Created by the Thomas Heatherwick Studio, the wall contains over 4,000 images of the history of the corporation as it expanded globally. The structure, thus, is both a functional history and a work of art.

Large Fortune 500 corporations also use formal museums, which are perhaps the most ambitious and expensive media for setting out a firm's rhetorical history (Griffiths, 1999). As we have noted, corporate museums are actively managed to communicate a clear depiction of organizational identity by selectively organizing a particular narrative structure of the organization's memory. While corporate museums are not a particularly new phenomenon (Wedgewood established its corporate museum in 1906), most were established in the late 1970s or later (Nissley and Casey, 2002). Although corporate museums appear to offer tremendous insight into the semiotic representation of how organizational memory is managed to generate identification, they remain a relatively understudied empirical site (Yanow, 1998).

Emergent re-membering, by contrast, is a much less deliberate, overt, and strategically organized type of rhetorical history than formal re-membering. Emergent re-membering refers to the rhetorical reconstruction of a firm's history through casual conversations and informal interactions. This type of re-membering typically occurs at the shop-floor level in which individuals employ historical narratives to create shared storylines that help foster a sense of community and belonging. These emergent narratives, thus, are somewhat ritualized practices (e.g., Dacin, Munir, and Tracey, 2010; Connerton, 1989) in which individuals collectively co-author a common identity by remembering together.

One of the best illustrations of the practice of narrating an emergent community by remembering together is offered by Orr (1997) who analyzed the narrative reconstructions of machine repair by photocopy technicians in a service organization. The stories they tell each other about past repairs, Orr concludes, serve a functional purpose of constructing an informal memory bank of technical information about arcane repair techniques, but also serve a more nuanced purpose of constructing communal values and professional identity through socio-historic continuity of a shared past. The creation of a technical memory, Orr (1997: 187) explains, had the unintended consequence of creating a communal memory and thus a shared identity:

> Service work really occurs in a triangular relationship of technicians, customers and machines. However the definition of a technician is pinned to the relationship between the technician and the machine; and, of the three, information about the machine is the most problematic. The identity of the technicians, then, is defined by the ability to do technical things to a machine. The skill that they demonstrate in fixing machine problems creates and proves this identity, and their stories celebrate this identity to themselves and to others, while creating another part of their identity: member of the community, contributor to community memory.

In her study of the use of narrative to construct institutional memory in a large Midwestern insurance company Linde (2009) compares the way in which narrative was used in both formal and emergent patterns to construct identity. Formal identity stories or "paradigmatic narratives" were stories, typically told by senior management to junior employees, that recounted the history of successful sales agents. Linde (1997: 223) describes these narratives as stories of the Everyman that reconstructed an ideal career from bits and pieces of past success stories, carefully omitting the failures, in a rhetorical history that says "You see the kind of career that Bob has had? You could do that too. You could be like him."

Linde also analyzed emergent re-membering in which individual employees spontaneously engaged in retrospective stories that carefully framed their own personal experiences within the context of valued stories of the corporation's history. As Linde

(1997: 224) observes, "learning the valued stories of the past, learning how to tell one's own story as a member, is part of the intimate work of the creation of identity."

Linde's analysis of the use of historical narrative as identity work is one of the few studies that presents and contrasts both formal and emergent approaches to organizational re-membering. Her detailed ethnography offers insight into how stories about the past, told both from the top down and from the bottom up, gradually filter away the pluralistic and polyphonic depictions of organizational and individual identity and begin to merge into a powerful shared historical narrative of a mnemonic community. History, thus, provides both a powerful legitimating agent as well as an incredibly persuasive source of shared social and temporal continuity.

CONCLUSION

There is an implicit historical element to identity. The construct of identity refers to those elements of an entity, an individual or an organization, that endure over time. While the relationship between identity and history has been at least implicitly acknowledged in management research, there has been a tendency to assume that history is a fixed and objective variable. This essay challenges that assumption. We introduce the term *organizational re-membering* to underscore the observation that membership in a mnemonic community is inherently dependent upon a subjectively interpreted and constantly revised shared past. History, in our view, is never objective. Rather, it is the practice of retelling and revising the narrative of the past, through the shared voices of the present that forms the essence of identification. Organizational identity work is based, largely, on rhetorical history or the strategic use of the past to foster a sense of shared values, places, and meanings. Organizations, thus, can be understood as a unique form of mnemonic community.

We identify two essential elements of re-membering: rhetoric or the skillful use of persuasive language, and historicity, or the skillful use of the present, past, and future to create a sense of commonality and co-presence among members, based upon a shared past, real or imagined (Anderson, 1983). We illustrate the concept in the context of practices of corporate re-membering, which, we argue, is a pervasive empirical phenomenon that has been, largely, ignored by academic research. We see many opportunities to extend our understanding of this emergent construct. For example, some theory and research has pointed to the important role of historically based emotions, such as nostalgia, in generating organizational identification and individual self-authorship (Brown and Humphreys, 2002; Cutcher, 2008; Gabriel, 1993). Yet this strand of research is still relatively unexplored.

Another promising thread of research, borrowed from the burgeoning interest in political science and sociology on how collective memory becomes contested, is based on the central research question of "who or what is entitled to speak for [the] past in the present" (Hodgkin and Radstone, 2003: 1). The process of using memory to construct mnemonic identity, as we have noted, requires a creative and sophisticated strategy of blending the varied and multiple versions of the past into a unified and meaningful master narrative. How this occurs in an organization is a mystery. What are the reasoning processes that underpin where a historical artifact should be located, or what content should be included and excluded in a corporate museum? How are embarrassing or compromising issues from the past reformulated for present consumption? These are critically important questions for understanding the complex and dynamic relationship between history, memory, and identity, and the process through which history is used to institutionalize identity (Suddaby, Foster, and Mills, 2014).

We conclude by returning to an observation made at the beginning of this essay— that memory and membership are linked activities. Individual memories are never completely individual. Rather, they are constructed in a communal context or a shared time and place. As we have argued, that shared time and place is rarely an objective fact. More commonly it is a narrative reconstruction of the past, made in the present, and with an eye toward an imagined future. Retelling stories of the past, however subjective or interpretive they might be, serves a critically important function in defining membership. Communities of identity are always based in a continuum of shared time and space. Considerable prior research has focused on how identity is constructed over variations in the terrain of space. Considerably more work, both theoretical and empirical, must be devoted to a comparable understanding of how identity is constructed over variations in the terrain of time and history.

REFERENCES

Albert, S. and Whetten, D. A. (1985). "Organizational Identity." In *Research in Organizational Behavior*, vol. 8, edited by L. L. Cummings and B. M. Staw, 263–95. Greenwich, CT: JAI Press.

Anderson, B. R. O. G. (1983). *Imagined Communities: Reflections on the Origin and Spread of Nationalism.* London: Verso Editions/NLB.

Anteby, M. and Molnar, V. (2012). "Collective Identity Meets Organizational Memory: Remembering to Forget in a Firm's Rhetorical History." *Academy of Management Journal* 55(3): 515–40.

Ashforth, B. E., Harrison, S. H., and Corley, K. G. (2008). "Identification in Organizations: An Examination of Four Fundamental Questions." *Journal of Management* 34(3): 325–74.

Ashforth, B. E., Joshi, M., Anand, V., and O'Leary-Kelly, A. M. (2013). "Extending the Expanded Model of Organizational Identification to Occupations." *Journal of Applied Social Psychology* 43: 2426–28.

Ashforth, B. and Mael, F. (1989). "Social Identity Theory and the Organization." *Academy of Management Review* 14: 20–39.

Aust, P. J. (2004). "Communicated Values as Indicators of Organizational Identity: A Method for Organizational Assessment and its Application in Case Study." *Communication Studies* 55: 515–34.

Beech, N., MacIntosh, R., and McInnes, P. (2008). "Identity Work: Processes and Dynamics of Identity Formations." *International Journal of Public Administration* 31(9): 957–70.

Brickson, S. (2000). "Exploring Identity: Where Are We Now?" *Academy of Management Review* 25(1): 147–8.

Brickson, S. L. (2013). "Athletes, Best Friends, and Social Activists: An Integrative Model Accounting for the Role of Identity in Organizational Identification." *Organization Science* 24(1): 226–45.

Brown, A. D. and Humphreys, M. (2002). "Nostalgia and Narrativization: A Turkish Case Study." *British Journal of Management* 13: 141–59.

Burke, K. (1969). *A Rhetoric of Motives*. Chicago: University of Chicago Press.

Burke, K. (1937/1984). *Attitudes toward History*. Berkeley, CA: University of California Press.

Cheney, G. (1983). "The Rhetoric of Identification and the Study of Organizational Communication." *Quarterly Journal of Speech* 69: 143–58.

Christianson, M. K., Farkas, M. T., Sutcliffe, K. M., and Weick, K. (2009). "Learning through Rare Events: Significant Interruptions at the Baltimore and Ohio Railroad Museum." *Organization Science* 20(5): 846–60.

Connerton, P. (1989). *How Societies Remember*. Cambridge; New York: Cambridge University Press.

Cutcher, L. (2008). "Creating Something: Using Nostalgia to Build a Branch Network." *Journal of Consumer Culture* 8(3): 369–87.

Dacin, M. T., Munir, K., and Tracey, P. (2010). "Formal Dining at Cambridge Colleges: Linking Ritual Performance and Institutional Maintenance." *Academy of Management Journal* 53(6): 1393–418.

Douglas, M. (1986). *How Institutions Think*, 1st edn. Syracuse, NY: Syracuse University Press.

Dutton, J., and Dukerich, J. M. (1991). "Keeping an Eye on the Mirror: Image and Identity in Organizational Adaptation." *Academy of Management Journal* 34(3): 517–54.

Dutton, J., Dukerich, J. M., and Harquail, C. V. (1994). "Organizational Images and Member Identification." *Administrative Science Quarterly* 39: 239–63.

Elsbach, K. D. (1999). "An Expanded Model of Organizational Identification." *Research in Organizational Behavior* 21: 163–200.

Fiol, C. M. (2002). "Capitalizing on Paradox: The Role of Language in Transforming Organizational Identities." *Organization Science* 13(6): 653–66.

Foster, W. M. and Hyatt, C. (2007). "I Despise Them! I Detest Them! Franchise Relocation and the Expanded Model of Organizational Identification." *Journal of Sport Management* 21(2): 194–212.

Foster, W. M., Suddaby, R., Minkus, A., and Wiebe, E. (2011). "History as Social Memory Assets: The Example of Tim Hortons." *Management and Organizational History* 6(1): 101–20.

Fournier, S. and Lee, L. (2009). "Getting Brand Communities Right." *Harvard Business Review* 87(4): 105–11.

Freud, S. (1938). "The Interpretation of Dreams." In *The Basic Writings of Sigmund Freud*, edited by A. A. Brill, 183–549. New York: Modern Library.

Gabriel, Y. (1993). "Organizational Nostalgia: Reflections on 'The Golden Age.'" In *Emotion in Organizations*, edited by S. Fineman, 118–41. London: SAGE.

Gioia, D. A., Corley, K. G., and Fabbri, T. (2002). "Revising the Past (while Thinking in the Future Perfect Tense)." *Journal of Organizational Change Management* 15(6): 622–34.

Gioia, D. A., Patvardhan, S. D., Hamilton, A. L., and Corley, K. G. (2013). "Organizational Identity Formation and Change." *The Academy of Management Annals* 7(1): 123–92.

Golden-Biddle, K. and Rao, H. (1997). "Breaches in the Boardroom: Organizational Identity and Conflicts of Commitment in a Non-Profit Organization." *Organization Science* 8(6): 593–611.

Griffiths, J. (1999). "In Good Company? What's the Point of Corporate Museums?" *Museums Journal* 10: 35–8.

Halbwachs, M. (1992/1950). *On Collective Memory*, translated by L. A. Coser. Chicago: University of Chicago Press.

He, H. and Brown, A. D. (2013). "Organizational Identity and Organizational Identification: A Review of the Literature and Suggestions for Future Research." *Group & Organization Management* 38(1): 3–35.

Hobsbawm, E. J. and Ranger, T. O. (1983). *The Invention of Tradition*. Cambridge; New York: Cambridge University Press.

Hodgkin, K. and Radstone, S. (2003). "Introduction: Contested Pasts." In *Contested Pasts: The Politics of Memory*, edited by K. Hodgkin and S. Radstone, 1–22. London: Routledge.

Howard-Grenville, J., Metzger, M. L., and Meyer, A. D. (2013). "Rekindling the Old Flame: Processes of Identity Resurrection." *Academy of Management Journal* 56(1): 113–36.

Kreiner, G. E., Hollensbe, E. C., and Sheep, M. L. (2006). "Where Is the 'We' among the 'Me'? Identity Work and the Search for Optimal Balance." *Academy of Management Journal* 49(5): 1031–57.

Kuhn, T. (1997). "The Discourse of Issues Management: A Genre of Organizational Communication." *Communication Quarterly* 45: 188–210.

Lawrence, T. and Suddaby, R. (2006). "Institutions and Institutional Work." In *The SAGE Handbook of Organization Studies*, 2nd edn., edited by S. Clegg, C. Hardy, T. Lawrence, and W. R. Nord, 211–54. London: SAGE Publications Ltd.

Linde, C. (2009). *Working the Past: Narrative and Institutional Memory*. Oxford: Oxford University Press.

Lowenthal, D. 1985. *The Past Is a Foreign Country*. Cambridge; New York: Cambridge University Press.

Marquis, C. and Tilcsik, A. (2013). "Imprinting: Toward a Multilevel Theory." *The Academy of Management Annals* 7(1): 193–243.

McGaughey, S. L. (2012). "Institutional Entrepreneurship in North American Lightning Protection Standards: Rhetorical History and Unintended Consequences of Failure." *Business History* 55(1): 73–97.

Melewar, T. C. and Karaosmanoglu, E. (2007). "Dimensions of Corporate Identity." *European Journal of Marketing* 40(7/8): 846–69.

Moingeon, B. and Ramanantsoa, B. (1997). "Understanding Corporate Identity: The French School of Thought." *European Journal of Marketing* 31(5): 383–95.

Mosse, G. L. (1975). *The Nationalization of the Masses: Political Symbolism and Mass Movements in Germany from the Napoleonic Wars through the Third Reich*. New York: H. Fertig.

Nissley, N. and Casey, A. (2002). "The Politics of the Exhibition: Viewing Corporate Museums through the Paradigmatic Lens of Organizational Memory." *British Journal of Management* 13(S2), S35–S45.

Olick, J. K. (1999). "Collective Memory: The Two Cultures." *Sociological Theory* 17(3): 333–48.

Olick, J. K. and Robbins, J. (1998). "Social Memory Studies: From 'Collective Memory' to the Historical Sociology of Mnemonic Practices." *Annual Review of Sociology* 24(1): 105.

Orlikowski, W. J. and Yates, J. (1994). "Genre Repertoire: The Structuring of Communicative Practices in Organizations." *Administrative Science Quarterly* 39(4): 541–74.

Orr, J. E. (1997). "Sharing Knowledge, Celebrating Identity: Community Memory in a Service Culture." In *Collective Remembering*, edited by D. Middleton and D. Edwards, 169–89. London: SAGE.

Pratt, M. G. (1998). "To Be or Not to Be? Central Questions in Organiztional Identification." In *Identity in Organizations: Building Theory through Conversations*, edited by D. A. Whetten and P. C. Godfrey, 171–207. Thousand Oaks, CA: SAGE.

Pratt, M. G. (2000). "The Good, the Bad, and the Ambivalent: Managing Identification among Amway Distributors." *Administrative Science Quarterly* 45(3): 456–93.

Pratt, M. (2012). "Rethinking Identity Construction Processes in Organizations: Three Questions to Consider." In *Constructing Organizational Identity in and around Organizations*, edited by M. Schultz, S. Maguire, A. Langley, and H. Tsoukas, 21–49. Oxford: Oxford University Press.

Pratt, M. G. and Foreman, P. O. (2000). "Classifying Managerial Responses to Multiple Organizational Identities." *Academy of Management Review* 25(1): 18–42.

Ravasi, D. and Phillips, N. (2011). "Strategies of Alignment Organizational Identity Management and Strategic Change at Bang & Olufsen." *Strategic Organization* 9(2): 103–35.

Roowaan, Ries (2009). *A Business Case for Business History: How Companies Can Profit from their Past*. Amsterdam: Uitgeverij Boom.

Rowlinson, M. (2002). "Public History Review Essay: Cadbury World." *Labour History Review* 67(1): 101–19.

Rowlinson, M. and Hassard, J. (1993). "The Invention of Corporate Culture: A History of the Histories of Cadbury." *Human Relations* 46: 299–326.

Schultz, M. and Hernes, T. (2012). "A Temporal Perspective on Organizational Identity." *Organization Science* 24(1): 1–21.

Schumpeter (2012). "Museums of Mammon: Company Museums Are not as Dull as they Sound." *Economist*, November 17, p. 64.

Scott, S. G. and Lane, V. R. (2000). "A Stakeholder Approach to Organizational Identity." *Academy of Management Review* 25(1): 43–62.

Snow, D. A. and Anderson, L. (1987). "Identity Work among the Homeless: The Verbal Construction and Avowal of Personal Identities." *American Journal of Sociology* 92(6): 1336–71.

Snow, D. A. and McAdam, D. (2000). "Identity Work Processes in the Context of Social Movements: Clarifying the Identity/Movement Nexus." In *Self, Identity, and Social Movements*, vol. 13, edited by S. Stryker, T. Owens, and R. White, 41–67. Minneapolis: University of Minnesota Press.

Squire, L. R. (1987). *Memory and Brain*. New York: Oxford University Press.

Stigliani, I. and Ravasi, D. (2007). "Organizational Artefacts and the Expression of Identity in Corporate Museums at Alfa Romeo, Kartell and Piaggio." In *Organizational Identity in Practice*, edited by L. Lerpold, D. Ravasi, and J. Van Rekom, 197–214. London; New York: Routledge.

Stinchcombe, A. L. (1965). "Social Structure and Organizations." In *Handbook of Organizations*, edited by J. G. March, 142–93. Chicago: Rand McNally.

Suddaby, R., Foster, W. M., and Mills, A. J. (2014). "History and Institutions." In *Organization Studies: Historical Perspectives*, edited by M. Bucheli and D. Wadhwani, 100–23. Oxford: Oxford University Press.

Suddaby, R., Foster, W. M., and Quinn-Trank, C. (2010). "Rhetorical History as a Source of Competitive Advantage." In *Advances in Strategic Management: The Globalization of Strategy Research*, vol. 27, edited by J. Baum and J. Lampel, 147–73. Bingley: Emerald Group Publishing.

Suddaby, R. and Greenwood, R. (2005). "Rhetorical Strategies of Legitimacy." *Administrative Science Quarterly* 50(1): 35–67.

Sveningsson, S. and Alvesson, M. (2003). "Managing Managerial Identities: Organizational Fragmentation, Discourse and Identity Struggle." *Human Relations* 56(10): 1163–93.

Tulving, E. (1985). "Memory and Consciousness." *Canadian Psychology* 26: 1–12.

Vadera, A. K. and Pratt, M. G. (2013). "Love, Hate, Ambivalence, or Indifference? A Conceptual Examination of Workplace Crimes and Organizational Identification." *Organization Science* 24(1): 172–88.

Walsh, I. J. and Glynn, M. A. (2008). "The Way We Were: Legacy Organizational Identity and the Role of Leadership." *Corporate Reputation Review* 11(3): 262–76.

Watson, T. J. (2008). "Managing Identity: Identity Work, Personal Predicaments and Structural Circumstances." *Organization* 15(1): 121–43.

Weschler, D. (1945). "A Standardized Memory Scale for Clinical Use." *The Journal of Psychology: Interdisciplinary and Applied* 19(1): 87–95.

Yanow, D. (1998). "Space Stories: Studying Museum Buildings as Organizational Spaces while Reflecting on Interpretive Methods and their Narration." *Journal of Management Inquiry* 7(3): 215–39.

Yates, J. and Orlikowski, W. J. (1992). "Genres of Organizational Communication: A Structurational Approach to Studying Communication and Media." *Academy of Management Review* 2(2): 299–326.

Ybema, S. (2010). "Talk of Change: Temporal Contrasts and Collective Identities." *Organization Studies* 31: 481–503.

Zerubavel, E. (1996). "Social Memories: Steps to a Sociology of the Past." *Qualitative Sociology* 19(3): 283–299.

Zerubavel, E. (2003). *Time Maps: Collective Memory and the Social Shape of the Past.* Chicago: University of Chicago Press.

CHAPTER 17

....

MATERIALITY
AND IDENTITY

how organizational products, artifacts,
and practices instantiate organizational identity

....

LEE WATKISS AND MARY ANN GLYNN

SINCE the publication of Albert and Whetten's influential article, *Organizational Identity,* in 1985, research on the topic has been a growth industry in the management literature (Corley et al., 2006). The preponderance of this research has emphasized the importance of intangible factors, especially language, rhetoric, and symbolization in organizational identity construction (e.g., Corley and Gioia, 2004; Glynn and Abzug, 2002; Glynn, 2000; Pratt and Foreman, 2000; Rindova, Dalpiaz, and Ravasi, 2011), to the relative neglect of more tangible, physical, or material factors.

Ironically, research on the topic of identity prior to 1985 had occurred largely in the field of marketing under the label of corporate identity (e.g., Olins, 1978; Selame and Selame, 1975); this work focused on the visual manifestations of an organization for the purposes of corporate branding and strategy. Concerned with the ways in which organizations project themselves to external audiences, corporate identity emphasized the visual aspects of an organization's identity in the form of corporate logos, trademarks, colors, organizational name, and public statements (Abratt, 1989; Balmer, 1995; Cornelissen, Haslam, and Balmer, 2007; Olins, 1990; van Riel and Balmer, 1999). It also included more physical structures in the form of "buildings, corporate architecture, design, and décor of retail outlets, and aspects of products and services such as product design, packaging, and ritualized behavior" (Hatch and Schultz, 2000: 13). Interestingly, Albert and Whetten (1985: 270) similarly emphasized how organizational identity is instantiated and disseminated via tangible objects such as "logos and sales slogans, product packaging, and the location and appearance of the corporate headquarters."

In recent years, there has been a reinvigoration of interest in materiality across many disciplines in the social sciences, arising from a growing dissatisfaction with reducing "things to meanings, or else to social relations" (Hicks and Beaudry, 2010a: 2). This new wave of materiality research has emphasized material practices, but not simply material objects; rather, "we enact knowledge of the world, rather than straightforwardly represent it" (Hicks, 2010: 95). Thus, greater insight into the social world can be gleaned by explicitly focusing on materiality and, as a result, collapsing the arbitrary divisions among the actions, actors, and materials that are often the subject of study (e.g., Orlikowski and Scott, 2008; Orlikowski, 2007).

Organizational identity studies are beginning to pick up traces of materiality that can be found in the early work on organizational identity (e.g., Albert and Whetten, 1985), as well as corporate identity (e.g., Olins, 1990) and organizational culture (e.g., Gagliardi, 1990; Schein, 1990). Researchers have pointed to the importance of professional or employee clothing (Pratt and Rafaeli, 1997), material memories (Schultz and Hernes, 2013), office layout (Elsbach, 2003, 2004, 2006; Hatch, 1987), organizational practices (Canato, Ravasi, and Phillips, 2013), technological capabilities (Tripsas, 2009), technological use (Kaplan, 2011), product offerings (Navis and Glynn, 2010; Ravasi and Schultz, 2006), and institutional field re-emergence (Raffaelli, 2013). Yet, there has been relatively little systematic investigation into the relationship between materiality and organizational identity (for notable exceptions, see Canato et al., 2013; Ravasi and Canato, 2010; Ravasi and Stigliani, 2012; Schultz and Hernes, 2013). We seek to address this gap.

To focus our attention in this chapter, we concentrate on explaining the relationship between materiality and organizational identity, with the belief that the ways in which organizations and their members interact with material objects and engage in practices are consequential for answering the identity questions of *who we are* and *what we do*. In line with a broader "material turn" that is occurring within the social sciences (Bechky, 2003; Bijker and Law, 1992; Carlile, Nicolini, Langley, and Tsoukas, 2013a; Carlile, 2002; Hicks and Beaudry, 2010b; Knorr Cetina, 1997; Latour, 1996; Orlikowski and Scott, 2008; Ravasi and Stigliani, 2012), we turn our attention to how materiality affects organizational identity construction. Although materiality can refer to consequentiality and significance, the organizational literature has emphasized materiality in terms of tangibility or having "material existence" (Carlile, Nicolini, Langley, and Tsoukas, 2013b: 4). How materiality impacts organizational identity construction has been largely unacknowledged in the extant literature; there are, however, hints that it plays an important role. In particular, materiality seems to have the potential to shape organizational identity construction through its instantiation in organizational products, organizational artifacts, and organizational practices.

Our goal is to encourage a research agenda that foregrounds the processes and mechanisms by which materiality affects organizational identity construction. We begin by offering a conceptual framework that delineates the ways in which materiality and organizational identity are linked. Specifically, we posit that there are three elements of materiality that are important for the instantiation of organizational identity: *organizational products*, *organizational artifacts*, and *organizational practices*. Adopting a mechanism-based approach (Davis and Marquis, 2005), we theorize how these three elements of materiality instantiate organizational identity via mechanisms that are hinged to *categorization, symbolization*, and the development of *repertoires for performance*. We conclude with a discussion of these ideas and suggestions for directions for future research.

Organizational Identity Instantiation and Materiality

Organizational identity consists of both self-referential claims about central, distinctive, and enduring attributes of the collective (e.g., Albert and Whetten, 1985), as well as claims to legitimate membership in social categories (e.g., Navis and Glynn, 2010). In short, these claims give meaning to addressing questions of "who we are" and "what we do" as an organization (Glynn and Watkiss, 2012; Nag, Corley, and Gioia, 2007; Navis and Glynn, 2010). We emphasize a meta-conceptualization of organizational identity—in terms of both attributes and categorical membership—because we seek to advance a general theory on the relationship between organizational identity and materiality.

There are multiple conceptualizations of organizational identity that are drawn from related literatures in psychology, social psychology, and sociology, and that emphasize different aspects of the organization, different levels of analysis, and different roles for agency in claiming an identity for the organization. These multiple conceptualizations hint at different implications for the role of materiality. The pioneering research of Albert and Whetten (1985), sometimes referred to as a social actor approach to organizational identity, is anchored on a psychological perspective. They defined organizational identity in terms of three core criteria claimed by the organization: central character, distinctiveness, and temporal continuity. In this view, organizational identity is a property of the organization (Cerulo, 1997). Work in this area has studied materiality in the form of organizational artifacts such as names (Glynn and Abzug, 1998, 2002; Glynn and Marquis, 2006), or corporate museums (Ravasi, Rindova, and Stigliani, 2012; Schultz and Hernes, 2013) and their role as carriers of organizational identity.

An alternative viewpoint argues that the locus of identity resides in the interpretive schemas of the various organizational members (Corley et al., 2006; Gioia and Hamilton, 2014), thereby allowing for greater multivocality. Here, researchers place greater emphasis on the material practices of organizational members to instantiate identity (Dutton and Dukerich, 1991; Nag et al., 2007), focusing on organizational artifacts, but emphasizes those that have a bearing on the members themselves, such as corporate dress (Pratt and Rafaeli, 1997, 2006) or office layout (Elsbach, 2003, 2004, 2006).

These psychological approaches to identity stand in contrast to sociological and institutional perspectives that emphasize how identity is defined by an organization's categorization in broad classification systems; thus, identity is a "set of claims to a social category, such as an industry grouping, a status ranking or an interest set" (Glynn, 2008: 363). In this perspective, the emphasis is less on the unique central character or distinctiveness of an organization, but, instead, how it fits within a category, aligning with the prototype and membership. Within a category, organizational identities come to resemble each other through their adherence to a common set of institutionalized norms (Albert and Whetten, 1985; Glynn and Watkiss, 2012) and their display of social fitness in processes of inter-organizational comparison (Ravasi and Canato, 2010). As a result of categorization, organizations are able to claim an identity of an haute cuisine restaurant (Rao, Monin, and Durand, 2003), a Scottish knitwear manufacturer (Porac, Thomas, and Baden-Fuller, 1989), or a satellite radio producer (Navis and Glynn, 2010). Identity here is manifest in a different aspect of materiality: the product portfolios of organizations.

At the heart of organizational identity is a collective sense of "what we do" as an organization (Gioia, Schultz, and Corley, 2000; Glynn and Watkiss, 2012; Hatch and Schultz, 1997; Nag et al., 2007; Navis and Glynn, 2010). Inviting a consideration of materiality, this includes what we (as an organization) produce, how we (as an organization) encode our values and who we are, and how we (as an organization) deliver our products and services to our customers. Thus, organizational products are material, values are encoded in organizational artifacts, and market activities that are consequential to the organization involve material practices. We next discuss the role of how each of these—organizational products, organizational artifacts, and organizational practices—instantiates organizational identity.

Materiality and Organizational Products

Materiality is perhaps most evident in the tangible or physical products of an organization. Product identity consists of those unique attributes of a product's architecture, design, and function that flow from the particular arrangement and interrelationships of physical components, functional elements, and user interface (Ulrich, 1995). Raffaelli (2013: 93 drawing from Bayazit, 2004) argues that product identity is "concerned with the physical embodiment of man-made things, how these things perform their jobs, and how they work." By considering the product's uniqueness (in architectural design, function, and user interface) as well as its comparison to other available products in the marketplace, organizations have been able to craft product identities in both new or emerging products, for example, satellite radio (Navis and Glynn, 2010), and in long existing products, for example mechanical watches (Raffaelli, 2013).

Organizational products, as a public form of organizational artifact, provide a key link between the internal and external stakeholders regarding an organization's identity. As such, artifacts act as a cognitive anchor in giving meaning to the organization's identity in different and unique ways (Ravasi and Canato, 2010). When an organization is known for offering a particular product, the identity of that product is inextricably linked to the identity of the organization (Tripsas and Gavetti, 2000; Tripsas, 2009). For instance, consider our daily commute: we place our Dell laptop in our bag, walk out to our Honda car, drive to the Exxon mobile gas station to fill up the tank, followed by a trip to Starbucks for our morning coffee before going to work. The identities of these organizations—Dell, Exxon Mobile, Honda, and Starbucks—are made visible in their flagship products; it is how we come to understand their identities.

This tight coupling between the identities of the organization and its products can affect the development of new products (Tripsas and Gavetti, 2000). In the case of LEGO, the identity coupling can be enabling of innovation. Schultz and Hernes (2013) found that organizational leaders use legacy products so that current product design teams will be inspired to construct "LEGO" products consistent with the company's historical identity. But, tight coupling can also be constraining. Tripsas and Gavetti (2000) show that the product identity of the iconic Polaroid camera was such a strong cognitive anchor that it constrained the ability of senior management to see beyond it and take advantage of the new digital camera technology that, ironically, it had designed. An alternative to the film camera was literally unthinkable, because it would have necessitated reassessing and altering the sense of who Polaroid was and what Polaroid did. However, Ravasi and Canato (2010) illustrate how loosening the coupling just a little so that it focuses on only one design aspect of a product can be beneficial. These authors found that Piaggio, an Italian manufacturer of motorcycles and scooters, best known for its prototypical scooter, *Vespa*, features its iconic metallic design throughout the entirety of its product line, thereby making product materiality reflective of its organizational identity.

When products are novel and organizations are new, there tends to be a tighter coupling between the product's identity and that of the organization. Navis and Glynn (2010) show how the development of satellite radio was fueled by the collective orientation of the two producers (XM and Sirius) as they claimed an identity for the newly emerging market category. With the legitimation and establishment of the product identity established, then XM and Sirius differentiated their products and claimed unique organizational identities. Thus, the product and organizational identities were inextricably linked, serving to define each other until the product category was legitimated. The tight coupling between product identity and organizational identity has implications for change: when one changes, the other is bound to change, too. Raffaelli (2013) found that the historical identity of the mechanical watch, long tied to traditions of *precision* and *craftsmanship*, was coupled to the identities of the Swiss watchmaking organizations; however, when the introduction of the more precise quartz technology challenged the *precision* identity element, it also threatened that element of the identity of the Swiss craftsman. It took a re-conceptualization of watches as luxurious accessories to shift this organizational identity to luxury, exemplified today by Swiss watchmakers such as Patek Philippe or Rolex.

Materiality and Organizational Artifacts

Artifacts are "material manifestations encoding social meanings" (Bechky, 2008: 99). In organizations, artifacts can encompass "everything from the physical layout, the dress code, the manner in which people address each other, the smell and feel of the place, its emotional intensity, and other phenomena, to the more permanent archival manifestations such as company records, products, statements of philosophy, and annual reports" (Schein, 1990: 111). Researchers have demonstrated the importance of artifacts in organizational identity (Gagliardi, 1990). Ravasi, Rindova, and Stigliani (2012) show how artifacts act as organizational identity markers. In their study of corporate museums, they found that organizational artifacts are used to affirm desired and distinctive features of the organization. Thus, the materiality of artifacts aids in the construction of the meanings attached to both the artifact and the organization (Hatch, 1993; Ortner, 1973). It is through the mechanism of translation, where the literal meaning of the artifact becomes associated with the symbolic meaning, that artifacts represent organizational identity; as Pratt and Rafaeli (2006) put it, artifacts mediate organizational activity.

A series of studies by Elsbach (2003, 2004, 2006) shows artifacts, such as office layout, décor (including personal possessions), and an individual's dress, can come to represent the distinctive identities of organizational members and groups (see also Bechky, 2008; Hatch, 1990). Moreover, the empirical settings studied were replete with other artifacts that symbolized identity for its members, including an office layout with non-territorial or "hoteling" work arrangements (Doxtater, 1990).

Pratt and Rafaeli (1997: 888) find that organizational artifacts "not only represent *core values and beliefs* but may also come to represent a variety of *event-driven issues* within an organization." They show how medical professionals and administrators used their clothing to represent the identity of the rehabilitation unit in which they worked. Specifically, dress "came to signify the complex set of issues that the notion of rehabilitation represented, including the unit's mission, patients, and employee roles" (Pratt and Rafaeli, 1997: 888). The authors report that organizational members who wore street clothes understood their role in the unit to be one of rehabilitation; street clothes symbolized the transition their charges would make from being a dependent patient to an independent member of society. By contrast, organizational members who wore hospital scrubs understood their role as one of acute care. Scrubs were a way to highlight that many of the unit's activities were the same as those in intensive care units. The materiality of organizational dress provided a "concrete representation and an accessible communication medium about otherwise abstract and threatening contradictions" (Pratt and Rafaeli, 1997: 889).

For the organization as a whole, Glynn, in a series of studies (Glynn and Abzug, 1998, 2002; Glynn and Marquis, 2006), shows that the artifact of the organizational name is a potent carrier of identity. When organizations change their names, they tend not to draw on their historical legacy but to claim membership in their new market

category. Conformity to the categorical imperative (Zuckerman, 1999) increased legitimacy, as well as ease of comprehension and acceptance, particularly for external
audiences. And, from the organizational culture literature, we know these physical
settings, together with external design, logos, colors, uniforms, products, and product
packaging symbolize the "basic traits of the organization inhabiting them" (Berg and
Kreiner, 1990: 42).

And, for both internal and external stakeholders, artifacts provide a way for the
organization to link its past to its present and a desired future. In their study of the
LEGO Group, Schultz and Hernes (2013) found that artifacts act as forms of organizational memory, providing cues to linking present and future organizational identities.
This study also demonstrated that the materiality of artifacts enabled LEGO's identity
to reflect a revised sense of "who we are" and accommodate its changing competitive
environment to a limit that was bounded by the identity. The organization was able
to alter the subjective meanings of the artifacts to reflect a changing identity, but the
literal meanings of those artifacts (Hatch, 1993) remained constant. Artifacts function
to provide a temporal continuity for identity while allowing for a degree of mutability of meanings (Gioia et al., 2000). This mutability enables organizational artifacts
to resonate with both the past and present, thereby acting as powerful symbols for
organizational identity.

Thus, material artifacts offer a vehicle through which organizational identity is understood and evaluated. By symbolizing key elements, issues, or membership, artifacts
can act as powerful representations of organizational identity as well as the means
through which that identity can be constructed.

Materiality and Organizational Practices

Organizational practices are "bundle[s] of behavioral routines, tools, and concepts
used to accomplish a certain [organizational] task" (Canato et al., 2013: 1725). In many
of the foundational papers on organizational identity, claims to organizational identity were viewed as being mediated through practices. Albert and Whetten (1985)
argued, persuasively, that it is often when organizational members are engaged in discussions about organizational practices that issues of organizational identity arise.
And, Dutton and Dukerich (1991) made clear that it was when those practices were
challenged that issues of identity became particularly salient. More generally, organizational practices are part of the identity element of "what we do."

Scholars have begun to reconsider the relationship between material practices
and organizational identity. Nag and colleagues (2007), in their study of how a high-
technology research and development organization attempted to change its identity,
show that "organizational identity inheres in work practices" (Nag et al., 2007: 842).
And, a robust finding in the organizational culture and identity literatures is that any
attempt to change practices that clash with an organization's sense of who it is or what

it does is likely to encounter resistance (Albert and Whetten, 1985; Bartunek, 1984; Schein, 2004), to the extent that practices will be altered only when they reflect the prevailing identity of the organization (Ansari, Fiss, and Zajac, 2010). However, the relationship between practice and identity may be more complicated.

Canato and colleagues (2013), for instance, argue for a recursive relationship between the cognitive and practice dimensions of identity, such that the prolonged exposure to new practices, even in the presence of long-standing cognitive beliefs about the identity of the organization, will have the effect of altering the organization's identity. This is not to say that identity merely adapts to reflect the changes in practices, but the more that practices are deeply embedded in an organization's identity, the more that changes in fundamental organizational practices are likely to result in the adaptation of identity. The key argument, here, is that the materiality of the practices mediates between the actions and their meanings.

This relationship is made clearer when we look at material objects and the ways organizational members interact with them. Matter is not merely an "object but rather is implicated in a set of practices" (Kaplan, 2011: 323). In an empirical a study of how organizational members use technology to formulate corporate strategy, Kaplan (2011) finds that PowerPoint software provides the materiality to make intangible ideas tangible by displaying those ideas in a form that provides a medium through which they can be seen, understood, and manipulated; in many ways, the software is performative of the identity. By providing a public and material record of the ideas, PowerPoint enables organizational members to generate a broadly shared understanding that facilitates the development of corporate strategy. Other work shows how materiality may not change an identity, but, instead, reinforce it. In a study of an international design consultancy, Stigliani and Ravasi (2012: 1253) find that material objects serve as "evolving material representations of emerging collective interpretations" that helped organizational members gain a better sense of who they were and what they did.

Identity, in the form of organizational practices, is not so much a unified or coherent set of claims or values but a "cache of ideas" (Small, Harding, and Lamont, 2010: 16), or a "repertoire" (Swidler, 1986: 277) that actors can draw from to understand, not only what the organization does, but also who the organization is. Taken together, this suggests that the organizational practices act as performative repertoires from which organizational identity is constructed.

In sum, these three elements of materiality—organizational products, organizational artifacts, and organizational practices—are important to organizational identity. Next, we elaborate the mechanisms that connect materiality to identity (see Figure 17.1): categorization, symbolization, and performative repertoires. For the sake of parsimony, we have modeled materiality, mechanisms, and processes of organizational identity construction as distinct, with separate and largely independent paths of influence. However, there are likely interdependencies among the factors; we discuss this possibility following our presentation of the conceptual framework.

Theorizing Mechanisms Linking Materiality to Organizational Identity

Organizations and their members interact with material objects and practices in order to construct identities that define "who we are" and "what we do." In our theoretical framework (Figure 17.1), we focus on how three elements of materiality in organizations—products, artifacts, and practices—function as mechanisms driving identity construction. In particular, we theorize that 1) organizational products *categorize* organizations as one type of an organization and not another (e.g., a film camera producer and not a digital one); 2) organizational artifacts *symbolize* organizational values, character, and attributes that substantiate identity claims; and, 3) organizational practices afford a *performative repertoire* from which organizations construct strategies of action in the marketplace.

Mechanisms, as inherently processual (Davis and Marquis, 2005), offer explanations as to how materiality can affect organizational identity construction. Thus, our theorizing is explanatory, and not predictive. We will illustrate our theorizing, using one specific organization, Apple, Inc. Apple is a multinational corporation that designs, develops, and sells consumer products. It is a widely recognizable organization with a strong identity; its offerings such as iPod, iPhone, iPad, and iMac are some of the best-known and most successful products in the marketplace today. Its patented

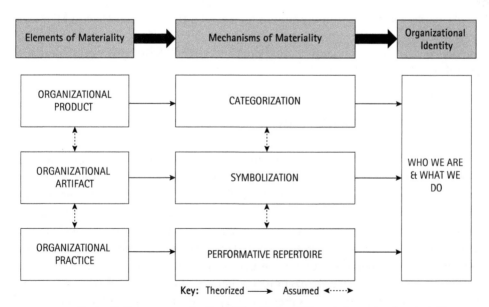

FIGURE 17.1 Instantiating an organizational identity by different elements of materiality

store designs provide a plethora of organizational artifacts, and its award-winning supply chain affords a window onto its organizational practices.

Categorization as a Mechanism

This mechanism focuses on how an organization's products serve to categorize organizations as one type of an organization and not another, for example as a manufacturing firm and not a consultancy. By drawing attention to specific products, and overlooking or diminishing others, this mechanism allocates the organization to a particular market category (e.g., Navis and Glynn, 2010; Raffaelli, 2013). By classifying an organization as one type and not another, organizational products provide the salient elements that give meaning to the organization's identity (Glynn, 2008). Furthermore, key products (Benner and Tripsas, 2012; Tripsas and Gavetti, 2000), and even elements of key products (Ravasi and Canato, 2010), serve as touchstones that categorize the types of products that are legitimate for a particular organization to create.

For instance, Apple Computer was for years understood in terms of its Mac computer products (and proprietary operating systems). The effect was to identify Apple as a computer manufacturer (like Hewlett Packard) and an operating systems producer (like Microsoft). However, with the introduction of iPod in 2001 and iPhone in 2007, Apple had by 2010 become the largest (by revenue) producer of mobile devices in the world. With the introduction of iPad in 2010 and the dropping of "Computer" from the organization's name in 2007, Apple re-categorized itself as a mobile devices organization. By drawing attention to its three "iP" products—iPod, iPhone, and iPad—Apple viewed its identity as more similar to Samsung and Motorola than to Microsoft or Hewlett Packard. This has been reinforced by Apple's subsequent additions to its mobile devices' product lines including smaller iPads and larger iPhones, all of which include similar technologies.

Symbolization as a Mechanism

In contrast to the broad membership concerns of categorization, symbolization is more local in orientation, focusing on how organizational artifacts encode the organizational values, character, and attributes that substantiate identity claims (Schein, 1990). By providing material form, organizational artifacts enable actors to comprehend (Ortner, 1973) and construct the meanings of the artifact. As Hatch (1993) makes clear, it is in the process of symbolization that organizational artifacts become infused with meanings beyond the literal meanings of the artifact. As a result, an actor can assess the legitimacy of an organization's membership in a particular market category, link the organization's past to its present, and provide a focal point for discussion of areas of interest and concern by representing a variety of event-driven issues.

Apple's patented store design is a classic example of how organizational artifacts can encode organizational values and character. With more than 400 stores worldwide, the consistent design of a glass storefront, recessed lighting and displays, cantilevered shelving, and rectangular tables (United States Patent and Trademark Office) enables Apple to construct an organizational identity that suggests both beautiful aesthetics and cutting-edge design. It also symbolizes that Apple is in control of its products from design to point-of-sale as evidenced by its closed-source software model and its unique strategy of producing both the software and hardware for its products. Moreover, the stores provide ample opportunity for customers to test drive products prior to purchase, thereby symbolizing the user-centric aspects of Apple. And, with the iconic logo of a stylized apple ever-present on products since 1976, Apple is able to symbolize the temporal continuity of its focus on beautiful aesthetics and cutting-edge design.

Performative Repertoires as a Mechanism

Theorizing organizational practices as performative repertoires from which organizations can construct strategies of action that instantiate their identity, we focus on how organizations and their members engage in material practices and utilize material objects in persistent ways over time (Swidler, 1986). The identity of the organization inheres in the materiality of these practices (Nag et al., 2007) because of this persistence. Thus, these performative repertoires direct attention toward organizational practices, but only those for which the organization is culturally equipped (Small et al., 2010).

Apple's identity is understood with respect to high-quality manufacturing processes. Gartner, the world's leading information technology research and advisory company, has named Apple the "world's best supply chain" for the last seven years (http://www.gartner.com/newsroom/id/2747417). It has received this accolade in part because it has spent $10.5 billon to develop robots to keep it ahead of its rivals (http://www.bloomberg.com/news/2013-11-13/apple-s-10-5b-on-robots-to-lasers-shores-up-supply-chain.html). These robots and the patented processes for using them (e.g., the use of a robotic arm for finishing the current generation of iPhone or the use of a robotic arm to degrease, anodize, and chemically polish the iMac) form part of Apple's repertoire from which the organization and its members can construct strategies of action in the marketplace. Anyone watching Apple's periodic keynote presentations that launch new products cannot fail to notice the same careful attention to detail, that inheres in both its product design practices and in the way the presenters seamlessly interact with the material objects on stage and the precise, consistent, and aesthetically pleasing content they convey. Returning to the Apple Store, the sales clerks' use of iPad as a point-of-sales terminal and subsequent emailing of the sales receipt to the customer is another illustration of how the act of conducting a sales transaction is mediated by materiality in a way that embodies the organization's identity as an innovative organization and is drawn from its repertoire of beliefs and skills that aims to maximize user experience.

DISCUSSION

In this chapter, we have called for greater attention to the relationship between materiality and organizational identity. We have argued that there are three elements of materiality that are important for the instantiation of organizational identity and that these elements are related to identity via three specific mechanisms: 1) the mechanism of categorization focuses on how an organizational product serves to classify an organization as a particular type; 2) the mechanism of symbolization encodes organizational artifacts with meanings that facilitate the substantiation of identity claims and, especially, "who we are"; and 3) the mechanism of performative repertoires provides the resources from which organizations construct organizational practices that reflect "what we do." More research is clearly warranted to understanding the nuances of such processes, and the inter-relationships among the various material properties and mechanisms. Here, we offer some ideas for future work.

For the sake of theoretical parsimony, we have treated the relationships among the various aspects of materiality and the mechanisms that drive organizational identity construction as if they were separate and independent processes. However, although this distinction is conceptually useful, it tends to mask the dynamics and interrelatedness of these processes. We represent these dynamics in our model (Figure 17.1) with broken line bi-directional arrows to reflect these assumptions. The feasibility of these assumptions is reflected in our use of similar examples to illustrate the various aspects of materiality. For instance, the material practices of consulting firms are mediated by software programs such as PowerPoint, but as Kaplan (2011) shows, PowerPoint also has implications for a consulting firm's product offerings. Similarly, we showed that the dropping of the word "Computer" from the name of Apple in recognition of its shift in the identities of its product offerings re-categorized Apple as a mobile devices organization. However, we could just as easily have considered the firm's name as an organizational artifact, highlighting the processes by which the name change symbolized a shift from Apple as a computer company to that of a mobile devices organization.

In a similar vein, we recognize the interdependence of the three mechanisms at the heart of our framework. For instance, in addition to categorizing Apple as a mobile devices organization, iPhone and iPad also acted as organizational artifacts to symbolize Apple as an innovative organization. Thus, it is possible that the various mechanisms may be affected by more than one aspect of materiality. As well as this, each mechanism may amplify each other when they function in concert. Symbolization and categorization have often been considered as complementary processes (e.g., Navis and Glynn, 2010), but little is currently known about how these mechanisms relate to an organization's performative repertoire. Little is also known about what happens if these mechanisms conflict with or contradict one other. For instance, as the innovative products of Apple are increasingly produced by the material practices (of suppliers), it is unclear what are the implications for the organization's identity. How these different and potentially conflicting material aspects and mechanisms' elements come together to construct an identity, and the impact on the potency of that identity are interesting areas for exploration, and await future scholarship.

To craft a general theoretical framework with respect to the relationship between materiality and organizational identity we have used a broad conceptualization of organizational identity. Admittedly, however, this masks some issues that might lead to more nuanced applications of our framework. For instance, our literature review suggests that an organization's institutional claims to a social category are more likely to favor mechanisms of categorization. And, it hints that identity elements focusing on organizational members' subjective meanings are more likely to emphasize artifacts and practices rather than products. Thus, empirical work is required to examine the specific conditions under which different aspects of materiality are brought to bear on different conceptualizations or elements of organizational identity.

Implicit in our discussion is the idea that material practices and objects do not have inherent meaning, but rather derive meaning from the categories in which they are embedded, through the actors who interpret them, and in the ways in which they are put into practice. This suggests that the various elements of materiality and their associated mechanisms may vary with the contexts in which they are located. As we have noted, emerging product identities have different relationships with organizational identity depending on the age of the organization or the maturity of the market category. Satellite radio was created by de novo firms in a nascent market producing a single product; thus, the product identity had a strong influence on the identity of the organizations (Navis and Glynn, 2010). It was not until a clear product identity emerged and the market category legitimated that the organizations began to claim their own differentiated identities, whereas, when a product identity emerged as a result of the activities of a number of firms, the organizational identity had greater influence on the identity of the product (Benner and Tripsas, 2012; Tripsas, 2009). This hints at the role of the external environment in relating materiality to the organizational identity, such that the relationship may differ during periods of organizational crisis, change, or conflict, or different moments of organizational transition. We can speculate, for instance, that focusing on the symbolization of organizational artifacts in terms of their historicity and semi-permanence may be useful when considering minor changes to an organization's identity, whereas for organizations wishing to initiate radical and long-term changes to their identities, a focus on reshaping their material practices may be more fruitful (e.g., Canato et al., 2013).

A material perspective provides a range of opportunistic levers for managers to use to shape the organization's identity. As a visible manifestation of identity, materiality makes identity more vivid. Materiality provides a point of reference, providing premises for action, around which managers can rally employees' identification and behaviors. For instance, managers can explicitly choose to represent the organization's identity in the products or design features emphasized (Ravasi and Canato, 2010; Tripsas, 2009). Simple changes such as altering office layout can have a powerful symbolic effect. For example, a move to open plan offices, from private offices with windows for managers and from cubicles lacking natural light for everyone else, symbolizes a more democratic and less hierarchical organization (Elsbach, 2003, 2004, 2006; Hatch, 1987). Managers may also make more resource-intensive and permanent decisions to represent the organizational identity in structures such as corporate museums (Ravasi et al., 2012; Schultz and Hernes, 2013) or by changing the name of the organization (Glynn and Abzug, 1998, 2002; Glynn and Marquis, 2006). But, both can be symbolically powerful to internal and external stakeholders. And, finally, managers can influence identity by altering their practices. Organizations such as 3M which adopted Six Sigma practices to enhance efficiency provided not only technical solutions but also symbolic ones (Zbaracki, 1998); as such they affected the identity of the organization (Canato et al., 2013) in several ways, altering 3M's concern for control, accountability, and risk management by providing alternative performance repertoires. And, as this study shows, managers cannot simply implant their own interpretation of a desired identity on the organization; rather, identity is instantiated in a negotiation with both internal and external key stakeholders.

CONCLUSION

We began by observing that, despite the growth in research into organizational identity construction, there is only limited research into the role of materiality in that process. We outlined a rudimentary conceptual framework that shows how organizational products, organizational artifacts, and organizational practices can instantiate organizational identity. We theorized that each of the three elements of materiality was related to organizational identity via a particular mechanism: organizational products via categorization; organizational artifacts via symbolization; and organizational practices via performative repertoires. It is our hope that the articulation of these mechanisms provides an opportunity for a more systematic and empirically driven research agenda into the role of materiality in instantiating organizational identity.

REFERENCES

Abratt, R. (1989). "A New Approach to the Corporate Image Management Process." *Journal of Marketing Management* 5(1): 63–76.

Albert, S. and Whetten, D. A. (1985). "Organizational Identity." *Research in Organizational Behavior* 7: 263–95.

Ansari, S. M., Fiss, P. C., and Zajac, E. J. (2010). "Made to Fit: How Practices Vary as They Diffuse." *Academy of Management Review* 35: 67–92.

Balmer, J. M. T. (1995). "Corporate Branding and Connoisseurship." *Journal of General Management* 21: 22–46.

Bartunek, J. M. (1984). "Changing Interpretive Schemes and Organizational Restructuring: The Example of a Religious Order." *Administrative Science Quarterly* 29: 355–72.

Bechky, B. A. (2003). "Sharing Meaning across Occupational Communities: The Transformation of Understanding on a Production Floor." *Organization Science* 14(3): 312–30.

Bechky, B. A. (2008). "Analyzing Artifacts: Material Methods for Understanding Identity, Status, and Knowledge in Organizational Life." In *The SAGE Handbook of New Approaches in Management and Organization*, edited by D. Barry and H. Hansen, 98–109. London: SAGE.

Benner, M. J. and Tripsas, M. (2012). "The Influence of Prior Industry Affiliation on Framing in Nascent Industries: The Evolution of Digital Cameras." *Strategic Management Journal* 33: 277–302.

Berg, P. O. and Kreiner, K. (1990). "Corporate Architecture: Turning Physical Settings into Symbolic Resources." In *Symbols and Artifacts: Views of the Corporate Landscape*, edited by P. Gagliardi, 41–67. New York, NY: Aldine de Gruyter.

Bijker, W. E. and Law, J. (eds.) (1992). *Shaping Technology/Building Society: Studies in Sociotechnical Change*. Cambridge, MA: MIT Press.

Canato, A., Ravasi, D., and Phillips, N. (2013). "Coerced Practice Implementation in Cases of Low Cultural Fit: Cultural Change and Practice Adaptation during the Implementation of Six Sigma at 3M." *Academy of Management Journal* 56: 1724–53.

Carlile, P. R. (2002). "A Pragmatic View of Knowledge and Boundaries: Boundary Objects in New Product Development." *Organization Science* 13(4): 442–55.

Carlile, P. R., Nicolini, D., Langley, A., and Tsoukas, H. (eds.) (2013a). *How Matter Matters: Objects, Artifacts, and Materiality in Organization Studies*. Oxford: Oxford University Press.

Carlile, P. R., Nicolini, D., Langley, A., and Tsoukas, H. (2013b). "How Matter Matters: Objects, Artifacts, and Materiality in Organization Studies: Introducing the Third Volume of Perspectives on Organization Studies." In *How Matter Matters: Objects, Artifacts, and Materiality in Organization Studies*, edited by P. R. Carlile, D. Nicolini, A. Langley, and H. Tsoukas, 1–15. Oxford: Oxford University Press.

Cerulo, K. A. (1997). "Identity Construction: New Issues, New Directions." *Annual Review of Sociology* 23: 385–409.

Corley, K. G. and Gioia, D. A. (2004). "Identity Ambiguity and Change in the Wake of a Corporate Spin-Off." *Administrative Science Quarterly* 49: 173–208.

Corley, K. G., Harquail, C. V., Pratt, M. G., Glynn, M. A., Fiol, C. M., and Hatch, M. J. (2006). "Guiding Organizational Identity through Aged Adolescence." *Journal of Management Inquiry* 15: 85–99.

Cornelissen, J. P., Haslam, S. A., and Balmer, J. M. T. (2007). "Social Identity, Organizational Identity and Corporate Identity: Towards an Integrated Understanding of Processes, Patternings and Products." *British Journal of Management* 18: S1–S16.

Davis, G. F. and Marquis, C. (2005). "Prospects for Organization Theory in the Early Twenty-First Century: Institutional Fields and Mechanisms." *Organization Science* 16: 332–43.

Doxtater, D. (1990). "Meaning of the Workplace: Using Ideas of Ritual Space in Design." In *Symbols and Artifacts: Views of the Corporate Landscape*, edited by P. Gagliardi, 108–27. New York, NY: Aldine de Gruyter.

Dutton, J. E. and Dukerich, J. M. (1991). "Keeping an Eye on the Mirror: Image and Identity in Organizational Adaptation." *Academy of Management Journal* 34: 517–54.

Elsbach, K. D. (2003). "Relating Physical Environment to Self-Categorizations: Identity Threat and Affirmation in a Non-Territorial Office Space." *Administrative Science Quarterly* 48: 622–54.

Elsbach, K. D. (2004). "Interpreting Workplace Identities: The Role of Office Décor." *Journal of Organizational Behavior* 25: 99–128.

Elsbach, K. D. (2006). "Perceptual Biases and Mis-interpretation of Artifacts." In *Artifacts and Organizations: Beyond Mere Symbolism*, edited by A. Rafaeli and M. G. Pratt, 61–81. Mahwah, NJ: Lawrence Erlbaum.

Gagliardi, P. (1990). "Artifacts as Pathways and Remains of Organizational Life." In *Symbols and Artifacts: Views of the Corporate Landscape*, edited by P. Gagliardi, 3–38. New York, NY: Aldine de Gruyter.

Gioia, D. A. and Hamilton, A. L. (2016). "Great Debates in Organizational Identity Study." In *The Oxford Handbook of Organizational Identity*, edited by M. G. Pratt, M. Schultz, D. Ravasi, and B. E. Ashforth, 21–38. Oxford: Oxford University Press.

Gioia, D. A., Schultz, M., and Corley, K. G. (2000). "Organizational Identity, Image, and Adaptive Instability." *Academy of Management Review* 25: 63–81.

Glynn, M. A. (2000). "When Cymbals Become Symbols: Conflict over Organizational Identity within a Symphony Orchestra." *Organization Science* 11: 285–98.

Glynn, M. A. (2008). "Beyond Constraint: How Institutions Enable Identities." In *The SAGE Handbook of Organizational Institutionalism*, edited by R. Greenwood, C. Oliver, K. Sahlin, and R. Suddaby, 357–74. Thousand Oaks, CA: SAGE.

Glynn, M. A. and Abzug, R. (1998). "Isomorphism and Competitive Differentiation in the Organizational Name Game." *Advances in Strategic Management* 15: 105–28.

Glynn, M. A. and Abzug, R. (2002). "Institutionalizing Identity: Symbolic Isomorphism and Organizational Names." *Academy of Management Journal* 45: 267–80.

Glynn, M. A. and Marquis, C. (2006). "Fred's Bank: How Institutional Norms and Individual Preferences Legitimate Organizational Names." In *Artifacts and Organizations: Beyond Mere Symbolism*, edited by A. Rafaeli and M. G. Pratt, 223–40. Mahwah, NJ: Erlbaum.

Glynn, M. A. and Watkiss, L. (2012). "Exploring Cultural Mechanisms of Organizational Identity Construction." In *Constructing Identity in and around Organizations*, edited by M. Schultz, S. Maguire, A. Langley, and H. Tsoukas, 63–88. New York, NY: Oxford University Press.

Hatch, M. J. (1987). "Physical Barriers, Task Characteristics, and Interaction Activity in Research and Development Firms." *Administrative Science Quarterly* 32: 387–99.

Hatch, M. J. (1990). "The Symbolics of Office Design: An Empirical Exploration." In *Symbols and Artifacts: Views of the Corporate Landscape*, edited by P. Gagliardi, 129–46. New York, NY: Aldine de Gruyter.

Hatch, M. J. (1993). "The Dynamics of Organizational Culture." *Academy of Management Review* 18: 657–93.

Hatch, M. J. and Schultz, M. (1997). "Relations between Organizational Culture, Identity and Image." *European Journal of Marketing* 31: 356–65.

Hatch, M. J. and Schultz, M. (2000). "Scaling the Tower of Babel: Relational Differences between Identity, Image and Culture in Organizations." In *The Expressive Organization: Linking Identity, Reputation, and the Corporate Brand*, edited by M. Schultz, M. J. Hatch, and M. H. Larsen, 11–35. Oxford: Oxford University Press.

Hicks, D. (2010). "The Material-Cultural Turn: Event and Effect." In *The Oxford Handbook of Material Culture Studies*, edited by D. Hicks and M. C. Beaudry, 25–98. Oxford: Oxford University Press.

Hicks, D. and Beaudry, M. C. (2010a). "Introduction." In *The Oxford Handbook of Material Culture Studies*, edited by D. Hicks and M. C. Beaudry, 1–21. Oxford: Oxford University Press.

Hicks, D. and Beaudry, M. C. (eds.) (2010b). *The Oxford Handbook of Material Culture Studies*. Oxford: Oxford University Press.

Kaplan, S. (2011). "Strategy and PowerPoint: An Inquiry into the Epistemic Culture and Machinery of Strategy Making." *Organization Science* 22: 320–46.

Knorr Cetina, K. (1997). "Sociality with Objects: Social Relations in Postsocial Knowledge Societies." *Theory, Culture and Society* 14(4): 1–30.

Latour, B. (1996). "On Interobjectivity." *Mind, Culture, and Activity* 3: 228–45.

Nag, R., Corley, K. G., and Gioia, D. A. (2007). "The Intersection of Organizational Identity, Knowledge, and Practice: Attempting Strategic Change via Knowledge Grafting." *Academy of Management Journal* 50: 821–47.

Navis, C. and Glynn, M. A. (2010). "How New Market Categories Emerge: Temporal Dynamics of Legitimacy, Identity, and Entrepreneurship in Satellite Radio, 1990-2005." *Administrative Science Quarterly* 55: 439–71.

Olins, W. (1978). *The Corporate Personality: An Inquiry into the Nature of Corporate Identity*. London: Mayflower Books.

Olins, W. (1990). *Corporate Identity: Making Business Strategy Visible through Design*. Cambridge, MA: Harvard Business School Press.

Orlikowski, W. J. (2007). "Sociomaterial Practices: Exploring Technology at Work." *Organization Studies* 28(9): 1435–48.

Orlikowski, W. J. and Scott, S. V. (2008). "Chapter 10: Sociomateriality: Challenging the Separation of Technology, Work, and Organization." *Academy of Management Annals* 2: 433–74.

Ortner, S. B. (1973). "On Key Symbols." *American Anthropologist* 75: 1338–46.

Porac, J. F., Thomas, H., and Baden-Fuller, C. (1989). "Competitive Groups as Cognitive Communities: The Case of Scottish Knitwear Manufacturers." *Journal of Management Studies* 26: 397–416.

Pratt, M. G. and Foreman, P. O. (2000). "Classifying Managerial Responses to Multiple Organizational Identities." *Academy of Management Review* 25: 18–42.

Pratt, M. G. and Rafaeli, A. (1997). "Organizational Dress as a Symbol of Multilayered Social Indentities." *Academy of Management Journal* 40: 862–98.

Pratt, M. G. and Rafaeli, A. (2006). "Artifacts and Organizations: Understanding our "Object-ive" Reality." In *Artifacts and Organizations: Beyond Mere Symbolism*, edited by M. G. Pratt and A. Rafaeli, 279–88. Mahwah, NJ: Lawrence Erlbaum.

Raffaelli, R. (2013). "Identity and Institutional Change in a Mature Field: The Re-Emergence of the Swiss Watchmaking Industry, 1970-2008." Unpublished Doctoral Dissertation, Boston College, Chestnut Hill, MA.

Rao, H., Monin, P., and Durand, R. (2003). "Institutional Change in Toque Ville: Nouvelle Cuisine as an Identity Movement in French Gastronomy." *American Journal of Sociology* 108: 795–843.

Ravasi, D. and Canato, A. (2010). "We Are What We Do (and How We Do It): Organizational Technologies and the Construction of Organizational Identity." *Research in the Sociology of Organizations* 29: 49–78.

Ravasi, D., Rindova, V. P., and Stigliani, I. (2012). "The Stuff of Legends: Mnemonic Practices and the Construction of Organizational Identity in Corporate Museums." (Unpublished article in progress).

Ravasi, D. and Schultz, M. (2006). "Responding to Organizational Identity Threats: Exploring the Role of Organizational Culture." *Academy of Management Journal* 49: 433–58.

Ravasi, D. and Stigliani, I. (2012). "Product Design: A Review and Research Agenda for Management Studies." *International Journal of Management Reviews* 14(4): 464–88.

Rindova, V., Dalpiaz, E., and Ravasi, D. (2011). "A Cultural Quest: A Study of Organizational Use of New Cultural Resources in Strategy Formation." *Organization Science* 22: 413–31.

Schein, E. H. (1990). "Organizational Culture." *American Psychologist* 45: 109–19.

Schein, E. H. (2004). *Organizational Culture and Leadership*, 3rd edn. San Francisco, CA: Jossey-Bass.

Schultz, M. and Hernes, T. (2013). "A Temporal Perspective on Organizational Identity." *Organization Science* 24: 1–21.

Selame, E. and Selame, J. (1975). *Developing a Corporate Identity: How to Stand out in the Crowd*. New York: Chain Store Publishing.

Small, M. L., Harding, D. J., and Lamont, M. (2010). "Reconsidering Culture and Poverty." *The Annals of the American Academy of Political and Social Science* 629: 6–27.

Stigliani, I. and Ravasi, D. (2012). "Organizing Thoughts and Connecting Brains: Material Practices and the Transition from Individual to Group-Level Prospective Sensemaking." *Academy of Management Journal* 55: 1232–59.

Swidler, A. (1986). "Culture in Action: Symbols and Strategies." *American Sociological Review* 51: 273–86.

Tripsas, M. (2009). "Technology, Identity, and Inertia through the Lens of 'The Digital Photography Company.'" *Organization Science* 20: 441–60.

Tripsas, M. and Gavetti, G. (2000). "Capabilities, Cognition, and Inertia: Evidence from Digital Imaging." *Strategic Management Journal* 21: 1147–61.

Ulrich, K. (1995). "The Role of Product Architecture in the Manufacturing Firm." *Research Policy* 24: 419–40.

van Riel, C. B. M. and Balmer, J. M. T. (1999). "Corporate Identity: The Concept, its Measurement and Management." *European Journal of Marketing* 31: 340–55.

Zbaracki, M. J. (1998). "The Rhetoric and Reality of Total Quality Management." *Administrative Science Quarterly* 43: 602–36.

Zuckerman, E. W. (1999). "The Categorical Imperative: Securities Analysts and the Illegitimacy Discount." *American Journal of Sociology* 104: 1398–438.

CHAPTER 18

MAKING SENSE OF WHO WE ARE

leadership and organizational identity

DAAN VAN KNIPPENBERG

As research in organizational identity has unfolded over the years, it has become increasingly clear that organizational identity—those aspects of the organization that its members perceive to be central, enduring, and distinctive (Albert and Whetten, 1985)—matters. Research in organizational identity suggests that what is seen as central, enduring, and distinctive to an organization is important for a number of reasons. It may motivate resistance to change when the change is seen as a threat to organizational identity (Fiol, 2002; Rousseau, 1998), but also make employees accepting of change when the change is understood to guarantee continuity of organizational identity (van Knippenberg, van Knippenberg, and Bobbio, 2008; van Knippenberg, van Knippenberg, Monden, and de Lima, 2002; cf. Shamir, 1999) or motivate change when the change is framed as progress toward a situation closer to the ideal-type of the organization's identity (Gioia, Schultz, and Corley, 2000; Ravasi and Schultz, 2006; Stam, Lord, van Knippenberg, and Wisse, 2014; van Knippenberg and Hogg, 2003). Through organizational identification (i.e., self-definition in terms of the organizational identity; Ashforth and Mael, 1989; Pratt, 1998), organizational identity reflects on the self. As a result, more attractive organizational identities (e.g., those associated with higher prestige; Mael and Ashforth, 1992, or those that are more distinctive; Dutton, Dukerich, and Harquail, 1994) inspire more organizational identification, and thus greater loyalty and motivation to pursue the organization's interests (Ashforth and Mael, 1989; van Knippenberg, 2000). Both in times of stability and in times of change well-articulated and attractive organizational identities may therefore contribute to an organization's competitive advantage.

Research in organizational identity also makes abundantly clear that organizational identity is neither a given nor set in stone. What is central, enduring, and distinctive is not a hard fact—who we are as an organization ultimately is a perception.

Even when there will be constraints (e.g., it will be easier to claim a distinctive identity when one offers a unique product or service than when one operates in a context with competitor offerings being highly similar: it will be easier to claim a positive identity as a charity organization than as a tobacco company), organizational identity as a perception is socially constructed—it is subject to sensegiving influences from organizational leadership as well as sensemaking efforts from organizational members (Ashforth, Rogers, and Corley, 2011; Ravasi and Schultz, 2006). What this implies is that organizations that are able to shape a more appealing and shared understanding of organizational identity that is aligned with (envisioned) organizational strategy and objectives stand to benefit from the identity dynamics captured in research in organizational identity and organizational identification. Both from the perspective of harvesting the benefits of a strong organizational identity and from the perspective of a push for change and innovation, these considerations render the question of how people's understanding of organizational identity can be shaped and changed a particularly relevant one.

In this chapter, I address this question from one specific angle—that of leadership. Other chapters in this handbook offer excellent discussions of what organizational identity is and why it matters. Rather than rehearsing these issues, I take as a starting point the widely accepted understanding that organizational identity captures those aspects of the organization that are central, enduring, and distinctive (Albert and Whetten, 1985; Dutton et al., 1994; Gioia et al., 2000; Pratt and Foreman, 2000), and the evidence that organizational identity matters in times of stability as well as change to address the question of how leadership may affect employee understanding of organizational identity. From the more "micro" perspective of organizational behavior, leadership probably is the most direct and flexible influence on employees' understanding of their job and the organization, and shaping employees' understanding of the job and the work context is often seen as a key leadership function (Hackman, 2002)—shaping an understanding of organizational identity should be no exception (cf. Chreim, 2005; Gioia and Chittipeddi, 1991).

Perhaps not surprisingly given the more "macro" focus of much of the research in organizational identity, however, our understanding of the influence of leadership in shaping organizational identity is underdeveloped (this holds especially from the behavioral perspective of leadership research in which leadership is understood first and foremost as an influence process between leaders and followers as opposed to the influence of managerial decisions on firm outcomes such as is studied under the label of strategic leadership; cf. van Knippenberg, 2014). This is not to say that organizational identity research has not touched upon the role of leadership. It has, and part of this chapter thus can be a review of what we have learned from studies of leadership and organizational identity. At the same time, the modest number of studies in leadership and organizational identity leave important questions unanswered. The most fundamental of these questions perhaps is what positions leaders to have credibility and legitimacy in their attempts to change members' understanding of organizational identity.

I propose that to address this question it is useful to adopt the more micro be-havioral perspective provided by the social identity analysis of leadership (Hogg, van Knippenberg, and Rast, 2012a; van Knippenberg and Hogg, 2003). This perspective sees the shared identity of leaders and followers as an important anchor in leader-ship processes, and points to a key role in leadership effectiveness for the extent to which the leader is perceived to be *group prototypical*—to embody the shared identity. I argue that leader group prototypicality is key to leaders' ability to influence mem-bers' understanding of organizational identity. This role of leader group prototypical-ity in shaping shared identity has, however, hardly been studied, and that only in the political domain (Reicher and Hopkins, 2001, 2003). The second part of this chapter, thus, is not a review of studies directly addressing the issue of leader group prototypi-cality and organizational identity but rather an analysis extending the social identity perspective of leadership to apply to leadership and organizational identity. The core conclusion here is that leaders' claims about organizational identity are more effective in influencing organization members' understanding of organizational identity the more they are perceived to be prototypical of the organizational identity—a process of simultaneously creating a desired image of identity and of the leader as embodying that identity.

LEADERSHIP AND ORGANIZATIONAL IDENTITY: A REVIEW

Research in organizational identity has recognized a variety of reasons why an organi-zation's leadership may desire to influence employees' perception of organizational identity. For instance, changes in the environment such as changing competitors, may invite strategic changes that have implications for organizational identity (Ravasi and Schultz, 2006), organizational identity may have drifted from what leadership believes it should be (Ravasi and Phillips, 2011; Ravasi and Schultz, 2006), or major structural changes such as a spin-off (Corley and Gioia, 2004) or a merger (Clark, Gioia, Ketchen, and Thomas, 2010), may create a new organization with a relatively undefined identity. Changing identity may also be seen as conducive to, or even a requirement for, stra-tegic change (Clark et al., 2010; Gioia and Thomas, 1996), even when identity change may also follow the enactment of strategic change (Kjærgaard, Morsing, and Ravasi, 2011; Rindova, Dalpiaz, and Ravasi, 2011). For a variety of reasons then, organizational leaders may attempt to influence perceptions of organizational identity.

Research on changing organizational identities has not only highlighted that lead-ership may actively try to change organizational identity, it also speaks to some of the ways in which leaders may do so. Perhaps the most obvious element in such leadership is the communication of the desired understanding of organizational identity: the consistent communication of the desired identity may cause this identity to be shared among the organization's members. Communicating the envisioned identity, for example in the form of a vision of organizational change that also captures how organizational identity would change (Corley and Gioia, 2004), could be seen as a specific instance of visionary leadership (Stam et al., 2014). Identity is a complex and abstract concept, and leaders most likely do not easily define such a desired identity. Indeed, as Gioia and Chittipeddi (1991) argue, there is substantial leadership effort required in sensemaking—understanding how, for instance, changes in the environment of the organization necessitate changes in the organization that would also be reflected in identity—before leaders can engage in sensegiving to influence employee understanding of identity.

This sensegiving notion is consistent with a broader analysis of leadership that recognizes that a key function of leadership is to shape followers' understanding of team or organizational objectives, mission, or vision, and individual or team task performance (Hackman, 2002; Marks, Zaccaro, and Mathieu, 2001; van Knippenberg and Stam, 2014; van Knippenberg, van Ginkel, and Homan, 2013). This work underscores the importance of leadership shaping an understanding of what we do, why we do it, and how we (should) do it. Even when some of this is cast in non-identity terms, it is but a small step from this emphasis on the what, why, and how of what we do to the identity question of who we are. Indeed a number of analyses have emphasized the role of leadership in shaping a sense of collective identity from this perspective (even when analyses that cast this leadership role in terms of charismatic–transformational leadership, e.g., Bass and Riggio, 2006; Conger and Kanungo, 1987; Shamir, House, and Arthur, 1993, have been criticized as invalid; van Knippenberg and Sitkin, 2013). Arguably, in an organizational context, who we are cannot be seen as independent from what we do and why we do it (cf. the observation that strategic change goes hand in hand with identity change; Gioia and Chittipeddi, 1991; Rindova et al., 2011). Who we are—or want to be—often is an important part of the reason why we do things (Stam et al., 2014). The understanding of leadership sensegiving as a means to shape and change the social construction of organizational identity thus is well aligned with the broader leadership literature.

To be successful in influencing identity perceptions, such attempts to convey an envisioned identity would, more or less by definition, need to speak to how the envisioned identity captures what is central, distinctive, and enduring about the organization. One important element in this identity rhetoric would be to establish a clear link between an existing understanding of organizational identity and the envisioned understanding. A relatively straightforward example is found in Ravasi and Schultz's (2006; Ravasi and Phillips, 2011) analysis of strategic and identity change at Bang & Olufsen. A key issue here was that the organization's leadership perceived the organizational identity as having drifted away from what it once was and was supposed to be. This allowed leadership to advocate a "return to true identity" that clearly speaks to the notion of enduring quality. A more complex twist is when a given concept that is seen to capture a core aspect of identity can be influenced to gradually take on a different meaning. Chreim (2005) describes an insightful example in this respect for the case of Bank of Montreal. Bank of Montreal is known as First Bank, referring historically to the fact that the bank was the first bank in Canada. Chreim describes how the First Bank notion over time and under the influence of different CEOs' framing, shifted in meaning from historically the first, to both historically the first and the first in the sense of being innovative (i.e., the first to do something), to only capturing the notion of first in the sense of innovative. This was no trivial change because the bank's strategy was more served by an understanding of organizational identity in terms of innovation than by the original historic sense of First Bank.

References to the collective's history or mythology have been recognized as an effective way of invoking collective identity (Shamir et al., 1993), and they are well aligned with notions of organizational culture advanced by Schein (1992) that culture is conveyed through stories about key events in the organization's history. Extending this analysis, we can see that in identity change linkage between current and envisioned understandings of identity is important, because it speaks to a sense of continuity of identity (i.e., the enduring nature of organizational identity)—it conveys the message that despite changes in the organization, its defining aspects are not violated. Conveying such a sense of continuity is important in building legitimacy of identity claims. Continuity is a valued aspect of identity, because it is an important element in identity's ability to give meaning to situations and reduce uncertainties. Conversely, a sense of discontinuity of identity (i.e., a violation of enduring qualities) is often what inspires resistance to organizational change (Rousseau, 1998; van Knippenberg et al., 2008).

It should also be easier to convince people of a change in organizational identity when the envisioned identity is perceived as attractive—and more attractive than the "old" identity—because people are more likely to embrace identities that reflect positively on the self (Ashforth and Mael, 1989; Tajfel and Turner, 1986). Gioia and Chittipeddi (1991; Gioia and Thomas, 1996), for instance, report a case analysis of a university pursuing the vision of being a "top 10 public university," and describe how this identity vision was construed as attractive, and as more attractive than the old identity that was less ambitious. Less explicit in the existing body of evidence but obviously implied by the conceptualization of organizational identity, leader identity rhetoric should also be more successful in changing identity perceptions the more it paints a picture of the envisioned identity as distinctive, and the more it stakes a claim that the elements of identity it highlights are central to the organization's being. As an illustration of how distinctiveness may be claimed, consider the famous Apple "1984" Super Bowl commercial as a clear instance of a claim of distinctiveness on the part of Apple vis-à-vis its competitors. This commercial called on the dystopia sketched in George's Orwell's novel 1984 to contrast the grey uniformity of other personal computer manufacturers' products with Apple's new personal computer. It thus also worked to contrast Apple as a company with all its competitors, flagging Apple's distinct and positive identity within this intergroup comparative context. Case evidence seems to suggest that at the time Apple's founder, Steve Jobs, used similar rhetoric internally to convey a message of Apple's identity to its employees (Isaacson, 2011).

A challenge that leaders may face in shaping an understanding of organizational membership that members would embrace and internalize is that it is not always easy to paint a positive picture of organizational identity. Prestigious organizations should find it relatively easy to invite members to embrace and internalize organizational identity (Ashforth and Mael, 1989; cf. Tajfel and Turner, 1986), but some organizations are involved in work that is unprestigious or that even has stigmatized connotations—nobody would feel ashamed working for UNICEF, but people might feel distinctly more ambivalent about working as a garbage collector or gravedigger. Ashforth and colleagues' analysis of identity claims in so-called "dirty" or stigmatized work (Ashforth and Kreiner, 1999; Kreiner, Ashforth, and Sluss, 2006) speaks to the identity implications of such more stigmatized professions. Particularly relevant to the present discussion is that they also outline how people in such professions may creatively reframe their professional identity to imbue it with more positive qualities (e.g., only a select few have what it takes to do this kind of work needed by society). Research in intergroup relations suggests that such social creativity generalizes beyond stigmatized work (Tajfel and Turner, 1986). It seems only a small step to propose that leadership in organizations characterized by stigmatized work or otherwise by lower-status connotations (e.g., being a "B brand") may likewise effectively frame organizational identity in ways that put a spin to organizational identity that is more positive than the organization's typical association may be.

Identity change is unlikely to thrive on leader communication of the envisioned identity alone, however. Corley and Gioia (2004) described how role modeling behavior that is consistent with the envisioned identity—"walking the talk"—adds to leaders' ability to influence perceptions of organizational identity. It is also important to get organization members to enact the envisioned identity, because this can be expected to foster the internalization of that identity (Ashforth, 2001; Ashforth et al., 2011; cf. Ravasi and Schultz, 2006). These notions are more generally consistent with the proposition that leadership is more effective when it not only advocates a certain understanding or course of action, but also role-models the enactment of this understanding or course of action (cf. van Ginkel and van Knippenberg, 2012).

In a related vein, changes or actions implemented in the course of a change process can also have a symbolic function in representing the envisioned identity change (arguably, these are also the consequence of leader behavior, but more in the sense of the outcome of decision-making than in the traditional sense of leader behavior vis-à-vis followers; cf. van Knippenberg, 2014). Gioia and Chittipeddi (1991), for instance, describe such a symbolic function for a strategic task force that was composed to support the change process toward realizing the "top 10 public university" vision (also see Gioia, Thomas, Clark, and Chittipeddi, 1994; Ravasi and Schultz, 2006; Rindova et al., 2011). In a similar vein, Isaacson (2011) described how Steve Jobs insisted on an expensive coating for the inside of an Apple computer's casing that no one would see, to convey a message about Apple quality standards, a message that seemed well aligned with his claims for Apple's identity and for which the inside coating seemed to fulfill a symbolic role. For organizations that capture substantial publication attention (e.g., media attention), leaders may also work to change the perceived external image, the perception of how the organization is seen by people outside of the organization (Dutton, Dukerich, and Harquail, 1994; think for instance of Apple's *1984* commercial), and such changes in perceived external image may subsequently impact employee perceptions of organizational identity (Kjærgaard et al., 2011).

Identity change is not a solo job for (for instance) the CEO either. Gioia and Chittipeddi (1991) describe how the university's "CEO" first influenced senior management and then in a sense enlisted senior management to help convey the message of envisioned structural and identity change. Although not explicit in their analysis, one may presume that one of the advantages of such a strategy of relying on an expanding identity coalition (cf. Hogg, van Knippenberg, and Rast, 2012b) is that it conveys broader support for this understanding of identity, and thus implies that it is not one person's idiosyncratic take but rather something more representative of how members of the organization more broadly (could) understand organizational identity. Conversely, and as another case in point, Voss, Cable, and Voss' (2006) analysis of a case in which organizational leaders' opposing views of identity were disruptive to organizational functioning suggests that inconsistent identity claims from an organization's leadership can be highly dysfunctional.

The existing body of evidence thus suggests that the core of leadership to influence employee perceptions of organizational identity is the communication of the desired identity—sensegiving to influence the social construction of identity. Other leadership actions can support these persuasive attempts (i.e., role modeling, symbolic changes, building an identity coalition), but probably are less likely to have a substantive effect on identity perceptions without the element of leader sensegiving. This conclusion then points to perhaps the most important question *not* answered by the current body of evidence—what gives leaders credibility and legitimacy in staking identity claims other than the content of the claim itself (e.g., its suggestions of enduring identity)?

It seems unrealistic that everyone appointed to a senior leadership position can stake claims about organizational identity to successfully influence employee identity perceptions—at least not without identity work to support those claims. The question of what gives leaders credibility and legitimacy in their organizational identity claims is not answered by the current empirical body of research, but there is a well-supported perspective on identity and leadership that I propose holds all the building blocks to construe the answer to this question: the social identity theory of leadership (Hogg, 2001; Hogg et al., 2012a; van Knippenberg, 2011; van Knippenberg and Hogg, 2003). In a nutshell, the answer that I propose revolves around the triangle of anchors in recognized parts of organizational identity, identity claims the leader wishes to establish, and positioning of the leader as prototypical of both the envisioned identity and of employees' current sense of organizational identity.

LEADER GROUP PROTOTYPICALITY
AND IDENTITY LEADERSHIP

It is not my intention to unpack the social identity theory of leadership and its supportive evidence here in full. Recent reviews are available elsewhere (Hogg et al., 2012a; van Knippenberg, 2011). Rather, I aim to highlight those aspects of the analysis that are particularly relevant in building an understanding of the influence of leadership in shaping organizational identity.

Core to the social identity theory of leadership is the concept of *prototypicality*—a concept for which the theory draws on categorization theory in cognitive psychology and its development in self-categorization theory in social psychology (Turner, Hogg, Oakes, Reicher, and Wetherell, 1987). In this analysis of social categorization processes group prototypes refer to mental representations that capture what group members have in common and differentiate the group from other groups. In reference to the notion of organizational identity, group prototypes thus can be understood to capture who we are—group identity as what is central and distinctive (and by implication enduring) about us. Importantly, for social groups such prototypes do not necessarily capture physical characteristics, but include what is held true and dear by the group. Group prototypes capture the shared social reality of the group, including values, attitudes, and behaviors, as well as group objectives and ambitions that are central and distinctive to the group. Prototypes thus have a clear normative component. In capturing group-normative positions, group prototypes are a source of influence in that they may inspire conformity to values, attitudes, and behaviors that are perceived to be group-normative (Turner et al., 1987). Group prototypes do not just capture what group members believe, value, and do, but also what they *should* believe, value, and do.

Note that this has clear overlap with the conceptualization of organizational identity as capturing those characteristics that are central, distinctive, and enduring. Indeed, in terms of the social identity analysis, organizational identity can be conceptualized as the perceived group (i.e., organization) prototype with very little deviation from the current conceptualization of organizational identity implied. Put differently, the social identity theory of leadership complements the existing analyses of leadership of organizational identity in a coherent and integrative fashion.

A key insight of the social identity theory of leadership for the analysis of leadership is that group members can be judged in terms of the extent to which they are group *prototypical* (i.e., resemble one's mental representation of the group identity). Some members are (perceived to be) more group prototypical than others. Because of the group-defining nature of group prototypes, the perception that an individual is group prototypical positions that individual to be more influential (van Knippenberg, Lossie, and Wilke, 1994). From this, it is a small step to the core of the social identity theory of leadership: the proposition that group prototypicality gives leaders a basis to be influential and effective (Hogg, 2001). Leader group prototypicality invites the perception that the leader represents the shared social reality of the group and has the group's best interest at heart (van Knippenberg and Hogg, 2003), and thus positions the leader to be more effective, provided members identify with the group (i.e., if the group identity is not part of their self-definition, the group prototype is no reference point in their responses to leadership; Hogg, 2001). This role of leader group proto-typicality in leadership effectiveness has been supported across experimental studies and surveys, including both organizational and non-organizational samples, across behavioral and attitudinal indicators of leadership effectiveness, and across countries and continents (van Knippenberg, 2011).

Leader group prototypicality is broadly relevant for leadership effectiveness, but it may be nowhere more relevant than in reference to leaders' ability to successfully stake claims about shared identity. There is perhaps nothing that gives greater credibility and legitimacy to identity claims than the perception that one embodies the shared identity, because it is this very perception that gives one legitimacy and credibility in one's claims about the nature of that identity. This is not to say that leaders who are not perceived as group prototypical are inevitably without legitimacy or credibility in their identity claims. There are many bases from which legitimacy as a leader can derive, including the formal leadership position (e.g., the fact that one is the CEO in and of itself), and to a greater or lesser extent these should also add to the effectiveness of leader identity claims. Rather, my proposition here is that, all other things being equal, more group prototypical leaders (i.e., more seen as embodying the organiza-tional identity) will be more effective in influencing organizational identity percep-tions, and moreover that being perceived to be the embodiment of the shared identity is likely to be one of the most influential leader characteristics in this respect.

Organizational identity is socially constructed, and it thus is no surprise that leader group prototypicality is too. A first element in this is that leaders or followers may construe organizational identity in such a way that an organizational leader would be more or less prototypical of the organizational identity. A second element is that leaders may actively construe how they are perceived vis-à-vis the shared identity. In combination, this allows leaders to stake stronger identity claims than when they did not position themselves as prototypical of that identity.

Examples of this process are easily observed in the political domain. Mahatma Ghandi, for instance, adopted the attire and lifestyle typical of rural India to convey his connection to the Indian identity as he envisioned it (Lelyveld, 2011), and Nelson Mandela made a point of appearing for trial in traditional Xhosa tribal attire—presumably at least in part to make a point about the roots of South African identity as he saw it (Sampson, 1999). In similar vein, Reicher and Hopkins (2001, 2003) outline how political leaders throughout history have called on national history and mythol-ogy to support their claims about national identity, and of themselves as represent-ing that identity. Reicher and Hopkins discuss for instance how former Indonesian President Sukharno referenced through symbols Indonesian mythology to present himself as a true embodiment of the Indonesian nation, and how Scottish politicians made claims about the national identity based on national history and the natural environment of Scotland to suggest that they and their party's core values were pro-totypically Scottish.

What holds for political leadership does not necessarily hold for organizational leadership, but research by Giessner, van Knippenberg, and Sleebos (2009; Giessner and van Knippenberg, 2008) suggests that the role of leader group prototypicality at least generalizes across political and organizational domains. As a more anecdotal example in this respect, Steve Jobs seems to always have staked strong claims about Apple identity, and it would seem that as a founder who was also the embodiment of Apple identity to the outside world—the embodiment of the group prototype—Jobs could stake such strong identity claims for Apple with undisputed legitimacy.

There is a complication here, however, in that for leadership to influence identity perceptions, more or less by definition, is focused on effectuating *change*—it makes less sense to try to convince employees of an image of organizational identity that they already share. For perceptions that the leader is group prototypical to be conducive to leadership effectiveness in changing identity, then, the leader would need to be seen as prototypical of the envisioned identity (the "new identity") as well as of the cur-rent understanding of organizational identity (the "old identity"). Most likely this is a matter of the leader's active construal of an image of group prototypicality that is anchored in the new as well as in the old identity. This is sensegiving all over, but the emphasis is not just on sensegiving to convey a message regarding an understanding of (envisioned) organizational identity, but also sensegiving in terms of conveying an image of the leader as prototypical of that identity.

The challenge may be less than the notion of new and old identities suggests, how-ever. As already discussed, there is a good case to be made that attempts to influence employees' understanding of organizational identity are more successful if there is a clear linkage between the new and the old—if the envisioned identity suggests a continuity rather than a discontinuity of identity. This linkage of new and old identity would also provide the basis for the leader's self-presentation as group prototypical to be anchored both in current and envisioned aspects of identity. There is a good case to be made that such identity claims and prototypicality claims co-evolve and mutually influence each other's effectiveness. On the one hand, identity claims that position the new identity as a clear continuation of the old identity make it easier for leaders to position themselves as prototypical of the shared identity (i.e., because the two identi-ties are not in opposition). At the same time, there is also evidence that leaders who are perceived to be more group prototypical are more successful in inspiring a sense of continuity of identity in times of change, because their group prototypicality leads them to be perceived, not just as agents of change, but also as "agents of continuity" of identity (van Knippenberg et al., 2008; cf. Shamir, 1999). Put differently, it would seem that leaders who build their identity claims and their prototypicality claims in conjunction and largely simultaneously will be more effective in their identity claims.

In sum then, an integration of the social identity analysis of leadership with analyses of leadership to influence organizational identity suggests that leader group prototypi-cality is an important element in leaders' ability to influence the social construction of organizational identity. I propose that to mobilize this influence of group prototypicality perceptions, leaders should stake identity claims that establish clear linkages between current and envisioned understandings of identity, and present themselves as prototypical of the envisioned identity, with clear anchors in these linkages. None of this is based on direct evidence, however; all this is extending conceptual reasoning. An obvious conclusion to this chapter thus is framed as much in what it implies in terms of a research agenda as in terms of what we know from the empirical evidence base.

LEADERSHIP AND ORGANIZATIONAL IDENTITY: A RESEARCH AGENDA

The research I reviewed in this chapter suggests that leaders may shape perceptions of organizational identity through the combination of communicating the identity they envision (supported by role modeling and symbolic changes) and presenting themselves as prototypical of that identity, provided both are anchored in an existing sense of what is central, distinctive, and enduring about the organization. This is a conclusion at a high level of abstraction, and future research would be required to speak in more detail to how leader identity claims may be framed to have the desired effect, and to how leaders may present themselves as prototypical of the envisioned identity.

Obviously, at a more detailed level, this may vary considerably from situation to situation, but there are likely to be some further specifications of the more general conclusion that holds across situations. To take one example, even when it stands to reason that effective identity rhetoric includes claims to centrality, enduringness, and distinctiveness, the importance of each is likely to differ as a function of context. A context of organizational change in which leadership desires to link organizational identity to the envisioned change, for instance, is likely to place greater demands on rhetoric regarding continuity of identity (i.e., enduring) than a context of stability. In a related vein, fierce competition with other companies is likely to bring distinctiveness more to the fore. Research to capture how such influences shape leaders' identity claims and their effectiveness in influencing the social construction of organizational identity would be valuable in developing our understanding of the leadership dynamics of organizational identity.

Whereas the number of studies of leadership influences on organizational identity is modest, research on the role of leader group prototypicality in this process is essentially nonexistent. An important avenue for future research would thus also be to develop a better understanding of how leaders may position themselves as prototypical of the organizational identity they envision. Available examples suggest some ways that are not easy to replicate. For instance, Steve Jobs' position as founder of Apple clearly positioned him to be seen as an embodiment of Apple's identity in ways that non-founding leaders would find hard to copy (although the distinctly lower profile of Jobs' co-founder, Steve Wozniak, illustrates that being a founder in and of itself does not provide a strong leadership basis). In a related vein, former Philips CEO Gerard Kleisterlee was recognized as a "real Philips man" after having worked in several Philips divisions for 27 years before becoming the company's CEO (not to mention the fact that Kleisterlee's father was also employed by Philips). Such instances of "leading by biography" where one's life history feeds into one's effectiveness as a leader (Shamir, Dayan-Horesh, and Adler, 2005) seem hard to replicate—and indeed in the literal sense they are when one is not the founder of Apple or has not worked for close to three decades for Philips. In a broader sense, however, elements of one's personal history may connect with the elements of organizational identity that the leader seeks to highlight. For instance, an emphasis on innovativeness as a key element of organizational identity may be backed up by the leader's personal history of innovation. Moreover, one does not need to just rely on history; one can also enact the envisioned identity in the present to speak to this issue. Leaders would presumably gain credibility, however, when the first instances of their acting in line with the espoused identity were in the past rather than in the present. None of these propositions currently can build on more than anecdotal evidence, extrapolating from research in other domains, or common sense, and here too lies a clear challenge for future research in leadership and identity.

Methodologically, there are also some real challenges here. It is noteworthy that the existing research in leadership of organizational identity is qualitative in nature and speaks at a relatively abstract level at leaders' actions and their effects on followers. The behavioral analysis of leadership ideally relies on evidence about leader behavior that can be linked to follower psychological states and behavior, and moreover evidence that is not only qualitative but also quantitative to complement Grounded Theory development with theory testing. These are serious challenges when studying leadership aimed at changing identity perceptions at the level of the organization, but there would be great value added if future research could meet these challenges, at least to some extent.

On the qualitative side, there should be scope for more fine-grained analyses of leader communications regarding organizational identity, ideally both as they appear in written statements and as they are communicated orally. The former could be achieved with archival information, but the latter would probably require more active involvement during the process such as in participant observation (cf. Gioia and Chittipeddi, 1991). On the quantitative side, the ideal set-up would perhaps be a repeated measures study that would allow for some kind of event analysis (e.g., plotting changes in leadership perceptions and identity perceptions over time as a function of the leadership attempts, if any, at influencing these perceptions)—a set-up that would require that researchers have access to the organization during the change process (a tall order indeed, but not a priori impossible). In this respect, it is also important to realize than even when the ultimate leadership goal would be engendering a shared sense of the envisioned organizational identity throughout the organization, theory-testing can to a certain extent rely on the individual level of analysis, where individual perceptions of leadership identity communication and prototypicality are treated as predictors of individual perceptions of organizational identity. Coming up with insightful quantitative measures—measures that tap into the content of the envisioned identity—would, however, require a decent level of case-specific knowledge that suggests grounding of such quantitative efforts in initial qualitative efforts (e.g., to get a clear sense from the CEO how he or she envisions organizational identity and him or herself vis-à-vis that identity as a basis for quantitative measurement).

These are no small challenges, but further development toward a more full-blown theory of leadership of organizational identity would require more explicit behavioral evidence to link leadership to follower responses, and triangulation of methods to optimally benefit from the interplay of theory development and theory testing. Given the importance of organizational identity and organizational identity change in a changing world, these seem challenges worth the investment for research in management.

REFERENCES

Albert, S. and Whetten, D. A. (1985). "Organizational Identity." In *Research in Organizational Behavior*, vol. 7, edited by L. L. Cummings and B. M. Staw, 263–95. Greenwich, CT: JAI Press.

Ashforth, B. E. (2001). *Role Transitions in Organizational Life: An Identity-Based Perspective*. Mahwah, NJ: Erlbaum.

Ashforth, B. E. and Kreiner, G. E. (1999). "'How Can You Do It?': Dirty Work and the Challenge of Constructing a Positive Identity." *Academy of Management Review* 24: 413–34.

Ashforth, B. E. and Mael, F. (1989). "Social Identity Theory and the Organization." *Academy of Management Review* 14: 20–39.

Ashforth, B. E., Rogers, K. M., and Corley, K. G. (2011). "Identity in Organizations: Exploring Cross-Level Dynamics." *Organization Science* 22: 1144–56.

Bass, B. M. and Riggio, R. E. (2006). *Transformational Leadership*. Mahwah, NJ: Erlbaum.

Chreim, S. (2005). "The Continuity-Change Duality in Narrative Texts of Organizational Identity." *Journal of Management Studies* 42: 567–93.

Clark, S. M., Gioia, D. A., Ketchen, D. J. Jr., and Thomas, J. B. (2010). "Transitional Identity as a Facilitator of Organizational Identity Change during a Merger." *Administrative Science Quarterly* 55: 397–438.

Conger, J. A. and Kanungo, R. N. (1987). "Towards a Behavioral Theory of Charismatic Leadership in Organizational Settings." *Academy of Management Review* 12: 637–47.

Corley, K. G. and Gioia, D. A. (2004). "Identity Ambiguity and Change in the Wake of a Corporate Spin-Off." *Administrative Science Quarterly* 49: 173–208.

Dutton, J. E., Dukerich, J. M., and Harquail, C. V. (1994). "Organizational Images and Member Identification." *Administrative Science Quarterly* 39: 239–63.

Fiol, C. M. (2002). "Capitalizing on Paradox: The Role of Language in Transforming Organizational Identities." *Organization Science* 13: 653–66.

Giessner, S. R., and van Knippenberg, D. (2008) "'License to Fail': Goal Definition, Leader Group Prototypicality, and Perceptions of Leadership Effectiveness after Leader Failure." *Organizational Behavior and Human Decision Processes* 105: 14–35.

Giessner, S. R., van Knippenberg, D., and Sleebos, E. (2009). "License to Fail?: How Leader Group Prototypicality Moderates the Effects of Leader Performance on Perceptions of Leadership Effectiveness." *The Leadership Quarterly* 20: 434–51.

Gioia, D. A. and Chittipeddi, K. (1991). "Sensemaking and Sensegiving in Strategic Change Initiation." *Strategic Management Journal* 12: 433–48.

Gioia, D. A., Schulz, M., and Corley, K. G. (2000). "Organizational Identity, Image, and Adaptive Instability." *Academy of Management Review* 25: 63–81.

Gioia, D. A. and Thomas, J. B. (1996). "Identity, Image, and Issue Interpretation: Sensemaking during Strategic Change." *Administrative Science Quarterly* 41: 370–403.

Gioia, D. A., Thomas, J. B., Clark, S. W., and Chittipeddi, K. (1994). "Symbolism and Strategic Change in Academia: The Dynamics of Sensemaking and Influence." *Organization Science* 5: 363–83.

Hackman, J. R. (2002). *Leading Teams: Setting the Stage for Great Performances.* Cambridge, MA: Harvard Business Press.

Hogg, M. A. (2001). "A Social Identity Theory of Leadership." *Personality and Social Psychology Review* 5: 184–200.

Hogg, M. A., van Knippenberg, D., and Rast, D. E. III (2012b). "Intergroup Leadership in Organizations: Leading across Group and Organizational Boundaries." *Academy of Management Review* 37: 232–55.

Isaacson, W. (2011). *Steve Jobs.* New York: Simon and Schuster.

Kjærgaard, A., Morsing, M., and Ravasi, D. (2011). "Mediating Identity: A Study of Media Influence on Organizational Identity Construction in a Celebrity Firm." *Journal of Management Studies* 48: 514–43.

Kreiner, G. E., Ashforth, B. E., and Sluss, D. M. (2006). "Identity Dynamics in Occupational Dirty Work: Integrating Social Identity and System Justification Perspectives." *Organization Science* 17: 619–36.

Lelyveld, J. (2011). *Great Soul: Mahatma Ghandi and his Struggle with India.* New York: Vintage Books.

Mael, F. and Ashforth, B. E. (1992). "Alumni and their Alma Mater: A Partial Test of the Reformulated Model of Organizational Identification." *Journal of Organizational Behavior* 13: 103–23.

Marks, M. A., Mathieu, J. E., and Zaccaro, S. J. (2001). "A Temporally Based Framework and Taxonomy of Team Processes." *Academy of Management Review* 26: 356–76.

Pratt, M. G. (1998). "To Be or Not to Be? Central Questions in Organizational Identification." In *Identity in Organizations: Building Theory through Conversations*, edited by D. A. Whetten, and P. C. Godfrey, 171–207. Thousand Oaks, CA: SAGE.

Pratt, M. G. and Foreman, P. O. (2000). "Classifying Managerial Responses to Multiple Organizational Identities." *Academy of Management Review* 25: 18–42.

Ravasi, D. and Phillips, N. (2011). "Strategies of Alignment: Organizational Identity Management and Strategic Change at Bang & Olufsen." *Strategic Organization* 9: 103–35.

Ravasi, D. and Schultz, M. (2006). "Responding to Organizational Identity Threats: Exploring the Role of Organizational Culture." *Academy of Management Journal* 49: 433–58.

Rindova, V., Dalpiaz, E., and Ravasi, D. (2011). "A Cultural Quest: A Study of Organizational Use of New Cultural Resources in Strategy Formation." *Organization Science* 22: 413–31.

Reicher, S. and Hopkins, N. (2001). *Self and Nation.* London: SAGE.

Reicher, S. and Hopkins, N. (2003). "On the Science and Art of Leadership." In *Leadership and Power: Identity Processes in Groups and Organizations*, edited by D. van Knippenberg and M. A. Hogg, 197–209. London: SAGE.

Rousseau, D. M. (1998). "Why Workers Still Identify with Organizations." *Journal of Organizational Behavior* 19: 217–33.

Sampson, A. (1999). *Mandela: The Authorised Biography.* London: HarperPress.

Schein, E. H. (1992). *Organizational Culture and Leadership*. San Francisco, CA: Jossey-Bass.

Shamir, B. (1999). "Leadership in Boundaryless Organizations: Disposable or Indispensable?" *European Journal of Work and Organizational Psychology* 8: 49–71.

Shamir, B., Dayan-Horesh, H., and Adler, D. (2005). "Leading by Biography: Toward a Life-Story Approach to the Study of Leadership." *Leadership* 1: 13–30.

Shamir, B., House, R., and Arthur, M. B. (1993). "The Motivational Effects of Charismatic Leadership: A Self-Concept Based Theory." *Organization Science* 4: 577–94.

Stam, D., Lord, R. G., van Knippenberg, D., and Wisse, B. (2014). "An Image of Who We Might Become: Vision Communication, Possible Selves, and Vision Pursuit." *Organization Science* 25: 1172–94.

Tajfel, H. and Turner, J. C. (1986). "The Social Identity Theory of Intergroup Behavior." In *Psychology of Intergroup Relations*, edited by S. Worchel and W. Austin, 7–24. Chicago: Nelson-Hall.

Turner, J. C., Hogg, M. A., Oakes, P. J., Reicher, S. D., and Wetherell, M. S. (1987). *Rediscovering the Social Group: A Self-Categorization Theory*. Oxford: Blackwell.

van Ginkel, W. P. and van Knippenberg, D. (2012). "Group Leadership and Shared Task Representations in Decision-Making Groups." *The Leadership Quarterly* 23: 94–106.

van Knippenberg, D. (2000). "Work Motivation and Performance: A Social Identity Perspective." *Applied Psychology: An International Review* 49: 357–71.

van Knippenberg, D. (2011). "Embodying Who We Are: Leader Group Prototypicality and Leadership Effectiveness." *The Leadership Quarterly* 22: 1078–91.

van Knippenberg, D. (2014). "Leadership and Decision Making: Defining a Field." In *Judgment and Decision Making at Work*, edited by S. Highhouse, R. S. Dalal, and E. Salas, 140–58. New York; London: Routledge.

van Knippenberg, D. and Hogg, M. A. (2003). "A Social Identity Model of Leadership Effectiveness in Organizations." *Research in Organizational Behavior* 25: 243–95.

van Knippenberg, D., Lossie, N., and Wilke, H. (1994). "In-Group Prototypicality and Persuasion: Determinants of Heuristic and Systematic Message Processing." *British Journal of Social Psychology* 33: 289–300.

van Knippenberg, D. and Sitkin, S. B. (2013). "A Critical Assessment of Charismatic-Transformational Leadership Research: Back to the Drawing Board?" *Academy of Management Annals* 7: 1–60.

van Knippenberg, D., and Stam, D. (2014). "Visionary Leadership." In *Oxford Handbook of Leadership and Organizations*, edited by D. V. Day, 241–59. New York: Oxford University Press.

van Knippenberg, D., van Ginkel, W. P., and Homan, A. C. (2013). "Diversity Mindsets and the Performance of Diverse Teams." *Organizational Behavior and Human Decision Processes* 121: 183–93.

van Knippenberg, D., van Knippenberg, B., and Bobbio, A. (2008). "Leaders as Agents of Continuity: Self Continuity and Resistance to Collective Change." In *Self-Continuity: Individual and Collective Perspectives*, edited by F. Sani, 175–86. New York: Psychology Press.

van Knippenberg, D., van Knippenberg, B., Monden, L., and de Lima, F. (2002). "Organizational Identification after a Merger: A Social Identity Perspective." *British Journal of Social Psychology* 41: 233–52.

Voss, Z. G., Cable, D. M., and Voss, G. B. (2006). "Organizational Identity and Firm Performance: What Happens when Leaders Disagree about 'Who We Are?'". *Organization Science* 17: 741–55.

SECTION VI

OI AND THE ENVIRONMENT

ORGANIZATIONAL IDENTITY IN INSTITUTIONAL THEORY

taking stock and moving forward

NELSON PHILLIPS, PAUL TRACEY,
AND MATT KRAATZ

INTRODUCTION

INSTITUTIONAL theory has, at its core, a concern with the effects of the broad social context of organizations. This has manifested itself most obviously in a focus on how structures and practices become shared among groups of organizations, but institutional theorists have also had an ongoing interest in organizational identity. However, despite repeated acknowledgments by institutional theorists of the importance of identity, there remains limited agreement within institutional theory as to the precise nature of organizational identity. This lack of agreement is exacerbated by the fact that the way in which institutional theorists have understood organizational identity has shifted dramatically over time as the focus of institutional theory has evolved.

In this chapter, we will attempt to provide an accessible overview of institutional discussions of organizational identity that we hope identity scholars will find useful and thought provoking. Our goal is to summarize the discussions of organizational identity that have taken place in institutional theory and to connect these with the concerns of organizational identity scholars. We will situate our discussions of organizational identity in institutional theory within the wider evolution that has characterized the institutional perspective on organizations, and provide some specific suggestions for how insights from institutional theory can be usefully brought into studies of organizational identity.

OVERVIEW OF HISTORY OF INSTITUTIONAL
THEORY AND ORGANIZATIONAL IDENTITY

In this section, we will examine how the concept of organizational identity has been used over time in institutional theory. We will present our arguments in three subsections reflecting the broad phases that characterize the evolution of institutional theory (see Table 19.1 for a summary).

Table 19.1 Summary of organizational identity in institutional theory

	Old Institutionalism	New Institutionalism	Agentic Institutionalism
Core Idea	"Organizations" (i.e., formally structured entities with fixed and limited goals) gradually take on lives of their own and become "institutions" (social collectivities with complex social structures and broader, self-defined purposes).	Organizations seek legitimacy by conforming to institutional demands for isomorphism. Institutions are a field-level phenomena.	Organizations become legitimate by altering strategically their institutional context and/or by drawing on aspects of their institutional context to position themselves in particular ways to different audiences.
Core Concepts	Institution Values	Institutional Field Institutional Logic Isomorphism	Institutional Entrepreneur Institutional Work Institutional Complexity
Key Works	Selznick, 1949	Dimaggio and Powell, 1983; Meyer and Rowan, 1977	Maguire et al., 2004; Lawrence and Suddaby, 2006; Greenwood et al., 2011
Conceptualization of Org. Identity	Organizational identity formation is the end product of institutionalization. As an organization becomes an institution, it acquires an identity and becomes something more than a socially engineered tool.	Organizations adopt organizational identities that are available in their field (or, alternatively, are associated with the logic of their field) in order to increase legitimacy through a process of isomorphism.	Organizations shape the identities of particular organizational forms in a field, and/or build their own distinctive identity by drawing on or managing aspects of their institutional environment.
Primary Level of Analysis	The Organization	The Field	Individual/Organization/ Field

Selznick's Theory of Institutionalization and Identity Formation

Philip Selznick is widely recognized as a founder of institutional theory, and the perspective's first insights about the nature, origins, and functions of organizational identity are found in the work that he published in the 1940s and 1950s (Selznick, 1949, 1952, 1957). In order to adequately explain these insights, it is necessary to first say a few words about the focus of Selznick's larger theory and the context in which it was developed.

Selznick and institutions. Selznick's institutional theory emerged from his in-depth study of one particular government agency, the Tennessee Valley Authority. Selznick's 1949 analysis of the TVA documented a remarkable process of organizational change—one that essentially transformed the entire agency and altered its basic purposes. The study also identified the (previously overlooked) social and political processes that were responsible for this transformation, and suggested that such processes were largely endemic to bureaucracy itself. The larger theory that Selznick subsequently developed can be understood as a direct effort to elaborate the implications of this early study and to address the many troubling questions that it presented.[1] Later in his life, Selznick described his institutional theory in these very terms (Selznick, 1992, 1996, 2000).

The theory's more specific aim was to explain the process through which "organizations" (i.e., formally structured entities with fixed and limited goals) gradually take on lives of their own and become "institutions" (more distinctly social collectivities with complex social structures and broader, self-defined purposes). This transformational process, which Selznick describes as "institutionalization," is most completely explained in *Leadership in Administration* (1957). Selznick describes this process as a complex and multifaceted one that is affected by a wide variety of social and political influences operating in and around the organization, and gives much attention to its various pathologies and ironies. But, he also emphasizes that the process is readily interpretable (and even intuitive) when properly viewed, and says a great deal about its more positive outcomes and potentialities.

Selznick and organizational identity. With this basic understanding of Selznick's institutional theory established, its insights about the nature and origins of organizational identity are easily explained. Specifically, Selznick saw organizational identity formation as the end product of institutionalization. In fact, from his perspective, the "terms 'institution', 'organizational character', and 'distinctive competence' all refer to

---

[1] Selznick's TVA study was especially disturbing to progressive reformers who then had great confidence in the possibilities of formal organization as a solution to various social problems. See Gouldner (1955) for such a response and Krygier (2002; 2012) for a discussion of Selznick's responses to Gouldner's criticism.

the same basic process—the transformation of an engineered technical arrangement of building blocks into a social organism" (1957:139).

As an organization becomes an institution, it acquires an identity (or "character") and turns into something more than a socially engineered tool:

> Organizations become institutions as they are infused with value ... This infusion produces a distinct identity for the organization.
>
> (1957: 40)

Put differently, it "takes on a life of its own" and becomes valued as "an end in itself" (rather than a mere means). This outcome is by no means a peripheral side effect of the process. In Selznick's view, institutionalization and character formation are two different names for the very same thing. Understanding this general process—and the very particular and unique identities that it produces—is the central aim of the theory itself.

While space constraints prohibit a full elaboration of this theory's many implications for identity, there are a few particularly important consequences that merit discussion. The first of these concerns the observability of organizational identity and its tangible, empirical content. As we have explained, Selznick saw organizational identity formation as a social and political process that occurs over an organization's life course and leaves deep marks on its internal social structure. These aspects of identity are readily observable, and Selznick strongly emphasizes the need to examine them (for example, by looking at the "critical decisions," "political compromises," and "character-defining commitments" that brought the organization to its current state). He does not suggest that this historical information can provide a complete or unambiguous indication of an organization's "true" identity. But, he does see it as at least a critical starting point for analysts and managers who are in search of such knowledge.

The second issue concerns the complexity and fungibility of organizational identity. Selznick's theory treats identity formation as an adaptive, evolutionary process that limits alternatives and precludes many subsequent choices. But, he does not see it as deterministic or closed-ended in a way that would shut off all options. The organizational identities that emerge from institutionalization are necessarily complex, multifaceted, and subject to interpretation. As such, they are open to revision and expansion within reasonable bounds: "[a]n organization's true commitments are not unchanging. They must be reassessed continuously" (Selznick, 1957: 73).

The third issue concerns the role that organizational inhabitants (and especially leaders) play within the ongoing institutionalization process. Selznick saw institutionalization as a naturally occurring phenomenon that tended to happen with or without conscious and deliberate human influence. But, his theory left a very wide space for human intervention and explicitly discussed the many different ways that individuals could affect the process (for better or worse). *Leadership in Administration* is full of examples that reveal this human influence (and the book's very title underscores their centrality in Selznick's thought).

Finally, and relatedly, it is also necessary to comment on the explicitly normative and prescriptive character of Selznick's theory. In his view, identity is not just a reflection of organizational history (or of members' interpretations of that history). It is also the metaphorical "soul" of the organization and the ultimate guide to strategic decision-making. The values that are "infused" through the process of institutionalization are genuinely valuable—things that leaders "ought" to pursue for reasons that are both moral and practical:

> The protection of integrity is more than an aesthetic or expressive exercise, more than an attempt to preserve a comforting, familiar environment. It is a practical concern of the first importance because the defense of integrity is also a defense of the organization's distinctive competence.
>
> (1957: 139)

This aspect of Selznick's perspective is one of its most intriguing—and challenging—features. We shall have much more to say about it in our discussion of the theory's contemporary applications.

In sum, Selznick's initial formulation of the institutional perspective saw organizational identity as the end product of the institutionalization process. He suggested that this process was best understood by studying the individual organization over its life course, and attending to the commitments and critical decisions that, taken together, formed the organization's "character." The identities that emerge from institutionalization were seen to "breathe life" into purely technical organizations and to make them distinctive among their peers. While these historically accreted identities clearly impose constraints, they also remain open to revision and create new possibilities and energies. Organizations are expendable. Institutionalization engenders a new concern with self-perpetuation.

New Institutional Theory

New institutional theory began with a deceptively simple question: why are there so few kinds of organizations? Or to put it another way, what is it that leads groups of organizations to look more and more similar over time? A number of papers reflecting on this question appeared in the late 1970s and early 1980s and form the foundation of what came to be known as "new institutional theory"[2] (Greenwood et al., 2008).

These papers sought to refocus attention from a single organization as an institution to organizational fields populated with institutions that are drawn from the broader

---

[2] This is, of course, as opposed to the "old institutional theory" of Selznick described in the preceding section.

societal context and that act to shape organizations and their activities through pressures for isomorphism. Central to this perspective is the idea of legitimacy and a simple but powerful mechanism: the need for organizations to conform to their institutional context in order to ensure flows of resources and support.

Institutions, fields, and logics. In the most general sense, institutions are self-policing conventions (e.g., Douglas, 1986). Within the tradition of new institutional theory, institutions are defined more specifically as "historical accretions of past practices and understandings that set conditions on action" through the way in which they "gradually acquire the moral and ontological status of taken-for-granted facts which, in turn, shape future interactions and negotiations" (Barley and Tolbert, 1997: 99). Institutions influence behavior due to the fact that departures from them "are counteracted in a regulated fashion, by repetitively activated, socially constructed, controls" (Jepperson, 1991: 145).

In other words, institutions shape behavior because deviations from the accepted institutional order are costly. This non-conformity can be associated with increased costs in several different ways: "economically (it increases risk), cognitively (it requires more thought), and socially (it reduces legitimacy and the access to resources that accompany legitimacy)" (Phillips, Lawrence, and Hardy, 2000: 28). Institutionalization is a matter of degree, and the more highly institutionalized a social pattern becomes, the more costly any deviations from it will be.

In addition to a new understanding of institutions, new institutional theory brought with it a new focus on the organizational field. Organizational fields are an intermediate analytical category between the firm level of analysis and the broader societal level, and play a central role in this form of institutional analysis. Fields include the organizations that make up an industry, but also include key customers, suppliers, regulators, and other actors that "constitute a recognized area of institutional life" (DiMaggio and Powell, 1983: 148). As a consequence, studies of institutional processes are no longer single case studies of large organizations, but instead become quantitative studies of populations of organizations within fields.

Organizational fields develop through processes of structuration where patterns of social action produce and reproduce the institutions and networks that constitute the field (Barley and Tolbert, 1997). Through repeated interaction, groups of organizations develop common understandings and practices that form the institutions that define the field and, at the same time, these institutions shape the ongoing patterns of interaction from which they are produced. In other words, the institutional context experienced by members of the field is uniform and shared, and, importantly, different from that which develops in other fields.

Furthermore, institutional fields are characterized by institutional logics (Friedland and Alford, 1991; Thornton and Ocasio, 1999). Institutional logics are the taken-for-granted rules that shape interests and action at the field level by furnishing "assumptions and values, usually implicit, about how to interpret organizational reality, what constitutes appropriate behavior, and how to succeed" (Thornton, 2004). In particular, they provide social actors with formal and informal rules of action and interaction, cultural norms and beliefs for interpretation, and implicit principles about what constitute legitimate goals and how they may be achieved.

New institutional theory and organizational identity. From a new institutional perspective, organizational identity is not so much an organizational phenomenon, but rather something that exists at the field level. It is not something that is created inside the organization and differentiates one organization from another, but is rather an organizational type that is created through processes of social construction within a field (or in society more broadly), and that sets of organizations associate themselves with in order to be understood and to increase their legitimacy.

One way that this new approach to institutions is theorized is through the notion of a collective identity. Scholars have defined collective identities "as groups of actors that can be strategically constructed and fluid, organized around a shared purpose and similar outputs" (Wry, Lounsbury, and Glynn, 2011: 449). In other words, a collective identity emerges when a group of organizations come to be understood as being organizations of the same kind in the sense that they do the same thing and share important characteristics. Examples include industrial versus craft brewers (Carroll and Swaminathan, 2000), classical versus nouvelle cuisine chefs (Rao et al., 2003), and Boston trustees versus New York money managers (Lounsbury, 2007).

Collective identities define the boundary between organizations that are external to the group and those that share an identity and are valued and judged to be legitimate or not on the basis of their membership. They also function to provide legitimacy ("dry cleaners are a legitimate type of organization and we are a dry cleaner"), setting decision premises ("what would a dry cleaner do in this circumstance?"), compel certain actions ("we have to do that, we are a dry cleaner"), and proscribing others ("we can't do that, we are a dry cleaner").

The idea that identities are externally determined is most developed in the literature on categories. From this perspective, the possible types of organization are limited to those available in the institutional context, and organizations that fail to "fit" into a category lose legitimacy and support from their environments. This idea is nicely summarized in Zuckerman's (1999) notion of the "categorical imperative" where organizations that span categories lose legitimacy (by, for example, trying to be a dry cleaner and a restaurant at the same time). Not only do organizations need to fit with the categories that exist in a field, but trying to combine aspects of different types of firms results in a penalty in terms of legitimacy and support.

The notion of categories has been the focus of much recent attention as various researchers have extended and developed the idea of a category and moved beyond the product categories that were the initial focus of attention. In the process, the idea of a category has evolved, and the focus has moved from the understanding of categories to understanding categorization as "a complex process that can span multiple levels of analysis (from individuals through organizations and markets), and that has been linked to a variety of organizational phenomena" (Glynn and Navis, 2013: 1124). Categories are not pre-given and obvious constructions, and how social objects are assigned to categories (for example, types of organization) is a complex social process that requires more investigation (Durand and Paolella, 2013). We will discuss this more agentic and processual view in detail in the next section.

Contemporary Developments: The Agentic Turn in Institutional Theory

From the late 1990s onwards, the nature of institutional scholarship changed markedly once again. More specifically, the focus on conformity and isomorphism that dominated the previous phase of institutional theory gave way to a focus on action and strategic intent. After a decade of new institutional theory, many researchers began to feel that agency was an important part of the institutional story, but one that was underemphasized due to new institutional theory's narrow focus on structure and constraint (Hirsch and Lounsbury, 1997; Selznick, 1996).

Associated with this change in focus was a change in the dominant research methods adopted by institutional theorists. With this new interest in agency, many researchers eschewed the quantitative approach that traditionally characterized the discipline (which focused on patterns across an organizational field), and began instead to rely on the detailed analysis of single cases in which the role and influence of individual and organizational actors was more apparent.

As part of this evolution, the focus of attention in institutional theory research moved to three new topics: institutional entreprencurship, institutional work, and institutional complexity. In this section we look at each in turn (see also Besharov and Brickson, Ch. 21 in this handbook).

Institutional entrepreneurship. The term "institutional entrepreneurship" was first used in institutional theory by DiMaggio (1988) who complained that institutional research was in danger of becoming irrelevant because of its neglect of "the reality of purposive, interest driven, and conflictual behaviour" (1988: 5). But it was not until some 15 years later that institutional theorists answered his call and began to focus on the intentional aspects of institutional change. The early part of this century saw a series of influential studies rooted in the concept of institutional entrepreneurship, defined as "the activities of actors who have an interest in particular institutional arrangements and who leverage resources to create new institutions or transform existing ones (Maguire et al., 2004: 657). For example, researchers have considered the role of institutional entrepreneurs in creating change in the "Big Five" accounting firms (Greenwood and Suddaby, 2006), legitimating new technological standards (Garud et al., 2002), and creating new categories of photography (Munir and Phillips, 2005).

Building explicitly on the concept of institutional entrepreneurship, Lawrence and Suddaby (2006) developed the notion of institutional work, which they defined as "the purposive action of individuals and organizations aimed at creating, maintaining or disrupting institutions" (Lawrence and Suddaby, 2006: 215). These authors noted that, while much research on institutional entrepreneurship had focused on how actors create new institutions, much strategic action with respect to institutions was actually concerned with how institutions are maintained, or how they are undermined and dismantled.

Moreover, institutional entrepreneurship had been criticized for assuming that actors are "disembedded" from their context and can therefore act freely. Institutional work, on the other hand, is explicitly focused on the so-called paradox of embedded agency: that is, "How can actors envision and enact changes in institutions if their actions, intentions, and rationality are all conditioned by the very institutions they wish to change?" (Holm, 1995: 398). A series of influential papers has been published using the institutional work perspective, including studies of the British Columbia coastal forest industry (Zietsma and Lawrence, 2010), conflict between leaders and students at San Francisco State College (Rojas, 2010), and responsible investing (Slager et al., 2010).

More recently, the concept of institutional pluralism (Kraatz and Block, 2008) or institutional complexity (Greenwood et al., 2011) has gained increasing attention in institutional theory. Organizations operate under conditions of institutional complexity when, rather than existing in a field characterized by a single logic as discussed in the previous section, "they confront incompatible prescriptions from multiple institutional logics" (Greenwood et al., 2011). In these circumstances, organizations face a series of tensions that they need to manage in order to survive. A number of different strategies have been identified for managing these tensions, including acquiescence, compromise, avoidance, defiance, and manipulation (Oliver, 1991; Pache and Santos, 2013).

While most organizations face institutional complexity to a greater or lesser degree, some organizations are actually designed to straddle two or more distinct logics. Such organizations, which include, for example, social enterprises (that combine the logic of the market and the logic of social welfare), and private hospitals (that combine the logic of the market and distinct professional logics), have been termed "hybrid organizations" (Battilana and Lee, 2014). Interestingly, the concept of institutional complexity assumes a markedly different conception of institutional logics than the previous phase, we have outlined. Rather than rules that shape interests and action, from this perspective, logics are seen as "tool kits" (Swidler, 1986) that actors can use to influence their institutional context externally and shape their organizational context internally.

The agentic turn and organizational identity. As we have noted, new institutionalists have traditionally considered organizational identity as something that exists at the level of a field; organizations draw on collective identities that are rooted in categories in order to become more legitimate. More recent work following the agentic turn has seen the conceptualization of organizational identity: 1) shift from a focus on the field level to include a focus on the organization; and 2) include the idea that field processes lead to pressures for the adoption of identities *and* enable actors to shape how these identities are adopted to the extent that they can even customize them in important ways.

Two sets of ideas are particularly worth highlighting here. One is the idea that organizations can draw on different collective identities (or logics) that exist in an organizational field, select particular elements from each of them, and combine them in new ways in order to construct a distinctive organizational identity (Kraatz and Block, 2008; Pratt and Kraatz, 2009). For example, Tracey et al. (2011) argued that the founders of Aspire—a social enterprise that supported homeless people by employing them in a business venture—engaged in institutional work to create a distinct organizational identity by drawing on elements from the logic of commerce and elements from the logic of charity. The logic of commerce emphasized the importance of concepts such as competitiveness, customer service, and efficiency. The logic of charity emphasized the importance of concepts such as social welfare, social justice, and fairness. This led to the emergence of a discrete type of hybrid organization with an identity that resonated with aspects of for-profit firms and aspects of non-profit homeless support charities, but that was different from each of them.

A second influential idea is the notion of legitimate distinctiveness (Navis and Glynn, 2011), which parallels the notion of optimal distinctiveness in social identity theory (Brewer, 1991). At the core of this idea is that organizations need to be similar enough to others of the same type so that they are legitimate in the eyes of key stakeholders, but different enough from them in order to be seen as characterized by some idiosyncratic features that render them worthy of support. For example, Navis and Glynn (2010) argue that in the long run entrepreneurs are more likely to receive support from audiences if they craft an identity for their venture that is legitimately distinctive. Through a study of the emergence of satellite radio as a new market category from the mid-1990s to the end of 2005, they develop a framework that conceptualizes market category formation, taking into account the role of actors in organizations and relevant external stakeholders. They show that when a market category reaches a particular "legitimacy threshold," this precipitates an "attentional shift" in the focus of both member firms and key audiences away from the collective and toward the differentiating features of individual firms.

In sum, we have traced the evolution of institutional theory from its roots in Selznick's research on institutionalization at the organizational level, to the work in new institutional theory on conformity at the field level, and finally to new institutional theory's agentic turn which has focused on the role and importance of strategic intent and institutional change. Doing so has allowed us to track how the notion of identity has shifted over time within institutional theory—from identity as the end product of institutionalization, to identity as category affiliation, to identity as a source of differentiation.

New Directions

In this section we would like to turn our attention to the future and discuss some of the areas that we feel show particular promise for institutional theory to contribute to thinking about organizational identity and, in some cases, where organizational identity research might be able to contribute to institutional theory.

Selznick and Contemporary Organizational Identity Scholarship

Selznick's various insights about organizational identity cannot be easily detached from their theoretical moorings. He did not set out to develop a theory of organizational identity, and his arguments about identity's nature, origins, and functions are part and parcel of a much larger research program that aimed to accomplish something else entirely. Nevertheless, we believe his work does offer a number of discrete insights that may be of use to the broader identity literature. We will elaborate these implications in this section.

Historical and diachronic orientation. Selznick's theory emerged directly from historical case studies of individual organizations, and is explicitly diachronic in nature. It is like other institutional approaches in that it situates the organization in society and emphasizes the latter's profound influence on the former's identity. But, it is highly distinctive in that it also situates the organization within its own developmental history and draws attention to the formative events, crises, and "critical decisions" that occur therein. It is through these events and choices that society leaves its mark on the organization—and from them that an identity ultimately emerges (see Gioia and Hamilton, Ch. 1 in this volume for a discussion of this point as it relates to identity).

This diachronic and organization-centric approach is not necessarily superior to the synchronic, field-centric one that is most common in contemporary institutional research. But, it does point to a void in this recent literature and offers a rather different picture of identity. Organizations are indeed evaluated according to categorical standards and these categories clearly do shape their self-understandings and decisions (increasingly, so it would seem). But, as Selznick reminds us, each organization is also "hostage to its own history" in ways that are both good and bad. Bringing these insights together seems a critical task and a key opportunity for institutionalists in particular (Kraatz and Flores, 2015; King, 2015). In emphasizing the importance of history, Selznick's theory parallels other recent work in the larger identity literature (Schultz and Hernes, 2013; Suddaby, Foster, and Trank, Ch. 16, this volume).

Holistic view of identity. Selznick's perspective is also attractive because it compels attention to the organization's entire social structure (e.g., its official and unofficial goals, its power structure, its culture, its demographic composition, its internal fault lines, etc.). The theory stresses that identity is a real and tangible phenomenon, and Selznick suggests that we can gain a deep understanding of any organization's identity if we approach it in the right way and collect sufficient information about its history and character. But, he does not imply that this identity can be assessed through any single empirical indicator, or make the mistake of equating identity with group affiliations or category memberships. These memberships are only one aspect of a much more complex phenomenon, and their perceived importance also varies substantially from one organization to the next. While these subtleties are not especially salient when we approach identity from a top-down societal perspective, they are very difficult to miss when we conceptualize organizations as "organic wholes" and assume a central concern with their historical development and evolution. This complex and empirically grounded understanding of identity is also likely to be more useful to managers and practitioners (who were a key audience for Selznick's pragmatically oriented theory).

Embrace of dualities. Selznick's perspective also provides a model for coping with many of the dualisms that typically arise in discussions of foundational concepts like identity (e.g., between structure and agency, stability and change, realism and interpretivism, etc.). The institutionalization process that he theorizes is a deeply constraining one that is largely driven by societal forces, and it produces empirically anchored identities that have "central, distinctive, and enduring" properties. However, these properties are by no means fixed, final, or essential; and society's influence on the organization is always mediated through the mechanism of human choice. These choices—which are clearly visible when one examines the organization over its life course—are sometimes careless, myopic, and ill considered. Indeed, they may not even be recognized as choices in the moment they unfold. But, they often become more deliberate and foresightful as the organization and its leaders develop a greater sense of self-awareness. Promoting this awareness was a key goal of *Leadership in Administration* and of much of what Selznick wrote thereafter.

Organizations as self-acting subjects. Selznick suggests a strong analogy between individual and organizational processes of identity formation, and his theory is rife with anthropomorphic language (e.g., organizations taking on "lives of their own," developing characters, possessing values, striving for integrity, etc.). While these characterizations are philosophically and politically debatable, they remain remarkably useful for at least three key reasons: first, many organizational members perceive their organizations in just this way (as a partial result of the process we have just described); second, external audiences commonly attribute human traits to organizations and view their actions as evidence thereof (whether rightly or wrongly); and, finally, human imagery is also valuable in that it discourages reductionism, encourages analytic humility, and maintains possibilities that object-focused theories rule out by assumption (e.g., consciousness, intentionality, responsibility, moral agency, etc.).

Values. Finally, identity scholars may also wish to revisit Selznick's arguments about institutional values and consider the role that they may play in identity-related processes (e.g., formation, change, external evaluations). It is certainly possible to navigate around this unconventional and outwardly problematic element of Selznick's theory, and most recent work that has drawn upon his perspective appears to have done just this (Kraatz and Flores, 2015; Hinings and Greenwood, 2015).

But, the fact remains that values are the single most central concept in Selznick's institutionalism and in his larger social theory (Selznick, 1992; 2008; Krygier, 2012). Kraatz and Flores (2015) have recently made a thoroughgoing effort to "reinfuse" values into the contemporary institutional conversation, and suggested a number of possible avenues for future research. These include studies that examine the value-infusion process and treat values as outcomes, studies that examine values' effects on organizational change and performance, and studies that examine value-realization and value-subversion (consistent with Selznick's overarching vision for "humanist science"). Because Selznick's theory posits such a close connection between values and organizational identity, research examining these "value-focused" questions may also deliver critical insights about the latter.

Institutions, Organizational Identities, and Social Construction

Another important area where organizational identity and institutional theory can be productively brought together is around their shared and growing interest in processes of social construction. This is not to say that the interest in social construction is either uniform across the two literatures or that all of the researchers that work in these areas would describe their own epistemological position as constructivist. However, there is a longstanding social constructivist current in both streams of research, and a parallel increase in interest recently among researchers in the two areas in using linguistic methods of various kinds to explore how identities and institutions are constructed. This shared interest provides an important potential connection where institutional theory and organizational identity researchers can work together and develop important insights that neither could develop alone.

Social construction of identity and institutions. Among researchers in organizational identity there is growing interest in how organizational identities are constructed by organizational members (e.g. Gioia et al., 2010). These researchers see "organization members as meaning creators—as the ultimate generators of the labels, meanings, and other cognitive features that produce the 'understandings' that constitute the essence of organizational identity" (Gioia et al., 2013: 170). From this perspective, organizational identities are produced and maintained by the ongoing meaningful interactions of organizational members, and understanding these processes is a necessary step in fully understanding organizational identities.

Interestingly, in institutional theory there has also been a growing interest how institutions are socially constructed. While institutional theory has always been underpinned by a recognition of the socially constructed nature of institutions, in the last decade this interest has spilled over into an active interest in exploring the processes through which institutions are constructed. In order to do so, researchers began to focus on language (broadly defined) as the medium through which social construction takes place: "institutionalization occurs as actors interact and come to accept shared definitions of reality, and it is through linguistic processes that definitions of reality are constituted" (Phillips et al., 2004: 635). Researchers have deployed a number of linguistic methods to explore these processes, including discourse analysis (e.g., Phillips et al., 2004), semiotics (e.g., Zilber, 2006), and rhetoric (e.g., Green, Li, and Nohria, 2009).

Social construction as a point of contact. This shared interest in social construction, and more specifically in applying linguistic methods to understand these important processes, is both an important point of contact and an exciting area where the two bodies of theory can inform and support each other. Work on processes of social construction in institutional theory can help provide important insights into the formation and maintenance of organizational identities. As Gioia et al. (2013) argue: "Organizational identity links an organization to the institutions in its environment, and establishing an organizational identity is a crucial element of forming an organization as a viable entity."

The process through which an organizational identity is constructed and maintained, and how the institutional context is drawn on in this process, therefore requires a clear understanding of the nature of the institutional context in which the organization is embedded and how these resources can be drawn upon in the processes of social construction that underpin organizational identities. Institutional theory, particularly the developing body of work drawing on linguistic methods to explore the construction and maintenance of institutions, can contribute important insights that identity scholars can draw upon as they develop a deeper understanding of this important connection.

At the same time, the identity work that organizational members carry out in and around organizations has important institutional effects. As Gawer and Phillips (2013: 27) discuss:

> Our findings ... suggest that, while organizations may attempt to change practices in response to institutional changes in logics, it is through the prism of their identity that organizational members make sense of these practices. And, most importantly, organizational identities shape understandings of who can legitimately perform what practices. Therefore, the adoption of new practices may encounter

significant resistance when organizational members believe there is a conflict between a new practice and the organization's identity.

Their findings indicate that the institutional processes that create pressure for isomorphism in organizations are mediated by organizational identities, and the activities of organizations that attempt to act as institutional entrepreneurs may require extensive identity work internally to accomplish their goals. Furthermore, an organization's identity will play a key role in the degree to which (and when) the organization succumbs to institutional pressure. Understanding institutions and institutional change therefore requires a deeper connection between organizational identity, identity work, and institutional processes.

The Multilevel Nature of Organizational Identity

Another important area where organizational identity theory and institutional theory can be productively brought together is in a multi-level conceptualization of identity in organizations. As noted, organizational identity researchers have generally focused on the internal dynamics that underpin identity construction in organizations (e.g. Ravasi and Schultz, 2006), and how each organization builds and maintains an identity that is unique (Gioia et al., 2010). Institutional theorists, on the other hand, have tended to focus on the external dynamics that underpin identity construction, and how each organization builds and maintains an identity that conforms to other organizations of a particular type in order to garner legitimacy and resources.

Partial accounts. While both perspectives have offered powerful insights, there is increasing recognition that each of them offers only a partial account, and that a focus on both internal and external dynamics is critical for understanding identity dynamics in organizations: it is hard to sustain the argument that each organization's identity is unique in all aspects, and likewise that a given organization's identity is identical in every respect to other members of a particular category of organizations. While these are of course stylized interpretations of the relevant arguments (see, for example, the writing on "optimal distinctiveness" in organizational identity theory [e.g., Whetten, 2006] and "legitimate distinctiveness" in institutional theory [e.g., Navis and Glynn, 2011]), they nonetheless capture the central thrust of the two perspectives.

Bringing identity and institutions together. It is important to acknowledge, however, that there have been important attempts to bring together ideas from these two perspectives. For example, writing from an organizational identity perspective, Gioia et al.'s (2010) study of the creation of a college of interdisciplinary technology studies in an American university offers a powerful example of how institutional environments influence organizational identity processes and vice versa. These authors explicitly note that organizational identities are shaped in part by the "institutional claims" made by the organization.

From this perspective, organizational identities are constructed, not only through the interactions and interpretations of organizational members, but through communication with external actors designed to signal the organization's relationship to particular categories. But Gioia et al. go even further by suggesting that in seeking to develop an organizational identity that is optimally distinctive, organizational leaders may act as institutional entrepreneurs and seek to shape the nature of the organizational field to which they belong. As the authors note, "This raises interesting possibilities for adopting an identity-based approach to studying institutional entrepreneurship" (2010: 41). (See also Foreman and Whetten, 2002; Osborn and Ashforth, 1990; Ravasi and Schultz, 2006.)

And writing from an institutional theory perspective, Battilana and Dorado's (2010) important comparative study of two microfinance ventures shows that when organizations face multiple institutional pressures in their environments, building a shared identity may allow organizations to balance legitimacy pressures externally and competing templates for action internally. (See also, Glynn and Azburg, 2002; Wry, Lounsbury, and Glynn, 2011—also Kodeih and Greenwood, 2014).

Yet, in the contributions outlined above, scholars are clearly writing from a particular perspective: in the first example Gioia et al. (2010) are organizational identity scholars who draw selectively on ideas from institutional theory, while in the second example, Battilana and Dorado (2010) are institutional scholars who draw selectively from organizational identity theory. This is not intended as a criticism: such an approach is understandable, perhaps even desirable in some circumstances, and we readily admit to doing the same in our own work. But to really make sense of the multi-level nature of identity processes in organizations and to maximize the synergies between the two perspectives, we suggest that more balance is needed.

A multi-level theory of identity and institutions. So what would a properly integrated, multi-level perspective on organizational identity—which privileges neither institutional theory nor organizational identity theory—look like? Interestingly, Ashforth, Rogers, and Corley (2011) potentially offer a conceptual basis for such a perspective. They delineate a "nested" approach to the study of identity in organizations which links individual, dyadic, work group, and organizational levels. A particularly powerful feature of their model is its core assumption that social processes at each level of analysis "simultaneously enable and constrain identities at other levels" (p. 1152). In other words they do not privilege any particular level of analysis. However, while they invoke institutional ideas, the institutional or societal level of analysis is missing from their framework. Taking their core idea about identities being nested across levels, but incorporating and theorizing about the "missing" institutional level, offers an intriguing opportunity to integrate meaningfully organizational and institutional approaches to identity in organizations.

CONCLUSION

In this chapter, we have provided a roadmap that we hope identity scholars will find useful in understanding how thinking about organizational identity has evolved within institutional theory over the last several decades. Our intention is to show that organizational identity has been the focus of considerable interest in institutional theory and that the various ways that institutional theorists have conceptualized organizational identity both parallel many of the discussions that have animated organizational identity scholars (Gioia et al., 2014) and also have the potential to add further insights to discussions that are occurring among organizational identity scholars.

In particular, we hope that our discussions here point to the value of a deeper connection between organizational identity scholars and institutional theorists. While there has long been a group of organizational identity scholars who have worked from what Gioia et al. (2014) call an "institutional perspective," there is much more that can be gained from a closer engagement between the two bodies of literature. The recent increase in interest in identity among institutional theory is just one indicator that bodes well for the further deepening of this connection.

Finally, it is interesting to note that it is quite common for individual scholars to work in both areas (the authors of this chapter are a good case in point!). The similar philosophical assumptions and interpretivist epistemology that underpin the two areas makes working across the boundary between them reasonably straightforward. It also means that there are many existing links between these areas, and great potential for further building a productive research community. We hope scholars on both sides of the divide (and especially the ones who are spanning the two research areas) will take up the challenge!

REFERENCES

Ashforth, B. E., Rogers, K. M., and Corley, K. G. (2011). "Identity in Organizations: Exploring Cross-Level Dynamics." *Organization Science* 22(5): 1144–56.

Barley, S. R. and Tolbert, P. S. (1997). "Institutionalization and Structuration: Studying the Links between Action and Institution." *Organization Studies* 18: 93–117.

Battilana, J. and Dorado, S. (2010). "Building Sustainable Hybrid Organizations: The Case of Commercial Microfinance Organizations." *Academy of Management Journal* 6: 1419–40.

Battilana, J. and Lee, M. (2014). "Advancing Research on Hybrid Organizing: Insights from the Study of Social Enterprises." *The Academy of Management Annals* 8(1): 397–441.

Besharov, M. L. and Brickson, S. L. (2016). "Organizational Identity and Institutional Forces: Toward an Integrative Framework." In *The Oxford Handbook of Organizational Identity*, edited by M. G. Pratt, M. Schultz, B. E. Ashforth, and D. Ravasi, 396–414. Oxford: Oxford University Press.

Brewer, M. B. (1991). "The Social Self: On Being the Same and Different at the Same Time." *Personality and Social Psychology Bulletin* 17(5): 475–82.

Carroll, G. R. and Swaminathan, A. (2000). "Why the Microbrewery Movement? Organizational Dynamics of Resource Partitioning in the US Brewing Industry." *American Journal of Sociology* 106(3): 715–62.

Di Maggio, P. J. (1988). "Interest and Agency in Institutional Theory." In *Institutional Patterns and Organizations: Culture and Environment*, edited by L. G. Zucker, 3–22. Cambridge, MA: Ballinger.

Di Maggio, P. J. and Powell, W. W. (1983). "The Iron Cage Revisited: Institutional Isomorphism and Collective Rationality in Organizational Fields." *American Sociological Review* 48: 147–60.

Douglas, M. (1986). *How Institutions Think*. New York: Syracuse University Press.

Durand, R. and Paolella, L. (2013). "Category Stretching: Reorienting Research on Categories in Strategy, Entrepreneurship, and Organization Theory." *Journal of Management Studies* 50(6): 1100–23.

Foreman, P. and Whetten, D. A. (2002). "Members' Identification with Multiple-Identity Organizations." *Organization Science* 13(6): 618–35.

Friedland, R. and Alford, R. R. (1991). "Bringing Society back in: Symbols, Practices, and Institutional Contradictions." In *The New Institutionalism in Organizational Analysis*, edited by W. W. Powell, and P. J. DiMaggio, 232–66. Chicago: University of Chicago Press.

Garud, R., Jain, S., and Kumaraswamy, A. (2002). "Institutional Entrepreneurship in the Sponsorship of Common Technological Standards: The Case of Sun Microsystems and Java." *Academy of Management Journal* 45: 196–214.

Gawer, A. and Phillips, N. (2013). "Institutional Work as Logics Shift: The Case of Intel's Transformation to Platform Leader." *Organization Studies* 34(8): 1035–71.

Gioia, D. A. and Hamilton, A. L. (2016). "Great Debates in Organizational Identity Study." In *The Oxford Handbook of Organizational Identity*, edited by M. G. Pratt, M. Schultz, B. E. Ashforth, and D. Ravasi, 21–38. Oxford: Oxford University Press.

Gioia, D. A., Patvardhan, S. D., Hamilton, A. L., and Corley, K. G. (2013). "Organizational Identity Formation and Change." *The Academy of Management Annals* 7(1): 123–93.

Gioia, D. A., Price, K. N., Hamilton, A. L., and Thomas, J. B. (2010). "Forging an Identity: An Insider-Outsider Study of Processes Involved in the Formation of Organizational Identity." *Administrative Science Quarterly* 55: 1–46.

Glynn, M. and Abzug, R. (2002). "Institutionalized Identity: Symbolic Isomorphism and Organizational Names." *Academy of Management Journal* 45(1): 267–80.

Glynn, M. A. and Navis, C. (2013). "Categories, Identities, and Cultural Classification: Moving Beyond a Model of Categorical Constraint." *Journal of Management Studies* 50(6): 1124–37.

Gouldner, A. W. (1955). "Metaphysical Pathos and the Theory of Bureaucracy." *American Political Science Review* 49(2): 496–507.

Green, S. E., Li, Y., and Nohria, N. (2009). "Suspended in Self-Spun Webs of Significance: A Rhetorical Model of Institutionalization and Institutionally Embedded Agency." *Academy of Management Journal* 52(1): 11–36.

Greenwood, R., Oliver, C., Sahlin, K., and Suddaby, R. (2008). "Introduction." In *The SAGE Handbook of Organizational Institutionalism*, edited by R. Greenwood, C. Oliver, R. Suddaby, and K. Sahlin, 1–46. London: SAGE.

Greenwood, R., Raynard, M., Kodeih, F., Micelotta, E., and Lounsbury, M. (2011). "Institutional Complexity and Organizational Responses." *The Academy of Management Annals* 5(1): 317–71.

Greenwood, R. and Suddaby, R. (2006). "Institutional Entrepreneurship in Mature Fields: The Big Five Accounting Firms." *Academy of Management Journal* 49: 27–48.

Hinings, C. and Greenwood, R. (2015). "Missing in Action: The Further Contribution of Philip Selznick to Contemporary Institutional Theory." In *Institutions and Ideals: Philip Selznick's Legacy for Organizational Studies* (Research in the Sociology of Organizations, vol. 44), edited by Matthew S. Kraatz, 121–48. Bingley: Emerald Group Publishing.

Hirsch, P. and Lounsbury, M. (1997). "Ending the Family Quarrel: Toward a Reconciliation of 'Old' and 'New' Institutionalism", *American Behavioral Scientist* 40(4): 405–18.

Holm, P. (1995). "The Dynamics of Institutionalization: Transformation Processes in Norwegian Fisheries." *Administrative Science Quarterly*, 398–422.

Jepperson, R. L. (1991). "Institutions, Institutional Effects, and Institutionalism." In *The New Institutionalism in Organizational Analysis*, edited by W. W. Powell and P. J. DiMaggio, 143–63. Chicago: University of Chicago Press.

King, B. G. (2015). "Organizational Actors, Character and Selznick's Theory of Organizations." In *Institutions and Ideals: Philip Selznick's Legacy for Organizational Studies* (Research in the Sociology of Organizations, vol. 44), edited by M. Kraatz, 149–74. Bingley: Emerald Group Publishing.

Kodeih, F. and Greenwood, R. (2014). "Responding to Institutional Complexity: The Role of Identity." *Organization Studies* 35(1): 7–39.

Kraatz, M. S. and Block, E. S. (2008). "Organizational Implications of Institutional Pluralism." In *The SAGE Handbook of Organizational Institutionalism*, edited by R. Greenwood, C. Oliver, R. Suddaby, R. and K. Sahlin-Andresson, 243–75. London: SAGE.

Kraatz, M. S. and Flores, R. G. (2015). "Reinfusing Values." In *Institutions and Ideals: Philip Selznick's Legacy for Organizational Studies* (Research in the Sociology of Organizations, vol. 44), edited by M. S. Kraatz, 353–81. Bingley: Emerald Group Publishing.

Krygier, M. (2002). "Philip Selznick, Normative Theory, and the Rule of Law." In *Legality and Community: On the Intellectual Legacy of Philip Selznick*, edited by P. Selznick, R. A. Kagan, M. Krygier, and K. I. Winston, 19–48. Lanham, MD: Rowman and Littlefield.

Krygier, M. (2012). *Philip Selznick: Ideals in the World*. Stanford, CA: Stanford University Press.

Lawrence, T. B. and Suddaby, R. (2006). "Institutional Work." In *The SAGE Handbook of Organization Studies*, 2nd edn., edited by S. Clegg, C. Hardy, T. Lawrence, and W. Nord, 215–54. London: SAGE.

Lounsbury, M. (2007). "A Tale of Two Cities: Competing Logics and Practice Variation in the Professionalizing of Mutual Funds." *Academy of Management Journal* 50(2): 289–307.

Maguire, S., Hardy, C., and Lawrence, T. B. (2004). "Institutional Entrepreneurship in Emerging Fields: HIV/AIDS Treatment Advocacy in Canada." *Academy of Management Journal* 47: 657–79.

Meyer, J. W. and Rowan, B. (1977). "Institutionalized Organizations: Formal Structure as Myth and Ceremony." *American Journal of Sociology* 83: 340–63.

Munir, K. and Phillips, N. (2005). "The Birth of the Kodak Moment: Institutional Entrepreneurship and the Adoption of New Technologies." *Organization Studies* 26: 1665–87.

Navis, C. and Glynn, M. A. (2010). "How New Market Categories Emerge: Temporal Dynamics of Legitimacy, Identity, and Entrepreneurship in Satellite Radio, 1990–2005." *Administrative Science Quarterly* 55(3): 439–71.

Navis, C. and Glynn, M. A. (2011). "Legitimate Distinctiveness and the Entrepreneurial Identity: Influence on Investor Judgments of New Venture Plausibility." *Academy of Management Review* 36(3): 479–99.

Oliver, C. (1991). "Strategic Responses to Institutional Processes." *Academy of Management Review* 16(1): 145–79.

Osborn, R. N. and Ashforth, B. E. (1990). "Investigating the Challenges to Senior Leadership in Complex, High-Risk Technologies." *The Leadership Quarterly* 1(3): 147–63.

Pache, A. C. and Santos, F. (2013). "Inside the Hybrid Organization: Selective Coupling as a Response to Competing Institutional Logics." *Academy of Management Journal* 56(4): 972–1001.

Phillips, N., Lawrence, T. B., and Hardy, C. (2000). "Interorganizational Collaboration and the Dynamics of Institutional Fields." *Journal of Management Studies* 37(1): 23–45.

Phillips, N., Hardy, C., and Lawrence, T. (2004) "Discourse and Institutions." *Academy of Management Review* 29: 635–52.

Pratt, M. and Kraatz, M. (2009). "E Pluribus Unum: Multiple Identities and the Organizational Self." In *Exploring Positive Identities and Organizations*, edited by Jane Dutton and Laura Morgan Roberts, 385–410. Mahwah, NJ: Lawrence Erlbaum and Associates.

Rao, H., Monin, P., and Durand, R. (2003). "Institutional Change in Toque Ville: Nouvelle Cuisine as an Identity Movement in French Gastronomy." *American Journal of Sociology* 108(4): 795–843.

Ravasi, D. and Schultz, M. (2006) "Responding to Organizational Identity Threats: Exploring the Role of Organizational Culture." *Academy of Management Journal* 49: 433–58.

Rojas, F. (2010). "Power through Institutional Work: Acquiring Academic Authority in the 1968 Third World Strike." *Academy of Management Journal* 53(6): 1263–80.

Schultz, M. and Hernes, T. (2013). "A Temporal Perspective on Organizational Identity." *Organization Science* 24: 1–21.

Selznick, P. (1949). *TVA and the Grass Roots: A Study of Politics and Organization*, vol. 3. Berkeley, CA: University of California Press.

Selznick, P. (1952). *The Organizational Weapon*. New York, McGraw Hill.

Selznick, P. (1957). *Leadership in Administration: A Sociological Interpretation*. Evanston, IL: Row, Peterson.

Selznick, P. (1992). *The Moral Commonwealth: Social Theory and the Promise of Community*. Berkeley, CA: University of California Press.

Selznick, P. (1996). "Institutionalism 'Old' and 'New'," *Administrative Science Quarterly* 41(2): 270–7.

Selznick, P. (2000). "On Sustaining Research Agendas: Their Moral and Scientific Basis." *Journal of Management Inquiry* 9: 277–82.

Selznick, P. (2008). *A Humanist Science: Values and Ideals in Social Inquiry*. Stanford, CA: Stanford University Press.

Slager, R., Gond, J. P., and Moon, J. (2010). "What Gets Measured Gets Managed? The Impact of Sri Indices on Responsible Corporate Behaviour." In *Academy of Management Proceedings* 1: 1–6.

Suddaby, R., Foster, W., and Quinn Trank, C. (2016). "Re-Membering: Rhetorical History as Identity-Work." In *The Oxford Handbook of Organizational Identity*, edited by M. G. Pratt, M. Schultz, B. E. Ashforth, and D. Ravasi, 297–316. Oxford: Oxford University Press.

Swidler, A. (1986). "Culture in Action: Symbols and Strategies." *American Sociological Review* 51: 273–86.

Thornton, P. (2004) *Markets from Culture: Institutional Logics and Organizational Decisions in Higher Education Publishing*. Stanford, CA: Stanford University Press.

Thornton, P. H. and Ocasio, W. (1999). "Institutional Logics and the Historical Contingency of Power in Organizations: Executive Succession in the Higher Education Publishing Industry, 1958–1990." *American Journal of Sociology* 105: 801–43.

Tracey, P., Phillips, N., and Jarvis, O. (2011). "Bridging Institutional Entrepreneurship and the Creation of New Organizational Forms: A Multilevel Model."*Organization Science* 22(1): 60–80.

Whetten, D. A. (2006). "Albert and Whetten Revisited: Strengthening the Concept of Organizational Identity." *Journal of Management Inquiry* 15(3): 219–34.

Wry, T., Lounsbury, M., and Glynn, M. A. (2011). "Legitimating Nascent Collective Identities: Coordinating Cultural Entrepreneurship." *Organization Science* 22(2): 449–63.

Zietsma, C. and Lawrence, T. B. (2010). "Institutional Work in the Transformation of an Organizational Field: The Interplay of Boundary Work and Practice Work." *Administrative Science Quarterly* 55(2): 189–221.

Zilber, T. B. (2006). "The Work of the Symbolic in Institutional Processes: Translations of Rational Myths in Israeli High Tech." *Academy of Management Journal* 49(2): 281–303.

Zuckerman, E. W. (1999). "The Categorical Imperative: Securities Analysts and the Illegitimacy Discount." *American Journal of Sociology* 104(5): 1398–438.

CHAPTER 20

INSTITUTIONAL PLURALISM, INHABITANTS, AND THE CONSTRUCTION OF ORGANIZATIONAL AND PERSONAL IDENTITIES

RICH DEJORDY AND W. E. DOUGLAS CREED

In this chapter, we explore one very basic question: Why do organizational identities exist? Or, more precisely, why do people socially construct identities for organizations? As institutional theorists, our focus is on why and how constituents infuse organizational identities with shared meanings and values such that those organizational identities come to have the qualities of objective (yet socially constructed) realities which institutional inhabitants also employ as cultural resources in their ongoing personal identity projects. We motivate our discussion with the following thought experiment: Imagine that you are a newly minted PhD, fresh from the job market. This may not be so much of a thought experiment as an exercise in memory for many of you. Imagine further that, for whatever reason, you targeted a particular city with a high population of institutions of higher education. Now imagine that you have received job offers from four target schools with the following distinct organizational identities: a university in the Catholic Jesuit tradition; a practice-focused university modeled on experiential education; a campus of the state university providing affordable education for non-traditional and first generation students; and a large secular university renowned for both its scholarship and wealth. Finally, assume the offers are comparable in terms of compensation, opportunity, and expectations for tenure. Recognizing that we are now clearly in the realm of a thought experiment, under such conditions, what role might the identity of these organizations play in your decision of which offer to accept?

Of course, the ceteris paribus condition is, well, academic and choice is seldom as unconstrained as presented, but the exercise helps illuminate our basic premise that organizational identities are socially constructed around sets of values and claims which, when embraced by people through organizational affiliation become facets of their personal identity claims as well. Consequently, we argue that people embrace organizational identities and the particular sets of claims that come with them, at least in part because they serve their personal identity projects better than others; the organization's identity claims help the people make sense of their own identities both for themselves and for others.

Indeed, we contend that how people engage in the ongoing social construction of organizational identities—that is, how they produce, reproduce, alter, and employ these organizational identities in service of their personal identity projects—reflects their experience of and response to the complex, pluralistic institutional demands at play in their cultural contexts (Kraatz and Block, 2008). In this vein, we propose that organizational identities—socially constructed around sets of value claims—provide integrated solutions to pluralistic institutional demands in ways that are meaningful and that speak to issues of personal identity. There are two basic tenets underlying this proposition: First, identities of any sort, even those of collectives such as organizations, exist to serve the needs of the people (either jointly or individually) who are their constituents. Second, identity projects at the personal and organizational level are inherently about sensemaking (Weick, 1995). Therefore, we submit that organizational identities are constructed for the express purpose of assisting people in making sense of themselves, of others, and of their social contexts by providing a distinct assemblage of building blocks of meaning. At a given point in time, an organizational identity offers a distinct composite, an established and even legitimated response to a set of pluralistic institutional demands, which serves the organizational constituents' identity projects. For newcomers opting into organizations, organizational identities in effect represent pre-packaged integrated solutions to a particular subset of diverse institutional demands. More broadly, organizational identities provide cognitively efficient ways for institutional inhabitants to make sense of themselves and their institutional contexts and to communicate that to others.

We contend that what Pratt and Kraatz (2009) frame as integrated "Meadian" organizational selves (discussed below) are one particular type of resource or building block of meaning that institutional inhabitants employ in service to their own identity projects. It follows that organizational identities and selves are intertwined with individual identities in a recursive fashion as well. That is, membership, at least under conditions of personal choice, has meaning both for the members and to others, in the sense that it signals a commonality of values. In addition, changes to organizational identities are byproducts of the actions of individuals in and around organizations as they continually engage in making sense of their own identities for themselves and others.

Before embarking on this theoretical expedition, some words of caution. First, we believe that the social constructionist perspective, with its emphasis on how persons intersubjectively create the meanings, labels, and categories that are ascribed to organizations, and the social actor perspective, with its greater attention to organizational agency in claims-making and the appropriation of available categories, are not only complementary but symbiotic in explaining organizational identity (Covaleski, Dirsmith, Heian, and Samuel, 1998; Gioia, Patvardhan, Hamiliton, and Corley, 2013). At the same time, we acknowledge that our theorizing is more in line with the social constructionist perspective, as outlined in the opening paragraph.

Second, our theorizing resonates with the construct of "organizational self" proposed by Pratt and Kraatz (2009). This term is less common in the literature on organizational identity so it is important to understand the distinction they draw between organizational identity and organizational self. Consistent with the social actor model of organizational identity they employ the term *identity* to refer to particular identity claims anchored in a specific institutional domain. Such organizational identities are verified through symbolic exchanges within that specific domain. However, they also argue that because organizations exist in pluralistic institutional environments (Kraatz and Block, 2008), they may simultaneously have multiple identities peculiar to the various domains that comprise their institutional context. Pratt and Kraatz (2009) conceive of an *organizational self* as both an organization's collection of multiple domain-specific identities and the hierarchical structure that integrates and prioritizes these diverse identities. We adopt organizational self to refer to an organization's integration of its many constitutive and socially contextualized "identities" in a manner akin to the construct they label the "Meadian organizational self." We will expand on these constructs later in the chapter.

Third, in developing theoretical linkages across levels of analysis, we limit our consideration of the concepts of organizational identity and organizational self only to how they figure in the identity projects of organizational members. We realize both organizational identity and organizational self may have implications for a range of constituencies (members, customers, suppliers, etc.), but we believe the link between organizational self and personal identity is strongest for those with the clearest membership affiliations.

The chapter's structure reflects our own theoretical journey. We begin by revisiting the work on institutional pluralism (Kraatz and Block, 2008; Greenwood et al., 2011), which highlights the multifaceted nature of our contemporary social world, delineating what we see as the implications for organizational identity (Friedland and Alford, 1991). We then review the emerging stream of work that examines the macro-institutional pressures that affect personal identity and how that triggers identity work at the individual level (e.g., Creed, DeJordy, and Lok, 2010; Lok, 2010; Kellog, 2011). We close our literature review by considering the work that connects individual identity work with organizational identity. Based on those literatures, we develop a model linking the three levels (institutional, organizational, and individual). In particular, we draw on Pratt and Kraatz's (2009) translation of Mead's multiple identities conceptualization of the self (MICS) to argue that organizational identity projects and constituents' personal identity projects unfold in parallel and interpenetrating processes. We propose that an organizational self provides a resource that helps institutional inhabitants solve the problem of responding to pluralism by offering a legitimate, stable, and understandable response to aspects of their pluralistic institutional context. Through affiliation and membership, inhabitants appropriate these responses as resources for their identity projects. We then leverage the model to revisit the question of change in organizational identity and its links to the macro and micro contexts that it mediates. Next, we illustrate the example with a simple case of institutional pluralism by contrasting the organizational identities of a particular organizational form, specifically three different Christian denominations. Finally, we close the chapter with implications for theory, research, and practice.

INSTITUTIONAL PLURALISM AND OUR COMPLEX SOCIAL WORLD

A quarter century ago, Friedland and Alford argued that modern society is constituted through multiple institutional orders, and their associated logics, that together "shape individual preferences and organizational interests as well as the repertoire of behaviors by which they may attain them" (1991: 232). While they specifically mention how these institutions shape individual preferences, organizational scholars have focused far more on the impact of logics on organizations than on persons (e.g., Thornton, 2004; Thornton, Ocasio, and Lounsbury, 2012). In addition, while there is a long tradition of work that looks at the effects of unitary institutional orders on organizations (e.g., Fox-Wolfgrams, Boal, and Hunt, 1998; Hoffman, 1999; Lounsbury, 2007; Marquis and Lounsbury, 2007; van Wijk et al., 2013) or at the transition from one institutional logic or set of practices to another (e.g., Thornton, 2004; Greenwood and Suddaby, 2006), it is only much more recently that research has interrogated the complex, simultaneous effects of institutional pluralism (e.g., DeJordy et al., 2014; Zilber, 2002) and attended to the ongoing and simultaneous influence of pluralistic institutional prescriptions on institutional inhabitants (e.g., Creed et al., 2010; Kellogg, 2009).

Kraatz and Block define institutional pluralism as "the situation faced by an organization that operates within multiple institutional spheres" (2008: 243). Noting that prior research has already implicitly identified many cases where organizations faced and navigated such pluralism, they set about framing the theoretical and practical implications explicitly. Drawing on Mead (1934), they propose that an organization facing the demands of multiple institutional spheres may develop both multiple institutionally given "identities" and a "self." Pratt and Kraatz extend this work with a systematic translation of Mead's concepts to the organization level. Based in the Median notion of a Multiple Identities Conceptualization of the Self (MICS), they suggest organizations can have multiple "identities." These identities are akin to the "me's" in Mead's work, the one who is identifiable and known; the identity of such a "me" is socially defined through its commitments and through intersubjective verification in a particular social context. Verification of any me (a specific, known identity) at the interpersonal level finds its analog in legitimation conferred upon the organization in institutional contexts. However, Pratt and Kraatz also propose the concept of an "organizational self," an "integrative structure that orders ... various identities and binds them together" into a "hierarchy of identities" that "facilitates the management of identity plurality" (2009: 378, 381). This is akin to what Mead termed the "I"—the one who is knower and actor, who is the subject as opposed to the object of knowing and action. The "I" is the fount of agency.

Importantly, in their discussion of the implications of institutional pluralism, Kraatz and Block draw on Selznick's (1957) early work, noting that:

> some organizations can become institutions *in their own right*, as they harness the otherwise discordant forces in their pluralistic milieu. Selznick argues that such organizations are able to forge identities which are uniquely their own, and which integrate and transcend their various socially given identities.
>
> (Kraatz and Block, 2008: 246, emphasis theirs)

While Selznick originally conceptualized this process as institutionalization (thus, the suggestion that the organization become an institution in its own right), it resonates well with subsequent work on the tripartite enduring/distinctive/central characteristic of organizational identity (Albert and Whetten, 1985): enduring, through being viewed as "an institution in their own right"; distinctive, due to the unique hierarchical ordering and integration of the various socially given identities in a distinctive self; and central, because that pattern orders and transcends the particular set of pressures based on the specific values *infused* into the organization (Selznick, 1957). The implication of this for organizational institutionalism is that, while the organizations are shaped by the pluralistic environments in which they exist, they are not merely social instantiations of supra-organizational patterns of activity structured in terms of particular principles or logics (Greenwood, Raynard, Kodeih, Micelotta, and Lounsbury, 2011). Organizations also provide a social arena where people make sense of, interpret, and ultimately determine how to enact complex institutional prescriptions (Greenwood et al., 2011) as they engage in their personal identity projects. Figure 20.1 represents work in this stream.

As Kraatz and Block (2008) note, the literature tacitly offers significant evidence that organizations can forge unique integrative organizational selves that transcend the institutional constraints of any specific logic, but this capacity has not been the primary focus of research. For example, D'Aunno, Sutton, and Price (1991) find that conflicting demands from two spheres shaped many of the central aspects of drug-abuse treatment centers. The treatment centers internalized two sets of pressures emanating from overlapping spheres in which they operate—specifically the

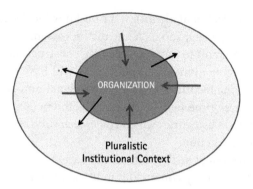

FIGURE 20.1 Organizational identity in a pluralistic institutional context

established mental health sector and the emerging drug-abuse treatment sector. The influence of two spheres reflects a particular form of expectation that Pratt and Kraatz (2009) identify in their work on organizational self and identity processes. They theorize that organizations may internalize multiple distinct sets of socially constructed expectations as "identities," along with the commitments, social bonds, and the context-specific standards that together set the conditions for verification of those identities. Further, they suggest organizations abstract those multiple identities and incumbent expectations into a "generalized other." Here, generalized other refers to an abstracted conceptualization of a unified external audience that serves as the "alter" for the organization's pulling together of its various identities (the knowable me's) into a coherent, agentic, and dynamic self (the I). (See also Pratt, 2012).

   Their argument points to a basic paradox encountered when attempting to integrate institutional theory with organizational identity. The latter is concerned, at least in part, with what is distinctive or unique about an organization (Albert and Whetten, 1985). In contrast, the so-called new institutionalism in organizational analysis sought explicitly to explain observed homogeneity, theorizing it resulted from socio-cultural pressures in the macro-sociological environment, acting on organizations (DiMaggio and Powell, 1983). Organizational isomorphism due to institutional pressures is antithetical to the distinctiveness associated with organizational identity. Glynn offers one approach to synthesis:

> Identities can be bricolaged or cobbled together from shared cultural elements and symbols and it is in this way that they can come to resemble each other. Although there may be shared elements, they are nonetheless combined in fairly unique and distinctive ways.
>
> (Glynn, 2008: 42)

Metaphorically, this is not unlike the DNA that defines biological identity. All DNA comprises the same four nucleic acids, but are put together in innumerable unique combinations. For organizational identities, the building blocks are cultural elements and symbols (Glynn and Abzug, 2002). While distinct assemblages are possible, there is still considerable constraint to any such identity construction. While there are innumerable possible combinations of DNA, species still have distinct genomes. For example, in a study of the identities of 54 environmental non-governmental organizations (ENGOs) in three time periods, Bertels, Hoffman, and DeJordy (2014) consistently find five common categories which coalesce around social position, strategic action, and identity construction.

The distinct "organizational self" (Pratt and Kraatz, 2009) provides a construct at a higher level of abstraction. By comprising multiple identities, each of which exists to meet the requirements of one set of institutional pressures, the organizational self addresses the diverse demands of pluralistic institutional settings. Each identity represents a set of commitments to others and can be subject to separate social verification or legitimation because each adheres to the expectations associated with that particular identity.

According to this stream of work (Kraatz and Block, 2008; Pratt and Kraatz, 2009; Pratt 2012), the paradox of organizations being both distinctive and isomorphic is resolved when, 1) the multiple internalized identities are integrated, and, 2) the commitments and expectations from the pluralistic institutional environment are recast into a generalized other. This allows for the dynamic, distinct, less constrained and more agentic "organizational self." Thus, different organizations may internalize the same forces in different ways, conceiving of the generalized other differently and, consequently, each developing a distinct organizational self, while still having individual constitutive identities which are responsive to and constrained by the demands of the various institutional pressures or logics they face.

This gives us a basis for understanding *how* organizations can escape, or at least bend, the iron cage of their institutional environments. But *why* does an organization adopt or develop the specific organizational self it does? To understand this, we need to look at what needs such a construct serves. Our contention is that, ultimately, organizational identities and the organizational self are "building blocks of meaning" employed by institutional inhabitants in their own identity projects.

INHABITANTS' EXPERIENCES OF INSTITUTIONAL PLURALISM

While most of the work on institutional pluralism focuses on organizational responses, recently work has begun to examine the responses of those inhabiting the institutional milieu. Drawing on the work of Seo and Creed (2002), a subset of research on institutional entrepreneurship focuses on how some individuals leverage the experience of institutional contradictions to effect changes in institutional arrangements. Initially, much of that work cast these institutional entrepreneurs as "hyper muscular change agents" who bend the macro institutional context to their interests (e.g., Greenwood and Suddaby, 2006; Rao, Monin, and Durand, 2003).

More recent work has explored how everyday institutional inhabitants (Hallett and Ventresca, 2006) engage in identity work in response to institutional pluralism and contradictions (Creed et al., 2010; Lok, 2010). Individuals are constantly exposed to a plurality of institutional forces which each prescribe appropriate ways of thinking and being. When these prescriptions conflict, the person experiences a dissonance and engages in work to resolve the contradiction through various forms of institutional work (Lawrence and Suddaby, 2006), including personal identity work which may have implications at higher levels of analysis. Figure 20.2 represents work in this stream.

One example of this is Creed, DeJordy, and Lok's (2010) examination of the identity work undertaken by gay and lesbian ministers in two mainline Protestant denominations who experienced salient contradiction between Christian values of inclusion and a manifest overarching societal heterosexism. This institutional contradiction also affected each denomination's development of a distinct organizational self (evident in divergent policies permitting and precluding LGBT ordination). Their study suggests not only that individual-level identity projects and institutional-level forces act upon each other, but also that organizational identities and selves (manifest in part in denomination policies and practices) are intertwined with personal identity projects (manifest in the LGBT ministers' pursuit of their vocations and denominational commitments) in a recursive fashion as well.

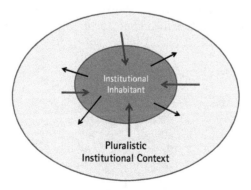

FIGURE 20.2 Personal identity in a pluralistic institutional context

INTERACTION OF ORGANIZATIONAL
IDENTITIES AND SELVES
WITH PERSONAL IDENTITIES

Within the large body of research on the interaction of personal and organizational identity, one stream focuses on how a person's "knowledge of his membership of a social group (or groups)—together with the value and emotional significance attached to that membership"—becomes imbricated in personal identity (Tajfel, 1978: 63). In this literature, organizational membership is examined as a specific case of group membership (Ashforth and Mael, 1989; Corley, Harquail, Pratt, Glynn, Fiol, and Hatch, 2006). For example, Pratt (2000) examines the process by which potential members of Amway come to internalize knowledge of the meanings associated with membership, delineating how candidates construct either positive, negative, or ambivalent identities vis-à-vis the organization. He finds that the link between personal and organizational identity is steeped in the personal experience of meaning and value such that organizational membership (with some exceptions) comes to signal an alignment of individual and organizational values. Membership, at least under conditions of personal choice, signals to both the self and others that the person shares the organization's values and identity claims.

Of course, organizations generally have many members and may make diverse value claims. Just as different organizations can respond to the same mix of institutional expectations by adopting a mix of different identities and forging distinct organizational selves from those identities, different organizational members can perceive and appropriate the organizational self and its associated value claims differently in their personal identity projects. In her study of the Atlanta Symphony Orchestra, Glynn (2000) shows how personal identity shaped organizational constituents' perceptions of organizational identity. Musician and non-musician constituents held different notions of what identities the ASO's organizational self prioritized vis-à-vis the business and artistic domains it faced. In addition, the differences in these groups' constructions of the ASO's organizational self reflected the distinctive demands of their constituents' own personal identity projects.

FIGURE 20.3 Interactions of personal and organizational identities

Further, in their classic study of the New York Port Authority, Dutton and Dukerich (1991), demonstrate how personal identification with the organization becomes integrated into the members' sense of self and self-evaluation, thereby affecting not only their action within the organization, but the organizational self's resolution to various institutional commitments through its varied organizational identities as well. Although the problem of homelessness was originally categorized as outside the functional domain of the Port Authority, organizational members reported being hurt by negative evaluations of the organization's handling of the homeless population in its facilities. Experienced as challenges to their personal character and human values, these evaluations spurred members to take actions that altered their understandings of the concept of professionalism at the heart of the Port Authority's organizational self. Dutton and Dukerich's work links members' sense of identity to actions that both respond to and, importantly, shape the organizational self and its meaning. Work connecting these constructs is depicted in Figure 20.3.

AN INHABITED VIEW OF ORGANIZATIONAL IDENTITY AND ORGANIZATIONAL SELF IN A PLURALISTIC INSTITUTIONAL WORLD

A basic premise of our theorizing is that individuals are embedded in highly complex social contexts that are experienced as pluralistic at all levels of analysis. Figure 20.4 illustrates how the organizational self mediates the relationship between pluralistic institutional environments and members' personal identity projects.

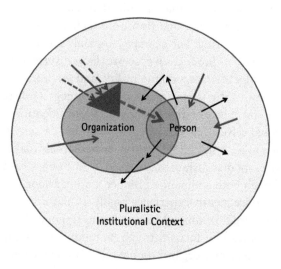

FIGURE 20.4 Composite model of personal and organization identity in a pluralistic institutional environment

We model the pluralistic institutional space as the outermost circle. All the arrows directed inward represent the forces arising from the many societal institutions at play in the particular institutional space. For example, institutional logics associated with the practices of religious faith and scientific inquiry are both at play in the institutional spaces occupied by colleges and research universities with salient religious affiliations (DeJordy et al., 2014). Both the logic of faith and the logic of scientific inquiry may bring normative, coercive, and mimetic pressures to bear on the organizational members of religiously affiliated colleges and universities.

The triangle within the organization represents a "reverse prism" through which an organization consolidates a particular, though not comprehensive, set of institutional pressures into a unified view of such pressures. Reversing the classic image of a prism differentially refracting white light into a rainbow of constituent colors, we conceptualize the organizational self as concentrating the variety of commitments to the pluralistic institutional environment (manifest in the varied organizational identities) into an integrated organizational self that is simultaneously unified (like white light), but still retains the individual identities that comprise it (the constituent spectrum of color), which remain accessible and can be activated as needed. Perhaps a more direct analogy is that of multiplexers used in communication technology, which combines multiple signals for efficient transmission, but without losing the individual signals, which happens when transmitting the video signals for multiple channels over a single cable, yet set-top boxes can still access the individual signals. In both analogies, the demands of institutional complexity is concentrated into a whole, or what Pratt and Kraatz (2009) call a singular "fluid gestalt" that manifests in the organizational self. This process is a form of integration, but not one that creates a unified whole at the expense of individual identities, or even a static hierarchical prioritization of identities, but more as providing an overarching coherence that transcends the composite identities in order to efficiently deal with multiple institutional pressures at once.

Here, Kraatz and Block's insight that organizations facing pluralistic environments "forge identities which ... integrate and transcend their various socially given identities" (2006: 246) bears repeating. For example, arguably any for-profit company that consumes raw materials in its production processes faces diverse institutional pressures relating to market competition, economic utility, and environmental sustainability. However, different organizations may respond to and integrate these pressures differently, facilitating the emergence of different organizational identities and, by extension, distinct organizational selves. For example, Interface Inc., a carpet-tile company renowned for its efforts to become carbon neutral, demonstrably makes stronger identity claims around environmental sustainability (Anderson, 2009; Creed et al., 2014) than Shaw Industries, though both companies produce modular flooring tile products and, theoretically should consequently experience highly similar institutional pressures.

The distinct way an organization understands and responds to a particular mix of institutional forces comes into focus through its unique positioning of constitutive identities, that is, its integrative organizational self. (This is indicated in the figure by the consolidated arrow emerging from the prism and influencing the person at the individual level.) For example, in the case of the Port Authority, society viewed the homelessness problem through diverse lenses, and not just in terms of the institutional logic of the transportation sector (Dutton and Dukerich, 1991). Port Authority employees were unable to resolve the dissonant identity implications of these pluralistic institutional expectations and felt that their families' and friends' judgments of Port Authority's prioritizing of those expectations reflected negatively on their personal identities. Importantly, the shift in the Port Authority's responses shows how the perceived threat to members' personal identity projects can trigger a reconstruction of the organizational self by renegotiating the internal coherence around relevant organizational identities.

We do not suggest the totality of institutional demands experienced by inhabitants is mediated through organizational selves, just that organizational selves are one mechanism by which inhabitants deal with institutional pluralism. We believe this mediation is distinct from and supplemental to the person's direct experience of institutional pluralism and contradiction. For example, Creed and his colleagues (2010) found that while the distinct organizational selves of the two denominations they studied, as manifested in their opposing stances on LGBT ordination, mediated the gay and lesbian ministers' experiences of institutional contradiction to varying degrees, all ministers nonetheless had highly personal and direct experiences of the contradictions between a theology of inclusion and societal heterosexism.

Thus, looking at the effects of macro-to-micro forces, we see institutional pressures exert influence on organizational identity claims, on organizations' integration of distinct identities into organizational selves, and on personal identities. In the case of personal identities, institutional pressures have both direct influence and influence that is mediated through an integrative organizational self. This mix of influences can be seen in what Creed et al. (2010) found to be the later phases of identity work among gay and lesbian ministers. Although all the ministers at first shared direct, personal experiences of the institutional contradiction between their callings and the dominant cultural messages about the ostensible incompatibility of ministry and gay and lesbian identity, in later phases, their identity work reflected their denominations' different identity claims with respect to the institutional pressures regarding Christian teaching, ministry, and sexual orientation. In effect, the denominations' distinct organizational selves, manifested in their different theological positions and denominational policies, mediated the ministers' experience of institutional contradiction in profoundly different ways.

However, taking an inhabited view of institutions, we propose it is not organizations, but persons engaging in their own identity projects who affect the institutional environment. As already discussed, research has shown that personal identity work can operate as a form of institutional work (Creed and Scully, 2000; Creed, Scully, and Austin, 2002) for the disruption of institutions (Rao et al., 2003). Likewise, Dutton and Dukerich (1991) and Elsbach and Kramer (1996) show how attending to personal identity projects affects organizational identity claims and, we would argue, the construction of integrative organizational selves.

Changes to organizational identities and integrative organizational selves are by-products of persons' efforts in and around organizations to make sense of their own identities for themselves and others. Put in the context of existing research, we suggest personal identity projects more congruent with business and market commitments than public service and accounting profession commitments are what motivated the leadership of the big five accounting firms to redefine the field dynamics surrounding public accounting and, importantly, the identities of their firms (Greenwood and Suddaby, 2006). With this insight, we next ask when and why do institutional inhabitants affect change to the identities they construct for organizations?

Organizational Selves: From Stable Solutions to Dynamic Processes

We have argued that an organization's stable integration of organization identities in its organizational self helps resolve the problems posed by institutional pluralism, and that these organizational selves exist to serve organizational members and other constituents in their personal identity projects. We now consider how inhabitants' identities projects and the enactment of organizational identities and integrative organizational selves are interpenetrating processes that are each doubly embedded in both a pluralistic institutional milieu and in person-level symbolic interactions (Hallett and Venteresca, 2006). To better understand efforts to construct and verify an organizational self, it is important to recall our earlier assertion that organizations are arenas "where people and groups make sense of, interpret, and enact institutional prescriptions" (Greenwood et al., 2011: 344). The persons, whether conceived of as members, constituents, or institutional inhabitants, who engage in the verification and reproduction or disconfirmation and change of organizational selves, are at the same time engaged in their own identity projects; their personal projects involve intersubjective processes which likewise entail the construction of selves and the inhabitants' quests for reciprocal ratification or verification of those selves. By applying, as Pratt and Kraatz (2009) propose, the Meadian multiple identities conceptualization of the self (MICS)—a conceptualization that emerged at the person level—simultaneously to organizations, and attending to the complementary nature of and tensions between the organization- and person-level processes, we propose a particular view of the processes of change in organizational identities and organizational selves.

In the MICS perspective, people constructing selves exercise agency in three ways: 1) choosing which roles to internalize and integrate as identities; 2) choosing communities or organizational memberships that increase the likelihood their selves will be verified; and three, choosing among and enacting multiple identities in ways that enable their full engagement in complex societies (Pratt and Kraatz, 2009). We argue that a person's decision to become a member of an organization may be based, at least in part, on his or her perception of the degree to which an organization's organizational self provides a workable way to view and respond to diverse social demands, that is, the demands of the generalized other. According to Meade, "a complete individual self involves understanding, internalizing, and creating an integrative whole out of a myriad of social demands" (Pratt and Kraatz, 2009: 393). That integrative whole is the person's "generalized other," which becomes a kind of avatar or proxy for the attitudes, demands, and desires of the whole community. In an analogous way, organizational members collectively create a generalized other out of a myriad of social demands and then create a commensurate organizational self which is not only a coherent organizational level response to that generalized other, but is also a building block for person-level identity projects to the extent that the organizational self provides the person a coherent solution to a particular set of identity commitment/verification dilemmas. In other words, organizations mediate institutional expectations for constituents through the construction of an organizational self by organizing, making sense of, and integrating pluralistic needs and desires into an abstracted generalized other and then offering responses to that generalized other in ways that enable its members to engage in their own ongoing identity projects of developing more coherent and unified selves.

However, in their translation of MICS to organizations, Praat and Kraatz (2009) emphasize that an organizational self is "a gestalt and fluid structure," that is produced through the organizational constituents' ongoing sensemaking and enactments. In addition, they argue that an organizational self needs to integrate constituents' needs and demands. This is a complex picture of the organizational self: it is simultaneously a resource for members' identity projects and an arena for the symbolic interactions in which those identity projects are embedded and through which identities are claimed, verified or disconfirmed, and ordered into persons' selves. With so much at stake, if the organizational self does not support their identity projects, constituents may change how they participate in its institutionalization and reproduction. The MICS perspective on how persons exercise agency in constructing selves suggests two conditions for their attempting to change constitutive organizational identities and the organizational self. In both conditions, the impetus is the organizational self's negative effect on the person's ongoing identity projects.

First, because people choose communities with an eye for likely verification of the self, if the organization ceases to be an arena where the person is likely to obtain verification of the self, then the person could either look for a more amenable arena or attempt to remediate the organizational self in order to recreate the conditions for personal self-verification. For example, Pradies (2014) found that veterinarians with a mismatch between their professional identities and the orientation of the clinics in which they worked were inclined to seek out other employment to resolve the contradictions. On the other hand, Port Authority employees, hurt by the perceived implications for their own identities, changed the organization's response to the problem (Dutton and Dukerich, 1990). Removing impediments to or changing the conditions for self-verification can entail recasting any of the constitutive organizational identities that are anchored in interpretations of community needs, desires, and prescriptions.

Alternatively, it can entail altering their relative importance or how they cohere with each other in the organizational self.

Second, the MICS perspective suggests that persons choose among and enact multiple identities in order to enable their full engagement in complex societies (Pratt and Kraatz, 2009). If membership in the organization undermines members' enacting of their chosen mix of identities, then members again may exit or attempt to alter the organizational conditions that are inhibiting their choices, enactments, and patterns of engagement in society. This situation could arise when the organizational self integrates and prioritizes its constituent identities unacceptably, for example by constraining or even misdirecting the ways its members can choose roles and integrate them into their personal selves. More simply, it may arise when the organizational self interferes with persons' exercise of agency in their identity projects. The extent to which participation in an organization may interfere with a members' enactment of multiple identities increases as the organization itself more completely mediates the pluralistic institutional environment. Greedy (Coser, 1974) or total (Goffman, 1961) institutions, for example, are enacted through organizations which mediate most, perhaps virtually all, aspects of social life for their members. Yet, in pluralistic institutional milieus, a person's identity project entails the choice, clustering, and prioritizing of roles. The choice of organizational memberships can be instrumental to these tasks if the organizational self provides a solution that coheres with the person's desired or more fully developed self. In contrast, constituents are likely to exit or work for change if the organizational self provides an inadequate solution, one that does not integrate an acceptable mix of pluralist community needs and desires for the purpose of the constituents' identity projects.

For example, at InterFace, the carpet-tile company with a mission of reaching a zero carbon footprint, CEO Ray Anderson's personal identity project evolved, in his words, as he became a "recovering plunderer of the earth." His personal commitments and those of his company had to accommodate simultaneous institutional pressures—from a financial market suspicious of sustainability and insistent on acceptable return on investment, and from a larger community of stakeholders increasingly concerned about climate change and degradation of the biosphere. As his awareness of his personal role in stewardship of the planet shifted, the salience of Ray's various "multiple identities"—CEO, entrepreneur, grandfather, industrial engineer, leader—were reordered in a new sense of self (Creed et al., 2014). Consequently, InterFace's reordered and reprioritized its practices and commitments (Anderson, 2009), forging a new organizational self.

ILLUSTRATING THE MODEL

We have proposed that organizational selves are meaning-making resources comprising multiple organizational identities that respond to institutional expectations and prescriptions. Further, distinct organizational selves are socially constructed precisely because they represent distinct bundles of meaning-making resources for persons' individual identity project needs. This suggests that organizations compete for members who are perpetually engaged in—even preoccupied with—their identity projects (Weick, 1995) in a marketplace of meaning where organizational preferences are determined, at least in part, by how closely the solution manifested in the organizational self matches the potential members' identity project needs.

To illustrate this concept, we consider three different Christian denominations with active memberships in the United States: the Roman Catholic Church (RCC), the United Church of Christ (UCC), and the Presbyterian Church USA (PCUSA). We look at how each of these deals with common, broad-stroke institutional pressures presented by central institutional orders identified by Friedland and Alford (1991)— religion, family, and bureaucracy. For the sake of this example, as a scope condition, we are considering not all people who claim affiliation with these denominations, such as congregants, but rather, only those who enter the organization in formal vocational roles, such as clergy. Also, we will assume that as Christian denominations, they all embrace a religious logic as the primary animating logic of their organizations, and so will not differentiate among them on that basis despite their many theological differences. In terms of how the other institutional orders are prioritized in their organizational selves, we believe there are clear differences.

Perhaps the most salient difference can be seen in the relative positioning in their organizational selves of "religion" and "family" as logics. While the RCC certainly supports many aspects of the institutional logic of the family through, for example, ascribing sacramental status to marriage, Roman Catholics entering the clergy or religious life more broadly must take vows of celibacy, foregoing marriage and its associated familial roles in lieu of service to the RCC. This is not true in either of the other two denominations. There are documented cases of men and women leaving religious life in the RCC as their personal commitments to the religious and the family logics shifted over time. This has taken at least two forms: leaving religious service, but remaining affiliated with the RCC, or converting and entering religious service in another denomination. These both represent forms of organizational exit that, presumably, could ultimately trigger changes in organizational identities and the RCC's organizational self, evident in the growing pressure in some Roman Catholic circles for permitting priests to marry. In contrast, most clergy in UCC and the PCUSA marry and have families.

While the relative primacy of religious logics over the family logic distinguishes Roman Catholicism from the two Protestant mainline denominations we chose, the way the logic of bureaucracy fits into their organizational selves strongly distinguishes them in a different way. For denominations, the logic of bureaucracy is reflected in church governance structures or what is called "ecclesiastical polity." The RCC has what is called an episcopal polity in which bishops have formal authority over sacramental practices and governance in regions of the church known as dioceses. In contrast, the UCC has a congregational polity, where each local congregation is self-governing; is bound together by its own uniquely forged congregational covenant and bylaws; and is free to associate, or not, with other congregations for the pursuit of shared denominational goals. The UCC is itself just such a voluntary association, but it exercises no authority over its member congregations. In short, under Congregational polity, even while in association with other congregations, each individual congregation remains autonomous with respect to all aspects of worship, mission, and operations.

The polity of the Presbyterian Church in the United Status of America (PCUSA) governs through a nested hierarchy of rigorously structured councils composed of clergy and democratically elected lay representatives (elders). While each council has authority over its constituents, the exercise of that authority is meant to be a matter of careful, collective deliberation, which is engaged in only in accordance with the practices and principles articulated in the denomination's constitution, known as the Book of Order. In addition, the decisions of a lower council can be appealed by a member to the next higher-level council, so the councils adjudicate as well as govern. While the PCUSA and the Catholic Church each have hierarchical, territorially centralized governance structures, the Presbyterian polity is arguably the apotheosis of democratic ecclesiastical governance, as seen in its lay participation in governance and in the constitutionalism of the ways in which members, parishes, and Presbyterians can contest interpretations of the Book of Order. In political terms, the Roman Catholic and Presbyterian Churches are arguably far more federalist in nature, with hierarchal authority, while the UCC is essentially a confederacy, based on local decisions to join in fellowship and association.

While traditionally many Christians remained members of the denominations they were brought up in, research on the careers of LGBT ministers suggests that considerations of church polity has figured in clerypersons' decisions to exercise forms of voice and exit in service of their personal identity projects (Creed et al., 2010). For example, during the 1980 and 1990s, many LGBT Protestant seminarians migrated to the UCC because its self-governing polity meant that any congregation that chose to, could call as its pastor a LGBT candidate. Once ordained, UCC clergy were free to officiate at same-sex marriages. In contrast, the PCUSA changed its Book of Order to allow gay and lesbian ordination only in 2011 and its General Assembly voted to permit PCUSA clergy to officiate at same-sex marriages only in 2014.

While our broadbrush treatment of these three denominations and how their organizational selves integrate and prioritize the logics of these central institutional orders does not do justice to the nuance of either the organizations nor the forces represented by these and other societal institutions, we do believe it illustrates how multiple organizations existing within a common, pluralistic institutional realm have adopted distinct organizational selves that uniquely respond to those pressures.

IMPLICATIONS FOR FUTURE RESEARCH

Envisioning organizational identities as "building blocks of meaning" that institutional inhabitants use to simplify the issues of institutional pluralism when engaged in their own identity projects offers several implications for future research on organizational identity.

First, it suggests that the root need organizational selves are created to meet is at the nexus of personal identity and institutional pluralism. Organizational identities are, in methodological terms, a form of data reduction—taking multiple, simultaneous institutional forces with their incumbent demands for commitments and verifications, and creating a gestalt that can be adopted effectively wholesale. Through affiliation, inhabitants convey some, although not necessarily perfect, alignment with the values manifest in the organizational self to both the self and others. Therefore, the construction and integration of organizational identities into organizational selves, and changes in those patterns, can be linked to members' needs in advancing their personal identity projects.

Organizational identity has, at times, been considered an organizational resource, but our model suggests that, ultimately, it is constituents' personal identity projects that drive the construction and reconstruction of organizational identities and selves. This suggests future research could examine the link between how personal identity projects both coalesce around organizational identities and selves and how they effect change. For example, what is the role of power (through elite status or numbers) in determining when and how misalignment between the organizational self and members' personal identity will translate into changes at the organizational level?

Second, we have focused primarily on the role of organizational members' identity projects, but there are additional categories of constituents (suppliers, customers, competitors) who inhabit the same pluralistic institutional context. For example, our model would suggest that for the two largest discount retailers in the United States—WalMart and Costco—employees who choose one organization over the other may do so because of different identity and value claims embedded in organizations' selves. But, we might ask, what about customers who freely choose to shop at one over the other purposefully? What are the implications that would follow from our theorizing for these constituents who are likely to be invested in different ways than organizational members in an organizational self? For example, there has been a rise in interest in socially responsible investing, an approach where investors choose organizations that place societal and environmental outcomes on a more equal footing with financial returns for their investment portfolio. This represents another form of identity alignment that may have different theoretical implications than identity claims associated with a strict membership approach we have focused on in this chapter.

Third, what is the role of personal perceptions in how the organizational self helps the person to address a set of pluralistic institutional demands? Not all members of an organization may agree on how well or even how the organizational self addresses competing demands. In fact, they may not even agree on what demands are, or should be, incorporated into the generalized other vis-à-vis the construction of the organizational self. To what extent does perceived ambiguity, crystallization, or dissent around how an organization selects, orders, prioritizes, and responds to institutional demands affect the way the organizational self arises and changes. The concept of decoupling (Meyer and Rowan, 1977) would suggest that, at a minimum, different constituencies might have different impressions of both the demands faced and the appropriate responses to them. This ambiguity may actually increase the stability of the identities and the organizational self, since it allows different parties to apprehend the organizational self in manners that are subjectively favorable vis-à-vis their own identity projects. For example, in any given university, different faculty members may view the same organization as emphasizing research or teaching in ways that better resonate with their own identities. This "robust" organizational self that can be different things to different people may be more stable and resilient than one that is more precisely delineated.

Finally, while the model suggests that the particular patterning of responses to pluralistic institutional pressures creates a unique organizational self, further inquiry should interrogate how that patterning emerges. What are the strategies for recognizing and satisfying pluralistic demands? An interesting line of inquiry might begin with Oliver's (1991) five strategies for strategic responses to institutional pressures, assessing them in terms of how they affect the integration of organizational identities into an organizational self.

REFERENCES

Albert, S. and Whetten, D. A. (1985). "Organizational Identity." *Research in Organizational Behavior*, vol. 7, edited by L. L. Cummings and B. M. Staw, 263–95. Greenwich, CT: JAI Press.

Anderson, Ray. (2009). *Confessions of a Radical Industrialist: Profits, People, Purpose—Doing Business by Respecting the Earth.* New York: St. Martins Press.

Ashforth, B. E. and Mael, F. (1989). "Social Identity Theory and the Organization." *Academy of Management Review*, 14: 20–39.

Bertels, S., Hoffman, A., and DeJordy, R. (2014). "The Varied Work of Challenger Movements: Identifying Challenger Roles in the US Environmental Movement." *Organization Studies* 35(8): 1171–210.

Corley, K., Harquail, A., Pratt, M., Glynn, M. A., Fiol, C. M., and Hatch, M. J. (2006). "Guiding Organizational Identity through Aged Adolescence." *Journal of Management Inquiry* 15: 85–99.

Coser, L. A. (1974). *Greedy Institutions: Patterns of Undivided Commitment.* New York: Free Press.

Covaleski, M., Dirsmith, M., Heian, J., and Samuel, S. (1998). "The Calculative and the Avowed: Techniques of Discipline and Struggles over Identity in Big Six Public Accounting Firms." *Administrative Science Quarterly* 43: 293–327.

Creed, W. E. D., DeJordy, R., and Lok, J. (2010). "Being the Change: Resolving Institutional Contradiction through Identity Work." *Academy of Management Journal* 56: 1336–64.

Creed, W. E. D., Lok, J., and DeJordy, R. (2014). "Myths to Work by: Redemptive Self-Narratives and Generative Agency for Organizational Change." *Research in the Sociology of Organizations* 41: 111–56.

Creed, W. D., and Scully, M. A. (2000). "Songs of Ourselves: Employees' Deployment of Social Identity." *Journal of Management Inquiry* 9: 391–412.

Creed, W. D., Scully, M. A., and Austin, J. R. (2002). "Clothes Make the Person? The Tailoring of Legitimating Accounts and the Social Construction of Identity." *Organization Science* 13(5): 475–96.

D'Aunno, T., Sutton, R. I., and Price, R. H. (1991). "Isomorphism and External Support in Conflicting Institutional Environments: A Study of Drug Abuse Treatment Units." *Academy of Management Journal* 34: 636–61.

DeJordy, R., Almond, B., Nielsen, R., and Creed, W. E. D. (2014). "Serving Two Masters: Transformative Resolutions to Institutional Contradictions." In *Religion and Organization Theory*, Research in the Sociology of Organizations, vol. 41, edited by P. Tracey, N. Phillips, and M. Lounsbury, 301–47. Bingley: Emerald Group Publishing.

DiMaggio, P. and Powell, W. W. (1983). "The Iron Cage Revisited: Institutional Isomorphism and Collective Rationality in Organizational Fields." *American Sociological Review* 48: 147–60.

Dutton, J. E. and Dukerich, J. M. (1991). "Keeping an Eye on the Mirror: Image and Identity in Organizational Adaptation." *Academy of Management Journal* 34: 517–54.

Elsbach, K. D. and Kramer, R. M. (1996). "Members' Responses to Organizational Identity Threats: Encountering and Countering the *Business Week* Rankings." *Administrative Science Quarterly* 41: 442–76.

Fox-Wolfgramm, S. J., Boal, K. B., and Hunt, J. G. (1998). "Organizational Adaptation to Institutional Change: A Comparative Study of First-Order Change in Prospector and Defender Banks." *Administrative Science Quarterly* 43: 87–126.

Friedland, R. and Alford, R. (1991). "Bringing Society back in: Symbols, Practices, and Institutional Contradictions." In *The New Institutionalism in Organizational Analysis*, edited by P. DiMaggio and W. Powell, 232–63. Chicago: University of Chicago Press.

Gioia, D. A., Patvardhan, S. D., Hamilton, A. L., and Corley, K. G. (2013). "Organizational Identity Formation and Change." *The Academy of Management Annals* 7(1): 123–93.

Glynn, M. A. (2000). "When Cymbals Become Symbols: Conflict over Organizational Identity within a Symphony Orchestra." *Organization Science* 11: 285–98.

Glynn, M. (2008). "Beyond Constraint: How Institutions Enable Identities." In *The SAGE Handbook of Organizational Institutionalism*, edited by R. Greenwood, C. Oliver, K. Sahlin, and R. Suddaby, 413–30. London: SAGE.

Glynn, M. A. and Abzug, R. 2002. "Institutionalizing Identity: Symbolic Isomorphism and Organizational Names." *Academy of Management Journal* 45: 267–80.

Goffman, E. (1961). "On the Characteristics of Total Institutions." In *Symposium on Preventive and Social Psychiatry*, edited by R. K. Cannan, 43–84. Washington, DC: Walter Reed.

Greenwood, R., Raynard, M., Kodeih, F., Micelotta, E. R., and Lounsbury, M. (2011). "Institutional Complexity and Organizational Responses." *The Academy of Management Annals* 5: 317–71.

Greenwood, R. and Suddaby, R. (2006). "Institutional Entrepreneurship in Mature Fields: The Big Five Accounting Firms." *Academy of Management Journal* 49(1): 27–48.

Hallett, T. and Ventresca, M. J. (2006). "Inhabited Institutions: Social Interactions and Organizational Forms in Gouldner's Patterns of Industrial Bureaucracy." *Theory and Society* 35: 213–36.

Hoffman, A. J. (1999). "Institutional Evolution and Change: Environmentalism and the US Chemical Industry." *Academy of Management Journal* 42(4): 351–71.

Kellogg, K. C. (2009). "Operating Room: Relational Spaces and Microinstitutional Change in Surgery." *American Journal of Sociology* 115(3): 657–711.

Kellogg, K. C. (2011). *Challenging Operations: Medical Reform and Resistance in Surgery.* Chicago: University of Chicago Press.

Kraatz, M. and Block, E. (2008). "Organizational Implications of Institutional Pluralism." In *The SAGE Handbook of Organizational Institutionalism*, edited by R. Greenwood, C. Oliver, K. Sahlin, and R. Suddaby, 413–30. London: SAGE.

Lawrence, T. B. and Suddaby, R. (2006). "Institutions and Institutional Work." In *The SAGE Handbook of Organization Studies*, edited by S. Clegg et al., 215–54. London: SAGE.

Lok, J. (2010). "Institutional Logics as Identity Projects." *Academy of Management Journal* 56: 1305–35.

Lounsbury, M. (2007) "A Tale of Two Cities: Competing Logics and Practice Variation in the Professionalizing of Mutual Funds." *Academy of Management Journal* 50(2): 289–307.

Marquis, C. and Lounsbury, M. (2007). "Vive la Résistance: Competing Logics and the Consolidation of US Community Banking." *Academy of Management Journal* 50(4): 799–820.

Mead, G. H. (1934) *Mind, Self, and Society.* Chicago: University of Chicago Press.

Meyer, J. W. and Rowan, B. (1977). "Institutionalized Organizations: Formal Structure as Myth and Ceremony." *American Journal of Sociology* 82: 340–63.

Oliver, C. (1991). "Strategic Responses to Institutional Processes." *Academy of Management Review* 16: 145–79.

Pradies, C. (2014). "Animal Doctors? Rug Sellers? Service Providers? Professionals' Identity Responses to a Regulatory Change Impacting the Nature of a Profession: The Case of French Veterinarians." Unpublished dissertation. Chestnut Hill, MA: Boston College.

Pratt, M. G. (2000). "The Good, the Bad, and the Ambivalent: Managing Identification among Amway Distributors." *Administrative Science Quarterly* 45: 456–93.

Pratt, M. (2012). "Rethinking Identity Construction Processes in Organizations: Three Questions to Consider." In *Constructing Identity in Organizations*, edited by M. Schultz, S. Maguire, A. Langley, and H. Tsoukas, 21–49. New York: Oxford University Press.

Pratt. M. and Kraatz, M. (2009). "E Pluribus Unum: Multiple Identities and the Organizational Self." In *Exploring Positive Identities: Building a Theoretical and Research Foundation*, edited by L. Morgan Roberts and J., Dutton, 385–410. New York: Taylor and Francis.

Rao, H., Monin, P., and Durand, R. (2003). "Institutional Change in Toque Ville: Nouvelle Cuisine as an Identity Movement in French Gastronomy." *American Journal of Sociology* 108: 795–843.

Selznick, P. (1957). *Leadership in Administration: A Sociological Interpretation.* Berkeley, CA: University of California Press.

Seo, M. G. and Creed, W. D. (2002). "Institutional Contradictions, Praxis, and Institutional Change: A Dialectical Perspective." *Academy of Management Review* 27: 222–47.

Tajfel, H. (1978). "Social Categorization, Social Identity and Social Comparison." In *Differentiation between Social Groups: Studies in the Social Psychology of Intergroup Relations*, edited by H. Tajfel, 61–76. London: Academic Press

Thornton, P. H. (2004). *Markets from Culture: Institutional Logics and Organizational Decisions in Higher Education Publishing*. San Francisco, CA: Stanford University Press.

Thornton, P. H., Ocasio, W., and Lounsbury, M. (2012). *The Institutional Logics Perspective: A New Approach to Culture, Structure, and Process*. London: Oxford University Press.

van Wijk, J., Stam, W., Elfring, T., Zietsma, C., and Den Hond, F. (2013). "Activists and Incumbents Tying for Change: The Interplay between Agency, Culture, and Networks in Field Evolution." *Academy of Management Journal* 56(2): 359–86.

Weick, K. (1995). *Sensemaking in Organizations*. Thousand Oaks, CA: SAGE

Zilber, T. B. (2002). "Institutionalization as an Interplay between Actions, Meanings, and Actors: The Case of a Rape Crisis Center in Israel." *Academy of Management Journal* 45(1): 234–54.

....

CHAPTER 21

ORGANIZATIONAL IDENTITY AND INSTITUTIONAL FORCES

toward an integrative framework

....

MARYA L. BESHAROV AND SHELLEY L. BRICKSON

IN today's complex and globalized world, organizations increasingly confront competing demands on their identities—on who they are and, indeed, on who they can be. These tensions stem in part from powerful and divergent external pulls. For example, external audiences increasingly expect for-profit corporations to be socially responsible while also meeting aggressive financial targets (Margolis and Walsh, 2003). Arts organizations encounter growing economic demands to be financially self-sustaining alongside long-standing aesthetic demands for cultural authenticity (Glynn, 2000; Glynn and Lounsbury, 2005). Meanwhile, as external forces grow in complexity and strength, tensions also appear to be mounting between external and internal pulls on organizations' identities. Universities face increasing pressures to operate like commercial businesses while remaining true to the research and teaching missions with which faculty strongly identify (Kraatz, Ventresca, and Deng, 2010; Kraatz and Block, 2008). Similarly, hospitals must compete in the marketplace while also preserving quality of care and advancing medical research, which medical professionals understand as core to their work (Dukerich, Golden, and Shortell, 2002; Reay and Hinings, 2009).

In this chapter, we explore the interplay between these competing tensions on organizational identity (OI). To do so, we first review existing literature on the intersection between OI and institutional forces—defined as the cognitive, normative, or regulative pressures that organizations confront in their external environments (Scott, 2008)—and we distinguish three perspectives. First, much of the OI literature emphasizes its internal determinants, characterizing OI as the product of social construction processes among members who may draw on institutional forces as they craft OI, but who retain substantial agency in doing so (e.g., Gioia,

Price, Hamilton, and Thomas, 2010; Ravasi and Schultz, 2006). Second, the institutional literature emphasizes the external determinants of OI, characterizing it as constructed out of and often highly constrained by institutional logics—the broader cultural value systems that establish the "rules of the game" for particular areas of social life (Thornton, Ocasio, and Lounsbury, 2012). Finally, in both literatures, we observed an alternative perspective that treats OI as a filter influencing how members interpret and respond to institutional forces (e.g., Dutton and Dukerich, 1991; Elsbach and Kramer, 1996; Gioia and Thomas, 1996; Greenwood, Raynard, Kodeih, Micelotta, and Lounsbury, 2011). Each of these perspectives offers valuable insight into the interface between OI and institutional forces. Yet they emphasize different aspects of this relationship. Moreover, there have been relatively few efforts within the OI or institutional literatures to bridge these perspectives (for an exception, see Glynn, 2008).

In the second half of our chapter, we seek to integrate these varied perspectives. To do so, we explore how they can be brought together by means of a distinction between content and structure. We suggest that the first two perspectives in the literature can be understood as referring to the content of OI and institutional forces and as anchoring two endpoints of a continuum. At one end, the content of OI—defined as an organization's central and distinctive attributes that have continuity over time (Albert and Whetten, 1985; Gioia, Patvardhan, Hamilton, and Corley, 2013)—is highly constrained by the content of institutional forces—the values, beliefs, and practices that are taken-for-granted as appropriate within a particular social context. At the other end of the continuum, the content of OI is more strongly influenced by internal forces and members' preferences. We then suggest that the third perspective in the literature can be understood as referring to structural features of OI and institutional forces, which act as filters influencing the extent to which institutional constraint or member agency shape OI. We conclude by considering how these ideas integrate previously disconnected perspectives on the relationship between OI and institutional forces and suggest new directions for future research, thereby building on and expanding scholarly conversations at the intersection of OI and institutional theory (see Glynn, 2008; Kraatz and Block, 2008).

ORGANIZATIONAL IDENTITY
AND INSTITUTIONAL FORCES

We adopt Albert and Whetten's (1985) definition of OI as an organization's central and distinctive characteristics that have continuity over time (see also Gioia, Patvardhan, Hamilton, and Corley, 2013). OI answers the question, "Who are we and what do we do as an organization?" Defined in this way, OI can be understood as influenced by both external and internal forces. Externally, social categories to which organizations belong (e.g., banks, schools) correspond with institutionalized meanings and expectations, consistent with the social actor view of OI (Whetten and Mackey, 2002; Whetten, 2006). Internally, members engage in sensemaking and sensegiving activities (Corley and Gioia, 2004; Gioia and Thomas, 1996) to develop a shared understanding of "who we are and what we do," consistent with the social construction view of OI. While OI research initially treated the social actor and social construction views as incongruous, scholars have recently attempted to integrate them by revealing their interdependent and mutually constitutive nature (Brickson, 2013; Gioia, Price, Hamilton, and Thomas, 2010; Ravasi and Schultz, 2006, see also Gioia and Hamilton, Ch. 1, this volume). We strive to further this effort by helping to reveal the conditions under which organizational members are imbued with greater versus lesser agency to shape OI.

We use the term "institutional forces" to refer to cognitive, normative, or regulative pressures that organizations confront in their external environments (Scott, 2008). They are "external cultural frameworks" (Scott, 2008) that influence the structures, practices, and identities of organizations and their members. To describe the distinct sets of institutional forces that organizations encounter, contemporary institutional scholars frequently draw on the concept of "institutional logics," defined as "socially constructed, historical patterns of material practices, assumptions, values, beliefs and rules" (Thornton and Ocasio, 1999: 804). Logics function as societal-level cultural meaning systems, each one providing a coherent set of organizing principles for a particular realm of social life: family, community, religion, state, market, profession, and corporation (Friedland and Alford, 1991; Thornton, 2004; Thornton, Ocasio, and Lounsbury, 2012). Specific variants or sub-types of these logics may develop within different industries or fields of activity. For example, science and care logics in medical education (Dunn and Jones, 2010) represent field-specific variants of a professional logic.

To understand how scholars have conceptualized the intersection between OI and institutional forces, we reviewed the published literature in both OI and institutional theory, from each field's conceptual foundations to the present. In the institutional literature, we included studies that described institutional forces, pressures, expectations, or demands confronting organizations and impacting their identity, whether or not these studies used the term "logics" to describe these forces. Our review surfaced three broad perspectives on the intersection between OI and institutional forces, which we describe in more detail below.

OI as Agentically Constructed

The first perspective related to the intersection between OI and institutional forces derives from the OI literature. Here, research tends to emphasize insiders' agentic role in constructing, maintaining, or adapting OI meanings. Much of this work highlights how collective understandings of OI are actively negotiated via "sensemaking" and "sensegiving" processes (e.g., Corley and Gioia, 2004; Dutton and Dukerich, 1991; Fiol, 1991; Ravasi and Schultz, 2006). Sensemaking refers to members' retrospective and prospective efforts to interpret reality (Weick, 1995), while sensegiving refers to efforts, often on the part of leaders, to shape members' OI interpretations (e.g., Gioia and Chittipeddi, 1991). One mechanism for these processes includes constructing narratives (Anteby and Molnar, 2012; Chreim, 2005; Sonenshein, 2010). Shared stories, even when "taken off the shelf" from a commonly available external stock, enable members to develop a common identity (Wertsch, 2012: 144). Leaders can also use stories to shift and change OI, for example by deleting and replacing old narratives (Humphreys and Brown, 2002), or by drawing on and reinterpreting stories from the past to construct a desired OI for the future (Schultz and Hernes, 2013). Another mechanism for sensemaking and sensegiving is identity enactment. Enactment of organizational policies and practices in the employment relationship and in external organizational relationships enables members to make sense of who the organization is (Ashforth and Rogers, 2012; Besharov, 2014; Brickson and Ackinlade, 2015; Petriglieri, 2015). Meanwhile, leaders wishing to change members' perceptions engage in internal and external actions designed to engender new interpretations of OI (e.g., Ravasi and Schultz, 2006).

Even as studies in the OI literature tend to foreground the role of members in socially constructing OI, some of this work describes OI as deriving in part from the institutional environment. This idea dates back to Albert and Whetten's (1985) foundational paper, in which they suggest that OI can be understood as a set of claims about an organization's membership in a set of social categories. Whetten and Mackey (2002) more explicitly state that "organizational identity is appropriately conceived of as a set of categorical identity claims (who or what we claim to be, categorically) in reference to a specified set of institutionally standardized social categories" (p. 397). Seen from this perspective, organizations construct their identity by drawing on institutionalized expectations about appropriate types (categories) of organizations and making claims to membership in one or more of these types.

OI studies that attend to the institutional environment often describe institutional forces as inputs into members' interpretive processes—material on which members may selectively draw as they construct OI (e.g., Czarniawska, 1997; Gioia, Price, Hamilton, and Thomas, 2010). For example, in their study of satellite radio, Navis and Glynn (2010) describe how both Sirius and XM initially constructed their identities by emphasizing their membership in the emerging market category, "satellite radio." Later, each differentiated its identity from that of the other through business partnerships and celebrity endorsements, while still retaining sufficient similarity to maintain membership in this overall category. Thus, drawing on institutional forces as building blocks, organizational members construct OI through a sort of "institutional bricolage" (Glynn, 2008). They pull from existing institutional elements so as to enable legitimacy in the external environment, yet they combine these into OI in unique ways, allowing organizations to also attain distinctiveness.

While the satellite radio example involves agreement among actors about the institutional expectations on which to draw, in many cases organizations encounter varied and potentially inconsistent institutional forces. Moreover, members may disagree about which forces are relevant in defining "who we are and what we do." The organization and its members thus confront and debate multiple possible institutional building blocks. Glynn's (2000) research on the Atlanta Symphony Orchestra illustrates this situation. As Glynn and Lounsbury (2005) explain, critics historically evaluated symphony orchestras according to an aesthetic logic. They expected them to be artistic organizations with a mission of producing high-quality musical performances emphasizing eighteenth- and nineteenth-century European repertoire. However, as audiences' tastes changed and concerns about orchestras' exclusivity and elitism mounted, critics started employing a market logic to evaluate orchestras, emphasizing the self-sufficiency and commercial viability of orchestras as economic organizations. Mirroring these two logics, members of the Atlanta Symphony Orchestra differed in their identity claims (Glynn, 2000). Musicians framed the orchestra as an artistic organization, drawing on the aesthetic logic, while administrators positioned it as an economic entity, consistent with the market logic, creating ongoing conflict over how to define OI.

OI as Institutionally Determined

The second perspective on the intersection between OI and institutional forces derives from the institutional literature. While much of the OI literature takes member agency in OI construction as an underlying assumption, the institutional literature generally emphasizes that external forces present in an organization's environment serve as OI constraints, even as it acknowledges the role of individuals in creating, maintaining, and changing institutions (Battilana and D'Aunno, 2009; Battilana, Leca, and Boxenbaum, 2009; Powell and Colyvas, 2008; Seo and Creed, 2002). Early institutional logics studies describe OI as almost entirely determined by the dominant logics in an organization's field or industry. In a study of higher education publishing, for example, Thornton (2002) describes how dominant editorial logics—initially "publishing as a profession" and later "publishing as a business"—influenced changes in publishing-house identities. Glynn and colleagues' research on organizational names as symbols of OI offers another illustration of how institutional forces strongly constrain OI construction. Glynn and Abzug (2002) show that, in changing their names, organizations tended to select those conforming to accepted practices in their institutional environment. Moreover, names that fit the institutionalized template for a particular field were seen as more understandable (Glynn and Abzug, 1998; Glynn and Abzug, 2002), and they enhanced organizational survival (Glynn and Marquis, 2004).

While many institutional studies portray OI as highly constrained by institutional forces present in an organization's environment, scholars have also recognized and examined the role that organizational members, particularly leaders, play in constructing OI by actively drawing on and interpreting institutional forces. This idea has roots in the "old institutional" work of Philip Selznick (1949; 1957). The central focus of Selznick's theory was how organizations, by which he meant formal structures of roles, relationships, and tasks, become transformed into institutions—adaptive social systems that embody the values of their members and of the communities and societies within which they operate. A key part of this process was the development of a distinctive organizational identity or "character" (see Phillips, Tracey, and Kraatz, Ch. 19, this volume). Selznick held that it was the role of leadership to create this identity by interpreting and weaving together the needs and expectations of diverse internal and external constituencies (Selznick, 1957; see also Besharov and Khurana, 2015; Kraatz, 2009). In this sense, Selznick viewed leaders as playing an active role in utilizing institutional building blocks to construct OI.

More recent work elaborates on these ideas. For example, Kraatz and Block (2008; see also Pratt and Foreman, 2000) theorize four possible responses to a pluralistic institutional environment in which different actors hold distinct expectations for the organization, including deleting the identities associated with one or more institutional constituencies, compartmentalizing them, aggregating them, and integrating them into a coherent whole. Battilana and Dorado (2010) illustrate an "integration" approach in their study of the Los Andes microfinance organization. Faced with competing expectations from commercial banking constituencies on the one hand and economic and social development constituencies on the other, Los Andes' leaders integrated these competing expectations into an identity based on operational excellence. Similarly, Christiansen and Lounsbury (2013) describe how members of Carlsberg, a global beer brewer, engaged in "institutional bricolage" to construct an identity around responsible drinking that combined elements of social responsibility and market logics.

In summary, the OI and institutional literatures addressing the intersection between OI and institutional forces often emphasize different things—the role of member agency versus that of institutional constraints on OI construction, respectively. Yet, the idea that insiders actively draw on institutional building blocks in constructing OI is evident in both literatures. We suggest, therefore, that it is fruitful to conceive of these two perspectives, not as completely independent, but as characterizing different points along a continuum representing OI construction, anchored by high member agency at one end and by high institutional constraint at the other.

OI as a Filter

While the first two perspectives might be arrayed along the same continuum of OI agency versus constraint, there is also a distinct third perspective that treats OI as a filter shaping how actors perceive, interpret, and respond to institutional forces. For example, studies show that OI influences how organizations respond to institutional change (Fox-Wolfgramm, Boal, and Hunt, 1998), adopt institutional standards and practices (Czarniawska and Sevón, 1996; Sahlin and Wedlin, 2008), and relate to stakeholders (Brickson, 2005; Brickson, 2007; Scott and Lane, 2000).

To date, most studies in both the OI and institutional literatures have considered one particular aspect of OI that influences its role as a filter—the extent to which the content of OI aligns with the content of the demands arising from the external environment. In both literatures, research suggests that greater alignment between OI content and institutional demands increases members' awareness of and responsiveness to those particular institutional influences. Within the OI literature, this finding dates back to Dutton and Dukerich's (1991) study of the Port Authority. This classic article revealed that members' beliefs about who they were as an organization influenced how they responded to external pressure to address the presence of homeless people in Port Authority facilities. Specifically, when organizational agents viewed the OI as centering on technical competence they addressed the homelessness problem reactively, resisting external pressure. In contrast, when they later came to understand public service as a central element of the Port Authority's OI, they responded to the homelessness problem more proactively. In this way, alignment between members' understandings of the content of the OI and external stakeholders' expectations regarding homelessness led to greater receptivity and responsiveness to the problem. As another example, Elsbach and Kramer (1996) show how members of business schools were more aware of, threatened by, and reactive to external evaluations of their school, as captured in the *Business Week* rankings, when those evaluations directly challenged key elements of their OI.

Similarly, in the institutional literature, scholars have described OI as one of several organizational characteristics that influence how organizations respond to institutional demands (see Greenwood, Raynard, Kodeih, Micelotta, and Lounsbury, 2011). Parallel with the OI literature, research in this domain generally suggests that greater alignment between institutional demands and OI enhances members' awareness of and responsiveness to those demands. As Raffaelli and Glynn (2013) write, drawing on Glynn (2008): "An organization's identity filters perceptions about the relevance and appropriateness of practices; practices that align with the organization's identity are perceived to be more appealing and legitimate." Consistent with this argument, Raffaelli and Glynn (2013) find that firms whose identities included a commitment to social and environmental issues were more likely to adopt customized volunteering practices prescribed by industry and professional associations, compared to firms without such a commitment. In another example, Kodeih and Greenwood (2013) describe how French business schools' current and aspired future OIs influenced the way they responded to external pressure to offer a more internationalized form of management education based on the model dominant in North America. Schools that aspired to become more international and raise their status embraced the external pressure as an opportunity to achieve a desired identity.

While most studies addressing the role of OI as a filter consider alignment between OI content and institutional demands, some work has begun to consider how other aspects of OI influence the extent to which members interpret and enact institutional forces. For example, Pratt and Kraatz (2009) and Kraatz and Block (2008) suggest that a coherent and integrated OI provides a means of interpreting and prioritizing competing institutional demands. In contrast, a fractured and multi-faceted OI leads members to disagree about the nature of the organization's central, enduring, and distinct features, creating divergent interpretations of institutional forces. Focusing on a different aspect of OI, Milliken (1990) found that OI "strength" led universities to be less concerned about demographic changes in the environment. Gioia and Thomas's (1996) study of strategic decision-making in universities modified this argument, showing that OI strength can lead a school to be *more* open and responsive to changes in the external environment, but that responsiveness also depends whether the OI is normative (i.e., focused on ideological and value-based concerns) or utilitarian (i.e., focused on economic factors). Strong identities, especially those of the utilitarian type, led schools to view environmental changes as strategic opportunities.

As this discussion suggests, different aspects of OI seem to have distinct implications for how members attend to and interpret institutional demands. While alignment between OI and institutional demands increases members' level of attention to and responsiveness toward institutional demands, allowing those demands to penetrate the organization relatively directly, other aspects of OI, such as integration and strength, seem to create more opportunities for members to actively interpret and modify institutional demands. In the next section we build on these ideas to suggest how structural features of OI can act as a filter influencing the extent to which the content of OI is constrained by institutional forces or more agentically constructed by organizational members.

INTEGRATION AND AVENUES FOR FUTURE DEVELOPMENT

We propose that the three perspectives described above can be integrated by distinguishing content-based as opposed to structure-based aspects of OI and institutional forces. We elaborate on this idea in the next section, and then suggest how it can be further developed in future research.

Integrating Perspectives by Disentangling Content and Structure

By "content," we mean the substance of OI and institutional forces. Specifically, OI content refers to the attributes that answer the question, "Who are we and what do we do as an organization?" Statements such as "we are a community bank," "we are a family business," "we are the best," or "we are caring," all describe OI content. OI content is important because it offers a blueprint for organizational action, outlining the goals and values that guide organizing efforts (Ashforth and Mael, 1996; Brickson and

Lemmon, 2009). For example, organizations that define themselves in terms of being "the best" organize very differently from those centered on being "caring" (Brickson, 2007; Brickson and Ackinlade, 2015).

Similarly, the content of institutional forces refers to the substance of the demands they impose on organizations. In the language of institutional logics, each logic is built around a distinct "root metaphor" and implies a particular type of legitimacy, strategy, identity, control mechanism, and so on (see Thornton, 2004; Thornton, Ocasio, and Lounsbury, 2012). For example, the emerging field of social enterprise is governed by two logics with markedly different content. The market logic prescribes a for-profit organizational form and the use of hired professionals to maximize efficiency, whereas the social welfare logic prescribes a non-profit organizational form and the use of volunteers to benefit from their deep commitment to a social mission (Pache and Santos, 2013).

The first two perspectives regarding the interface between OI and institutional forces, which treat OI as agentically constructed by organizational members or as more highly constrained by institutional forces, respectively, can be understood as referring primarily to the content of OI and the content of institutional forces. As we noted previously, rather than being seen as oppositional, these perspectives represent the endpoints of a continuum that describes the role of institutional content in the construction of OI content. At one end, organizational members actively interpret, enact, and recombine institutional content in a process of institutional bricolage. Here, institutional logics serve as a cultural toolkit (Swidler, 1986) on which actors may choose to draw, and which they may strategically manipulate, as they construct organizational identities. At the other end of the continuum, institutional forces salient in the external environment largely constrain OI content. Here, dominant institutional logics have considerable power to shape cognition and action, and OI content tends to reflect their prescriptions. In Figure 21.1, the two shaded shapes depict the content of OI and institutional forces. The shape representing OI content is characterized as a double-sided arrow reflecting the continuum between agency and constraint in OI construction.

By "structure," we mean the relationship or nature of the interplay between different content elements. Research adopting the third perspective we have outlined, which treats OI as a filter, suggests that the alignment between OI content and institutional content is a particularly important aspect of structure. Alignment can be characterized as high when an organization's central, enduring, and distinctive characteristics correspond to and are consistent with the institutional demands and expectations present in the external environment. For example, non-profit organizations face increasing external pressure to incorporate market demands and business-like practices in addition to their traditional charitable focus (Hwang and Powell, 2009). In this context, non-profits whose identities include both utilitarian (i.e., economic) and normative (i.e. ideological, value-based) components would have relatively high alignment, whereas those whose identity content is primarily normative in nature would have lower alignment.

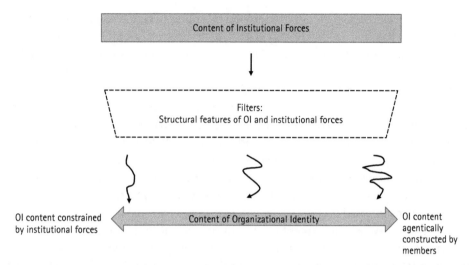

FIGURE 21.1 The filtering role of OI and institutional structure in influencing how institutional forces shape OI content

Building on the third perspective we outlined, we suggest this structural feature of OI and institutional forces can be understood as a filter influencing where along the agency/constraint continuum OI construction falls. Specifically, when the content of OI is aligned with the content of institutional forces, members tend to be more responsive to those forces (e.g., Dutton and Dukerich, 1991; Elsbach and Kramer, 1996; Gioia and Thomas, 1996) and are therefore more likely to incorporate them into OI. In this way, alignment with external forces reduces opportunities for novel interpretations in OI construction, shifting organizations toward the constraint end of the continuum. This filtering role is depicted in Figure 21.1 by the dotted-line shape and the arrows below it. The arrows become more distorted as one moves from left to right across the figure, indicating greater member agency in interpreting institutional content when constructing OI content.

Future Research Avenues: The Role of Additional Structural Filters

While existing research tends to focus on alignment between OI content and institutional content as an important aspect of structure, there are hints in the literature that other aspects of structure may also act as filters influencing where along the agency/constraint continuum OI construction falls. In particular, we believe it would be fruitful for future research to explore the internal alignment between OI content and the content of members' self-identities, the relationship among different elements of OI content, and the relationship among different elements of institutional content.

The concept of internal alignment between OI content and the content of members' self-identities has not been explicitly discussed in past research on the intersection between OI and institutional forces. However, it may offer a way of understanding the studies we described previously, which point to identity "strength" as an important dimension influencing members' responsiveness to external pressures (Gioia and Thomas, 1996; Milliken, 1990). OI strength has been defined in different ways, recently as the extent to which identity beliefs are widely shared and densely articulated among members (Ashforth, Harrison, and Corley, 2008). Stronger OIs are associated with greater organizational identification, which is often operationalized as overlap between the content elements that define the OI and those that define members' self-identities (Ashforth, Harrison, and Corley, 2008; Pratt, 1998; cf. Brickson, 2013). We refer to this as internal alignment, in contrast to the external alignment that arises from overlap between the content of OI and the content of institutional forces. The concept of internal alignment may help researchers explain mixed findings about the influence of OI strength on members' responsiveness to institutional forces (Gioia and Thomas, 1996; Milliken, 1990). In particular, studies could explore how and under what conditions an internally aligned OI makes members more or less likely to incorporate institutional forces in constructing OI content. For example, when members' own identities are strongly aligned with the OI, are they less open to external ideas due to their greater investment in existing OI content?

A second set of structural features that we believe merits further attention concerns the relationship among different elements of OI content—that is, the structure of OI itself. This relationship can be described in various potentially fruitful ways, including the number of different identities or identity attributes, their degree of compatibility, and their level of integration. Regarding the first of these possibilities, many organizations have multiple sets of central and distinctive features that endure over time (Albert and Whetten, 1985; Cheney, 1991). Pratt and Foreman (2000) use the term "plurality" to describe this aspect of OI structure. Plurality could refer to multiple categorical claims, as in the case of family businesses or religious universities that are situated in two distinct social categories. Alternatively, plurality could refer to multiple identity attributes, as in Dukerich, Golden, and Shortell's (2002) study of healthcare organizations, where physicians mentioned 37 distinct identity attributes when asked to describe their organization's identity.

A second possible way to conceptualize the relationship between different elements of OI content is in terms of compatibility, understood as the extent to which multiple identities or identity attributes are mutually consistent and reinforcing. Some research treats compatibility as an objective feature. For example, studies depict cooperatives (Ashforth and Reingen, 2014; Foreman and Whetten, 2002), universities (Albert and Whetten, 1985), and arts organizations (Glynn, 2000) as having relatively incompatible identities because they are simultaneously normative organizations pursuing cultural, educational, or expressive values as well as utilitarian organizations pursuing economic values. In contrast, research adopting a social construction perspective tends to treat compatibility as subjective, arising through members' negotiated understandings of the meaning of different identity labels (e.g., Corley and Gioia, 2004).

Yet another way in which the relationship between different elements of OI content could be described is in terms of integration, or the extent to which content elements are combined into a single, overarching identity or "organizational self" (Pratt and Kraatz, 2009), versus being compartmentalized and separated from one another. An integrated OI may retain multiple distinct facets, but they form a coherent whole and are embodied in unified structures and practices. In a family business, for example, being a family and being a business are often deeply intertwined within the organization's operations and core work activities, with family members occupying key leadership positions (Whetten, Foreman, and Dyer, 2014). Understood in this way, organizations high on integration might be considered "holographic" identity hybrids, whereas those low on integration might be deemed "ideographic" identity hybrids (Albert and Whetten, 1985).

Future research can examine these and other structural features of OI and their possible role as filters influencing the extent to which OI content is actively constructed by members or highly constrained by institutional content. As conceptualized here, plurality, compatibility, and integration of OI likely imply greater opportunities for member agency in constructing OI. For example, when the multiple attributes that comprise OI are highly integrated, this provides members with a single, unified lens through which to interpret institutional forces (see Kraatz and Block, 2008; Pratt and Kraatz, 2009), making it less likely that institutional forces will directly penetrate the organization and creating space for greater member agency in the construction of OI content. Yet other dimensions of OI structure could work the other way, increasing constraints on OI construction.

Finally, we encourage researchers to examine structural properties of institutional forces and the role they may play as a filter between the content of institutional forces and the content of OI. Just as the structure of OI can be described in terms of plurality, compatibility, and integration, so too might the structure of institutional forces. First, there can be one or multiple distinct institutional logics present in an organization's environment, creating variation in the plurality of institutional forces. For example, because they explicitly pursue social missions through commercial ventures, social enterprises confront both a market logic and a social welfare logic (Battilana and Lee, 2014; Smith, Gonin, and Besharov, 2013). In contrast, traditional entrepreneurial ventures typically confront just one primary logic, that of the market. Second, as with OI, institutional forces can differ in their degree of compatibility, or the extent to which distinct logics imply consistent and reinforcing organizational actions (Besharov and Smith, 2014). For example, Greenwood and colleagues' (2010) study of Spanish manufacturing firms suggests compatibility between religious and family logics, both of which proscribed organizational downsizing, yet incompatibility between these two logics and a market logic, under which downsizing was considered appropriate.

Third, like OI, institutional forces may differ in their degree of integration, which can be understood as the extent to which multiple logics are combined into a single blended logic or remain distinct and structurally separated. In the field of social enterprise, for example, professional institutions that train individuals to become social entrepreneurs initially represented either the market logic (e.g., business schools) or the social welfare logic (e.g., social work schools), creating a low degree of integration. As the field has developed, however, professional institutions such as Ashoka and the Schwab Foundation for Social Entrepreneurship started to combine market and social welfare logics, creating greater integration. There has also been a shift in legal institutions. While there remain distinct legal forms for businesses and charities, social enterprises can now adopt an integrated legal form such as the Benefit Corporation in the US and the Community Interest Company in the UK, which require the pursuit of both financial profits and a social mission (Haigh, Kennedy, and Walker, 2015).

Opportunities abound for future research to explore these structural properties of institutional forces and their filtering role in affecting how and to what extent organizational members actively interpret institutional demands as they construct OI content. For example, when the plurality of institutional forces is high, this may create greater opportunities for agency, because organizational members can pick and choose among multiple logics present in the environment (Seo and Creed, 2002). However, when these multiple logics offer relatively consistent and unified prescriptions for OI content, as would occur with high compatibility or high integration, this may reduce opportunities for members to agentically combine logics in novel ways, as there is less opportunity for different interpretations to surface among members. Meanwhile, other structural features of institutional forces may create greater constraints on OI construction.

CONCLUSION

In this chapter, we sought to both integrate extant work and suggest avenues for future research exploring the interface between OI and institutional forces. Distinguishing the content of OI and institutional forces from their structural features enabled us to bring together three existing perspectives in the literature. We described how the process of OI construction can be understood as varying along a continuum that reflects the extent to which organizational members have agency to craft an OI based on their interests and beliefs or are more constrained to enacting an OI that is strongly shaped by institutional forces. We further suggested that the location of an organization along this continuum may depend in part on structural features of OI and institutional forces, which act as filters influencing the extent to which agency is possible. While existing work implicitly highlights the relevance of one structural filter—alignment between the content of OI and that of institutional demands—we described how future research could examine additional structural features that may act as filters.

In conclusion, we want to highlight several theoretical and practical implications of our approach to understanding the intersection of OI and institutional forces. First, our approach suggests a need to disentangle content from structure, both when studying OI and when studying the institutional environment. OIs convey content-based information—about the organization's goals, values, beliefs, practices, and so on. Yet even organizations with similar identity content can differ in terms of the structural features of their identity—such as the extent to which OI content involves more than one set of central, enduring, and distinctive features, the compatibility between these features, their degree of integration, and the extent to which they are aligned with the content of institutional forces. Similarly, institutional forces convey specific content—prescriptions regarding appropriate organizational strategies, structures, and identities. At the same time, any particular institutional context can be described in structural terms—such as the number of logics present and their degree of integration and compatibility.

The divergent perspectives in the literature about the intersection between OI and institutional forces may stem in part from a lack of clarity about which aspects of OI and institutional forces are being described—their content or their structural features. Our chapter suggests that both content and structure matter, but in different ways. The content of the forces present in an organization's environment may influence the content of OI, while the structure of OI and institutional forces can help explain to what extent and how this occurs. Thus, to fully explain the interface between OI and institutional forces, future research will need to attend to content *and* structure, not just one or the other. Our chapter also creates opportunities for future research to examine *how* specific structural features may act as filters influencing the relationship between OI content and institutional content. We suggested a few structural features that may influence this intersection, and we encourage future research to explore in greater depth how they might do so, as well as to examine other structural features that may be important.

Second, beyond its relevance to researchers, our chapter also has implications for practicing managers. While OI is commonly understood as relevant to managers because it offers a solution to internal problems, our framework suggests it may offer a solution to external problems as well. When organizational members have greater agency to construct OI, they can interpret and recombine institutional forces in a way that enables them to accommodate multiple and potentially competing external demands. Moreover, our discussion of the filtering role of OI structure lends insight into what determines members' interpretations, and can thereby aid leaders in more effectively managing these interpretations. For example, inconsistent and fragmented interpretations may arise when OI involves incompatible elements that are not integrated into a coherent whole. By implication, leaders could foster more consistent and uniform interpretations by increasing compatibility and integration. In these and other ways, our chapter provides a foundation for both researchers and managers seeking to better understand and address the intersection of OI and institutional forces.

REFERENCES

Albert, S. and Whetten, D. A. (1985). "Organizational Identity." In *Research in Organizational Behavior*," vol. 7, edited by L. L. Cummings and B. M. Staw, 263–95. Greenwich, CT: JAI Press.

Anteby, M. and Molnar, V. (2012). "Collective Memory Meets Organizational Identity: Remembering to Forget in a Firm's Rhetorical History." *Academy of Management Journal* 55(3): 515–40.

Ashforth, B. E., Harrison, S. H., and Corley, K. G. (2008). "Identification in Organizations: An Examination of Four Fundamental Questions." *Journal of Management* 34(3): 325–74.

Ashforth, B. E., and Mael, F. (1996). "Organizational Identity and Strategy as a Context for the Individual." *Advances in Strategic Management* 13: 19–64.

Ashforth, B. E., and Reingen, P. H. (2014). "Functions of Dysfunction: Managing the Dynamics of an Organizational Duality in a Natural Food Cooperative." *Administrative Science Quarterly* 59(3): 474–516.

Ashforth, B. and Rogers, K. (2012). "Is the Employee–Organization Relationship Misspecified? The Centrality of Tribes in Experiencing the Organization." In *The Employee-Organization Relationship*, edited by L. M. Shore, J. A.-M. Coyle-Shapiro, and L. E. Tetrik, 23–53. Philadelphia, PA: Taylor & Francis.

Battilana, J. and D'Aunno, T. (2009). "Institutional Work and the Paradox of Embedded Agency." In *Institutional Work: Actors and Agency in Institutional Studies of Organizations*, edited by T. B. Lawrence, R. Suddaby, and B. Leca, 31–58. Cambridge: Cambridge University Press.

Battilana, J. and Dorado, S. (2010). "Building Sustainable Hybrid Organizations: The Case of Commercial Microfinance Organizations." *Academy of Management Journal* 53(6): 1419–40.

Battilana, J., Leca, B., and Boxenbaum, E. (2009). "How Actors Change Institutions: Towards a Theory of Institutional Entrepreneurship." *The Academy of Management Annals*, 3: 65–107.

Battilana, J. and Lee, M. (2014). "Advancing Research on Hybrid Organizing: Insights from the Study of Social Enterprises." *The Academy of Management Annals* 8(1): 397–441.

Besharov, M. L. (2014). "The Relational Ecology of Identification: How Organizational Identification Emerges when Individuals Hold Divergent Values." *Academy of Management Journal* 57(5): 1485–512.

Besharov, M. L. and Khurana, R. (2015). "Leading amidst Competing Technical and Institutional Demands: Revisiting Selznick's Conception of Leadership." In *Research in the Sociology of Organizations*, vol. 44, edited by M. S. Kraatz, 53–8. Bingley: Emerald Group Publishing.

Besharov, M. L. and Smith, W. K. (2014). "Multiple Institutional Logics in Organizations: Explaining their Varied Nature and Implications." *Academy of Management Review* 39(3): 364–81.

Brickson, S. L. (2005). "Organizational Identity Orientation: Forging a Link between Organizational Identity and Organizations' Relations with Stakeholders." *Administrative Science Quarterly* 50(4): 576–609.

Brickson, S. L. (2007). "Organizational Identity Orientation: The Genesis of the Role of the Firm and Distinct Forms of Social Value." *Academy of Management Review* 32(3): 864–88.

Brickson, S. L. (2013). "Athletes, Best Friends, and Social Activists: An Integrative Model Accounting for the Role of Identity in Organizational Identification." *Organization Science* 24: 226–45.

Brickson, S. L. and Ackinlade, D. (2015). *Organizations as Internal Value Creators: The Role of Organizational Identity in Shaping Resource Generation* (Working Paper ed.). Chicago: University of Illinois Chicago.

Brickson, S. L. and Lemmon, G. (2009). "Organizational Identity as a Stakeholder Resource." In *Exploring Positive Identities and Organizations: Building a Theoretical and Research Foundation*, edited by J. E. Dutton and L. M. Roberts, 411–34. New York: Psychology Press.

Cheney, G. (1991). *Rhetoric in an Organizational Society: Managing Multiple Identities.* Columbia, SC: University of South Carolina Press.

Chreim, S. (2005). "The Continuity–Change Duality in Narrative Texts of Organizational Identity." *Journal of Management Studies*, 42(3): 567–93.

Christiansen, L. H. and Lounsbury, M. (2013). "Strange Brew: Bridging Logics via Institutional Bricolage and the Reconstitution of Organizational Identity." *Research in the Sociology of Organizations* 39: 199–232.

Corley, K. G. and Gioia, D. A. (2004). "Identity Ambiguity and Change in the Wake of a Corporate Spin-Off." *Administrative Science Quarterly* 49(2): 173–208.

Czarniawska, B. (1997). *Narrating the Organization: Dramas of Institutional Identity.* Chicago: University of Chicago Press.

Czarniawska, B. and Sevón, G. (1996). *Translating Organizational Change.* Berlin: Walter de Gruyter.

Dukerich, J. M., Golden, B. R., and Shortell, S. M. (2002). "Beauty Is in the Eye of the Beholder: The Impact of Organizational Identification, Identity, and Image on the Cooperative Behaviors of Physicians." *Administrative Science Quarterly* 47(3): 507–33.

Dunn, M. B. and Jones, C. (2010). "Institutional Logics and Institutional Pluralism: The Contestation of Care and Science Logics in Medical Education, 1967–2005." *Administrative Science Quarterly* 55(1): 114–49.

Dutton, J. E. and Dukerich, J. M. (1991). "Keeping an Eye on the Mirror: Image and Identity in Organizational Adaptation." *The Academy of Management Journal* 34(3): 517–54.

Elsbach, K. D. and Kramer, R. M. (1996). "Members' Responses to Organizational Identity Threats: Encountering and Countering the *Business Week* Rankings." *Administrative Science Quarterly* 41(3): 442–76.

Fiol, C. M. (1991). "Managing Culture as a Competitive Resource: An Identity-Based View of Sustainable Competitive Advantage." *Journal of Management* 17(1): 191–211.

Fiol, C. M. (2002). "Capitalizing on Paradox: The Role of Language in Transforming Organizational Identities." *Organization Science* 13(6): 653–66.

Foreman, P. and Whetten, D. A. (2002). "Members' Identification with Multiple-Identity Organizations." *Organization Science* 13(6): 618–35.

Fox-Wolfgramm, S. J., Boal, K. B., and Hunt, J. G. (1998). "Organizational Adaptation to Institutional Change: A Comparative Study of First-Order Change in Prospector and Defender Banks." *Administrative Science Quarterly* 43(1): 87–126.

Friedland, R. and Alford, R. R. (1991). "Bringing Society back in: Symbols, Practices and Institutional Contradictions." In *The New Institutionalism in Organizational Analysis*, edited by W. W. Powell and P. J. DiMaggio, 232–63. Chicago: University of Chicago Press.

Gioia, D. A. and Chittipeddi, K. (1991). "Sensemaking and Sensegiving in Strategic Change Initiation." *Strategic Management Journal* 12: 433–48.

Gioia, D. A. and Hamilton, A. L. (2016). "Great Debates in Organizational Identity Study." In *The Oxford Handbook of Organizational Identity*, edited by M. G. Pratt, M. Schultz, B. E. Ashforth, and D. Ravasi, 21–38. Oxford: Oxford University Press.

Gioia, D. A., Patvardhan, S. D., Hamilton, A. L., and Corley, K. G. (2013). "Organizational Identity Formation and Change." *The Academy of Management Annals* 7(1): 123–92.

Gioia, D. A., Price, K. N., Hamilton, A. L., and Thomas, J. B. (2010). "Forging an Identity: An Insider-Outsider Study of Processes Involved in the Formation of Organizational Identity." *Administrative Science Quarterly* 55(1): 1–46.

Gioia, D. A. and Thomas, J. B. (1996). "Identity, Image, and Issue Interpretation: Sensemaking during Strategic Change in Academia." *Administrative Science Quarterly* 41(3): 370–403.

Glynn, M. A. (2000). "When Cymbals Become Symbols: Conflict over Organizational Identity within a Symphony Orchestra." *Organization Science* 11(3): 285–98.

Glynn, M. A. (2008). "Institutions and Identity Theory." In *The SAGE Handbook of Institutional Theory*, edited by R. Greenwood, C. Oliver, R. Suddaby, and K. Sahlin-Andersson, 413–30. Thousand Oaks, CA: SAGE.

Glynn, M. A. and Abzug, R. (1998). "Isomorphism and Competitive Differentiation in the Organizational Name Game." *Advances in Strategic Management* 15: 105–28.

Glynn, M. A. and Abzug, R. (2002). "Institutionalizing Identity: Symbolic Isomorphism and Organizational Names." *Academy of Management Journal* 45(1): 267–80.

Glynn, M. A. and Lounsbury, M. (2005). "From the Critics' Corner: Logic Blending, Discursive Change and Authenticity in a Cultural Production System." *Journal of Management Studies* 42(5): 1031–55.

Glynn, M. A. and Marquis, C. (2004). "When Good Names Go Bad: Symbolic Illegitimacy in Organizations." In *Research in the Sociology of Organizations*, vol. 22, edited by C. Johnson, 147–70. Bingley: Emerald Group Publishing.

Greenwood, R., Díaz, A. M., Li, S. X., and Lorente, J. C. (2010). "The Multiplicity of Institutional Logics and the Heterogeneity of Organizational Responses." *Organization Science* 21(2): 521–39.

Greenwood, R., Raynard, M., Kodeih, F., Micelotta, E. R., and Lounsbury, M. (2011). "Institutional Complexity and Organizational Responses." *The Academy of Management Annals* 5(1): 317–71.

Haigh, N., Kennedy, E. D., and Walker, J. (2015). "Hybrid Organizations as Shape-Shifters: Altering Legal Structure for Strategic Gain." *California Management Review* 57(3): 59–82.

Humphreys, M. and Brown, A. D. (2002). "Narratives of Organizational Identity and Identification: A Case Study of Hegemony and Resistance." *Organization Studies* 23: 421–47.

Hwang, H. and Powell, W. W. (2009). "The Rationalization of Charity: The Influences of Professionalism in the Nonprofit Sector." *Administrative Science Quarterly* 54(2): 268–98.

Kodeih, F. and Greenwood, R. (2013). "Responding to Institutional Complexity: The Role of Identity." *Organization Studies* 35: 7–39.

Kraatz, M. S. (2009). "Leadership as Institutional Work: A Bridge to the Other Side." In *Institutional Work: Actors and Agency in Institutional Studies of Organizations*, edited by T. B. Lawrence, R. Suddaby, and B. Leca, 59–91. New York: Cambridge University Press.

Kraatz, M. and Block, E. (2008). "Organizational Implications of Institutional Pluralism." In *The SAGE Handbook of Organizational Institutionalism*, edited by R. Greenwood, C. Oliver, R. Suddaby, and K. Sahlin-Andersson, 243–75. London: SAGE.

Kraatz, M. S., Ventresca, M. J., and Deng, L. (2010). "Precarious Values and Mundane Innovations: Enrollment Management in American Liberal Arts Colleges." *Academy of Management Journal* 53(6): 1521–45.

Margolis, J. D. and Walsh, J. P. (2003). "Misery Loves Companies: Rethinking Social Initiatives by Business." *Administrative Science Quarterly* 48(2): 268–305.

Milliken, F. J. (1990). "Perceiving and Interpreting Environmental Change: An Examination of College Administrators' Interpretation of Changing Demographics." *Academy of Management Journal* 33(1): 42–63.

Navis, C. and Glynn, M. A. (2010). "How New Market Categories Emerge: Temporal Dynamics of Legitimacy, Identity, and Entrepreneurship in Satellite Radio, 1990-2005." *Administrative Science Quarterly* 55(3): 439–71.

Pache, A. and Santos, F. (2013). "Inside the Hybrid Organization: Selective Coupling as a Response to Competing Institutional Logics." *Academy of Management Journal* 56(4): 972–1001.

Petriglieri, J. (2015). "Co-creating Relationship Repair: Pathways to Reconstructing Destablilized Organizational Identification." *Administrative Science Quarterly* 60(3): 518–57.

Phillips, N., Tracey, P., and Kraatz, M. (2016). "Organizational Identity in Institutional Theory: Taking Stock and Moving Forward." In *The Oxford Handbook of Organizational Identity*, edited by M. G. Pratt, M. Schultz, B. E. Ashforth, and D. Ravasi, 353–73. Oxford: Oxford University Press.

Powell, W., and Colyvas, J. (2008). "Microfoundations of Institutional Theory." In *The SAGE Handbook of Organizational Institutionalism*, edited by R. Greenwood, C. Oliver, K. Sahlin, and R. Suddaby, 276–98. London: SAGE.

Pratt, M. G. (1998). "To Be or Not to Be: Central Questions in Organizational Identification." In *Identity in Organizations: Building Theory through Conversations*, edited by D. A. Whetten and P. C. Godfrey, 171–207. Thousand Oaks, CA: SAGE.

Pratt, M. G. and Foreman, P. O. (2000). "Classifying Managerial Responses to Multiple Organizational Identities." *Academy of Management Review* 25(1): 18–42.

Pratt, M. G. and Kraatz, M. S. (2009). "E Pluribus Unum: Multiple Identities and the Organizational Self." In *Exploring Positive Identities and Organizations: Building a Theoretical and Research Foundation*, edited by L. M. Roberts and J. E. Dutton, 385–410. New York: Psychology Press.

Raffaelli, R. and Glynn, M. A. (2013). "Turnkey or Tailored? Relational Pluralism: Institutional Complexity, and the Organizational Adoption of More or Less Customized Practices." *Academy of Management Journal* 57(2): 541–62.

Ravasi, D. and Schultz, M. (2006). "Responding to Organizational Identity Threats: Exploring the Role of Organizational Culture." *Academy of Management Journal* 49(3): 433–58.

Reay, T., and Hinings, C. R. (2009). "Managing the Rivalry of Competing Institutional Logics." *Organization Studies* 30(6): 629–52.

Sahlin, K. and Wedlin, L. (2008). "Circulating Ideas: Imitation, Translation and Editing." *The Sage Handbook of Organizational Institutionalism*, edited by R. Greenwood, C. Oliver, K. Sahlin, and R. Suddaby, 218–42. Thousand Oaks, CA: SAGE.

Scott, S. G. and Lane, V. R. (2000). "A Stakeholder Approach to Organizational Identity." *The Academy of Management Review* 25(1): 43–62.

Scott, W. R. (2008). *Institutions and Organizations*, 3rd edn. Thousand Oaks, CA: SAGE.

Schultz, M., and Hernes, T. (2013). "A Temporal Perspective on Organizational Identity." *Organization Science* 24(1): 1–21.

Selznick, P. (1949). *TVA and the Grass Roots: A Study in the Sociology of Formal Organization.* Berkeley, CA: University of California Press.

Selznick, P. (1957). *Leadership in Administration: A Sociological Interpretation.* Evanston, IL: Row Peterson.

Seo, M. and Creed, W. E. D. (2002). "Institutional Contradictions, Praxis, and Institutional Change: A Dialectical Perspective." *The Academy of Management Review* 27(2): 222–47.

Smith, W. K., Gonin, M., and Besharov, M. L. (2013). "Managing Social-Business Tensions: A Review and Research Agenda for Social Enterprise." *Business Ethics Quarterly* 23(3): 407–42.

Sonenshein, S. (2010). "We're Changing—or Are We? Untangling the Role of Progressive, Regressive, and Stability Narratives during Strategic Change Implementation." *Academy of Management Journal* 53(3): 477–512.

Swidler, A. (1986). "Culture in Action: Symbols and Strategies." *American Sociological Review* 51(2): 273–86.

Thornton, P. H. (2002). "The Rise of the Corporation in a Craft Industry: Conflict and Conformity in Institutional Logics." *Academy of Management Journal* 45(1): 81–101.

Thornton, P. H. (2004). *Markets from Culture: Institutional Logics and Organizational Decisions in Higher Education Publishing.* Stanford, CA: Stanford University Press.

Thornton, P. H. and Ocasio, W. (1999). "Institutional Logics and the Historical Contingency of Power in Organizations: Executive Succession in the Higher Education Publishing Industry, 1958–1990." *American Journal of Sociology* 105: 801–43.

Thornton, P. H., Ocasio, W., and Lounsbury, M. (2012). *The Institutional Logics Perspective: A New Approach to Culture, Structure and Process.* Oxford: Oxford University Press.

Weick, K. (1995). *Sensemaking in Organizations.* Thousand Oaks, CA: SAGE.

Wertsch, J. V. (2012). "Narrative Tools and the Construction of Identity." In *Constructing Identity in and around Organizations*, edited by M. Schultz, S. Maguire, A. Langley, and H. Tsoukas, 128–46. New York: Oxford University Press.

Whetten, D. A. (2006). "Albert and Whetten Revisited: Strengthening the Concept of Organizational Identity." *Journal of Management Inquiry* 15(3): 219–34.

Whetten, D. A., Foreman, P. O., and Dyer, W. G. (2014). "Organizational Identity and Family Business." In *The SAGE Handbook of Family Business*, edited by L. Melin, M. Nordqvist, and P. Sharma, 480–97. Thousand Oaks, CA: SAGE.

Whetten, D. A. and Mackey, A. (2002). "A Social Actor Conception of Organizational Identity and its Implications for the Study of Organizational Reputation." *Business and Society* 41: 393–414.

SECTION VII

IMPLICATIONS OF OI

CHAPTER 22

....

ORGANIZATIONAL IDENTITY AND INNOVATION

....

CALLEN ANTHONY AND MARY TRIPSAS

INTRODUCTION

RESEARCH on organizational identity has had a tremendous impact on our understanding of organizational dynamics, starting with Albert and Whetten's seminal 1985 article. Organization identity influences business orientation and firm strategy (Nag, Corley, and Gioia, 2007), corporate structure (Corley and Gioia, 2004; Clark et al., 2010), and how employees relate to their organizations (Dutton, Dukerich, and Harquail, 1994; Glynn, 2000; Fiol, 2002; Pratt, 2000). Despite this extensive literature, the potential implications of organizational identity for the management of innovation and the implications of innovation on organizational identity remain underdeveloped. Yet innovation processes are central to sustaining the competitive position of many organizations, and organizational identity, which acts as a guidepost for organizational action (Kogut and Zander, 1996), likely influences which innovative activities are pursued. By its very nature, innovation is about exploring new terrain. Organizations search across boundaries (e.g., Rosenkopf and Nerkar, 2001) and absorb external knowledge (Cohen and Levinthal, 1990), adapting to and creating novel technologies and practices. Thus, at its core, innovation is about new things. In contrast, organizational identity is rooted in coherence and endurance (Albert and Whetten, 1985). While recent work has considered organizational identity as more emergent and subject to evolution and change, change is not easy (e.g., Fiol, 2002). This presents a fundamental tension between organizational identity and innovation. While innovation is about change, organizational identity is about stability and the difficulty of change. We argue these constructs reflect conflicting logics, which perhaps has contributed to what can largely be characterized as a lack of dialogue between the management of technology and organizational identity literatures. Our goal in this chapter is to explore this tension by explicating what we propose is a recursive relationship between organizational identity and innovation: identity influences the direction of innovative activities, and those activities, in turn, influence how organizational identity evolves.

We view organizational identity as a shared belief amongst organization members about "who we are," often articulated through claims about "what business we are in" (Watkiss and Glynn, Ch. 17, this volume; Navis and Glynn, 2010). In line with recent scholarship (e.g., Dutton and Dukerich, 1991; Gioia, Schultz, and Corley, 2000; Ravasi and Schultz, 2006; Schinoff, Rogers, and Corley, Ch. 12, this volume), we conceive of organizational identity as more fluid than Albert and Whetten's (1985) initial definition of organizational identity as attributes that are central, distinctive, and enduring. In fact, the potential for organizational identity to evolve incrementally or change discontinuously in correspondence with innovation is central to our arguments about how identity and innovation relate.

Associated with organizational identity is a shared understanding of what activities constitute appropriate action. Put differently, "who we are" has implications for "what we should do." Alignment between "who we are" and "what we do" is desirable, as conflict and dysfunction arise when organizational members engage in behaviors that violate the expectations of organizational identity (Elsbach and Kramer, 1996; Kraatz and Zajac, 1996). As a result, when identity is challenged, organizations attempt to re-establish alignment between organizational identity and the activities of organizational members (Dutton and Dukerich, 1991; Golden-Biddle and Rao, 1997). Since innovation is about doing new things, innovative activities are perhaps more likely to challenge the limits of identity than other activities. Despite this tension, we argue that innovation is not deterministically problematic to organizational identity. Instead, we propose that innovative activities can be placed on a continuum from identity-enhancing to identity-stretching to identity-challenging. We explore the dynamics associated with each of these types of innovations and the evolution of organizational identity. As background, we first discuss extant research on the management of innovation, which for the most part, is silent about organizational identity.

DRIVERS OF INNOVATION SUCCESS

An extensive literature has analyzed the challenges faced by established firms attempting to innovate. One line of research has focused on the factors that enable organizations to develop breakthrough, high-impact innovations that create opportunities for growth. A second line of research has focused on how well incumbent firms respond to radical innovations that transform their industries, often making existing technologies obsolete. Scholars in both traditions have, for the most part, ignored organizational identity (exceptions include Tripsas, 2009a; Tripsas, 2015; Altman and Tripsas, 2015).

Numerous scholars have attempted to explain what factors distinguish organizations that successfully develop important innovations. The primary finding of these studies is that organizations must reach beyond their existing knowledge base. By integrating knowledge that is distant organizationally (Rosenkopf and Nerkar, 2001), geographically (Jaffe et al., 1993), or technologically (Katila and Ahuja, 2002), firms are more likely to have innovation success. The explanations for why managers are blind to potentially distant opportunities have to do with cognitive and behavioral factors. Managers fall into competency traps (Levitt and March, 1988), core competencies become core rigidities (Leonard-Barton, 1992), and prior outdated mindsets influence the interpretation of opportunities (Tripsas and Gavetti, 2000). Organizational identity, as a possible explanation for innovative behavior, is simply absent from this literature.

A second stream of research focuses on explaining the performance of incumbent firms, vis à vis new entrants, when radically new technology results in a transition from one generation to another. Research in this tradition categorizes innovations based on different characteristics, and looks for systematic patterns of incumbent success or failure based on the type of technological innovation. Abernathy and Clark (1985) categorized innovations as being incremental or radical along technology and market dimensions, and, using data from the automotive industry, they proposed that established firms face the greatest challenges when an innovation is radical from both perspectives. Since then, scholars have deconstructed the technological dimension of innovations and found that incumbent organizations underperform new entrants when innovations build upon fundamentally different scientific knowledge that destroys the value of existing competencies (Tushman and Anderson, 1986), or destroys the value of architectural knowledge about product interfaces (Henderson and Clark, 1990). Researchers have also extended work on how non-technological aspects of innovations affect established firms. Using data on successive generations of disk drives, Christensen and Bower (1996) found that established organizations suffered when an innovation was disruptive, meaning that it initially targeted a new market segment that valued different performance criteria. Tripsas (1997) added another non-technological piece to the puzzle by examining the effect of an innovation on the value of an incumbent organization's complementary assets that are needed for commercialization. This line of research did not consider the effect of an innovation on an organizational identity until Tripsas (2009a) drew the distinction between identity-challenging and identity-enhancing innovations. Building upon that initial distinction, we next develop an extended typology that categorizes innovations in relation to identity and discusses the relationship between the constructs.

AN IDENTITY-BASED CATEGORIZATION
OF INNOVATIONS

Just as innovations can be categorized as competence-destroying, architectural, or disruptive, they can also be categorized by their relationship to organizational identity.

We propose that the dynamic between organizational identity and innovation varies depending upon whether the innovation is identity-enhancing, identity-stretching, or identity-challenging. An innovation is considered identity-enhancing when, by engaging in some innovative activity, the existing identity is enhanced or strengthened. This relationship results in a mutually constitutive dynamic between organizational identity and innovation, where identity guides innovation, and innovation reinforces organizational identity. Identity-stretching innovations do not fit with the core of an organization's identity, but are related enough that if the scope of organizational identity were expanded, these innovations would fit. In this case, broadening organizational identity enables innovation, and innovative activities stretch organizational identity. This can result in continuous cycles of incremental identity stretching and innovation. Finally, an innovation that is identity-challenging is in direct conflict with the existing organizational identity. In this instance, there is no reinforcing dynamic between identity and innovation. Instead, there is a lack of alignment that can result in significant organizational dysfunction. If pursued, these innovations challenge the core beliefs of organizational members, resulting in potential conflict. Alternatively, organizational identity may constrain innovative activity, precluding effective pursuit of an innovative opportunity. Below we discuss these dynamics with illustrations from the innovation and organizational identity literatures.

Identity-enhancing innovation. When organizations pursue identity-enhancing innovations, organizational identity and innovative activities are consistent with each other, resulting in a self re-enforcing positive feedback loop. Organizational members all "know" what actions are acceptable based on a shared understanding of what the organization represents, and this knowledge becomes codified in a set of heuristics about which innovative activities should be pursued and which should be dismissed; identity serves as a guidepost, providing focus to the organization's R&D and product-development activities. In turn, engagement in identity-enhancing innovations reinforces organizational identity, which becomes more deeply embedded in the routines and beliefs of organizational members. These *guiding* and *reinforcing* dynamics are illustrated in Figure 22.1.

The majority of innovation scholarship has focused on contexts in which organizations develop innovations that would be considered identity-enhancing using our categorization scheme (see Table 22.1 for a summary of identity-enhancing studies). Although the studies themselves do not consider identity, they look at firms within particular industries, and the boundaries of these industries remain intact despite innovation. Technological breakthroughs in pharmaceuticals, robotics (Katila and Ahuja, 2002), and optical disks (Rosenkopf and Nerkar, 2001) that resulted from the acquisition and integration of distant knowledge were challenging, but not from an identity standpoint. Identity did not have to stretch or change in order to accommodate these activities; rather, one could argue that the growth trajectory and associated exploratory innovations were guided by and benefited from the organizational routines and heuristics that resulted from a stable, unchanging identity. Similarly, the radical

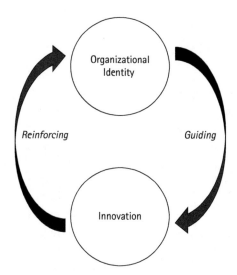

FIGURE 22.1 Identity-enhancing innovation

technological changes in cement and mini-computers (Tushman and Anderson, 1996), photolithography (Henderson and Clark, 1990), disk drives (Christensen and Bower, 1996), and typesetters (Tripsas, 1997) were identity-enhancing. For instance, cement companies remained cement companies across multiple technological generations.

In all of these instances, the direction of innovative activity was guided by identity, and identity was confirmed and strengthened through continued innovation. In this steady state, the relationship between organizational identity and innovation is continuous and iterative. Identity does not change to accommodate innovation, and innovation does not conflict with organizational identity.

Identity-stretching innovation. As with identity-enhancing innovations, the relationship between organizational identity and identity-stretching innovations is mutually constitutive and subject to a strong feedback dynamic. Though identity-enhancing innovations re-enforce existing identity, which in turn drives a narrow set of innovations, in the case of identity-stretching innovations, both identity and innovative activities incrementally broaden or shift as a result of the feedback dynamic. Managers can proactively encourage and facilitate a broader range of innovative activities by making incremental, fluid changes to identity, and innovations can, in turn help to stretch organizational identity. These *enabling* and *stretching* dynamics are illustrated in Figure 22.2.

Identity-stretching innovations often occur when organizations face a continuously shifting landscape (see Table 22.2 for an overview of studies of identity-stretching innovation). For example, the multiple identity changes that Ravasi and Schultz (2006) describe at Bang & Olufsen were in reaction to a series of environmental changes, including competitive dynamics, shifting consumer tastes, and variation in the economic climate. Managers recognized that innovations to the product line required a

Table 22.1 Studies of identity-enhancing innovation

Paper	Industry Setting	Identity-Enhancing Innovative Activity	Change in Organizational Identity	Key Findings Related to Innovation
Tushman and Anderson, 1986	Minicomputer, cement, and airline industries	Improvements in computer processing time, kiln capacity, passenger seat miles/year/plane	None	• Incumbents underperform new entrants when innovations are competence-destroying (destroy the value of existing scientific knowledge)
Henderson and Clark, 1990	Photolithographic alignment equipment industry	Architectural and component photolithograpy innovations	None	• Incumbents underperform new entrants when innovations are architectural (destroy an organization's knowledge of how technological components interface)
Christensen and Bower, 1996	Disk drive industry	Architectural innovations for different sized generations of disk drives	None	• Incumbents underperform new entrants when innovations are disruptive (appeal to new customers with different needs)
Tripsas, 1997	Typesetter industry	Photographic, digital CRT, and laser typesetters	None	• Incumbents outperform new entrants even if innovations are competence-destroying, if they don't destroy the value of complementary assets
Rosenkopf and Nerkar, 2001	Optical disk industry	Patents within the optical disk industry	None	• Exploration that spans both organizational and technological boundaries has a greater impact on innovation
Katila and Ahuja, 2002	Robotics industry	Design of an organization's robots	None	• Organizations that search more broadly from a technical viewpoint perform better

Table 22.2 Identity–stretching innovation

Paper	Industry Setting	Identity-Stretching Innovative Activity	Change in Organizational Identity	Key Findings Related to Innovation
Ravasi and Schultz, 2006	Bang & Olufsen, Danish audiovisual equipment producer	Design features, distribution channel and product display from multi-brand dealers to Bang & Olufsen "shops within shops" at high-end department stores	Successful changes from authentic, inventive high-end products to "unique combination of technological excellence and emotional appeal" to "excellence, synthesis, and poetry"	• Dynamic relationship between culture, identity, and image • Construed image and organizational culture provide cues for re-evaluating organizational identity
Rindova, Dalpiaz and Ravasi, 2011	Alessi, an Italian kitchen utensil company	Designers' creative freedom; new distribution channels (art galleries, merchants, and museums); resistance to putting plastic material into products	Successful changes from "publisher" to "artistic mediator" to "crafts workshop" to a "research laboratory in the field of applied arts" to "dream factory"	• Cultural resources from a firm's environment can be drawn upon to facilitate changing identity • Changing organizational identity followed the incorporation of new cultural resources, and vice-versa

newly shaped identity. Bang & Olufsen's identity was restated and stretched, which facilitated necessary innovations such as inventive design features that became important when Japanese players entered the market. Similarly, as competitors imitated the design of Bang & Olufsen's products in the mid-1990s, managers recognized a new identity was necessary in order to enable innovation in their distribution, relying on exclusive stores and "shops-in-shops" in upmarket department stores rather than selling through a range of dealers that would display their products next to other brands. Though these identity changes were punctuated, discontinuous shifts, they illustrate long-term evolution of organizational identity. This recursive enabling of innovation and stretching of organizational identity allowed Bang & Olufsen to continuously adapt to environmental changes.

Similarly, Rindova, Dalpiaz, and Ravasi (2011) show that the multiple identity changes at Alessi reflected ongoing cycles of enabling and stretching. Innovative activities across product development, production, and marketing stemmed from new cultural resources in the organization's environment, which then informed "identity redefinition," leading to both unconventional strategies and strategic versatility. Activities such as using artists to design and comment on products, as well as altering both production and distribution channels to incorporate galleries and museums were

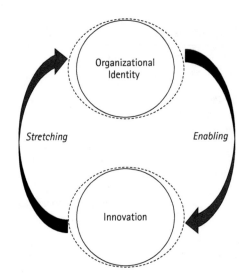

FIGURE 22.2 Identity-stretching innovation

reflected in Alessi's shifting organizational identity. As such, Alessi's identity evolved from "artistic mediator" to "crafts workshop" to "dream factory." These changes, in turn, enabled ongoing innovative activities.

Overall, the relationship between organizational identity and identity-stretching innovation reflects a recursive dynamic that is broadening. As organizations stretch their identity to enable innovation, cycles of enabling innovation further stretch and reconfigure identity. Though this category results in organizational identity change, innovation and identity do not challenge or threaten one another.

Identity-challenging innovation. Innovation is likely to be identity-challenging in two broad contexts. First, in extreme situations where technological innovation results in the obsolescence of a product market or the convergence of multiple product markets, established firms are likely to find the transition identity-challenging since their core business may cease to exist. For instance, the transformation of stand-alone copiers to sophisticated document management systems blurred the lines between copiers, printers, and computers, causing Xerox to redefine itself as a document company, not a copier company. Second, innovations may be identity-challenging when competitive imperatives or exploratory research lead to new products, product lines, or services (changes in "what we do") that do not fit clearly with the existing identity. Altman and Tripsas (2015) suggest that when product-based firms respond to the competitive environment by developing platform-based business models (such as an app store), the new set of innovative activities they engage in may be identity-challenging. For instance, product-based firms are often technology-driven and expect their developers to create the "best" product given customer needs. If, instead, members of a product-based firm that is developing a platform-based business start to emphasize expanding the size of the new platform-based network at the expense of developing quality products—something that would be consistent with a platform-based model—that activity would challenge the original product-based identity.

Identity-challenging innovations can pose major problems for organizations. When organizational identity constrains innovation and innovation threatens organizational identity, the reinforcing dynamic between organizational identity and innovation breaks down. This makes both innovation and identity change not only difficult for organizations to accomplish, but also puts organizational identity and innovation at odds with each other. Organizational identity can *constrain* innovation in response to environmental shifts, and be *threatened* in the face of innovation (see Figure 22.3).

As the organizational identity literature itself reflects a tension between identity as stable and identity as more fluid and changing, it is perhaps not surprising that much of the organizational identity literature that we consider as relevant to problems of innovation falls within this third category: innovation, or changes in "what we do", have been largely studied in contexts where these changes challenge organizational identity and result in some attempted identity change (See Table 22.3 for an overview of this work). Thus, our understanding of how organizations respond to identity-challenging innovations is much more developed and nuanced than our understanding of how organizational identity and innovation co-construct one another when innovations are identity-enhancing or identity-stretching. According to work in contexts where innovation threatens organizational identity, we find that organizations respond to identity-challenging innovation opportunities in three primary ways: they do not notice an innovation opportunity, they notice an opportunity but do not pursue it, or they notice and attempt to develop the innovation, in some cases failing to innovate, while in others implementing approaches for realigning the innovation and identity (what we refer to as "realignment mechanisms").

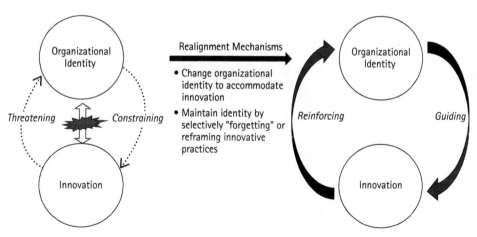

FIGURE 22.3 Identity-challenging innovation

Table 22.3 Studies of identity-challenging innovation

Paper	Industry Setting	Identity-Challenging Innovative Activity	Change in Organizational Identity	Key Findings Related to Innovation
Fiol, 2002	Data storage company	Move from developing data storage products to developing data storage solutions that emphasize services	Successful change from an engineering-driven data storage company to a "storage solution information-management company"	• Identity can constrain organizational ability to adapt and innovate; to successfully respond to a competitive imperative, an organization may need to change both activities and identity • Shifting member identification is crucial to an organizational identity change effort
Nag, Corley, and Gioia, 2007	High-tech R&D firm	Added business development personnel to improve commercialization capability	Failed change from R&D organization to "market-oriented organization"	• Consistency is needed between organizational identity and knowledge reflected in work practices for successful strategic change
Brunninge, 2007	Handelsbanken	Adoption of internet banking technology	Maintained the identity of the bank as "branch-centred"	• Tailoring new technology in implementation plan allows for organizational identity to remain intact
Tripsas, 2009a	Flash memory	Developed USB flash drives that extended the firm's product line beyond digital photography	Successful change from a "digital photography company" to a "memory company"	• Organizational identity filters what technological opportunities are noticed and shapes how they are interpreted • Considering whether innovations are identity-challenging or identity-enhancing helps explain why incremental technological innovations can be challenging
Anteby and Molnar, 2012	Snecma, France's largest aircraft engine manufacturer	Engaged in collaborations with German engineers and an external company GE	Maintained the "technological prowess and sovereignty" tied to French national identity	• Endurance of identity in the face of identity-challenging activities requires ongoing reconstruction of the past • Forgetting selective elements of the past helps organizational identity to endure
Schultz and Hernes, 2013	LEGO	Pursue "digital opportunities" by forming a business division to develop computer games and TV shows	Successful shift from "mass market producer of play material" to "idea-based company dedicated to 'systematic creativity'"	• Time horizons of the past used to articulate identity claims were mirrored in the time horizon of claims about the future

Organizational identity can color and restrict what possibilities are noticed, result-ing in managers being "blind" to some identity-challenging innovations (Fiol, 2002; Tripsas, 2009a). For example, Tripsas (2009a) describes how Linco's strong identity as a digital photography company making "digital film" restricted its recognition of innovative opportunities that its memory cards were well suited for. This was clearly evidenced by Linco employees' very use of the company's digital film memory cards as storage devices to transfer data files among themselves. The employees did not recog-nize the incremental innovation needed to re-package these memory cards into USB flash drives as a potential opportunity for the firm until a competitor produced such a flash drive. The identity of the firm constrained how employees saw the function of their memory devices, and in this case, the constraining role of organizational iden-tity was so strong that innovation was not even a consideration. And once the organ-ization did recognize the opportunity, it was initially rejected, precisely because it did not fit with how the organization saw itself.

If an organization decides to pursue identity-challenging innovations, the mis-match between identity and the innovative activities can create significant problems. In addition to constraining what gets noticed, organizational identity can also restrict the very realization of an attempted innovation. This can eventually lead to failure, as employees continue in their existing practices, which are guided by the old or-ganizational identity. For example, strategic change at Tekmar failed because the or-ganizational identity continued to constrain the practices of employees even after the decision to innovate and acquire new knowledge was made (Nag, Corley, and Gioia, 2007). The failed attempt to move from an R&D organization to a market-oriented organization was spurred by employees continuing to "solve the ... business develop-ment problems according to their own ways of thinking and doing" (Nag, Corley, and Gioia, 2007: 838). The old identity constrained employee practices, thwarting Tekmar's attempt at innovation.

In other cases, organizations were able to effectively realign organizational iden-tity and innovation after experiencing dysfunctional dynamics. Fiol (2002) describes a change in the competitive environment of the computer industry that required Tech-Co to develop service-oriented solutions innovations to complement its prod-uct strengths. Management recognized the need to move away from hardware, however, Tech-Co's "strong identity became a barrier, constraining organizational interpretations, actions, and potential for change" (Fiol, 2002: 655). By proactively leading a transition of Tech-Co's identity from an engineering-driven data storage company to a storage-solution information management company, management was able to shift the firm's focus from storage products to storage solutions. Managing the identification of employees, and in particular engineers, was key to this transi-tion. Through the interim process of employee reidentification to an experimental context, employees were better able to eventually identify with the new organiza-tional identity.

Innovation that challenges organizational identity can also be managed by draw-ing on organizational memory to legitimate a new identity. As Schultz and Hernes

(2013) discuss, changes at LEGO were driven by the digitization of the toy market in which LEGO competes. Initially the organization took several measures to adapt to this shifting competitive landscape, including creating a separate business unit to develop computer games. Yet digital innovations and the associated change in LEGO's capabilities "confus[ed] employees and consumers with respect to the identity of LEGO as both an organization and as a provider of play experiences" (Schultz and Hernes, 2013: 10). Drawing upon organizational memory in order to construct a desired future, ultimately LEGO worked to redefine its identity from a "mass market producer of play material" into a "premium idea-based company dedicated to 'systematic creativity'" in order to allow for the sustained pursuit of digital opportunities as core to LEGO's identity (Schultz and Hernes, 2013: 12). This new identity was in alignment with the new, innovative activities, but by building heavily upon LEGO's legacy as a firm that encouraged creative play, it allowed for a sense of continuity in the face of change.

Another tactic for re-establishing alignment is to selectively "forget" and ignore behavior that is inconsistent with organizational identity. This can allow for an organization to benefit from innovation without facing the challenges of behavior that does not "fit" with "who we are." For example, French aircraft manufacturer Snecma drew on expertise from German engineers in developing core technological capabilities, and also collaborated with other firms like GE to grow its technological competencies. These important ventures allowed Snecma to develop its products. However, as Anteby and Molnar (2012) discovered, such activities were inconsistent with how members of Snecma viewed the firm's organizational identity, which was closely linked with their perception of national identity. The shared belief amongst organization members was that "Frenchness" meant "technological prowess and sovereignty" (p. 519), and thus instances of foreign collaborations and reliance on technologies from foreign firms challenged what it meant to be a French technology firm. In order to bypass contradictions between these innovative activities and what organization members saw as "Frenchness," these activities were selectively forgotten, thus upholding conceptions of national identity within the firm (Anteby and Molnar, 2012).

Finally, to manage identity threats from innovation, organizations may implement the innovation in a way that mitigates the identity threat and leaves identity intact. For example, the decentralized identity at Handelsbanken was threatened with the emergence of internet banking (Brunninge, 2007). The new technology threatened to centralize the bank's operations, which was inconsistent with the belief that the local branch was "the most important organizational unit" and core to the bank's identity (Brunninge, 2007: 64). As a result, the bank allowed each branch to run its own systems, maintaining the identity of the organization while still adopting the innovation.

Identity-challenging innovations are the most studied within the organizational identity literature, potentially because of the orchestrated change in identity that this type of innovation requires. When innovation and identity are at odds with one another, we argue that unless they are brought back into alignment, organizational identity acts as a constraint, and decreases the ability of an organization to innovate effectively.

Implications

We suggest that these relationship dynamics have consequences for organizations. When innovative practices are identity-enhancing, organizational identity is strengthened. Having a strong identity can certainly be positive for an organization. A strong identity can help to filter and guide organizational action, giving organizational members frames to make sense of the environment with. It can also allow external audiences clarity for the purposes of evaluation (Zuckerman, 1999). Though identity-enhancing innovation can reinforce and strengthen organizational identity, which can lead to more enhancing innovation, it can also result in a loop that can turn an organization's focus increasingly inward. Thus organizational identity provides an alternative explanation for the managerial blinders that can cause important, "distant" innovations to be overlooked. When innovative activities are guided by and reinforce organizational identity, organizations can become stuck in a feedback cycle whereby change and adaptation become increasingly problematic. Organizations might fall into competency traps (Levitt and March, 1988), making it more difficult for management to even notice or take seriously innovation that does not align with their identity (Tripsas and Gavetti, 2000; Tripsas, 2009a).

When organizational identity is continuously confirmed and strengthened by innovative activites, it can create a situation where that same organization becomes threatened by identity-challenging innovation. Further, employees can become more strongly identified with an organization (Fiol, 2002), making it increasingly difficult to implement innovative changes altogether (eg., Nag, Corley, and Gioia, 2007). Thus, while identity-enhancing and identity-challenging innovations might first appear to be two ends of a spectrum (reinforcing versus threatening), in actuality, one might lead to an increased likelihood of the other.

While identity-enhancing dynamics can strengthen organizational identity, which makes it more difficult to change, identity-stretching innovation can help organizations adapt to shifting competitive landscapes. Such adaptation has been demonstrated as central to organizational survival (Levinthal, 1997). Too much identity-stretching, though, can confuse both an organization's members and audience. Not only has previous research shown that if a label is too ambiguous, others struggle to make sense of it (Padgett and Ansell, 1993), research has also demonstrated that audience members discount organizations that do not "fit" into product categories (Zuckerman, 1999). Thus, organizations whose relationship between identity and innovation is identity-stretching run the risk of broadening their identity too much, which can harm their perceived value.

Finally, taking organizational identity into account helps to explain why seemingly similar organizations may have different reactions to the same innovative opportunity: despite similarities, their firm-specific organizational identity may vary. For instance, Luxxotica, a leading provider of eyeglass frames, and Bausch and Lomb, a leading provider of contact lenses, were both engaged in vision correction. However, Luxxotica viewed itself as "an eyewear company," and Bausch and Lomb viewed itself as "an eye health company." The opportunity to engage in laser eye surgery was therefore identity-threatening to Luxxotica, and identity-enhancing to Bausch and Lomb. Luxottica's management decided against investing in laser eye surgery centers, commenting that "We are an eyewear company, and simply put, our best opportunities for growth going forward continue to be in our core business ... From this perspective, we passed on laser vision correction" (Tripsas, 2009b). In contrast, Bausch and Lomb diversified into laser eye surgery centers, an innovative activity consistent with and reinforcing of its organizational identity. Similarly, Tripsas's (2015) comparison of Fuji and Polaroid's reactions to digital imaging illustrates the importance of including organizational identity in studies of innovation. While on the surface Fuji and Polaroid were similar in that they both had film-based capabilities and were dependent on film sales when digital imaging emerged, they had different reactions to the technology, based to some extent on differences in managing identity. Fuji adopted a broad, robust identity as an "Information and Imaging" company, and explicitly included digital imaging in the set of activities encompassed by this phrase, whereas Polaroid maintained a narrower identity as an instant photography company. Digital imaging remained identity-challenging for Polaroid, contributing to the ultimate demise of the company.

CONCLUSIONS AND DIRECTIONS FOR FUTURE RESEARCH

Because such little research has directly studied the connection between organizational identity and innovation, much work remains to be done. In order for the management of technology and organizational identity literatures to engage in dialogue, there are some methodological differences that need to be overcome. Work in the innovation literature is dominated by quantitative, large-sample studies that often use patent data to measure innovative success. In contrast, the organizational identity literature that provides insight into the relationship between organizational identity and innovation is largely comprised of inductive, qualitative, single case studies.[1] We suggest that future work in this area could use multiple case studies, either as a compelling way to develop theory through comparison (Eisenhardt, 1991) or as a means for qualitative evidence to inform quantitative, deductive research (Eisenhardt and Graebner, 2007).

[1] Though our focus in this chapter has been on a set of studies that happen to be single case studies, other studies of organizational identity in not-for-profit sectors have utilized surveys (Dukerich et al., 2002; Foreman and Whetten, 2002; Martins, 2005; Voss et al., 2006).

We also suggest potential directions for future research across three levels of analysis: professional workers within an organization, firm strategic management of organizational identity, and organizational identity in relation to collective identity.

Organizations that innovate, including technology-driven firms, often employ individuals with strong professional and occupational identities, such as scientists, engineers (Fiol, 2002), and salespeople (Bubenzer and Foreman, 2014). Research has demonstrated the importance of understanding identity conflicts amongst administrators and professionals within organizations, but has predominately focused on not-for-profit sectors, such as nurses within a rehabilitation unit (Pratt and Rafaeli, 1997) and musicians within a symphony orchestra (Glynn, 2000). We propose that it is also important to understand professional identity conflicts between technologically oriented engineers and scientists, and business-focused sales and marketing representatives. How might such conflict affect the ability of organizations to innovate? Can organizational identity be managed in a way that minimizes conflict among professions? Further, future work might also explore how a technological innovation can affect professional or occupational identity, such as effect of internet search on the identity of librarians (Nelson and Irwin, 2014). How professionals incorporate and relate to technologies is a missing link that is important to understanding the role innovation plays in threatening professional and occupational identity, which can impact organizational outcomes.

The relationship between strategy, innovation, and organizational identity is also ripe for exploration. For instance, the strategy literature is inconclusive about whether diversification creates value, with some arguing that related diversification has a higher likelihood of success (Markides and Williamson, 1994; Villalonga, 2004). The manner in which "related" is defined, however, is primarily in terms of a firm's assets and capabilities (Silverman, 1999). In contrast, the preceding discussion implies that "related" can also be defined by how close potential diversification moves are to existing identity. Future research might examine whether diversification that involves identity-challenging innovation is less likely to succeed than identity-enhancing or identity-stretching diversification.

Although the identity literature acknowledges the importance of changing identity if identity-challenging activities are to be effectively pursued, it does not discuss how an organization should decide what new identity, if any, to pursue. However, some identities might fare better than others, especially in the context of innovation. A broader identity might allow for better adaptation to a shifting environment—in other words, an organization with a broad identity could be less likely to face an identity-challenging innovation. For example, in his classic piece on "marketing myopia," Levitt (1960) argues that one problem railroad companies faced when air transport emerged as a threat was their product-based identities. He suggests that if, instead of thinking of themselves as railroad companies, they had conceived of themselves as "transportation companies," they would have fared better. If the railroad companies had defined themselves as a broader function (transportation rather than mode of transportation), incorporating air travel into business practices would have "fit" with existing organizational identity. Thus, we suggest future research explore the question of which identities might do better than others, and under what conditions.

Another potential area for future exploration is at the intersection of organizational identity, collective identity, and the competitive landscape (Glynn, 2008; Livengood and Reger, 2010). In particular, little is known about how competitive dynamics might shape organizational identity, and how an organization might choose to define itself when innovating. Research has already demonstrated how crucial this is to organizations: organizations must appear as "fitting" within a categorical structure amongst other firms, lest they suffer a disadvantage from being seen as a misfit (Zuckerman, 1999; Benner, 2010). Further, firms within established categories must also balance the need to fit in with the need to be seen as distinctive from each other within the same category (Zuckerman, 1999, Navis and Glynn, 2011; Zuckerman, 2016). We suggest that competitive positioning choices are most salient during times of new industry emergence. Navis and Glynn (2010) show how Sirius and XM worked together to confer legitimacy to the innovation of satellite radio, and then shifted away from emphasizing collective identity to attempting to differentiate themselves from each other: Sirius began distinguishing itself on its coverage of sporting events and talk shows, whereas XM claimed itself as a "music purist" (Navis and Glynn, 2010: 457). Though this study illuminates that innovative organizations must be mindful of competitive dynamics when claiming their identity, much remains to be done in this area. For example, unlike the two satellite radio players, what happens when organizations in an emerging field do not agree on a collective identity that they jointly promote? When organizations from diverse fields with diverse identities converge on a new domain, they may have different perspectives on what the new product/service is and how it should be used (Benner and Tripsas, 2012). Future research could explore whether organizations innovating in a new domain need to converge upon a dominant design before they can promote a collective identity.

In conclusion, we believe that the intersection between organizational identity and innovation provides a rich domain for future research to explore. At present these bodies of literature have not engaged in much conversation, yet we believe they have much to say to each other.

References

Abernathy, W. J. and Clark, K. B. (1985). "Innovation: Mapping the Winds of Creative Destruction." *Research Policy* 14(1): 3–22.

Albert, S. and Whetten, D. A. (1985). "Organizational Identity." *Research in Organizational Behavior* 7: 263–95.

Altman, E. J. and Tripsas, M. (2015). "Product to Platform Transitions: Organizational Identity Implications." In *The Oxford Handbook of Creativity, Innovation, and Entrepreneurship: Multilevel Linkages*, edited by Christina Shalley, Michael Hitt, and Jing Zhou, 379–94. Oxford: Oxford University Press.

Anteby, M. and Molnár, V. (2012). "Collective Memory Meets Organizational Identity: Remembering to Forget in a Firm's Rhetorical History." *Academy of Management Journal* 55(3): 515–40.

Benner, M. J. (2010). "Securities Analysts and Incumbent Response to Radical Technological Change: Evidence from Digital Photography and Internet Telephony." *Organization Science* 21(1): 42–62.

Benner, M. J. and Tripsas, M. (2012). "The Influence of Prior Industry Affiliation on Framing in Nascent Industries: The Evolution of Digital Cameras." *Strategic Management Journal* 33(3): 277–302.

Brunninge, O. (2007). "Handelsbanken and Internet Banking." In *Organizational Identity in Practice*, edited by L. Lerpold, D. Ravasi, J. Van Rekorn, and G. Soenen, 63–78. London: Routledge.

Bubenzer, P. and Foreman, P. O. (2014). "The Effects of Hybrid Product and Organizational Identities on Organizational Identification." Working paper.

Christensen, C. M. and Bower, J. L. (1996). "Customer Power, Strategic Investment, and the Failure of Leading Firms." *Strategic Management Journal* 17(3): 197–218.

Clark, S. M., Gioia, D. A., Ketchen, D. J., and Thomas, J. B. (2010). "Transitional Identity as a Facilitator of Organizational Identity Change during a Merger." *Administrative Science Quarterly* 55(3): 397–438.

Cohen, W. M. and Levinthal, D. A. (1990). "Absorptive Capacity: A New Perspective on Learning and Innovation." *Administrative Science Quarterly* 35: 128–152.

Corley, K. G. and Gioia, D. A. (2004). "Identity Ambiguity and Change in the Wake of a Corporate Spin-Off." *Administrative Science Quarterly* 49(2): 173–208.

Dukerich, J. M., Golden, B. R., and Shortell, S. M. (2002). "Beauty Is in the Eye of the Beholder: The Impact of Organizational Identification, Identity, and Image on the Cooperative Behaviors of Physicians." *Administrative Science Quarterly* 47(3): 507–33.

Dutton, J. E. and Dukerich, J. M. (1991). "Keeping an Eye on the Mirror: Image and Identity in Organizational Adaptation." *Academy of Management Journal* 34(3): 517–54.

Dutton, J. E., Dukerich, J. M., and Harquail, C. V. (1994). "Organizational Images and Member Identification." *Administrative Science Quarterly* 39: 239–63.

Eisenhardt, K. M. (1991). "Better Stories and Better Constructs: The Case for Rigor and Comparative Logic." *Academy of Management Review* 16(3): 620–7.

Eisenhardt, K. M. and Graebner, M. E. (2007). "Theory Building from Cases: Opportunities and Challenges." *Academy of Management Journal* 50(1): 25–32.

Elsbach, K. D. and Kramer, R. M. (1996). "Members' Responses to Organizational Identity Threats: Encountering and Countering the *Business Week* Rankings." *Administrative Science Quarterly* 41: 442–76.

Fiol, C. M. (2002). "Capitalizing on Paradox: The Role of Language in Transforming Organizational Identities." *Organization Science* 13(6): 653–66.

Foreman, P. and Whetten, D. A. (2002). "Members' Identification with Multiple-Identity Organizations." *Organization Science* 13(6): 618–35.

Gioia, D. A., Schultz, M., and Corley, K. G. (2000). "Organizational Identity, Image, and Adaptive Instability." *Academy of Management Review* 25(1): 63–81.

Glynn, M. A. (2000). "When Cymbals Become Symbols: Conflict over Organizational Identity within a Symphony Orchestra." *Organization Science* 11(3): 285–98.

Glynn, M. A. (2008). "Beyond Constraint: How Institutions Enable Identities." In *The SAGE Handbook of Organizational Institutionalism*, edited by R. Greenwood, C. Oliver, K. Sahlin, and R. Suddaby, 413–30. London: SAGE.

Golden-Biddle, K. and Rao, H. (1997). "Breaches in the Boardroom: Organizational Identity and Conflicts of Commitment in a Nonprofit Organization." *Organization Science* 8(6): 593–611.

Henderson, R. M. and Clark, K. B. (1990). "Architectural Innovation: The Reconfiguration of Existing Product Technologies and the Failure of Established Firms." *Administrative Science Quarterly* 35(1): 9–30.

Jaffe, A., Trajtenberg, M. and Henderson, R. (1993). "Geographic Localization of Knowledge Spillovers as Evidenced by Patent Citations." *The Quarterly Journal of Economics* 108(3): 577–98.

Katila, R. and Ahuja, G. (2002). "Something Old, Something New: A Longitudinal Study of Search Behavior and New Product Introduction." *Academy of Management Journal* 45(6): 1183–94.

Kogut, B. and Zander, U. (1996). "What Firms Do? Coordination, Identity, and Learning." *Organization Science* 7(5): 502–18.

Kraatz, M. S. and Zajac, E. J. (1996). "Exploring the Limits of the New Institutionalism: The Causes and Consequences of Illegitimate Organizational Change." *American Sociological Review* 61(5): 812–36.

Leonard-Barton, D. (1992). "Core Capabilities and Core Rigidities: A Paradox in Managing New Product Development." *Strategic Management Journal* 13(S1): 111–25.

Levinthal, D. A. (1997). "Adaptation on Rugged Landscapes." *Management Science* 43(7): 934–50.

Levitt, B. and March, J. G. (1988). "Organizational Learning." *Annual Review of Sociology*: 319–40.

Levitt, T. (1960). "Marketing Myopia." *Harvard Business Review* 38(4): 24–47.

Livengood, R. S. and Reger, R. K. (2010). "That's our Turf! Identity Domains and Competitive Dynamics." *Academy of Management Review* 35(1): 48–66.

Markides, C. C. and Williamson, P. J. (1994). "Related Diversification, Core Competences and Corporate Performance." *Strategic Management Journal* 15(S2): 149–65.

Martins, L. L. (2005). "A Model of the Effects of Reputational Rankings on Organizational Change." *Organization Science* 16(6): 701–20.

Nag, R., Corley, K. G., and Gioia, D. A. (2007). "The Intersection of Organizational Identity, Knowledge, and Practice: Attempting Strategic Change via Knowledge Grafting." *Academy of Management Journal* 50(4): 821–47.

Navis, C. and Glynn, M. A. (2010). "How New Market Categories Emerge: Temporal Dynamics of Legitimacy, Identity, and Entrepreneurship in Satellite Radio, 1990–2005." *Administrative Science Quarterly* 55(3): 439–71.

Navis, C. and Glynn, M. A. (2011). "Legitimate Distinctiveness and the Entrepreneurial Identity: Influence on Investor Judgments of New Venture Plausibility." *Academy of Management Review* 36(3): 479–99.

Nelson, A. and Irwin, J. (2014). "'Defining What We Do—All Over Again': Occupational Identity, Technological Change, and the Librarian/Internet-Search Relationship." *Academy of Management Journal* 57(3): 892–928.

Padgett, J. F. and Ansell, C. K. (1993). "Robust Action and the Rise of the Medici, 1400–1434." *American Journal of Sociology* 98: 1259–319.

Pratt, M. G. (2000). "The Good, the Bad, and the Ambivalent: Managing Identification among Amway Distributors." *Administrative Science Quarterly* 45(3): 456–93.

Pratt, M. G. and Rafaeli, A. (1997). "Organizational Dress as a Symbol of Multilayered Social Identities." *Academy of Management Journal* 40(4): 862–98.

Ravasi, D. and Schultz, M. (2006). "Responding to Organizational Identity Threats: Exploring the Role of Organizational Culture." *Academy of Management Journal* 49(3): 433–58.

Rindova, V., Dalpiaz, E., and Ravasi, D. (2011). "A Cultural Quest: A Study of Organizational Use of New Cultural Resources in Strategy Formation." *Organization Science* 22(2): 413–31.

Rosenkopf, L. and Nerkar, A. (2001). "Beyond Local Search: Boundary-Spanning, Exploration, and Impact in the Optical Disk Industry." *Strategic Management Journal* 22(4): 287–306.

Schinoff, B., Rogers, K., and Corley, K. G. (2016). "How Do We Communicate Who We Are? Examining How Organizational Identity Is Conveyed to Members." In *The Oxford Handbook of Organizational Identity*, edited by M. G. Pratt, M. Schultz, B. E. Ashforth, and D. Ravasi, 219–38. Oxford: Oxford University Press.

Schultz, M. and Hernes, T. (2013). "A Temporal Perspective on Organizational Identity." *Organization Science* 24(1): 1–21.

Silverman, B. S. (1999). "Technological Resources and the Direction of Corporate Diversification: Toward an Integration of the Resource-Based View and Transaction Cost Economics." *Management Science* 45(8): 1109–24.

Tripsas, M. (1997). "Unraveling the Process of Creative Destruction: Complementary Assets and Incumbent Survival in the Typesetter Industry." *Strategic Management Journal* 18(1): 119–42.

Tripsas, M. (2009a). "Technology, Identity, and Inertia through the Lens of 'The Digital Photography Company.'" *Organization Science* 20(2): 441–60.

Tripsas, M. (2009b). "When Names Change to Protect the Future," *New York Times*, November 29.

Tripsas, M. (2015). "Exploring the Interaction between Organizational Identity and Organizational Design in Technology Transitions". Working paper. Boston, MA.

Tripsas, M. and Gavetti, G. (2000). "Capabilities, Cognition, and Inertia: Evidence from Digital Imaging." *Strategic Management Journal* 21(10–11): 1147–61.

Tushman, M. L. and Anderson, P. (1986). "Technological Discontinuities and Organizational Environments." *Administrative Science Quarterly* 31(3): 439–65.

Villalonga, B. (2004). "Diversification Discount or Premium? New Evidence from the Business Information Tracking Series." *The Journal of Finance* 59(2): 479–506.

Voss, Z. G., Cable, D. M., and Voss, G. B. (2006). "Organizational Identity and Firm Performance: What Happens when Leaders Disagree about 'Who We Are?'". *Organization Science* 17(6): 741–55.

Watkiss, L. and Glynn, M. A. (2016). "Materiality and Identity: How Organizational Products, Artifacts, and Practices Instantiate Organizational Identity." In *The Oxford Handbook of Organizational Identity*, edited by M. G. Pratt, M. Schultz, B. E. Ashforth, and D. Ravasi, 317–34. Oxford: Oxford University Press.

Zuckerman, E. W. (1999). "The Categorical Imperative: Securities Analysts and the Illegitimacy Discount." *American Journal of Sociology* 104(5): 1398–438.

Zuckerman, E. (2016). "Optimal Distinctiveness Revisited: An Integrative Framework for Understanding the Balance between Differentiation and Conformity in Individual and Organizational Identities." In *The Oxford Handbook of Organizational Identity*, edited by M. G. Pratt, M. Schultz, B. E. Ashforth, and D. Ravasi, 183–99. Oxford: Oxford University Press.

....

CHAPTER 23

PLANNED ORGANIZATIONAL IDENTITY CHANGE

insights from practice

....

MAMTA BHATT, CEES B. M. VAN RIEL,
AND MARIJKE BAUMANN

INTRODUCTION

....

ALBERT and Whetten (1985) defined identity as members' beliefs about what is central, enduring, and distinctive about their organization. Out of these three aspects, the one that has attracted a great deal of attention and debate is whether identity is enduring or not. While the early research emphasizes the enduring nature of identity (e.g., Whetten and Mackay, 2002), later research recognizes the idea that despite several barriers, under some circumstances identity may change (e.g., Corley and Gioia, 2004; Fiol, 2002; Gioia and Thomas, 1996; Kjærgaard, Morsing, and Ravasi, 2011; Ravasi and Schultz, 2006). Following this argument, extant research proposes that such an identity change can come about both as a result of a planned initiative by the leadership (e.g., Fiol, 2002; Tripsas, 2009) and as an emergent (unplanned) phenomena (e.g., Cook and Yanow, 1993).

In this chapter, we focus on the former, that is, planned organizational identity change, a phenomenon that has attracted much scholarly attention. However, even though it is a growing field of research, we still "need to garner a better understanding of its origins and its transitions" (Gioia, Patvardhan, Hamilton, and Corley, 2013: 184). In this regard, while pursuing applied research at the Corporate Communication Center, Erasmus University Rotterdam, we have come across several companies that have engaged in deliberate efforts to change their identity. Drawing from our observations at these companies and building upon past research, we develop a framework describing the phenomenon and illustrate the same with the example of a Dutch funeral insurance and care organization, DELA, which is one of the organizations where we observed change unfolding in this manner. In doing so, we shed light on how new identity claims are used in effecting a planned identity change. Further, we emphasize how such change is geared as much toward the external stakeholders (e.g., customers, suppliers, other institutional actors, etc.) as the internal stakeholders. We end with a discussion of avenues for future research on identity change and practical implications for managers.

ORGANIZATIONAL IDENTITY CHANGE: PAST RESEARCH

Over the past two decades, there has been an increased attention on understanding organizational identity change. As Corley, Harquail, Pratt, Glynn, Fiol, and Hatch (2006) summarized, this body of research has focused on various aspects of identity change such as its nature and process (Corley and Gioia, 2004; Fiol, 2002; Hatch and Schultz, 2002; Ravasi and Schultz, 2006), frequency (Biggart, 1977; Gioia and Thomas, 1996), origin (Corley and Gioia, 2004), speed (Fiol, 2002), and motives (Glynn and Marquis, 2007). Overall, these studies suggest that "organizational identity change is a difficult process laden with uncertainty and ambiguity" (Clark, Gioia, Ketchen, and Thomas, 2010: 400). Furthermore, past research also looks at how top management or organization's senior leadership plays a proactive role in bringing about identity change (e.g., Clarke et al., 2010; Corley and Gioia, 2004; Fiol, 2002; Ravasi and Schultz, 2006; Trispas, 2009).

To elaborate, one of the ways organizational leadership facilitates members' identity construction is through projection of desired organizational image (Gioia and Thomas, 1996). In particular, the top management addresses the ambiguity about changing organizational identity by "refinement of the desired future image, increased branding efforts, and modelling behaviours associated with the desired future image" (Corley and Gioia, 2004: 196). For instance, Humphreys and Brown (2002) found that the senior management tried to redefine organizational identity by authoring organizational identity narrative. Leaders may also use different rhetorical techniques to purposefully destroy old identity, make future image more attractive, and build consensus around the new identity (Fiol, 2002). Following a similar notion, past research in a merger context shows how leaders communicated a transitional identity—which is an interim sense of what the merged identity would stand for—to facilitate a transition toward a very different organizational identity post-merger (Clark et al., 2010). Further, top management resort to organizational culture and artifacts such as stories, objects, and practices to communicate new identity and facilitate how members interpret it (Ravasi and Schultz, 2006). Similarly, companies that are publicly visible often attract media coverage; in such organizations, leaders may attempt to take an advantage of positive media coverage to facilitate members' commitment toward the new identity (Kjærgaard et al., 2011).

However, despite an increased focus on studying organizational identity change, our understanding of this topic represents "only the tip of a very large iceberg" (Gioia et al., 2013: 177). For instance, while past research emphasizes the importance of communicating organizational identity to employees (Smidts, Pruyn, and van Riel, 2001), we do not know much about the goals that organizational leadership could pursue while doing so and what some of the concrete steps are that the top management can take in order to achieve such goals.

Furthermore, a majority of identity research is inward looking and focuses on employees or members of the organization (e.g., Corley, 2004; Dutton and Dukerich, 1991; Clark et al., 2010); relatively fewer studies look at how external stakeholders are taken into account while planning and implementing identity change (e.g., Ravasi and Schultz, 2006; Trispas, 2009). This is surprising since along with internal audiences, organizational identity has an impact on external audiences as well. On the one hand, identity bears upon how internal stakeholders interpret issues and make decisions (Dutton and Dukerich, 1991), shapes their commitment (Golden-Biddle and Rao, 1997), and is associated with their response to threats (Elsbach and Kramer, 1996); on the other, it helps external stakeholders associate certain characteristics with the organization, and form expectations about organizational actions (Hsu and Hannan, 2005). As such, this raises the question: how could leaders bring about an identity change that focuses on both internal and external stakeholders?

Building upon past research and our observations at different companies, we develop a framework that addresses these questions.

Organizational Identity Change in Practice: A Framework

Our framework suggests that there could be several triggers that may lead the senior leadership to bring about a change in organizational identity claims. Implementation of the changed identity claims would involve communication initiatives targeted at both internal and external audiences. Further, while these initiatives would aim at ensuring employee alignment in the internal audience (i.e., organizational members), the goal in the case of external audience would be managing reputation. Figure 23.1 depicts the framework and Illustrations 1–5 describe identity change at DELA.

Triggers of Identity Change

Past research identifies several triggers of organizational identity change (see Gioia et al., 2013 for a review). For instance, impetus for change includes an identity gap between the current identity and the organizational image (i.e., how we would like to be seen by

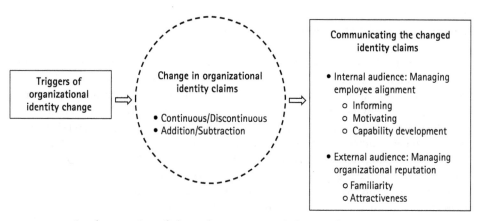

FIGURE 23.1 Implementation of planned organizational identity change

others), or a gap between the current identity and ideal identity (or the vision) (Gioia and Thomas, 1996). To illustrate, Gioia and Thomas (1996) observed that top management's perceptions of identity and image acted as a trigger of identity change. Likewise, Reger, Gustafson, Demarie, and Mullane (1994) found that an optimal identity gap provides

Illustration 1 DELA: History and Triggers of Change

DELA—a Dutch funeral insurance and care organization—was founded as a cooperative in 1937 in the southern part of the Netherlands. The four letters of DELA's corporate name stand for "Bear one another's burdens" (in Dutch: "Draagt Elkanders Lasten"). It was started by a group of people who believed that everyone has the right to a dignified funeral, regardless of rank, position, or income. Anyone could join the association for a limited monthly amount, and in return was guaranteed a dignified funeral. Within a decade, DELA became the largest and most appreciated funeral insurance and care organization in the Netherlands. Consolidating its initial success, DELA achieved a steady growth in the 80s and 90s as well by focusing on two mutually reinforcing pillars—insurance and funerals; accordingly the organization used the tagline DELA insures and organizes (Source: Annual report DELA, 2003). However, with the advent of the twenty-first century, the business, which till then seemed stable, predictable, and profitable, came under severe pressure.

In particular, there were two key changes that led leadership at DELA to broaden its existing product portfolio. First, the consumer's attitudes toward funerals began to change, and people started considering them, more and more, as family reunions. Thus, the focus of the funeral changed *from* showing glory to God and saying farewell to the deceased by shared rituals *to* continuity of life by emphasizing the shared memories around the life of the deceased. Second, in the beginning of the twenty-first century, the funeral insurance industry came under further pressure for reasons such as saturation of the market for funeral insurance, decline in the number of deaths (due to demographics and improved health case), and an increase in the number of new competitors due to low entry barriers in the funeral market. These environmental changes created, not only pressures on the prices for basic services, but also forced the organization to offer cheaper alternatives for burial and cremation packages.

Illustration 2 DELA: Changing Identity Claims

To deal with the changes in the external context, the new chairman of the company, Edzo Doeve, who took over in 2004, recalibrated DELA's strategy and product offerings. The company was known up to that point as a traditional funeral insurance and care organization; that is, in essence, its current identity focused on death. The leadership decided that the way forward was to extend the positioning with new products and services that focused on continuity of life (and not just death), while at the same time preserving the roots of the organization in the funeral business. In line with DELA's new emphasis on continuity of life, the organization started to offer related insurance products and services, for example life insurance policy, and funeral insurance policy offering care to relatives after a loved one passed away. At the same time, the organization strove to increase the funeral business by acquiring funeral homes in parts of the Netherlands where DELA did not yet have a presence (Source: Annual report DELA, 2004).

In line with the intended change, DELA also changed its identity claims and introduced a new mission. The changed mission statement emphasized the cooperative character of the organization, but also accentuated continuity of life and the three core values of commitment, integrity, and entrepreneurship. Further, the emphasis on continuity of life only increased with time. Accordingly, DELA reformulated its mission one more time with a heightened focus on involvement with, and responsibility for, the friends and family of the deceased. It stipulated that DELA had to go a step further in delivering on their promise to offer care, security, and continuity. In other words, there was both continuity and change in the new identity claims, that is, while DELA continued to stick to its core identity features, its identity also expanded to add features that were related and logical (yet were contrasting).

Illustration 3 DELA: Communicating the Changed Identity Claims to Internal Audience

To begin with, one of the ways DELA provided information about its new identity was through round-table sessions where people could have vibrant discussions with senior management and guests (Source: Annual report DELA, 2007). Further, on its 75th anniversary, DELA staged a musical, enacted by its employees, in which the story of DELA—how it originated and overcame the obstacles to grow into the present organization—was narrated to internal and external stakeholders (Source: Annual report DELA, 2012). In addition, the company started to modernize the head office, crematoria, and burial centers. Vibrant colors became a vital characteristic of DELA's buildings and house style, evoking a more attractive context for people to share memories during funerals.

Second, DELA motivated employees to support and contribute to the identity through dialogue and by implementing appropriate reward and recognition systems (Boswell et al., 2006; van Riel et al., 2009). An initiative in this regard was implementation of Result Oriented Work (ROW) in 2006 (Source: Annual report DELA, 2006). The round-table sessions were also used to discuss how result-oriented work can take place more effectively individually and in teams (Source: Annual report DELA, 2006). Further, more clarity was provided to the role of the supervisor in such work and, particularly, how one can strive for the right balance between caring and decisiveness (Source: Annual report DELA, 2008). Furthermore, in order to align funeral homes, and especially the more recently acquired funeral homes, with DELA's new direction, the company conducted interviews with customers about their recent experiences with the funeral home. These conversations were video-recorded and the employees from the funeral homes were confronted with the ones that showcased improvement areas related to DELA's core values—commitment, integrity, and entrepreneurship.

Third, employees were provided training for applying the new identity in daily practice. DELA instituted a special training program under the title "BIO-Scoop," which is the acronym of the first letters of the values in Dutch. The program included, among other things, a game in which employees had to explain to each other how they applied the values in their daily work. The game was well received and following the program, employees approached each other in the hallways to ask whether performed actions were in line with the core values (Source: Annual report DELA, 2005). Similarly, multiple training sessions were organized for employees and managers to assess internal improvement points, improve teamwork, and stimulate supportive behavior in line with the new identity. For instance, in 2009, much attention was paid on working in teams; a survey was conducted in internal teams and, based on its results, the improvement points and future action plan were decided (Source: Annual report DELA, 2009). In addition, funeral directors were trained to embed more social and emotional aspects in a funeral, adjust to personal circumstances, and improve teamwork (Source: Annual report DELA, 2009–2012).

Illustration 4 DELA: Communicating the Changed Identity Claims to External Audiences

DELA undertook several initiatives to communicate its new identity traits to the external stakeholders. One of the initiatives was the establishment of the DELA Foundation in 2005. Its aim was to strengthen DELA's original idea to "Bear one another's burdens" by offering a helping hand and doing good things for one another. To start the fund, DELA initially donated the operating profit of 2.0 million euro and subsequently half a million euro annually. By the end of 2007, over 150 projects that focused on remembering the deceased were submitted, out of which about a third received donations from the fund (Source: Annual Report DELA 2007). For example, in 2012, DELA's members could plant a bulb to remember a deceased love one at the Floriade (international exhibition of flowers and gardening) during DELA's first members' day.

Another initiative—sponsoring of the Dutch national ladies volleyball team in 2006—was aimed at expressing the idea that DELA was becoming more colorful and lively and that "continuing life" was the central aspect of its identity. Furthermore, the slogan "For one another" was printed on the shirts of the team—reconnecting yet again to DELA's roots to "Bear one another's burdens" (Source: Annual Report DELA 2006 and 2007). Similarly, in 2010, DELA developed a program called "Family Portrait." The objective of the program was to pass on life stories within families—connecting to DELA's positioning of continuity of life. After a successful season, a second episode was recorded and broadcast in 2011 (Source: Annual Report DELA 2010 and 2011).

Finally, in 2012, DELA developed a campaign "Why wait for something good to say as you can also say it now?" whose central theme was to express oneself to a loved one today (and not continuously postponing saying something beautiful to the people you love). The campaign started off with three commercials recorded with hidden cameras. In one commercial, a former refugee thanked her parents for the courage to leave their country of origin and enable her to start a new life in a safe country. In another commercial, a mother thanked her son for his extraordinary support during difficult periods (http://ogilvy.nl/werk/voor-elkaar/). Together with the commercials, DELA launched a website called "For one another." People could go to the website and leave a text for a loved one. In the following months, the texts of people were published in bus shelters of the local neighborhoods where those specific people were living. The campaign, like the other three initiatives, expressed DELA's new identity that focused on continuity of life and at the same time reconnected with DELA's roots, that is, being there for one another.

Illustration 5 DELA: Challenges Ahead

We conducted a survey a few years after DELA launched these change initiatives; this survey involved measuring employee alignment and the overall reputation of the company with the general public. Based on our results, in general, the employees responded favorably to the new identity and the related strategic initiatives, and the scores for both employee alignment and reputation were high. For instance, employees' contribution in applying changed identity to daily practice was satisfactory. Further, a similar proportion of managers and non-managers contributed to the identity and values, that is, the lower hierarchical levels did not have a lesser "line of sight" than managers.

However, the results indicated several challenges that lay ahead for DELA. For instance, the employees opined that the dialogue with the managers could be improved. Further, the employees of one of the functional areas (insurance) were less aligned with the new identity. As such, DELA needed to ensure that all the functional areas had a consistent experience, and needed to focus on training and empowering the employees from the insurance side.

Further, while, DELA enjoyed a good reputation with the general public, it still needed to work on its reputation among external stakeholders other than existing customers. Another challenge was to maintain a balance between its association with death and its foray into products and services emphasizing continuity of life. For instance, an informant from DELA mentioned, "What also remained, and therefore hinders us, is the categorization with death." Our survey results also indicated that respondents who categorized DELA as primarily a funeral insurance and funeral care organization had the most positive associations and least negative associations with it, and the ones who categorized it as being about other insurance products had more negative spontaneous associations and less positive associations. This perhaps indicates that both internal and external audiences take time to accept a new identity.

maximum motivation for identity change—when the gap is small, there is little incentive to change, and when it is too wide, there is cognitive opposition. Similarly, organizations strive to gain legitimacy by aligning the identity with the external environment (Glynn and Azbug, 2002), or respond to the pressures to improve financial performance (Tripsas, 2009). Finally, as also in the case of DELA (see Illustration 1), organizations may bring about a change in their identity following a change in the external environment (Elsbach and Kramer, 1996; Dutton and Dukerich, 1991; Ravasi and Schultz, 2006).

Change in Identity Claims

Past research has delved into the social actor and the social construction views of identity. The social construction perspective, on the one hand, regards organizational identity as shared understandings that result from members' sensemaking process about what an organization stands for (e.g., Gioia, Schultz, and Corley, 2000; Corley and Gioia, 2004). The social actor perspective, on the other hand, regards organizational identity as self-definitions or claims articulated by the organizational leaders (e.g., Whetten and Mackay, 2002). These, in essence, are "intended associations" (also referred to as projected image, desired organizational image, projected identity) that managers want stakeholders to have about the organization (Brown, Dacin, Pratt, and Whetten, 2006: 103).

As Figure 23.1 depicts, leaders respond to the triggers through a change in identity claims. In particular, when the changes in organization (e.g., due to change in external environment, identity gaps, etc.) "cannot be accommodated within the constraints of the existing identity," there may be a need to change it (Tripsas, 2009: 443). Further, in an organization going through change, existing understanding and narrative about what the organization stands for gets challenged, and stakeholders lack clarity about the organization's identity (Corley and Gioia, 2004; Ravasi and Schultz, 2006). For instance, Trispas (2009) found that during change, while claims about 'what identity is not' are well defined, there is ambiguity and uncertainty around what the organization is. At that point, top management's identity claims can reduce the uncertainty (Elstak, Bhatt, van Riel, Pratt, and Berens, 2015) and ambiguity, and help internal and external audiences "rebuild their sense of who they are as an organization" (Corley and Gioia, 2004; Ravasi and Schultz, 2006: 448). Thus, through a "claim-making process," organizational leadership may try to convince internal and external stakeholders about what the organization stands for (Glynn, 2000: 286). These new identity claims then help members reconstruct a collective sense of who they are as an organization (e.g., Corley and Gioia, 2004; Tripsas, 2009).

The change in organizational identity claims could involve continuity or discontinuity. Discontinuous change is radical—it is characterized by a break from the past where the old identity is substituted or replaced by a new identity (e.g., Biggart, 1977; Fiol, 2002). However, based on our observation from practice—which perhaps could also be implied by the number of studies on the topic—a majority of identity change efforts are characterized by a sense of continuity even when the identity is changing, that is, an organization may add new identity elements, instead of replacing the old identity completely (e.g., Chreim, 2005; Gioia et al., 2000; Gioia and Thomas, 1996; Ravasi and Philips, 2011; Ravasi and Schultz, 2006). For instance, at DELA too, change in identity claims involved both continuity and change (see Illustration 2).

Initiatives to Implement Organizational Identity Change

As organizations begin changing their organizational identity claims, the next step is to communicate this change to stakeholders. As our framework proposes (see Figure 23.1), the key goal of these communication efforts for internal audience is ensuring employee alignment, and for external audience it is managing organizational reputation.

Communicating the Identity Claims Internally: Managing Employee Alignment

As noted, there are two views of identity—the social actor view and the social constructionist view; the interplay of these two views—that is, the claims and the understandings—provides a more "accurate representation" of organizational identity (Ravasi and Schultz, 2006: 436). In particular, changing the identity claims (for instance, what DELA did by changing its mission statement) may not always result in a change in members' shared understanding of organizational identity; hence, how they come in line with each other could be an interesting empirical question to explore (Ravasi and Schultz, 2006).

One of the ways, the top management could try to get them in sync is through their communication initiatives aimed at ensuring employee alignment, which refers to employee actions that are consistent with the organization's strategy (van Riel, Berens, and Dijkstra, 2009). Specifically, such actions/behaviors could be seen as a subset of in-role and organizational citizenship behaviors that contribute to the realization of strategy (van Riel et al., 2009). Employee alignment could be promoted by "stimulating employee motivation, informing employees, and stimulating the development of their capabilities" (van Riel et al., 2009: 1197); the basic premise here is that organizations tend to perform well when employees are motivated and knowledgeable about how to behave in line with the organizational identity and its strategy (Colvin and Boswell, 2007).

Organizations can take several actions to motivate and inform the employees and stimulate their capability development (see Illustration 3 for DELA's initiatives). To begin with, leaders can provide information about the new strategic course and organizational identity to the employees (Boswell and Boudreau, 2001; Boswell, 2006). Second, a coherent, realistic story could be another way of communicating the new identity to employees (van Riel and van Hasselt, 2002). Third, the office architecture, visual, and material artifacts are the visible elements of organizational culture that may help demonstrate identity claims (Schein, 1996; Ravasi and Schultz, 2006). As Ravasi and Schultz (2006: 449) argued, "top managers turn ... to the culture of the organization to imbue revised identity claims with meaning, relying on a web of familiar stories, objects, and practices to facilitate interpretation of the new claims and illustrate their implications for action." Fourth, past research highlights that even when leaders communicate a shift in identity claims and make relevant structural changes in the organization, identity change is inhibited if the organization fails to change practices (i.e., how things are done) (Nag, Corley, and Gioia, 2007). As such, it is important, not just to make a claim of identity change, but also to bring about a change in routines and practices. Therefore, an organization could implement appropriate reward and recognition systems for motivating the employees to support and contribute to the new identity (Boswell, Bingham, and Colvin, 2006; van Riel et al., 2009). Finally, employees also need training to develop the right set of capabilities to be able to contribute to the new identity (Colvin and Boswell, 2007; Gottschalg and Zollo, 2007; van Riel et al., 2009).

Communicating the Identity Externally: Managing Organizational Reputation

Reputation refers to "perceptual representation of a company's past actions and future prospects that describe the firms' overall appeal to all its key constituents when compared with other leading rivals" (Fombrun, 1996: 72). It denotes stakeholders' feedback to an organization about whether they find its identity claims credible and appealing (Whetten and Mackay, 2002). Thus, as depicted in Figure 23.1, reputation includes, not just the extent to which audiences are familiar or aware about the organization, but also their judgments regarding the overall attractiveness of the firm and its products and services, etc. (Lange, Lee, and Dai, 2011). Thus, initiatives to manage reputation need to aim at establishing familiarity as well as attractiveness.

Further, these initiatives could be both substantive and symbolic (Highhouse, Brooks, and Gregarus, 2009). Substantive actions generally require a major change in company's goals and structures (Ashforth and Gibbs, 1990); these may include investments in human capital, product development, and diversification (Petkova, Rindova, and Gupta, 2008; Highhouse et al., 2009). For example, DELA's substantive actions included launching new products and services (see Illustration 2). Further, an organization's market performance and corporate social responsibility initiatives also affect its reputation positively (Fombrun and Shanley, 1990).

In contrast to substantive actions that include making key changes, symbolic activities include actions taken to express or convey an impression to the stakeholders (Ashforth and Gibbs, 1990). These initiatives should aim at facilitating familiarity and formulating an emotional connect with the external stakeholders; as van Riel (2012: 172) also suggested, "the power of communication is not in passing along facts but in evoking emotions." One of the most effective strategies for increasing audience's understanding about the company and increasing its appeal is advertising (Brady, Arndt, and Barrett, 2005; Highhouse et al., 2009). Other ways of communicating to external audience include new corporate slogans and logos, press releases, interviews published in media, educational material and brochures, annual reports and corporate websites, and public relations (Ravasi and Schultz, 2006; Trispas, 2009; Highhouse et al., 2009).

In sum, an organization may respond to triggers by changing its identity claims. These claims could be directed both toward internal and external audiences with the goals of managing employee alignment and organizational reputation respectively.

PLANNED IDENTITY CHANGE: IMPLICATIONS FOR RESEARCH

In the previous section, we proposed a framework of planned organizational identity change. The framework opens several avenues for future research.

Type of Identity Change

Identity change could be characterized by continuity (e.g., Corley and Gioia, 2004; Gioia and Thomas, 1996; Hatch and Schultz, 2002) or discontinuity (e.g., Biggart, 1977; Fiol, 2002); however, as Ravasi and Schultz (2006: 455) state, "the literature holds little evidence of successful radical changes of organizational identity." The implementation initiatives discussed in our framework also apply mostly in cases of continuous change; as such, an interesting question would be how an organization could implement a discontinuous change successfully. Understandably, implementing a radical change might involve a greater level of difficulty; and it would be interesting to look at how such a change varies in terms of process, organizational actions, and challenges that have to be addressed for implementing the change. For instance, Biggart (1977) proposed steps such as resocializing employees, changing their behavior, and even removing employees who continued to support the old identity. Since a discontinuous change may involve more drastic steps, future research may examine how the nature of initiatives used for aligning employees and managing reputation differ from those used in a change involving continuity.

Further, past research, in general, does not focus on differences between identity change involving expansion to add more elements, and one characterized by substitution or subtraction of certain elements. Addition and substitution may imply different challenges for employees. For instance, replacing an old identity with a new one involves a sense of loss (Albert and Whetten, 1985). Similarly, as Kjærgaard et al. (2011) opine, members may be more resistant to altering their identity beliefs when identity change involves substitution rather than addition. How, then, would an organization address members' sense of loss and modify its identity claims to ensure employee alignment and reputation? A case in point is Clark et al.'s (2010) study of top management teams implementing a major change—that is, a merger—where having an interim transitional identity helped in retaining some sense of current identity, along with facilitating a movement toward a new one.

Addition of identities, on the other hand, may lead to identity plurality or exist-ence of multiple identities which could be hybrid, that is, the identity may include ele-ments which are incompatible and not expected to go together (Albert and Whetten, 1985). As Pratt and Foreman (2000) argued, when different identity characterizations are compatible and synergistic, organizational members tend to aggregate them, that is, retain all of them and forge links between them. However, when these charac-terizations are hybrid or conflicting, organizational members resort to either identity compartmentalization (i.e., segregating them) or identity deletion (i.e., choosing to limit the expression of some of them) (Pratt and Foreman, 2000). As such, this raises a question: How would identity claims change to incorporate contrasting elements? And more importantly, how would an organization communicate such claims to in-ternal and external audiences? For instance, Humphreys and Brown (2002) suggested that senior managers tried to reduce identity plurality in the narratives by resorting to identity deletion. Further, past research on individual identities suggests that in-dividuals tend to ascribe "differential importance" to different self-aspects (Showers, Abrahmson, and Hogan, 1998). This could be true for an organization too; further, the relative emphasis on different elements may change over time and, perhaps, one iden-tity element may act as a deterrent to the other. For instance, while DELA aggregated its identities, its emphasis on "life" increased over time. Perhaps, future research could examine how organizational members deal with an organization's changing emphasis over time.

Barriers to Identity Change

There could be several barriers to identity change (Gioia et al., 2013). For instance, organizational members may resist change as a stable identity provides psycho-logical anchoring (Gustafson and Reger, 1995) and a way to preserve social identity (Ashforth and Mael, 1989). Other barriers to change include organizational prac-tices (Nag et al., 2007), cognitive inertia to accept the change (Trispas, 2009), and legitimacy imperatives (Glynn and Azbug, 2002). For instance, at DELA, the outsid-ers had a more positive association with the old identity (i.e., a funeral company) and less so with the new one (see Illustration 5). This is in line with Trispas' (2009) observation that the external audience took three to five years to perceive and re-spond to the changes in the firm's identity claims and associated business strategy. Thus, a possible question to investigate could be how leaders can address some of these barriers through their communication practices? Similarly, Corley and Gioia (2004) talked about employees' sense of overload during change, as they often have additional responsibilities and activities during such times. For instance, several of DELA's actions also required involvement of employees and perhaps, in effect, meant extra work for them. If so, at what point might these activities that facilitate change, instead, act as a barrier to change?

Cross-Level Identity Dynamics during Change

Ashorth, Rogers, and Corley (2011) drew our attention to cross-level identity dynamics. They suggested that, in general, core identity aspects tend to be isomorphic across levels; such isomorphism is usually reinforced by identity claims, narratives, and archetypes that are used by leaders for sensegiving to different stakeholders. At DELA too, we observed that employees at different hierarchical levels responded similarly to the new identity (see Illustration 5). However, identity differentiation across levels may also happen—for one, identities become more grounded and less abstract as one goes down levels, and two, different groups tend to emphasize different aspects of identity (Ashforth et al., 2011). As Corley (2004) observed, while the top management and those higher in the hierarchy were focused on changes in identity labels, those in the lower ranks were more concerned by the meaning behind the change in labels. Given that identity at one level may both constrain and enable identities at other levels (Ashforth et al., 2011), several questions become relevant for identity change. For instance, what are some of the challenges organizations encounter in aligning employees at different levels? At which level—the distal or the proximal—is it easier to implement identity change and why? Are the steps taken for these levels different? How does the lack of alignment at one level affect the alignment at another level?

Further, there is a possibility that members of some departments or functions are more receptive to identity change than the others; for instance, at DELA, we found that the employees of one of the functional areas were less aligned with the new identity (see Illustration 5). This raises several questions that could be examined in future research: does the change get implemented and also accepted or received similarly across the organization and different stakeholders? When and why is there an inconsistency in how different groups (e.g., different departments, functional groups, stakeholders, etc.) receive change? What are some implications of such an inconsistency? For instance, alignment in only some part(s) of the organization can create an insider–outsider dynamic, hampering value creation across the workforce (Colvin and Boswell, 2007). So, how can organizations ensure that all groups have a consistent experience? And finally, how can an organization manage such inconsistencies?

Similarly, the external stakeholders (e.g., customers, suppliers) may have a bearing on how organizational members make sense of top management's identity claims (Scott and Lane, 2000); however, as Ashforth et al. (2011: 1153) claim, "little consideration has been given to the interactions between the dynamics of image and the cross-level dynamics of identity." For instance, perhaps organizational members at the boundaries, that is, those who are interacting with the outsiders (e.g., salespeople) might be more affected by organizational reputation. How would organizational identity claims from top management and organizational reputation bear upon their sense of identity and alignment with the organization?

Identity Change and Reputation

Our framework suggests organizational actions that can be taken to communicate the new identity to outsiders with the goal of managing reputation. Past research argues for more research on how identity and reputation may be linked (e.g., Whetten and Mackey, 2002). Perhaps, these two streams could be integrated to examine several interesting and relevant questions. For instance, what does identity change mean for managing reputation in the short and long term? What are some of the challenges in managing reputation when the organization is going through identity change? What are some of the steps organizations take to manage reputation while going through change? Do these steps and challenges differ based on the type of identity change?

Further, as Whetten and Mackay (2002) argue, given that reputation denotes the feedback from external stakeholders about the credibility of the organization's identity, these two are naturally linked, and a mismatch between them may lead to identity crisis (e.g., Elsbach and Kramer, 1996). Perhaps, in future, one could longitudinally examine the reciprocal relationship between identity and reputation and how one feeds into the other. For instance, Kjærgaard et al. (2011: 536) suggested that organizational "members and the media are constantly engaged in an ongoing co-creation of meaning that provides media with appealing newsworthy stories, and addresses members' needs for self-enhancement." But then, how does an organization respond when the new identity claims are not received well by the external stakeholders? Further, how would an incongruence in substantive initiatives (e.g., change in products mix) and symbolic actions (e.g., communication of identity through advertisements, etc.) affect reputation?

Role of Context in Identity Change

Studies that focus on an organization's similarity with other organizations in a category (e.g., an industry grouping, status ranking, societal culture, nation-state, etc.) argue that "institutions—and processes of institutionalization—might surface more fully in the dynamics of identity construction, change, and performance" (Glynn, 2008: 363; Glynn and Abzug, 2002). To illustrate, Glynn and Abzug (2002) found that organizations chose their names such that the names aligned with the prevailing naming practices in the industry. It would be interesting to examine how category bears upon identity change efforts for managing alignment and reputation. For instance, one aspect of a category is "category currency" or the extent to which it has both "clear meaning and positive appeal" (Kennedy, Lo, and Lousbury, 2010: 372). Perhaps it would be interesting to examine if the identity change process looks different in different industry categories because of the difference in their appeal or reputation. As past research suggests, identification is easier to achieve in organizations with a higher perceived external prestige (Smidts et al., 2001). Drawing from this finding, perhaps it would be more difficult to implement organizational identity change in an industry category with low reputation.

As a related point, specific characteristics of the company, such as its size may have a bearing upon identity change process. DELA is a relatively small organization: would identity change look different in organizations in a large, global organization? In particular, bigger organizations have many more stakeholders: would that make reputation management more complex? Similarly, organizations that have a unique positioning and are more visible may encounter different advantages and challenges; as such, future research might look at how identity change takes place in such companies. For instance, Ravasi and Schultz (2006: 455) argued that perhaps people may had a more "heightened sense of self" due to the unique nature of product offering. Similarly, Kjærgaard et al.'s (2011) examination of identity change in a "celebrity firm" suggested that media coverage may both facilitate and impede identity reconstruction.

Identity Change and Strategy Change

Several scholars have raised our attention toward how strategic change may associate with identity change (e.g., Corley and Gioia, 2004; Gioia and Thomas, 1996; Kjærgaard et al., 2011; Ravasi and Phillips, 2011; Trispas, 2009). Yet, there is a need for more research on the relationship between strategy and identity (Trispas, 2009): for instance, Trispas (2009: 456) called for examination of "whether a change in strategy implies a change in identity and vice versa," and how "relationship between origins of strategy and origins of identity" looks. For instance, in the case of DELA, decisions related to product and services or business strategy more broadly, led to a change in identity claims; further, implementing this change required a communication strategy. Thus, in some sense, strategy and identity had a reciprocal relationship with one bearing upon the other and vice versa. Thus, an interesting question could be to examine the two longitudinally to understand how they are intertwined. More generally, one could investigate how existing structures (and a change in them) bear upon identity change and vice versa. Perhaps, Giddens' (1984) structuration theory would be a lens to draw from as one analyzes such change situations.

PLANNED IDENTITY CHANGE: IMPLICATIONS FOR PRACTICE

The framework offers several practical implications. First, while DELA went through a change in identity, it also preserved the origins of the organization. Past research in the merger context emphasizes that a sense of continuity, that is, "a general feeling that the post-merger organization is a continuation of the pre-merger organization" helps reduce the uncertainty surrounding the merger (e.g., Giessner, 2011: 1080; van Knippenberg and van Leeuwen, 2001). Perhaps even in a non-merger context, such continuity helps in ensuring employee alignment, and leaders should highlight it in their identity change initiatives.

Second, the framework discussed suggests how an organization could possibly align identity claims and understandings; further, we illustrate concrete steps that were taken by DELA's management to communicate and embed the new expanded identity in the organization. In particular, these included actions to inform the employees about the new identity, motivate them to imbue these claims in their daily activities, and capability development which involved training them to do so (see Illustration 3). Taking such actions might help organizations in ensuring employee alignment.

Third, in a deliberate organizational identity change effort, it is important to take both internal and external audiences into consideration. As discussed, several symbolic initiatives could be undertaken to communicate the change to the external stakeholders. In particular, a compelling and authentic story goes a long way in getting support for the intended change (van Riel, 2012). Further, the message needs to be appealing, understandable, and "summarized in a memorable way" (van Riel, 2012: 69). Top management should focus on crafting such a story in order to manage its reputation.

Fourth, we mention that both substantive and symbolic actions could be taken to manage reputation. For organizations bringing about change, the congruence between symbolic and substantive activities could be crucial. As van Halderen, Bhatt, Berens, van Riel, and Brown (2016) found, when stakeholders perceive that the symbolic actions were not aligned with the substantive ones, pressures from them increased; in response to growing stakeholder pressures, the organizations tried to bring them in line. In any case, times such as change are filled with ambiguity, and any incongruence would perhaps only add to the prevailing confusion. As such, leaders' change efforts should aim at keeping the two in sync.

Finally, once an identity change initiative is implemented, it is important to take stock of whether the organization has been able to achieve goals aspired to. Such an exercise may help in ensuring that the organization is able to reap the full benefits of change. For instance, we found that at DELA, while the change, in general, was implemented successfully, there were several areas that needed improvement. To ensure sustained success of identity change, DELA needed to address these issues.

References

Albert, S. and Whetten, D. (1985). "Organizational Identity." In *Research in Organizational Behavior*," vol. 7, edited by L. L. Cummings and B. M. Staw, 263–95. Greenwich, CT: JAI Press.

Ashforth, B. E. and Gibbs, W. G. (1990). "The Double-Edge of Organizational Legitimacy." *Organization Science* 1: 177–94.

Ashforth, B. E. and Mael, F. (1989). "Social Identity Theory and the Organization." *Academy of Management Review* 14: 20–39.

Ashforth, B. E., Rogers, K. M., and Corley, K. G. (2011). "Identity in Organizations: Exploring Cross-Level Dynamics." *Organization Science* 22: 1144–56.

Biggart, M. W. (1977). "The Creative Destruction Process of Organizational Change." *Administrative Science Quarterly* 22: 410–25.

Boswell, W. R. and Boudreau, J. W. (2001). "How Leading Companies Create, Measure, and Achieve Strategic Results through 'Line of Sight.'" *Management Decision* 39: 851–9.

Boswell, W. R. (2006). "Aligning Employees with the Organization's Strategic Objectives: Out of 'Line of Sight,' Out of Mind." *International Journal of Human Resource Management* 17: 1489–1511.

Boswell, W. R., Bingham, J. B., and Colvin, A. J. S. (2006). "Aligning Employees through 'Line of Sight.'" *Business Horizons* 49: 499–509.

Brady. D., Arndt, M., and Barrett, A. (2005). "When your Name Is Mud, Advertise." *Business Week* 3941: 56–8.

Brown, T., Dacin P., Pratt M., and Whetten, D. (2006). "Identity, Intended Image, Construed Image, and Reputation: An Interdisciplinary Framework and Suggested Methodology." *Journal of the Academy of Marketing Science* 34: 95–106.

Chreim, S. (2005). "The Continuity–Change Duality in Narrative Texts of Organizational Identity." *Journal of Management Studies* 42: 567–93.

Clark, S. M., Gioia, D. A., Ketchen, D. Jr., and Thomas, J. B. (2010). "Transitional Identity as a Facilitator of Organizational Identity Change during a Merger." *Administrative Science Quarterly* 55: 397–438.

Cook, S. D. N. and Yanow, D. (1993). "Culture and Organizational Learning." *Journal of Management Inquiry* 2: 373–90.

Corley, K. G. (2004). "Defined by our Strategy or our Culture? Hierarchical Differences in Perceptions of Organizational Identity and Change." *Human Relations* 57: 1145–77.

Corley, K. G. and Gioia, D. A. (2004). "Identity Ambiguity and Change in the Wake of a Corporate Spin-Off." *Administration Science Quarterly* 49: 173–208.

Corley, K. G., Harquail, C. V., Pratt, M. G., Glynn, M. A., Fiol, C. M., and Hatch, M. J. (2006). "Guiding Organizational Identity through Aged Adolescence." *Journal of Management Inquiry* 15: 85–99.

Colvin, A. J. S. and Boswell, W. R. (2007). "The Problem of Action and Interest Alignment: Beyond Job Requirements and Incentive Compensation." *Human Resource Management Review* 17: 38–51.

Dutton, J. E. and Dukerich, J. M. (1991). "Keeping an Eye on the Mirror: Image and Identity in Organizational Adaptation." *Academy of Management Journal* 34: 517–54.

Elsbach, K. D. and Kramer, R. M. (1996). "Members' Responses to Organizational Identity Threats: Encountering and Countering the *Business Week* Rankings." *Administrative Science Quarterly* 41: 442–76.

Elstak, M. N., Bhatt, M., van Riel, C. B. M., Pratt, M. G., and Berens, G. A. J. M. (2015). "Organizational Identification during a Merger: The Role of Self-Enhancement and Uncertainty Reduction Motives during a Major Organizational Change." *Journal of Management Studies* 52: 32–62.

Fiol, C. M. (2002). "Capitalizing on Paradox: The Role of Language in Transforming Organizational Identities." *Organization Science* 13: 653–66.

Fombrun, C. J. (1996). *Reputation: Realizing Value from the Corporate Image*. Boston: Harvard Business School Press.

Fombrun, C. J. and Shanley, M. (1990). "What's in a Name? Reputation Building and Corporate Strategy." *Academy of Management Journal* 33(2): 233–56.

Giddens, A. (1984). *The Constitution of Society*. Cambridge: Polity Press.

Giessner, S. R. (2011). "Is the Merger Necessary? The Interactive Effect of Perceived Necessity and Sense of Continuity on Post-Merger Identification." *Human Relations* 64: 1079–98.

Gioia, D. A. and Thomas, J. B. (1996). "Identity, Image and Issue Interpretation: Sensemaking during Strategic Change in Academia." *Administrative Science Quarterly* 41: 370–403.

Gioia, D. A., Patvardhan, S. D., Hamilton, A. L., and Corley, K. G. (2013). "Organizational Identity Formation and Change." *Academy of Management Annals* 7: 123–92.

Gioia, D. A., Schultz, M., and Corley, K. G. (2000). "Organizational Identity, Image, and Adaptive Instability." *Academy of Management Review* 25: 63–81.

Glynn, M. A. (2000). "When Cymbals Become Symbols: Conflict over Organizational Identity within a Symphony Orchestra." *Organization Science* 11: 285–98.

Glynn, M. A. (2008). "Beyond Constraint: How Institutions Enable Identities." In *The SAGE Handbook of Organizational Institutionalism*, edited by R. Greenwood, C. Oliver, R. Suddaby, and K. Sahlin, 413–30. Los Angeles, CA: SAGE.

Glynn, M. A. and Abzug, R. (2002). "Institutionalizing Identity: Symbolic Isomorphism and Organizational Names." *Academy of Management Journal* 45: 267–80.

Glynn, M. A. and Marquis, C. (2007). "Legitimating Identities: How Institutional Logics Motivate Organizational Name Choices." In *Identity and the Modern Organization*, edited by C. A. Bartel, S. Blader, and A. Wrzesniewski, 17–33. Mahwah, NJ: Lawrence Erlbaum.

Golden-Biddle, K. and Rao, H. (1997). "Breaches in the Boardroom: Organizational Identity and Conflicts of Commitment in a Non-Profit Organization." *Organization Science* 8: 593–611.

Gottschalg, O. and Zollo, M. (2007). "Interest Alignment and Competitive Advantage." *Academy of Management Review* 32: 418–37.

Gustafson, L. T. and Reger, R. K. (1995). "Using Organizational Identity to Achieve Stability and Change in High Velocity Environments." *Academy of Management Best Papers Proceedings* 464–8.

Hatch, M. J. and Schultz, M. (1997). "Relations between Organizational Culture, Identity and Image." *European Journal of Marketing* 35: 356–65.

Hatch, M. J. and Schultz, M. S. (2002). "The Dynamics of Organizational Identity." *Human Relations* 55: 989–1018.

Highhouse, S., Brooks, M. E. and Greguras, G. (2009). "An Organizational Impression Management Perspective on the Formation of Corporate Reputations." *Journal of Management* 35: 1481–93.

Hsu, G. and Hannan, M. T. (2005). "Identities, Genres and Organizational Forms." *Organization Science* 16: 474–90.

Humphreys, M., and Brown, A. D. (2002). "Narratives of Organizational Identity and Identification: A Case Study of Hegemony and Resistance." *Organization Studies* 23: 421–47.

Kennedy, M. T., Lo, J. Y., and Lounsbury, M. (2010). "Category Currency: The Changing Value of Conformity as a Function of Ongoing Meaning Construction." In *Categories in Markets: Origins and Evolution*, Research in the Sociology of Organizations, vol. 31, edited by G. Hsu, G. Negro, and Ö. Koçak, 369–97. Bingley: Emerald Group Publishing.

Kjærgaard, A., Morsing, M., and Ravasi, D. (2011). "Mediating Identity: A Study of Media Influence on Organizational Identity Construction in a Celebrity Firm." *Journal of Management Studies* 48: 514–43.

Lange, D., Lee, P. M., and Dai, Y. (2011). "Organizational Reputation: A Review." *Journal of Management* 37: 153–84.

Nag, R., Corley, K. G., and Gioia, D. A. (2007). "The Intersection of Organizational Identity, Knowledge, and Practice: Attempting Strategic Change via Knowledge Grafting." *Academy of Management Journal* 50: 821–47.

Petkova, A., Rindova, V., and Gupta, A. (2008). "How Can New Ventures Build Reputation? An Exploratory Study." *Corporate Reputation Review* 11: 320–34.

Pratt, M. and Foreman, P. (2000). "The Beauty of and Barriers to Organizational Theories of Identity." *Academy of Management Review* 25: 141–3.

Ravasi, D. and Phillips, N. (2011). "Strategies of Alignment: Organizational Identity Management and Strategic Change at Bang & Olufsen." *Strategic Organization* 9: 103–35;

Ravasi, D. and Schultz, M. (2006). "Responding to Organizational Identity Threats: Exploring the Role of Organizational Culture." *Academy of Management Journal* 49: 433–58.

Reger, R., Gustafson, L. T., Demarie, S. M., and Mullane, J. V. (1994). "Reframing the Organization: Why Implementing Total Quality Is Easier Said than Done." *Academy of Management Review* 19: 565–85.

Schein, E. H. (1996). "Culture: The Missing Concept in Organization Studies." *Administrative Science Quarterly* 41: 229–40.

Scott, S. G. and Lane, V. R. (2000). "A Stakeholder Approach to Organizational Identity." *Academy of Management Review* 25: 43–62.

Showers, C. L., Abramson, L. Y., and Hogan, M. E. (1998). "The Dynamic Self: How the Content and Structure of the Self-Concept Change with Mood." *Journal of Personality and Social Psychology* 75: 478–93.

Smidts, A., Pruyn, A. T. H., and van Riel, C. B. M. (2001). "The Impact of Employee Communication and Perceived External Prestige on Organizational Identification." *Academy of Management Journal* 49: 1051–62.

Tripsas, M. (2009). "Technology, Identity and Inertia through the Lens of 'The Digital Photography Company.'" *Organization Science* 20: 440–61.

van Halderen, M. D., Bhatt, M., Berens, G. A. J. M., Brown, and van Riel, C. B. M. (2016). "Managing Impressions in the Face of Rising Stakeholder Pressures: Examining Oil Companies' Shifting Stances in the Climate Change Debate." *Journal of Business Ethics* 133: 567–82.

van Knippenberg, D. and van Leeuwen, E. (2001). "Sense of Continuity as the Key to Post Merger Identification." In *Social Identity Processes in Organizational Context*, edited by M. A. Hogg and D. J. Terry, 249–63. Philadelphia, PA: Psychology Press.

van Riel, C. B. M. (2012). *The Alignment Factor*. New York: Routledge.

van Riel, C. B. M., Berens, G., and Dijkstra, M. (2009). "Stimulating Strategically Aligned Behaviour among Employees." *Journal of Management Studies* 46: 1197–226.

van Riel, C. B. M. and van Hasselt, J. J. (2002). "Conversion of Organizational Research Findings into Action." In *Corporate and Organizational Identities*, edited by G. Soenen and B. Moingeon, 156–74. London: Routledge.

Whetten, D. A. and Mackey, A. (2002). "A Social Actor Conception of Organizational Identity and its Implications for the Study of Organizational Reputation." *Business and Society* 41: 393–414.

CHAPTER 24

IDENTITY CONSTRUCTION IN MERGERS AND ACQUISITIONS

a discursive sensemaking perspective

JANNE TIENARI AND EERO VAARA

INTRODUCTION

In their groundbreaking treatise on organizational identity, Albert and Whetten (1985) encouraged us to study the specific contexts of mergers and acquisitions (M&As) that blur the boundaries between previously separate organizations, and challenge taken-for-granted assumptions about what is central, distinctive, and enduring about an organization. Subsequent research has established that M&As place acute demands on the employees of the merging organizations (Brown and Humphreys, 2003). Perhaps inevitably, M&As are characterized by confrontation, and identities can become entrenched and intractable when people are forced to search for a common future (Cartwright and Cooper, 1990; van Knippenberg and van Leeuwen, 2001; Empson, 2004; van Vuuren, Beelen, and de Jong, 2010). Hence, it has been argued that the ultimate success of an M&A depends on establishing a sense of continuity in the transition from pre- to post-merger identification. This has proven to be notoriously difficult, however, and extant research reports that mergers often fail to meet the initial objectives set by the strategists. "People-related issues" such as culture and identity are commonly cited as reasons for these disappointments (Teerikangas and Very, 2006).

In this chapter, we elucidate the processes by which organizations and organizational members engage in self-definitions during mergers and acquisitions. We will take stock of the literature on identity in M&As, highlight its shortcomings, and offer discursive sensemaking as an alternative conceptualization of identity construction. In this view, identities are construed in sensemaking (Weick, 1995; Weick, Sutcliffe, and Obstfeld, 2005) that draws from and mobilizes a variety of cultural and discursive resources (Swidler, 1986; Weber and Dacin, 2011) to construct, transform, and at times destruct senses of organizational identity. Discursive resources are understood here as language-based means used by individuals and groups in attempts to work on a sense of belonging to a collective in novel circumstances. We argue that this conceptualization also contributes more generally to our understanding of identities in radical or extreme organizational change. Although it is not exclusive and exhaustive, it offers an alternative perspective that complements the extant body of knowledge.

The chapter is structured as follows. We first locate studies of identity in M&As against the backdrop of the much debated concepts of culture and power, and go on to review research that focuses specifically on identity and identification in the merger setting. We then develop a framework for understanding identity construction in M&As and elaborate on the central role of stereotypes, tropes, narratives, and antenarratives as discursive resources mobilized in sensemaking as the merger unfolds. Finally, we outline avenues for future research.

Culture and Identity in M&As

Mergers involve a transfer of assets from two or more companies to a new one. Acquisitions involve the takeover of one or more companies by another. While the concepts of merger and acquisition are legally distinct, they are often treated interchangeably in academic research. This is because in practice one merger partner typically turns out to be more influential in shaping the new organization. In other words, most "mergers of equals" exist only on paper. As an empirical phenomenon, the transition from legacy organizations—the merger counterparts—to new, combined organizational entities has proved to be a fruitful setting for studying the ways in which human beings as individuals and groups think and act in radical change characterized by uncertainty.

Culture and Power

Extant research suggests that mergers and acquisitions involve two fundamental dynamics: culture and power. Cultural compatibility, incompatibility, and rivalry, as well as combinations of legacy cultures are frequently addressed topics in M&A literature. As radical change involving the amalgamation of two (or more) previously separate entities, mergers invite a heightened sense of belonging to a specific social group (the merging organizations), but also generate pressure to identify with a new group (the organization resulting from the merger). Cultural belonging becomes increasingly pronounced when one's "own" group and its unique qualities and characteristics are perceived to be under threat. This condition is typical of M&As where the present and the future become uncertain, and individuals experience anxiety, stress, and the perception of losing their sense of belonging to an organization (Cartwright and Cooper, 1990). At the same time, they may also fear losing their jobs and livelihoods.

Although the cultural perspective on M&As originally focused on "organizational cultures" (Buono et al., 1985; Nahavandi and Malekzadeh, 1988; Cartwright and Cooper, 1990), a stream of studies soon emerged with a focus on differences and contradictions in international M&As through the lens of "national cultures" (Olie, 1994; Calori, Lubatkin, and Véry, 1994). Socio-cultural integration of two (or more) previously separate entities was found to be of crucial importance in making mergers work, and culture became a useful heuristic device for singling out reasons for the various merger outcomes (Shrivastava, 1986; Haspeslagh and Jemison, 1991). The impact that "cultural" differences—and their management or lack thereof—have on merger performance has subsequently attracted substantial research interest (Stahl and Voigt, 2005).

It has become customary to assert that a significant proportion of mergers fail to fulfill the objectives initially set, and that "people-related" issues—typically culture and a lack of culture management—explain these disappointments to a significant extent (for contradictory findings, see Teerikangas and Véry, 2006). However, viewed from a social constructionist perspective, cultural manifestations are not clearly consistent or inconsistent; they are neither essentially harmonious nor in conflict, but are instead ambiguous, fragmented, and in flux (Risberg, 1997). Not surprisingly, then, singling out the cultural factors that explain merger performance has proven to be a quixotic task (Meglio and Risberg, 2011). Hence, following the development of cultural studies in organizations more generally (Weber and Dacin, 2011), research interest in M&As has focused on cultural and discursive resources and their mobilization in specific contexts, rather than on essential cultural characteristics and their effects on outcome factors such as performance (Vaara and Tienari, 2011).

In addition to culture, specific dynamics of power and resistance characterize M&As (Tienari and Vaara, 2012). Seminal studies of organizational culture were already acutely aware of the importance of perceptions of the "locus of power" in M&As (Buono et al., 1985) and of people's "heightened self-interest," which gives rise to confrontation in merger contexts (Marks, 1997). This also applies to studies of international M&As which have sought to understand the impact of the dominance of one national culture over another (Olie, 1994). In brief, cultural studies of M&As have typically framed power as the dominance of (the "culture" of) one merger party over the other, even in cases that are promoted as "mergers of equals" (Vaara, Tienari, Piekkari, and Säntti, 2005; Maguire and Phillips, 2008; Monin, Noorderhaven, Vaara, and Kroon, 2013).

However, the power-related dynamics of M&As are more complicated than a simple matrix of domination and subordination would imply. Various actors and groups with different interests and expectations are involved in the process and affect its unfolding. Perceptions of domination and subordination play out in struggles, resistance, and politicking, and the "locus of power" is negotiated and renegotiated over time

(Vaara et al., 2005; Tienari and Vaara, 2012). What is specific about the M&A context, however, is that the power struggles are enmeshed in cultural confrontation and ambivalence. Vaara (2003) argues that cultural confusion leads to the politicization of post-merger integration. Hence integration has been found to be contingent on the specific cultural and power-related characteristics of the merger process in hand. Brannen and Peterson (2009) talk about "pockets of alienation" in pinpointing reasons why certain localities in the organization following a cross-border merger report more alienation than others. These reasons include poor local cross-cultural management by representatives of the "stronger" merger counterpart. Overall, research on culture in M&As has proliferated to the extent that it has been argued that culture has become a shorthand with which both researchers and practitioners frame and simplify complex social phenomena (Riad, 2005).

Identities and Identification

Different emphases notwithstanding, research addressing identities and identification in M&As has emerged on the back of studies of cultures and cultural differences. The formation of self-definitions in merging organizations has been addressed at various levels of analysis. Much of the seminal research has focused on individuals as members of social groups confronted by mergers. In line with these social psychological studies, van Knippenberg and van Leeuwen (2001) assert that the more employees perceive the merged organization to be a continuation of their pre-merger group, the closer is the association they make between pre-merger and post-merger identification. Their research also suggests that employees whose pre-merger organizational identification is strong tend to feel more threatened by merger processes. The postulation that mergers may fail "because of 'us' versus 'them' dynamics that prevail if employees do not relinquish their old identities" is also typical (Hogg and Terry, 2000: 133). Arguments on distinct rival "cultures" are thus extended to a new domain of identity and identification.

Van Knippenberg, van Knippenberg, Monden, and De Lima (2002) suggest that pre- and post-merger identification are more positively related for members of dominant as opposed to dominated groups, and that perceived differences between the merger partners are more negatively related to post-merger identification for members of dominated groups. Considerations of domination and subordination figure in the analyses—as they do in cultural studies of M&As—as perceptions of domination/subordination and the relative status of the merger counterparts are deemed critical for understanding how people identify or fail to identify with the new organization (Terry, Carey, and Callan, 2001). Researchers have also found that the permeability of intergroup boundaries in the new organization—in other words the perceptions of employees regarding how freely they can pass from one status group to another—plays a significant role in post-merger identification (Terry, Carey, and Callan, 2001). To summarize, the crucial elements in this line of inquiry on organizational identity in M&As are, first, how members of the merging organizations (as members of distinct social groups) are able to develop a sense of continuity in the process and, second, their perception of the influence they have over the unfolding events.

Recent contributions share these concerns, albeit with a focus on the top echelons of the merging organizations. Clark, Gioia, Ketchen, and Thomas (2010: 397) find that "a transitional identity—an interim sense held by members about what their organizations were becoming—was critical to moving the change process forward." It is suggested that this transitional state allows top managers to work toward a new shared organizational identity. Clark et al. (2010) argue that a functioning transitional identity must be ambiguous enough to allow multiple interpretations of what the merged organization is becoming, but "not so ambiguous as to be threateningly unfamiliar." In a similar vein, Drori, Wrzesniewski, and Ellis (2013) suggest that what they call boundary negotiation is an engine for identity creation in post-merger integration. They argue that identity creation takes place in two stages: first, the boundaries between organizations are negotiated to leverage and import practices and values of the pre-merger firms and, second, the boundaries become blurred as managers build on imported practices and values to impose further systems that define the post-integration firm. Both Clark et al. (2010) and Drori et al. (2013) seem to argue that senior managers are gradually able to leave the past behind and identify with the new merged entity. In the case of Drori et al. (2013) this pertains specifically to international mergers and national identification.

Leaving the past behind may, however, be more complicated for those employees who have no control over merger planning and implementation. This is implied by Hogg and Terry (2000), van Knippenberg et al. (2002), and others who highlighted the power- and status-related problematics of identity in M&As. This overarching work has been complemented by specific thematic foci. Maguire and Phillips (2008), for example, introduce the notion of institutional trust in M&As, taking a longitudinal perspective on the subject matter. They focus on how issues of organizational identity and identification contribute to the loss of institutional trust—the trust that members have in their organization—in a group of employees. Maguire and Phillips (2008) argue that this involves two mechanisms. First, the ambiguity surrounding the identity of the newly merged organization can undermine trust. Second, over time, as ambiguity is reduced, those employees who closely identify with their legacy organization may continue to experience low institutional trust because they do not identify with the new organization. Maguire and Phillips' (2008) contribution is in line with Hogg and Terry (2000) and van Knippenberg et al. (2002) in suggesting that perceived domination and subordination are crucial for understanding identities and identification in M&As, and that (depending on the perceptions) people may continue to identify with their legacy organization—the pre-merger group—for quite some time.

Finally, the temporal element in identity construction in M&As has also been highlighted. While most studies emphasize a sense of continuity from the past to the present, Ullrich, Wieseke, and Van Dick (2005) address questions of the future in the here-and-now. They differentiate between "observable" and "projected" continuity in

M&As, and make explicit "how the subjective experience of continuity after a merger is determined, not only by the link between past and present, but also by the road map into the future" (p. 1555). Ulrich et al. (2005) argue that projected continuity is a "determinant of organizational identification and is as such as important as observable continuity" (p. 1562). They conclude that "projected continuity answers the questions of where are *we* going to and what can *we* do to make it happen" (Ulrich et al., 2005). Communicating a collective vision, then, is the key management challenge in M&As, and "a sense of projected continuity would arise if the *process* leading to a well-defined goal is sufficiently clear and accepted by managers" (Ulrich et al., 2005).

In summary, while the stock of knowledge on identities and identification is more limited than the wide and varied literature on culture in M&A, some parallels can be drawn. Most often, the analyses have looked at managers and employees as distinct social groups that make up the organizations facing the merger, and focused on particular post-merger dynamics—such as domination and subordination, status, trust, and managerial communication—that affect how group members establish or fail to establish a sense of continuity in the changing circumstances. However, this literature ignores the multi-level dynamics of identity construction, and the impact of language and power relations, as well as the broader socio-cultural context where M&As take place. Drawing on a different research tradition, we suggest an alternative, arguably more dynamic and contextually sensitive approach to studying identity construction in M&As.

IDENTITY CONSTRUCTION AS DISCURSIVE SENSEMAKING IN M&AS

Identity Construction as Discursive Sensemaking

How people make sense of their experiences in organizational life has emerged as a popular topic in organization and management studies. Karl Weick (1995) refers to sensemaking as the ways with which people constantly seek to cope with experiences that are surprising, complex, or confusing. Sensemaking is about people interpreting phenomena and producing intersubjective accounts and meanings that help them in understanding and dealing with their experiences. It is argued to be a significant process of organizing that "involves an ongoing retrospective development of plausible images that rationalize what people are doing" (Weick et al., 2005: 409). It has also been argued that sensemaking is grounded in identity construction (Dutton and Dukerich, 1991) and that "who we think we are (identity) as organizational actors shapes what we enact and how we interpret, which affects what outsiders think we are (image) and how they treat us, which stabilizes or destabilizes our identity" (Weick et al., 2005). In other words, "sensemaking describes a process of identity construction whereby individuals project their identities into an environment and see it reflected back" (Helms Mills, Thurlow, and Mills, 2010: 188).

Sensemaking is an issue of language, talk, and communication as "situations, organizations, and environments are talked into existence" (Weick et al., 2005: 409). Among others, Cornelissen (2012: 131) talks about discursive sensemaking that "considers language as a resource that individuals use to make novel circumstances understood," and we will use this notion here. In particular, it is well established that stories and narratives offer people discursive resources for making sense of self (and others) in changing circumstances. A growing literature builds on the premise that sensemaking involves language: narrativization or narrative-making[1] (Brown, Stacey, and Nandhakumar, 2008; cf. Bruner, 1990).

Viewing identity construction as discursive sensemaking alerts us to three key points, all of which indicate that it is a dynamic phenomenon in constant flux. Sensemaking cuts across levels of analysis, it is related to power struggles, and it takes place in specific contexts that influence its very nature. First, sensemaking and identity construction as inherently language-related activities cut across various levels of analysis: those of individuals, groups, organizations, and beyond (Ashforth, Rogers, and Corley, 2011). Individuals' narrative accounts of self provide an ongoing stream of sensemaking (Brown, 2006) into which they fit their selective perceptions of new experiences (Sims, 2005). However, while sensemaking occurs in the idiosyncratic efforts of individuals in identity construction, it is through shared stories and narratives that this construction becomes meaningful (Polkinghorne, 1988; Brown et al., 2008). It has, in fact, been suggested that the performance of stories is a primary means of collective sensemaking in organizations (Boje, 1995) to the extent that shared stories and narratives carry an organization's "common-sensical stock of knowledge" (Patriotta, 2003). Tapping into this stock of knowledge is how people in organizations "get to hear what is going on" and how they "persuade others that they know what is going on" (Sims, 2005: 1633). Hence, subjectively conceived identities are not "subjective" after all. They are grounded in processes of socialization that come into being through storytelling and narration. In this way, identities become "nested" in terms of individuals, groups, and organizations (Ashforth et al., 2011).

Shared stories and narratives can be seen as discursive resources in and through which identities in organizations become available to individuals. These may comprise written texts and visual images as well as spoken words in conversations (Brown et al., 2008). They "not only provide members with an agreed understanding of [the organization's] history but are constantly modified and updated, sometimes subtly and at other times profoundly, to account for recent and current occurrences" (Brown and Humphreys, 2003: 124). Discursive resources "often assume a mythic quality, embodying an idealized past and … hopes for the organization's future" (Ashforth et al., 2011: 1149). Sensemaking and identity construction, then, draw flexibly from senses of

---

[1] In this chapter, we treat story and narrative as synonymous. "Discursive" is used as an overarching concept that incorporates all kinds of language-based communication.

the past and the future in the present. Sensemaking is shaped by past experiences that condition how people understand what they experience in the present (Helms Mills et al., 2010). It is also filtered by what people expect to happen in the future (cf. Ulrich et al., 2005).

Second, power relations condition sensemaking and identity construction in organizations, not as clear-cut and static configurations of dominance and submission, but as struggles where different versions of social reality evolve and compete for position and attention. The various stories and narratives carrying these realities are often connected to specific groups or communities with specific interests in the organization. Although dominant individuals and groups are better positioned to impose their own versions of social reality on others (Helms Mills, 2010), more often than not people have simultaneous commitments to multiple groups (e.g., organizational units or professional groups) and thus different loci of identification. This tempers sensemaking as a collective activity.

Organizations constitute a complex of stories and narratives that are "susceptible to a potentially limitless number of interpretations" (Brown, 2006: 739). On the one hand, people become exposed to—and interpret and draw on—stories and narratives that may diverge to the extent that they offer competing versions of social reality. On the other, discursive resources such as stories and narratives (that make particular "subjectively" conceived identities available) have constitutive effects as they position people in organizations in specific ways. Production and reproduction of power relations in organizations can be understood to take place in and through such positioning and related struggles.

One way to make sense of this proliferation and struggle is through the concept of antenarrative. According to Boje (2008), these are not narratives in the traditional sense—with a beginning, plot, and ending—but stories-in-the-making. They are bets on the future that may (or may not) be widely used in sensemaking. In effect, they are different versions of social reality that jockey for position, and may (or may not) develop into fully fledged narratives. Antenarratives are nevertheless carriers of power relations as they represent and give meaning to social reality in specific ways, and discursive or narrative identities in organizations are complexes of "in-progress stories and story-fragments, which are in a perpetual state of becoming, and suffused with power" (Brown, 2006: 732). Configurations of dominance and submission in organizations are not stable and fixed, but fluid and under constant negotiation.

Third, identities in organizations "are not constructed in a vacuum" (Ashforth et al., 2011: 1147). Sensemaking and identity construction reach beyond the focal organization to comprise more general (or more broadly shared) socio-cultural resources. Stories in-the-making may, for example, build on stereotypes and tropes such as metaphors that draw their meaning from the wider historical, socio-cultural, and societal context (Brown and Humphries, 2003). Stereotypes are widely held popular beliefs about social groups or types of individuals, standardized and simplified conceptions based on prior assumptions that are often deeply held. Stereotypes tend to come in two basic forms: auto-stereotypes that are idealized images of the self and hetero-stereotypes that are images of others (Vaara and Tienari, 2007). Metaphors are figurative expressions that represent one thing in terms of another, and which allow the transfer of meaning across different life domains. They can be used to "build and conventionalize understanding by compressing novel, complex, and at times emotionally anxious circumstances into familiar and coherent positions, frames, or narratives" (Cornelissen, 2012: 131). All these socio-cultural resources offer opportunities for people in organizations to craft stories and narratives that make distinctions between "us" and "them" on the one hand, and forge a new common identity on the other. In other words, identies in organizations are "nested," not only in terms of individuals, groups, and organizations, but also beyond organizational boundaries and in the wider environment (Ashforth et al., 2011).

In all, identities are constitutive of organizations, and not intrinsic to them. Also, organizational identities are not uniform and monolithic, and their relationship with individual and group identities is not clear-cut; in effect, organizational identities are hybrids (Albert and Whetten, 1985; Glynn, 2000).[2] From a discursive sensemaking perspective, an organization's identities are "constituted by the multiple identity-relevant narratives that their participants author" about the organization (Brown, 2006: 731). While resources such as stereotypes, tropes, and (ante)narratives offer material for sensemaking and identity construction, they are also in constant need of sensemaking. They are reproduced in ever more elaborated forms.

How do M&As figure in such a conceptualization of discursive sensemaking and identity construction? In the light of extant research, the answer is that extreme and radical cases of organizational change such as M&As break established patterns of sensemaking and narration and trigger new ones. They are "organizational shocks" (Weick, 1995): important events that force people "to make sense of things differently" (Helms Mills et al., 2010: 191). They disrupt identity construction and force people to reconsider their belonging to an organization. In brief, M&As disrupt the collective's established answers to the question "who are we as an organization?" (Albert and Whetten, 1985).

Discursive Sensemaking and Identity Construction in M&As

On the basis of the discussion in this chapter, we conceptualize identity construction in M&As as discursive sensemaking where discursive resources such as stereotypes, tropes, narratives, and antenarratives are mobilized to construct, transform, and at

---

[2] In addressing dual and multiple identities in the organization, Albert and Whetten (1985) considered the notion of "hybrid identity" as well as the potential for conflict when identities were not seen as compatible or complementary. In a study of a cultural organization, Glynn (2000) illustrated such a hybrid identity characterized by conflict where two professional groups (artists and administrators) made sovereign organizational claims over each other.

times destruct senses of organizational identity. Figure 24.1 below summarizes our framework.

Recent contributions have explored the multi-level dynamics of organizational identity construction in M&As. They have also detailed the complexity of power relations and highlighted the importance of the broader socio-cultural context in discursive sensemaking. These studies argue that mergers and acquisitions cast people in a position "betwixt and between" identities (Turner, 1967). They also address this transitional state in a variety of ways and have suggested that the notion of liminality helps individuals to transition between identities (Ashforth, 2001) and to cope between two identity constructions (Beech, 2011). Liminality can be understood as "a reconstruction of identity (in which the sense of self is significantly disrupted) in such a way that the new identity is meaningful for the individual and the community" (Beech, 2011: 296–7). Liminality may be triggered by events such as M&As, which destabilize the social context for individuals and offer an abundance of ambiguous meanings. These events are also characterized by a perceived lack of resolution.

Applying a narrative perspective to identity construction, Brown and Humphreys (2003) study how groups of people—"senior managers and two distinct cohorts of their subordinates"—make sense of a merger. They argue that identities in M&As are authored in stories and narratives, which—when shared and repeated—become essential means of constructing existing and future identities in the uncertain and political spaces that are M&As. In the studied merger, Brown and Humphreys (2003) found that while the merger strategists offered a heroic narrative of epic change, their subordinates authored tragic narratives. While the strategists identified with a change initiative that they deemed crucial, others contested it. While the strategists envisioned a future full of opportunities, others foresaw a bleak future where their work was not appreciated. Rather than forcing the two merging organizations into confrontation, the merger developed into a configuration where the top management emerged as a distinct group with a particular version of social reality that differed markedly from those narrated by other organizational groups.

Van Vuuren et al. (2010) combine a sensemaking approach with insights from social identity theory to highlight the importance of several foci of identification in M&As. They argue that professional identities affect how organizational identities are construed in post-merger settings. In the university merger examined in their study, this refers to the vital importance of disciplinary identities. Empson (2004) similarly

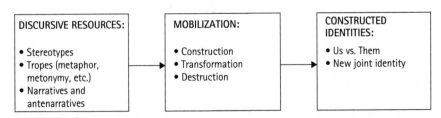

FIGURE 24.1 The discursive sensemaking approach to identity construction

underscores interactions between professional and organizational identities and suggests in her research on acquisitions in the context of accounting firms that strong identities based on complex relationships between the "professional" and the "organizational" may coexist in the post-acquisition phase. The key issue in both studies is that these constructions are not static. The identifications of organizational members change as the organizations evolve in response to shifts in their competitive environment. The implication of these insights for identity construction in M&As is that several loci of identification affect sensemaking simultaneously and that these constructions are in flux.

Crucially, the construction of identities in M&As is conditioned—and complicated—by the broader socio-cultural context. Van Vuuren et al. (2010) present an example of this in their examination of perceived status differences and domination in a merger of two universities. The authors found that members of both merging partners felt dominated in the merger, although there was relative consensus with regard to the difference in status between the pre-merger organizations. Van Vuuren et al.'s (2010) study not only shows that domination and status can be viewed as distinct and separate constructs in M&As, but also that how idiosyncratic contextual conditions play into sensemaking is important. The studied merger took place between a "black" and a "white" university in post-apartheid South Africa. The former university was favored by current legislation, whereas the latter was historically superior in terms of funding and academic development. In the post-merger ambiguity, talk about domination by the latter merger party emerged as a form of politicking. Van Vuuren et al. (2010: 639) conclude that "claiming to be the dominated partner … may be a way to distance oneself from the organizational level of identification and turn to other foci." This distancing provides different groups with resources for negotiating the future on their own terms and, it seems, to prepare for merger failure. The authors concluded as follows: "As an out-group they can criticize the organization from within, cope with the perceived negative reputation of the merged organization, and be proud of their identity as professionals" (p. 640).

In a similar vein, Brown and Humphreys (2003) argue that groups' narrations of their working lives in M&As are influenced, not only by psychological processes (such as categorization, self-enhancement, and uncertainty reduction), but by broadly available cultural resources. The epic narrative featuring top strategists as heroes is an example of this. It was suggested that "the availability of the heroic frame, combined with the self-enhancing rewards associated with a plot form that encourages simplification, in-group idealization, and stereotyping" accounts for the structure and tone of this narrative (p. 136). The tragic narrative authored by the other groups is similarly based on the cultural resources available to participants in (Western) organizations. The co-existence of the two narratives is perhaps not surprising per se, as it confirms that "people tend to attribute positive outcomes internally, as a result of their own actions, and negative outcomes to external agents and forces" (p. 136). However, Brown and Humphreys' (2003) study sheds new light on how these constructions affect senses of power relations in M&As.

The importance of socio-cultural context in M&As is further highlighted by Vaara et al. (2005), who discuss it in terms of international relations. The authors found that the choice of corporate language became a source of confrontation in a Finnish–Swedish merger. The top management in the newly merged organization decided on Swedish as the "official" corporate language. This became a heated issue in the Finnish legacy organization where it not only brought about practical problems but came to symbolize Swedish domination.[3] It led to perceptions of inferiority among Finns, and evoked post-colonial identities in the merging organization. The language decision encouraged sensemaking that drew on nationalist sentiment and cast ideas about a common future in a dubious light. Vaara et al.'s (2005) study shows how the socio-cultural context that is relevant for understanding identity construction in M&As transcends national boundaries to comprise particular historically developed relations between nations (see Riad, Vaara, and Zhang, 2012, for the case of USA and China). Incidentally, it was immediately announced in a subsequent merger undertaken by the Finnish–Swedish company with a Danish company that the corporate language would be English. The top management had learnt an important lesson regarding the delicate nature of (national) identity constructions and the entanglement of these constructions in efforts to make sense of power relations in the merging organization. As a result, top management began to advocate a joint regional Nordic identity for the new Finnish–Swedish–Danish organization (Vaara, Tienari, and Irrman, 2007).

To summarize, identification in M&As is complicated by the co-existence of senses of organizational, professional, and, at times, national identities. Actors can mobilize a variety of discursive resources to convey an image of belonging or not belonging to a specific social group. Although discursive sensemaking can be deliberate—as in organizational identity-building, sensegiving, or storytelling orchestrated by top management—less deliberate sensemaking also involves mobilization of discursive resources. These resources can be used both to construe a sense of a new joint organizational identity and to develop senses of "us" and "them" between the merging parties.

National Identity as a Case in Point

National identity illustrates what the dynamics of discursive sensemaking in M&As entail more specifically. In keeping with the considerations above, our point of departure here is that the construct of nationality is often reproduced in mundane habits of

---

[3] The language question in the merger only becomes understandable against the backdrop of the socio-historical context, the joint history of the two nations. Until 1809, Finland was part of the Kingdom of Sweden. There remains a small Swedish-speaking minority in Finland, and Swedish is the second official language. Sweden continues to serve as a point of comparison for Finns, who tend to consider themselves the "little brother" in the relationship. Hence it was especially important for them to feel like equal partners in the merger.

language and symbolism. Billig (1995) calls this banal nationalism. In international M&As this is often accompanied by what we call banal globalism, which may take the form of references to allegedly unavoidable processes of globalization that render national boundaries obsolete and offer unprecedented opportunities for business (Tienari, Vaara, and Björkman, 2003). The outcome is a struggle where stereotypes, tropes, narratives, and antenarratives play a central role.

As discursive resources, stereotypes come in two basic forms—auto- and hetero-stereotypes—which are evoked to make sense of encounters with the other merger party. Such stereotyping tends to present itself easily and automatically to people as they draw on past constructions to navigate the ambiguity of the present (Vaara, Risberg, Søderberg, and Tienari 2003). Used as sensemaking devices, the two forms of stereotypes offer different vantage points: auto-stereotypes tend to be markedly more positive than hetero-stereotypes. In their study of a US–Israeli merger, Ailon-Souday and Kunda (2003) demonstrate how national stereotypes on the Israeli side were used as a symbolic resource in politicized sensemaking, leading to complex constructions of distinction and sameness in the post-merger turmoil. Crucially, the authors show that national identities and international or global organizational identities are not mutually exclusive, but can be simultaneously embraced in M&As.

Tropes in general and metaphors in particular offer resources for making sense of M&As. An example is offered by Tienari (2000) in his study of the merger of two rival banks in Finland. The merger took place in 1995, when ethnic groups in the former Yugoslavia were at war, and media images of the confrontation and violence there were much to the fore. In the early days of the bank merger, people in the two organizations—which were considered to be fierce rivals—began to refer to themselves as "Serbs" and "Croats." This crude analogy served as a metaphor that conveyed particular meanings to the merger. It enabled organizational members to make sense of the dramatic nature of the endeavor. However, while the metaphor initially depicted a state of war between the merger parties, it gradually took on more ironic meanings and eventually settled into a shared story among other stories in the organization. It was initially destructive, but turned into a collective discursive resource that lost its clout when the bank engaged in further M&As, now across national boundaries. "Serbs" and "Croats" began to embrace their common Finnishness vis-à-vis others.

These findings cohere with those of Riad and Vaara (2011), who focused on the role of metonymy (a figure of speech in which a concept is not called by its own name but by the name of another concept with a related meaning) in national identity-building in M&As. In their analysis of media sensemaking in the acquisition of the American IBM Personal Computer Division by the Chinese company Lenovo and the acquisition of the American Anheuser-Busch by the Belgian–Brazilian company InBev, they demonstrated that metonymy is a central linguistic resource through which sense is made of national identities. They illustrated how metonymy could be combined with metaphors to generate evocative imagery, engaging wit, and subversive irony in M&As. For example, "once-red China takes a bite out of Big Blue" includes metonyms (red for communism, China for Lenovo, and Big Blue for IBM) but also the metaphor "takes a bite," and thus constructs specific organizational and national identities for the actors involved in the merger.

Tropes can also be used deliberately by corporate managers. Vaara, Tienari, and Säntti (2003) studied how metaphors were used in culture seminars in the Finnish–Swedish merger that was the next step in the Finnish merger involving "Serbs" and "Croats." The authors elucidate how these seminars offered opportunities for employees to make explicit and confront their often unconscious assumptions about self and the other, and to construe a new joint organizational identity. This was accomplished by first acknowledging that notions of "us" and "them" would affect the merger process and, second, by dealing with these identity constructions by making them visible in carefully orchestrated interactions. Metaphors were turned into a constructive force. Conveyed in metaphors, the self-images of Finns vis-à-vis Swedes and vice versa were brought into the open so that they could be discussed and challenged. National identities were not left behind. Instead, perceptions of national differences—and inevitably points of convergence and sameness as well—provided resources for Finns and Swedes to make sense of a joint future that would benefit both parties. Perceptions of dominance and subordination between the national groups were tempered by open dialogue.

Furthermore, antenarratives (Boje, 2008) can be mobilized in organizational storytelling both to promote and question the organizational identity imposed. The analysis by Vaara and Tienari (2011) of international M&As reveals how antenarratives are mobilized in organizational storytelling to legitimate or resist change. In their example, globalist storytelling was used to legitimate a merger and to create MNC identity, nationalist storytelling was used to re-legitimate national interests and identities, regional storytelling was used to create a joint regional identity (here Nordic), and globalist storytelling was used critically to challenge the regional identity. This analysis underscores the dialogical dynamics or dialogisms (Boje, 2008) involved in sensemaking. In particular, the globalist, nationalist, and regional (Nordic) antenarratives provided very different kinds of grounds for defining what was seen as appropriate, legitimate, and natural in constructing the identity of the new organization.

CONCLUSION

This chapter has conceptualized identity construction in M&As as sensemaking in which discursive resources are mobilized to construct, transform, and at times destruct senses of organizational identity. Mergers and acquisitions have been offered as a specific setting in which resources such as stereotypes, tropes, narratives, and antenarratives are drawn on to make sense of self in the transition from legacy organizations to new combined organizational entities. As such, we argue that a dual process can be at play in the merger context. Organizational members are likely to *both* cling to the past *and* work for a common future as they struggle to make sense of the uncertainty and ambiguity that characterize M&As. Identities and identification are dynamic, ongoing, and negotiated—they are contingent on the available discursive resources in the specific socio-cultural context, rather than simple either–or questions. This supports the argument that hybrid identities (Albert and Whetten, 1985; Glynn, 2000) prevail in organizations undergoing change, including M&As. The discursive sensemaking approach developed in this chapter is well positioned to make this dynamic visible.

The ideas discussed in this chapter suggest a number of avenues for future research on organizational identities. First, and in general, future research could go further in examining the contradictions and ambiguities in organizational identity construction. That is, there are always alternative and competing ways to make sense of, or give sense to, radical change that disrupts established patterns of identity construction. At the same time, various (new) identities are available. This simultaneity results in a great deal of contradiction and ambiguity that warrants more attention from the perspective of multiple levels of analysis, complex power relations, and the impact of socio-cultural context.

Second, how actors resist the organizational identities imposed upon them in M&As calls for more research. In conditions of uncertainty and ambiguity resistance may involve the use of irony, sarcasm, or cynicism in collective sensemaking. Such research could draw attention to self-doubt, dis-identification, and alienation (Collinson, 2003; Costas and Fleming, 2009) in M&As. How individuals reflect upon and challenge their socially ascribed identities and how dynamics between identity (who I am) and anti-identity (who I am not) play out (Holmer-Nadesan, 1996; Meriläinen, Tienari, Thomas and Davies, 2004) in discursive sensemaking in M&As are topics for future research. Uncovering the dynamics of power and resistance would perhaps also help us to better understand the linkages between organization-level identity constructions and individual identity work in organizations more generally (Ashforth et al., 2011).

Third, temporality is a key issue in organizational identity constructions that has to date received surprisingly little research attention (Schultz and Hernes, 2013). It would be important to investigate how identities in M&As develop over time and to explore how past- or future-oriented these identities become. Such research could focus on organizational nostalgia in highlighting how the past is evoked to make sense of the present and to make claims for future identity. Times of radical change are apt for "making active use of memory" to articulate alternative futures (Schultz and Hernes, 2013: 1). While the importance of establishing a sense of continuity from the past to the present has been extensively cited as a prerequisite for making M&As work, our discursive sensemaking approach suggests that assumed continuities between past, present, and future will become blurred. There is much to be elaborated in terms of Ulrich et al.'s (2005) notion of "projected continuity" in M&As.

Fourth, socio-materiality deserves more attention in sensemaking and identity construction. Analyses of organizational identity and identification tend to be relatively general and abstract, and disconnected from the material realities of people's lives in the midst of merger turmoil. This is also the case with our approach, which focuses on language, discourse, and discursive resources. While we know a great deal about the use of texts and visual images in organizational identity-building, more in-depth study is called for on how they—as material artefacts—play into the identity work of individuals and groups in radical change such as M&As. Such research could explore, for example, how people in the merging organization appropriate or fail to appropriate the new organizational brand and branding materials and practices in their everyday lives. We need to better understand sensemaking and identity construction as socio-material performances in organizations undergoing radical change.

Finally, and relatedly, the classic question of reciprocity between identity and image in organizations should be revitalized from the perspective of discursive sensemaking (Dutton and Dukerich, 1991; Weick et al., 2005; Ashforth et al., 2011). While it is often assumed that identity construction takes place in organizations with relatively clear boundaries, in today's world much of what happens in and around organizations is mediated and mediatized. In M&As, achievements in construing a new identity or image outside the organization, among customers and other stakeholders, have been found to be reflected back on the sensemaking and identity construction of organizational members (Vaara and Tienari, 2011). Social media warrant special attention in understanding organizational identity constructions as they provide unprecedented means for discursive sensemaking in online environments that are devoid of time and place in the traditional sense (Rokka, Karlsson, and Tienari, 2014). Social media remains to a large extent unexplored in the M&A context.

References

Ailon-Souday G. and Kunda, G. (2003). "The Local Selves of Global Workers: The Social Construction of National Identity in the Face of Organizational Globalization." *Organization Studies* 24: 1073–96.

Albert, S. and Whetten, D. A. (1985). "Organizational Identity." *Research in Organizational Behavior* 7: 263–95.

Ashforth, B. E. (2001). *Role Transitions in Organizational Life: An Identity-Based Perspective.* Mahwah, NJ: Lawrence Erlbaum Associates.

Ashforth, B. E., Rogers, K. M., and Corley, K. G. (2011). "Identity in Organizations: Exploring Cross-Level Dynamics." *Organization Science* 22(5): 1144–56.

Beech, N. (2011). "Liminality and the Practices of Identity Reconstruction." *Human Relations* 64(2): 285–302.

Billig, M. (1995). *Banal Nationalism.* London: SAGE.

Boje, D. M. (1995). "Stories of the Storytelling Organization: A Postmodern Analysis of Disney as 'Tamara-Land.'" *Academy of Management Journal* 38: 997–1035.

Boje, D. M. (2008). *Storytelling Organizations.* London: SAGE.

Brannen, M. Y. and Peterson, M. F. (2009). "Merging without Alienating: Interventions Promoting Cross-Cultural Organizational Integration and their Limitations." *Journal of International Business Studies* 40: 468–89.

Brown, A. D. (2006). "A Narrative Approach to Collective Identities." *Journal of Management Studies* 43(4): 731–53.

Brown, A. D. and Humphreys, M. (2003). "Epic and Tragic Tales: Making Sense of a Change." *The Journal of Applied Behavioral Science* 39(2): 121–44.

Brown, A. D., Stacey, P., and Nandhakumar, J. (2008). "Making Sense of Sensemaking Narratives." *Human Relations* 61(8): 1035–62.

Bruner, J. (1990). *Acts of Meaning*. Cambridge, MA: Harvard University Press.

Buono, A. F., Bowditch, J. L., and Lewis, J. W., III (1985). "When Cultures Collide: The Anatomy of a Merger." *Human Relations* 38(5): 477–500.

Calori, R., Lubatkin, M., and Véry, P. (1994). "Control Mechanisms in Cross-Border Acquisitions: An International Comparison." *Organization Studies* 15(3): 361–79.

Cartwright, S. and Cooper, C. L. (1990). "The Impact of Mergers and Acquisitions on People at Work: Existing Research and Issues." *British Journal of Management* 1(1): 65–76.

Clark, S. M., Gioia, D. A., Ketchen, D. J., and Thomas, J. B. (2010). "Transitional Identity as a Facilitator of Organizational Identity Change during a Merger." *Administrative Science Quarterly* 55, 397–438.

Collinson, D. (2003). "Identities and Insecurities: Selves at Work." *Organization* 10: 527–47.

Cornelissen, J. (2012). "Sensemaking under Pressure: The Influence of Professional Roles and Social Accountability on the Creation of Sense." *Organization Science* 23(1): 118–37.

Costas, J. and Fleming, P. (2009). "Beyond Dis-identification: A Discursive Approach to Self-Alienation in Contemporary Organizations." *Human Relations* 62(3): 353–78.

Drori, I., Wrzesniewski, A., and Ellis, S. (2013). "One out of Many? Boundary Negotiation and Identity Formation in Postmerger Integration." *Organization Science*, 24(6): 1717–41.

Dutton, J. E. and Dukerich, J. M. (1991). "Keeping an Eye on the Mirror: Image and Identiy in Organizational Adaptation." *Academy of Management Journal* 34(3): 517–54.

Empson, L. (2004). "Organizational Identity Change: Managerial Regulation and Member Identification in an Accounting Firm Acquisition." *Accounting, Organizations and Society* 29: 759–81.

Glynn, M. A. (2000). "When Cymbals Become Symbols: Conflict over Organizational Identity within a Symphony Orchestra." *Organization Science* 11(3): 285–98.

Haspeslagh, P. and Jemison, D. B. (1991). *Managing Acquisitions: Creating Value through Corporate Renewal*. New York: Free Press.

Helms Mills, J., Thurlow, A. and Mills, A. J. (2010). "Making Sense of Sensemaking: The Critical Sensemaking Approach." *Qualitative Research in Organizations and Management: An International Journal* 5(2): 182–95.

Hogg, M. A. and Terry, D. J. (2000). "Social Identity and Self-Categorization Processes in Organizational Contexts." *Academy of Management Review* 25(1): 121–140.

Holmer-Nadesan, M. (1996). "Organizational Identity and Space of Action." *Organization Studies* 17(1): 49–81.

Maguire, S. and Phillips, N. (2008). "'Citibankers' at Citigroup: A Study of the Loss of Institutional Trust after a Merger." *Journal of Management Studies* 45(2): 372–401.

Marks, M. L. (1997). "Consulting in Mergers and Acquisitions: Interventions Spawned by Recent Trends." *Journal of Organizational Change* 10: 267–79.

Meglio, O. and Risberg, A. (2011). "The (Mis)measurement of M&A Performance: A Systematic Narrative Literature Review." *Scandinavian Journal of Management* 27(4): 418–33.

Meriläinen, S., Tienari, J., Thomas, R., and Davies, A. (2004). "Management Consultant Talk: A Cross-Cultural Comparison of Normalising Discourse and Resistance." *Organization* 11(4): 539–64.

Monin, P., Noorderhaven, N., Vaara, E., and Kroon, D. (2013). "Giving Sense to and Making Sense of Norms of Justice in Post-Merger Integration." *Academy of Management Journal* 56(1): 256–84.

Nahavandi, A. and Malekzadeh, A. R. (1988). "Acculturation in Mergers and Acquisitions." *Academy of Management Review* 13(1): 79–90.

Olie, R. (1994). "Shades of Culture and Institutions in International Mergers." *Organization Studies* 15(3): 381–405.

Polkinghorne, D. E. (1988). *Narrative Knowing and the Human Sciences.* Albany, NY: State University of New York.

Riad, S. (2005). "The Power of 'Organizational Culture' as a Discursive Formation in Merger Integration." *Organization Studies* 26(10): 1529–54.

Riad, S. and Vaara, E. (2011). "Varieties of Metonymy in Media Accounts of Mergers and Acquisitions." *Journal of Management Studies* 48(4): 737–71.

Riad, S., Vaara, E., and Zhang, N. (2012). "The Intertextual Production of International Relations in Mergers and Acquisitions." *Organization Studies* 33(1): 121–48.

Risberg, A (1997). "Ambiguity and Communication in Cross-Cultural Acquisitions: Towards a Conceptual Framework." *Leadership & Organization Development Journal* 18(5): 257–66.

Rokka, J., Karlsson, K., and Tienari, J. (2014). "Balancing Acts: Managing Employees and Reputation in Social Media." *Journal of Marketing Management* 30(7–8): 802–27.

Schultz, M. and Hernes, T. (2013). "A Temporal Perspective on Organizational Identity." *Organization Science* 24(1): 1–21.

Shrivastava, P. (1986). "Post-Merger Integration." *Journal of Business Strategy* 7(1): 65–71.

Sims, D. (2005). "You Bastard: A Narrative Exploration of the Experience of Indignation within Organizations." *Organization Studies* 26: 1625–40.

Stahl, G. and Voigt, A. (2005). "Impact of Cultural Differences on Merger and Acquisition Performance: A Critical Research Review and an Integrative Model." *Advances in Mergers and Acquisitions* 4: 51–82.

Swidler, A. (1986). "Culture in Action: Symbols and Strategies." *American Sociological Review* 51: 273–86.

Teerikangas, S. and Véry, P. (2006). "The Culture-Performance Relationship in M&A: From Yes/No to How." *British Journal of Management* 17(S1): 31–48.

Terry, D. J., Carey, C. J., and Callan, V. J. (2001). "Employee Adjustment to an Organizational Merger: An Intergroup Perspective." *Personality and Social Psychology Bulletin* 27(3): 267–80.

Tienari, J. (2000). "Gender Segregation in the Making of a Merger." *Scandinavian Journal of Management* 16(2): 111–44.

Tienari, J. and Vaara, E. (2012). "Power and Politics in Mergers and Acquisitions." In *The Handbook of Mergers & Acquisitions*, edited by D. Faulkner, S. Teerikangas, and R. Joseph, 495–516. Oxford: Oxford University Press.

Tienari, J., Vaara, E., and Björkman, I. (2003). "Global Capitalism Meets National Spirit: Discourses in Media Texts on a Cross-Border Acquisition." *Journal of Management Inquiry* 12(4): 377–93.

Turner, V. (1967). *The Forest of Symbols: Aspects of Ndembu Ritual.* Ithaca, NY: Cornell University Press.

Ulrich, J., Wieseke, J., and Van Dick, R. (2005). "Continuity and Change in Mergers and Acquisitions: A Social Identity Case Study of a German Industrial Merger." *Journal of Management Studies* 42(8): 1549–69.

Vaara, E. (2003). "Post-Acquisition Integration as Sensemaking: Glimpses of Ambiguity, Confusion, Hypocrisy, and Politicization." *Journal of Management Studies* 40(4): 859–94.

Vaara, E., Risberg, A., Søderberg, A.-M., and Tienari, J. (2003). "Nation Talk: Reconstructing National Stereotypes in a Merging Multinational." In *Merging across Borders: People, Cultures and Politics*, edited by A.-M. Søderberg and E. Vaara, 61–86. Copenhagen: Copenhagen Business School Press.

Vaara, E. and Tienari, J. (2007). "M&As as Stereotypes: Banal Ideas and Self-Serving Explanations." In *Mergers and Acquisitions*, edited by D. Angwin, 256–75. Oxford: Blackwell Publishing.

Vaara, E. and Tienari, J. (2011). "On the Narrative Construction of MNCs: An Antenarrative Analysis of Legitimation and Resistance in a Cross-Border Merger." *Organization Science* 22(2): 370–90.

Vaara, E., Tienari, J., and Irrmann, O. (2007). "Crafting an Inter-National Identity: The Nordea Case." In *Organizational Identity in Practice*, edited by L. Lerpold, D. Ravasi, J. van Rekom, and G. Soenen, 215–31. London: Routledge.

Vaara, E., Tienari, J., Piekkari, R., and Säntti, R. (2005). "Language and the Circuits of Power in a Merging Multinational Corporation." *Journal of Management Studies* 42(3): 595–623.

Vaara, E., Tienari, J., and Säntti, R. (2003). "The International Match: Metaphors as Vehicles of Social Identity-Building in Cross-Border Mergers." *Human Relations* 56(4): 419–52.

van Knippenberg, D. and van Leeuwen, E. (2001). "Organizational Identity after a Merger: Sense of Continuity as the Key to Postmerger Identification." In *Social Identity Processes in Organizational Contexts*, edited by M. A. Hogg and D. J. Terry, 249–64. Ann Arbor, MI: Taylor and Francis.

van Knippenberg, D., van Knippenberg, B., Monden, L., and De Lima, F. (2002). "Organizational Identification after a Merger: A Social Identity Perspective." *British Journal of Social Psychology* 41: 233–52.

van Vuuren, M., Beelen, P., and de Jong, M. D. T. (2010). "Speaking of Dominance, Status Differences, and Identification: Making Sense of a Merger." *Journal of Occupational and Organizational Psychology* 83: 627–43.

Weber, K. and Dacin, T. (2011). "The Cultural Construction of Organizational Life." *Organization Science* 22(2): 286–98.

Weick, K. E. (1995). *Sensemaking in Organizations*. Thousand Oaks, CA: SAGE.

Weick, K. E., Sutcliffe, K. M., and Obstfeld, D. (2005). "Organizing and the Process of Sensemaking." *Organization Science* 16(4): 409–21.

....

CHAPTER 25

FOSTERING STAKEHOLDER IDENTIFICATION THROUGH EXPRESSED ORGANIZATIONAL IDENTITIES

....

CAROLINE A. BARTEL, CINDI BALDI, AND JANET M. DUKERICH

CREATING positive first impressions is vital for organizations looking to establish productive relationships with external stakeholders. Initial impressions of an organization can influence, for example, whether job seekers pursue employment opportunities (Barber, 1998; Gatewood, Gowan, and Lautenschlager, 2003), prospective consumers choose particular products or services (Ahearne, Bhattacharya, and Gruen, 2005), or potential donors or investors make financial contributions (Navis and Glynn, 2011). Yet, creating positive first impressions is no small task. It not only requires generating a positive attitude toward the organization and toward forming a relationship with the organization, but also doing so quickly, often in just minutes, while using relatively lean means of communication such as written statements or documents appearing on the company website (e.g., "about us" descriptions, annual reports, and media releases).

Without question, people are relying more and more on technology to interact with the world around them. Increasing dependence on the Internet for both instrumental and recreational purposes means that external stakeholders' initial impressions of organizations often come from their online presence. Indeed, members of consumer groups (e.g., customers and clients), financial communities (e.g., donors, investors, and financiers) and the general public (e.g., job seekers and volunteers) often gain their first exposure to organizations via company websites. For example, a prospective investor perusing company websites might visit GoPro.com and view the following "About Us" page that highlights what the company does, what it values and who its members are:

GoPro "About Us"

Think it. See it. Do it.

- We dream. We have passionate ideas about what's possible in this world. Our passions lead us to create experiences and realities that expand our world and inspire those around us.
- GoPro helps people capture and share their lives' most meaningful experiences with others—to celebrate them together. Like how a day on the mountain with friends is more meaningful than one spent alone, the sharing of our collective experiences makes our lives more fun.
- The world's most versatile cameras are what we make.
- Enabling you to share your life through incredible photos and videos is what we do.
- This is your life ...GoPro.

(GoPro "About Us," 2016)

From a modest amount of text on the GoPro.com website, prospective investors can begin to construct a perception of the organization that captures its essence or character (e.g., an innovative product from a company that recognizes the power of social connections in making everyday life meaningful), which may sway their investment decisions.

Company websites are a form of symbolic management—an effort to portray the organization in a certain way to particular audiences (Bromley, 2000; Cheney, 1983; Whetten and Godfrey, 1998). Most company websites have "About Us" ("Our Story") and "Careers" pages that provide background information on, for example, the organization's history and mission, and products or services, as well as its values and culture. This information provides a window into the *organizational identity* (Alessandri, 2001)—the central, distinctive, and relatively enduring features that organizational members use to define what the organization represents and stands for (Albert and Whetten, 1985). How aspects of the internally held organizational identity are expressed on company websites constitute purposeful efforts to craft a *desired or intended organizational image*—the attributes and characteristics that organizational leaders communicate and want external stakeholders to strongly associate with the organization (Brown, Dacin, Pratt, and Whetten, 2006; Scott and Lane, 2000). It is this organizational image that provides a basis for external stakeholders' initial evaluations of an organization's attractiveness. An essential task, therefore, for organizations is to translate their internally held organizational identity into an intended organizational image that external stakeholders will likely find attractive.

How organizations craft intended organizational images in online contexts is not well understood. Research cutting across diverse domains, including communication

(Cheney, 1983), marketing and consumer behavior (Ahearne et al., 2005; Bhattacharya and Sen, 2003), and organizational behavior (Scott and Lane, 2000), has speculated more generally on the mechanisms through which intended organizational images influence organizational attraction among external stakeholders; namely, perceptions of organizational legitimacy and positive distinctiveness, and congruence in personal and organizational values. Importantly, such perceptions also occupy prominent roles in theories of how people identify with organizations (Ashforth and Mael, 1989; Dutton, Dukerich, and Harquail, 1994). Arguably, then, the intended organizational images communicated to external stakeholders in online contexts may initiate feelings of identification with the organization (Scott and Lane, 2000). Focusing on how external stakeholders come to feel the psychological connection with an organization that underlies identification, thus, may provide insight into how organizations can best craft their online communication. That is, the task of creating attractive, intended, organizational images may be construed more broadly as a process of creating *stakeholder identification.*

Stakeholder identification refers to a perception of belonging such that a stakeholder's affiliation with an organization becomes an important part of his or her self-definition (Scott and Lane, 2000). In essence, stakeholder identification answers the question *Who am I in relation to the organization?* (Balmer, 2008). Even though they are not organizational members, prior research has asserted that external stakeholders can identify with organizations (Bhattacharya and Elsbach, 2002; Cardador and Pratt, 2006;), including alumni (Mael and Ashforth, 1992), art museum patrons (Bhattacharya, Rao, and Glynn, 1995), donors (Arnett, German, and Hunt, 2003), boards of directors (Golden-Biddle and Rao, 1997), customers (Ahearne et al., 2005; Bhattacharya and Sen, 2003), and sports fans (Fisher and Wakefield, 1998; Laverie and Arnett, 2000). This chapter provides a review and conceptual synthesis of prior research to elaborate how organizational communication in online contexts might spark this sense of connectedness that fuels stakeholder identification.

The potential for organizational communication to influence individuals' identification with an organization has long been part of conventional wisdom (e.g., Ashforth and Mael, 1996; Cheney, 1983; Pratt, 2003; Vaughn, 1997). Nonetheless, organizational research has given greater consideration to communication aimed at current members than that aimed at external stakeholders. Cheney's (1983) seminal work on organizational identification examined the primacy of organizational communication in how employees come to understand the organizational identity, define who they are in relation to the organization, and build identification with the organization. Other work similarly has elaborated the sensegiving function of organizational communication in defining for employees the organization's essential goals, values, and beliefs, and in building or intensifying their organizational identification (e.g., Corley and Gioia, 2004; DiSanza and Bullis, 1999; Gioia and Thomas, 1996; Postmes, Tanis, and De Wit, 2001; Pratt, 2000; Smidts, Pruyn, and van Riel, 2001).

External stakeholders, however, differ from organizational members in important ways. External stakeholders refer to individuals who are objectively non-members of the organization but who can affect or be affected by the organization's successful performance (Donaldson and Preston, 1995; Jones, 1995). In this chapter we focus on "expectant stakeholders" (Mitchell, Agle, and Wood, 1997) who are in a *potential* relationship with the organization: that is, stakeholders who might be influenced by, or potentially are influencers of, the organization (Starik, 1994: 90). Expectant stakeholders' first exposure to an organization often comprises the formal communications they encounter on the company website. In contrast, for employees, these same organizational communications occur against a backdrop of prior knowledge of, and experience with the organization. Employees thus relate identity-relevant information in these communications to their current perceptions of the organizational identity. For expectant stakeholders, a lack of personal knowledge of, and experience with an organization suggests a corresponding lack of a priori perceptions of the organizational identity. While some organizations receive considerable media attention and even become part of popular culture (e.g., Google and Whole Foods Market), for the vast majority of organizations it is usually not the case that expectant stakeholders have a clear image of the organizational identity before initiating a relationship with it. Ultimately, creating stakeholder identification via online communication necessitates consideration of these circumstances. Precisely which communication strategies may effectively induce feelings of belonging to an organization is the main focus of this chapter.

We focus on company websites as a mass communication channel (see Ch. 12 by Schinoff, Rogers, and Corley). Company websites provide the organizational leadership a platform for one-way, vertical (top-down) communication with external audiences. This communication is intentional or otherwise endorsed by senior management, and provides information about the organization as a whole. Our review concerns text statements. Company websites often contain an array of text-based content, including formal mission or vision statements, annual reports, press releases, media articles, and descriptions of different facets of the organization, such as its culture. While company websites can vary in their richness (Daft and Lengel, 1984): for example, leaner websites contain only text while richer websites tend to include hypertext, pictures, sounds, and video clips; text nonetheless, is the most elemental form of communication on company websites (Allen, Biggane, Pitts, Otondo, and Van Scotter, 2013).

This chapter is organized as follows. First, we introduce stakeholder identification as an outcome of organizations' efforts to communicate their organizational identity. Second, we organize prior research to outline how stakeholder identification develops in an online context, highlighting the critical motives that may shape expectant stakeholders' perceptions of an organization's attractiveness. Then, we outline how distinct organizational communication strategies tap into these motives to trigger stakeholder identification. We conclude with speculation on how organizational communication aimed at stakeholder identification connects to other management practices, such as corporate branding, organizational image management, and corporate identity communication.

ORGANIZATIONAL IDENTITY ATTRACTIVENESS AND STAKEHOLDER IDENTIFICATION

At first blush, it seems unusual that expectant stakeholders could anticipate feelings of identification with organizations with which they are not actually in a relationship. Yet, social identity theory (Tajfel and Turner, 1979) maintains that people need not interact with, nor possess strong interpersonal ties, to perceive themselves as having a connection to a group. In line with this premise, research has asserted that job seekers pursue particular employment opportunities (Kristof-Brown, Reeves, and Follmer, 2014) and consumers choose to patronize certain organizations (Bhattacharya and Sen, 2003) precisely because of a perceived sense of connectedness and belonging to an organization. Scott and Lane (2000) proposed that external stakeholders, like all individuals, seek to define for themselves and others who they are, and may identify with an organization because doing so satisfies certain self-definitional needs. For example, potential donors, although objectively non-members of PETA, may identify with that organization because they define both themselves and PETA (People for the Ethical Treatment of Animals) as animal rights' advocates. Conversely, non-members may disidentify with an organization—such as the NRA (National Rifle Association)—because this disidentification explains who they are by contrasting who they are not (Elsbach, 1999; Elsbach and Bhattacharya, 2001).

To articulate more precisely how expectant stakeholders develop a sense of belonging to an organization, we draw upon Rousseau's (1998) work that distinguished two levels of identification: situated and deep-structure identification. Our view is that stakeholder identification likely resides between these levels. Situated identification is an elementary form of identification; that is, a perception of belonging to an organization, created by situational cues signaling shared interests, that remains salient as long as the cues persist (Meyer, Becker, and Van Dick, 2006; Rousseau, 1998). In essence, situated identification captures categorical membership (Hogg and Terry, 2000; Turner, Hogg, Oakes, Reicher, and Wetherell, 1987). Organizations intentionally craft messages to prompt a perception of membership among expectant stakeholders. Membership is a label that can be evoked to pull non-members into an organization (see Bhattacharya et al., 1995): for example, corporate philanthropy and cause-related marketing programs use the vocabulary of membership to invite consumers into the organization, nonprofit organizations offer membership to donors and other supporters, for-profit businesses create membership opportunities to draw in customers (e.g., American Express extends "membership privileges"), and employment announcements often frame the application process as "becoming a member" for job seekers. By implication, we assert that expectant stakeholders for whom the organization enables such claims of membership are the most likely to experience situated identification.

Deep structure identification, in contrast, is a more meaningful connection between the individual and organization, a perception of congruence between one's sense of self in a work role and broader self-concept (Rousseau, 1998). Deep structure identification corresponds to conventional definitions of organizational identification that implicate a redefinition of the self (Hogg and Abrams, 1988; Turner, 1982)—that is, when an individual's perceptions of an organization's qualities become self-referential or self-defining (Dutton et al., 1994; Pratt, 1998). Situated and deep structure identification are distinct yet interrelated in that the former necessarily precedes the latter (Ashforth, Harrison, and Corley, 2008; Rousseau, 1998). Stakeholder identification reflects the progression that occurs when a person moves beyond simply imagining whether he/she could enter into a relationship with an organization and claim membership (yes or no) to anticipating how much this relationship could define his/her broader sense of self.

How expectant stakeholders come to anticipate feelings of identification in their initial exposures to an organization is not well understood. Research on organizational identification has focused largely on current members (for reviews, see Ashforth et al., 2008; Dutton et al., 1994; Pratt, 1998); in contrast, processes driving non-members' identification with an organization are relatively understudied. There is ample reason to believe that identification among members and non-members unfolds in parallel fashion because the target of identification—the organization—is the same. For example, work on relationship marketing and consumer-company identification (e.g., Ahearne et al., 2005; Bhattacharya and Sen, 2003) leverages social identity theory to implicate conventional self-definitional needs (e.g., similarity, distinctiveness, and prestige) as critical antecedents. Nonetheless, unique considerations arise because expectant stakeholders are outsiders who often lack substantive information about an organization and its members. Below we outline these considerations as related to three motivational forces that may drive stakeholder identification: uncertainty reduction, self-continuity, and self-enhancement.

Is This a Legitimate Organization? The Need for Uncertainty Reduction

Decisions about whether to pursue a relationship with an organization can evoke considerable uncertainty for expectant stakeholders. For example, feelings of uncertainty may loom large for job seekers considering an employment opportunity (Ibarra, 2003) and prospective investors evaluating the investment worthiness of an entrepreneurial proposal (Navis and Glynn, 2011). Expectant stakeholders ultimately want to partner with credible organizations that will remain viable entities in the future. An important task for organizations is to communicate their organizational identity in ways that mitigate expectant stakeholders' felt uncertainty. Uncertainty reduction is a core human motivation (Hogg and Mullin, 1999), and individuals tend to identify strongly with groups that help satisfy this elemental need (Hogg and Terry, 2000).

Organizational legitimacy may be an especially potent factor for mitigating expectant stakeholders' felt uncertainty. Legitimacy is a generalized perception that an organization is desirable or proper according to some culturally shared definition of what constitutes appropriate organizational norms, values, beliefs, and intentions (Suchman, 1995: 574). While legitimacy captures collective approval and endorsement for an organization among a group of actors, individual stakeholders nonetheless form their own perceptions of how relevant others (e.g., other stakeholders and public audiences) assess an organization (Suchman, 1995). Scott and Lane (2000) proposed that such perceptions of legitimacy are a prerequisite for stakeholder identification. Expanding this idea, we suggest that organizations perceived as more legitimate may yield stronger stakeholder identification because such perceptions operate to reduce uncertainty.

The value of legitimacy for expectant stakeholders may derive from the fact that legitimate organizations provide an enhanced sense of security. More concretely, individuals who perceive an organization as legitimate are likely to view it as possessing more capacity for collective action than an organization with questionable legitimacy (see Deephouse and Suchman, 2008). Moreover, perceptions of agency and potency associated with legitimacy should foster expectations that the organization's capacity to act will be stable and consistent for at least some period of time. Consistent with this idea, Gioia and colleagues (Gioia, Price, Hamilton, and Thomas, 2010) noted in their study of the founding of a new college that it was essential for the new entity to provide some reassurances to prospective employees that they were a legitimate school with recognizable promotion and tenure procedures. Relatedly, organizational research on new entrepreneurial ventures highlights how legitimizing the organizational identity provides assurances of future viability to external audiences (Navis and Glynn, 2011; Wry, Lounsbury, and Glynn, 2011). Together, this evidence suggests that intended organizational images that convey greater legitimacy are likely to be evaluated as more attractive among expectant stakeholders.

Do I Fit in This Organization? The Need for Self-Continuity

People also identify more strongly with an organization when their organizational affiliation promotes a coherent sense of self (Pratt, 1998). Defined as the need for self-continuity, people are attracted to organizations when the characteristics comprising the organizational identity are consistent with their own self-perceptions (Dutton et al., 1994), and enacting the identity provides opportunities for self-expression (Swann, Johnson, and Bosson, 2009). Expectant stakeholders considering a possible relationship with an organization often are highly attentive to whether its goals and values are consistent with their own.

For example, research on recruitment has shown that part of the search process involves locating organizations with which a job seeker perceives a fit (Cable and Judge, 1996; Chapman et al., 2005; Judge and Cable, 1997; Kristof-Brown, Zimmerman, and Johnson, 2005). Cable and Edwards (2004) refer to "supplementary fit," or value congruence, as the perceived similarity between an individual's values and the cultural values of an organization or its members (Chatman, 1991; Kristof, 1996). Assessments of fit can extend beyond values to include other organizational attributes such as goals, beliefs, and attitudes (Ashforth and Saks, 1996). The desire for consistency in personal and organizational attributes will likely be salient for other expectant stakeholders as well, such as donors (Arnett et al., 2003; Mael and Ashforth, 1992) and consumers (Bhattacharya and Sen, 2003). For instance, the sense of self-continuity that expectant stakeholders can derive from organizational membership is apparent for an environmentalist who donates to Greenpeace or makes financial investments in Whole Foods, and a patriot who volunteers for an army recruiting office.

While the pursuit of self-continuity often is a matter of continuity per se (i.e., sameness), it also can be a matter of desired growth. The need for self-continuity is satisfied not only when there are opportunities to affirm current self-perceptions, but also perceptions of who one might become, would like to become, or should become in the future (i.e., joining the army will make me into the kind of person I wish to be). For example, Strauss, Griffin, and Parker (2012) use the term "future work self" to refer to a future-oriented self-image that includes work-related hopes and aspirations. Future work selves are based on the concept of hoped for "possible selves" (Markus and Nurius, 1986), and can motivate proactive career behaviors when the future self is salient (i.e., clear and easy to imagine) and meaningfully different from a person's current self (i.e., a clear discrepancy exists). The pursuit of future work selves may not only propel a job search but also explain why some job seekers enter the labor market in the first place (Ibarra and Barbulescu, 2010). Similar ideas appear in research on consumer behavior (Cardador and Pratt, 2006; Fombelle, Burke Jarvis, Ward, and Ostrom, 2012). Consumers often are initially attracted to organizations whose organizational identity comprises attributes related to desired or dormant aspects of the self (Bagozzi, Bergami, Marzocchi, and Morandin, 2012), such as a prospective customer who is drawn to Harley Davidson or Ducati because he/she aspires to be a rebel and to be associated with powerful motorbikes and the freedom of the road. The pursuit of self-continuity, therefore, can involve aspects of the self across different life domains (continuity in work and non-work roles) and over time (past-present-future self). Intended organizational images that satisfy such self-continuity needs will likely be evaluated as more attractive among expectant stakeholders.

How Does This Organization Measure Up? The Need for Self-Enhancement

Expectant stakeholders considering a potential relationship with an organization are attuned to how it is comparatively different and, ideally, better than other organizations. Individuals generally are attracted to organizations that have a desirable organizational identity, because those positive attributes reflect back onto the individual (Cialdini et al., 1976; Cialdini and De Nicholas, 1989). Indeed, employees tend to identify with organizations with high social status or socially desirable features relative to other groups to elevate their own sense of self-esteem (Ashforth and Mael, 1989). The need for self-enhancement is one of the most powerful motives underlying employees' identification with their organizations (Dutton et al., 1994; Pratt, 1998).

Similarly, perceived opportunities for self-enhancement should also be a consideration in expectant stakeholders' initial evaluations of organizations. Research has found that job seekers, for example, are attracted to prestigious organizations with positive reputations (i.e., a positive evaluation made by other external stakeholders), or that otherwise convey a positive intended image (Lievens and Highhouse, 2003; Lievens, Hoye, and Schreurs, 2005; Turban and Keon, 1993). Prospective consumers also are attracted to organizations that enable self-enhancement (Belk, 1988): for example, Bhattacharya and colleagues (1995) showed that purchasing a membership in a prestigious museum was associated with stronger stakeholder identification, presumably because of the boost to self-esteem that membership afforded. Therefore, intended organizational images that emphasize what is positive and distinct about an organization will likely be evaluated as more attractive among expectant stakeholders.

COMMUNICATING ORGANIZATIONAL IDENTITY: ONLINE COMMUNICATION STRATEGIES AND INTENDED ORGANIZATIONAL IMAGE

Generating organizational images that will be attractive to expectant stakeholders can be a complicated task. Organizational leaders and members often find it difficult to articulate and represent effectively the organizational identity. Shared beliefs and values comprising the organizational identity can be abstract, complex, and/or highly subjective (e.g., Corley and Gioia, 2004; Fiol, 1991, 2002; Hatch and Schultz, 2002; Rindova and Schultz, 1998). Representing the organizational identity in ways that are not only comprehensible to expectant stakeholders, but also induce feelings of identification, is further complicated when using mass communication channels, such as company websites. Mass communication channels allow for broad-based announcements, rather than customized exchanges with specific stakeholders, and one-way exchanges (organization to stakeholders) that are primarily text descriptions. To be sure, the use of this less rich, less personal communication medium poses constraints on what organizations can do to effectively convey who they are to non-members. Yet, it may also pose some advantages, as leaner communication can be easier to sort through, and therefore preferable to expectant stakeholders who are considering a potential relationship with an organization (cf. Daft and Lengel, 1984).

Much of what we know today about organizations' strategic use of communication to construct attractive organizational images comes from Cheney's (1983) seminal work on *identification inducements*. Cheney (1983) defined identification inducements as intentional and unintentional attempts by an organization to create a common set of shared meanings about the organization that provides members with a sense of belonging and identity. Identification inducements take different forms, but share a common aim of persuading employees to accept the organization's values and interests as their own. Cheney (1983) examined the rhetorical techniques used in internal company newsletters and concluded that two distinct processes underlie identification inducements: association and dissociation. Association processes aim to establish a connection between the organization and the employee, whereas dissociation processes aim to unite employees by calling attention to a common enemy. We extend work on identification inducements (Cheney, 1983; Cheney and Christensen, 2001; DiSanza and Bullis, 1999) to organizations' external communications via mass communication channels such as the company website, and explore the roles of association and dissociation strategies in building stakeholder identification. Notably, we call out how these strategies can trigger stakeholder identification by tapping into individual needs likely to be salient to expectant stakeholders—uncertainty reduction, self-continuity, and self-enhancement.

Identification Inducement via Association Strategies

Organizational communication that is associational in nature attempts to convey the content of the organizational identity (i.e., the organization's central, distinctive, and relatively enduring features) and, critically, how members have embraced this identity as their own. Association strategies include the "common ground" and "transcendent we" techniques (Cheney, 1983). The "common ground" technique is an explicit effort to establish how the organization and individual presumably share the same values, goals, and interests (Cheney, 1983). This technique can involve expressing concern for the individual as an integral part of the organization, recognizing individual contributions to the organization, espousing "shared" values, and offering testimonials highlighting individuals' dedication to and affection for the organization (Cheney 1983; DiSanza and Bullis, 1999). For example, consider the following excerpt from the Careers page of Whole Foods Market, a retailer of natural and organic foods:

Working At Whole Foods Market

Whole Foods Market attracts people who are passionate—about great food, about the communities they live in, about how we treat our planet and our fellow humans—and who want to bring their passion into the workplace and make a difference. Our Team Members make us who we are by being who they are.... our

> Team Members are the secret to our continued success. As the saying goes around here, without our Team Members, "We're just four walls and food."
>
> ("Whole Foods Careers," 2013)

This excerpt illustrates the common ground technique: particularly, the positive connection that exists between employees and the organization due to commonly shared values and interests; and to individuals' unique contributions that enable the organization to survive and prosper. Offering an account of what unifies employees as a collective whole sends an important signal to expectant stakeholders about uniformity and order inside the company.

In contrast to the common ground technique, the "transcendent we" technique is a more subtle effort to show how the organization and its members are unified with regard to particular values, goals and interests. It involves using pronouns such as "we" or "us" to signal a shared organizational identity. Consider the following excerpt from the About Us page of Gorilla Coffee, an independently owned and operated coffee shop and micro-roastery in Brooklyn, New York:

> Gorilla Coffee—About Us
>
> We began in 2002 with the dream of bringing great coffee to the people of NYC. Our approach reflects the people we serve. We are passionate yet practical. We understand the value of things. We love our history while keeping our eyes on the future. We are diverse yet the same. The city's energy binds us together. It drives us to be the best. When we set up shop with an espresso machine up front and a roaster in the back, we hoped to someday be a part of New York's rich tradition of service and culinary achievement. Everyday this aspiration drives us. We are committed to quality. From the coffee we source, to the precision with which it is roasted and packaged, to our constant training and pursuit of knowledge. We love what we do.
>
> ("About Us," 2016)

In this example it is apparent how the "transcendent we" technique can imbue an organization with coherence and order, enabling expectant stakeholders to form an image of what unifies the organization and its members.

Association strategies are potent triggers of stakeholder identification. Such strategies tap into fundamental needs for uncertainty reduction and self-continuity that will likely be especially salient to expectant stakeholders. Association strategies aim to establish for expectant stakeholders a coherent image of the organizational identity— the goals, values, and interests that define the organization and enable members to act with order and purpose. Armed with this image, expectant stakeholders can infer motives and objectives for the organization, and are likely to consider the organization as having collective decision-making capacity and responsibility. By virtue of discussing "who we are" as though "we" were a single unit and not a collection of individual employees, the organization thus presents an image of being a unified entity. Discussing "who we are" therefore establishes entitativity (Campbell, 1958; Lickel et al., 2000) and implies legitimacy. Association strategies therefore may operate to reduce uncertainty among expectant stakeholders, thereby generating attractive organizational images that promote stakeholder identification.

Association strategies may also address expectant stakeholders' need for self-continuity. Association strategies convey precisely what unites its members—that is, the substance of the organizational identity. Such information is essential: expectant stakeholders need an awareness of the organization's defining characteristics before they form an impression of whether the organizational identity is generally consistent with their own self-perceptions (Dutton et al., 1994; Hogg and Terry, 2000). To this point, marketing research describes how organizations hope to become positive reference groups for consumers—that is, a group with which a consumer desires an association due to actual or aspired similarities (i.e., when a consumer is actually similar to a group in some way or aspires to be similar to the group in some way) (White and Dahl, 2006).

Whether intended organizational images are actually consistent with expectant stakeholders' self-perceptions will vary. Association strategies potentially create perceived opportunities for self-expression for some, but not all, expectant stakeholders. Ultimately, though, the goal is to attract expectant stakeholders with a particular set of qualities and entice them to enter into a relationship with the organization. Association strategies provide a means to this end. Association strategies thus appear instrumental to generating intended organizational images that expectant stakeholders may find attractive and identify with.

Identification Inducement via Dissociation Strategies

Identification inducements also use dissociation processes as a means of persuading individuals to take on the organization's values, goals, and interests as their own. Dissociation strategies aim to unite individuals by creating a common threat or enemy and fostering an "us versus them" mindset. "Identification through antithesis" is a technique that involves invoking an external threat to promote a sense of solidarity among internal members to rally together and defeat the threat. For instance, Cheney (1983) highlights several examples from internal corporate newsletters where the federal government is portrayed as a threat—an enemy of commerce.

A critical feature of the identification-through-antithesis technique, aside from specifying the nature of the threat, is that the organization also simultaneously expresses how it is superior in some significant way to the source of threat (Cheney, 1983). Such expressions of superiority imply a sense of righteousness and purpose, and offer a focal point around which organizational members unite against their enemy. To this point, Cheney (1983) asserts that the "transcendent we" technique operates by dissociation as well as association. Critically, the use of "we" and "us" necessarily implicates a real or imagined "they" (symbolizing outsiders) as an unfavorable point of comparison. Cheney's (1983) primary argument concerning the relationship between dissociation strategies and identification is that by specifying a threat, the organization simultaneously offers an intended image of what it is (its essential values, goals, and interests), as well as an image of what it is not (or will not become), thereby bringing a boundary into sharper focus. Consistent with this idea, marketing research implicates dissociation techniques in efforts to convey a "comparative corporate identity" (e.g., Sony vis-à-vis Samsung, Sun Microsystems vis-à-vis Microsoft) (Balmer, 2008: 888) as a means to articulate an organization's essential qualities to key stakeholders. Relatedly, marketing research points to the value of invoking dissociative reference groups—groups with which a consumer wishes to avoid being associated and feels a sense of disidentification with—as a means for building a sense of connection to an organization and its brands (Englis and Solomon, 1995; Escalas and Bettman, 2005; White and Dahl, 2007).

Dissociation strategies are potent triggers of stakeholder identification. Such strategies are particularly well suited to addressing needs for uncertainty reduction and positive distinctiveness (Tajfel and Turner, 1979). Dissociation strategies offer an intergroup comparison involving the organization and a real or implied out-group. By invoking a boundary through such "us versus them" comparisons, perceptions of coherence as well as efficacy are established as attention is drawn to what unites the organization. At the same time, dissociation strategies intentionally offer comparative information that directs attention toward positive organizational features that affirm the integrity and desirability of the organization. Dissociation strategies, thus, may address needs for self-enhancement as expectant stakeholders envision the beneficial implications for the self that will likely result from entering into a relationship with the organization. Dissociation strategies, therefore, may generate attractive intended organizational images that promote stakeholder identification.

Future Directions for Research on Organizational Identity and Stakeholder Identification

Expectant stakeholders' decision to pursue a relationship with an organization often begins with their initial impressions of the organizational identity. Organizations, therefore, need to translate their internally held organizational identity into an intended organizational image that external stakeholders will likely find attractive (Hatch and Schultz, 2001). This provides conditions conducive to stakeholder identification, which we suggest is a mechanism that partly accounts for *why* expectant stakeholders decide to pursue a relationship or to look elsewhere. Indeed, prior work suggests that employees with stronger organizational identification will seek out opportunities for increased contact with the organization (Dutton et al., 1994), and we similarly suggest that stronger stakeholder identification will lead expectant stakeholders to initiate formal relationships with the organization—for example, by applying for employment, becoming a donor or investor, or consuming products.

Mass communication platforms (the Internet—i.e., company websites) provide a means for influencing expectant stakeholders' initial impressions of an organization. To be sure, how organizations construct written statements appearing on these platforms matters a great deal for creating stakeholder identification. Yet, research that has begun to integrate communication and stakeholder identification is fairly limited. Critically, an organization's attractiveness seems to hinge on whether such communication taps into expectant stakeholders' fundamental needs (Cornelissen, Haslam, and Balmer, 2007; Scott and Lane, 2000), such as uncertainty reduction, self-continuity, or self-enhancement. We outlined how association and dissociation communication strategies may address these needs, generating intended organizational images that expectant stakeholders consider attractive and providing sparks for stakeholder identification.

We see several promising avenues for future research on organizational identity, organizational communication, and stakeholder identification. Beyond the use of association and dissociation tactics, how the content of these communications shapes stakeholder identification could benefit from additional investigation. Translating the organizational identity into an intended image for stakeholders necessarily involves conveying "what the organization is"—the combination of qualities that gives the organization stability, coherence, and character. Yet, how might an organization best signify these qualities—for example, through explicit (and relatively context-free) statements of espoused values (and/or values they do not endorse), or through more contextualized statements that embed essential qualities in descriptions of strategies, culture, company history, structure, leadership team, or employment practices? Without awareness of how the content of communications affects expectant stakeholders, the organizational identity may get lost in translation.

Opportunities also exist to enrich current conceptualizations of the antecedents of stakeholder identification. Our review points to how the motivational bases for identification may be more or less central at different points in time in an individual's relationship with an organization. For example, research on organizational identification among employees, by and large, emphasizes self-enhancement (e.g., Dutton et al., 1994)—particularly for explaining changes in the strength of employees' organizational identification (Bartel, 2001). Relatively less attention has been focused on uncertainty reduction and self-continuity, yet we infer that these are essential motivational drivers in the case of expectant stakeholders. Intuitively this makes sense. Whether an organization comes across as legitimate and also offers opportunities for self-expression are fundamental concerns that are likely to occur in the early stages of a stakeholder's relationship with an organization. Once a relationship is established, such concerns may recede to the background, while concerns about how the organization continually reinforces a positive sense of self move to the foreground. To this point, future research could explore these temporal aspects to assess how the motivational bases for stakeholder identification may evolve over time.

Relatedly, we also see value in diving deeper into the nature of expectant stakeholders' motives—namely, the need for self-consistency. We called attention to how stakeholder identification may offer opportunities to attain self-consistency—not for a current (actual) sense of self but for a future imagined self (Markus and Nurius, 1986). It is an interesting proposition that stakeholders might bring to life a particular self-image based on an affiliation with an organization in which they do not possess a formal membership. This idea may connect to research that touches upon issues of self-definition, especially in regard to who a person could possibly become (e.g., Ibarra, 1999; Ibarra and Barbulescu, 2010; Pratt, 2000; Thompson and Bunderson, 2001), would ideally like to be (Higgins, 1987), or thinks he or she should (ought to) be (Higgins, 1987). Other connections to explore include marketing research on brand identity and identification (e.g., Balmer, 2001; He, Li, and Harris, 2012): specifically, research that has positioned consumer identification to a specific brand as a means to fulfill needs for self-expression, particularly uniqueness (Berger and Heath, 2007; Ruvio, 2008; Tian et al., 2001).

This chapter emphasized a vital task for organizations—communicating their organizational identity in ways that generate intended organizational images that expectant stakeholders deem attractive. Such favorable evaluations create conditions conducive to feelings of connectedness to an organization that act as strong pull forces on expectant stakeholders. The benefit of considering how organizational communication can induce identification is that most organizations now share a common platform from which to speak directly to non-members—the Internet. Indeed, a relationship between expectant stakeholders and organizations can begin in initial encounters with communication directly from the organization. In an era where expectant stakeholders are better able to screen potential organizations with which to partner, organizations that fail to craft appealing expressions of their organizational identity that spark stakeholder identification will quickly lose ground in the battle to secure productive partnerships that affect their performance and future viability.

References

Ahearne, M., Bhattacharya, C. B., and Gruen, T. (2005). "Antecedents and Consequences of Customer-Company Identification." *Journal of Applied Psychology* 90(3): 574–85.

Albert, S. and Whetten, D. A. (1985). "Organizational Identity." *Research in Organizational Behavior* 7: 263–95.

Alessandri, S. W. (2001). "Modeling Corporate Identity: A Concept Explication and Theoretical Explanation." *Corporate Communications: An International Journal* 6(4): 173–82.

Allen, D. G., Biggane, J. E., Pitts, M., Otondo, R., and Van Scotter, J. (2013). "Reactions to Recruitment Web Sites: Visual and Verbal Attention, Attraction, and Intentions to Pursue Employment." *Journal of Business and Psychology* 28(3): 263–85.

Arnett, D. B., German, S. D., and Hunt, S. D. (2003). "The Identity Salience Model of Relationship Marketing Success: The Case of Nonprofit Marketing." *Journal of Marketing* 67(2): 89–105.

Ashforth, B. E., Harrison, S. H., and Corley, K. G. (2008). "Identification in Organizations: An Examination of Four Fundamental Questions." *Journal of Management* 34(3): 325–74.

Ashforth, B. E. and Mael, F. (1989). "Social Identity Theory and the Organization." *Academy of Management Review* 14(1): 20–39.

Ashforth, B. E. and Mael, F. A. (1996). "Organizational Identity and Strategy as a Context for the Individual." *Advances in Strategic Management* 13: 19–64.

Ashforth, B. E. and Saks, A. M. (1996). "Socialization Tactics: Longitudinal Effects on Newcomer Adjustment." *Academy of Management Journal* 39(1): 149–78.

Bagozzi, R. P., Bergami, M., Marzocchi, G. L., and Morandin, G. (2012). "Customer-Organization Relationships: Development and Test of a Theory of Extended Identities." *Journal of Applied Psychology* 97(1): 63–76.

Balmer, J. M. T. (2001). "Corporate Identity, Corporate Branding and Corporate Marketing: Seeing through the Fog." *European Journal of Marketing* 35(3/4): 248–91.

Balmer, J. M. T. (2008). "Identity Based Views of the Corporation: Insights from Corporate Identity, Organisational Identity, Social Identity, Visual Identity, Corporate Brand Identity and Corporate Image." *European Journal of Marketing* 42(9–10): 879–906.

Barber, A. E. (1998). *Recruiting Employees: Individual and Organizational Perspectives.* Thousand Oaks, CA: SAGE.

Bartel, C. A. (2001). "Social Comparisons in Boundary-Spanning Work: Effects of Community Outreach on Members' Organizational Identity and Identification." *Administrative Science Quarterly* 46: 379–413.

Belk, R. W. (1988). "Possessions and the Extended Self." *Journal of Consumer Research* 15: 139–68.

Berger, J. and Heath, C. (2007). "Where Consumers Diverge from Others: Identity Signaling and Product Domains." *Journal of Consumer Research* 34(2): 121–34.

Bhattacharya, C. B. and Elsbach, K. D. (2002). "Us and Them: The Roles of Organizational Identification and Disidentification in Social Marketing Initiatives." *Journal of Public Policy and Marketing* 21: 26–36.

Bhattacharya, C. B., Rao, H., and Glynn, M. A. (1995). "Understanding the Bond of Identification: An Investigation of its Correlates among Art Museum Members." *Journal of Marketing* 54(4): 46–57.

Bhattacharya, C. B. and Sen, S. (2003). "Consumer-Company Identification: A Framework for Understanding Consumers' Relationships with Companies." *Journal of Marketing* 67(2): 76–88.

Bromley, D. B. (2000). "Psychological Aspects of Corporate Identity, Image and Reputation." *Corporate Reputation Review* 3(2): 240–52.

Brown, T., Dacin, P., Pratt, M. G., and Whetten, D. (2006). "Identity, Intended Image, Construed Image, and Reputation: An Interdisciplinary Framework and Suggested Terminology." *Journal of the Academy of Marketing Science* 34(2): 95–106.

Cable, D. M. and Edwards, J. R. (2004). "Complementary and Supplementary Fit: A Theoretical and Empirical Integration." *Journal of Applied Psychology* 89(5): 822–34.

Cable, D. M. and Judge, T. A. (1996). "Person–Organization Fit, Job Choice Decisions, and Organizational Entry." *Organizational Behavior and Human Decision Processes* 67(3): 294–311.

Campbell, D. T. (1958). "Common Fate, Similarity, and Other Indices of the Status of Aggregates of Persons as Social Entities." *Behavioral Science* 3: 14–25.

Cardador, T. M. and Pratt, M. G. (2006). "Identification Management and its Bases: Bridging Management and Marketing Perspectives through Focus on Affiliation Dimensions." *Journal of the Academy of Marketing Science* 34(2): 174–84.

Chapman, D. S., Uggerslev, K. L., Carroll, S. A., Piasentin, K. A., and Jones, D. A. (2005). "Applicant Attraction to Organizations and Job Choice: A Meta-Analytic Review of the Correlates of Recruiting Outcomes." *Journal of Applied Psychology* 90(5): 928–44.

Chatman, J. A. (1991). "Matching People and Organizations: Selection and Socialization in Public Accounting Firms." *Administrative Science Quarterly* 36: 459–84.

Cheney, G. (1983). "The Rhetoric of Identification and the Study of Organizational Communication." *Quarterly Journal of Speech* 69(2): 143–58.

Cheney, G. and Christensen, L. T. (2001). "Organizational Identity: Linkages between 'Internal' and 'External' Organizational Communication." In *The New Handbook of Organizational Communication,* edited by F. M. Jablin and L. L. Putnam, 231–69. Thousand Oaks, CA: SAGE.

Cialdini, R. B., Borden, R. J., Thorne, A., Walker, M. R., Freeman, S., and Sloan, L. R. (1976). "Basking in Reflected Glory: Three (Football) Field Studies." *Journal of Personality and Social Psychology* 34(3): 366–75.

Cialdini, R. B. and De Nicholas, M. E. (1989). "Self-Presentation by Association." *Journal of Personality and Social Psychology* 57(4): 626–31.

Corley, K. G. and Gioia, D. A. (2004). "Identity Ambiguity and Change in the Wake of a Corporate Spin-Off." *Administrative Science Quarterly* 49: 173–208.

Cornelissen, J. P., Haslam, S. A., and Balmer, J. M. T. (2007). "Social Identity, Organizational Identity and Corporate Identity: Towards an Integrated Understanding of Processes, Patternings and Products." *British Journal of Management* 18: 1–16.

Daft, R. L. and Lengel, R. H. (1984). "Information Richness: A New Approach to Manager Information Processing and Organisational Design." In *Research in Organizational Behavior,* vol. 6, edited by L. L. Cummings and B. M. Staw, 191–233. Greenwich: JAI Press.

Deephouse, D. L. and Suchman, M. C. (2008). "Legitimacy in Organizational Institutionalism." In *The SAGE Handbook of Organizational Institutionalism,* edited by R. Greenwood, C. Oliver, K. Sahlin, and R. Suddaby, 49–77. Thousand Oaks, CA: SAGE.

DiSanza, J. R. and Bullis, C. (1999). "'Everybody Identifies with Smokey the Bear' Employee Responses to Newsletter Identification Inducements at the US Forest Service." *Management Communication Quarterly* 12(3): 347–99.

Donaldson, T. and Preston, L. E. (1995). The Stakeholder Theory of the Corporation: Concepts, Evidence, and Implications." *Academy of Management Review* 20: 65–91.

Dutton, J. E., Dukerich, J. M., and Harquail, C. V. (1994). "Organizational Images and Member Identification." *Administrative Science Quarterly* 39(2): 239–63.

Elsbach, K. D. (1999). "An Expanded Model of Organizational Identification." In *Research in Organizational Behavior,* vol. 21, edited by B. M. Staw and R. I. Sutton, 163–200. Oxford: Elsevier.

Elsbach, K. D. and Bhattacharya, C. B. (2001). "Defining Who You Are by What You're Not: Organizational Disidentification and the National Rifle Association." *Organization Science* 12: 393–413.

Englis, B. G. and Solomon, M. R. (1995). "To Be and Not to Be: Lifestyle Imagery, Reference Groups, and the Clustering of America." *Journal of Advertising* 24(1): 13–28.

Escalas, J. E. and Bettman, J. R. (2005). "Self-Construal, Reference Groups, and Brand Meaning." *Journal of Consumer Research* 32(3): 378–89.

Fiol, C. M. (1991). "Managing Culture as a Competitive Resource: An Identity-Based View of Sustainable Competitive Advantage." *Journal of Management* 17(1): 191–211.

Fiol, C. M. (2002). "Capitalizing on Paradox: The Role of Language in Transforming Organizational Identities." *Organization Science* 13(6): 653–66.

Fisher, R. J. and Wakefield, K. (1998). "Factors Leading to Group Identification: A Field Study of Winners and Losers." *Psychology and Marketing* 15(1): 23–40.

Fombelle, P., Jarvis, C. B., Ward, J., and Ostrom, L. (2012). "Leveraging Customers' Multiple Identities: Identity Synergy as a Driver of Organizational Identification." *Journal of the Academy of Marketing Science* 40(4): 587–604.

Gatewood, R. D., Gowan, M. A., and Lautenschlager, G. J. (1993). "Corporate Image, Recruitment Image, and Initial Job Choice Decisions." *Academy of Management Journal* 36(2): 414–27.

Gioia, D. A., Price, K. N., Hamilton, A. L., and Thomas, J. B. (2010). "Forging an Identity: An Insider-Outsider Study of Processes Involved in the Formation of Organizational Identity." *Administrative Science Quarterly* 55(1): 1–46.

Gioia, D. A. and Thomas, J. B. (1996). "Identity, Image, and Issue Interpretation: Sensemaking during Strategic Change in Academia." *Administrative Science Quarterly* 41(3): 370–403.

GoPro (2016). *About Us.* Last accessed March 21, 2016. https://gopro.com/about-us.

Golden-Biddle, K. and Rao, H. V. (1997). "Breaches in the Boardroom: Organizational Identity and Conflicts of Commitment in a Non-Profit Organization." *Organization Science* 8(6): 593–611.

Gorilla Coffee (2016). *About Us.* Last accessed March 5, 2016. http://www.gorillacoffee.com/pages/about-us.

Hatch, M. J. and Schultz, M. (2002). "The Dynamics of Organizational Identity." *Human Relations* 55(8): 989–1018.

He, H., Li, Y., and Harris, L. (2012). "Social Identity Perspective on Brand Loyalty." *Journal of Business Research* 65(5): 648–57.

Higgins, E. T. (1987). "Self-Discrepancy: A Theory Relating Self and Affect." *Psychological Review* 94: 319–40.

Hogg, M. A. and Abrams, D. (1988). *Social Identifications: A Social Psychology of Intergroup Relations and Group Processes.* London: Routledge.

Hogg, M. A. and Mullin, B. A. (1999). "Joining Groups to Reduce Uncertainty: Subjective Uncertainty Reduction and Group Identification." In *Social Identity and Social Cognition,* edited by D. Abrams and M. A. Hogg, 249–79. Oxford: Blackwell.

Hogg, M. A. and Terry, D. I. (2000). "Social Identity and Self-Categorization Processes in Organizational Contexts." *Academy of Management Review* 25(1): 121–40.

Ibarra, H. (1999). "Provisional Selves: Experimenting with Image and Identity in Professional Adaptation." *Administrative Science Quarterly* 44: 764–91.

Ibarra, H. (2003). *Working Identity: Unconventional Strategies for Reinventing your Career.* Boston: Harvard Business School Press.

Ibarra, H. and Barbulescu, R. (2010). "Identity as Narrative: Prevalence, Effectiveness, and Consequences of Narrative Identity Work in Macro Work Role Transitions." *Academy of Management Review* 35(1): 135–54.

Jones, T. M. (1995). "Instrumental Stakeholder Theory: A Synthesis of Ethics and Economics." *Academy of Management Review* 20: 404–37.

Judge, T. A. and Cable, D. M. (1997). "Applicant Personality, Organizational Culture, and Organization Attraction." *Personnel Psychology* 50(2): 359–94.

Kristof, A. L. (1996). "Person-Organization Fit: An Integrative Review of Its Conceptualizations, Measurement, and Implications." *Personnel Psychology* 49(1): 1–49.

Kristof-Brown, A. L., Reeves, C., and Follmer, E. (2014). "Organizational Fit and Recruitment." In *The Oxford Handbook of Recruitment*, edited by D. Cable and T. Yu, 437–43. New York: Oxford University Press.

Kristof-Brown, A. L., Zimmerman, R. D., and Johnson, E. C. (2005). "Consequences of Individuals' Fit at Work: A Meta-Analysis of Person-Job, Person-Organization, Person-Group, and Person-Supervisor Fit." *Personnel Psychology* 58(2): 281–342.

Laverie, D. A. and Arnett, D. (2000). "Factors Affecting Fan Attendance: The Influence of Identity Salience and Satisfaction." *Journal of Leisure Research*, 32(2): 225–46.

Lickel, B., Hamilton, D. L., Wieczorkowska, G., Lewis, A., Sherman, S. J., and Uhles, A. N. (2000). "Varieties of Groups and the Perception of Group Entitativity." *Journal of Personality and Social Psychology* 78(2): 223–45.

Lievens, F. and Highhouse, S. (2003). "The Relation of Instrumental and Symbolic Attributes to a Company's Attractiveness as an Employer." *Personnel Psychology* 56(1): 75–102.

Lievens, F., Hoye, G., and Schreurs, B. (2005). "Examining the Relationship between Employer Knowledge Dimensions and Organizational Attractiveness: An Application in a Military Context." *Journal of Occupational and Organizational Psychology* 78(4): 553–72.

Mael, F. A. and Ashforth, B. E. (1992). "Alumni and their Alma Mater: A Partial Test of the Reformulated Model of Organizational Identification." *Journal of Organizational Behavior* 13(2): 103–23.

Markus, H. and Nurius, P. (1986). "Possible Selves." *American Psychologist* 41(9): 954–69.

Meyer, J. P., Becker, T. E., and Van Dick, R. (2006). "Social Identities and Commitments at Work: Toward an Integrative Model." *Journal of Organizational Behavior* 27(5): 665–83.

Mitchell, R. K., Agle, B. R., and Wood, D. J. (1997). "Toward a Theory of Stakeholder Identification and Salience: Defining the Principle of Who and What Really Counts." *Academy of Management Review* 22: 853–86.

Navis, C. and Glynn, M. A. (2011). "Legitimate Distinctiveness and the Entrepreneurial Identity: Influence on Investor Judgments of New Venture Plausibility." *Academy of Management Review* 36(3): 479–99.

Postmes, T., Tanis, M., and De Wit, B. (2001). "Communication and Commitment in Organizations: A Social Identity Approach." *Group Processes & Intergroup Relations* 4(3): 227–46.

Pratt, M. G. (1998). "To Be or Not to Be: Central Questions in Organizational Identification." In *Identity in Organizations: Building Theory through Conversations*, edited by D. A. Whetten and P. C. Godfrey, 171–207. Thousand Oaks, CA: SAGE.

Pratt, M. G. (2000). "The Good, the Bad, and the Ambivalent: Managing Identification among Amway Distributors." *Administrative Science Quarterly* 45(3): 456–93.

Pratt, M. G. (2003). "Disentangling Collective Identities." *Research on Managing Groups and Teams* 5: 161–88.

Rindova, V. P. and Schultz, M. (1998). "Identity within and Identity without: Lessons from Corporate and Organizational Identity." In *Identity in Organizations: Building Theory through Conversations*, edited by D. A. Whetten and P. C. Godfrey, 46–62. Thousand Oaks, CA: SAGE.

Rousseau, D. M. (1998). "Why Workers Still Identify with Organizations." *Journal of Organizational Behavior* 19(3): 217–33.

Ruvio, A. (2008). "Unique Like Everybody Else? The Dual Role of Consumers' Need for Uniqueness." *Psychology & Marketing* 25(5): 444–64.

Schinoff, B., Rogers, K., and Corley, K. G. (2016). "How Do We Communicate Who We Are? Examining How Organizational Identity Is Conveyed to Members." In *The Oxford Handbook of Organizational Identity*, edited by M. G. Pratt, M. Schultz, B. E. Ashforth, and D. Ravasi, 219–38. Oxford: Oxford University Press.

Scott, S. G. and Lane, V. R. (2000). "A Stakeholder Approach to Organizational Identity." *Academy of Management Review* 25(1): 43–62.

Smidts, A., Pruyn, A., and Van Riel, C. B. M. (2001). "The Impact Of Employee Communication and Perceived External Prestige on Organizational Identification." *Academy of Management Journal* 44(5): 1051–62.

Suchman, M. C. (1995). "Managing Legitimacy: Strategic and Institutional Approaches." *Academy of Management Review* 20: 571–610.

Starik, M. (1994). "Toronto Conference: Reflections on Stakeholder Theory (Essays by Mark Starik)." *Business & Society* 33(1): 89–95.

Strauss, K., Griffin, M. A., and Parker, S. K. (2012). "Future Work Selves: How Salient Hoped-For Identities Motivate Proactive Career Behaviors." *Journal of Applied Psychology* 97: 580–98.

Swann Jr, W. B., Johnson, R. E., and Bosson, J. K. (2009). "Identity Negotiation at Work." *Research in Organizational Behavior* 29: 81–109.

Tajfel, H. and Turner, J. C. (1979). "An Integrative Theory of Intergroup Conflict." In *The Social Psychology of Intergroup Relations*, edited by W. G. Austin and S. Worchel, 33–47. Pacific Grove, CA: Brooks/Cole Publishing.

Thompson, J. A. and Bunderson, J. S. (2001). "Work/Nonwork Conflict and the Phenomenology of Time: Beyond the Balance Metaphor." *Work and Occupations* 28(1): 17–39.

Tian, K. T., Bearden, W. O., and Hunter, G. L. (2001). "Consumers' Need for Uniqueness: Scale Development and Validation." *Journal of Consumer Research* 28(1): 50–66.

Turban, D. B. and Keon, T. L. (1993). "Organizational Attractiveness: An Interactionist Perspective." *Journal of Applied Psychology* 78(2): 184–193.

Turner, J. C. (1982). "Towards a Cognitive Redefinition of the Social Group." In *Social Identity and Intergroup Relations*, edited by H. Tajfel, 93–118. Cambridge: Cambridge University Press.

Turner, J. C., Hogg, M. A., Oakes, P. J., Reicher, S. D., and Wetherell, M. S. (1987). *Rediscovering the Social Group: A Self-Categorization Theory*. New York: Blackwell Publishing.

Vaughn, M. A. (1997). "Organizational Identification Strategies and Values in High Technology Industries: A Rhetorical-Organizational Approach to the Analysis of Socialization Processes in Corporate Discourse." *Journal of Public Relations Research* 9(2): 119–39.

Whetten, D. A. and Godfrey, P. (eds.) (1998). *Identity in Organizations: Developing Theory through Conversations*. Thousand Oaks, CA: SAGE.

White, K. and Dahl, D. W. (2006). "To Be or Not to Be: The Influence of Dissociative Reference Groups on Consumer Preferences." *Journal of Consumer Psychology* 16(4): 404–13.

White, K. and Dahl, D. W. (2007). "Are All Outgroups Created Equal? Consumer Identity and Dissociative Influence." *Journal of Consumer Research* 34(4): 525–36.

Whole Foods Market. "Careers at Whole Foods Market" (2013). Last accessed March 5, 2016. http://www.wholefoodsmarket.com/careers.

Wry, T., Lounsbury, M., and Glynn, M. A. (2011). "Legitimating Nascent Collective Identities: Coordinating Cultural Entrepreneurship." *Organization Science* 22: 449–63.

CONCLUSION: ON THE IDENTITY OF ORGANIZATIONAL IDENTITY

looking backward toward the future

MICHAEL G. PRATT, BLAKE E. ASHFORTH, MAJKEN SCHULTZ, AND DAVIDE RAVASI

The past may dictate who we are, but we get to determine what we become.

(Unknown)

HANDBOOKS, by their very nature, use present understandings to (re)interpret the past in order to peer forward into the future. Such future glimpses, however, are inevitably obscured by those very backward glances. How we view "who we have been" as an intellectual community of organizational identity (OI) scholars shapes "who we will be" and "who we can become." Moreover, it is not only "how we view ourselves" but "who views" that plays a role in self-definitions. We have endeavored to include a myriad of voices in our handbook, including those scholars who have been writing about OI for decades, as well as those who are relatively new to the field. We have also deliberately invited authors from "both sides of the pond"—North America and Europe—as research on the topic seems most active in these areas. Based on this constellation of thinkers, OI today seems quite different from what it was in at least three major respects. Indeed, these differences appear to map out some important paths forward:

1. *Moving beyond "definition wars."* In September of 1994, David Whetten hosted the first of three conferences in Utah on the topic of OI. It is fair to say that much of the discussion was about "what is OI?" In the years that followed, several views have emerged, including social actor, social constructionist, institutional,

narrative, and critical (see Gioia and Hamilton, Ch. 1, and Foreman and Whetten, Ch. 2; see also Brown, 2006). The debate regarding whether organizational identity is best typified by any of these perspectives has at times generated more heat than light—although there have been voices arguing for the complementarity of perspectives (Gioia, Price, Hamilton, and Thomas, 2010; Ravasi and Schultz, 2006). As certain chapters elaborate and confirm (e.g., Gioia and Hamilton, Ch. 1; Cornelissen, Haslam, and Werner, Ch. 11), some perspectives can be quite complementary. However, because each addresses different research questions (entailing different methodologies), scholars need not use all of them in a given study. That said, it is very important that scholars clearly articulate which perspectives they are implicitly or explicitly using, and how they are combining them, if that is the case (see Pratt and Foreman, 2000 for a similar call).

One implication of moving beyond definition wars is that it has allowed scholars to put their energies toward other areas, such as why OI is important and matters to organizations. Intuitively, it makes a great deal of sense that stakeholders need a reasonably clear sense of what is central, distinctive, and more or less enduring about an organization to know how—or even whether—to engage with it. However, we have barely scratched the surface regarding why OI may be important to those who lead, manage, and otherwise participate in the continuous construction of what the organization is about, as discussed in chapters on identity work and the multiple levels of identity (e.g., Ashforth, Ch. 4; Kreiner and Murphy, Ch. 15). Fortunately, various chapters provide promising leads, suggesting for example, that OI can underpin and direct strategy both as intention (what we want to do) and as practice (how we do it), can strongly affect sensemaking and how organizational members come to see themselves, and can facilitate innovation (DeJordy and Creed, Ch. 20; Anthony and Tripsas, Ch. 22; Bhatt, van Riel, and Baumann, Ch. 23).

2. *Moving toward process.* In our original plans for this handbook, we had allocated one section for OI processes. However, after receiving chapter outlines from our authors, it was clear that many of them viewed OI as a "work in process" rather than as a more stable entity. Indeed, the role of history and other elements of time are viewed as increasingly integral to how collectives continuously view "who we were" and "who we are in the process of becoming" (e.g., Schultz, Ch. 5; Suddaby, Foster, and Quinn Trank, Ch. 16). Thus, we abandoned the idea of a specific section dedicated to these topics; instead you will find those who take a process view throughout the handbook.

The move toward process opens new views on identity change and stability. It may be that OI change itself is not that difficult (if OI is indeed a "momentary accomplishment"), though "planned" change certainly can be. It further suggests that we need to look not only at the process of change but also at the processes through which OI is maintained. Indeed, we appear to be rediscovering Lewin's

(1951) argument that seemingly stable states are really vacillating equilibria that are roughly suspended between dynamic but opposing forces. If so, what are the multilevel forces that allow an OI to be momentarily accomplished?

A renewed attention to organizational history and historical analysis (Rowlinson, Hassard, and Decker, 2014) also encourages us to expand the scope of our analysis of change from episodic events—when identities are challenged, reconsidered, or redefined—to long-term processes of adaptation and evolution. How and why do organizational identities change over extended periods of time, possibly tacitly, gradually, and without explicit recognition? What forces—inside and outside the organization—cause these changes and, over time, bring members to view their organization very differently than what they used to? Consistent with the narrative perspective on OI (e.g., Brown, 2006), a process view challenges the very ontology of OI as an entity, and instead conceives of OI as an ongoing flow of self-definitions—always in the making (e.g., Gioia and Hamilton, Ch. 1; see also Langley et al., 2013, and Hernes, 2014). Such a view questions how actors construct continuity in the midst of constant change, and sets out to explore how OI as flow points both backward and forward in time. These issues, in turn, raise questions about how to study OI processes and how to empirically distinguish them from processes associated with other constructs, such as culture (see Ravasi, Ch. 3).

Critical management scholars have further suggested that such processes involve the application of power. If we assume that individuals do not come into the organization thinking that there is one way to view OI, then establishing an OI may involve political, and often top-down, exercises of normative control to ensure a coherent view of "who we are." Such control may become buttressed by institutional norms or logics and reified in structures and practices. As we move forward, we may want to pay more explicit attention, not only to top-down exercises of power in the establishment, maintenance, and change of OI, but to bottom-up and middle-outward exercises as well (cf. Watson, Ch. 7; Kenny, Whittle, and Willmott, Ch. 8; Alvesson and Robertson, Ch. 9).

3. *Moving toward a deeper understanding of OI plurality and complexity.* As noted, we have known since OI was first conceptualized that the collective answer to the question, "who are we?" may have different answers. While the field has moved from hybrid OIs to include multiple OIs, how OI plurality comes about and is enacted in organizations remains under-explored. Clearly, insights from power and politics, institutional theory, sensemaking, and other perspectives that have come to influence our understanding of OI can help us deepen our understanding of OI plurality. But as noted by our authors (Foreman and Whetten, Ch. 2; Pratt, Ch. 6), empirical work in this area is sorely lacking.

Our understandings of OI are becoming increasingly complex, not only as we tackle the issue of "how many" identities, but also as our knowledge of the multilevel nature of OI continues to evolve. Indeed several core questions remain. To what extent are identities at different levels of analysis isomorphic? (see Phillips, Tracey, and Kraatz, Ch. 19, and Besharov and Brickson, Ch. 21). While the individual, subunit, and organization levels are the most commonly studied, it's also worthwhile to consider dyad, team, occupation, industry, institution, nation, and geographic region. Are there challenges, dynamics, and constraints that help foster level-specific identities? To what extent can multilevel identities be described as supplementary (as the organization strives for consistency) versus complementary (as the organization grows and becomes increasingly differentiated)? How prevalent are "identity foils" (Ashforth, Rogers, and Corley, 2011), where one level defines itself at least partly in opposition to another level (e.g., Elsbach and Dukerich, Ch. 14)?

Such questions multiply when we take a process perspective on OI. For example, how do identities at different levels of analysis interact—in terms of initial identity formation, identity stabilization/maintenance, and identity change? While the literature seems to tacitly view formation and stabilization as relatively unproblematic, to what extent can we describe these processes—and especially identity change—as conflicted/politicized? What happens when organizations with different identity histories merge and their identities become intertwined in a new joint future? Which dimensions of identity formation/stabilization/change are intentional versus unintentional, directed (via leadership) versus emergent?

But the future of OI may also veer in new and unexpected directions. As noted, most of our contributing scholars are from North America and Europe. How might societal cultures be influencing how we think about OI? Research suggests that conceptualizations of identity in Western cultures vary greatly from those in Eastern cultures (e.g., independent versus interdependent; Markus and Kitayama, 1991). Might there be an Eastern perspective on OI, and if so, in what ways might it differ from Western social actor, social construction, institutional, narrative, and critical perspectives? How is our theorizing about OI influenced by the societies we are living in and the identity problems facing our local organizations? How might the processes through which OIs form, stabilize, and change vary across cultures? The vast majority of empirical studies have been conducted within national contexts, and there is a profound need for research reflecting the globalized world in which more and more organizations are operating.

Organizations themselves are becoming more distributed, with functions being outsourced, networks replacing traditional hierarchies, and employees being displaced by contractors. In what ways may these trends influence the very nature of OIs and how they emerge and change? As the average lifespan of companies continues to decrease (Foster and Kaplan, 2001), might the life-cycle metaphor—once so prominent in organization theory—provide renewed insight for OI dynamics and take us in the direction of the metaphor of constant flow? Or will an explosion in the "shared economy" take us even further, seeing OI as shifting intersections of small streams? Intriguing questions also remain regarding how OI unfolds in global settings and the relationship between OI and social media, which transforms the pace and distribution of how multiple "others" see "us."

We also know more about the people inhabiting organizations. Indeed, research in psychology in the past 20 years has shown the power of implicit and otherwise nonconscious processes in how we think, feel, and make decisions (Pratt and Crosina, 2016). Research also suggests that nonconscious processes can occur at the group and organizational level (e.g., systems psychodynamic perspectives; Gould, Stapley, and Stein, 2001). In what ways are nonconscious processes associated with OI? As careers become increasingly turbulent, how might the psychological contracts—the core expectations—of employees change, and what impact will that have on how organizations define themselves vis-à-vis their employees? Organizations have already become far less paternalistic, tending to view themselves less as permanent homes for their employees and more as temporary platforms for skill development and resumé burnishing. And individuals, for their part, increasingly look to their occupations and networks of relationships for self-definition rather than to their current employer. As a new generation, with its own evolving portfolio of wants, enters the workplace, how might OIs and organizational identification continue to change?

Finally, as the world becomes more densely interconnected and corporations increasingly fulfill what were once thought to be mainly governmental responsibilities (as through, for example, triple bottom line concerns and privatized schools), one also wonders how other societal institutions will come to bear on OI. Beyond government, how might the cultural institution of family influence OI, especially given the preponderance of family businesses? How might other cultural institutions, such as religion, impact our understanding of OI? These trends indicate that organizations are increasingly transposing fundamental norms, beliefs, and expectations—the "logics" that characterize different institutions such as the state, the family, or the church (see Phillips et al., Ch. 19, and DeJordy and Creed, Ch. 20)—from one field to another. Some are induced to do so by changing societal expectations; others do so strategically to explore new market opportunities. Both produce new hybrids and other multiple-identity forms of organizing that raise tensions between old and new understandings of "who we are." How can organizations reconcile these tensions? Are these changes fundamentally altering the way we view the organizations we inhabit?

These considerations suggest that while OI research has been thriving and growing in the past few decades, much remains to explore. We look forward to seeing and participating in what the future will bring, and what the field will become.

References

Alvesson, M. and Robertson, M. (2016). "Organizational Identity: A Critique." In *The Oxford Handbook of Organizational Identity*, edited by M. G. Pratt, M. Schultz, B. E. Ashforth, and D. Ravasi, 160–80. Oxford: Oxford University Press.

Anthony, C. and Tripsas, M. (2016). "Organizational Identity and Innovation." In *The Oxford Handbook of Organizational Identity*, edited by M. G. Pratt, M. Schultz, B. E. Ashforth, and D. Ravasi, 417–35. (Oxford: Oxford University Press.

Ashforth, B. E. (2016). "Organizational, Subunit, and Individual Identities: Multilevel Linkages." In *The Oxford Handbook of Organizational Identity*, edited by M. G. Pratt, M. Schultz, B. E. Ashforth, and D. Ravasi, 79–92. Oxford: Oxford University Press.

Ashforth, B. E., Rogers, K. M., and Corley, K. G. (2011). "Identity in Organizations: Exploring Cross-level Dynamics." *Organization Science* 22(5): 1144–56.

Besharov, M. L. and Brickson, S. L. (2016). "Organizational Identity and Institutional Forces: Toward an Integrative Framework." In *The Oxford Handbook of Organizational Identity*, edited by M. G. Pratt, M. Schultz, B. E. Ashforth, and D. Ravasi, 396–414. Oxford: Oxford University Press.

Bhatt, M., van Riel, C. B. M., and Baumann, M. (2016). "Planned Organizational Identity Change: Insights from Practice." In *The Oxford Handbook of Organizational Identity*, edited by M. G. Pratt, M. Schultz, B. E. Ashforth, and D. Ravasi, 436–54. Oxford: Oxford University Press.

Brown, A. D. (2006). "A Narrative Approach to Collective Identities." *Journal of Management Studies* 43(4): 731–53.

Cornelissen, J. P., Haslam, S. A., and Werner, M. D. (2016). "Bridging and Integrating Theories on Organizational Identity: A Social Interactionist Model of Organizational Identity Formation and Change." In *The Oxford Handbook of Organizational Identity*, edited by M. G. Pratt, M. Schultz, B. E. Ashforth, and D. Ravasi, 200–15. Oxford: Oxford University Press.

DeJordy, R. and Creed, W. E. D. (2016). "Institutional Pluralism, Inhabitants, and the Construction of Organizational and Personal Identities." In *The Oxford Handbook of Organizational Identity*, edited by M. G. Pratt, M. Schultz, B. E. Ashforth, and D. Ravasi, 374–95. Oxford: Oxford University Press.

Elsbach, K. D. and Dukerich, J. M. (2016). "Organizational Identity and the Undesired Self." In *The Oxford Handbook of Organizational Identity*, edited by M. G. Pratt, M. Schultz, B. E. Ashforth, and D. Ravasi. 257–75. Oxford: Oxford University Press.

Foreman, P. O. and Whetten, D. A. (2016). "Measuring Organizational Identity: Taking Stock and Looking Forward." In *The Oxford Handbook of Organizational Identity*, edited by M. G. Pratt, M. Schultz, B. E. Ashforth, and D. Ravasi, 39–64. Oxford: Oxford University Press.

Foster, R. and Kaplan, S. (2001). *Creative Destruction: Why Companies that are Built to Last Underperform the Market—and How to Successfully Transform Them*. New York: Doubleday.

Gioia, D. A. and Hamilton, A. L. (2016). "Great Debates in Organizational Identity Study." In *The Oxford Handbook of Organizational Identity*, edited by M. G. Pratt, M. Schultz, B. E. Ashforth, and D. Ravasi, 21–38. Oxford: Oxford University Press.

Gioia, D. A., Price, K. N., Hamilton, A. L., and Thomas, J. B. (2010). Forging an Identity: An Insider-Outsider Study of Processes Involved in the Formation of Organizational Identity." *Administrative Science Quarterly* 55(1): 1–46.

Gould, L. J., Stapley, L. F., and Stein, M. (2001). *The Systems Psychodynamics of Organizations: Integrating the Group Relations Approach, Psychoanalytic, and Open Systems Perspectives*. London: Karnac.

Hernes, T. (2014). *A Process Theory of Organization*. Oxford: Oxford University Press.

Kenny, K., Whittle, A., and Willmott, H. (2016). "Organizational Identity: The Significance of Power and Politics." In *The Oxford Handbook of Organizational Identity*, edited by M. G. Pratt, M. Schultz, B. E. Ashforth, and D. Ravasi, 140–59. Oxford: Oxford University Press.

Kreiner, G. E. and Murphy, C. (2016). "Organizational Identity Work." In *The Oxford Handbook of Organizational Identity*, edited by M. G. Pratt, M. Schultz, B. E. Ashforth, and D. Ravasi, 276–93. Oxford: Oxford University Press.

Langley, A. N. N., Smallman, C., Tsoukas, H., and Van de Ven, A. H. (2013). "Process Studies of Change in Organization and Management: Unveiling Temporality, Activity, and Flow." *Academy of Management Journal* 56(1): 1–13.

Lewin K. (1951). *Field Theory in Social Science: Selected Theoretical Papers*, edited by D. Cartwright. New York: Harper & Brothers.

Markus, H. R. and Kitayama, S. (1991). "Culture and the Self: Implications for Cognition, Emotion, and Motivation." *Psychological Review* 98(2): 224–53.

Phillips, N., Tracey, P., and Kraatz, M. (2016). "Organizational Identity in Institutional Theory: Taking Stock and Moving Forward." In *The Oxford Handbook of Organizational Identity*, edited by M. G. Pratt, M. Schultz, B. E. Ashforth, and D. Ravasi, 353–73. Oxford: Oxford University Press.

Pratt, M. G. (2016). "Hybrid and Multiple Organizational Identities." In *The Oxford Handbook of Organizational Identity*, edited by M. G. Pratt, M. Schultz, B. E. Ashforth, and D. Ravasi, 106–20. Oxford: Oxford University Press.

Pratt, M. G., and Crosina, E. (2016). "The Nonconscious at Work." *Annual Review of Organizational Psychology and Organizational Behavior* 3: 321–47.

Pratt, M. and Foreman, P. (2000). "The Beauty of and Barriers to Organizational Theories of Identity." *Academy of Management Review* 25: 141–3.

Ravasi, D. (2016). "Organizational Identity, Culture, and Image." In *The Oxford Handbook of Organizational Identity*, edited by M. G. Pratt, M. Schultz, B. E. Ashforth, and D. Ravasi, 65–78. Oxford: Oxford University Press.

Ravasi, D. and Schultz, M. (2006). "Responding to Organizational Identity Threats: Exploring the Role of Organizational Culture." *Academy of Management Journal*, 49(3): 433–58.

Rowlinson, M., Hassard, J., and Decker, S. (2014). "Research Strategies for Organizational History: A Dialogue between Historical Theory and Organization Theory." *Academy of Management Review* 39(3): 250–74.

Schultz, M. (2016). "Organizational Identity Change and Temporality." In *The Oxford Handbook of Organizational Identity*, edited by M. G. Pratt, M. Schultz, B. E. Ashforth, and D. Ravasi, 93–105. Oxford: Oxford University Press.

Suddaby, R., Foster, W. M., and Quinn Trank, C. (2016). "Re-Membering: Rhetorical History as Identity Work." In *The Oxford Handbook of Organizational Identity*, edited by M. G. Pratt, M. Schultz, B. E. Ashforth, and D. Ravasi, 297–316. Oxford: Oxford University Press.

Watson, T. J. (2016). "Organizational Identity and Organizational Identity Work as Valuable Analytical Resources." In *The Oxford Handbook of Organizational Identity*, edited by M. G. Pratt, M. Schultz, B. E. Ashforth, and D. Ravasi, 123–39. Oxford: Oxford University Press.

Author Index

Abzug, R. 400, 449
Ahuja, G. 422
Ailon-Souday, G. 467
Albert, S. 1, 8, 15, 28, 39, 55, 57, 68, 71, 80, 94, 97, 106–10, 112, 114, 123–6, 131, 169, 170, 206, 317, 319, 397, 399, 422, 436, 455
Alford, R. 377
Altman, E. J. 424
Alvesson, M. 4, 7, 8, 82, 150, 168, 277, 278, 286
Anderson, L. 276, 278
Anderson, P. 422
Anteby, M. 4, 97, 280, 287, 426, 428
Anthony, C. 5, 14, 100
Ashforth, B. E. 4, 5, 7, 12, 14, 80, 100, 109, 116, 169, 207–8, 211, 232, 270, 288, 340, 368, 448

Bailey, K. D. 41
Barbulescu, R. 278
Bardi, C. 4, 15
Bartel, C. 4, 15
Bateson, G. 32
Battilana, J. 109, 116, 368, 401
Baumann, M. 5, 14
Berens, G.A.J. M. 451
Berger, J. 192
Berger, P. L. 277
Besharov, M. L. 4, 13, 112
Bhatt, M. 5, 14, 451
Bhattacharya, C. B. 482
Biggart, M. W. 446
Billig, M. 467
Birnholtz, J. P. 223
Block, E. 112, 377, 378, 384, 402
Boje, D. M. 462
Bouchikhi, H. 143
Bower, J. L. 419, 422
Brannen, M. Y. 458
Brewer, M. B. 25, 27

Brickson, S. L. 4, 13
Brown, A. D. 143, 267, 280, 437, 447, 464, 465
Brown, T. 451
Brunninge, O. 426
Burke, K. 298, 299

Cable, D. M. 231, 349
Canato, A. 4, 162, 321, 324
Cheney, G. 299, 476, 483, 485
Chia, R. 28, 30, 32
Chittipeddi, K. 338, 339, 340, 341
Chreim, S. 83, 100, 338
Christensen, C. M. 419, 422
Christiansen, L. H. 401
Christianson, M. K. 304
Clark, B. R. 1
Clark, K. B. 422
Clark, S. M. 446, 459
Clegg, S. R. 279
Cohen, M. D. 223
Colquitt, J. A. 56
Cook, S. D. N. 229
Corley, K. G. 4, 25, 65, 69, 80, 85, 86, 94, 98, 99, 308, 340, 368, 426, 437, 448
Cornelissen, J. P. 3, 9, 127–8, 130, 461
Covaleski, M. A. 224
Creed, W. E. D. 3, 4, 8, 13, 380, 381, 385
Csikszentmihalyi, M. 287
Cyert, R. M. 132, 133
Czarniawska-Joerges, B. 167

De Lima, F. 458
DeJordy, R. 3, 4, 8, 13, 381
Demarie, S. M. 439
Denton, P. 1
Devine, B. A. 4, 10, 264
DiMaggio, P. M. 192
Dirsmith, M. W. 224

Dolpiaz, E. 423, 425
Dorado, S. 109, 116, 368, 401
Drori, I. 459
Dukerich, J. 4, 5, 11, 15, 47, 66, 116, 144, 163, 225, 252, 323, 382–3, 385, 402, 406
Dutton, J. E. 4, 5, 47, 66, 116, 144, 163, 169, 225, 252, 323, 382–3, 385, 402

Edmonson, A. C. 56
Ellis, S. 459
Elsbach, K. D. 4, 11, 23, 66, 75, 116, 261, 262, 263, 269, 322, 385, 402
Empson, L. 82, 150

Fabbri, T. 308
Farkas, M. T. 304
Feldman, M. S. 28, 32
Fiol, C. M. 5, 70, 71, 426, 427, 437
Flores, R. G. 365
Foreman, P. 3, 6, 21, 107, 110, 112, 114, 166, 447
Foster, W. 3
Foucault, M. 147–8, 154
Fournier, S. 304
Friedland, R. 377

Garbett, T. 143
Gavetti, G. 321
Gawer, A. 366
Gersick, C. 98
Giddens, A. 277, 450
Giessner, S. R. 344
Gino, F. 231
Gioia, D. A. 3, 6, 24, 25, 31, 65, 66, 86, 94, 98, 99, 123, 126, 127–8, 130, 143, 161, 162, 166, 167, 169–71, 221, 287, 308, 338, 339, 340, 341, 366, 367, 368, 369, 403, 426, 439, 459, 480
Glynn, M. A. 5, 12, 24, 26, 99, 108, 241, 261, 303, 305, 321, 322, 362, 382, 400, 402, 432, 437, 449
Golden, B. R. 406
Golden-Biddle, K. 5, 108, 146
Greenwood, R. 27, 302, 402, 407
Griffin, M. A. 481
Gustafson, L. T. 439

Hackley, C. 262, 267
Halbwachs, M. 301

Hamilton, A. L. 3, 6, 25, 100, 130, 161
Hardy, C. 283
Harquail, C. 163, 437
Haslam, S. A. 3, 9
Hatch, M. J. 4, 73, 100, 114, 170, 326, 437
Heath, C. 192
Heian, J. B. 224
Henderson, R. M. 422
Hernes, T. 4, 100, 223, 298, 303, 305, 321, 323, 426, 427
Hinings, C. R. 83
Hirsch, P. M. 41
Hoch, S. V. 223
Hofmann, D. A. 81
Hogg, M. A. 459
Hollensbe, E. C. 284
Hopkins, N. 343
Howard-Grenville, J. 304
Hsu, G. 116
Humphreys, M. 143, 437, 447, 464, 465

Ibarra, H. 262, 278
Isaacson , W. 340

Kaplan, S. 328
Karaosmanoglu, E. 308
Kärreman, D. 143
Katherine, A. 284
Katila, R. 422
Kaufman, J. B. 265
Kellogg, K. C. 249
Kenney, K. 4, 5, 8
Kenny, K. 161
Ketchen, D. J. 459
Kimberley, J. R. 143
Kjaergaard, A. 164, 449, 450
Klein, K. J. 81, 82
Kodeih, F. 402
Kornberger, M. 279
Kover, A. J. 262, 267
Kozlowski, S. W. J. 81, 82
Kraatz, M. 13, 98, 112, 113, 116, 371, 375, 376, 377, 378, 379, 384, 386, 387, 402
Kramer, R. M. 66, 385, 402
Kreiner, G. E. 3, 8, 11, 101, 135, 265, 284, 285
Kunda, G. 467

Laclau, E. 149–50, 154, 155
Lane, V. R. 134
Lawrence, T. B. 282, 286, 360
Lee, L. 304
Levin, D. Z. 41
Levitt, T. 431
Lewin, K. 495
Linde, C. 307, 310–11
Lok, J. 381
Lounsbury, M. 400, 401
Lowenthal, D. 301
Luckman, T. 277
Lukes, Steven 145–55

Mackey, A. 399, 449
Maguire, S. 283, 459
March, J. G. 132, 133
Marquis, C. 99
Martin, J. 170
Mason-Schrock, D. 279
McGinn, K. L. 224
McManus, S. E. 56
Mead, G. H. 4, 377
Melewar, T. C. 308
Metzger, M. L. 304
Meyer, A. D. 304
Meyerson, D. 170
Milliken, F. J. 403
Molnár, V. 4, 97, 280, 287, 426, 428
Monden, L. 458
Morgeson, F. P. 81
Mouffe, C. 149–50, 154, 155
Mullane, J. V. 439
Murphy, C. 3, 8, 11, 101, 135

Nag, R. 323, 426
Navis, C. 321, 362, 432
Nerkar, A. 422
Nippert-Eng, C. E. 284

Obukhova, E. 192
O'Connor, E. J. 5
Olick, J. K. 301
Orlikowski, W. J. 299
Orr, J. E. 310

Panico, P. 5
Parker, S. K. 481
Patvardhan, S. 161, 287
Peterson, M. F. 458
Petriglieri, J. 4, 10, 264, 265
Phillips, N. 13, 98, 286, 366, 459
Porac, J. F. 194
Powell, W. W. 192
Pradies, C. 387
Pratt, M. G. 4, 5, 6, 7, 13, 33, 107, 109, 110, 112, 113, 114, 115, 149, 166, 223, 225, 231, 265, 280, 322, 375, 376, 377, 378, 379, 382, 384, 386, 387, 402, 437, 447
Price, K. 25

Quinn, R. E. 30
Quinn Trank, C. 3

Rafaeli, A. 5, 109, 115, 149, 322
Raffaelli, R. 32, 322, 402
Rao, H. 5, 108, 146
Ravasi, D. 4, 5, 7, 24, 25, 31, 84, 162, 207, 209, 221, 233, 321, 322, 421, 422, 425, 444, 450
Reed, M. I. 277
Reger, R. 439
Reicher, S. 343
Reingen, P. H. 5, 109, 116
Rhodes, C. 279
Riad, S. 467
Rindova, V. 322, 423, 425
Robertson, M. 4, 7, 8
Rockman, K. W. 265
Rogers, K. 4, 80, 85, 368, 448
Romanelli, E. 98
Roowan, R. 307, 308, 309
Rosenkopf, L. 422
Rousseau, D. M. 478
Rylander, A. 143

Samuel, S. 224
Säntti, R. 468
Schein, E. H. 69, 72, 339
Schinoff, B. 4, 10, 85
Schoenberger, E. 133

Schultz, M. 3, 4, 5, 7, 24, 25, 31, 65, 73, 84, 94, 99, 100, 114, 170, 207, 209, 221, 223, 233, 298, 303, 305, 321, 323, 421, 425, 426, 427, 444, 450
Schwalbe, M. L. 279
Scott, S. G. 134
Selznick, P. 13, 107, 203, 355–7, 362–5, 378, 400–1
Seo, M. G. 380
Sheep, M. L. 284
Shortell, S. M. 406
Skov, A. M. 100
Sleebos, E. 344
Smith, W. K. 112
Snow, D. A. 276, 278
Staats, B. R. 231
Stigliani, I. 322
Stinchcombe, A. L. 203
Strauss, A. 134
Strauss, K. 481
Suddaby, R. 3, 4, 12, 282, 302, 360
Sundaramurthy, C. 285
Sutcliffe, K. M. 304
Svenningsson, S. 278

Tajfel, H. 5
Tanz, J. 266
Terry, D. J. 459
Thomas, J. B. 25, 161, 403, 439, 459
Thornton, P. H. 400
Tienari, J. 4, 5, 14, 98, 279, 467, 468
Tracey, P. 13, 98
Tripsas, M. 5, 14, 97, 100, 321, 419, 424, 426, 427, 430, 447, 450
Tsoukas, H. 28, 30, 32
Turner, J. C. 5
Tushman, M. 98, 422

Ulrich, J. 459, 460

Vaara, E. 4, 5, 14, 98, 279, 458, 466, 467, 468
Van Dick, R. 459
van Haldern, M. D. 451
van Knippenberg, D. 4, 12, 344, 458
van Knippenberg, E. 458
van Leeuwen, E. 458
van Riel, C.B. M. 5, 14, 451
van Vuuren, M. 464, 465
Voss, G. B. 341
Voss, Z. G. 341

Walsh, I. J. 302, 305
Watkiss, L. 5, 12, 261
Watson, T. J. 5, 8, 278
Weick, K. 30, 304, 460
Werner, M. D. 3, 9
Whetten, D. A. 1, 3, 6, 8, 15, 21, 24, 28, 39, 55, 57, 68, 69, 71, 80, 94, 97, 106–10, 112, 114, 123–6, 131, 166, 170, 171, 203, 206, 317, 319, 397, 399, 436, 449, 455, 494
Whittle, A. 4, 161
Wieseke, J. 459
Williams, B. E. 83
Wilmott, H. 4, 161, 168, 277, 286
Wrzesniewski, A. 459

Yanow, D. 229
Yates, J. 299
Ybema, S. 279, 280, 303

Zald, M. N. 1
Zapata-Phelan, C. P. 56
Zerubavel, E. 301
Zhang, J. 192
Zuckerman, E. 3, 9, 13, 47, 66, 192, 359

Subject Index

ACID (aggregation, compartmentalization, integration, and deletion) 112
actual self 258
adaptive instability 99
agency
  and history 305
  in institutional theory 360–2
  and organizational identity
    work 279
agentic construction, of OI 398–400, 404
agentic turn, and OI 361–2
aggregation strategy 111
alienation 458
alliance networks 249
antenarratives 462, 463, 468
anthropomorphic view, of
    organizations 166–7
Apple 5, 12
artifacts 319, 322–3
association strategies, and identification
    inducement 483–5
assumptions, on OI 8–9, 220–2
audience selection process 190–4
audience types 193, 443
authenticity paradox 195–7
auto-stereotypes 462–3, 467

beliefs and perceptions, fluidity of 174
between-level dynamics 7
bottom-up processes 7, 86, 205
boundary negotiation 459
boundary theory 283
boundary work, in organizational identity
    work 283–6
branding 150–5
bridging OI theories 200–12
business school branding 150–5

case study measurement 49, 54
categorical identity claims 399
categorical imperatives 191
categorical membership 71, 194, 399
categorical self-descriptors/claims 71
categorization
  and materiality 319, 320
  as mechanism 326, 328
  OI as 203
  of organizations 325–8
categorization metaphor 203, 206
categorization stage 190
categorization theory 7, 12, 13, 359
category currency 449
CED (central, enduring, distinctive)
    definition 23, 28, 94–101
central characteristics 162, 165, 378
centrality 112, 163
centrality component, in organizational
    identity work 281
character formation 356
Christian denominations, as organizational
    selves 388–90
claim-making process 443
clarification points, of OI 220–2
classification mechanisms 41, 56, 71–3
cluster analysis, in OI 47–53
collective beliefs 24
collective identity or self 13, 204, 220, 359
  and leadership 338, 339
  and OI/competitive landscape 432
collective identity work 279–81, 297
collective memory 301, 303
collectives, defining 3
commonality of values 13
communicating OI 219–34, 482–6
communication ambiguity 230

communication strategies, online 474–7, 482–6, 487
communication typology 226–32
comparative corporate identity 206, 486
compartmentalization 111
compatibility, and OI content 406
competitiveness, and OI 12, 432
complexity, of OI 496
concepts, as instruments 127–9
conceptualizing OI *see* definitions/ concepts of OI
conflict
  internal 23
  and OI 5
conformity, and differentiation 9, 183–97
consciousness, in organizational identity work 286–7
construction
  of OI 142–5, 374–92
  of personal identities 374
constructionist *see* social constructionist
construed external image 152
content vs. process theme, and organizational identity work 279–81
contextual understanding, of cultural norms 70–1
continuity
  and history 303
  in M&As 460–1
continuity/change duality 100
continuously dynamic identity 27–30
co-optation 142
core attributes, of organizations 202
core values 73
  changes 72
  incompatibility 24
  and organizational artifacts 322
corporate branding 143, 317
corporate goals/objectives 130–1
corporate historians 307
corporate museums 308–9
Corporate Social Responsibility (CSR) 108, 115
corporate structure 417
critical hermeneutics 169
Critical Management Studies (CMS) perspective 160–77
  critical perspectives, on OI 8–9

critical perspectives, on OI 8–9
cultural institutions, and OI 498
cultural norms, contextual understanding of 70–1
culture 161, 339
  as identity referent 68–70
  inconsistencies in 170
  in M&As 456–60
  and OI 14, 67–73, 169–74
    dynamic interrelation between 71–3
  OI as foundation of 173
  similarities with OI 14, 67–73, 169–74
  visual elements of 444
culture analysis 175
custodian perception of OI 220

data analysis 44–5
data reduction, and OI 391
debates, in OI study 21–34
deep processes, and OI 167
deep-structure identification 478–9
definitions/concepts of OI 2–3, 4, 6, 8, 28–9, 39, 44, 123–5, 127, 131, 140–2, 172, 202, 206, 241, 257, 319, 397–8, 418, 494–5, 497
deviance, and audiences 192–3
different audience theory 184, 188–93
differentiation, and conformity 9, 183–97
differentiation strategy 190
discontinuous change 443
discourse analysis 49
discursive approach 278–9
  to identity work 278–9
discursive sensemaking, as identity construction 460–8
dissociation strategies, and identification inducement 485–6
distinctive competence 355
distinctiveness, and OI 142, 165, 378
distinctiveness component, in organizational identity work 281
divergence, of root metaphors 204–12
dominant coalition 132, 133
Dragon Man sketch 185–9, 195–6
dynamic processes, and organizational selves 386–8

emergent identity 80, 81–4, 87
emergent re-membering 310–11
emotional labor 287–8
emotions, in organizational identity
        work 287–8
employee, *see also* members
encapsulation 231
endurance component, in organizational
        identity work 281
enduring identity 7, 24–5, 94–101, 378
enduring vs. fluid theme, and organizational
        identity work 279–81
enduringness 57
epistemological debate, on OI 21, 22–7,
        30–1, 137
espoused identities 82
espoused values 73
essentialism, and OI 165–7
essentialist perspective 116
explicit identity 114
extended metaphor analysis 39
external cultural frameworks 398
external determinants/forces, and OI 26,
        397, 400
external identity boundaries 285–6
external stakeholders 15, 448, 449,
        474–88
    and identity change 438
externalized other 116
extra-organizational context 83

filtering role, of OI 401–3, 404–5
first impressions 474
fluid gestalt, as OI 384, 387
fluid vs. enduring theme, and organizational
        identity work 279–81
frame of reference, OI as 202
framework, of OI change 438–46
future work self 481

genres, and identity 300
GLBT, and identity work 381
grounded theory measurement 49, 50,
        51, 54, 55

hegemony, and power 146, 149–50, 155
hierarchy of identities 378

high clarity/high intent OI
        communication 226, 230–1
high clarity/low intent OI
        communication 226, 228–9
historical memory, and identity 300–1
historical narrative, and identity work 311
historical strategies 303–4
history
    and agency 305
    and breach of identity 304
    as continuity 303
    and identity/continuity change 302–3
    and identity resurrection 304
    and identity work 298
    and rhetorical identification 300–5
history/language relationship 12
holographic hybrid organizational
        identities 107–8, 407
homogenous vs. heterogeneous beliefs 167
horizontal differentiation 190
human needs, and optimal
        distinctiveness 193–5
hybrid identity 7–8, 55, 85, 106–17, 165, 407,
        447, 463
hybrid organizations 107, 361
hybrid vs. multiple OI conceptualizations 113

ideal self 258
identification
    as process 297
    through rhetoric 299–300
identification inducement 483
    and association/dissociation
        strategies 483–6
identification through antithesis 485
identification types 478–9
identity 1, 4
    attribute-focused descriptions 32
    CED (central, enduring, distinctive)
        definition 23, 28, 94–101
    cognitive/practice relationship 324
    comparative nature of 206
    definition/meaning of 8, 11, 28–9, 39
    distinctiveness of 26
    as entity vs. process 27–30, 161
    and expressed values 170
    hierarchy of 378

identity (*Cont.*)
  and history 298–305
  holistic view of 364
  and image 470
  implications of 14-15
  inherent usefulness of OI 5
  and innovations *see* innovations
  internal/external determinants 116
  interrelations between organizational
      identity, image, culture 74
  as it relates to OI 494–8
  levels of analysis 79–88
  and mergers and acquisitions (M&As) 14,
      450–1, 455–70
  as ongoing change 7, 94–101
  organizational identity work 11, 135-7
  and organizational practices 324
  and the organization's environment 12–14
  as periodic/partial change 7, 94–101
  processual aspects 31
  psychological approaches 319–20
  roadmap to OI 6-15
  sense of 69
  substantiveness of 27–30, 31
  see also social identity
identity activation 100
identity affirmation/undesired self
      framework 267–8
identity alignment 391
identity ambiguity 25
identity boundaries, as cognitively
      constructed 284
identity cascades 80, 84, 85, 87
identity change 7, 93–101, 340, 436–51
  barriers to 447
  and context 449–50
  and continuity/discontinuity 446
  cross-level identity dynamics and 448
  planned 436–51
  and reputation 449, 451
  and strategy change 450
  triggers of 438–43
  types of 446–7
identity claims
  change in 443–4
  internal communication of 444–6, 451
identity clarity 226–32

identity coalition 341
identity conflicts 431
identity construction
      as discursive sensemaking 460–8
      and mergers and acquisitions (M&As) 14,
          450–1, 455–70
identity content 232
identity custodians 10, 85, 86, 221–32
      OI content clarity 226–32
      OI content communication 226–32
identity deletion 447
identity destabilization 86
identity differentiation 448
identity drift 86
identity dynamics 7
identity emergence 80, 81–4, 87
identity flow 100
identity formation 81, 356
identity function 81
identity hybrids 7–8, 55, 85, 106–17, 165, 407
identity and identification, in M&As 458–60
identity inertia 97
identity leadership 12
identity management responses,
          classification scheme 111
identity perception 240–1, 344
identity plurality 7–8, 106, 115, 117, 378, 447
identity protection 265
identity question 68
identity reconstruction 11
identity referent 23
      as organizational culture 68–70
identity regulation, and management 168
identity restructuring 265
identity rhetoric 338, 339
identity structure 81
identity struggles 72
identity studies 305
identity synergy 112
identity theory 106
identity threat 23–4, 239–53
      coping responses 265
identity transformation organizations
          (ITOs) 231
identity work 11, 135-7, 265, 276–89, 297–8
      and historical narrative 311
identity workspaces 244

identity-as-content 32
identity-as-flow 30, 34
identity-challenging activities 100
identity-consistent thinking 282
identity-defining beliefs 72–3
identity-enhancing activities 100
identity-stretching activities 100
identity/image/culture interrelations 74, 100
ideographic hybrid organizational
       identities 107–8
image, and OI 65–74, 164, 470
implementing OI change, initiatives 444–6
implicit vs. espoused beliefs 167
individual identity work 277–81
individualism, myth of 196
individuals
    alliance networks 249
    hierarchical power and
        mobilization 248–9
    and institutional pluralism of 380–1
    and organizations 166–7
    relating to OI 10–11
    responses to threat 245–50
    and uniqueness 194
innovations
    categorization of 419–29
    drivers of success 418–19
    identity-challenging 420, 424–9, 431
    identity-enhancing 420–2, 429, 431
    identity-stretching 420, 421–5, 429, 431
    implications 429–30
    and non-technical aspects 419
    and OI 14, 417–32
    realignment mechanisms 424, 425, 428
institutional bricolage 26, 401, 404
institutional change, outsider-driven 283
institutional claims 368
institutional complexity 384
institutional conformity 99
institutional determination, of OI 400–1
institutional entrepreneurship 13, 360–1
institutional expectations 382, 387
institutional forces
    divergent perspectives 409
    implications of 408–9
    integrating perspectives 403–5, 407
    and OI 13, 396–409

OI as filter of actors' perceptions 401–3
    and OI members responses 397
    structural properties of 407
institutional inhabitants
    effects on OI 386–8
    experiences of institutional pluralism
        of 380–1, 391
institutional isomorphism 192, 367
institutional logics 27, 358–9, 398, 400, 404
institutional memory 310
institutional perspective 22, 26–7, 30, 369
institutional pluralism 7–8, 27, 106, 132,
       361, 377–92
    and institutional inhabitants 380–1, 391
institutional structure, filtering role 404–5
institutional theory, and OI 98, 353–69, 379
    agentic turn in 360–2
    conceptualization of 354
    contemporary developments 360–2
    core ideas 354
    diachronic orientation 363
    dualisms in 364
    historical orientation 363
    history overview of 354–62
    and legitimacy 358
    new directions in 363–8
    new institutional theory 357–60
    non-conformity 358
    Selznick's institutional theory 355–7,
       363–5, 400–1
    social construction of identity and
       institutions 365–7
    summary of 354
    synchronic orientation 363
institutional trust 459
institutional values 365
institutional work, in organizational identity
       work 276, 281–3
institutionalization 355–7
integration, and OI content 407
integrative framework, of OI
       theories 200–12
integrative models, of OI 9–10, 111
intentionality, in organizational identity
       work 286–7
internal alignment, OI and members'
       identities 406

internal determinants, of OI 396–7
internal identity boundaries 285–6
internal stakeholders 15, 438
interpretive schemas 319
intersubjective identity 82
intrasubjective identity 82
isomorphic identity 26, 165, 379

language, and identity 298, 305
language/history relationship 12
latent identity 114
leadership/management
    and asymmetrical relations 168
    and collective identity 338
    communications and OI 346
    and employee perceptions of OI 341
    and identity regulation 168
    identity rhetoric 338, 339
    leader group prototypicality 337, 342–5
    and members' identity construction 437–8
    and OI 12, 172, 335–47
    social identity theory of 337, 342–5
    and stigmatized work 340
    visionary 338
legacy identities 114
legitimacy 113
legitimacy threshold 362
legitimate distinctiveness 362, 367
legitimate OIs, and undesired selves 261
levels of analysis
    interaction 79–88
    and OI 4
liminality 464
logics compatibility 112
low clarity/high intent OI
        communication 226, 229–30
low clarity/low intent OI
        communication 226–8

M&As see mergers and acquisitions
management-centric view, of OI 176
manager-stakeholder view 134
managerial power, and OI 167–9
mapping OI field 6–8
material practices, and OI 323
material turn 318
materiality

and categorization 319, 320
elements of 319–20, 324
and OI 317–30
and OI instantiation 319–24
and organizational artifacts 322–3
and organizational practices 323–4
and organizational products 320–1
performative repertoires 319
and symbolization 319, 325–8
theorizing mechanisms relating to OI 325–8
Meadian organizational self 375–6, 386
    see also multiple identity
        conceptualization of the self
measuring OI 39–60
    article coding scheme 44–6
member agency, and institutional
        constraints 400–1
members or employees
    alignment 444–5, 448
    beliefs/perceptions 164–165
    identification, and organizational
        image 163–165
        assumptions about 163
        communicating OI to 219–34
        identity construction and
            organizational leadership 437
        identity-related perceptions 219, 240–1
        and institutional forces 397, 402–3
        interpretation of reality 399
        interpretation of structure 409
        interpretive processes 399
        and mergers 458–9
        relating to organization 175, 477
        response to threats to OI 239–53
        self-concepts and OI 268–9
        self-esteem 245
        sense of membership 163
        and social construction of OI 399
members' identities and OI, internal
        alignment 406
membership, as social construction 298
membership norms 194
membership opportunities 478
memory
    collective 301, 303
    and identity 300–1
    and individual analysis 300

and mnemonic communities 301, 312
as social construction 298
mentoring relationships 224
mergers and acquisitions (M&As), and
    identity 14, 450–1, 455–70
metaphors 127–8, 130, 201–4, 205, 467–8
methodological research issues 40–1
  in leadership/identity 346
  measuring OI 44–5
  methods used 41–8
  perspective 44
  qualitative v. quantitative analyses
      comparison 53, 56
  representative selected articles 43
  research clusters 47–50
  use of OI 45
  see also research
middle-status conformity 194
mimetic isomorphism 192
mnemonic communities 301, 312
moral authenticity 195–7
multilevel linkages over time 81–7
multilevel nature, of OI 367–8
multiple identities 7–8, 21, 55, 59, 106–17, 166,
      230, 388
  individuals' boundary work 285
  of people 244
Multiple identity conceptualization of self
      (MICS) 377–8, 386–8
multiple institutional orders 377
multiple vs. hybrid OI conceptualizations 113

narrative, and identity 305
narrative identity work 278
narrative interpretations 462
narrative perspective, on OI 32–3, 223
narrative/discourse analysis 48, 49, 51, 54, 55
narrativization, and sensemaking 461
national identity, and M&As 466–8
nested identities 84–7
new institutional theory 357–60, 379
nomological issues, in OI 7
normative isomorphism 192

OI (organizational identity) see identity
online communication strategies 474–7,
      482–6, 487

ontological debate, on OI 21–2, 27–33, 137
optimal distinctiveness 27, 59, 82, 88, 167,
      183–97, 362, 367
organization environment, and
    identity 12–14
organizational artifacts 319, 325–8
  and materiality 322–3, 324
organizational character 1, 355, 401
organizational communication 476
organizational conformity 9, 183–97
organizational culture see culture
organizational differentiation 9, 183–97
organizational groups, political mobilization
      of 249–50
organizational hybridity 107–17
organizational identity see identity
organizational image
  changing nature of 165
  and employee identification 163–5
  intended 482-6
  online 474–7, 482–6
  and stakeholders 474–86
organizational isomorphism 26, 165, 379, 380
organizational leadership see leadership
organizational legacy 303
organizational legitimacy 479–80
organizational names, and OI 400
organizational personification 131
organizational practices 319
  and identity 324
  and materiality 323–4, 325
  and performance repertoire 319, 325–8
organizational products 319, 325–8
  and materiality 320–1, 324
organizational re-membering 101, 297–312
  actor groups 308–9
  and corporate identity 307
  definition 306–8
  emergent 309–11
  formal 309–11
organizational response, to identity
      threat 239–53
organizational self-identity 133, 136, 137
organizational selves 116, 375–7, 378, 380,
      381–92, 407
organizational shocks 463
organizational structuration 358

organizations
    actors' expectations for 401
    anthropomorphic view of 166–7
    classifying of 71–3
    concept of 32
    distributed nature of 497
    and individuals 166–7
    members' communication with 219–34
    mobilization and threat 246–53
    as organic wholes 364
    as political systems 175
    as self-acting subjects 364
    as superpowers 167
ought self 258

paradigmatic narratives 310
perceptions
    of OI 239–53
    of OI threat 246
    of own identity 244
performance, firm 419
performative repertoires
    as mechanism 326–7, 328
    and organizational practices 319, 325–8
personal identities
    construction of 374
    interaction with OIs 381–6
    in pluralist institutionalist context 381
personal identity work 11, 135–7, 278
personal perception, and organizational
        self 392
personification, OI as 203–4
personification metaphor 206
phantom limb identities 114
planned identity change 436–51, see also
        identity change
pluralism
    institutional 7–8, 27, 106, 361, 374–92
    in management 132
pluralist institutionalist context, and
        personal identities 381
pluralistic context, in OI 379
pluralistic demands 13
pluralistic environments, and OI/
        organizational self 383–6
pluralistic research methodology 50
plurality, and OI 406, 496

political dynamics, of OI 8
political mobilization, of organizational
        groups 249–50
possible selves 481
power
    and actors' preferences 146
    and discourse 146, 147–8
    and hegemony 146, 149–50, 155
    and interests 145–7
    managerial power and OI 167–9
    in mergers and acquisitions 456–60
    and politics, and OI 146
    qualities of 147
    as relational 147
    and subjectivity 146, 147–8
    three dimensions of 152–6
power dynamics, of OI 8
power and OI, framework for analysis 146
power and politics, and OI 140–56
power relations, and sensemaking/identity
        construction 462
pragmatic instrumentalism 126
pragmatic realism 126
pragmatism, and research 125–7, 137
preservation, of OI 142–5
process model, of OI 201, 207
process sensitivity 160–77
process thinking 99
process vs. content theme, and
        organizational identity work 279–81
processes and sources, of OI 11–12,
        495–6, 498
product identity 320
promotion focus 259
prototypicality 337, 342–5
provisional selves 262
psychological approaches, to identity 319–20
punctuated equilibrium 98

realism, and research 125–7
reality, members' interpretation of 399
regulative isomorphism 192
reification, and OI 165–7, 176, 204
relational construct, OI as 3–4, 8
religious logics 388–90
re-membering see organizational
        re-membering

rhetoric, and identity 338
rhetorical history 298–312
rhetorical identification 299–300
  and history 300–1
role-consistent behaviour 267
roles
  non-investment in 266–7
  re-defining meaning 266
  self-ambivalence 271
root metaphors 204–12
routines 225

saying, as communication 10, 85, 220,
    222–3, 230
segmentation-integration, in boundary
    theory 284
self-coherence 244
self-concepts, of organizational
    members 258, 268–9
self-continuity 244–5
  and stakeholder identification 480–1
self-definition 14, 245
  and strategic choice 70
self-discrepancy theory/research 259
self-enhancement 245
  and stakeholder identification 481–2
self-esteem 245
self-identity 133, 136, 137, 143
self-process 100
self-states 258
self-understanding 270
sensegiving 9, 24, 84, 142, 210, 338, 399
sensemaking 25, 84, 142, 338, 398–9, 460–8
showing, as communication 10, 85, 220, 222,
    223–4, 230
situated identification 478–9
social actor perspective/theory 3, 6, 9–10, 22,
    23–4, 49, 84, 113, 114, 200–12, 220–2,
    319, 376, 398, 443
social construction
  of identity and institutions 365–7,
    374–92
  as point of contact 366–7
social constructionist perspective/theory 3,
    6, 9–10, 22, 24–6, 30, 48, 49, 84, 114,
    126, 142, 200–12, 220–2, 336, 343,
    398, 443

social existence, and OI 3
social identity theory/perspective 9–10, 12,
    106, 163, 200–12
  formation 210
  of leadership 337, 342–5
social identity work 278
social interactionist model, of OI formation
    and change (SIMOI) 207–12
social memory studies 301
socio-cultural context, and mergers and
    acquisitions 466
socio-materiality 469–70
source terminology 209
sources and processes, of OI 11–12
stable solutions, and organizational
    selves 386–8
staging, as communication 10, 85, 220, 222,
    224–6, 230
stakeholder identification 474–88
  and dissociation strategies 486
  and OI attractiveness 478–82
  and self-consistency 488
  and self-continuity 480–1
  and self-enhancement 481–2
  and uncertainty reduction 479–80
stakeholders 15, 134, 309, 323
  expectant 477, 479-86, 487
status hierarchy 194
stereotypes 14, 462–3, 467
strategic choice, and self-definition 70
strategy, innovation and OI 431
structural feature, of OI 404–6
structural filters, and OI 403–8
structural properties, of institutional
    forces 407
structurational thinking 31, 34
symbolic management 85
symbolization
  and materiality 319, 325–8
  mechanism of 326–7, 328

taken-for-granted OI 161–3, 169
temporal continuity/
    discontinuity 93–101, 303
temporality, in OI construction 469
tensions, in OI work 279–81
theories, associated with OI 4

threat
  aftereffects of 252
  classifying 241–3
  external 23
  external events 242–3
  individuals' responses to 245–50
    bottom-up critical mass 247–8, 251
    top-down hierarchical 248–9, 251
  internal events/changes 242
  organizational responses to 246–50, 251
  political mobilization of organizational
      groups 249–50
  strength 243
  to OI members 10–11, 244–6
top-down dynamics 7, 277
transcendent we 484, 485
transformation, of OI 142–5
transitional identity 25, 459
translation, and OI 283
tropes, and megers and acquisitions 467–8
turn to work 277, 278
two-stage valuation theory 9, 184–5,
    188–91, 195

uncertainty reduction, and stakeholder
      identification 479–80
undesired self 257–71
  actual/ideal/ought self 258
  and corporate professionals 262
  and distinctive OIs 263–4
  imposition on members 264–7
  and legitimate OIs 261–4
  and OI affirmations 260–4
  theoretical overview 258–60
undesired self/OI affirmation
      framework 267–8
unified OI 5
unitary conceptualizations, of OI 8
unity, and OI 142

valuation risk 194
valuation theory, two-stage 9
values 365
vertical differentiation 190

weak process perspective 163–4
  who we are? communication 219–34